Early German Philosophy

Ariſtoteles Philoſophorum princeps.

An Augsburg woodcut, ca. 1480

Early German Philosophy

Kant and His Predecessors

Lewis White Beck

The Belknap Press of
Harvard University Press
Cambridge, Massachusetts
1969

To Leroy E. Loemker
[Aber] ich weiss das Land nicht zu finden

Preface

This book was originally intended to be a history of German philosophy down to our own days. I hoped to begin it by saying that here is the first such history since Eduard Zeller's *Geschichte der deutschen Philosophie seit Leibniz* (1873). I must begin it instead by saying that here is only the first part of such a book and I do not know whether I shall have the time, which would permit me, and the approbation of readers, which would encourage me, to write about the last century and a half.

It is worth noting that it has been nearly a hundred years since a German has written a large history of German philosophy. It suggests that it may be presumptuous of a non-German to write one. The German who has not essayed such a task may be wiser than the non-German who does attempt it. Natural endowments which could be confidently counted on by a German tracing the evolution of a body of teaching of which he himself is a product are lacking to anyone outside the tradition, however much he may attempt to penetrate into it. But though the native resources required for such an undertaking as mine were regrettably exiguous, I was singularly blessed with the external resources needed. I would not have had the temerity to begin such a work had I not known that I would be given every assistance possible; and, when I put my hand to it, help came in generous measure.

The University of Rochester provided the ideal environment, viz., one in which hard work is a pleasure. The University also gave me a sabbatical leave and several travel and research grants.

The American Council of Learned Societies gave me a travel grant and a fellowship. The American Philosophical Society made a grant in aid (Grant 2684) for some related studies which were later useful when I decided to expand my work. Except for the research supported by a fellowship from the John Simon Guggenheim Foundation in 1957–1958, I am sure I would not have embarked upon this larger project; it was my study of Kant's ethical theory which showed me the need for understanding the pre-Kantian period of German philosophy.

I cannot forget the selfless, but I regret to say often anonymous, services of members of the staffs of the libraries where I worked: in Rochester, The Rush Rhees Library of the University of Rochester and The Ambrose Swasey Library of the Colgate-Rochester Divinity School; in England, The Bodleian, the British Museum, the Warburg Institute, and the Institute of Germanic Studies of the University of London; in Germany, the philosophical seminars of the Universities of Heidelberg, Marburg, and Tübingen.

These generous but critical scholars read and commented upon parts of my manuscript: Professor William F. Eberlein, Professor Paul Edwards, Professor Alfred Geier, Professor William Hamilton, Professor Winthrop S. Hudson, Professor Leroy E. Loemker, Rev. Professor Robert G. Miller, C. S. B., Professor Charles Nielsen, Mr. Martin J. Scott-Taggart, and Professor Hayden V. White.

Mr. Charles Mills was an inexhaustible source of information on German dynastic history. Professor Kurt Weinberg answered many questions. Professor Harmon R. Holcomb helped me to sources of important information. Professor Ingeborg Heidemann and Professor Giorgio Tonelli procured rare books for me. Mr. John Dennison Moore saved the book twice. Miss M. Kathleen Ahern insisted, and made me see, that obscurity in German philosophy neither entails nor excuses obscurity in a history of German philosophy. M. Jacques Rodbertus helped me most when he knew it least. Three graduate research assistants really assisted: Mr. (now Dr.) Jeffrie G. Murphy, Mr. (now Dr.) George Hole, and Mr. Peter Laska.

Mrs. Beatrice Burch and Miss Karen Ewell prepared copies of manuscripts, in many stages of disorder, with skill, expedition, and cheerful good humor. Mrs. Ruth Spall, my secretary, made many things easy which without her would have been impossible. And my family gave the comfort and tranquillity without which all the other help would have been of no avail.

To each of these institutions and individuals, my genuine thanks. Looking back over the long list, I wonder what in the book is my own. The old formula is not used perfunctorily when I say: I alone am responsible for the errors.

L. W. B.

The University of Rochester
July 1968

Contents

Early German Philosophy

I

A National History of Philosophy?

Deutschland? aber wo liegt es? Ich weiss das Land nicht zu finden.
Wo das gelehrte beginnt, hört das politische auf.[1]

Thus Goethe, Hegel, on the contrary, believed that the march of philosophy was the special burden, and the glory, of the Germanic people:

Philosophy, excepting in name, has sunk even from memory [in other countries] . . . and . . . it is in the German nation that it has been retained as a peculiar possession. We have received the higher call of Nature to be the conservers of this holy flame . . . We have already got so far, and have attained to a seriousness so much greater and a consciousness so much deeper, that for us ideas, and that which our reason justifies, can alone have weight; to speak more plainly, the Prussian State is a State constituted on principles of intelligence.[2]

Can there be, should there be, a history of *German* philosophy?

Nations are, in different degrees, proper subjects for histories of philosophy. No one objects to there being histories of Greek philosophy and his-

---

[1] *Xenien*, 85 ("Germany? Where is it? I don't know how to find that country. Where the learned begins, the political ends.") Goethe was making fun of a new journal with the title "Das gelehrte Deutschland," but it is much more than a criticism of this title; it is a criticism of spiritual nationalism.

[2] Inaugural Lecture, Heidelberg, 1816, in *Lectures on the History of Philosophy*, trans. E. S. Haldane (London: Routledge & Kegan Paul, 1892), I, xii. (Last clause added in Berlin!)

tories of Roman philosophy. The Greeks, for a long period, alone effected the historical development of philosophy; the Romans, for almost equally long, supplied from Greek springs the whole stream of European thought. Histories of Greek philosophy and of Roman philosophy are justified geographically, linguistically, and temporally.

A history of philosophy of the Middle Ages, however, cannot avoid having a broader geographical base. While the philosophical movements of the East, Africa, and Western Europe had so few contacts with each other for many centuries that we do not need knowledge of one in order to understand the others, within Europe there was a common culture. Any division along lines of political and ethnic differences reads back into earlier centuries distinctions and differences which were of decisive importance only much later.

In modern philosophy, however, the situation is very different. A thousand years from now, "Western philosophy" may seem to name a single complex historical phenomenon just as "Greek philosophy" does today. But today, many will feel that "Western philosophy" is as poor a name for a complex and variegated historical phenomenon as we are coming to see "Oriental philosophy" to be—a name that suggests a unity where there is none, and overlooks great internal diversity. If even as broad a term as "European philosophy" is objectionable to the extent that it suggests some distinct system of thought cut off from others and internally integrated, how much more objectionable is the thought of a history of German philosophy!

Within the history of European culture we see thoughts expressed in various languages by men from different parts of the Continent. But these components are hardly well-formed unities with sharp edges. None of them is comprehensible by itself. In every one of them, important men and ideas from another must be included. No history of English or German philosophy can be understood without Descartes; no history of French or German philosophy can be understood without Locke; no history of French thought can be understood without Leibniz. If we add to this caution the recollection that few countries are now geographically what they were five centuries ago and that up to three centuries ago most philosophical works were written in a single language and passed, more freely than they do now, from one part of Europe to another, a national history of philosophy may appear at best episodic, at worst arbitrary. Why not write a history of philosophy mentioning only men whose names begin with the letter "p"?

And yet . . . There are good histories of French literature, German literature, English literature, even if there are and perhaps can be no good histories of French science, German science, English science. And, though most philosophy strives to be a "science" and not *belles lettres*, even among the most "scientific" philosophers do we not see national differences? Is there not something unmistakably French about Descartes, English about Locke, German about Kant, besides their languages? Something besides geographical accident that connects Albertus Magnus, Meister Eckhart, and Nicholas of Cusa; something without which the very idea of a national history of philosophy would be absurd?

It may well be the case, of course, that there are not well-formed categories of distinctively English, French, or German national characters which we know in some way independently of the history of thought, so that we could define this elusive something and then find it in men who represented each. For who can doubt that much of our common conception of the English character is based upon the fact that Bacon, Locke, and Mill are its representative thinkers? Who can doubt that the vaunted French clarté is a fruit of Montaigne's and Descartes' work and not just a pre-existent ideal they exemplified? The great thinkers of Germany are not just spokesmen for the national consciousness; they helped fashion it. In no case can we take as given a national spirit and explain national philosophy in terms of it, any more than we can explain the spirit of a nation in terms of the thoughts of men supposed, in some way, not to be *products* of their place and time.

But whatever we think about the etiology of the philosophy or the public mind of a nation, it is not at all easy to be sure that there are common traits, or to say what they are should we find them. Certainly all the philosophers of a given nation possess no single common, peculiar, and interesting trait; wherein would one find a common trait of Melanchthon and Fichte that would have any bearing upon their philosophizing? After reading a vast amount of writings purporting to list the distinctive and peculiar traits of German philosophy, I must report that I have found no generalization to which many important exceptions cannot be found in a moment's reflection. Perhaps the notion of an ideal type or of family resemblances may help us find the nongeographical meaning of "German philosophy." But my experience of attempts to do this is little more encouraging. Physiognomies of German philosophy by German apologists are hardly more than lists of philosophical virtues; by critics of German philosophy hardly more than lists of philosophical vices. It does not help us, I think, to read that German philosophy rests on a synthesis of the personal and the objective, that it always strives for the whole, that it is attentive to the very large and the very small, that it is free individuality realizing itself in the community, that it is irrationalism which favors the will over knowledge and ethics over logic, that it comes from the Germans' "unusual ability to see both sides of a problem and to synthesize them," or from a preference for intuition over thought or from an emphasis upon becoming over being. I am not edified by the claim that the German, a creature of deep feeling and rich fantasy, requires of himself such a degree of vigorous intellectual control that he ends either in pedantic discipline or untrammeled speculation.[3] No more does it help to be treated to a denial that there is a "German philosophy" because each racial component in Germany has produced its own philosophy.[4] None of this helps, for most of it is not true, and what is true in it is probably equally true of most non-German philosophers too.

[3] For the sources of this *Allerlei*, see the books and articles listed in the Bibliography.
[4] This egregious theory is defended by Max Wundt in *Die Wurzeln der deutschen Philosophie in Stamm und Rasse* (Berlin: Junker und Dunnhaupt, 1944), a bar on the escutcheon of a distinguished historian of German philosophy whose other works are of great value.

I am less presumptuous than I would have to be to attempt to give a brief and memorable description of German philosophy *überhaupt*. If, however, we introduce a temporal dimension which is often omitted from both pro-German and anti-German typologies, the problem becomes easier. While philosophers are supposed to survey all time and all existence, each one, even the greatest, like a Leibnizian monad surveys it from a peculiar point of view. His point of view may have the originality of genius or mere idiosyncrasy, and thereby escape the limits of consensus imposed by common social, political, scientific, and religious forces which shape him and his fellows. But though he escapes this uniformity—otherwise he does not appear in history—the path of his escape at least begins from a common terrain of ideas, institutions, and problems; and this terrain is temporally and geographically restricted. There will be ideas in it from far away and long ago, ideas which come out of other cultures; but there is a common stock of ideas and challenges facing neighboring thinkers contemporaneous with each other. Hence, though it is difficult or impossible to characterize German philosophy *überhaupt*, it may be easier to characterize, say, "German philosophy of the Baroque period" or "philosophy of the German Enlightenment." Because periods like "the Baroque" and "the Enlightenment" have a sequence, a continuity, and an intelligible order, a history of many ideas and complexes of ideas can show their connection with national interests and conflicts in politics, society, religion, literature, and art. A national history of philosophy can at least be parasitic upon a study of these interests and conflicts.

Though the abstractness of Hegel's history of philosophy makes the problem appear to him to be far simpler than it in fact is, there is truth in his statement which justifies a history of philosophy along national lines:

Philosophy which arises among a people, and the definite character of the standpoint of thought, is the same character which permeates all the other historical sides of the spirit of the people, which is most intimately related to them, and which constitutes their foundation. The particular form of philosophy is thus contemporaneous with a particular constitution of the people amongst whom it makes its appearance, with their institutions and forms of government, their morality, their social life and capabilities, customs, and enjoyments of them; it is so with their attempts and achievements in art and science, with their religions, warfares, and external relationships.[5]

Hegel compares the "mind of a people" to a cathedral, all of whose vaults, passages, pillars, and vestibules "have proceeded out of one whole and are directed to one end"; but it would be more apt to compare it to actual cathedrals built over centuries in different styles, yet, as a whole, producing a unitary impression upon the onlooker who sees here a Gothic mysticism, there a Prussian rationalism, yonder a South German romanticism, but all contributing to a unitary effect not describable in the language of any one period or any one style. To add to such a complex description the adjective "German" is to locate it historically and geo-

---

[5] *Lectures on the History of Philosophy,* trans. E. S. Haldane, I, 53.

graphically; it is not to explain it except by calling attention to the fact that some of the extra-philosophical determinants were events and states of affairs more or less unique to Germany. The "German spirit" is not something brooding over a thousand years of philosophy; it is a name for immensely rich and varied responses to the mysteries of existence, some of which were refracted through the variegated historical experiences of the German people, so that many of the responses were different from those made by Dutchmen, Frenchmen, Britons, and Italians. Unless this variety is kept in mind, conceptions of German philosophy will be so simple that they will seem to explain it, but will be in fact so simple that they explain nothing.

This conception of "German philosophy" directs our attention to historical facts about which there need be little dispute and away from the obscurities of Volksgeist about which there is bound to be unending dispute. Can we not find historical events and circumstances which could be expected to affect the shape of popular thought and thereby to characterize philosophy in Germany in very much the same way other events have affected popular thought and philosophy in other countries? Can we not in these events and circumstances find some relation of fittingness—I do not speak of determination—between the powers effective in various periods, the problems these powers provoked, and the kind of philosophizing which grew out of these problems?

Before suggesting what some of these complexes of powers, problems, and philosophy have been, let me comment upon one obvious complex of them at some length, for the purpose of illustration: To a greater extent than in any other country, important German philosophy has been the product of university teachers. Most of the great German philosophers since the establishment of universities in the fourteenth century have been professors in the universities. The exceptions—for example, Nicholas of Cusa, Leibniz, Lessing, Herder, Schopenhauer, Marx, and Nietzsche—are important, but they are so few that they readily appear to be exceptions.[6] In England and France, on the other hand, most important philosophical movements have taken place outside the universities and against their opposition. Why is this? And what effect has the fact that German philosophy is largely university-philosophy had on its content and style?

At least one reason for the important role of the universities has been their proliferation in Germany. Unlike France and England, with their few and powerful universities, Germany has never had one dominant university center; because of particularism (Kleinstaaterei), universities multiplied almost as in America. Universities existed, and competed, with the backing

6 "To us Germans, who, by a philosopher, understand a professor standing with raised finger before his chair, it must necessarily appear striking that among the English philosophers there have been so many statesmen; nay, what is almost remarkable, that in England the statesmen are sometimes philosophers" (F. H. Lange, History of Materialism, trans. E. C. Thomas [London: Routledge & Kegan Paul, 1957], II, 160). While there is much to bear out this stereotype, Lange has overlooked Nicholas of Cusa, Leibniz, and Frederick the Great who, in their political activity, compare very well indeed with Bacon, Locke, Mill, and (a little later) Lord Balfour and Lord Haldane.

of forces in conflict with each other: after the sixteenth century Lutheran, Calvinist, Catholic, and secular universities existed side by side. During much of their history, scholars have freely moved from one to another. A good man driven out of one by persecution could almost always find a position and often an enthusiastic welcome in rival university (as Wolff did in Marburg when he was driven out of Halle, and as Thomasius did in Halle when driven out of Leipzig). Each great new intellectual movement in Germany has produced its own university, which nurtured the new movement. Thus we have nominalist universities (like Heidelberg and Tübingen) over against realist universities (like Cologne and Louvain); Lutheran universities (like Wittenberg, Jena, and Königsberg) over against universities that remained Catholic (Freiburg, Innsbruck, Breslau); Calvinist universities (like Heidelberg and Marburg) over against the Lutheran; Halle the Pietist university and Göttingen that of the secular Enlightenment; Berlin and Jena the universities of German idealism, classicism, and romanticism. Again and again we see philosophical movements closely associated with a single university—for example, Wittenberg remained the orthodox Lutheran university, and Leipzig was the eighteenth-century stronghold against Wolffianism; and in the nineteenth and twentieth centuries each school of Kant-interpretation was known by the name of the university which professed it, as "Marburg neo-Kantianism" and "Heidelberg neo-Kantianism." For most important philosophizing there has been a university in existence, and, if not, one was founded to be its center.[7] The important philosophers who have stood outside the university community have, by that very fact, lessened or at least delayed their influence (as can most easily be seen in the cases of Leibniz and Schopenhauer). Here we have a historical situation which has had an important philosophical effect; particularism and the lack of a single strong political and cultural center have given a variety to university thought that it did not have in other countries.

The effect of this situation on philosophy in Germany is clear. The mainstream of German philosophy has had a scholastic shape; Catholic scholasticism was replaced by Protestant scholasticism, and this in turn was replaced by the scholasticism of the Wolffians in the eighteenth century. A German who tried to escape from scholasticism, as Bacon, Descartes, and Locke tried to do, found that if he was successful at all his followers, as it were, scholasticized *him*. (This is very clear in the relations between Leibniz and Wolff, though Leibniz himself did not even profess to move against scholasticism as much as his non-German peers did.) Because of the strength of German universities in the intellectual life of the seventeenth century, they may have inhibited the growth of non-university philosophy and kept Germany from participating on a large scale in the revolutionary philosophical movements from the time of Bacon to near the end of the century. The German universities were then no more backward than the

[7] The two universities in Berlin at the present time are striking reminders of the manner in which German intellectual life institutionalizes itself along lines of political and ideological division.

English and French (but more so than the Dutch); it was their strength, not their modernity, which kept them in step with their times, for they held the times back. But when German universities—at least a few of them—became research institutions before foreign universities did, their teaching kept up with the progress of philosophy instead of remaining, as in France especially, behind the times. Philosophy became a *Fach* and a liberal profession in Germany sooner than it did in other countries. Textbooks, histories, lexicons, encyclopedias, and even periodicals devoted to philosophy, appear in Germany earlier, and in greater numbers, than in other countries. German academies had philosophical classes long before foreign academies. This professionalization of philosophy may have much to do with the prosaic, prolix, and architectonic styles which seem characteristic of much German philosophical writing. Various schools of philosophy develop their own orthodoxies, with private technical (but seldom precise) vocabularies, and a strong sense of difference between the "ins" and the "outs." One who reads the lives of Melanchthon, Wolff, and Hegel gets the impression that these professors must have spent an inordinate amount of time placing their students in this or that university chair, and seeking the support of the respective ministries of education for signs of official approval. Sometimes this is not a pretty sight.

Because the universities were state institutions, political criticism, which has been one of the important functions of French and English philosophy, was either absent or highly disguised in Germany. Since there was little of the new science in most German universities until the nineteenth century, German philosophers had less occasion to concern themselves with the problems which were changing the whole shape of philosophy in the seventeenth century. While the development of science in other countries was at the expense of speculative philosophy, in the philosophical faculties of Germany this was a reason for excluding science from the institutions which formed the popular mind. Because of the universities, the term "schools of thought" in Germany has an institutional meaning which it often lacks in other countries; there is a kind of legitimacy established through a series of teacher–student relations (Rüdiger taught Hoffmann, Hoffmann taught Crusius, Crusius taught Gellert; Darjes taught Eschenbach, Eschenbach taught Tetens; Carl Leonhard Reinhold, Kant's disciple, taught Trendelenburg, Trendelenburg taught Cohen, Cohen taught Natorp, Natorp taught Nicolai Hartmann . . .). However much Schopenhauer and Nietzsche disliked the fact that the main stream of German philosophy flowed through the universities, it is a fact, and an important one, for the style and content of German philosophy.

Every institutional mode of thought generates an antithesis to both its content and style. Hence it would be a serious mistake to regard German philosophy as if it were the product of the universities only. But the strength and continuity of this peculiar institution give a strength and a continuity to its antithesis as well—not a temporal continuity, but a continuity of like reactions to philosophy as a university specialty. Non-university philosophy, as a reaction to academic philosophy in all its various forms from Albertus Magnus to Hegel and beyond, tends toward those forms which invite or perhaps require a visionary obscurity. Pantheisms, humanisms, vitalisms, mysticisms, recur again and again in Germany, as if from time to time German thinkers need an intellectual holiday from arid technicalities, and need to soak themselves in ambient fantasy to recover from academic desiccation. Mysticisms, humanisms, and pietisms make their repeated appearances first outside and against dominant intellectual-isms and orthodoxies, each time taking local color from what they rise against, each time returning to a vaguely defined but recognizable existential center, each time eventually becoming respectable in safe university chairs where they await counterrevolutions against their own orthodoxies. The great dialectic of German philosophy is that between school philosophy and what are felt to be the interests of humanity, allegedly forgotten in the elaboration and overelaboration of systems.[8] No doubt such a dialectic is common to all philosophy, but it is perhaps clearer in Germany than else-where because one pole, the intellectually systematic, is pushed so far in one direction by being concretized in institutions that the counterthrust comes with almost predictable regularity: Mysticism in the fourteenth cen-tury, Nicholas of Cusa in the fifteenth; humanism and much Reformation and Protestant Counter Reformation thought in the sixteenth; Paracelsian and Böhmean vitalism and mysticism in the sixteenth and early seven-teenth; Pietism in the late seventeenth and early eighteenth; Counter-En-lightenment, *Sturm und Drang,* and Romanticism in the late eighteenth and nineteenth centuries—all are examples of such antitheses to dominant systems of university philosophy. It does not much matter whether the greatest thinkers—Nicholas, Leibniz, Kant—were professors or not; they kept these antithetical elements in hand, and not only harmonized them for a while, but gave each a new strength for its next appearance.

I have expanded on this fact largely to exemplify the kinds of social forces in philosophy that a historian of a national philosophy must be interested in. We should now turn to more specific and limited factors of this kind which have, I think, had effects on German philosophy in various periods. I shall mention twelve, the first eight of which are relevant to the periods to be discussed in this book.

1. The lack of universities in Germany until the fourteenth century required German thinkers to go to Italy and France for their education. We can hardly speak of German philosophy except as a series of isolated episodes before that time. Only in Cologne after Albertus Magnus can we speak of schools of thought being built around continuing concerns and maintained by self-perpetuating bodies of scholars establishing a style and tradition, as these can be found in Paris, Chartres, Padua, and Oxford. Hence German philosophy before the thirteenth century tends to be idiosyncratic and discontinuous, or to merge without any trace of national identity into the general stream of European thought.

2. When universities were founded in the fourteenth century, historical accidents (which we shall study in Chapter V) peopled them with dissi-

---

[8] "The monopoly of the schools" and "the interests of humanity," Kant calls them, in *Critique of Pure Reason,* Preface to 2nd ed., p. xxxii.

dents from the University of Paris, thereby favoring the development of a single line (it happened to be the *via moderna*) of scholastic philosophy. But the *via moderna* was not equally favored everywhere; and where the *via moderna* competed side by side with the *via antiqua* for the same students, the two systems were organized almost as separate faculties in the universities.

3. The Protestant Reformation, initiated by followers of the *via moderna,* left Germany permanently divided into approximately equally strong religious sects, and these sects were politically protected because the lines of religious division coincided (generally) with political divisions. Political divisions exacerbated religious divisions; philosophical defenses of these religious differences generally left local political practices and abuses uncriticized and uncorrected, and philosophy was forced into a preoccupation with religious to the exclusion of political and moral questions. For a longer time than in other countries, philosophy remained an *ancilla theologiae,* a handmaiden to theology; in fact, it was *ancilla theologorum,* a handmaiden to quarreling theologians.

4. During much of the seventeenth century Germany was the battleground in long and devastating wars among its own princes. The wealth of the nation was destroyed; the German population was more than decimated by starvation and plague and rapine. Thus, during the most important formative years of modern philosophy in France, England, and Holland, Germany was doing little or nothing in philosophy, and did not begin to philosophize "in the modern manner" until nearly fifty years after Descartes' death. Battles won in England and France in the seventeenth century had to be fought anew in Germany in the eighteenth.

5. In few countries has the *furor theologorum* been less inhibited than in Germany. Religious wars, fought with both pen and sword, have been a major part of German history. But facts of political life in some states, especially those with large religious minorities and those in which the ruling family belonged to one confession and the populace to another, contributed to the development of a practical toleration which favored and was favored by ecumenical and irenic philosophical theologies. It is astonishing how little difference there has been in the philosophies associated with the Catholic, Lutheran, and Calvinist confessions, considering the bitterness of their opposition. There were, in fact, differences in the way philosophy was practiced by adherents of each—they had somewhat different interests and differences in tone—but there were few theological issues which made any significant difference within philosophy itself. Disputes about space and substance tended for a time to separate philosophers who held divergent beliefs about the Eucharist, but these differences were relatively minor compared to the much greater similarities among them all—similarities derived from the common use philosophers in all three confessions made of a common scholastic tradition throughout the seventeenth century. Most philosophers were also theologians, and their *ex officio* oppositions were on credal rather than philosophical issues.

6. The variety of religions in Germany from the sixteenth century onward had another effect. It was not only possible, it apparently was not

very difficult, for Germans to change from one church to another. Princes did so for the sake of a favorable marriage or a disputed inheritance. Academic men driven out of one university, when (as happened twice in Heidelberg within a short time) the civil government changed from one church party to another, simply migrated to a neighboring university where their adherence to one or the other of the churches was not held to incapacitate them for teaching. One remarkable effect of this was that there was little polarization of the intellectual life between a religious and an antireligious attitude. Germany did not produce many skeptics, free thinkers, and infidels. Unlike France, there was room enough in the complex of German churches—if not in any single one of them—for a considerable variety of religious attitudes, and dissenters were pushed not in the direction of an anti-Christian or an anti-clerical attitude, but simply into another church.

7. The variety of political forms in Germany had a somewhat similar effect. A man persecuted in one state could find refuge in another just a few miles away, as a philosophical skeptic of a triumphant political ideology in France could not. This situation in Germany, because it was not altogether too uncomfortable, discouraged deep and critical political thinking. Germany produced as few keen and radical critics of government as of religion, and for much the same reason. Religious and political respectability was to be found even among the leaders of the eighteenth-century Enlightenment in Germany. Elsewhere I have described this unique feature and attempted to explain it:

To see why the French had *philosophes* instead of philosophers in the English or German (and modern) sense, we should briefly compare the intellectual and social situation in France with that in England and Germany about 1750. England had had her revolution; Germany was not to have hers for another century; France was moving towards hers. Germany had had her religious awakening in Pietism, and a Pietistic patina spread over almost all of German culture; England was beginning to have (in Methodism) a popular, emotional, and anti-intellectualistic religious awakening; France had had hers, in Jansenism, but it was now a thing of the past. Put these two facts about each country together, and one can go far towards understanding the characteristics of the intellectual life of each country. In France, religious and political dissent was practiced and persecuted; in England, practiced but not persecuted; in Germany, not practiced and therefore not persecuted (except in rare instances).[9]

8. The role of dynastic accidents is large on the stage of German philosophy. There was little in the relationship of France and England to Germany, through much of their history, to make Germans want to think like Frenchmen or Englishmen when to do so meant to think as a Baconian, a Cartesian, a Lockean, or a Newtonian—in a word, to think like a modern man. But when in the eighteenth century there was a Francophile on the throne of Prussia and one man was both Elector of Hanover and King of

---

[9] *Eighteenth-Century Philosophy* (New York: The Free Press, 1966), p. 9.

England, and each established a university or an academy, the way was open through which Germany entered the modern, Newtonian, Voltairean, world.

The foregoing historical factors, in my opinion, deeply influenced the style, content, and direction of philosophy in Germany in the thousand years ending about 1800. The philosophy of the nineteenth and twentieth centuries presents an even more complicated phenomenon, and it is harder to estimate the contribution of various historical and cultural factors to its later course. But the following four seem to be among the most portentous, for good or ill.

9. National enthusiasm against Napoleon, led by Romantic patriots, became naturally associated with a rejection of the ideas and ideals of the Enlightenment, which were commonly identified with those of the French Revolution and the Empire (though it is hard to see how they could be converted into *both*). German thinking became conspicuously and self-consciously nationalistic even before there was a nation. It turned against the cosmopolitan and largely nonpolitical ideals of the German Enlightenment and immunized itself against the ideas dominant in the Western countries. A political opposition to France became an intellectual opposition to the eighteenth century. French and English philosophical ideas, which had deeply influenced German thought first in the eighteenth century, were vehemently renounced in the nineteenth. What we shall call the Counter-Enlightenment of the eighteenth century, an opposition movement to the main line of thought from Leibniz to Kant, came to victory in the nineteenth.

10. The political system, after some simplification, survived the attack and temporary domination by Napoleon, but what was left did not at first free itself from the abuses characteristic of the *ancien régime*. The continuing political situation of *Kleinstaaterei* was little improved by the elimination of the feeblest states, because the one center of unity, the Empire, was destroyed at the same time; the units became larger, but no more representative of the whole. Nonconstitutional monarchies did not provide an environment favorable to the Romantic enthusiasms for liberty and German unity which Napoleon had stirred up and which destroyed his German system. Metternich was no more what young Germans wanted than Napoleon had been. Constitutional freedom and national unity were delayed, and the price eventually paid for the latter was a weakening of the ideals and instrumentalities for the former. The unification of the Reich in 1870, as it was actually accomplished, was predicated upon the failure of the Revolution of 1848. Liberal political thought and criticism were repressed by the political system established by the Congress of Vienna, and though the Metternichian system and the Carlsbad Decrees were opposed up to 1848, Germans came to see themselves as political failures and prided themselves on Germany as the land of poets and philosophers and musicians. Novalis' epigram, "To the French, God has given the land, to the English the sea, to the Germans only the air," gave voice to a political disillusionment which favored the conjunction of "the greatest boldness of

thought [and] the most obedient character," which Madame de Stael saw in Germany. What in the twentieth century has been called an "internal emigration," viz., a political alienation of philosophers, occurred with a high degree of self-consciousness and even pride. Those who did not share the popular illusions of a land of poets and thinkers,—Feuerbach, Marx, and Heine among them—emigrated either intellectually or geographically.[10]

11. In the Wilhelmine and Bismarkian period this internal emigration of philosophical thinkers from the problems of parvenue government and the consequences of the industrial revolution continued. Unlike the defeated Germany of the first decade of the nineteenth century, and the divided Germany of the next half-century, the German Reich at the end of the century was a glittering success, with a tame and well-fed intellectual elite. Wagner, no longer a revolutionary, was a hero; Nietzsche, who despised the new Reich,[11] furnished it with a vague but inspirational vocabulary so heady that his contempt for the "Berlin system" was overlooked. While socialist thought flourished in some universities and on the periphery of others, *Kathedersozialismus*—"socialism of the chair"—was not sufficiently effective to strengthen social democracy against being swept away by militarism and attempts at empire-building; and the institutions and practices of democracy were not sufficiently strong to inspire the respect of many philosophers who might have buttressed it.

After the defeat of Germany in 1918 had brought about a political revolution for which neither the people nor their institutions had been prepared, philosophers outside the universities despised the Weimar Republic and wrote widely read and even more widely quoted books of blood and doom against it. The intellectuals in the universities were unable or unwilling to provide support for the new regime to enable it to withstand the Hitlerian attack, and those who did try to maintain the liberal ideals

---

[10] Heine's awareness of the explosive hazards of a nonalienated German philosophy is eloquently expressed in his *Religion and Philosophy in Germany* (trans. John Snodgrass [1882], Boston: The Beacon Press, 1959), especially pt. III. "German philosophy is an important fact; it concerns the whole human race, and only our latest descendants will be in a position to decide whether we are to be praised or blamed for having first worked out our philosophy and afterwards our revolution. It seems to me that a methodical people, such as we are, must begin with the reformation, must then occupy itself with systems of philosophy, and that only after their completion could it pass to the political revolution. [The systems of Kant, Fichte, and Schelling] served to develop revolutionary forces that only await their time to break forth and fill the world with terror and with admiration . . . Smile not at my counsel, at the counsel of a dreamer, who warns you against Kantians, Fichteans, Philosophers of Nature. Smile not at the fantasy of one who foresees in the region of reality the same outburst of revolution that has taken place in the region of intellect. The thought precedes the deed as the lightning the thunder . . . When ye hear a crashing such as never before has been heard in the world's history, then know that at last the German thunderbolt has fallen. At this commotion the eagles will drop dead from the skies and the lions in the farthest waste of Africa will bite their tails and creep into their royal lairs. There will be played in Germany a drama compared to which the French Revolution will seem but an innocent idyl" (pp. 158, 159, 160).

[11] Nietzsche in almost all his books, but especially *Morgenröte* §§ 167, 190–207, and 481; *Joyful Wisdom*, §§ 146 and 357.

without which that government could not survive were forced into silence, conformity, exile, or death. The Thousand Year Reich caused a thirteen-year hiatus in the history of German philosophy.

12. Alone among the great powers, Germany achieved its highest technological development and political integration under a regime barbarous in its anti-intellectualism and in its trampling upon humane values. Not only was philosophy *gleichgeschaltet* (coordinated),[12] there were "philosophers," and even some philosophers, who had helped prepare the way for Hitler through their own hostility to democratic and liberal values. Intellectual scum floated to the surface and poisoned much of what was below it.

This is not the place to evaluate or even to describe what has happened in Germany since 1946. Let it suffice to say that German philosophers have returned to Germany or emerged out of silence; that walls between German thought and the West have come down while new ones have been erected to the East, and that once again German philosophy is a part of the republic of letters which, over eleven centuries, it had helped to found and support. But a history of its latest chapter is a task for the next generation, not this one.

I do not insist upon this brief listing of factors which have impinged upon German philosophical thought. Several of them may be debatable; some are so mixed up with others that different analysis might give a longer or a shorter list. And I do not mention at all the fact, alleged by many, that some of these may be products of a pattern of philosophical thought and *Weltanschauung* instead of factors in determining the *Weltanschauung* and the shape of philosophy. But each of them is typical of the kinds of events and circumstances which the historian of the national tradition in philosophy must keep in mind when he attempts to discern a national pattern in the philosophy of various periods; and the sequence of these conditions provides a continuity which would otherwise seem to be lost in the larger turnings and twistings of European philosophical thought as a whole.

The traditions so formed appear in the history of philosophy in various ways. There are men who are remembered because their thought was the self-conscious expression of the most effective of these factors in their time; in them, philosophy is, in Hegel's language, their culture come to self-consciousness. These are the men who are remembered not for any originality that speaks to us across the centuries, but for the exemplary manner

[12] Thus Gerhard Lehmann's *Die deutsche Philosophie der Gegenwart*, (Stuttgart: A. Kröner, 1943) a learned and informative book, does not treat of any important Jewish philosophers, but has a flattering chapter on Rosenberg. A good collection of documents on the *Gleichschaltung* of German philosophy is found in Léon Poliakow and Josef Wulf, *Das Dritte Reich und seine Denker* (Berlin: arani Verlag, 1959). An especially valuable brief study of the interlude is "German Philosophy and National Socialism," by Helmut Kuhn in *Encyclopedia of Philosophy* (New York: Macmillan, 1967), III, 309–316.

in which they gave expression to the needs and purposes of their time. Such a typical spokesman for his age was Melanchthon; perhaps Fichte can be seen playing a similar role in his. There are others who are remembered for precisely the opposite reason because they rebelled against their time and fought the conditions which were shaping the thought of their fellows. They were "[men] of tomorrow and the day after tomorrow . . . in contradiction to their today"; they were "the bad conscience of their time" in Nietzsche's memorable description.[13] Among the philosophers who can be best understood as such critics and opponents of the established cultural values were Erasmus, Thomasius, and Nietzsche himself. Finally, there are those who were a great deal of both: men who were at home in their time, but sensitive to questionable issues which they themselves brought to full consciousness. They were thus discoverers of problems for their time and their followers, and of solutions which would be the groundwork for new problems and new solutions in coming generations. Of this most noble type, one thinks necessarily of Nicholas of Cusa, Leibniz, and Kant. These are men who are heroes of the history of philosophy; yet they are those least understood in the categories of a national history of philosophy. It is no discredit to the greatness of German philosophy to say that they are somehow diminished if seen as belonging, by anything but accident, to Germany. It is by its greatest men that the thousand-year labor of philosophy in Germany is justified, and what can be explained historically, and *a fortiori* what can be explained in the categories of a *national* history of philosophy, is not what is loftiest in their achievement.

A history of the philosophy of a single nation (unless it be Greece) requires a radical shift from the style and pattern of the history of philosophy in general. Some will disapprove of this shift, but there is no way to avoid it, and it is my hope that it will bring some interesting and generally neglected features of the history of philosophy to light.

It is a shift from one kind of continuity to another. Ordinarily the history of philosophy is a history of philosophical problems and ideas embodied in the work of the two or three dozen most important philosophers, far apart from each other both spatially and temporally. In a national history of philosophy, on the other hand, one must deal with many more philosophers, few of whom can be considered world figures. The continuities of a national history, therefore, are spatial and temporal as well as intellectual. Because, at any time, the main burden of the history of philosophy may be borne by philosophers who are outside this spatio-temporal continuum of any national history, there is also a different kind of discontinuity which must be accepted in such a history. Sometimes the chief actors in philosophy are off the stage of any one national history, and insistence upon spatio-temporal continuities leads to an underestimate of their role, while insistence upon their intellectual importance distorts the shape of a national history.[14] I have tried to meet this problem by treating the leading

13 *Beyond Good and Evil*, § 212.
14 An outstanding example of such distortion is in Émile Boutroux's *La Philosophie allemande au xviie siècle* (Paris: Vrin, 1948), where Leibniz is the only German philosopher who gets more than passing mention. The opposite distortion is found in a recent history of Kant's ideas, in which Hume is not mentioned at all!

philosophers in other countries who influenced German philosophy as well-known men whose thought is familiar to my readers. No doubt this has led to some distortion too; for example, I have had to give more space to Cornelius Martini than to Suarez, more to Joachim Jungius than to Descartes, more to Lambert than to Hume, though there can be little doubt that these "foreigners" had more influence on the go of German philosophy than these natives did.

If the reader will bear these considerations in mind, I may hope that such incongruities, unexpected discontinuities, and unsuspected continuities will not throw him off the track of the long story I am about to tell.

One
German Philosophy Before The Reformation

II

From the Beginnings to Albertus Magnus

The first thinker born in Germany and known to the historian of philosophy provides us with an instance of the kinds of problems that are met again and again in writing a history of German philosophy in the Middle Ages. St. Ambrose was born in Trier in 340, educated in Rome and consecrated as Bishop of Milan, and died in 397. In his writings the philosophical cannot be separated or even clearly distinguished from the theological; he was not concerned to think new thoughts but to bring to bear upon Christianity the lessons learned from classical writers and philosophers, and though born in the region we now know as Germany, there is no other reason than this accident of birth to consider him German.

The foregoing pattern will apply to most German philosophers of the next nine centuries, and of each of them we have to ask, in a history of German philosophy: Was he a philosopher? If so, was his philosophy original? And even: Was he German? Of many of them we shall have to answer one or more of these questions in the negative. Until we come to men of whom affirmative answers to all three can be given, and until they form a tradition of agreement with each other or of development of one from another or at the very least a polemical group, we shall have only intermittent philosophic episodes which happen to have occurred on German soil or in the minds of German-born thinkers living in France or Italy. But we shall not have anything properly called German philosophy.

German philosophy, in this respect, is far from unique. If we were writing a history of British, or even of French, philosophy, we should have to wait almost as long into the Christian era for the first dawning of national traditions in philosophy which could be handled historically and not merely in the manner of a chronicle. But though we should not succumb to the patriotic illusions of some German historians of philosophy who see in Hugo of St. Victor, for example, essential and peculiar German traits—and certainly not to those of German propagandists who find Meister Eckhart to be a forerunner of National Socialism—neither should we think that philosophizing began in Germany without precedent.

Even in the thirteenth century it is not easy always to decide whether a man was a philosopher, whether he was a good (that is, to some extent, original) philosopher, or whether he was German by anything more than accident of birth. This last question becomes easy to answer only in the fourteenth century, when the universities were established and gave professional homes in Germany to German-born thinkers; only then does "German philosophy" begin to denote a corpus and a tradition.

Another reason why a history of German philosophy in the period before the fourteenth century is intermittent and episodic lies in the intellectual and theological unity of Europe. Of course there was no political entity that could be called Germany, with boundaries approximately those of what we call Germany today. But much more important than this is the fact that until the end of the ninth century there was not even much regionalism anywhere in the cultural life of continental Europe. The one viable institution was the Church, and what was not in the Church (for instance, eastern Germany) was not a part of Europe either culturally or politically, except as a threat.

Ideas now know no walls that keep them long within the region of their birth, and the history of philosophy of any country cannot be understood without constant attention to what is being done in other countries, even though each has its own traditions which predominate and determine the use that will be made of foreign importations. But in Medieval Europe there were few walls of any kind—not even linguistic barriers—and the intellectual tradition of the small literate population of one region was almost exactly the same as that of any other. Hence what we call "German philosophy," simply because we have no better name for it, is at first hardly more than a series of episodes in what is now Germany, whose intellectual connections must be found in what was going on in other regions. In this respect, German philosophy was even more of an accidental conglomeration of apparently isolated thoughts than French philosophy or English philosophy, and European philosophy would probably have been little different from St. Ambrose to St. Albert the Great had the region between the Rhine and the Oder been a wasteland; in fact the Rhineland itself could have been empty, without serious loss to philosophy.

With these forebodings of what is to come, let us return for a moment to St. Ambrose. Though he adapted Cicero's *De officiis* to Christian purposes, making the reward of mundane virtue to lie in eternal blessedness and not the Stoic happiness of Tully, his principal contribution to the history of philosophy was a direct product of his pastoral work, though an unphilosophical head could not have accomplished this piece of pastoral work: It was St. Ambrose's sermons which did more than any other one thing to bring Augustine into the Christian fold. Thus was brought into the Christian intellectual tradition the most formidable philosophical mind of the first millennium of Christianity. The conversion of Augustine from the Manichaean heresy and Neoplatonism to Christianity was as significant for the fifth to the twelfth centuries as the Christian use of Aristotle was for the thirteenth to the sixteenth centuries.

For though Augustine no longer considered himself a Platonist after he became a Christian, or indeed a philosopher at all—because he had transcended the limits of the natural philosophic intellect—he claimed that Plato had approached more nearly to Christianity than any other classical writer, and he could not help thinking as a Platonist in theology. Until Europe was ready to learn from another equally great classical philosopher, to the extent that it was able and willing to use philosophy it used Plato, and in so doing it had the comforting precedent and irresistible authority of the greatest of the Fathers.

The wealth of classical learning and the skill in classical philosophizing made available to Europe by Boethius (d. 524) was hardly less than that which it owed to Augustine. But it is significant that the Platonism of Augustine seems to have blinded Europe to the Aristotelianism present in Boethius. Boethius' thought was almost as Aristotelian as it was Platonic, but he was not so good a Christian as Augustine, and in his imprisonment he found consolation in philosophy, not in anything specifically Christian. But Boethius had translated parts of Aristotle's *Organon* into Latin and had written a commentary on Porphyry and thus made available to Europe these methodologies. No one seems to have noticed, however—incredible though it may seem to us—how much metaphysics that was not Platonic was included in Boethius' writings, and six centuries later European thinkers had to settle by themselves issues which Aristotle had already settled. Boethius was the first of the Latin philosophers to be translated into German, in the eleventh century, when the knowledge of Latin had fallen so low that even he was no longer understandable in the original. But for centuries his *Consolation of Philosophy* was the most widely read book; and together with the works of his pupil Cassiodorus (d. 565?), who formalized the liberal arts under the rubrics *quadrivium* (the four theoretical ways to wisdom: arithmetic, astronomy, geometry, and music), practical philosophy (ethics, politics, and economics), and the *trivium* (grammar, rhetoric, and logic), this book was a central part of the curriculum of the Middle Ages.

Pope Gregory the Great (d. 604), however, made Christianity available to the lowliest by overthrowing, as superfluous, classic learning and philosophic dialectic. While, on the one hand, he popularized Augustine, on the other his break with pagan antiquity destroyed any conception of an independent philosophy from the seventh to the ninth century. Without his simplicism in liturgical matters, which appealed to the concrete imagist thinking of semi-barbarians and made it possible for them to enter into

Christian mysteries oblivious of how mysterious they were, perhaps Christianity could not have spread in Germany, which entered the fold of the Church only in the eighth century. But his simplicism, anti-intellectualism, and anti-philosophy characterized the age known, rightly or wrongly, as the Dark Ages. Learning fell to the lowest point in its up-and-down history, and nothing was left for the exiguous schooling of monks and priests except a little Latin, the encyclopedias of Isadore of Seville and Martianus Capella, and the *trivium* and a smattering of the *quadrivium* from Cassiodorus. Only the Irish monasteries in the West preserved the riches of antiquity for a later revival. The Church, which was later to claim philosophy as a handmaiden of theology, could and did succeed for two centuries in making all learning an *ancilla Ecclesiae* if not *ancilla theologiae* —for this was a depressed period even in theology.

When Charlemagne, in Aachen, established his schools at the beginning of the ninth century with the help of Alcuin, whom he brought over from Britain, they had two tasks instead of the one which the rudimentary schools of the preceding centuries had had. For though Charlemagne did not, perhaps, clearly discern the differences between the Church and his empire, the actual effect of his school reform was felt in the improved education not only of the clergy but of the political agents Charlemagne needed for his vast empire. The philosophical innocence of Gregorian ecclesiasticism proved incapable of meeting the demands of the new empire, and the indifference to the higher works of the mind made them inadequate to the manifold functions he assigned to the ecclesiastics and, hence, to his schools. The very name "Holy Roman Empire of the German Nation" suggests a complexity which was no longer compatible with Gregorianism in learning and Benedictinism in the management of the Church: it was sacred, not secular, but it was an empire, not a church; and it was German, but also Roman (and French), and it was Roman in both the classical and the Christian sense. Even the name seems to include several contradictions, but they were not seen:

In the early immature middle ages the very nature of Christianity and culture made men regard them as identical and co-extensive. . . . [The name 'Middle Ages'] could be used to signify the period which stands as an intermediate age between an epoch which had not yet arrived at such a conception of the world or such a program of culture, and an age which no longer took them into account.[1]

Escaping from the inhibitions of Benedictine practicality and Gregorian simplicism, the empire of Charlemagne enjoyed the brief period known as the Carolingian Renaissance. There was at least a temporary improvement in the schools attached to the great abbeys; there was a sudden blooming of secular literature and humane culture; there was even a little philosophy.

Alcuin's pupil, Rabanus Maurus, bishop of Mainz (b. Mainz, 776 or 784,

---

[1] Max Seidlmayer, *Currents of Medieval Thought with Special Reference to Germany* (Oxford: Basil Blackwell, 1960), p. 26.

d. 856), devoted himself to the improvement of clerical education and won the epithet *praeceptor Germaniae*. He engaged in what was perhaps the first philosophical debate in Germany. His opponent was a recalcitrant monk who had tried unsuccessfully to withdraw from Rabanus' abbey at Fulda. This monk, Gotescalc (Gottschalk) of Saxony (808–867 [?]), took Augustine's doctrine of predestination to mean, at least according to Gotescalc's opponents, that there was a double predestination, an election of some to heaven and some to damnation. We do not know exactly what he taught, since much of what he said has come down to us only through reports by his critics and the findings of various ecclesiastical courts, which presumably reported only what they condemned. But at least this much is certain: he accused his superiors of diverging from Augustine, and was so deeply convinced of predestination that much that the Church regarded as necessary to salvation he regarded as indifferent, as *adiaphora*. Rabanus thought that Gotescalc's teachings, which seem to have enjoyed a widespread and sympathetic audience among French, German, and even Italian theologians, threatened the Christian regimen and made Christian teaching futile. In his attack on the rebellious monk he had the help of a greater philosoper who had come into the Frankish kingdom from Britain, John Scotus Erigena, in his *De predestinatione* (851). But that the controversy was carried on with the help of such arguments as imprisonment, torture, and the burning of Gotescalc's books shows some of the difficulty Dame Philosophy had to face in that still barbarous land and time.

Rabanus' successor in the school at Fulda was Canidus (original name: Brunn), who has been given credit for the first philosophical proof in the Middle Ages for the existence of God: man knows that he stands at the apex of a hierarchy of natural being (mere existence, life, mind), but he also knows he is not omnipotent, as he would be if the natural hierarchy were the only reality; hence there must be a being who stands above him. This is an argument which is at least philosophic in spirit, even if not very convincing; it is one of the many forms of argument based upon the idea of the Great Chain of Being, or perhaps we should say it is an inversion of that metaphor.

The educational reforms introduced by Charlemagne and the humanistic culture which attended them did not last long in the regions east of the Rhine, which had not the advantage of having been long under the Latin influence. The intellectual and cultural consequences of the Carolingian reform were more significant and continuous in the western part of the Empire. By the time of the Treaty of Verdun (843)—which is perhaps as good a date as any to give for the origin of Germany as a political entity, since this Treaty marked the effective dismantling of Charlemagne's Empire by the splitting off of France—the difference between Tours and Paris, the principal French schools, and Fulda and St. Gallen is easily recognizable. The intellectual center of Europe moved from Aachen west, not east, though the tenth century is not a time of which either French or German philosophers need be proud. In St. Gallen, Notker Labeo (952–1022) translated Boethius and Capella and some Aristotle into Old High German "out of love of my students," who were no longer able to read them in Latin.[2] The liberal arts were hardly adequate to the most necessary business of the Church and the warring kingdoms; by the twelfth century apparently all the monks at St. Gallen were illiterate. This decline in literacy did not go hand in hand with an increase in piety; the Cluniac reforms, which did much to revive the religious life of France, were resisted in Germany out of love of "the good old days" of easy living in the abbeys and monasteries, which provided a refuge from the hard life of the villeins without requiring also a renunciation of its delectable temptations.

The few Germans with ecclesiastical aspirations, religious ideals, or intellectual interests had to go to France for their education—a practice to be continued until the establishment of the German universities in the fourteenth century. The most notable of these was Hugo of Blankenburg, known to history as Hugo of St. Victor (1096–1140 or 1141), and certainly one of the most attractive and likable of medieval thinkers. He received his elementary education in the monastery of Hamersleben, Saxony, but spent most of his life in the Abbey of St. Victor in Paris, where he composed his *Didascalicon* (ca. 1126).[3] The *Didascalicon* is a manual of the liberal arts, carefully distinguished from theology, but oriented according to Neoplatonic ideals of knowledge and thus leading to theology according to the program of St. Anselm (b. 1033): *credo ut intelligam*—" I believe in order that I may understand." Hugo belongs to the history of early scholasticism, with a clear distinction between what could be seen by the *oculus carnis* and *oculus rationis* and what could be seen only by the *oculus meditationis* had it not been blinded by sin.[4] Having lost the original knowledge of his Creator, man works himself upward through five stages: denial, doubt, conjecture, faith, and knowing. The content of faith is capable of being known; we can believe only what, in some sense, we can know, for faith is not object-less. Faith is as much an act of will as it is of cognition; but it is directed to what can be known. Reason cannot comprehend God; faith is beyond reason. In the order of cognition, faith is less than knowledge, though in terms of merit it is not below knowledge. The objects of knowledge which can be objects of faith are things that can be known indirectly, such as the proper interpretation of a text or a miracle; or they are

[2] Notker, it must be remembered, was not just translating from Latin into German; he was putting his own language to new uses, and he had to invent new words or put old words together in ways in which they had never before been combined, in order to get the meanings of Boethius and Aristotle. Rudolf Eucken (*Geschichte der philosophischen Terminologie* [Leipzig, 1879], pp. 116–118) gives enthusiastic praise to his success, and points out that when philosophy was later written in German, many neologisms had to be invented again since later writers did not know Notker's vocabulary; but many of their decisions conformed, quite independently, to Notker's. Among Notker's happy inventions Eucken cites: *begrifen* (New High German *begreifen* = *comprehendere*), *gewizeda* (NHG *Gewissen* = *conscientia*), *sinnig ding* (NHG *sinnliches Ding* = *substantia sensibilis*).

[3] *Eruditionis didascalicae libri septem*. English translation by Jerome Taylor: *Didascalicon* (New York: Columbia University Press, 1961).

[4] *De sacramentis christianae fidei*. English translation by R. J. Deferrari: *Sacraments of the Christian Faith*, (Cambridge, Mass.: Medieval Academy of America, 1951), bk. I, pt. vi, § 14, p. 103.

things that can be known or comprehended by the *oculus meditationis* by their very presence to the mind.[5] God can be known in this way, by his presence to us in a mystical revelation which is beyond even faith (for faith is the evidence of things not seen); God can be seen. Direct experience of God, therefore, can answer questions left unanswered by the dialectic of *sic et non*.[6]

Yet because Hugo has an essentially cognitive conception of the contents of faith (i.e., that which is an object of faith can be also an object of knowledge), the rationalism of earlier scholasticism is little changed by the fact that the highest form of knowledge of God is mystical, intuitive, rather than intellectual, dialectical. The major difference between faith and knowledge lies in their psychological foundations: faith and knowledge differ in the manner in which they involve the will and the emotions, not with respect to their objects. While it seems odd to speak of an unemotional mysticism, which would be needed if a sharp distinction between faith and knowledge is to be made, the vision of God is a cognitive act; that it elevates man and fills his heart with peace and joy is true, but this does not mean that it is itself an emotional ecstasy. In Hugo, therefore, the division and contrast of rational and mystical theology, of scholasticism and mysticism, has not yet been made.

Hugo had a wide influence and raised the school of St. Victor to an eminent position. But his influence was in France, not in Germany. He was German only in the sense that St. Ambrose was:

The man who finds his homeland sweet is still a tender beginner; he to whom every soil is as his native one is already strong; but he is perfect to whom the entire world is as a foreign land . . . From boyhood I have dwelt on foreign soil, and I know with what grief the mind takes leave of the narrow hearth of a peasant's hut; and I know, too, how frankly it afterwards disdains marble firesides and panelled rooms.[7]

If philosophy be the critique of abstractions current in one's culture, as Whitehead defines it, two conditions seem to be necessary for its continuous growth, though a philosophy may arise sporadically without either. These two conditions seem incompatible, but they can exist together on different levels: an outward peace, and an inward struggle. The former is necessary if the difficult work of philosophy is to be done; the latter is necessary if it is to be recognized that there is work to be done. Internal turmoil is the cause or the effect of the clash of ideals in society, the resolution of which is one of the works of philosophy. Without this, there may be mystical contemplation or undisciplined speculation, but the occasion for dialectic —the soul's converse or argument with itself, as Socrates called it—is miss-

---

[5] *Ibid.*, bk. I. pt. x, §§ 2, 3, pp. 167–169.
[6] In the use of *sic et non* in its simplest form—collecting contradictory sentences of the Fathers and reconciling them—Abelard was anticipated by Bernold of Constance (d. 1100). On Bernold, see Martin Grabmann, *Geschichte der scholastischen Methode* (Freiburg: Herder, 1911), I, 234–239; Grabmann calls him "one of the most significant theological writers of Germany in the last decades of the eleventh century" (p. 234).
[7] *Didascalicon*, trans. Taylor, p. 101.

ing. In the Germanies of the eleventh century there was little outward peace, and what struggle there was in men's souls that did not find expression in war and politics was quieted in piety instead of articulated in philosophy.

Consider the wandering scholars called *philosophi* or *peripatetici* who came to Germany from Italy in the eleventh century, like the Sophists who came to Athens in the fourth Century B.C. They practiced their dialectical arts to the wonderment and puzzlement of the people; they argued by the craft of dialectic against theological dogmas such as the Virgin Birth and immortality, and thus brought even dialectic, a part of the *trivium*, into disrepute. When Anselm the Peripatetic appeared in Germany (we know that he was in Basel, Augsburg, Bamberg, and Mainz) about the middle of the century, there emerged the problem that had not been important in Germany before this, but one that was to dominate its thought henceforth, namely, that of the respective claims of faith and reason. The German response was typically to take refuge in Gregorian simplicism again, in Cluniac and Cistercian asceticism, or in a morbid sense of sin. Otloh of St. Emmeram (1010–1070), a monk in Regensburg, and Manegold (1060–1104), of the monastery at Lautenbach, have left records of their struggle with the doubts instilled by the Peripatetic dialecticians. Both tried to close their minds to dialectic and took refuge in prayer and meditation; they accused the dialecticians of putting Boethius above the Scriptures, and they ascribed to the devil the variety of philosophies which puzzled and plagued them. They sought answers in the simplicity of Christian faith when philosophy created rather than stilled their doubts: and they rejected philosophy and worldly wisdom as useless and dangerous to Christians. Otloh, who has left us an autobiography (*Liber de tentionibus suis*), did try to answer his doubts with rational proofs of the existence of God, but they were not strong enough for or proper to a monk who had put away worldly wisdom. Manegold, however, is remembered for his casuistry (which showed high dialectical skill worthy of a Peripatetic dialectician) in the investiture conflict.

But in the eleventh century, as in every other, it was useless to defend Christianity against reason when it was possible—through the work of men like Anselm, Hugo, and Abelard—to put reason to work for Christianity. The *peripatetici* had no lasting influence, and scholasticism—natural reason, working through dialectic, in the service of faith—triumphed during the twelfth and thirteenth centuries. In this, however, one danger had to be avoided if heresy was not to be committed: natural reason had to remain the servant of theology, not its master or judge. Dialectic had repeatedly to be disciplined to prevent it from completely rationalizing theology and changing it into natural metaphysics; rationalism, polytheism, and pantheism were constant dangers to dialecticians who wished to remain orthodox. In the twelfth century, however, mysticism and something like humanism were open as escapes from dialectic which might back theology to the wall.

Humanism is not the name of a philosophy in the Middle Ages, though some thinkers who turned away from dialectic subtleties to consider man's actual state, or to enjoy what this world offers in intellectual and cultural goods, seem to be ancestors of the later humanists who rejected dialectic as an instrument of theology when they did not reject theology itself. A good example of such a protohumanist is Otto of Freising (1114–1158), an uncle of Frederick I. Hugo of St. Victor may have been one of his teachers in Paris, and at Chartres Otto came into contact with theologians imbued with the love of classical antiquity. In the controversy over universals, in which every schoolman had to participate since decisions on theological questions (such as the Trinity and original sin) depended upon the theory of the relation of the one to the many (as Socrates described the analogous problem), Otto seems to have been a moderate realist, but his position is subject to some doubt, and legend has it that he renounced his theory on his deathbed. But Otto is well remembered for two certain accomplishments. First, he introduced into Germany for the first time the *logica nova*, that is, the study of logic based on the whole of Aristotle's *Organon* and not merely on the parts that had been translated into Latin by Boethius and into German by Notker (*logica vetus*). The translations he introduced were probably imported from the south of Italy, though he erroneously believed they were by Boethius. They became widely known in Germany, Otto having established a school for their study in Freising. This may help explain the fact that Germany was in the forefront of the Aristotelian movement in the thirteenth century. The *Organon* was all Otto knew of Aristotle; it was Plato who was for him "the philosopher."

Since he knew none of Aristotle's metaphysical writings, Otto took his metaphysical teachings from Augustine, Scotus Erigena, and Gilbert of Poiret, who may have been one of his teachers. The result was a somewhat unoriginal mixture of Aristotelian and Neoplatonic doctrines. Second, Otto was the greatest historian in medieval Germany. His *Chronicle*, or *History of the Two Cities* (the title is sometimes translated *Chronicle of Universal History*),[8] was written in the years 1143 to 1146, and its philosophy is based largely on Augustine's conception in *The City of God*. Not only is Otto an important source of historical information and a naive but earnest historian of philosophy; his concern with the struggles between the Hohenstaufens and the popes was motivated by deep philosophical consideration of the "two cities" confronting each other; he did not write like a member of the warring family—though his pride in family and nation becomes evident in his later *Deeds of Frederick Barbarossa*.

If it be true that the philosophy of history flourishes only when the historical record itself becomes unintelligible because it conflicts with historical expectations—when, in short, historical evils require a new theodicy—then the times required a philosophy of history like Otto's. For Otto faced the breakdown of the Carolingian synthesis of *imperium* and *sacerdotium* (see p. 22); the Church and the Empire, the two swords of God, had become, in the investiture conflict, the arms of opposing forces, of the City of God and the City of Man. It was essential to re-establish an alliance between them.

[8] Translated by C. C. Mierow (New York: Columbia University Press, 1928).

Otto thought that the Empire had a divine mission to protect the Church, which was its superior; but he feared that the Church would destroy the Empire and thus itself be left helpless. Before Dante, he held to the ideal of universal peace secured through a single monarch serving Christian purposes, but actual history made him deeply pessimistic, and he foresaw the end of the world if the papacy won in its conflict with the Empire. In his Ghibelline conception of the state, Otto has been seen as a forerunner of Hegel and other characteristic German philosophers of history.

Otto's concern with this world and its practical problems, however, was not common in the philosophical thought at this time. More common was degeneration into an arid dialectic which was to give scholasticism a bad name in future centuries. The earliest important antidote to this desiccation was not practical worldly concern, but the warmth of mysticism. Though the mystics themselves were often in actual heresy, and were even more often suspect simply because they could not be counted on to conform to the traditions of ecclesiastical discipline, most of the great schoolmen thought of dialectic and mysticism as complementary. For them, mystical experience, or at least acts of profound and direct contemplative faith, were either the beginning or the end of their philosophic exercises. The philosophy in question in the twelfth century was, of course, Platonic or Neoplatonic, on the authority of Augustine and Boethius, and its method was the dialectic based principally on the *Prior Analytics* of Aristotle, as this was known through Boethius. Internal criticism of this philosophy on the problem of universals had forced changes from the extreme realism of Anselm and William of Champeaux to the conceptualism of Abelard; but there was no serious difficulty experienced by the early scholastics in making a transition from reason to faith since reason had been infused with faith from the beginning (*Credo ut intelligam*).

Hugo may be mentioned again not merely because he was, accidentally, a German, but because he was so typical of the argument of twelfth-century scholasticism. "Philosophy," he says, "is the discipline which investigates comprehensively the ideas of all things human and divine," where "human" refers to the mechanical arts and "divine" to the theoretical and practical (moral) arts (not theology). But because of the philosophy he embraces, philosophy is destined from the beginning to serve in fact a theological aim; for Hugo also gives another definition of philosophy which he thinks is perfectly compatible with the one just quoted: it is the love "of that Wisdom in which the form of the perfect Good stands fixed"[9]—a Boethian statement of the Christian interpretation of the *logos*.

The transition from the secular to the sacred arts, from philosophy to theology, from reason to faith, from intellectual analysis to mystical synthesis, as found in Hugo and most Christian philosophers of the twelfth century was altogether too simple to satisfy the more stringent demands made on the Church by the momentous development of philosophy in the thirteenth. I refer to the rediscovery of the whole Aristotle, a philosopher

[9] *Didascalicon*, trans. Taylor, pp. 51, 183.

whose teaching could not be claimed to have been infused with faith. Putting Aristotle in the service of Christianity was the greatest accomplishment of the thirteenth century, and in this a German played for the first time a significant role in the history of European philosophy.

The First Wave of Aristotelianism

Europe hitherto had known only Aristotle the logician; even Otto of Freising had thought of Plato as the philosopher in the pair of men he thought were fellow pupils of Socrates. Those who thought of Aristotle as a philosopher did so because Neoplatonic writings were falsely ascribed to him.

One effect of the Crusades was to upset the complacency of Europe by bringing it into invidious contrast with the thought and culture of Islam. In science, medicine, and the amenities of life, Western Europe suddenly and to its surprise found itself backward. Whatever we may think of our ancestors of that time, they certainly had not seen themselves as just waiting around for the Renaissance. Their intellectual self-confidence received a shock when they saw how little they knew compared to their neighbors. In appropriating the riches of the South and East, if they did not find the Holy Grail, they at least discovered the products of an uninterrupted intellectual tradition which was older than their own. The most important of these were the Arabic translations and commentaries on Aristotle and original scientific works. The latter, perhaps the easiest to appreciate and assimilate, were the first to be translated into Latin, largely in Spain where the two cultures were closest together.[10] Then came the works of Aristotle and commentaries by Avicenna and Averroes; and about the same time there began to flow from South Italy translations of Aristotle made directly from the Greek instead of the Arabic. The Aristotle thus presented was no mere logician, and not a Neoplatonic philosopher either. His scientific writings were immeasurably superior to the poor efforts of the northern Europeans—so far superior to them that it is almost incredible that two centuries later they would prove to be a hindrance to the work of Europeans. This part of Aristotle's work was welcomed because it had no rivals and it filled a vacuum.

Those of Aristotle's writings which had direct theological import, however, did have rivals in the current scholastic philosophy of the Church. His *Physics* was condemned in Paris in 1209, and in 1215 the *Metaphysics* was banned, while the *Logic* was required and the *Ethics* permitted. But the prohibitions were not observed. By 1230 Arnold of Saxony had composed an entire encyclopedia based on Aristotle's writings on nature, and the use of the books was so widespread that efforts were made to extend the ban from Paris to other schools. In 1231 Pope Gregory IX appointed a commission to censor Aristotle's works and eliminate their errors, so that the remainder could be used with safety; but nothing seems to have been

10 Some of the translations were by Germans, e.g., Hermannus Alemanus in Toledo.

done by this commission. In 1263 Urban IV renewed the original prohibition, and in 1277 the Paris school of Aristotelians was condemned[11] in such a way that the teachings of Thomas Aquinas, who had just died, were likewise made suspect. But all in vain; Aristotle triumphed.

The Averroists in the arts faculty at Paris claimed to be the impartial interpreters of Aristotle. When they found heretical teachings in Aristotle, such as the doctrine of the eternity of the world, they claimed that they were merely pointing out what was the teaching of philosophers working without the aid of revelation. They were interpreted to mean, however, that there were two kinds of truth, philosophical and theological, and that something could be true philosophically and false theologically. This dualism of truths is either a triviality or an absurdity, depending upon the way one takes it. It could even be made to subserve scholastic functions if it was thought of as a way of pointing out the impotence of reason working without revelation—a line of thought to be exploited in the fourteenth century; and it was a sound principle for the historical reconstruction of Aristotle's philosophy, which had not been formulated for Christian apologetic purposes.

While such Franciscans as Alexander Hales (d. 1245) and St. Bonaventure (d. 1274) took cognizance of Aristotelianism but remained true to their Augustinian heritage, it was the Dominicans in Cologne who established an orthodox Christian Aristotelianism. Their teaching was that the exercise of natural reason led up to the truths of faith which could be known only by revelation. Thus natural reason could prove the existence of God, but revelation was necessary for us to know, for example, the Incarnation. Once again philosophy was *ancilla theologiae* but, as such, subject to direction and correction by faith and autonomous and independent only where no issue of faith was raised. Still, there were those philosophical arguments in Aristotle which the Church could not accept; the Christian Aristotelian's response here was to say that they were not good even as philosophy. Instead of two kinds of truth which might conflict and yet be true, as the Averroists were accused of believing, there was only one truth, for faith and reason had to be consistent; even though faith went beyond the things of reason, it did not go against them, and in case of apparent conflict, the heretical doctrine was not true even philosophically.

Just to say this, of course, required no philosophical talent. But to show where Aristotle was wrong and how he fell into error, to separate the arguments of Aristotle that led to faith and were good from those that did not and were false—all this required the talent of philosophers of the first rank. The Church for the first time since it had assimilated Alexandrian and Athenian elements was faced with a body of teachings independent of its own doctrines, of a magnitude and profundity and accuracy that nothing could rival, and of an authority that could not be ignored. In dealing with it, the Church had to develop talents and skills that history showed would

---

[11] The condemnation exists in English translation in Joseph Katz and R. H. Weinhartner, *Philosophy in the West* (New York: Harcourt Brace, 1965), pp. 532–543.

not long remain humble servants of her own purposes.[12] Philosophy as an independent and autonomous intellectual discipline concerning things of this world was about to be born again. Aristotle was its father, and Albertus Magnus the midwife.

Albertus Magnus

Albert, known in his lifetime as Albertus Coloniensis or Albertus Teutonicus, and since at least the middle of the fourteenth century as Albertus Magnus, was born to the noble family of Bollstedt in Lauingen on the Danube in 1193 (though some authorities prefer the date 1206). Two visions are believed to have guided his life: the Virgin Mary is said to have ordered him to go to Padua (or perhaps Pavia) to study Aristotle, and the devil (uncharacteristically, to be sure) is said to have later tried unsuccessfully to frighten him from the study of Aristotle back to theology and divine wisdom.

In 1223 he became a member of the Dominican Order as a result of the preaching of Jordan of Saxony, the superior of the order who was so persuasive in drawing men to him and girls to the convents that it was said to be wise for families to lock up their children when he came to town. This conversion seems to have taken place in Padua, but some claim that it took place in Cologne. Albert studied in Bologna for several years before returning to Germany. We know that by 1227 he was in Cologne teaching the arts in the Dominican monastery, which stood on the street now known as "An die Dominikaner." For nearly twenty years he was in Cologne or traveling over western Germany, establishing Dominican schools and visiting libraries, the latter perhaps making it possible for him to know more Aristotle texts than anyone else of his time. His wide travels, and the fact that the Dominican discipline required that all travel should be by foot, would justify us in calling him the peripatetic philosopher of the century, even if he had not been an Aristotelian.

In 1245 he went to Paris as a lecturer in the theology faculty and was the first German to take the doctor's degree there. (It is sometimes stated that he took the master's degree, but at that time there seems to have been no difference between them.) His lectures, according to legend at least, were delivered in a house on what is now known as "Place Maubert," but this may be only a fanciful explanation of the name of that square (Place M. Albert → M. Aubert).

Thomas Aquinas heard Albert lecture in Paris from 1245 to 1248 and in Cologne from 1248 to 1252. The mutual esteem and love of the two men was well known and memorable. Philosophically they were close to each other in that both drew upon Aristotle and made a similar distinction between faith and reason. What chiefly separated their views was Albert's closer adherence to Arabic interpretations of Aristotle. These brought

---

[12] This is Nietzsche's explanation of the rise of philosophy against Christianity; see *Genealogy of Morals*, Third Essay, § 27; and *Joyful Wisdom*, § 357.

with them an admixture of Neoplatonic speculation which Albert was not always able to distinguish from genuine Aristotelianism.

From 1254 to 1257 Albert was provincial of the Dominicans in Germany; from 1260 to 1262 he was bishop of Regensburg; in 1263–1264 he was papal legate in Bohemia and eastern Germany. From 1264 to 1269 he lived in Würzburg and Strassburg; from 1270 to his death on November 15, 1280, he lived again in Cologne. Three times he acted as peacemaker between the citizens of Cologne and their archbishops in conflicts which grew out of political and commercial rivalries between them and which led from time to time to military action between them.

In 1259 Albert was at Valenciennes participating in conferences with Thomas Aquinas and others on the constitution and curriculum of Dominican schools. He participated in the synod of Anagni in 1256, and the Council of Lyons in 1274 (where he backed Rudolf of Hapsburg for election as emperor); and it is believed that in 1277 he was in Paris defending the teaching of the recently deceased Thomas Aquinas from the consequences of the condemnation of the Averroists by the Archbishop of Paris, Stephen Tempier.

The trips to Anagni and Paris had some philosophical significance. In Paris there had long been a dispute between the secular faculty and the mendicant orders on the number of monks who could have seats in the faculty. It had led to a temporary strike in the faculty in 1229, and later had prevented Bonaventure and Thomas Aquinas from becoming members. The struggle grew from hostility among the masters and the rival claims of the bishops of Paris and the popes—the secular masters being responsible to the bishops and the mendicants somewhat more directly responsible to Rome. Questions concerning the primitive communism of the church and the poverty of the Disciples and their bearing upon the property of the Church and the mendicancy of the orders were also involved.[13] But there was a philosophical dimension to the quarrel, and when Albert at Anagni defended the rights of the mendicants, he did so by attacking the Averroism of the secular faculty. When Averroism was about to be condemned in 1277—three years after the death of Thomas—Albert, at least according to legend, went to Paris to defend his deceased pupil because the condemnation of Averroism could not but put into jeopardy the Aristotelianism he and his pupil had espoused. Perhaps through Albert's efforts, the official condemnation exempted Thomas.

Albert is, I believe, the only philosopher to be called "the Great." He was also known as *Doctor universalis* and was recognized even by his enemies (Roger Bacon among them) as the most universal polyhistor of his century. He was German by birth but not solely by birth; his interest in German customs and politics and his knowledge of the fauna and flora of Germany were unsurpassed; his involvement in German affairs was as great as that of Otto of Freising.

---

[13] See D. L. Douie, *The Conflict between the Seculars and the Mendicants at the University of Paris* (London; Blackfriars, 1954).

Of his importance in the history of philosophy, and not merely in German history, there can be no question. He was the first man in Europe to be able to survey the whole (or almost the whole) of the Aristotelian corpus; he was the commentator and paraphraser who made Aristotle universally accessible; and he was the first who clearly discerned the possibility and function of an orthodox Christian Aristotelianism. This last entailed the necessity of his being more than a commentator and transmitter, for Aristotelianism taken by itself simply does not fit neatly into Christian thought. To establish Christian Aristotelianism, Albert had also to be a critic of Aristotle. But because of the very variety of the sources of his thought (which he could not always differentiate, since they had become confused in the transmission of the manuscripts he used)—Al-Farabi, Augustine, Avicenna, Averroes, Avicebron, Moses Maimonides, Dionysius the Areopagite, Proclus—it is little wonder that he was not able to make a consistent structure of his own philosophy and that there are in his version of Christian Aristotelianism many doctrines by no means Aristotelian. He claimed that he did not try to present his own thoughts in his philosophical works; except where Aristotle had not written on a subject, his professed purpose was to report what Aristotle had said, adding information Aristotle had not possessed. Only in his theological writings did he feel free to go against Aristotle. But in this statement of his limited purpose he is not entirely fair to himself, for he did not merely report Aristotle, he also judged him. He was no slavish follower of Aristotle in his descriptions of nature, but depended upon his own eyes to correct Aristotle's errors and to report observations (as, for example, on German plants and animals) which the earlier philosopher could not make. Nor was he a slavish follower of Aristotle in metaphysics, nor of the Neoplatonism which was confounded with Aristotle in Albert's sources, because he had, he thought, in faith a standard to which he could appeal when he believed they were in error.

With these cautionary remarks, which should keep us from expecting much originality in this first north-European Aristotelian, we can briefly describe his works.[14] They are divided into four large parts: Logic, *Philosophia realis*, Moral Philosophy, and Theology. In the first, we find almost nothing except commentaries on the *Organon* influenced by Avicenna and thus tending away from the conception of logic as a science of language (*scientia sermocinalis*) and making it rather a science of reason. In the third, there are commentaries on the *Ethics* and *Politics*. The last is divided into three parts, the dogmatic, exegetical, and ascetic works. Albert is no enemy of mysticism, and there is a certain mystical cast to his writings; on the other hand, *On Cleaving to God*, which has generally been considered

14 The division given here is both a classification of the major writings of Albert (as they will be found listed, for example, in *Ueberwegs Grundriss der Geschichte der Philosophie*, 12th ed., II, 405–406 [1924], and Albert's own division of the modes and genera of knowledge in *Metaphysica* (Book VI, Tract. I, chap. 2: "Quod tres sunt theoricae essentiales.") The definition of physics is on p. 303 of the Bernhard Geyer edition (*Opera omnia*, vol. XVI, pt. ii [Aschendorff, 1964]).

to be his principal mystical writing, is now known not to be by him at all. Here we must be concerned mostly with the writings of the second part.

Philosophia realis is divided into three parts, as in Aristotle. There is first the *Physica*, which contains Albert's commentaries on Aristotle's scientific works and reports of his own observation. Second, there is mathematics, which is knowledge of that which can be presented in the imagination but without empirical observation as its verification. Physics is defined, as Aristotle defined it, as dealing with substance in which there is a principle of motion and rest. The third division, *Metaphysica*, also called *prima philosophia*, or *divina philosophia*, and sometimes simply *theologia*, is knowledge of intelligible being by the exercise of reason alone.

There are two ways of knowing intelligible being—by the exercise of reason alone, and by revelation. Reason, though it conceives of God as the first cause of the world, cannot adequately conceive him because it is finite and complex and God is infinite and simple. This principle of the likeness of the intellect to what it knows is fundamental throughout Albert's work. Our conception of God is by analogy; the predicates we apply to God and to creatures are not univocal, but they are applied by analogy. It is by analogy that we call God first cause, but even this is not literally correct. Even the word "cause"—indeed, even the word "first"—is applied only by analogy. The thesis that God transcends all categories, such as cause and even being, is one of the clearest evidences we have of the Neoplatonic restrictions in Albert's Aristotelianism. Yet he follows Aristotle in proving the existence and causality of God from the existence of motion. Aristotelian, Neoplatonic, and purely Christian elements are inextricably woven together in Albert's account of the relation of God to the world.

The inadequacies of our rational knowledge of God are filled out by revelation. Reason cannot demonstrate the mysteries of Incarnation, Trinity, and Resurrection, but can only serve in the defense of their super-rational truth. Here, then, is the dividing line between philosophy and theology. We can make the division clear by comparing several views of this principle.

The Averroists held—or were believed to hold—that a principle could by true in philosophy but false in theology. Now this opinion may be interpreted in two ways: (a) Some Averroists claimed that "true in philosophy" meant only "really present in Aristotle," who worked solely from natural reason; hence such a principle is *really* false, but known to be false only by faith, which Aristotle did not have. The effect of this is to set philosophy and theology against each other, so that the former makes no autonomous contribution to the latter. Another—unwanted—effect was to make philosophy a threat to theology, since it presents doctrines false in theology. (b) Some insinuated, at least, that philosophy was superior to theology; that if a principle was true philosophically, it was true without qualification, and hence theological alternatives to it were false, even if "found in the Fathers." The times were not ready for this interpretation, however, and the historical effect of Averroism was based upon the first interpretation.

Still others said that theology may be held to be superior to philosophy, but not in opposition to it. The scholastics before the thirteenth century, such as St. Anselm, would say that the eternity of the world is false because we accept on faith that the world was created. But though we accept its falsity on faith, we can then demonstrate its falsity by reason. Hence, though faith is temporally prior to philosophical knowledge, all the truths of faith are also truths of philosophy or may become so. This rationalism, however, put too great a burden on philosophy—one it could not, looked at honestly, actually support; but such rationalism is an irrepressible tendency that appears again and again in the history of philosophy, and is repressed again and again. For the modest claim of philosophy to support articles of faith leads inevitably to the presumption of philosophy to be the judge of faith; repeatedly in the history of German philosophy we find theologians rejecting the help offered by reason and philosophy because of the danger that the handmaiden will become the mistress. In the eleventh century this danger was seldom seen at the highest levels; but the rationalism that claimed to help and support theology led to a dry and arid theology which offered little to humble faith and conceded nothing to the aspect of mystery in Christianity.

Between these two attitudes—one rationalistic, which merged philosophy and theology, and one Averroistic, which separated them and left them potential rivals—there is the Albertine solution. We can decide whether any thesis is philosophical or theological, and if the former we can try to prove or disprove it philosophically; if the latter we have revelation to support or reject it. If the thesis cannot be decided by philosophy, faith guided by revelation and tradition may and must make the decision. We shall consider two examples of Albert's conciliation of philosophical claims and religious truths.

The first is found in his attitude to the Aristotelian thesis of the eternity of the world. Albert finds the proof of this wanting, but in fact he says he cannot refute it. But we have clear revelation that the world was created; hence, we may reject Aristotle's proof in spite of the fact that we cannot refute it philosophically. Thus the discrepancy between Aristotle and Christian theology is too great for Albert to resolve by a purely philosophical argument, and he seeks to render it innocuous by adjusting the line between faith and reason.

Albert's treatment of the problem of the unity of agent intellect is perhaps a more subtle example. Aristotle, we must remember, defined the soul as the form of the living body; but with apparent disregard of this he argued also that the agent intellect might separate from the body as a pilot from his ship. The Averroists argued, quite correctly, that if the agent intellect is a form and is separable, then what is separable is not individual but is one and the same for all ("monopsychism"). Thus there can be no personal immortality, no immortality of Peter or Paul, but, at most, of their manhood. Hence Averroism, taken by some in Paris to be equivalent to Aristotelianism, conflicted with the Christian teaching of the immortality of the individual soul and the resurrection of the body.

One way to escape from the Averroistic conclusion is to reject the identification of soul with form, as Plato had done, and as Descartes was later to do. But the Averroists could not do this, for then the soul, as individual, could not know forms. Here then, is Albert's problem: how can the soul know forms (and thus be a form) and yet be immortal (as an individual)?

Albert solves the problem by availing himself of the concept of substantial form, that is, a substance that can be the indwelling form of another being. He believes, with Aristotle and Avicenna, that the soul is a form. But, like the Aristotle of the metaphor of the ship's pilot, he holds that the soul is also a complete substance, capable of existing apart from the body which it forms. Such also, according to the teachings of Augustine, is the angelic soul, which is not an embodied soul; but the human soul has an "inclination" to the body. This inclination makes it possible for the human soul to be embodied, and after it is disembodied it will be reunited with the body at the final resurrection.

The soul has, as its highest power or part the agent intellect, i.e., the active intellect, and as its lower part the possible intellect, i.e., the passive part which merely receives the forms in things. Each is individuated and single, and not merely individuated by connection with the material body, for even angelic souls have both agent and possible intellects. But, in man, only the latter is so connected with the body that it receives knowledge through the senses. But even our sensuous knowledge of things is not produced by the possible intellect alone; it would give us only images of things, or sense data. Only as illuminated by the agent intellect can the forms which are in individual material things be discerned, abstracted, and universalized. The agent intellect which thus works on the material of the possible intellect to enable us to know the things of this world—as in mathematical knowledge, which is knowledge of embodied forms—is not, however, restricted to working with the data of the senses. Without the mediation of the possible intellect and the sense organs of the body, the agent intellect produces knowledge of metaphysical and divine realities when it, in turn, is guided by the divine light. Indeed, in all its operations, even those exercised upon the possible intellect in producing knowledge of nature, the agent intellect is divinely illuminated, though in our knowledge of empirical things the illumination is called the *natural* light.

This brief account of the levels and functions of the soul has adumbrated two more difficult considerations, to which I now turn. They are Albert's theory of universals and Albert's metaphysics of light.

On the surface, Albert's solution of the problem of universals is close to the logical conceptualism of Abelard. Abelard had reached an anti-Platonic position in his controversy with the Platonist, William of Champeaux. He did not, however, have the Aristotelian metaphysics to support what was in many respects an Aristotelian solution to a logical and ontological problem. Albert did, and in this he was preceded by Avicenna, whose theory he largely accepted.

Albert held that the universal exists in the intellect of God as the *esse*, or intellectual cause of things, since the intellect of God is the source of all beings. The universal in this sense is absolute *in se* as the essence or nature of the thing. It is an intelligible reality which informs particular things, making them to be what they are with respect to their form or genus. Considered *in se*, the form is one, a unity present in, or communicable to, many things. Simply as a nature it is indifferent with respect to the distinction between unity and plurality; it is a unity in God's mind, but a universal with respect to the many things which it may inform.

This *natura* is the formal cause existing in many things and is universal because it is univocal in all. Yet it is distributed among them; in each singular thing, it is singular. The agent intellect discerns the formal cause of each of the single things and abstracts it from the many. Thereby, the form is a universal in the sense in which the term "universal" is used in logic, and Albert quotes the Peripatetics in saying the universal exists only in the intellect (*universale non est nisi in intellectu*). Still, that which is signified by the logical universal is a universal *in rem* and *ante rem*, the form in the thing and the form prior to the thing. In the thing, it is the principle, or ground, of being (*principium essendi*). The thing perceived or known produces in the mind (in the passive intellect) a phantasm, and the agent intellect imposes upon this phantasm the form which is identically in, prior to, and posterior to the thing known. By virtue of the knowledge the agent intellect has of the nature or essense or form of the thing, the passive intellect sees the particular thing as informed with that which is universal (the *natura in se*) and thus knows it.

The universal, therefore, has a different status in the intellect from that which it has in the mind of God and in the particular thing. It does not exist in the intellect as a form of matter, as it does in the particular thing, for there is no matter in the soul. It exists in the mind rather as an "intention" or "sign," as truly universal and not individuated by the individuality of the soul in which it is, any more than light is specificated and individuated by an object which it illuminates. In the mind of God, *ante rem*, it is unitary; in things (*in rem*) it is distributed and individuated; in the intellect (*post rem*) it is made universal by abstraction and by being used as a single sign, or mark, for the many.

This theory of the ontological status of the form and the universal is intimately connected with the metaphysics of light. This theory, taken from Neoplatonism, gives an analogous theory of knowledge by showing the *operations* of the intellect, while the theory of universals itself is more concerned with the status of the *objects* of the intellect. The agent intellect is the image of God in us, that is, it is a God-like power. It illuminates and gives form to the phantasms of things produced in the passive intellect; but it does so only when aided by the greater light of the divine intellect. Nothing, he says, can be known unless the light of God strengthens the light of the agent intellect. These two lights, which he compares to that of the sun and that of the stars, are present in all knowing; even the "natural light" by which we know things which affect our senses is, ultimately, a divine light. But the illumination of the agent intellect by God extends beyond the limits of what can be seen by the passive intellect. When so illuminated there is revealed to the agent intellect forms and truths which extend beyond the world of the senses; thus we know metaphysical truths and the truths of faith. The distinction between natural and supernatural knowledge, therefore, is a difference in their objects, for both kinds of knowledge are possible only by the grace of God, who illuminates all things and guides all our mental operations.

Thus we see the intimate mixture of Neoplatonic metaphysics and an Avicennan Aristotelianism in Albert's theory of knowledge. Even this brief account suffices to show how far removed in fact he was from Aristotle, because of both his Augustinianism and his Neoplatonism. He did not attain the accuracy of interpretation of Aristotle which was achieved by his pupil Thomas. But, more importantly, he did not achieve the same degree of naturalism in his conception of reason. In all knowledge, including that of nature, there is for Albert an illumination from God, and in metaphysics divine illumination and not sensuous abstraction is the way to and guarantor of knowledge. The radical distinction between supernatural faith and natural reason, between Christian faith and natural philosophy, did not exist for him; hence he did not need to bridge the gap between them in the systematic way which Thomas was to attempt. The epistemology of Albertus Magnus, therefore, was carried on not by Thomas Aquinas but by the German Dominicans, and especially the mystics among them who shared his Neoplatonic background.

The Albertists

Though Thomas Aquinas was a student in Cologne, he belongs to European, not German, philosophy. When his work seemed threatened by the Paris condemnation of the Averroists, the Dominicans responded by making him the official doctor of their order. By a favorable regimen, which permitted Dominicans time for uninterrupted study—uninterrupted even by routine religious observances—the scholarly work of the Dominicans progressed. The most important Thomists, however, were not in Germany but in Italy. Quite naturally, German Dominicans were much more directly influenced by Albertus Magnus, and were more particularly attracted by the remnants of his Neoplatonism than by his Aristotelianism. Thomas and the stricter Thomists outside Germany developed the Aristotelian and neglected the Neoplatonic aspects of Albert's work. The "orthodox" Albertists, if we may call them that, were Berthold of Mosburg, Hugo and Ulrich of Strassburg, and Johannes of Freiburg. There was, according to Meersseman,[15] a flourishing school of *Albertistae* in Paris at the beginning of the fifteenth century, led by Johannes de Nova Domo of the arts faculty, who carried the main burden of the attacks on the nominalists among his arts colleagues and on the Thomists in the theological faculty, the principal issue at stake among them being the reality of universals, with the Thomists occupying a position between the extremes of Albertism and Occamism. His pupil Heymeric van den Velde or Heymeric de Campo (1395–1460) led the fight against the same groups in Cologne after his appointment there in 1423.

[15] Gilles Meersseman, O.P., *Geschichte des Albertismus*, I, 4–30, esp. 14–15; II, 11–22. (For full bibliographical details see Bibliography for Chapter II.)

With the exception of Meister Eckhart, to whom we devote the next chapter, the most important follower of Albertus Magnus was Dietrich of Freiberg (in Saxony), also called Theodoric of Freiberg and Theodoricus Teutonicus de Vriberg (ca. 1250–ca. 1311). Dietrich was probably a pupil of Albert's in Cologne, and like him was Provincial of the Dominican Order in Germany. All the elements found in the somewhat eclectic Albert are to be found again in Dietrich. His theory of the relation of the agent intellect to the possible intellect is taken from his teacher, but he uses it directly in the development of his theory of mysticism. The light of God, given by grace, illuminates the possible intellect, which has been darkened by sin. In consequence, the agent intellect is freed from the limitations of the sensory phantasms of the possible intellect and thereby enabled to enjoy the beatific vision without the encumbrance of the body. Above all names stands God; but as the next hypostasis there is the One, or the Word, which in turn transmits or transfuses being into the many levels of existence, shining in man as the agent intellect which is the image of the One. By knowing itself, the agent intellect knows all things because it is potentially all things which it knows. Much of this is more Neoplatonic than anything to be found in Albert, and may be attributed to the influence of Proclus, whose work became available about this time in translations by William of Moerbecke.

Such expressions as the "divine light" and the "light of nature" were commonly used by philosophers of all persuasions, but they were used literally by Neoplatonists. They thought of light as the basic constituent of the world, a substance taking many forms or an agent effecting changes in all things. Though in many respects a typical Neoplatonist, Dietrich did not adopt the metaphysics of light into his physical theory as was done in England, for instance, by Robert Grosseteste. For Dietrich, on the contrary, light is an accidental quality of the translucent medium, the *diaphanum*, and a carrier of active powers, such as heat, for example, but not itself directly and dynamically active upon things it illuminates. Building on the work of the Polish student of nature, Witelo (born ca. 1230), in which the nature of refraction and its angles were studied, Dietrich produced the most advanced explanation of the rainbow achieved up to that time. He worked experimentally with glass globes filled with water and saw that the rainbow, or at least the dispersion of the spectrum in it, must be explained in terms of the individual drop of water. Though he had an erroneous theory of colors (derived from Averroes) and did not achieve genuinely quantitative results, his geometrical constructions were essentially correct,[16] and Father William Wallace has shown in detail how Dietrich followed Aristotelian methodology in his discovery of the cause of the rainbow.[17] Dietrich's work must be considered the first important contribution of lasting value by any German to the sciences of nature.

Among the successors of Albertus Magnus we thus find a division according to the directions they took from his own combination of Aristotelianism

[16] A clear exposition of Dietrich's theory, with his own diagrams, will be found in A. C. Crombie, *Augustine to Galileo* (London: Falcon Press, 1952), pp. 77–81.

[17] William A. Wallace, O.P., *The Scientific Methodology of Theodoric of Freiberg* (Fribourg [Switzerland]: The University Press, 1959).

and Neoplatonism. First, there were those who developed his Aristotelianism; and, of course, Thomas ranks above all the rest in this respect. But there were few in Germany who took this direction; the main development of Thomism was in Italy and France. The most important German Thomists were Johannes Versor (d. 1485) and Heinrich of Gorichen (= Gorkum; d. 1431), the first of whom was the author of the most important commentaries on Aristotle's metaphysics and logic (*Quaestiones super metaphysicam Aristotelis, Super omnes libros novae logicae*) of the fifteenth century. The latter wrote a commentary on Thomas' *De Énte et essentia* and *Quaestiones in omnes partes S. Thomae*. Second, there was the Neoplatonic line running through the Dominican mystics in Germany.

But there were also those who kept the Aristotelian elements, inhibited by the condemnation of 1277, out of theology, while they furthered their use in secular learning. This division between theology and Aristotelian philosophy was not adopted by the German Dominicans, but was prominent not only among the so-called Latin Averroists but also among Franciscans influenced by William of Occam. From the standpoint of logically possible alternative developments from Albert, this third movement deserves mention in a brief historical schematization, but it was not the alternative chosen by those whose actual historical inspiration was Albertus Magnus.

III

Mysticism

The Situation in the Fourteenth Century

The delicate compromises between—or rather adjudications of—the rival claims of faith and reason, as achieved by Albertus Magnus and Thomas Aquinas, were too delicate to stand the theological storms of the fourteenth century, which has been called the "century of heresy." The papal monarchy established by Innocent III, which led to an increase in ultramontanism, external bureaucracy, and alienation from the religious instincts of the layman, left open a wide field for schism, heresy, and, with the development of the towns, anticlericalism. In the struggles between Ludwig II and John XXII, Germany was riven by divided loyalties. Cities and whole provinces were placed under papal ban. Essential clerical services had to be performed, and were performed by priests and laymen acting under political authorization, not authorization from Avignon. When, as in the case of Frankfort, the ban lasted nearly a generation, it was not surprising that there should have arisen decentralized religious organs responsive to local political powers and to laymen's thirst for the consolations of religion. The old discipline broke down; there was social unrest and civil discord which might have been inhibited had the sacred and secular swords been used in unison. The Rhineland, a principal scene of these social, political, and religious conflicts, was a refuge for heretics who had suffered elsewhere and a home for not-quite-orthodox separatist and quietist movements, as well as for some spectacular heresies native to the region. It was fertile soil for mysticism, which sought direct access to God and thus appealed to those who could not reconcile imperial and papal claims but who suffered from both. Mysticism, even when not itself heretical, was tainted by association with the heretical and the anarchic.

But we must try to understand mysticism as an intellectual movement and not merely as a response to the troubled state of the Church, the Empire, and the cities.

The condemnation of Averroism in 1277 did not stop the spread of Aristotelianism, but it made the post-Aquinian philosophers reexamine the issue of the kinds of truth and the ways to reach it. There were several alternatives possible. Dominican scholastics maintained the doctrine of the consistency of theological and philosophical truth while claiming pre-eminent position for the transrational truths of theology as fixed in dogma. The Franciscans either carried the rights of speculation further into theological realms (Duns Scotus) or denied power to natural reason and philosophy in ever-expanding regions of theology (William of Occam). The first of these Franciscan policies did not flourish in Germany; Duns Scotus died almost immediately after he came to Cologne in 1309 and left few followers, and speculative philosophical theology was the preserve of the Dominicans influenced by the Neoplatonism which passed to them through Albertus Magnus and the Albertian opponents of Thomas Aquinas. The second Franciscan policy, however, was to dominate German university philosophy for the next century and a half, under the name of the *via moderna*.

The *via moderna*, however, was subject to two interpretations. First, it could be regarded as an opportunity to theologize without the necessity of showing that theology was consistent with, though independent of, natural reason and philosophy; and thus it could lead to a dominant emphasis upon faith at the expense of reason, emphasizing the independence of theology from philosophical criticism. This line of thought was not blocked until the revival of the Thomistic solution in the sixteenth century by Suarez, after it had already been carried to extremes by Luther. Second, it could be regarded as an opportunity for an independent philosophy, philosophy freed of the burden of serving theology. This line of development is traced in those genealogies of science which see it as arising from the separation of theology and philosophy by the followers of Occam. The most important feature of German philosophy of the fourteenth and fifteenth centuries is that it almost without exception followed the first of these paths, not the second. It was Luther, not students of nature, who brought the strategy of the *via moderna* to fruition.

Mysticism provided another set of alternatives open to those troubled by the problem of the relation of reason to faith, of philosophy to theology. This problem had not been one of such overwhelming importance before the philosophical member of these pairs had become Aristotelian. If the naturalism of Aristotelian philosophy created this problem, then Aristotle should be supplemented *within* philosophy and not just at its upper limit.

Hence recourse was taken to the Platonism and Neoplatonism of Augustine, the pseudo-Dionysius, and John Scotus Erigena. The Neoplatonic elements of Albert's thought were emphasized at the expense of the Aristotelian. In all these doctrines, the radical distinction between the conception of metaphysical and that of theological truth was denied. Such denial in the fourteenth century meant a restriction upon Aristotle and the development of the suprarational supplement of faith into outright mysticism in which both metaphysical and theological truth was contained. Mysticism had never been entirely absent from scholasticism, but had always been admitted, if not actually practiced, as one phase of scholastic theory of religious knowledge and faith. But the inversion of their order of importance was the decisive step taken by Meister Eckhart.

In its turn, the condemnation of Eckhart by the papacy left open two alternatives. First, the speculative and intellectualistic articulation of mystical metaphysics could be altogether eschewed and in its place there could be a practical mysticism with little philosophical content and pretension. Or, second, in some way within mystical theology a place could be found for philosophy and the philosophical study of nature, without risking the heresies condemned in 1277 and 1329.

This division into two kinds of mysticism is easily seen by comparing each according to its relation to nominalism, which was condemned at about the same time. Nominalism precluded the possibility of a rational theology. In the eyes of the deeply religious, this was a depreciation of the value of philosophy—she was an incompetent handmaiden to theology. Mystics of the first kind, therefore, turned against philosophy and largely disappeared from the history of philosophy; some of these mystics were followers of Eckhart; others turned to mysticism as a consequence of their nominalism. On the other hand, if nominalism itself was rejected, a philosophical mysticism of a very different kind might still be possible. It would be mysticism in which faith and the intensification of religious experience would be less prominent than naturalistic and rationalistic Neoplatonism.

The first of these alternatives was accepted by the groups known as the Friends of God, who established a pietistic lay movement known as the *devotio moderna* and disappeared from the history of philosophy except insofar as their exemplary educational efforts influenced men who were not —or who were more than—practical mystics. The second alternative was the one chosen by Nicholas of Cusa, but had no other followers until after the Reformation.

An account of the various alternatives is necessary to show the pattern we shall follow in depicting the course of German philosophy in the period generally known as the "decline of scholasticism." All of these movements led to, or at least made their contribution, unwittingly, to the Reformation. We shall first discuss Eckhart in some detail, give a brief account of practical mysticism and the *devotio moderna*, and then come to Nicholas of Cusa. Thereafter we shall go back more than a hundred years, to the newly established universities, and recount the further history of scholasticism as it separated theology and philosophy.

Mysticism before Eckhart

Mysticism in the thirteenth century has frequently been regarded as anti-scholastic and even anti-Catholic; some speak of a "pre-Reformation" in the fourteenth century. While it is true that Luther was influenced by the *devotio moderna* and sometimes despised the Aristotelian scholasticism in which he was trained, we must not read Protestantism back into the fourteenth century, nor must we think of mysticism, even in its greatest figure, as a new rival of scholasticism. Neoplatonism—the intellectual source of mystical thought and vocabulary—had been an important ingredient in most earlier scholastic thinking; and revelation as a kind of direct access to God had been seen either as an essential foundation for reason (as in Anselm) or as an essential supplement to it (as in Thomas). Revelation itself, of course, was institutionalized, in the sense that there were established standards and traditions for it; revelation was not a private and ineffable experience of truth standing over against reason as the only public source and standard. Nonphilosophical mystics in Germany in the thirteenth century, such as Mechthilde of Magdeburg, were, to be sure, subjectivisitic; but when philosophers like Meister Eckhart achieved the mystical union, they used the public language of reason and philosophy to convey their insights to others, and they submitted their findings to examination by the received wisdom of the Church, both in matters of reason and of faith. That Eckhart was found to have taught heretical doctrines is indeed true; but it is significant that a finding of error was sufficient to teach him that he had committed theological error. Eckhart was no heretic, since heresy—he repeatedly says in defending his views—is not the same as error, but is error persisted in after it is shown to be error. He did not persist in his teaching; nor is there any reason for us to think that this was a hypocritical act on his part; he was no heretic, no proto-Protestant, no irrationalist, and no anti-scholastic.

Nevertheless it would be a mistake to think of mysticism as merely filling the "empty place" (to borrow Kant's language for this scholastic situation) left by knowledge to faith; mysticism does not claim to supply objects for faith, but to supply a higher kind of *knowledge*. That which was to go beyond natural reason was not, for the mystics, something presented ready-made in Scripture and the writings of the Fathers, and thus to be received secondhand as something to be learned and believed even though reason did not warrant it. Rather, what went beyond the scholastic truths of reason as we find them in Thomas was something to be actively sought; mystical vision was a dynamic act involving the will as well as the reason, not a passive reception of the Word of God to be followed by our willing. The mystical union is an illumination of reason.

Mysticism in the Rhineland originated in the devotions and writings of several remarkable women; hence the name *Frauenmystik*. But while the intense devotional ecstasies of the *Frauenmystik* were often expressed in erotic symbolism, some of which was used again later among the Friends of God, we should call Meister Eckhart an objective, even a rational, mystic if that did not sound too much like an oxymoron. His language is not theirs.

Yet this does not mean that the *Frauenmystik*—and, indeed, women who were not mystics at all—did not have an import for the philosophical movement. In a peculiar historical way, they were perhaps responsible for its flourishing just when it did. Convents and orders of Beguines in Germany increased in size and wealth at this time—some say because of an increase in piety; but others point to the catastrophes of the fourteenth century and to the great excess of women over men, largely as a consequence of the Crusades. Whatever the reason, women took the veil in unprecedented numbers. Their instruction had been committed in 1267 to the Dominicans, the most philosophical and scholarly of the religious at this time. The instruction of pious women was regarded generally as an unwelcome chore; but because the well-educated Dominicans had this responsibility, the teachings (in Latin) were conveyed to their students in German, and in a form less rigorously scholastic than that practiced in the universities of France and the schools in Germany. In these circumstances it was perhaps to be expected that the traditions and lore of the *Frauenmystik*, now de-eroticized and intellectualized, would be exploited intellectually, and that there would be a fruitful meeting of Neoplatonism and scholasticism with individual mystical raptures. There is talk at this time of the teaching of priests by mystical laymen; but this is perhaps better evidence of the growing anticlericalism than it is an explanation of how the mystical element came into the Church—for most of these stories are clearly fraudulent. Be that as it may, whether Eckhart learned from his charges or not, he undoubtedly buffered his teaching for their untutored ears, and this meant a homiletic mysticism and not intellectual scholasticism. His effort is quite understandable; but it may be wondered how successful it was, considering the intellectual demands his form of mysticism makes, and considering the fact that he had repeatedly to defend himself on the grounds that he had not made statements attributed to him.

Meister Eckhart

Johannes Eckhart, known also as Eckardus Coloniensis, was born in Hochcim, near Gotha, about 1260. He studied in Erfurt and Cologne and may have been a pupil of Albertus Magnus; at least the works of Albert were well known to him and often cited and used in his formal teaching. The Neoplatonism of those works reappears in magnified form in Eckhart's, though he had none of the interest in nature which was so characteristic of Albert. In 1302 he received the master's degree (hence the title, Meister) in Paris. He was provincial of the Dominicans in Saxony and then vicar general of Bohemia until 1311, when he returned to Paris for three years. In 1314 he was sent to Strassburg, one of the centers of both mysticism and conventual life, and from then until 1326 he divided his time between Cologne and Strassburg, preaching primarily to the nuns. His scholastic works were written in Latin; most of his sermons were in German. His sermons contain most of the mystical teachings. Eckhart was the first great philosopher to think and write in German, and Eucken has written that "much of what we think is a gift of nature to the German language is the invention of Eckhart." [1]

In July 1326 charges of heresy were brought against him by Heinrich von Virnenburg, Archbishop of Cologne. The popularity of the Dominican preacher, the continuing debate over universals, and the pill the Franciscans had had to swallow with the canonization of Thomas Aquinas (1323), had aroused the envy of the Franciscans against him, and he claimed that only ignorant and envious men would have brought such charges. Furthermore, the Dominicans' faithful adherence to the pope while the archbishop was an ally of the emperor did not make Eckhart beloved in the new cathedral at Cologne. Finally, and perhaps most importantly, the Beghards and the Brethren of the Free Spirit, as well as other heretical sects whom Virnenburg was attempting to stamp out, seem to have repeatedly cited Meister Eckhart's teaching as the foundation of their own beliefs, and all during the subsequent trial there were repeated accusations that his doctrines had misled the uneducated who (according to Eckhart) must have misunderstood him.

Eckhart was first cleared of the charges by Nicholas of Strassburg, a Thomist, who was inquisitor of the Dominican Province of Germany, and who was himself tried before the episcopal court in 1327. But the charges against Eckhart were reopened by the archbishop and prosecuted by three Franciscans. Eckhart first denied (September 26, 1326) the competence of the episcopal court but nevertheless replied to the charges. To meet the clamor stirred up against the Dominicans by the trial, Eckhart appealed from the episcopal court to the pope and defended himself in a sermon preached in Latin on February 13, 1327, having his sermon repeated in German so that all could understand his defense and his asseveration that he would retract any teachings found by competent authority to be in error. (The outcome of the Cologne trial is not known.) Eckhart himself went to Avignon, and the documents from Cologne were examined by John XXII and Cardinal Fournier (who was a judge also in the concurrent trial of William of Occam). On March 27, 1329, after Eckhart's death, the bull *In Agro Domenico* was issued, condemning as heretical seventeen, and as suspect eleven propositions, but stating that before he died Eckhart had recanted on these propositions. The date and place of his death are not known, but it probably occurred in 1327.

The effect of this bull on the history of philosophy was to frighten Eckhart's pupils away from speculative and dogmatic questions, for speculative mysticism using philosophical terminology can hardly fail to sound pantheistic, no matter how much orthodoxy is claimed. So other Friends of God, as mystics were called, turned almost wholly to practical rather than theoretical problems. Since mysticism, when it is not speculatively philosophical, has an immediate appeal to the pious, the scholastic teaching— which had never been for the layman—had less and less effect on the monastics, and mysticism became effective in the teaching office of the Church while scholasticism went down the path of the *via moderna.*

[1] Rudolf Eucken, *Geschichte der philosophischen Terminologie* (Leipzig, 1879), p. 118.

As mentioned earlier when describing the general pattern of fourteenth-century thought and placing Eckhart's mysticism in relation to its scholastic background, even his scholastic writings are affected by mystical Neoplatonism. He stands closer to Albert than to Thomas, and closer to Augustine than either of them did. It would be difficult for a mystic to warm up to an Aristotelian deity. Aristotle left in the minds of Christian Aristotelians an empty place to be occupied by faith or—*in extremis*—mystical insight. Neoplatonism, however, did not erect a philosophical barrier to be overcome by a different kind of cognitive act. In its Christian form, it provided a negative theology which inevitably drew personal and devotional cathexis to it—cathexis working in a homogeneous medium without discontinuities between natural reason and supernatural faith, in a medium that was a world already (at least by Aristotelian standards) supernaturalized. The vision of God which was reached along this path of ascent within philosophy was not one that had to be filled out by totally different kinds of experience, as faith was to supplement knowledge in Aristotelian scholasticism. For the God arrived at by philosophy of the Christian Neoplatonic kind was much closer to the God required by innocent and earnest Christian piety than the Aristotelian-Thomistic God. The philosophy of the Christian Neoplatonic kind was a much less natural, rational philosophy than that of Aristotelian scholasticism. And the world of Christian Neoplatonism, which emanated from God, was a very different world from that which, according to Thomism and Christian orthodoxy in general, God created *ex nihilo*.

To help make clearer the distinction between the two philosophical paths to God, consider the difference between the existence of the world in a creation-theory and in an emanation-theory. The former is clearly incompatible with any pantheism; it is radically dualistic—there is God and the world, and though the world owes its being to an act of God, as created being it exists in its own right and is not reducible to a mode of God. A theory of emanation, on the other hand, does not, as it were, *give* being to the world; it *lends* God's being, in a restricted form, to creatures, and the loan can be called at any time. All the capital funds of existence are in God's name. Hence it follows that whatever exists exists in an eternal contingency, not autonomously and in its own right. If a thing exists, it exists in God, or God exists in it. Read in this way, emanationism is pantheistic. But it can be read in another way just as well. To say that whatever exists has the mode of existence we have just been describing can also mean that *nothing but God* truly exists. So far from being pantheistic, this reading of emanationism is implicitly acosmic. Meister Eckhart prefers the latter interpretation, since his whole interest is in God, not in the world.

Thus he says, "Everything that is created is nothing,"[2] not "everything that is created is God." Yet there is a sense in which the latter is true too. "Being is God" is true, and this proposition is convertible, is an identity.

---

[2] J. M. Clark, *Meister Eckhart. An Introduction to the Study of His Works with an Anthology of His Sermons* (New York and London: Nelson, 1957), Sermon XX, p. 225. This work is hereafter cited as Clark. On the difficult point raised here, see B. J. Muller-Thym, *The Establishment of the University of Being in the Doctrine of Meister Eckhart of Hochheim* (New York and London: Sheed, Ward, 1939), pp. 86–88.

If it were false, God would not be; and if there were a being other than God, it would have to derive its being from something other than God, and this is impossible. In an absolute sense, therefore, apart from God there is indeed nothing. It was this reading which was the basis for the charge against Eckhart that he was a pantheist. But in defending himself from this accusation, he distinguished between the meanings of *esse* in *Esse est Deus*, which is absolute being (*esse absolutum*) and inherent being (*esse formaliter inhaerens*) which is God penetrating and giving being to the creature. If the latter sense of *esse* is equated with the former, then Eckhart's theory is pantheistic, for God would be merely the form of the world; but Eckhart insists on the distinction, and then insists that the *esse* inhering in the world is not intrinsic to the world and the creatures in it. Just as Albertus Magnus had distinguished between the soul as substance and the soul as the form inherent in the body, Eckhart distinguishes God as equivalent to absolute being from God as the being which pervades, penetrates, forms, causes, and lends being to the world. Then by analogy with the Albertine theory, he then can say that God is in the world as the soul is in the body. He says this because, like Nicholas of Cusa later, he wants to bring God and the world into maximum immediacy to each other, yet does not want to identify them with each other in every respect.

A theory which is so delicately balanced between saying that the world is nothing and that the world is divine is sensitive to the tension and polarity felt in man's own relation to God: for the starting point for Neoplatonic Christian mysticism is the religious paradox of the nothingness of man (the acosmic pole) and of his divine being (the pantheistic pole). The pathos of the mystic is his alienation from God, who is, paradoxically, closer to him than breathing and nearer than hands and feet. The solution to this paradox is to be found in the ontological structure corresponding to the dynamism of emanation, the structure being that of the great chain of being descending from God, from the ineffable being of God to the nearly absolute non-being of the creature. In this static structure each link is a level of being, whose dignity depends upon its distance from God or Plotinus' The One. Man is in this chain, and he returns to God by going up this chain; the highest link is reached in a mystic union with the unnameable One which Christians call God. Much of Neoplatonism is easily accommodated in Christianity; the levels of being can be seen as the ranks of angels (like the Greek intelligences of the various heavenly spheres), and the ascetic movement upward along the chain is quite congruent with the ideals of Christian living. But the doctrine of emanation was not acceptable to Christianity, which had a doctrine of creation *ex nihilo* as given in Genesis. The Aristotelian doctrine of the eternity of the world was rejected for the same reason. Neoplatonism brought an added difficulty, not present in Aristotle—that of the world's immanence in God. This is a difficulty inherent in pantheism (a difficulty not clearly represented in the metaphor of the chain). While much of the metaphysics and cosmology of Neoplatonism were rejected by scholastics after the metaphysics and cosmology of Aristotle became known, there still remained, to quicken religious devotion and aspiration, all the rich symbolism of man's participation in God ("in whom we live and move and have our being,") and of God's emanation and illumination of the world (which lent itself more easily to iconographic representation than creation by a transcendent God *ex nihilo* did). Seeing the world as the body or symbol of God himself was closer to Christian sacramental conceptions of the world than seeing it as a creation of a transcendent and hidden God. The problem was to use this symbolism which was available to both the common man and the adepts at *Frauenmystik* without, as it were, taking the world itself too seriously and without falling into the heresies which this symbolism might generate if taken literally.

Eckhart, preaching to the uneducated pious, attempted to use this symbolism and these metaphors, and he did fall into errors condemned by the Church. His attempts to use it and to avoid collision with dogma led him to short and memorable statements which are *prima facie* heretical, followed by long and obscure demonstrations that they are not heretical after all; but the former were the ones remembered, even if misunderstood (and one may well wonder if indeed they were misunderstood), and the latter were neither remembered nor understood. Sermons to the uneducated on matters which require the highest philosophical subtlety are not perhaps the best vehicles for profound philosophy. It is easy to find inconsistencies in the sermons of Eckhart, and not all the inconsistencies are likely to be the responsibility of his hearers who wrote them down from memory. Often enough the hearers and their limitations must have been forgotten when Eckhart was most deeply immersed in his speculations: "If anyone has understood this sermon," he says at the close of one of them, "I wish him well. If no one had been here, I should have had to preach to this alms box."[3]

Earlier in this chapter I suggested that Eckhart might be called an "objective mystic." It is now time to try to explain this apparent *contradictio in adjecto*. We do not find in any of his works descriptions of the mystic raptures which he may, for all we know, have experienced. He tells his hearers nothing of his mystical experiences, except charming little anecdotes that show wit and humor; he prescribes for his hearers no regimen, no ascetic practices, which will secure them mystical raptures; he says that each person must find God in his own way, in abandoning himself in his own way; sacraments may help, but they are not essential; sin may hurt, but it is not disabling. Mercy, self-forgetfulness, detachment, and love of God— the Christian virtues within the reach of all, whether in the church or in the street—lead to an insight that we are or may be God-like, that God is in us, that God loves us when we love Him, that the things of this world are evil when they stand between us and God, that by self-forgetfulness we may be taken up into God's all-encompassing love, that we should love our brother not in his natural brotherliness to us but in his divine sonship to our Father. But Eckhart promised no rapture with a thinly veiled eroticism in which his pious nuns, after harrowing ascetic practices, will cry out, as Mechtilde of Magdeburg did: "O thou God pouring out thy gift! O thou

[3] Sermon XII (Clark, p. 184).

God burning in thy longing! O thou melting God, melting so Thou canst unite Thy loves! O thou God resting on my breast! O thou Sun, beautiful in thy splendor! O thou Full Moon in thy rising up (*Stande*)!" No: he tells us simply that we are sons of God and ought to recognize it and act as if we were. Instead of debasing humanity before God—Eckhart even says we ought not to pray for anything from God, for that makes us his slave, and him our master, and we are closer to him than that—Eckhart was accused of deifying man.

I shall describe Eckhart's theory under three headings, though it will not be possible to separate them sharply. We shall present his theory of God and the Godhead, his theory of the power and functions of the soul, and his theory of the relation between God and the soul.

From Neoplatonism Eckhart derived his theory of the Godhead, the fountain of being, the absent God (*deus absconditus*). He did not always consistently call this the Godhead, but sometimes called it God; but the context usually shows which he meant. This Eleatic conception equates the Godhead with Being, and denies to the Godhead all other predicates; for if I say Godhead, which is Being, is for example white, or even good, then I am saying that what is not-white or not-good has no being at all and cannot even be mentioned. Every predicate is a negation of another, but Godhead is the negation of negations: "He is one and denies every other, for outside of God[head] there is nothing."[4] "Being is God[head]. This proposition is obvious . . . because if being were something different from God, God [would not] exist and there [would be] no God[head]. For how can he exist, or how can anything exist, if there is another existence foreign and distinct from being?"[5] "Whatever one says that God[head] is, he is not; he is what one does not say of him, rather than what one says he is."[6]

Even Being cannot be predicated of Godhead univocally with other things, but only by analogy;[7] for when I say X is, I am denying non-X; yet both X and non-X must be affirmed of the Godhead as the common root of what we ordinarily call both being and non-being. Godhead is the coincidence of opposites, as Erigena before Eckhart and Nicholas of Cusa after him express it; theology can only be negative theology.

No one who writes or talks at all, of course, can say anything about such a negation of all negations; it has been vainly attempted from Parmenides to the present day. And if one remains silent about it, it can play no role in philosophical debate and cannot even function as an object in theology, however much it may be adumbrated in silent devotion. Now one thing that philosophers seem unable to do is remain silent about the unnameable, the indescribable, the ineffable. They may prescribe ways of experiencing

---

[4] Sermon XXI (Clark, p. 230).

[5] *Meister Eckhart. A Modern Translation*, trans. R. M. Blackney (New York and London: Harper, 1941; hereafter cited as Blackney), p. 278. The passage quoted is from Eckhart's "Defense."

[6] Sermon VII (Clark, p. 159).

[7] *Expositio sancti evangelii secundum Johannem*, in *Die lateinischen Werke*, ed. Karl Christ and Josef Koch (Stuttgart: Kohlammer, 1936), vol. III, fascicle 1, p. 43: "Everything apart from God is a definite being of one sort or another and not an absolute being or existence; such absolute being or existence belongs solely to the prime cause, which is God."

it in raptures; they may use metaphors and symbolism; but talk about it they must. And Meister Eckhart preached about it.

Two attributes are assigned by him to the Godhead, at least analogically: being and knowing. Godhead is and knows. If the literal sense be the one in which I know and am, then it is at least closer to the truth to say that he is and knows than to say that he is not and knows not. Because of the absolute oneness of the Godhead, Eckhart thinks of being and knowing in this one instance as identical. But since pure intellect can only be one, it is more fundamental to say that the Godhead knows than to say that the Godhead is being. The Godhead is an absolutely unitary spiritual being.

Intelligere is the basic ontological attribute of God. God *is* because God *understands*; God is above Being, God is the One of the Neoplatonists whose absolute ontological unity is that of spirit, which must be one, and not of being, which can be plural, dispersed, diverse. Hence Eckhart can even say of God that he *is not*; but he cannot say of God that he *knows not*.

This is the doctrine expressed in the *Questiones Parisiensis*, but in the *Opus tripartitum* and in the German sermons, which will be cited in detail later, this extreme position is modified and the equation is set up: God = *esse* = *intelligere*. Even then, however, the last term remains the decisive one: "The nature of God is intellect, and his being is to know himself (*sibi esse est intelligere*). Therefore he produces things in being by intellect."[8]

The Aristotelian form-matter distinction is applicable to this Being. Its actuality is consciousness, reflection, thought, or expression whereby its being is dirempted into subject and object. Like Aristotle's God, too, the Godhead has nothing to think but his own thought; like Spinoza's God, he has only himself as the object of his infinite intellectual love. But as the object of his thought and love, he is distinguishable from himself as thinker or lover. Therefore the undifferentiated being of the Godhead becomes internally differentiated and thus there arises (not temporally, but logically and eternally) the Trinity. (This overflowing, or differentiation of being I shall call "trinitation;" but this word is my own, not Eckhart's, and I apologize for it; but it will be useful from time to time.) Godhead becomes God the Father in expressing his being in knowing another; Being becomes the Son as the Logos, or the Word, which is its expression, like the *nous* of Plotinus, and the Son's return into the Father by will and love is the Holy Spirit. The Trinity, therefore, is the form in which Godhead is articulated as three persons in one. The attributes of God are the attributes of God as one aspect of the triune person; the will (which corresponds to the Son) apprehends God as good, but the intellect (which corresponds to God the Father) presses on to the Godhead itself: "The intellect pierces through and is not satisfied with wisdom or goodness or truth or even God *Himself*. She is as truly little satisfied with God as with a stone or tree. She never rests; she breaks into the ground out of which goodness and truth break forth and apprehends it *in principio*, in the beginning, where goodness [the Father] and truth [the Son] issue forth."[9]

[8] *Expositio libri Genesis* (*Die lateinischen Werke*, vol. I, fascicle 1, p. 52.
[9] Sermon XI (Clark, p. 181).

In quite human terms, Eckhart is saying that in begetting, a child is created and the person who begat him becomes a father; Father and Son logically require each other, and hence the existence of the Son is necessary to the existence of the Father. Eckhart speaks of the Son's begetting the Father in the same act that the Father begets the Son. God's being "depends upon His begetting the Son."[10] "When all creatures pronounce his name, God comes into being."[11] In Aristotle's theory of reproduction, also, the efficient cause (the father) must have the same form as the son; hence in form the begetter and the begotten, God and Son and each one of us as sons of God, are identical in form, though different in accidents. Charged with having taught that man *is* God, Eckhart defended himself by using an analogy with the Eucharist:

For just as many loaves on different altars are converted into one true body of Christ, conceived and born of the Virgin, suffered under Pilate, while the accidental properties of the loaves still remain, so our minds, through the grace of adoption, and we ourselves are made one with the true Son of God, parts of the head of the church who is Christ.

Again:

In the sacrament on the altar the whole is changed into the whole, but is not so in us. Whence it does not follow that we are God, as in Christ the first-born man is God, begotten the idea and likeness of the Father-God—for we are *after* the idea and likeness, and created.[12]

The creation of the world and of man by this process did not take place in time, for there was no time before it. Time came into being with the creation of the world. But the Aristotelian theory of the eternity of the world is denied, because such a theory means the world was not created at all. But Eckhart has little interest (in his mystical works, at least) in the world; he is interested in the soul.

With one most important exception, Eckhart's theory of the soul is taken from earlier scholastics, especially from Albertus Magnus, and, ultimately, from Augustine and Aristotle. From Aristotle, *via* Albertus Magnus, he derives the distinction between the lower faculties of the soul by which it digests, moves the body, grows, desires, sees, and the like. From Augustine he derives the trinitarian analogy of the soul whereby the higher faculties (memory, intellect, and will) are seen as representative of the Father, Son, and Holy Spirit. So much is not original with him; but now comes the uniquely Neoplatonic conception of the intellect not merely as a faculty of the soul but as the *image* of God in us. (And since the Image of God in the Trinity is the Son, by virtue of the Image in us we bear the Son of God in ourselves.)

God has implanted or begotten an image of himself which in Aristotelian form is identical with him; it is an image without a medium.[13] God does

---

[10] Sermon X (Clark, p. 174).
[11] Sermon XII (Clark, p. 184).
[12] "Defence" (Blackney, pp. 268, 297).
[13] Sermon IV (Clark, p. 147) But sometimes it is said to have a medium, and then man's vision is cut off (Clark, pp. 177, 223).

not come into man; he is in us virtually or essentially as God's image, man's form.[14] This image of God in man is what Eckhart calls the ground of the soul, the citadel of the soul, the guardian, or, most often, the *spark*. It is uncreated and eternal;[15] it is not known to us as the other faculties of the soul but only by God's revelation, his grace, which makes it possible for us to perceive it. As we perceive and understand it, it seems to be a power of the soul, and Eckhart often calls it simply the intellect and disputes the Franciscans for thinking the will is the highest faculty; but in fact it is "to be identified with God."[16] "There is something in the soul that is so akin to God that it is one [with him] and not united [to him]. It is one, it has nothing in common with anything; in fact it has nothing in common with anything that is created. Everything that is created is nothing. If man were entirely of this nature, he would be wholly uncreated and uncreatable."[17] "Not God himself [but only the Godhead] can gaze upon it . . . or enter the citadel of the soul."[18]

The spark is ontologically like the Son in the Trinity; it is for this reason possible for us to know God. "The Scriptures say: 'No one knoweth the Father save the Son.' Hence if you wish to know God, you should not merely be like the Son, you must be the Son Himself."[19] But the spark does not know merely God the Father; it presses on to the blinding light (or darkness) of the wilderness or the ground of the Godhead: "When I [through this spark] enter the ground, the bottom, the stream and the source of the Godhead [that is, the Godhead as the ground, and so on] no one asks me where I came from or where I have been. No one missed me there, for there even God disappears."[20] This is the mystical losing of oneself in the dark wilderness of God, in which the self becomes detached, disinterested, de-individualized, and finds its rest in the Godhead . . . It falls into its nothingness, falling so far from the created something into Nothing that it cannot by any means return of its own strength into its created Something. And God[head]in His uncreated nature upholds the nothingness of the soul and preserves it in His Something [as God]. The Soul has desired to become nothing and cannot of itself return to itself (for it has escaped so far from itself) until God supports it."[21] Thus man is reborn; he loses himself, and God gives him his self back again, by a kind of trinitation process.

Many quotations from Eckhart's sermons which are known to be authentic come near saying that man *is* God; and many in sermons of dubious authenticity do say it. It is indeed hard for him not to say it or seem to say it, for the sense in which man is not God is more difficult to convey than the sense in which he is. But Eckhart, in his defense, explicitly denies that he said it, and the papal bull does not attribute the saying to him. Yet again and again he asserts and means quite literally that God is in the soul as in God's Only Begotten Son, and is in the world as the soul (the separable substantial form) is in the body. The spark is the Son begotten in us by God: "The Father begets His Son in the eternal knowledge [i.e., in the

[14] Sermon XVI (Clark, p. 200).
[15] Sermon XX (Clark, p. 225).
[16] Fragment 39 (Blackney, p. 246).
[17] Sermon XX (Clark, p. 225)

[18] Sermon II (Clark, p. 137).
[19] Sermon IV (Clark, p. 147; cf. p. 153).
[20] Sermon XII (Clark, p. 184).
[21] Sermon I (Clark, p. 130).

trinitation] and in the same way the Father begets His Son in the soul as in His own Nature, and begets Him as His own in the soul."[22] Like the Son in the Trinity, "I well forth in the Holy Spirit . . . God and I are one. Through knowledge [the Son in the Trinity] I enter into Him."[23] When God sees that I am His Only Begotten Son, he hastens to me to reveal "the whole abyss of his Godhead and the fullness of His being and His nature."[24] I open myself to God, God opens himself to me; he cannot do otherwise; even the humble man can compel God to this revelation, as the son when born "compels" his begetter to be a father.

This opening of the dark wilderness of the Godhead to man is not to be gained only by ascetic practices but by turning away from non-being, that is, from creatures. A commonplace of ascetic piety,

If, therefore, you want to have and find full joy and consolation in God, see to it that you are stripped of all creatures, of all consolation from creatures. For certainly, as long as creatures comfort and are able to comfort you, you will never find true comfort . . . if you are consoled by what is not God, you will have comfort neither here nor there . . .[25]

becomes an heretical metaphysical thesis: "All creatures are a mere nothing. I do not say that they are insignificant or something; they are a mere nothing."[26] They are nothing, except insofar as they are manifestations of God's being, and we turn away from them in their creatureliness by loving them as Sons of God.

One person who mastered life is better than a thousand persons who have mastered only the contents of books, but no one can get anything out of life without God. If I were looking for a master of learning, I should go to Paris to the colleges where the higher studies are pursued. But if I wanted to know about the perfection of life, they could not tell me there.[27]

Some will find the path in one way and some in another—some in asceticism and other in learning, some in the church, some in the streets, and some as hermits. Those who cannot find it in wisdom will find it in faith.

Eckhart's efforts to show that he was not a pantheist were futile. Had he not taught that God needs the world and had to give it his being? That God wills the evil we do, because we are parts of God, and therefore we ought not to repent our sins, which may, in their way, show forth the glory and plenum of God? That the soul, or a part of it, is uncreated? That the world is uncreated in time, since time began with it? That the sacraments are not directly ordained by God? For these heretical errors are natural consequences of his philosophy, and it were better, from the standpoint of the Church, to have remained silent than to preach heresies and call them only paradoxes. Negative theology—a theology which denies any knowledge of

[22] Sermon X (Clark, p. 174).   [24] Sermon XX (Clark, p. 225).
[23] Sermon XIII (Clark, p. 189).
[25] *Book of Divine Consolation*, quoted from Jean Ancelet-Hustache, *Meister Eckhart and the Rhineland Mystics* (London: Longmans, 1957), p. 94.
[26] Sermon X (Clark, p. 173).   [27] Fragment IX (Blackney, p. 236).

God—is safer than a paradoxical theology that tries to preach incompatibilities which only confuse the uneducated and lead them into mortal sin.

Yet even if one removes such a metaphysics from the context of a theology which is quite explicit in what it claims we can know about God, the consequence of its paradoxy is to show mysteries which not only conflict with dogma but transcend mundane reason. Still, it is important to remember that though the language of Eckhart is that of mysticism, there are no ecstatic deliverances in his writings; for all we know, Meister Eckhart may not have been a mystic, if in calling a man a mystic we mean that he had direct experiences of a mystical union with God. We shall find the same to be true of Nicholas of Cusa, who deserves even less than Eckhart to be called a mystic. In both these writers, the ascent to God is an intellectual process, even if its fruition may be an ecstatic union. But unlike the normal scholastic path to God, whereupon reason completes its work, which is that of man, and there is added to this work a revelation and faith, which is the work of God, neither Eckhart nor Nicholas finds a smooth path from the world of creatures to the Creator. The paradoxical element in the world— a religious paradox for Eckhart, an intellectual paradox for the Cusan— keeps them from the easy scholastic solution.

Later Rhineland Mysticism

The papacy condemned Meister Eckhart for heretical teachings and other doctrines offensive to orthodoxy, if not actually heretical. Among the condemned doctrines was the teaching that the unity of God is above all hypostatic distinctions, that the world is eternal, that creatures are nought, that no predicates apply univocally to God, and that we are "wholly transformed into God."

The condemnation of errors in the works of Eckhart by John XXII came just before the interdict by the papacy on those parts of Germany adhering to the cause of Ludwig II as Holy Roman Emperor. In 1334 Jacques Fournier, who had prosecuted both William of Occam and Meister Eckhart, became Pope Benedict XII, and Germany was to all intents and purposes declared in schism. The Dominicans were especially hard hit by this, and many of them migrated from Cologne and Strassburg to Basel and the Netherlands. The interdict was an unusually heavy burden in Germany, especially because of various catastrophes, including the Black Death, which befell Germany at this time. The condemnation of Eckhart had the effect of turning mysticism from its speculative metaphysics to a practice of devotion which was little concerned with philosophical issues and theological subtleties; and the alienation of the pious from the Church as a result of the interdict reduced the clerical and sacramental aspects of religion to such an extent that a movement of lay-mysticism flourished among the Friends of God, which was the name taken by monks and laymen who banded together for pious living and mystical devotion.

Johann Tauler (1300–1361), in Cologne, Basel, and Strassburg, and Heinrich Suso (= Seuse, ca. 1300–1366), the former probably, and the latter certainly, direct pupils of Meister Eckhart, continued the mysticism of the master but without the near-pantheism of his metaphysics, tending to treat psychologically and subjectively what had been for him ontological distinctions and relations. They were far more widely studied than Eckhart himself, partly because of their unchallenged orthodoxy. In the Low Countries the mystical theology of Jan de Ruysbroeck (1293–1381) was put into social practice by Gerard Groot (b. 1340), who established in Deventer the School of the Brethren of the Common Life. Similar schools were established also in the Rhineland in Germany. The piety practiced there was expressed in two of the most important devotional books of Christendom, the *Imitation of Christ*, attributed to Thomas of Kempen (1380–1471), and the wholly anonymous *Theologia Germanica*, composed between 1400 and 1430 and first published by Luther in 1516. The piety of the Friends of God and the Brethren of the Common Life was called the *devotio moderna*. It renounced philosophy for the sake of a simple religion: "I am weary often to read and hear many things; in Thee is all I desire and long for. Let all the doctors hold their peace; let all creatures be silent in Thy sight; speak Thou alone unto me."[28] Ritual and theological good works were rejected for simple faith and love, which overflowed in good works to one's fellows without the spur or bridle of laws and rewards and punishment.[29] Many of the ascetic ideals and devotional expressions in these two books can be traced back to Eckhart's sermons. But Ruysbroeck and Groot and others in Holland repeatedly warned against Eckhart's heresies. Since it was the heresies—especially Eckhart's belief in the indwelling of God in man and his denial of the reality of creatures—which were philosophically original and interesting, however, Eckhart's characteristic contributions to metaphysics were not developed.

Even so, the influence of the *devotio moderna* on philosophy was profound though indirect, exercised through two men who had been students at Deventer, Nicholas of Cusa and Erasmus. Nicholas was the last great metaphysician of the medieval world, and it is noteworthy that he himself felt constrained to emphasize the divergence between his teachings and those of the master. Erasmus, in his "Christian philosophy," continued the *devotio moderna* without the metaphysics and the mysticism and with little of the actual asceticism. Yet the very concept and name, "Christian philosophy," was characteristic of the teaching of the school of Deventer, which Erasmus secularized and humanistically interpreted.

More important than these two perhaps accidental contributions to later philosophy, however, is the fact that the *devotio moderna* represents one pole in a recurring tension between the intellectual and speculative, on the one hand, and the emotional and the practical on the other.

28 *The Imitation of Christ*, III, i.
29 *Theologia Germanica* (*The Way to a Sinless Life*), ed. Thomas S. Kepler (New York: World Publishing Co., 1952), Chap. xxx.

IV

Nicholas of Cusa

Nicholas of Cusa is the most puzzling of the great German philosophers. Just how much he has puzzled historians can be seen most easily from tables of contents of their books, where the reader will sometimes find him in the chapters on medieval philosophy, sometimes in chapters on modern philosophy, and sometimes in a chapter by himself as a "transitional figure." He is discussed as a mystic, as a philosopher of nature, as a humanist, and as an orthodox theologian. All these classifications refer to some important aspect of his work, but each is wrong if taken to be exclusive; the Cusan was all these things, but without knowing it, because he did not have our chronology and our professional categories which assign a man to one age and to one discipline rather than another. No one disputes his importance; but few agree as to why he was important. "Any study that seeks to view the philosophy of the Renaissance as a systematic unity," Cassirer writes in the opening sentence of his book,[1] "must take as its point of departure the doctrines of Nicholas Cusanus." But point of departure for what destination? For no one claims that Nicholas was historically important in the sense of having initiated characteristic and decisive changes in the state of

---

[1] Ernst Cassirer, *The Individual and the Cosmos in Renaissance Philosophy*, trans. Mario Domandi (New York: Harper, 1964), p. 7.

mind of his and the following century. Until he was rediscovered in the nineteenth century, the only influence we know he had on another philosopher was on Bruno, over a century later. Yet there is truth in Cassirer's statement, and a truth which I think Cusanus would have been able to appreciate: the truth of a symbol to a complex reality which cannot be directly categorized. For it is appropriate that Nicholas should be all things to all men; he believed that man himself is a microcosm, reflecting in partial ways what cannot be reflected as a whole. For a man who taught that all things are involved in everything, it is appropriate that he himself should be almost all things—church statesman, theologian, mathematician, humanist, metaphysician, scientist. In the manifoldness of his interests and abilities, only two men in German intellectual history are his equals: Leibniz and Goethe. It is a remarkable fact, difficult to interpret, that these three men, alike in their universal genius, should have been so much alike in the contents of their philosophies. The resemblance between Leibniz and Nicholas is especially marked in their lives, personalities, and teachings; the most marked resemblance between their philosophies is found in the way each gives a scientific cosmology appropriate to his Pythagoreanism. Both sought unity everywhere, whether in church, or state, or the cosmos. For each, the world is isotropic, both geometrically and intellectually. It does not matter where one begins, for each part reflects the whole, as a mirror or a microcosm, and the intellectual and cosmological bonds which connect each part with all the others and with the whole are organic or mathematical, or both. But the differences between them are no less marked: Leibniz often writes as if he were a cardinal, privily acquainted with the plans and stratagems of God, while Nicholas, actual cardinal, is a theologian on the negative path, continuously reminding us of our ignorance, though learned ignorance, of God.

And this brings us to the question: was Nicholas a mystic? This has been denied. If he were, one would not expect learned ignorance to be man's final stance before God; and one would expect something more ecstatic than the somewhat modest language of the *devotio moderna*. It has been said that Nicholas himself had no mystical experiences; yet he speaks of the "mental trance" in which he saw God. I do not see how or why one should wish to deny that the author of the *Visio dei* was a mystic in the fullest sense of the word, provided we remember that a mystic in the fifteenth century could be many things besides.

The "vision of God" is *meant* to be equivocal. It is man's vision of God, and it is God's vision. Nicholas brings this fully intended equivocation to a vivid presentation by talking of pictures by Roger van der Weyden, which he had seen in Brussels, and others he possessed. These he takes as "ikons of omnivoyance," because the eyes seem to look directly at every viewer, wherever he stands. God sees the world as the subjects of these paintings see it, not as we men see it; for we men see first one thing and then another, and in seeing one thing cannot see something else in a different direction. Yet of course the picture does not literally see anything; that it seems to do so depends upon *our* vision *of* it. In human perspective, to see and to be seen are different; for the infinite God, to be seen and to see are identical.[2] Even in seeing God, man sees himself in and through God's eyes: "O Lord, how marvelous is thy face, which a young man, if he strove to imagine it, would conceive as a youth's; a full-grown man, as manly; an aged man, as an aged man's!"[3] But the picture is (or rather suggests, by an un-geometrical extension of the metaphor) all these things, without letting them be contrary to each other:

I behold in the face of the picture a figure of infinity, for its gaze is not limited to one object or place, and is thus infinite, seeing that it is not more turned to one than to another of them that look upon it. Yet, albeit its gaze is infinite in itself, it seemeth to one regarding it to be limited, since it looketh so fixedly on any beholding it as if it looked on him alone and on nought else.[4]

Naturally, then, a discursive non-iconic theology must be negative, since it uses the language in which a word means one thing and not another, in which a perspective must be fixed. Compared to our learning about things, our knowledge of God is ignorance; but on the path to our knowledge of God, our reason itself erects barriers of ignorance: "The door of Paradise is guarded by the most proud Spirit of Reason, and unless he be vanquished, the way will not lie open."[5]

German mystics take one of two attitudes (or a mixture of two attitudes) toward the world. While admitting that God makes the world out of his own substance, and that the world is an emanation of God instead of a separate being over against him, mystics avoid pantheism by refusing to apply natural categories like space and time to God, while applying them to the world. Man is a part of the world, and so neither do human categories apply to God. Because of this categorial dualism, both the world and man seem alienated from God even though the Neoplatonic mystic knows that world and man are derived from God and are inexplicable and nonexistent without him.

But here the two paths diverge, and the dividing point is the question of the relation of man to the *natural* world. The alienation of nature from God may not weigh heavily on the mind of a mystic like Meister Eckhart, who is little interested in nature; but the alienation of man's soul from God, arising from his being a part of an alienated world, is the root of the mystical agony. By a denial of the world's autonomy, man can gain a sense of his now lost oneness with God. Such a mystical path of withdrawal from the world the better to approach God cannot lead to pantheism for a far deeper reason than that mentioned in the previous paragraph. It does not lead to pantheism because the natural world is not worth deification. Nature is a barrier between man and God; it is something to be negated, forgotten, or overcome. The danger in mysticism of this kind is not that it is akin to pantheism, but that it may lead to acosmism and solipsism. Instead

2 *The Vision of God*, trans. Emma G. Salter (London: J. M. Dent & Sons, 1928), chap. X, p. 47.
3 *Ibid.*, chap, vi, p. 25.   5 *Ibid.*, chap. ix, p. 44.
4 *Ibid.*, chap. xv, p. 70.

of depending on the teachings of the church derived from another's revelations, mystics of this kind see the self in the world as one with God in a direct and unmediated experience of union. To describe the experience, they use the language of love and vision, not that of cosmology and discursive logic. They make use of the vocabulary and ritual of their religious tradition, but it is the experience that sanctifies the vocabulary and ritual, not the sacramental which authenticates the experience. That is why the mystic is never safely orthodox and is always a threat to a fixed system of dogma.

The alternative path to God, the one followed by Nicholas, does lead to, or close to, pantheism. Nicholas' kind of mysticism is kept from pantheism only by the categorial dualism which is common both to him and Eckhart. But for Nicholas, nature is neither something to be deeply distrusted as an obstacle to be overcome along man's path to God nor is it something that the soul may, in a fit of mystical absentmindedness, simply ignore because it is not God. Instead of a withdrawal from the world for the sake of a hypostatic union with God—a union in which the world simply drops into non-being, leaving no rack or trace behind—Nicholas teaches a hypostatic union of nature itself with God. The near-deification of the world brings with it a deification of the soul. The soul is not alienated from God by its natural status. The tensions that led some mystics along the first path to transcend nature for the sake of union with God were like the tensions that led others along the second path. These latter wanted the world related to God in much the same way that the soul alone was related to God by Eckhart. Instead of acosmism, there is something very close to pantheism. Instead of mystical ecstasy, there is natural dialectic. Instead of the spiritual anthropomorphism of a holy family in the Godhead, there is negative theology based only on paradox.

Such negative theology tears apart a stable systematic network of dogma just as surely as ecstatic experience does. But Nicholas' dialectic carries the world with it when it escapes this network; man in his relation to God has no specially privileged position over the world and the church in their relation to God. All things are equally an epiphany; the soul of man is no better gateway to divinity than a geometrical figure.

Let us call this second path that of nature-mysticism, to contrast it with the soul-mysticism of Eckhart and his followers. German mystics after the fifteenth century frequently try to follow both paths. They want the world to be an epiphany, but they want their souls to have privileged access to its source. They are not satisfied with negative theology or an autonomous science of nature; they fill both with human-all-too-human fantasies, of the kind we shall find in Böhme. They see nothing paradoxical in nature, but see God himself as the paradigm of paradox, conflict, contradiction, tension, and agony.

Nicholas, however, with much more single-mindedness, follows the second path (in fact, he did not so much follow it as lay it out), and his path from the world and man to God might seem to be very much smoother. But in fact it is not. For though God and the world are in union, they are also polar opposites within it. Without God, we could say nothing true about the world; but there is nothing that we can say which is true about both of them. There is no comparison, no proportion, between the world and God, nothing common to them—this basic conviction is endlessly repeated by Nicholas. This much he might have learned from his nominalist teachers at Heidelberg, where he was a student at the time they dominated the university (1416); for they drew the conclusion from Occam that faith and reason were sharply separated. But Nicholas did not draw this conclusion, which led to a separation of theology from philosophy (and opened the way to a nominalist mysticism uncontrolled by any philosophic discipline). For, holding to the thesis of Neoplatonism, which teaches that the world is necessarily derived from God's infinite being, Nicholas taught, as much as any scholastic, that knowledge of the world leads to knowledge of God. But—and here is where he parted from all Aristotelian scholasticism—it leads to knowledge of God not by extrapolation or analogy, but by way of paradox. The incompleteness of natural knowledge is not merely a quantitative incompleteness, to be corrected by more and more knowledge, or to be complemented by faith; its incompleteness is radical, and it is shown by the manner in which paradoxes arise in its most secure part, mathematics. Our knowledge of the world depends upon a knowledge which is not like any other knowledge we have, but on a knowledge to which we are brought by the paradoxes we discover in our knowledge: it is knowledge with the paradoxical name of "learned ignorance." Regarded as a gift of God, this knowledge is wisdom or, at least, human participation in divine wisdom; it is faith which the understanding unfolds but which may be possessed by the simple, and will be possessed by them in higher degree than by the scholastic philosopher who thinks there is a straight logical road to the deity.

The author of this remarkable strategy, Nikolaus Krypffs (= Krebs), was born in Kues on the Mosel in 1401, the son of a winegrower and bargemaster. He was educated at the school in Deventer and the universities of Heidelberg, Cologne, and Padua. He began his career as a canon lawyer and became a priest in 1430. As a leading exponent of the conciliar theory of church government he was present at the Council of Basel (1431–1433), but in the course of the long dispute between the papacy and the bishops he changed to the papal party when he saw that the disunion in the conciliar party would not lead to union but to continued discord and to threat of a renewal of the Great Schism. He was sent to Constantinople in 1437 to accompany the delegates of the Eastern Church to the ecumenical council at Ferrara (later moved to Florence), the purpose of which was to heal the breach between the two halves of Christendom. Thereafter he was sent as papal legate to Germany, working to have the empire accept the election of Nicholas V as pope. His success was rewarded with the cardinalate in 1448. In 1450 he was made bishop of Brixen (Bressanone) in the Tyrol, a see in strife with the Archduke of Austria. He was not able to resolve this dispute, and while in Austria he was subject to dangers and repeated indignities to his person and office. While bishop of Brixen he traveled also in Germany, seeking to introduce reforms and to help organize a crusade against the Turks, who had taken Constantinople in 1453.

In 1459 he was recalled to Rome by his old friend Aeneas Sylvius Piccolomini, now Pope Pius II, as a curial counselor. He died in Rome in 1464 and left his considerable estate (which he had augmented by what have been called "shady dealings in livings") to found a hospital for the elderly and to house his magnificent library in Kues. This foundation still exists. His body is buried in his titular church of San Pietro in Vincole in Rome, and his heart is buried in the Cusanus-Stift in Kues.

The writings of Nicholas of Cusa may be divided into several groups, though few of his books fall under only one rubric. His chief works, primarily concerned with Church polity and religious concord, are *De concordantia catholica* (1433) which is his defense of conciliar theory against papal authority, and *De pace fidei* (1453), on the unification of all religions. The principal religious (devotional) writings are *The Vision of God* (1453) and sermons and letters. His scientific writings are the *Reparatio calendarii* (1436), *De quadratura circuli* (1452) and *De staticis experimentis* (1453). Finally there are the philosophical works proper. By far the most important is the first *De docta ignorantia* (*Of Learned Ignorance*) and *De coniecturis*, both finished apparently in 1440. There are many smaller philosophical works, including the dialogues *De sapientia* and *De mente* (together with the *De staticis experimentis* they constitute the work *Idiota*, finished in 1450), *De possest* (1460), and *De non aliud* (1462). In addition, there is *De venatione sapientiae* of 1463, a somewhat autobiographical work describing his and others' "hunt for wisdom"; this is perhaps the best introduction, after *Of Learned Ignorance*, to his work as a whole.

Nicholas' Latin falls between that of the Italian humanists and that of the scholastics. In larger questions of rhetoric, style, and organization, however, he is definitely a humanist, with his writings in the form of essays, dialogues, and letters instead of great encyclopedic *summae*. His technical vocabulary is a mixture of those of scholasticism and Neoplatonism, together with a number of strange coinages of his own. In general the difficulty of understanding him comes from the intrinsic complexity of his thought rather than from any culpable failure on his part to write as clearly as his subject permitted.

Nicholas' vastly complex philosophy is obscure in many details, but its principal features, which give unity to its many complications and diverse applications in every field from church polity to cosmology, are repeated so often that they can be comprehended without great difficulty, though there will always be puzzling fragments left over that do not seem to fit into any unitary pattern. These main features can be summarized under the rubrics: the coincidence of opposites, learned ignorance, complication and explication, conjecture, the cosmological structure, and the dignity of man.

The Coincidence of Opposites (*Coincidentia oppositorum*)

The first of these doctrines, which leads directly into the next two, derives from the Neoplatonic tradition and John Scotus Erigena in particular. God, according to this teaching, is the coincidence of opposites, the one being to which contradictory predicates can and must be ascribed. The function of God in this metaphysics is to be the ground, source, and unity of all beings; as preeminent, unitary, and infinite being, he must be the metaphysical cause—efficient, final, formal, and material—of all the diversity of finite beings. God, therefore, provides the ground for differences in the world, which are not contradictory because they are ascribed to different things; but the oneness and unity of God require that these contraries be ascribed to him as one being, which then must have contradictory predicates. If, for example, God is white, then black things, which really exist, have no ground in being; hence God cannot be white. But if God is not white, then white things do not exist, . . . and so on for every pair of contrary predicates. Let us suppose, further, for a moment that God is white. But he cannot be white in the manner in which white *things* are white because, among other reasons, they are visible and he is not; hence to say that he is white is not to use the term univocally of him and things. Thus Nicholas concludes: "In theology negative propositions are true, and affirmative ones are inadequate."[6] We can at best say what God it not; we cannot adequately say what he is. When we are able to see that God transcends every concept we form of him, we see that we cannot know him; we see that our knowledge of God is a knowledge of our ignorance of him.

Learned Ignorance (*Docta ignorantia*)

In our ignorance, we do not apply predicates, or we misapply them. A man is ignorant if he says of something that it is a stone and not a stone, or if he can say neither that it is a stone nor that it is not a stone. This ignorance can be corrected; from sense experience we make abstraction of the concept of stone which our understanding (*ratio*) learns to apply to some things and not to others, and which it never applies to the things to which it applies the concept of "living." But because God is the coincidence of opposites—and incidentally because we have no sense experience of God—the understanding cannot correct its ignorance. For the ignorance we have of God is the same as the knowledge we have of things, since we are ignorant if we say God is white and do not add that he is also not white. The knowledge we have of God, that he is both white and non-white, is what we would call ignorance and error if we were talking of any other being. The only knowledge we have of God is that we are ignorant of him and that our ignorance is inescapable: this is learned ignorance, not the corrigible ignorance of inadvertence or neglect. When we learn that we do not know (in the sense in which we do know other things) we thereby reach another kind of knowledge which in the eyes of the world is ignorance. Those philosophers who have tried to know God by the natural intellect have failed; they have failed because they hunted in the wrong field, this

[6] *Of Learned Ignorance*, bk. I, chap. xxv; in the translation by Germain Heron (New Haven: Yale University Press, 1954), p. 61.

side of the fence erected by the law of contradiction.[7] It is an astonishing fact (astonishing to these philosophers), says Nicholas, that

reason strives for knowledge and yet this natural striving is not adequate to the knowledge of the essence of its God but only to the knowledge that God is so great that his greatness acknowledges no limit and thus is great beyond all conception and knowledge. But reason would not be satisfied with itself if it were the image (*similitudo*) of so poor and imperfect a creator that he could be greater and more perfect.[8]

While now, when the Aristotelian sect prevails, the coincidence of opposites is counted a heresy, to admit it is to begin the ascent into mystical theology.[9]

It seems to be a professional vice of philosophers, met with even before the Cusan, to say a great deal about what is unknowable, to speak of that whereof they ought to be silent; and though Nicholas warns that "this our search for inexpressible wisdom . . . is found in silence and looking rather than in loquacity and listening." [10] he tells us a great deal about the inexpressible being. He is too much a Neoplatonist to be democratic about all predicates: "It is truer . . . to deny that God is a stone than to deny that He is life or intelligence—truer to deny that He is intemperate than to deny that He is virtuous." [11] He is also too much a Christian to do so, for "understanding is the unfolding of what was wrapped up in faith; the intelligence is directed by faith, and faith is extended by understanding." [12]

The doctrines of learned ignorance and of the coincidence of opposites in God are epistemological and ontological sides of the same coin. But let us return now to the ontological side and ask: What are the contradictory predicates of God which are metaphysically interesting? They are the attributes which will help us to understand ("in an incomprehensible way," Nicholas often adds) the relation of God to the world.

The most interesting of these attributes is that of magnitude. The ontological argument depends upon the conception of God as maximum of reality or perfection, and this conception gives Nicholas the occasion for working out his theory of infinity. Medieval science agreed with Neoplatonism in a theory of intensive magnitudes by which qualities could be manifested in a thing by the degree of participation in a Platonic idea, so that as a body becomes hotter, for instance, it approaches a maximum of hotness and a minimum of coldness. God must be the highest number of

---

[7] *De venatione sapientiae*, chap. xiii; in the bilingual (Latin and German) edition by Paul Wilpert (Hamburg: Felix Meiner, 1964), p. 57; and in the Paris edition of *Opera* (1514; reprinted, Frankfurt; Minerva, 1962), vol. I, folio ccvi^r. N. B. The critical edition by the Heidelberg Academy (Leipzig, 1932–) is not yet complete. I therefore cite as follows: (a) If there is an English translation, that is cited. (b) If there is no English translation, and the work has appeared in Academy edition or the Wilpert edition, I cite one or the other of those. (c) Otherwise I cite the Paris edition.

[8] *De venatione sapientiae*, chap. xii (Wilpert, p. 49).

[9] *Apologia doctae ignorantiae*, ed. Raymond Klibansky (Heidelberg Academy edition), II, 6.

[10] *De venatione sapientiae*, chap. xxxiii (Wilpert, p. 153).

[11] *Of Learned Ignorance*, I, chap. xxvi (Heron, p. 61).

[12] *Ibid.*, III, chap. xl (Heron, p. 160).

a hierarchy, the most perfect or maximum being in any such series. But Nicholas saw two things wrong with this view that one could reach the conception of God by a series of gradations. First, the coincidence of opposites required him to say that God was not only the Maximum but also that he was the Minimum, for since the Maximum is everything it can be, it is also as small as it can be.[13] Second, there is an ambiguity in the concept of "maximum" as it is applied to God and to the things in the world. There is no absolute maximum in the world, for there always could be added another unit to make it larger; but when we say of God that he is the Maximum, we mean that no more perfect being can be conceived. Hence infinite magnitude in God is not a quantitative concept at all but simply a name for a superlative (just as "minimum" is another name for a superlative). The physical concept of degrees of intensive magnitude, therefore, fails to lead to the metaphysical concept of the Maximum. The mathematical concept of the infinite, however, gives us, according to Nicholas, an analogy to the coincidence of opposites in the absolute Maximum.

Nicholas' mathematical illustration throws light on almost every part of his philosophy, so it is well to consider it in some detail. "If we want to reach the Absolute Maximum through the finite," he writes,[14] "we must, in the first place, study finite, mathematical figures as they are, namely a mixture of potency and act; then we must attribute the respective perfections to the corresponding infinite figures, and finally we must, in a much more sublime way, attribute the perfections of the infinite figures to the simple Infinite, which cannot possibly be expressed by any figure."

The first purpose of this illustration is to show that the coincidence of opposites arises within the mathematics of the quantitative infinite and thus can illuminate the paradoxes in the simple infinite magnitude. Repeatedly, but most fully in *Of Learned Ignorance* (Chaps. 12 to 23), he argues as follows: Take any geometrical figure, such as a triangle or circle, and imagine it extended to infinity. In a circle, make the diameter infinite, and you reduce the curvature of the circumference to zero; it becomes a straight line infinite in length. In a triangle, make one side infinite, but the other two sides are longer than it, and hence they must become infinite also. But "it is impossible to have more than one infinite; therefore our transcendental conclusion is that the infinite triangle, though it is a perfect model of all triangles, is not composed of a plurality of lines, is not in any sense a compound, but is most perfectly indivisible; and since it is the perfect model triangle, it must have three sides; therefore the one infinite line is itself three lines, and these three lines are one perfectly indivisible line." [15] Generalizing, from several such examples, he says: "I maintain that if there were an infinite line, it would be at once a straight line, a triangle, a circle, a sphere; similarly if there were an infinite sphere, it would at once be a circle, triangle, and line; and it would be likewise with the infinite triangle and circle." [16] These truths are seen by the *intellectus*

[13] *Ibid.*, I, chap. iv (Heron, p. 12).
[14] *Ibid.*, I, chap. xii (Heron, p. 27).
[15] *Ibid.*, I, chap. xiv (Heron, p. 31).
[16] *Ibid.*

even in mathematics, where we go beyond the classificatory logic of the *ratio;* and they are not, Nicholas thinks, arbitrary puzzles, but involved in the nature of mathematical objects.

The second pair of interesting coincident opposites is actuality and possibility. God is the infinite actuality of all that is possible, not merely of all that exists. To name this pair, Nicholas coins the word *possest* and applies it to the one infinitely perfect being; he contrasts it to *posse fieri,* which is the opposite of *esse* when applied to things in the world. (We might try to put this in English by saying that he contrasts the "can be" of God, which is equivalent to "being" and "possibility," with the "can become" of finite things, which is precisely what they can be but are not.)

With these conceptions of God's attributes—a Maximum which is also a Minimum and therefore not quantitative (plural) but simple, and an actuality which is not contrasted with a possibility—we are ready to try to see how Nicholas interprets his mathematical examples to explain "in a mysterious way," as he confesses, the relation of God to the world.

Contraction and explication (*contractio et explicatio*)

Nicholas sometimes[17] uses the Neoplatonic term "emanation" to refer to the timeless unfolding (*explicatio*) of God in the world, but more often he uses his mathematical analogy. Just as the infinite line is, or contains, implicitly (*complicatio*) the triangle, circle, and sphere of which it is the limit as they are infinitely expanded, so also God as absolute unity and infinity contains implicitly the plurality of things contracted (*contracte*) into unity. Out of the *coincidentia oppositorum,* opposites emerge by explication. Nicholas' examples are drawn from geometry, but perhaps we will not be unfaithful to his teaching if we use examples of which he could know nothing. We can express a number in two ways: as a single term, for example, log x,—or as a series whose sum approaches the value of the term asymptotically as the series is extended. The *explicatio* of the number is the series; the *contractio* or *complicatio* of the series is the number.

Following this analogy,[18] Nicholas says that the world is in God "contractedly" (*contracte*) as the line is in the point *contracte;* or God is in the world spread out (*explicate*) as the line is made explicit by motion of the point. What is true of the relation of God to the world is true of the relation of the world to the individual things in it: each individual thing is the whole universe in condensed form (*contracte*). Everything is in everything, *contracte;*[19] this is "the same as saying that God, by the intermediary of the universe, is in all things, and that the universe, by the intermediary of all things, is in God."[20]

---

[17] *Ibid.,* III, chap. iv (Heron, p. 82).

[18] Nicholas is not consistent in his use of words drawn from the mathematical analogy. Sometimes the world is the *explicatio* of God—the expansion of God, as it were; sometimes it is the *contractio* of God—the limitation of God to this and not that. Occasionally he indicates that in any one instance it does not matter which we say.

[19] *Of Learned Ignorance,* II, chap. iv (Heron, p. 82).

[20] *Ibid.,* II, chap. v (Heron, p. 84).

There are many examples of the use of this analogy. In one example[21] he begins with the simple infinite as the Minimum and compares its explications to the development of point to solid body or of numbers from 1 to 2, 3, 4, 10 (the sum of the first four) and 100 and 1000 (the second and third powers of ten), these being the numbers "corresponding to" the infinite one, the *intellectus* (the power of seeing the coincidence of opposites), the soul (an individual), the body, and the world. Each of these participates in the higher and is superseded by the higher; each is a concretization of the higher and a limit upon it. Another example[22] is the contraction of God into the universe in its infinite plurality, of the universe into its genera, of these into species, and finally of species into individuals, only the first and last of which actually exist. Again, he sees our mental acts as explications of our faculties. Genera and species are human constructions, i.e., mental abstractions, but they reproduce inadequately the essential likeness and differences of things, which are explications of God. Nicholas' view of universals is closer to conceptualism than to nominalism: our conceptions are not universals in things, but human constructions or conjectures.

Conjectures (*Coniecturae*)

Nicholas uses the words "conjecture" and "conjectural" in two different but related senses. Epistemologically, they refer to the mode of man's knowledge before the level at which he attains a knowledge of the coincidence of opposites and hence of his own ignorance, and to the images or pictures men make to themselves of the simple infinite being which is not adequately represented by any of their concepts. The ontological use of "conjectural" refers to the status of the world of things which are known by conjecture. The being of the world is partial, not genuine or independent; it is characterized by otherness, plurality, non-being, and imprecision. We shall have more to say of the ontological meaning when we come to speak of Nicholas' cosmology, since the world itself has "conjectural being"; but we can indicate what Nicholas means by analogy; he calls the visible church (with all its imperfections, compared to its divine model) a "conjectural church" (*ecclesia coniecturalis*).[23]

Nicholas seems to have been led to this important conception again by his meditations upon mathematics.[24] Pure mathematical knowledge is a knowledge of our own mental creations and is perfect; we know the essential properties of a triangle because we made it, and it has no properties except those which are essential to it. There is no imprecision, no more or less, no probability, in our knowledge of mathematical entities. But our knowledge of the world, even when it has mathematical form, is imprecise; we know not only what a triangle is, we know also that there is no perfect triangle actually in existence. Hence our knowledge of visible

---

[21] *De coniecturis* I, chaps. vi–x, (Paris ed., folio xlii^d–xlvi^r).

[22] *Of Learned Ignorance*, II, chaps. iii, vi; III, chap. i.

[23] Cited from Karl Jaspers, *Nikolaus Cusanus* (Munich: R. Piper, 1964), p. 14.

[24] *De coniecturis*, I, chap. xiii (Paris ed., folio xlviii^r).

figures and physical things in the world is conjectural, like the second level in Plato's account of the levels of knowledge.

Our knowledge begins with sense experience of physical things which awakens our reason (*ratio*);[25] reason conceptualizes the plurality of things by abstraction of common properties and classifies them. But the classifications do not adequately repeat the essential likenesses of things and our measurements do not give numbers which accurately fit them; for what we call a sphere is actually not quite a sphere, and is also many other things which we neglect or tacitly deny when we call it a sphere. There is nothing in the reason which was not first in the senses,[26] and hence our rational knowledge cannot be brought to perfect correspondence (*adequatio*) with the things. Each of the conjectures we make depends upon the limited position of man, and Nicholas develops very pleasingly the analogy between our perspectives on God and the world to the portrait by Roger van der Weyden, to which I referred earlier.

Our best knowledge is knowledge of the measure of things; Nicholas suggests that the noun *mens* is derived from the verb *mensurare*;[27] but our measurements are conjectural only, for there is no fixed point in the world, no actual maxima and minima, no absolute rest, no two things exactly alike (and therefore no absolute equalities), no absolute center, no perfect sphere (of the earth) or perfect circle (of planetary movements). The imprecision or conjectural status of the world is illustrated by many examples drawn from astronomy, geometry, and music.[28]

The metaphysics, aside from the mathematical analogies, is medieval; but the applications and conclusions are Renaissance. We shall summarize Nicholas' remarkable conclusions under two headings: the world and man.

The Cosmological Structure

Perhaps Nicholas is best known as the man who is said to have anticipated by over a century Copernicus' theory of the motion of the earth. This is hardly true. Though he said that the earth moved and that it did not have a position in the center of the universe, he did not argue that the earth moved around the sun, and he denied what Copernicus was to teach, that the sun is in the center of the universe. But what keeps Nicholas from being in the line of the great astronomers is that his conclusions were reached entirely as a consequence of a metaphysical speculation and not at all as a result of empirical observation and calculation. And we cannot well imagine Nicholas taking the deviations from a circular orbit seriously, as Kepler did, for though he denied a purely circular movement, he did so on grounds of the "imprecision" of all things physical and not because he thought, as Kepler did, that whatever positions and movements the

---

[25] *Ibid.*, II, chap. xvi (Paris ed., folio lxii[d]).
[26] *Idiota de mente*, chap. ii (Heidelberg Academy ed. [Ludovicus Bauer, ed.] Leipzig, 1937, V, 53).
[27] *Ibid.*, chap. i (Heidelberg Academy ed., V, 48.)
[28] *Of Learned Ignorance*, bk. chaps. xi and xii. Thus Nicholas has an a priori argument for the irregular movement of the earth.

heavenly bodies had, they were susceptible to exact mathematical treatment. Had Nicholas been more influential in his time, we might think that he in some way prepared the stage for Copernicus, but not even that can be claimed in his favor. Copernicus was a scientist and very little a philosopher; Nicholas was a philosopher and very little a scientist.

Not only did Nicholas fail to anticipate Copernicus in any significant way; he did not have a workable theory of science which a scientist could have used. For he did not see the function of conjectures to be that of hypotheses that could be checked and submitted to experimental control; they were pictures which, to be sure, had alternatives, but the alternatives were simply different ways of seeing the same thing. The measurements he insisted should be made were left as isolated numbers; they were not values to be put into hypotheses or laws. His measurements and counting sometimes touched on important and fruitful questions, such as the determination of specific gravities of different kinds of bodies, but they also were devoted to such numerological computations as determining the date of the end of the world. We can easily imagine him doing much that Kepler did—from casting horoscopes to writing on the harmony of the spheres; but we cannot think of him as formulating, testing, and rejecting innumerable hypotheses because they did not fit by an error of eight minutes of arc the data on the orbit of Mars. He had one conception which has proved essential in modern science—that measurement is important. But he lacked two other conceptions without which measurement is not able to fulfill its function. He did not conceive of mathematical laws by which the number assigned to one thing is a function of numbers assigned to others, and he did not conceive of alternative hypothetical connections of one measured quantity with another, so that experimental observation could choose among the alternative mathematical conjectures.

In spite of all this, however, Nicholas is important in the history of science at least as a symbol, if not a cause, of what was to characterize the study of nature. He, like Albertus Magnus before him, had respect for nature; nature was a worthy object of study. Those who believed that the world is vile because it is a world of change and corruption, those who separated it from God by intermediaries such as the world-soul, and those who saw it as a barrier between men and God could not see it as a worthy object of study; on the other hand, those who gave it a permanent and privileged status as the center of the universe were simply wrong. Nicholas denies the privileged status of the world; the universe has no center and no circumference; the earth is not the only inhabited star; it is not made of baser matter than the rest of the universe, and change and corruption are characteristic of all things and not just of the earth. The most significant and symbolic way in which Nicholas anticipated Copernicus was in moving away from anthropocentrism and geocentrism, in breaking the connection between the apparent geometry of the world and theology.

In another respect, Nicholas' theory of mathematical knowledge was rich in implications which have been repeatedly explored by philosophers since his day. If his conception that nature is mathematical and that God created the universe by figure and number was ancient, his theory of mathematics as a human creation was genuinely new. Man's mind creates mathematical figures and numbers; that is why they are completely transparent to us. Man's mind is an image of God's, and that is why our applied mathematics is as nearly accurate as it is. God's thought creates things, man's mind creates images or conjectures of things. Man is the creator of a spiritual world which more or less conforms to the actual world. Man is a little god; and the clue to wisdom is found in the streets where men measure, weigh, and count, and not in the books of the schools.[29]

The Dignity of Man

Man shows his divine nature in his creative activity in mathematics, as we have seen, and also in art and craft. Art is not an imitation of nature, for the spoon-maker (the principal speaker in the dialogue *De mente*) creates by an idea in his mind something that has no counterpart in nature, just as God and the mathematician do. "These capacities lying in him lead him to esteem himself and let him believe that he can approach all things by his own measure. Man is a god, though not in an absolute sense because he is still man: he is a human god. Man is also the world, though not concretely, because he is still man. He is a microcosm, a miniature world or a human world. The realm of humanity comprehends God and the cosmos within the power of man. Man can be a human God and a God in a human manner; he can be a human angel, a human brute, a human lion or bear, or anything else, for he has within his power to be all things in a human manner."[30]

Only one man can reach the fullest perfection and rise to complete union with the Maximum: "This man would so be man as to be God, would so be God as to be man, the perfection of all things and in all things holding the primacy."[31] This God-man is Christ.

But we are all little gods, reflecting, in the conjectures and images we create, the universe and God, with varying degrees of adequacy. Each religion, for instance, is a human conjecture about that which is above our power of knowing accurately. This is the ecumenical consequence of the theory of conjecture as Nicholas drew it in his *De pace fidei*, whose theme has been repeated again and again by almost believers in rational religion, including Lessing in *Nathan the Wise*.

At the end of this exposition, the reader will appreciate the difficulties pointed out in classifying our Cusan. I said his metaphysics was medieval,

---

[29] *Idiota de sapientia*, bk. I (Heidelberg Academy ed., V, 6).

[30] *De coniecturis*, II, chap. xiii (Paris ed., folio lxʳ).

[31] *Of Learned Ignorance*, bk. III, chap. iii (Heron, p. 135). The position of Christ in Nicholas's philosophy is subject to dispute. He is the "bracket of the world," a mediator between man and God. But Nicholas has repeatedly denied that there is any need of mediation, and has denied the Neoplatonic World Soul in order to maintain the direct inherence of God in the world. But he accepts Christ on faith and attempts to make this intelligible. His arguments are sometimes quasi-numerological (trinitarian); but here he is arguing that the perfections he has been ascribing to man are true of men in their plurality, and he is praising humanity and not man. These perfections are not perfect if not realized in an individual, since only individuals exist. Therefore there must be one man who is truly god-like.

but his conclusions Renaissance. I meant that he drew his metaphysical inspiration from Dionysius the Areopagite, John Scotus Erigena, and Meister Eckhart, but he came back to earth close to the students of nature and the humanists who were praising the power and dignity of man. But in the Renaissance we often contrast the philosophy of nature and humanism; no such contrast can be applied to Nicholas, because to him man is a microcosm and without knowledge of him we cannot understand nature. And he is unintelligible except as an image of God and the natural world *contracte*. If we give up vain efforts at classification and do not seek direct influences on the philosophers who followed him, we can appreciate Nicholas of Cusa for presenting, in the earliest full form, various attitudes which have been repeated in German philosophies in the succeeding centuries. His theory of conjectures suggests Leibniz' view that we and all things are living mirrors of the universe. His theory of the creativity of the mind in making world-pictures in mathematics and science is not wholly unlike Kant's. His theory of the polarity but unity of man, God, and nature is elaborated by Schelling (who, we know, was actually influenced by reading Nicholas). Nicholas' denial of a gradual transition ("approximation") between the finite and the infinite has made him a favorite among existential philosophers.

But the misfortune was that he had no followers. Bruno, a century later, complained that the Germans had forgotten him. What was rich and suggestive in his work was neglected. The points at which he was a harbinger of future philosophy were so inextricably connected with a metaphysics drawn from the past that when Germany began to move in humanistic and scientific directions it did so under foreign (Italian and French) influences and threw away his metaphysics. If any stream of thought can be traced, even intermittently, back to Nicholas it was that of the philosophy of nature, theosophy, and Protestant mysticism; and this stream did not lead to the most significant work in philosophy.

V

Nominalism and the Rise of University-Philosophy

Mysticism, while not necessarily incompatible with scholasticism, developed mostly outside the universities and was even, in part, a lay movement. The intellectual movement we are about to survey, nominalism, occurred within the scholastic tradition. Though nominalism of the fourteenth and fifteenth centuries is sometimes considered to show "the decline of scholasticism," this is an apt description only from one specific point of view. If by scholasticism we mean dialectical philosophy in the service of theology (*ancilla theologiae*), then nominalism is a decline from the conception that Albertus Magnus and Thomas Aquinas had. If, on the other hand, we consider scholasticism to be the philosophy of the arts faculties, its growing independence of theology can be seen as a strengthening, or at least as an opportunity for strengthening, the discipline of philosophy and the autonomy of a slightly more secular learning than that possible in the days of the great *summae*. It would, however, be dangerous to exaggerate either the degree to which theology was ill-served by the new movement, or the degree to which philosophers actually enjoyed a freedom from concern with the questions of faith and an immunity to theological censure. In Germany, particularly, the potentialities of nominalism in these directions were not realized.

Germany had no universities in the thirteenth century. German students in arts and theology generally went to Paris, occasionally to Italy, after completing their preliminary studies in the cathedral and monastic schools in their homeland. While some remained in France (as Hugo of St. Victor did) and others returned to Germany as officials in their orders or teachers in their schools (as Albertus Magnus and Meister Eckhart did), the main center of philosophical and theological work was Paris. We have found, for this reason, that the history of philosophy in Germany during this period was discontinuous and episodic; again and again, what happened in Paris determined what, if anything, happened in Germany. Philosophy, being essentially scholastic in the sense of being the arts preparation for theological study, could take root and flourish only in the intellectual life of a university or *studium generale*. In the thirteenth century, only Cologne approached offering such an environment, and the Albertist teachings were continued there in competition with the new intellectual movements introduced elsewhere when universities were established. Through a series of political contingencies, the new universities were to stand opposed to both the Albertist and Aquinian teachings; and though these teachings continued in Cologne, Louvain, and a few other centers, and sometimes were professed side by side with the newer doctrines, the main features of German intellectual life were to be determined by nominalist teachers, until the entire scholastic enterprise was successfully attacked by the humanists, and Catholic polity and theology by Luther. Only in the Counter Reformation was there a scholastic turn away from nominalism toward the realism represented by Aquinas, and subsequently Protestant scholasticism itself followed Aquinas and Suarez.

Before we speak of the political events and their effects on institutions in Germany, however, we must speak briefly of nominalism itself, even though this takes us for a time outside the boundaries of Germany. Platonic realism, in St Anselm, had had to fight against the nominalism of Roscellinus; the realism of William of Champeaux had been defeated by the moderate conceptualism of Abelard; Albertus Magnus, availing himself of most of Aristotle's works and the teachings of Avicenna, had established a moderate realism. But the condemnation of the Averroists in Paris in 1277 and the associated threat to the use of Aristotle, though intended to restrict autonomous philosophy, had had the ironic effect of breaking up the subservience of philosophy to theology, without, however, letting them stand in opposition to each other as the Averroists had seemed to permit.

It is in William of Occam that we see the beginnings of this divorce insofar as it is not predicated, as it were, upon an adulterous relation with Aristotle himself. In his career during the struggles between the papacy and the empire, leading to the Great Schism, we see the beginnings of both German university life and German scholasticism. William was born in England in 1290 and became a Franciscan. He completed his study in Paris in 1324 but did not assume a teaching post in the university because he was called to Avignon by Pope John XXII to answer charges of heresy. His trial lasted three years, and some of his teachings were condemned. In 1329 he escaped from Avignon and took refuge first in Pisa and then in Munich with Ludwig of Bavaria, who claimed to be Holy Roman Emperor and had been excommunicated by Pope John. Thenceforth, until his death in the plague of 1349 or 1350, William defended the imperial position against the papacy. Legend has him saying to Ludwig, "Protect me with the sword, and I will protect you with the pen." In his campaign for the Emperor he condemned the corruption of the papacy and defended the right of a church council to judge a pope and, if necessary, to depose him. He challenged the pope's authority in political matters, and placed the authority of the Bible, tradition, and revelation above that of pope and curia. In these controversies Occam stood beside Marsilius of Padua, author of *Defensor pacis*, who also had taken refuge with Ludwig. Because he was at a court instead of a school, William does not seem to have had direct followers of his philosophy in Germany; the schools in Germany, like the one at Cologne, were taught by Dominicans, who adhered to the pope against the emperor. But William left disciples in Paris. These disciples were condemned by acts of the arts faculty in 1339 and 1340 for departing from the established traditions in the expositions of the texts, in which logic-chopping and oversubtlety were principal faults.[1] Though nominalism itself was not officially proscribed, it was declared an error punishable by exclusion from the university to teach that "things which are not signs, which are not terms or propositions, are not a part of science. [For] in the sciences, if we use certain terms, this is solely to take the place of things which we cannot introduce into our discussions; it is, therefore, of things of which we possess science, although we have it by the intermediary of terms and phrases."[2] The nominalistic emphasis upon words and terms, and not upon things, and the tendency to turn and twist terms and phrases for their own use and to multiply distinctions was present in both the Scotists and the Occamists, and this gave their pedagogies more points of similarity than their philosophies would suggest.

William of Occam was a nominalist in philosophy. For him, universals are names, but not names of real things, whether essences, natures, real species, or Platonic ideas. Universal terms mean individual things, for nothing but individual things exist. Universals—or, rather, universal terms —arise when we judge and apply a single predicate to a plurality of individuals. "Socrates and Plato are men" predicates manhood of Socrates and Plato; the judgment is about Socrates and Plato, but the manhood predicated of them is not universal man; there is no such thing, and realism is wrong. Nor does the predicate name something they have in common, for there is no common thing, nor an idea in the mind of God prior to the existence of Plato and Socrates (as the Neoplatonist scholastics held). Rather, the universal term is a single term used for many individual things, this use having been determined by convention. The so-called "concept of man" is not a universal idea in our minds (*post rem*, as the earlier nominalists had believed) but is a particular though confused idea that indiscriminately applies to several individuals without regard to their actual uniqueness. Hence a universal term can apply to several things, whereas

---

[1] Pierre Duhem (*Le Système du monde* [Paris: Hermann, 1954–59], VI, 693) sees rivalry between the spirit of Oxford and the spirit of Paris in the condemnation. Even then, there were veiled warnings against the influence of Oxford on perennial philosophy. *Nullumst iam dictum quod non sit dictum prius.*

[2] Quoted from Duhem, *ibid.*, p. 691,

the particular subject term may apply to only one. Furthermore, if we ask why the term "man" can be applied to both Plato and Socrates, we must not answer that it is because of something they have in common. There is no such thing; they are simply sufficiently alike to be denoted by one term that does not denote univocally the specific and unique characteristics of either. We should not explain their likeness and difference in terms of *quidditas* and *haecceitas*, as the Scotists did; Occam's razor cuts away these entities.

Since the only things that exist are unique individuals, our knowledge must begin with direct apprehension of individuals. William calls this apprehension intuitive. It is by abstractive knowledge that we make the universal terms which apply to many particulars in intuition, or by which we know individuals which we do not directly intuit. By abstractive knowledge we do not know that an individual thing exists, but only what possible things might exist; our whole instruction about existence is intuitive, since we cannot demonstrate, by the law of contradiction, the existence of one thing from the premise that something else exists. William does not identify intuition with sense perception, as later empiricists do; we may also have intellectual intuitions of things we cannot sense and, what is worse, we may have intuitions of things that do not in fact exist at all.

From all this it follows that we cannot prove that God exists. No proof of the existence of one thing from the existence of another is valid, and hence no proof of God's existence can be given. Moreover, an intuition of God might be incorrect. Our conviction of the existence of God is only probable if based upon philosophy, but its certainty comes from faith and the teachings of the Church.

Since universals do not exist *ante rem* in the mind of God, William concluded that the world is an absolutely free and arbitrary creation of God. God's will is prior to his intellect and is not limited by any necessary ideas except the law of contradiction; we cannot know his will by any reasoning, for that would show that God was constrained to create in one way rather than another. God has ordained that adultery is wrong, but he could have commanded it, and then it would have been right; God chose to appear as a man, but he could have appeared as a donkey. We know by experience that fire heats water, but God could have ordained that it would cool it. Our knowledge of the actual state of the world, then, can be got only by experience and probable reasonings based upon it. Whatever the state of the world, it tells us nothing about God's absolute power or perfection.

Let us now consider Occam's place in the long-continued debates about faith and reason, theology and philosophy, which agitated Europe for centuries. So long as it was believed that theology was a science the question of the relationship between the truths of theology and the truths of philosophy could not be avoided. Nor could it be solved without a subordination of one to the other, or a doctrine of a double truth (what is true in one may be false in the other), or a pious hope and effort to show that they never conflict, either in fact or in principle. Each of these expedients was employed, or at least there were accusations by philosophers who used one of them that there were other philosophers wrongly employing one of the others. But with Occam, theology is not a science, and philosophy is a science only of words and terms (*scientia sermocinalis*), or a science of the empirical and probable. Hence they talk about different things and never conflict either in their respective objects or in their epistemological procedures. Philosophy can offer probable arguments for the existence of God, and that is all. Could it not have done so, nothing would have had to be changed either in it or in theology. The only valid function that philosophy performs for theology is to systematize it and deduce consequences from dogmas of faith; and in this the sermocinal sciences are of more use than real philosophy (*philosophia realis*). Theology can thereby gain a systematic structure that seems to be that of a science, but since the premises are neither demonstrable nor intuitive, the superstructure built upon them is not, strictly speaking, a science. A theological sentence, therefore, even though it be a deductive consequence of others, is finally based upon faith.

Occam reached this conclusion about the status of theology not only from his logic and epistemology, but also from his conception of the nature of God. For Occam was no skeptic, but a fideist in his acceptance of dogma. The dogma he accepted was that of an omnipotent God—omnipotent and therefore not bound by any rule, moral or logical. God is defined by His omnipotent will. This voluntaristic theology strengthened the conclusion that could have been reached on epistemological grounds alone, viz., that reason cannot penetrate to the nature of God and his fiat and purposes, and that the existence of things in the world is not to be understood rationally simply because it was God who created and disposed them. This conclusion means that theology is free from philosophical criticism, while able to use philosophical analysis and synthesis. It also means that philosophy is free from theological limitation and, as natural knowledge, must be empirical in method and probabilistic in outcome.

From Occam's teachings, therefore, there flowed four streams that fed philosophical and theological thought for more than a century and a half. They were (a) the development of the *scientiae sermocinales*—logic, grammar, and rhetoric—untrammeled by any metaphysical or ontological presuppositions except that of the individuality of all beings; (b) a theology of faith, using philosophy and the sermocinal sciences just mentioned, but not threatened by any possible collision between metaphysical and theological claims; (c) empiricism in natural science, in principle but not in historical fact free from metaphysical and theological assumptions; and (d) skepticism issuing from the third of these streams. The first of these spread all over Europe. The second also spread throughout Europe, but was the only one of very much importance in Germany. The third was primarily a French phenomenon, though derivatives of it were found in Germany, in the scientific work of Albert of Saxony and Marsilius of Inghen, who were concerned with the theory of impetus and the explanation of motion, though they contributed nothing significantly beyond what Jean Buridan, of the arts faculty in Paris, had already done. In fact, it is positively painful to see how nominalists, armed with a theory of empirical knowledge, again and again failed to take advantage of it and instead solved their problems by an appeal to earlier authority. (Thus, for example, in their discussions of the motions of the earth, the plurality of worlds, and the possibility of a vacuum, Conrad Summenhart of Tübingen (d. 1502) and Friedrich Sunczell of Ingolstadt (d. ca. 1499) appealed to the condemnation of Averroistic errors by Tempier in Paris in 1277.)[3] Here, then, it was unlikely that the skeptical conclusion would be drawn from nominalism; in fact, the fourth of these possible outcomes of nominalism was seen only in France.

But "streams of thought" do not really flow. Ideas have to be taken from one place to another, or men with ideas have to go from one place to another. How nominalism came to Germany, therefore, is a straightforward question of historical fact.

Followers of Occam continued their own work in Paris after his excommunication in 1329 and his exile in Munich. They were themselves censured in 1339, but this censure seems to have had little force except against the skeptical views of Nicolas of Autrecourt and Jean de Mirecourt. Certainly Buridan was able to proceed without interference, and such logic-choppers as Jean de Ripa set the tone for a long time to come. The Great Schism of 1378 made for the spread of nominalism in Germany in spite of the condemnations of 1339 and 1340.

The Great Schism of 1378 placed the Germans in Paris in a difficult position. Since France accepted Clement VII as pope and Germany accepted the Italian Urban VI, those who belonged to the French party could not expect ecclesiastic preferment in Germany; nor could they well remain in Paris if they were not adherents of Clement. They were held to be in schism, and in 1381 Paris refused to grant them degrees. They were compelled to leave Paris and they took with them the Occamist teachings, especially in the form given to them by Jean Buridan. (Some Germans went so far as to see Buridan, not Occam, as their master and called their period the *saeculum Buridani*.) Some went to the University of Prague, which had been founded by the Emperor Rudolf in 1347, when the papacy was opposing the establishment of new theological faculties; others went to the University of Vienna (founded 1365). Universities were established in Heidelberg and Cologne in 1385 and 1388 respectively, partly at least to make the Rhineland a bulwark against the French and Avignon influence. Marsilius of Inghen, who had left Paris in 1378, became the first rector in Heidelberg. Albert of Saxony (1316–1390), who was rector in Paris in 1353, became rector in Vienna and continued his work in optics and mechanics. He was followed by Heinrich of Hainbuch (1325–1397), also called Heinrich of Langenstein, who left Paris in 1376 and developed still further the conciliar theory of William of Occam.[4] In 1409 there was an exodus of

---

[3] *Ibid.*, X, 183–187, 189; see also p. 246.

[4] One should not fail to mention at least one Heinrich of Oyter (b. ca. 1330?), who came to Vienna from Paris via Prague. But there is such confusion between Heinrich Otting, Heinrich Olting, and Heinrich Totting, and between the town-names of Oyta, Euta, Otha, and Huncta from which one or more of these Heinrichs may have sprung, that one does not know what to attribute to one of them and what to another, assuming,

over a thousand Germans from the University of Prague because of dissatisfaction with the predominance there of the realistic teachings of Jan Hus and discrimination against the Occamists who came from Paris—a discrimination which seems to have been compounded against them because they were Germans and not Czechs. They formed themselves into the University of Leipzig and strengthened the Occamist part in Heidelberg and Vienna.

By the Occamist party I mean those teachers of logic who used Occam's commentary on the logic of Peter of Spain, the standard logic text throughout the universities. They followed the methods of teaching and expounding the texts which we have seen condemned in Paris and were generally nominalists in their theory of knowledge and metaphysics. Because their body of teaching constituted a curriculum for a degree in the universities, this complex of new doctrine, new text, and new method of exposition was called the *via moderna*, in contrast to the *via antiqua* in which the commentaries of Albertus Magnus and Thomas Aquinas were used. This *via* prided itself on dealing with real things (*realia*) and not with words (*termini*), under the motto: *Nos imus ad res, de terminis non curamus*: "We ourselves go to things; we do not concern ourselves with terms."

Heidelberg was the chief bastion of the *via moderna*, and Cologne of the *via antiqua*. Heidelberg, however, was less successful than Cologne in maintaining the purity of its teaching. In 1406 Jerome of Prague, a follower of Hus, presented himself in Heidelberg for appointment and attacked the Occamists so strongly, calling them "logical heretics," that he was forbidden the right to lecture (though he continued to lecture, but in a cemetery!); and every other teacher coming from another university was required to pass a test of his "logical orthodoxy"—to show himself to be a follower of the traditions established by Marsilius of Inghen[5]—before being given the licence to teach (*venia legendi*). Some realists from Cologne succeeded in infiltrating Heidelberg, and the faculty later decided that every member should take an oath to teach only in "the accepted way established by Marsilius" at the founding of the university. The Elector, however, hoping apparently to gain an advantage over Cologne and to draw students from it, abrogated this faculty legislation and split the university into two faculties, one practicing the *via antiqua* and the other one the *via moderna*. Four months later he forbade vituperation between the parties and required that the students be permitted to attend lectures in either *via*. The faculties in 1455, however, made it difficult for a student to "transfer credits" (to use the modern terminology) from one to another. (There was a similar policy in Tübingen.) But by 1481 students in one *via* were required to attend lectures in the other when his own *via* did not have a qualified master on the specific work of Aristotle on which the lectures were

of course, that they were not all one and the same man. For a good piece of detective work in philosophical historiography, see Albert Lang, "Heinrich Totting von Oyta. Ein Beitrag zur Entstehungsgeschichte der ersten deutschen Universitäten und zur Problemgeschichte der Spätscholastik," in *Beiträge zur Geschichte der Philosophie und Theologie des Mittelalters*, 33 (1937), pts. 4 and 5.

[5] The *via moderna* was sometimes called the *via Marsilia* in Heidelberg.

to be held. Much of the controversy seems to have turned not on philosophical issues but on faculty politics and economic rivalry (there were certain emoluments that could be received only by members of one or the other of the *viae*). It was not to be expected, therefore, that the radical consequences of Occamism for theology and the sciences would be drawn in Heidelberg, and even Marsilius of Inghen, who followed Occam in logic and Buridan in cosmology (theory of impetus), followed Duns Scotus instead of Occam in metaphysics and theology, and offered a metaphysical argument for the existence of God.

Cologne, on the other hand, remained a fortress of realism by defying the wishes of the city fathers (who had converted the Dominican *studium generale* into the city university), expressed in 1425, that the teaching should follow the "new masters" Buridan and Marsilius instead of the "old doctors" Albert and Thomas. The officials claimed that the students were not able to understand the older writers as well as the new, and that realism was heretical,[6] having been condemned by the Council of Constance. This was not true; and the faculty responded that both *viae* were in fact followed; that in condemning Hus for heresy, the Council had not condemned his realism, and that the realism of Hus was not, in fact, the root of his heresy. Perhaps the most effective defense of the faculty, however, was their pointing out that the university would lose its students (to Paris, perhaps to Louvain?) if they changed their course. (It is interesting to note that the Elector Palatine was one of the counsel who had advised the civic authorities to request the change; the faculty, perhaps correctly, saw the request as a trick in the rivalry between Cologne and Heidelberg.)

I have gone into some detail on these squabbles in order to put the realist–nominalist controversy into focus, and to answer the question as to why the rivalry between the two schools did not have happier consequences in the clarification of a fundamental philosophical issue. Occamists should have maintained their master's clear-cut division between faith and reason and developed a clear-cut empiricism rather than a quasi-rationalism and Aristotelian authoritarianism in the knowledge of the world. To be sure, one cannot become an empiricist overnight, and it might have been expected that the authority of other students of nature, preeminently Aristotle, would have continued side by side with a gradually growing reliance on one's own observations. At least nominalism, consistently developed, would have gone as far as Buridan, if not all the way to Nicolas of Autrecourt, "the medieval Hume." Instead of this, in Germany we find independence from theology meaning little more than the new sophisticated way of reading texts, whether religious or secular. And we have seen how German nominalists thought the condemnation of Averroism in 1277 to be authoritative for their cosmological conclusions. Even if we disagree with the thesis that nominalism led, historically, to the science of the sixteenth and seventeenth centuries, and that realism, through its concern with the spirit of the texts instead of their letter, led to Humanism—two theses

---

[6] In Erfurt, there was no formally recognized distinction between the two *viae*, but Scotists were not admitted to the faculty because of their alleged connection with the Hussite heresy.

equally extreme, and equally to be rejected—we cannot hide the fact that nominalism in Germany did not properly exploit its own resources and, in science and philosophy, did not lead anywhere.

Though Stephen Hoest, the vice-chancellor of Heidelberg in 1499, said explicitly that all the disputes between the *viae* turned on the question of the status of universals,[7] Prantl, the most learned but least sympathetic historian of medieval logic,[8] came to the conclusion that the controversy over universals was not the dividing line, or not a dividing line as important as differences in the manner of expounding texts. More recent scholarship does not seem to me to have shown Prantl to be wrong on this point; in fact, more recent studies have shown that there was no *single* distinction by which men were then, and are now, assigned to one path instead of the other. The method of teaching, the texts and commentaries used, even a preference for an "a priori method" over an "a posteriori method"—from time to time any one of these might be decisive, and what was decisive in one university was not necessarily decisive in another, where different administrative arrangements and distinctions were in force. Perhaps the most generally valid distinction lies in the different weights attached to the sermocinal sciences (logic and rhetoric) and to the "real" sciences included under metaphysics. Naturally the last-named distinction had some correlation with that between nominalism and realism, but the adherents of the Occamist party rejected the name *nominalistae*, which was originally a term of abuse. Some leading members of the *via moderna* adhered to Thomistic or Scotistic theories in metaphysics and theology; no one clearly drew the conclusions implied by Occam's theory—conclusions which were very early drawn (and condemned) in France. Even the meaning of the terms *via moderna* and *via antiqua* varied, so that sometimes, for instance, Scotists were counted in one and sometimes in the other. The neatness of the dividing line was obscured also by the multiplication of *viae: antiqui* (Thomists), *moderni* (Scotists and Occamists), *Guilielmi* (Occamists), the latter sometimes called also *Gregorii*, after Gregory of Rimini.

Aside from the scientific work of Buridan, Nicolas of Oresme, and Albert of Saxony, the empirical opportunities opened by nominalism were not exploited. The adherents of science and of Humanism in the sixteenth century seem to some modern historians to be following the directions pointed out by the *via moderna* and *via antiqua* respectively. While the connection between the *via antiqua* and Humanism is hardly more than a fancy, a good a priori case might be made to show that empirical science arose out of nominalism and thus that the *via moderna* led to what *we* think of as modern. But the facts are rather different; the Renaissance opponents of scholasticism who worked in the name of science did not draw a nice dis-

---

[7] Quoted from Gerhard Ritter, *Studien zur Spätscholastik*, vol. II, *Via antiqua und Via moderna auf den deutschen Universitäten des XV. Jahrhunderts* (*Sitzungsberichte der Heidelberger Akademie der Wissenschaften*, phil.-hist. Klasse, 1922. (Volume II of this work is now reprinted with identical pagination (Darmstadt: Wissenschaftliche Buchgesellschaft, 1963.)

[8] Karl Prantl, *Geschichte der Logik* (1885–1890; reprint, Leipzig: Fock, 1927), I, 53, 193.

tinction between the *viae*, or hunt for scholastic predecessors. And in Germany, where the opposition to the *via moderna* was most moderate, there was the least disposition to follow it into the empirical study of nature. It was not until nominalism was established among some Protestant scholastics of the seventeenth century that Germany produced epistemologies congenial to the empirical study of nature. Hence we can only conclude that the *via moderna* in Germany did not lead to the emancipation of philosophy and science from theology to anything like the degree to which this occurred in other countries.

How little Occamism in Germany meant a reform of philosophy, how little it implied a vigorous effort toward setting it free or, rather, toward enjoying and using its freedom, is well illustrated by its most important representative there. He was Gabriel Biel (ca. 1430–1495), professor of theology in Tübingen, who was more important for his direct influence upon Luther than for any originality in his philosophizing. Biel distinguished between philosophy and theology, reason and faith, in the long-familiar manner. Philosophy is available to natural reason and experience, and it is adequate to our knowledge of nature and it shows that God does exist. There is no breath of the skepticism found in French Occamism here. Theology, on the other hand, is based on faith, revelation, and tradition and not on empirical or intuitive knowledge and reason; but it is not opposed to reason, because God, the object of faith, is mysteriously but inherently rational. Our failure to achieve rational and intuitive knowledge of him is a consequence of our creaturely status, not of God's irrationality; evidence of this is Biel's belief that angels and the beatified do possess actual knowledge of God, which is denied to us. For us, however, in our theology, when there is no directly revealed answer to a specific question, probable reasoning is allowed, and logic can be used in the organization of the articles of faith. But each article of faith stands alone, the object of a separate and independent revelation; each is consistent with the rest, but our acceptance of them is not based upon any insight we have into their connection with each other. In the natural world, reason does act independently of faith in the divine sphere. Faith seeks reason, but because of human limitations it achieves only probabilities where the voice of revelation does not categorically decide for us.

It might appear that the Occamist potentialities for skepticism, which were exploited in the theory of natural knowledge in France, were here confined to theology. But this was not so. For Biel believed that faith is no less certain than natural knowledge; in fact, it is more reliable than natural knowledge because the objects of faith are inherently rational. God's nature is not arbitrary or whimsical; there is reason in God and in his creation of this world. Our natural knowledge is predicated upon and directed toward what God actually created, and why he created thus we do not know rationally. For knowledge of his creation we have to go to experience (whose adequacy to support natural knowledge Biel did not challenge, any more than Buridan did). The extreme consequences of nominalism—skepticism of our knowledge of nature, blind faith in an inscrutable God who could by fiat have produced different moral and natural laws, even a willingness to accept a theory of double truth like that ascribed to the Averroists, and a sharp distinction leading to a divorce between theology and philosophy—were not drawn by Biel.

Such moderation was possible because Biel, like Occam, but unlike some of Occam's followers, did not accept a sharp division of the faculties of the soul. It is one soul that thinks and wills; there is a volitional element in knowledge, a cognitive element in willing. But in both man and God, it is the volitional act that is basic and explanatory of the other.

Much of Biel's moderate Occamism passed over into Protestant theology in the following century. Even the mode of religious life which fits into this framework resembles Luther's. We approach God not intellectually but through an affective submission to his will. Here the *devotio moderna* (Biel, too, had been a member of the Brethren of the Common Life), with its "self-justifying piety,"[9] provided a quasi-mystical supplement to the limitations of human reason in its search for God. The *devotio moderna* and the *via moderna* both led to the Reformation, once the political times were ripe for it.

[9] H. A. Oberman, *The Harvest of Medieval Theology* (Cambridge: Harvard University Press, 1963), p. 352.

Two

From Luther To Leibniz

VI

Philosophy of the Reformation

Introduction

Between Nicholas of Cusa in the fifteenth century and Leibniz at the end of the seventeenth, there was no one in Germany who shared the stage of world philosophy with men like Bacon, Hobbes, Descartes, and Spinoza.

During the sixteenth century Germany was torn by religious strife that repeatedly broke out into armed conflict, and thought was constantly affected by persecution. During the seventeenth century Germany was the scene of the Thirty Years' War (1618–1648), which more than decimated its population, destroyed its wealth, and closed many of its universities. A civil war, continued by foreign intervention aiming in part at territorial booty and in part at simply continuing devastation in order to weaken the country as a whole, was blundered into for no constitutional or moral principle. Bribery and disloyalty prevented the development of even any consistent ideological commitments out of which philosophical thought on human well-being might have developed. The Thirty Years' War was a disaster of almost incomparable magnitude; it left the country devastated and it did not solve a single political problem which was not narrowly dynastic in origin and scope. The War is perhaps unique among the great civil wars of modern history in its failure to rise into a moral dimension, to mobilize ideologies which might—say in men like a Dante, a Hobbes, a Milton, a Fichte, or a Lenin—produce philosophy. One can read almost the whole corpus of German philosophy of the period without seeing any clues that a savage war was being fought, perhaps in the next town. One sees the effect of the war in philosophy, if at all, only in the lack of first-rate talent devoted to it.

In spite of Humanism and the Reformation, without which the birth of the modern world, not only in Germany, is almost unthinkable, however one defines the medieval and modern worlds one looks in vain for characteristic traits of modern civilization and world-view in Germany before the end of the period we are about to discuss. Religious toleration that was more than an act of political desperation; the development of a centralized and stable political power able to handle in dependable ways the provision of the necessities of civil life; an acceptance of secular political institutions justified by more than divine right and dynastic pretensions; the recognition of the practical importance of science and the organization of institutions for exploiting it; the provision of education for gentlemen as well as for priests and bureaucrats—the failure to achieve any of these delayed the birth of the characteristic features of the modern world in Germany. This delayed birth was followed by a delayed adolescence; and Germany went through spiritual experiences in the eighteenth century that had already been lived through by France, England, and Holland in the late sixteenth and seventeenth centuries.

Bacon, Hobbes, Descartes, Spinoza, Galileo, and Newton were either already dead or had at least accomplished all their major work before a man who was their equal appeared in Germany. Had there been no German theologian except Luther and no German scientist except Kepler, and no German philosopher at all between Nicholas of Cusa and Leibniz, it is unlikely that things would be different today. From the standpoint of world history, philosophy in this period in Germany simply does not count. This is the Dark Ages of German philosophy.

Yet in a history of Germany, two centuries cannot be skipped because they made no important contribution to world-philosophy. For they were not a hiatus in German intellectual history itself, and the beginnings of the world-historical philosophers of the later period can be found in them. Some of the issues which were agitating the philosophers of the rest of Europe were agitating the theologians of Germany. But the ideas and attitudes in these controversies which were on the whole triumphant in Germany were those which were being abandoned elsewhere.

The situation is highly complex, and it is necessary to explain how we shall treat the various overlapping and contrasting topics. The present chapter will deal with Humanism and the Reformation down to about the time of the Heidelberg Catechism of 1562 and the Formula of Concord of 1577. The principal figures to be considered are Erasmus, Luther, Calvin, and Melanchthon.

Chapter VII, "The Philosophy of Protestant Orthodoxy," will deal with the reactions against the Melanchthonian synthesis of humanistic philosophy and a diluted form of Lutheran dogmatism, the chief of these reactions being the development of a system of Protestant scholasticism which dominated German university life during most of the seventeenth century.

In Chapter VIII, "Occultism, Spiritualism, and Pietism," we shall consider the religious thinkers and two of the natural philosophers who opposed the Lutheran and Calvinist dogmatisms and academic philosophers, and Chapter IX will discuss the philosophers, some within and some outside the universities, who were more concerned with the problems of the philosophy of nature than humanistic or theological questions.

The Reformation is the most important event in the history of Germany, but it is not an event that belongs intrinsically to the history of philosophy. And yet we must speak of "the philosophy of the Reformation" because the philosophical work was done in new Protestant institutions and directly or indirectly for the sake of Protestant theology and regimen. The issues separating Lutheran, Calvinist and Catholic philosophers were not primarily philosophical; they were theological and political, and the competence of philosophy to settle theological issues had long since been surrendered, not to be reclaimed until the eighteenth century. Within philosophy there were differences of interest and emphasis, to be sure; but the most important differences among the three confessions lay not on the surface of opposing philosophies but were deeper and less conceptual. Philosophy sprang, in each communion, from different intellectual, political, and moral purposes. In spite of nominalism the long subservience of philosophy to the needs of theology continued, and when new theological and ecclesiastical institutions were established, naturally each complex of intellectual, political, and theological doctrines and practice had its own philosophical substructure or elaboration. Since the original differences between them were strictly theological, being dependent upon different practices and interpretations of revelation and of what lay beyond reason, it would be expected that the philosophical differences would not be very great; but inasmuch as the great confessions developed in conflict with each other, it would also be expected that whatever differences there were would be polemically magnified. This expectation can be confirmed; yet in spite of this, philosophy during the seventeenth century became to a surprising degree interconfessional, providing the polemical tools for both sides in the theological debate while remaining largely unaligned in the debate between the orthodox in each confession. Naturally this statement must be modified when we consider the fact that many men united in themselves the two professions of theologian and philosopher; but the separation of philosophy from theology—indeed their opposition in principle—had become so wide that even in these cases we can discern common philosophical bases for diverse theological positions.

This is not to say, of course, that there were no differences when we consider the movements as a whole, even though they may be hard to pick out when we look at a few individuals. Catholic philosophy turned against the later scholastic nominalism which was thought to have sown the seeds of the Protestant revolt, and Thomas Aquinas came into his own. Counter Reformation thought was largely influenced by Fonseca and Suarez, in their modernization of Thomas, and no important original work was done by German Catholic philosophers, who were content simply to follow Suarez instead of using him for further work as the Protestants did. Calvinism had a vigorous life only on the periphery of Germany, and never gained dominance for any long period of time in any part of Germany. But its theology favored a freer development of philosophy, its congregational organization permitted a more various and variegated intellectual life, and its exposed position on the western boundary of Germany made it more permeable to intellectual currents from the West than we find to be the case with Lutheranism. The main burden of philosophical work in Germany, therefore, was carried by Lutherans, who had to contend with a theological and ecclesiastical system which was often inimical to free philosophizing. Though most German philosophers since that time have been Lutheran in their personal affiliation, there was actually a greater contribution by the Calvinist minority of the sixteenth and seventeenth centuries to the philosophical movements of the eighteenth, than there was by the Lutheran majority. (In the nineteenth century, on the other hand, not only were most of the philosophers personally Lutheran, but a Lutheran turn of mind replaced the typically Calvinistic thought-system of the Enlightenment.) How a country largely Lutheran in its composition could, for about a century, think as if it were Calvinistic is to be explained by the influence of Western (French, Dutch, and English) thought which made itself felt from just before Leibniz to the time of Kant. This does not mean that Western thought was confessionally Calvinistic—neither Descartes nor Spinoza nor Locke was a Calvinist!—but only that Calvinism, especially in some of its heretical offshoots, was contrasted with Lutheranism in many of the same ways that the Enlightenment was contrasted with the Age of Reformation and Orthodoxy. How this came about is one of the most interesting features of the philosophy of the Reformation, but before it can be explained we must go back to the beginnings of the Reformation.

Humanism

No one set of facts—political, economic, theological, intellectual—explains the Reformation; but given the facts in all these categories, it seems almost self-explanatory. Some of them are perhaps more important in explaining its initiation, others in explaining its success. Since what we call the Reformation was not a homogeneous movement, did not start from a single geographical or intellectual point, and did not at all times have the same goal, any simple explanation is bound to apply to only a small part of it. We have spoken of the contribution of mysticism, a constant threat to ecclesiastic solidarity even when practiced in the bosom of the church, and of nominalism, which robbed theology of much of its intellectual support in metaphysics. In a few isolated individuals (almost all of them outside Germany) the empirical study of nature had the effect of threatening Catholic theology indirectly, but effectively, by an attack on its greatest secular authority, Aristotle. The most important of the factors, in Germany, however, was humanism, which had little mystical and no nominalistic scientific inspiration.

"Humanism" means many things in the history of philosophy, and it is too easy to read the meaning it had in one country and in one century into others where it has a quite different meaning. In Germany we speak of "Carolingian humanism," which meant hardly more than a broadening of interest beyond the narrow confines of monastic education, and of classical humanism in the beginning of the nineteenth century, which was a reaction against the alleged narrowness of Enlightenment ideals. But one thing humanisms always have in common: they are always against doctrines, practices, and institutions which seem to confine human interests and talents; they are protests of the whole man against the partial man produced by and for institutions and systems of thought which seem for that very reason to be oppressive and restrictive. Twice in German history the ideal of such protest has been found in Greece. In the fifteenth and sixteenth centuries it was an appeal to the Greece of Plato, Aristotle, the Stoics, the dramatists, the poets, and the historians against a medieval Aristotle. The initiative for this humanistic movement came from Italy, which was at this time going through a process of assimilating Plato again, of studying nature through Platonic eyes, of rediscovering and praising the dignity of man.

The founder of German humanism (or shall we say its chief importer?) was Rudolf Agricola (1443–1485), "the German Petrarch," who brought humanist teachings from Italy to Heidelberg, where he taught. Agricola brought Petrarch's critical attitude toward scholasticism into Germany. He remained a good Catholic, and there is but little discomfort in his mind about the features of the Church which were to exercise later humanists. His most lasting influence in Germany was not on the other humanists, who soon turned to criticism of the Church, but on Protestant thinkers of the next century who modified scholastic teaching to make it of service to their theology. His principal work, *De inventione dialectica*, was the original source of the logical treatises of both Melanchthon and Peter Ramus. In it, he opposed scholasticism for all the intellectual and pedagogical sins that were to be broadcast for the next fifty years; but more important was his breaking the monopoly of the scholastic logic represented by the most widely used textbook of that century, the logic of Petrus Hispanus (after 1276, Pope John XXI). Against this logic he proposed a logic or dialectic which would be an efficient means of instruction instead of an arid science of proofs. This meant a turn to the rhetorical writings of antiquity—chiefly those of Cicero—to replace Aristotle's analytics, and an emphasis upon the ways of leading to firm opinion or probabilities instead of striving after demonstrable truths. The connection of logic, both in theory and in pedagogical practice, with theology and metaphysics was broken, and a new connection with humane and profane letters was established. This instrumental and rhetorical logic reappears especially in the work of Melanchthon, who called the *Inventione* the best new work in logic of that period. Melanchthon's friend Johannes Sturm (1507–1589), of Heidelberg and Strassburg, introduced it in Paris, where it was heard by and had an unmistakable influence on Ramus.

Humanist circles outside the universities sprang up in almost all parts of Germany in the late fifteenth century. Petty courts had resident humanists as their showpieces, and humanists secured chairs in some universities.

Most universities, however, resisted the invasion because humanism represented a new method of teaching from classical sources which were neglected by the schoolmen. The humanists were not seen, nor did they see themselves, as defenders of one *via* against the other; they were opposed to the entire scholastic apparatus and method of learning and teaching. Originally hardly more than a program for the reform of universities through improvements in the arts curriculum, humanism soon became a source of widespread attack on things medieval—openly an attack on the universities and the scholastics, who resisted them, and on monasticism; covertly an attack on the Church through criticism of what the humanists considered its abuses, such as the veneration of relics, pilgrimages, monastic and clerical luxury, the exploitation of the German people by foreigners, and superstition. Sebastian Brandt's *Ship of Fools* (1494), the *Letters of Obscure Men* (1515), and Eramus's *The Praise of Folly* and some of his *Colloquies* typify this protest of humanists, who were making serious fun of the features of Catholic life which Luther was to fight against. In the writings on German history by Conrad Wimpfeling and in the nationalistic propaganda of Ulrich von Hutten a patriotic element was injected into humanist criticism, and this likewise helped set the stage for Luther's Reformation, which would have been impossible had there not been a peculiar conjunction of political issues between Christendom and the Turks and between Rome, the Emperor, and the College of Electors.

German humanism, unlike Italian, did not produce any important system of philosophy; but German humanists deserve a place in the history of philosophy they did not earn by their eclectic and unoriginal concern with issues which belong at least on the periphery of philosophy. For their satires, lampoons, orations, and editions had a greater effect on German thought than any continuation of philosophic subtleties could have had. Yet, had it not been for Luther's Reformation, their work would have been futile and known only to historians of literature. By themselves, they represented either a too precious modification of Catholic thought (for example, in the efforts of Mutianus Rufus to assimilate Catholic theology and Greek mythology) or too radical a change in theological values to be effective without some institution to create a *cultus* to carry their teaching.

Italian humanism did not contribute to any fundamental religious revolution; German humanism did. While Italian humanism carried through a return to classical sources and the inspiration of Greece and Rome, in Germany there was also a return to two other phases of antiquity, primitive Germany before it was Christianized, and primitive Christianity. By the former, national and patriotic ideals which were to be portentous for the Reformation were vivified; by the latter, the first steps were taken toward the Reformer's program of wiping out twelve or fifteen centuries of decline from Augustinian Christianity. Though all the German humanists, like their Italian confrères, were inspired by classical antiquity, there was a religious seriousness in most of them which was deeper than that of the Italian humanists, with the exception of Dante. Petrarch was pious and orthodox, but saw little conflict between humanism and current Church polity; Boccaccio made fun of the foibles of churchmen; but with humanist cardinals and popes befriending and patronizing them, Italian humanists did not stand for Church reform as strongly as German humanists did.

In Germany the opposition to the ecclesiastical system and to scholasticism had the fervor of religion as well as the love of good Latin and Greek to nourish its agitation. It was not for nothing that Erasmus had been brought up in the *devotio moderna*. German humanism opposed the scholastic and monastic and ecclesiastical system because it was judged to be alien to the spirit of Christianity itself, and not merely because its Latin was bad, its teaching mechanical, and its ideals out of touch with the new times. Humanists wanted reform within the Church; they begot rebellion against it. The rebellion contemned their halfway efforts at reform and their classical manners as well as their half-Hellenic, half-Catholic religiosity. The humanists prepared the way for a religious revolution which swept them into it, or swept them aside.

Nothing shows better the difference between Italian and German humanists, and why Germany and not Italy was the home of the Reformation, than the difference between the two most significant literary efforts by humanists to bring the ancient world to the modern. In Italy it was Ficino's translation of Plato. In Germany it was Erasmus' critical edition of the New Testament.

Erasmus brought the craft and learning of humanism to bear on Scripture. Though he recognized its divine origin and (generally) its sole authority, treating it in his humanistic way brought it down to a human level where, like the classics of antiquity, it spoke to man as man—perhaps to man as a victim of folly, but not to man as a helpless and depraved creature. Unwilling to remain with unabridged dualisms between the secular and the sacred and between the things of reason and the things of faith, opposing scholasticism, which had made clefts between them, and being enough of a skeptic to believe in tolerance, Erasmus tried to bring the extremes together in what he called "Christian philosophy." But Erasmus was more a polyhistor and a moralistic critic of his times than he was a philosopher or theologian. His goal was original Christianity, which he thought stood without any need of support from speculative metaphysics. He thought it recoverable in the way in which another humanist might seek to restore the original, "primitive" Platonism of which medieval Platonism was only a degenerate form. But it should not be surprising that this modest-sounding goal was more easily seen than achieved; the most difficult goals require more philosophy, not less. Adherence to eudaemonistic morals, tempered by both Stoicism and Christian pathos of original sin and hope of resurrection; recognition of the sole authority of the Bible, but with a sophisticated humanistic awareness that a text does not always mean what its says, and with a ready subjection to the teaching authority of the Church; reverent acceptance of Jesus as the greatest teacher, but cognizance of the teaching function of pagan philosophers and Christian heretics—Erasmus's *philosophia Christi* is neither exclusively Christian nor consistently philosophical. Nor does it even comprehend all of Erasmus' own teachings, which contained many deposits of Patristic and scholastic thought. The most eloquent statement of it, the *Enchiridion milites Christiani (Handbook for the Christian Soldier,* 1501)[1] comes directly from the *devotio moderna* with humanist overtones—the Christian as a man in the world—and without the mysticism.

Erasmus wished, through his Christian philosophy, to reform the Church, but he had no thought of destroying it. He denounced Luther because Luther would not temper his theology with humanistic half-measures. While Luther wished for collaboration with Erasmus or endorsement by him, Erasmus had no influence on his thought except through his biblical scholarship. Erasmus did, however, have significant influence upon Melanchthon and Zwingli, who were humanists before they became reformers. They gave institutional substance to his Christian humanism even if they could do nothing with his ethereal thought of a philosophy of Christ. Melanchthon's Christian-German humanism was the basis of his great educational reform by which, it was believed, the historical (and not the Catholic) Aristotle and other classical heroes of the humanists (for instance, Cicero and Galen) could be brought into the service of Protestant theology and the Lutheran church.

Luther

Luther's theological training at Erfurt was in nominalistic scholasticism. He called himself a Gabrielist—that is, a follower of Gabriel Biel—even though in theological matters he later criticized Biel and Occam and other nominalists just as much as he did the realists. He could be this indiscriminate in his attack because he rejected, or tried to reject, the entire scholastic theological project of making reason serve theology, even to the minimum extent that the German nominalists had attempted to make it. The only recent theology he approved was that of the *Theologia Germanica,* which he issued in 1516, saying in the Preface that there had been no book since Augustine from which he had learned so much; "It proves that German theologians are the best theologians."[2] Luther really meant this; he not only rejected the "sophists" (his least abusive term for the schoolmen, borrowed from the humanists) but also the teaching authority of popes, councils, and saints—one of whom, St. Jerome, he thought deserved to be in hell and, in fact, to *be* in hell if not saved by some extraordinary grace.[3] The root error of three centuries of Christian theology, he asserted, is to be found in trying to use the philosophy of a "beast," of a "damned, arrogant, pagan rascal," and in introducing the "Greek whore" into the interpretation of the simple and evident message of Scripture. The beast and pagan rascal, of course, was Aristotle; the whore, reason. The only

[1] *The Enchiridion of Erasmus,* trans. Raymond Himelick from the edition of 1503 (Bloomington: Indiana University Press, 1963).
[2] *Vorrede zur deutschen Theologie* (*Werke,* [ed. Arnold Berger, Leipzig: Bibliographisches Institut, 1917]) I, 7–8.
[3] *The Bondage of the Will* (*De servo arbitrio*), trans. J. I. Packer and O. R. Johnston (Westwood, N.J.: Revell; London: James D. Clarke & Co., 1957), p. 284. This view of St. Jerome's fate is hardly consistent with Luther's eschatology and probably expresses more of his choler than his theology or Christian charity.

uncertainty Luther seemed to feel about Aristotle was whether God plagues us with him because of our sins, or Satan introduced the study of him in order to lead us away from God.[4] Nominalist though he is, Luther is carried away by his hatred of Aristotle to condemn him even for opposing Plato's theory of ideas.[5] Only if Plato is thought of in terms of Neoplatonism, and Neoplatonism is seen through the eyes of Christian mystics, is such a strange judgment intelligible at all in a man like Luther.

In spite of these uncompromising statements, however, Luther, no doubt under the influence of Melanchthon, did not always condemn Aristotle and reason. They do have a right and proper use. He recommended the logical works and the *Rhetoric* as important in secular learning, and even granted that an Aristotle purified of scholastic errors of interpretation would be a valuable ally in theological debate in spite of his naturalism, which was incompatible with Christian supernaturalism. In fact, he even desiderated an accurate text of Aristotle, and thus came into line with all those philosophers who condemned the scholastic Aristotle in the name of the authentic Aristotle—though, as we have seen, he had plenty of spleen left for the authentic Aristotle too. In the things of the world, reason is a gift of God and even Aristotle is of help. This less extreme attitude toward Aristotle does not reflect any change in Luther's view of the proper and improper use of secular learning. Salvation is not gained or understood by philosophical reason—Luther never changed this opinion—but he came to see the magnitude of the task of secular education when the Catholic schools were dissolved and the new church had to assume the burden of training in the arts faculties as well as the theological.

In his opposition to scholasticism and what he regarded as ecclesiastical abuses—for at first Luther held the Erasmian view that it was not the Roman theological system, but abuses in it that must be opposed—Luther was in essential agreement with Erasmus. But events, his combative nature, and his theological originality pushed him so much further that he came to a complete break with Erasmus and regarded the humanist himself as guilty of most of the intellectual sins of the schoolmen and of the clerisy. Luther shared with Erasmus and other humanists an antipathy to abuses in the Church, but Luther was brought to this—and then to the more extreme position—by a theological revolution within himself that convinced him of the falsity of the Catholic doctrine of tradition as a source of authority supplemental to Scripture, and of good works as bringing salvation. The attack on indulgences was only a consequence of this theological reorientation to the problem of Christian works. The Erasmian attack, on the other hand, was directed against the practices, not the doctrine, of the Roman Church; it was founded upon a more humane—one might almost say a more common-sense—rejection of various forms of folly in life, not

---

[4] *The Babylonian Captivity of the Church*, in *Luther's Reformation Writings*, 2 vols., trans. B. L. Woolf (London: Lutterworth Press, 1952), I, 229. This collection of Luther's works is hereafter cited as "Woolf." *Appeal to the German Nobility* in Woolf, I, 184–85.

[5] *Heidelberg Disputation*, Thesis 36 (*Early Theological Writings*, trans. James Atkinson (Philadelphia: Westminster Press, 1962), p. 281.

upon errors in dogma. The difference in their motives—one lying in an unappeased sense of loss and sin, the other in a civil and sophisticated sense of the folly he saw in others and in the church—made Luther the great Reformer and kept Erasmus timidly standing aside. Except for some later agreement on secular education (insofar as anything was secular to Dr. Martin), and except for a desire to plough under at least twelve centuries of theology in order to get to an Augustinian or even more pristine form of Christianity, Luther and Erasmus were united only by having a common opponent, the "Roman system." They did not agree on fundamental theological principles. On most points, Luther was as much opposed to the humanist ideal as he was to the Catholic system except in questions of polity, where, in fact, he was more Catholic than Erasmus. His sacramental view of the church and his view of the supreme role of dogma were closer to the Catholic than to Erasmian conceptions. In his other-worldliness, combined with earthy coarseness and his cry of "*Sola fide!*," Luther stood against a worldly rational church and the worldly rational humanist.

Occamism, especially as it was developed by Biel, and the *devotio moderna* provided room for unphilosophical, nonrational theology based solely on revelation. Luther started with Occamistic and Augustinian conceptions of the priority of faith over reason, and indeed of a faith to which man can be brought by no human effort or learning but a faith which is the gratuitous gift some men receive from God. All the instruction man needs is vouchsafed to him in Scripture, and it is a "shameless blasphemy" to teach that Scripture is obscure or that it needs to be interpreted allegorically or philosophically before it can be followed.[6] The Christian does not need the pope or councils or even the Fathers to know what it is that he need believe. Natural theology, scholasticism, and Aristotelianism are not needed even by theologians, and certainly not by Christians.[7] When they "prove the existence of God" they establish only an idolatry of the human mind.

At that time in Germany, to reject Aristotle was the same as to reject secular reason and philosophy. It was to deny any transition from the empirical or rational study of nature to the awareness of what is beyond nature. To reach that awareness, Luther needed no transitional steps; in fact, he needed to take no steps at all, for in the transaction of faith, all the action is on God's side, not on man's. God reveals himself to man; man is a passive receptacle of grace. Faith gives an immediate contact with the supernatural. It is not acquired by thinking and seeking, but is gratuitously given by God to the man in despair who has been struck down into an awareness of his wormlike impotence. If God does not freely choose to reveal himself to that man, his access to God is forever blocked. Luther accepted the lesson of nominalism, and pushed it so far that it meant the end of supernatural philosophy; while the lesson of the *devotio moderna*

[6] *Bondage of the Will*, p. 128; see also pp. 72 and 125. Luther, of course, admits that there are philological obscurities and esteems Erasmus' work in clarifying them.

[7] "The truth is, a man cannot become a theologian unless he becomes one without Aristotle." *Disputation against Scholastic Theology*, Thesis 44 (*Early Theological Writings*, trans. Atkinson, p. 269).

was accepted for the sake of a theology closed to natural reason but given first in scriptural and then in mystical form.

At various times in his career, Luther held slightly different views of the relation of faith to reason and of theology to philosophy, varying, as we have seen, from outright denials of the validity of reason in theology to the acknowledgment that philosophy had an important propaedeutic function. Luther had two conceptions of reason—reason informed with faith and a useful servant to theology (reason *post fidem*) and reason the work of the devil, claiming truth on its own (reason *ante fidem*). One must respect philosophy more than Luther did to hold a theory of twofold truth, a theory that a statement can be true in philosophy and false in theology. Luther distrusts the devilish reason even when it is not used in theology. When Luther attacked the Sorbonne ("*Mater errorum*") for teaching (in its condemnation of Averroism in 1277 and often since) that there is one truth in philosophy and theology, he was not asserting the allegedly Averroistic doctrine of twofold truth. He anathematized the Parisian position because it "brought articles of faith under judgment by human reason." He is asserting that there is only one truth, and that one truth is theological. Theology is the judge of philosophy, and faith that of reason; nothing, not even philosophy, can claim a truth of its own which escapes the theological prerogative. "All truth is compatible [*consonat*] . . . Contraries cannot belong to the same subject. Philosophy and theology are in the same subject, viz., the human soul. Therefore philosophy and theology are not contraries. But I concede that they are different."[8] They are different in subject matter sometimes, in "method" always.

Rather than a doctrine of twofold truth against the Paris condemnation, therefore, this is a theory of the subjection of partial (philosophical) truth to the whole truth, of inherently but not completely corrupt reason to faith. The philosophers' error lay in pushing philosophy into a field where it is not competent, and where all is a matter of faith. Aristotle himself was not guilty of this, but his scholastic followers sinned in this way; and Luther likes to hold himself up as a better Aristotelian than his Catholic opponents. Certainly Aristotle did teach things incompatible with faith (such as the eternity of the world), and there of course, he was in error. Autonomous philosophy is possible and permissible only where there is no question of salvation at stake, only where faith has not spoken. The arrogance of philosophical reason is to be humbled by its having to accept as *true* what is philosophically and rationally "false and absurd."[9]

One may well hesitate, in view of all this, to speak of "Luther's philosophy," even when insisting upon the massive effect his acts and thoughts had on men who did not so limit philosophy. Yet it would be a thin and

---

[8] "Die Disputation de sentenia: Verbum caro factum est," (1539) in *Kritische Gesamtausgabe* (Weimar: Böhlaus, 1932), vol. 39[ii], pp. 1–33. Almost the entire disputation is relevant; the quotations are from Thesis 1 (p. 3), Thesis 6 (p. 4) and Argument 27 (p. 27).

[9] On the whole matter, see the many quotations in B. A. Gerrish, *Grace and Reason* (Oxford: Clarendon Press, 1962), which the author collects and reconciles by reference to the exigencies of the diverse polemics in which Luther expressed a variety of views.

sickly conception of philosophy which would deny this title to Luther's
De servo arbitrio (*The Bondage of the Will*). This is the most original
work on a philosophical question to come out strictly orthodox Lutheranism.

Luther had denied freedom of the will in various tracts published early
in his career.[10] Erasmus, though sympathetic with some of Luther's complaints against the Church, urged caution on both sides, and by so doing
involved himself in the dangers of being a man without a party. Catholics
and reformers alike gradually came to see him as adhering to their opponent. To make sure that he would not be burned along with the
uncouth and heretical Luther, Erasmus wrote the *Diatribe or Sermon Concerning Free Will* in 1524, in which he argued that such a metaphysical
subtlety was of no concern to the pious Christian. Debates about it divided Christians, who ought to be at one; as for himself, he preferred the
skeptical position "wherever the inviolable authority of Scripture and the
decision of the Church permit."[11] But, as befitting a moralistic humanist,
Erasmus could not adhere to a doctrine of utter impotence; so he defended
the freedom of the will as "the power of the human will whereby man can
apply to or turn away from that which leads unto eternal salvation."[12]
Pelagius, he asserted, attributed too much to the will, as though it could
through its freedom effect salvation; but Luther erred even more in denying it altogether.[13] Erasmus then defended his views with a medley of
arguments taken from classical writers and from passages in Scripture in
which men are interpreted as having had a free choice to accept or reject
God's commands. The book as a whole is a typical Christian-Humanist
tract—irenic, polite, and erudite.

Luther's reply published in 1525, is erudite, but it has nothing else in
common with Erasmus' essay. It belongs in the genre of common flyte
laced with Christian exhortation. To anyone who admires Erasmus, or has
a taste for good manners in argument, it is not an unmixed pleasure to read.

Luther proposes to show that man unaided by God's grace can do no
good work, whether moral or sacramental, that could merit him salvation.
Man's will is in bondage to sin, and he can do nothing to change its
direction. He is bent upon damnation, and unaided by God he will be—
and always has been—damned. Through no merit of man (for he has none)
God inscrutably gives grace to some men and saves them by an act of mercy
from their just eternal torment. The others are not treated with injustice;
they simply get what they deserved from eternity, to eternity. As long as
a man believes he can save himself by his works, i.e., that he is free to
choose to do things that will constrain or incline God to save him, even
if this act be nothing but a cry for the faith that will save him, he is
utterly blocked from what he seeks. The belief that he can do anything
to save himself is the belief that his will is free; and this belief is an il-

[10] *Disputation against Scholastic Theology*, Theses 5, 6, 20, 28; *Heidelberg Disputation*, Thesis 13.

[11] *Discourse on Free Will*, trans. E. F. Winter, (New York: Frederick Ungar, 1961),
p. 6.

[12] *Ibid.*, p. 20.   [13] *Ibid.*, p. 92.

lusion created in him by Satan to keep him from God.[14] Only the contrite soul that sees its own absolute impotence and sinfulness and thereby suffers a bottomless depair can receive the faith which is the sign of God's grace. Such a soul cannot even desire that it be free:

I frankly confess that, for myself, even if it could be, I should not want "free-will" given to me, nor anything be left in my own hands to enable me to endeavour after salvation; not merely because in face of so many dangers, and adversities, and assaults of devils, I could not stand my ground and hold fast my "free-will" . . . but because . . . I should still be forced to labour with no guarantee of success, and to beat my fists at the air. If I lived and worked to all eternity, my conscience would never reach comfortable certainty as to how much it must do to satisfy God. Whatever work I had done, there would still be a nagging doubt as to whether it pleased God, or whether He required something more. The experience of all who seek righteousness by works proves that.[15]

To support this doctrine, Luther uses several types of arguments, some well known in the history of philosophy and a few interestingly different. The most arresting is his answer to Erasmus' thesis that "ought" implies "can," and "can" means "freely can." Erasmus cites many texts in which God commands a man to do something, and says that God's command is nugatory if the man either must or cannot follow it. Not so, replies Luther: "ought" does not imply "can," but may, on the contrary, be merely a way of bringing a man to a vivid consciousness of his impotence, of bringing him to give up the presumption that he can, by an act of will, do what is commanded, and thus to bring him to submit to God's will. It is as if one commanded a bound man to leave his prison cell as a way of convincing him that escape was indeed impossible.[16]

A less perverse argument is that from God's foreknowledge.[17] Luther distinguishes between the necessity of infallibility and the necessity of force.[18] The former is the necessity that Judas sin because God knew infallibly that he would do so; the latter is necessity arising from coercion. The former does not imply the latter, and while the former is true, only the latter is exculpatory. Judas did not, indeed, freely sin since no one can do anything, even sin, freely; but God did not coerce Judas into sinning, for Judas was a passive, though willing, instrument, his will being bent upon sinning and only sinning.[19]

The odd turn of these two classical arguments, where Luther draws quite different conclusions from accepted premises, leads directly to the question of theodicy. Erasmus introduced this question in his interpreta-

14 *Bondage of the Will*, p. 162.
15 *Ibid.*, pp. 313–314.
16 *Ibid.*, pp. 153, 157, 159, 161.
17 *Ibid.*, pp. 217–222.
18 The conclusion for the sake of which this distinction is usually made is that the necessity of infallibility does not entail the denial of freedom. Luther uses it, however, for a very different purpose, viz., to show that unfree actions are not actions forced.
19 There is a pervasive ambiguity in the whole debate, for Luther always argues that man's will is not free to do any action that will merit salvation or damnation, and sometimes that he has no freedom of indifference with respect to things that do not count. The latter is sometimes explicitly affirmed (*Heidelberg Disputation*, p. 296) but often seems to be tacitly denied.

tion of Romans 9:21–23, in which God is compared to the potter and the pot complains that it was poorly made.[20] Luther answers with one of his most important distinctions; that between "the God preached" and "the God not preached," or the Word of God and God Himself, or the God revealed and the God concealed (*deus absconditus*). To the scriptural God is added a mystical God, like Eckhart's Godhead, which transcended the Person of God. But while Eckhart gave religious priority to the transcendent hidden Godhead, Luther puts the emphasis upon the God preached in the Scripture: "God does not will the death of a sinner—that is, in his Word," from which (i.e., the Bible) Erasmus chose the semi-Pelagian passage about the spoiled pot; "but he wills it by his inscrutable will."

God in His own nature and majesty is to be left alone; in this regard, we have nothing to do with Him, nor does He wish us to deal with Him. We have to do with Him as clothed and displayed in His word, (by which He presents Himself to us . . . God preached works to the end that sin and death may be taken away, and we may be saved . . . But God hidden in Majesty neither deplores nor takes away death, but works life, and death, and all in all; nor has He set bounds to Himself by His word, but has kept Himself free over all things.[21]

With respect to the God preached, a semi-Pelagianism is permissible, for the fault of those who are not saved lies in their will,[22] that they do not receive God into themselves; but

why the Majesty does not remove or change this fault in every man (for it is not in the power of man to change it), or why He lays this fault to the charge of the will, when man cannot avoid it, it is not lawful to ask.[23]

By his inscrutable will God chose to manifest himself in the Word, which commands and blesses or damns. God could have manifested himself in a form other than that in which he actually expressed himself (as Occam taught), but "it is enough for us to know that God so wills, and it becomes us to worship, love, and adore his will, bridling the presumption of reason."[24] Our human judgment of what is right and wrong, just and unjust, is based upon God's revelation in the preached Word; but these distinctions are not antecedent to God's decisions in creating the world. In strict Occamist manner, Luther argues

What God wills is not right because He ought, or was bound, so to will; on the contrary, what takes place must be right, because He so wills it. Causes and grounds are laid down for the will of the creature, but not for the will of the Creator—unless you set another Creator over him!"[25]

By the light of nature, God is unjust in not punishing the sinner and rewarding the good man in this world; by the light of grace, based on God's

---

[20] Erasmus, *Discourse on Free Will*, pp. 55–58; Luther, *Bondage of the Will*, pp. 229–235.

[21] *Bondage of the Will*, p. 170.

[22] *Ibid.*, p. 171.

[23] *Ibid.*, p. 184.

[24] *Ibid.*

[25] *Ibid.*, p. 209.

Word, this injustice is explained away by the revealed distributive justice of the after-life. But even the light of grace will not illuminate the problem of why the evil are permitted to be evil. By the light of grace

it is inexplicable how God can damn him who by his own strength can do nothing but sin and become guilty . . . But the light of glory insists otherwise, and will one day reveal God, to whom alone belongs a judgment whose justice is incomprehensible, as a God Whose justice is most righteous and evident— provided only that in the meanwhile we believe it."[26]

This is Luther's theodicy. It is the source of the strict Lutheran sense of the helplessness of man, the futility of practice, and the indifference or even evil of works. Luther teaches that faith does not free us from the necessity of works, but only from false opinions about works.[27] But he was not always interpreted in this way; works came to be seen by some later Lutherans (e.g., Nicolaus von Amsdorf [1483–1565], one of Melanchthon's bitterest opponents) as evil because they sprang from and fed presumption and pride.

When the followers of Luther, including Melanchthon, relinquished predestinarianism, they retained the passivity of man in the face of God. When the followers of Calvin retained predestinarianism, they added to it a doctrine of man's duty to glorify God by obedience, which was practically equivalent to that of justification by works. If man is predestined to good works—and what Calvinist ever thought he was not doing good works?—predestinarianism strengthens his good right arm; but if a man is predestined to sin—and what Lutheran ever thought he was not in imminent danger of sinning?—and can be saved from it by nothing that he can do, the motor of action is inhibited. The modern world, with its emphasis on practice, required Arminianism, a polite Protestant name for the Pelagian heresy; hence Luther's denial of man's freedom did not make fruitful contact with humane activism, while Calvin's did. This is the reason why Lutherans in the Enlightenment acted more like Calvinists than like orthodox Lutherans. And the greatest of these crypto-Calvinistic theodicies is that of Leibniz. Leibniz set out to destroy the irrationalism of the light of glory by extending the principle of sufficient reason into the acts of God. He drew the conclusion from such arguments as those from God's foresight and "ought implies can," that a predestinarian system does *not* entail the denial of freedom. The German Enlightenment was secularized Calvinism, not Lutheranism, even though almost every German philosopher from Leibniz to Kant was confessionally Lutheran.

Luther's own form of theodicy could have had quite different consequences, depending upon the relative weights assigned to the Majesty and to the Word of God. A mystical quietism would flow from the predominance of the former, and Luther explicitly warned against that. For the life of man on earth, only the Word of God counts. The Word of God is to be found in plain Scripture and nowhere else, and by the conscientious, seeking individual who may need teachers, but who does not need inter-

[26] *Ibid.*, p. 317.
[27] *The Freedom of a Christian Man* (Woolf, I, 374).

mediaries. Holding that all men are equally close to or equally distant from God, Luther moved against the aristocratic ideal of the humanists and the hierarchical conception of the Church. Rather, by the doctrine of each man a priest—a doctrine whose practical consequences Luther brutally opposed —Luther broke the moral monopoly claimed by the humanists and the eschatological monopoly claimed by the Church; he broadened the moral and eschatological economy to include men in every walk of life. The denial of the saving power of works had, as its paradoxical other side, the importance of every piece of work for man, who could serve God better by human than by most sacramental works. Secularization was not what Luther wanted; but his omnisacerdotalism was a long step in that direction.

Omnisacerdotalism was paired with an "omniroyalism": every man a king.[28] It is the freedom of the Christian man that, in things that matter, he has no man above him. The Christian man does not need the state. If all men were Christians, there would be needed "no prince, king, lord, sword, or law."[29] But if the Christian man does not need the state, others who are not Christians do need it, and obedience to the service of the state by the Christian is a duty of love.[30] Service to the state, even that of the soldier and hangman,[31] is a divine service. There is no right to revolt against tyranny. "One must not resist government with force, but only with the knowledge of truth."[32] On the other hand, the power of the state is limited to things temporal. It does not extend to belief or heresy. "Every man is responsible for his own faith," and "Heresy can never be prevented by force."[33]

Luther tried to keep two realms separated: that of the law and that of the Gospel. He thought that the Catholic Church had confused them by becoming itself a legalistic and political system, and that the Anabaptists and radicals had confused them in thinking that the religious man could by-pass the law and reject the political magistracy. In the religious sphere the individual has direct access to God, but this does not mean that in the political he has direct access to power. The priestly powers had to be removed from man's religious path; hence the Catholic Church had to be dismantled in order that Christian man might be free. But this did not, in Luther's thought, imply any political liberty.

The political powers had no sacramental function, and they could not touch man's soul or stand in the way of his salvation. That they could make man's life difficult and unpleasant was, for Luther, a matter of religious indifference. Hence Luther could consistently make peace with whatever political powers there might be, while at the same time defying the ecclesiastical. He thereby acknowledged the validity of the political system. The German princes had not meekly acceded to the demands of the papacy even when they formally acknowledged its authority. They were less likely to see in Lutheranism a threat to their own authority, especially when they found in Luther a strong political ally in suppressing the Peasants' Revolt.

---

[28] *Ibid.*, pp. 357–366.
[29] *Treatise on Secular Authority* (Woolf, I, 369).
[30] *Ibid.*, p. 373.
[31] *Ibid.*, pp. 374, 381.
[32] *Ibid.*, p. 398.
[33] *Ibid.*, pp. 385, 389.

But because of political threats to his movement, Luther was unable to establish the kind of church his theology required, and he left the civil authority in a less vulnerable position than when the Roman Church, at least in principle and often in practice, had provided a theological and moral counterbalance to its presumptions. Without defense by the secular power of some of the German princes, both against Rome and against the emperor, Luther would have had no defense against either. The Reformation, therefore, was almost from the beginning a compromise between a theological radicalism and a political necessity. Medieval forms of political control lasted into the time when the theological foundations for this control had been exposed and destroyed. Luther's and Melanchthon's weasel words about the bigamy of Philip of Hesse showed where the power lay, and showed that they were as helpless as some of their Catholic confrères in the face of other royal misbehavior.

Hence the Reformation, though it caused and was in part caused by political turmoil, did not bring about a political revolution or reformation in Germany. Those who thought it could, such as Ulrich von Hutten, the Peasants in 1525, and the Anabaptists, were put down. So successfully was this done, and so successful (politically) was the system of territorial churches in which the prince was bishop in all but name, that the philosophical doctrines of natural law did not come to effective political status in the Lutheran states until much later, and even then it was achieved under Calvinist influence. Since neither a science of nature nor a science of man was called for, and philosophical instruments were not developed to adjust the deep tension between the secular and the sacred powers, Luther's immediate effect on the content of philosophizing was negligible. Philosophy grows from a conflict of values and a conflict of opinions only when these conflicts are examined in the light of reason. When they are not, there is no dialectic; there is heresy-hunting but no philosophy. For the latter, Germany had to turn to others, and it turned first to Luther's lieutenant.

Philipp Melanchthon: the Second *Praeceptor Germaniae*

The kind of philosophy—which is to say, the kind of study and use of Aristotle—which Luther gradually came to see his movement must have if it was to be intellectually stable and defensible—was provided by his closest disciple, Philipp Melanchthon (= Schwartzerd; 1497–1560). Melanchthon was a grandnephew of arch-humanist Johann Reuchlin and himself a brilliantly promising humanist, first in Heidelberg and then in Tübingen, from which he was called to the professorship of Greek at Wittenberg in 1518. This call, made on the recommendation of Erasmus and Reuchlin, was accepted by Melanchthon not because he wanted to be at Luther's side, but because of his disgust with the scholasticism of Tübingen: "The method of teaching which ought to improve both the understanding and manners is neglected [here]," he wrote a friend. "What is called philosophy is a weak and empty speculation, which produces strife and contention. The true wisdom come down from Heaven to regulate the affections of men is banished."[34] He came to Wittenberg as a humanist, not as a reformer of anything other than the university curriculum. His inaugural address, *De corrigendis adolescentia studii*, was a courageous humanistic diatribe against the current learning in the universities. His prescriptions for the education of youth fully accorded with those of Erasmus and other humanists; he emphasized the importance of the classics, to be read in the original languages, and the "new learning." He alluded to a plan he had already made in Tübingen to prepare a new edition of Aristotle which would be free of the errors introduced by the scholastics, who generally used only Latin translations. The lecture was enthusiastically received and widely read. What is surprising is that it delighted Luther, who was in the audience. Thus began the friendship and collaboration of the two men. The streams of Humanism and Reformation flowed together as they had never done for Luther and Erasmus.

The friendship of two such different men is not easy to understand. Their relationship was not always easy, especially for the more sensitive Melanchthon. But as long as he played Wagner to Luther's Faust, all went well; and Melanchthon faithfully tried to keep to this role. Melanchthon, "the little master," as Luther sometimes called him, was of a mild and irenic disposition. He had not the titanic theological passion of his colleague, the professor of theology, nor the wit of Erasmus; nor was he a very good philosopher. But he was the right man to be at Luther's right hand (or fist) because he had talents that Luther lacked, and Luther knew not only that he lacked them but that his movement required them.

We have seen that Luther, so far as we know under the influence of Melanchthon, became aware of the importance of secular learning once his movement had gained sufficient momentum to have to provide institutions (especially schools) to secure its advances. But the effect of Luther on Melanchthon was immediate and profound and lasting. Luther made Melanchthon into a theologian, but Melanchthon never made Luther a humanist. For several years Melanchthon was hardly more than a mouthpiece for Luther. Instead of a new edition of Aristotle, there was in 1520 a new edition of Aristophanes' *The Clouds*, chosen by Melanchthon "to show that philosophy contains nothing but silly disputes about frivolous opinions."

In the writings of the next few years we find Melanchthon's abuse of Aristotle only a little less strong than that of Luther himself: "That hag who smells of Greece," that is, philosophy, is not fit to be the servant of theology. But in his *Loci* of 1521, the first formal doctrinal textbook of Lutheran theology, which put an end to what is sometimes called the "normless" period of the new movement, Melanchthon expressed a view we find later in Luther, though Melanchthon no doubt meant its affirmative part more fervently: philosophy is one thing, and a very good thing in its proper realm of worldly wisdom, but it is not a basis for theology, and philosophasters must not be permitted to meddle in theology. But the positive evaluation of worldly wisdom, and hence of Aristotle as the greatest

[34] Quoted from J. W. Richard, *Philipp Melanchthon, The Protestant Preceptor of Germany* (New York: Putnam, 1907), p. 27.

of the philosophers, introduced a new note into Protestant thought, and one that manifested Melanchthon's humanist conviction of the "dignity and power of man" as against Luther's view of human impotence—moral, intellectual, and eschatological. This humanist conviction, which was never again to be given up by Melanchthon, was the source of the revival of philosophy within Lutheranism. Christian humanism became an effective educational practice.

Through the *Loci* of 1521, the Marburg colloquy with Zwingli of 1528, and the Augsburg Confession of 1530, Melanchthon became the chief codifier of and apologist for Lutheran doctrine. With the establishment of the new church, there was need for a Protestant educational system to prepare its ministers. The University of Marburg was established in 1527, Königsberg in 1544, and Jena in 1556; other older universities became Protestant during Melanchthon's lifetime. Their curricula and most of their textbooks came from Melanchthon. His *Instructions for the Visitation* (1528) provided almost an "accreditation system" for Protestant schools, and he, like Rabanus Maurus, was honored with the apothegm *praeceptor Germaniae*.

But the irony of Melanchthon's fate was that, beginning as a humanist critic of scholasticism and a Lutheran critic of Catholicism, he produced an educational system which finally differed very little from that of the Catholics. For both, philosophy existed in the arts faculty as a propaedeutic to theology in the higher faculty. Without philosophy, Melanchthon saw theology as *inerudita*, confused knowledge unable to defend itself and thus an occasion for skepticism and heresy. But before the final outcome of Melanchthon's educational reforms had been reached in Protestant scholasticism, Melanchthon had been renounced by his fellow Lutherans, who divided on the question as to whether he had been too philosophical and had perverted Luther's theology with Aristotelianism, or whether he had not been philosophical enough and had left Lutheranism without the metaphysics it needed in its polemics with Calvinism and Catholicism. His humanism led him to Aristotle, but kept him from appreciating Aristotle's metaphysics. To some he seemed to have gone too far, to others, not far enough.

When Luther himself saw the need of a revival of the liberal arts, which had suffered under his own attacks on learning and which came to be neglected in Wittenberg especially, it was Melanchthon's task to re-establish them. Since the liberal arts were taught primarily in the form of commentaries on the classical writers, Melanchthon had consciously to choose between the various ancient models that were available. I mean "choose" a philosophy in a quite literal sense; the idea of setting out on his own to develop a philosophy did not occur to Melanchthon, not merely because he was a modest man, but because he was a humanist, to whom it seemed that human wisdom was already to be found in some classical writers who needed only to be supplemented by Christian revelation. "Choosing a philosophy" was hardly for him more than choosing a textbook in the experience of a modern teacher who wants to use the books which come closest to presenting ideas he calls his own without any claim that he formulated them—books which are most suitable to his hearers, and which contain the fewest errors he will have to correct. So in a quite ingenuous way Melanchthon ran through the available philosophical corpus. He evaluated the classical schools of philosophy in the light of Christian experience and the needs of his time. He rejected Epicureanism because of its atheism, Stoicism because of its fatalism, the Academic form of Platonism because of its skepticism.[35] He was then left with Aristotelianism, to which he thought he could easily add what was needed from natural theology and revelation. In spite of his official adherence to Aristotle, however, there was far more Stoicism in Melanchthon's thought than could be tolerated in a strict Aristotelianism; and even Stoic fatalism is not further removed from one part of Melanchthon's solution to the problem of freedom than Aristotle's theory of the will is from the other. The thoughts of Cicero were as important as the thoughts of Aristotle to Melanchthon; but Justus Lipsius (1547–1606), who was to hawk Stoicism as a basis of educational reform for both Calvinism and Catholicism, did not have a comprehensive corpus of doctrine on every subject to fall back upon and exploit, while almost everything Melanchthon needed could be found ready-made in Aristotle. Hence Aristotle was, in Melanchthon's eyes, the philosopher who had most to contribute to Protestant education, and Melanchthon's philosophical writings took the form of commentaries on Aristotle with appropriate use of other masters. But his humanistic training and interests led him back to the original sources, and not to the late medieval conceptions, of these writers. His commentaries are written in good humanist Latin, not in scholastic style, and with close attention to making them "teachable" without the rote learning that had become characteristic of scholastic instruction. His humanism made him neglect some parts of Aristotle's work, most notably the *Metaphysics*; his Lutheranism made him reject those parts of Aristotle which were incompatible with theology—the parts which had already been handled in the same way by Catholic theologians, such as the teaching of the eternity of the world and the tripartite division of the human soul. Like Catholic scholastics, he always made Aristotelianism subservient to the demands of theology, or at least, as in his treatment of the *Ethics* and *Politics*, to regard them as secondary to Christian teachings in these fields. In only one important respect did Melanchthon correct the theology with which he started—he accepted Aristotle's doctrine of will and freedom into his theory of natural virtue (though he supplemented it, as the Catholics had done, with a theory of theological and infused virtues, and added astrological influences to the other natural causal factors in the determination of human dispositions). By these changes, some of the positive humanist teaching concerning the power and dignity of man was introduced into Lutheran theology against Luther's own denial of human power to work toward salvation and happiness, for Melanchthon was unwilling to accept any theological doctrine that conflicted with the moral improvement of mankind.

[35] *Erotemata dialectices* chap. iv (1547) in *Corpus reformatorum* (ed. C. G. Bretschneider, Halle, 1834–1860), XIII, cols. 655–657.

The first of his textbooks was the *Commentaria dialectices ratio*, published in 1520, which was based largely on Agricola. It was followed by two other editions, the one of 1547, under the title of *Erotomata dialectices*, being much more Aristotelian and less Agricolan than the first two. This work became the standard logic textbook of the Lutheran schools until about 1600. In it Melanchthon made a sharp distinction between rhetoric and dialectic, which had been dealt with together by Agricola. Dialectic begins with the theory of definition and division and then goes into logic proper—the art of argument which aims at truth and ways of discovering it through syllogism, enthymeme, example, and induction. While definition and division belong also to rhetoric, logic is apart from rhetoric, which aims at persuasive probability and not necessarily at truth and proof. Obviously only a logic conceived in this way could be of service to theology, but Melanchthon made no contribution to logic itself and meant his logical writings to be of use only to students.

According to Melanchthon, there are four sources of knowledge. The first three—innate ideas implanted in the mind by God, experience, and logical inference—he took from a common Stoic doctrine. By innate ideas (*noticia natae*) he meant such principles as the equality of equals, but broadened their scope to include the basic principles of every science, both theoretical and practical.[36] In this he followed Plato and the Stoics, not Aristotle and the scholastics. He explicitly accepted the principle that nothing is in the intellect that was not first in the senses—but took back what he had granted by insistence upon the innate principles. By experience, he meant not controlled sense experience, and certainly not the raw experience of later empiricists, but the general experience of mankind as in the third level of knowledge in Aristotle.[37] To these three classical epistemological roots he added revelation. The scope of revelation is narrow, but it has absolute priority over the others, so much so that Melanchthon accepts what is almost a doctrine of the twofold truth. Theological questions cannot be settled by appeal to the first three kinds of knowledge. Nevertheless, there is no inclination to limit the power of reason in theology, and Melanchthon gives philosophical arguments for the existence of God· from the common agreement of mankind, from external and internal teleology (Providence and the design of nature), and from conscience as the voice of God.[38]

In his *Initia doctrina physicae* Melanchthon describes the physical world. For him, it is a thoroughly teleological world, in which the teleological features are drawn from three sources: Christian providence, Aristotelian explanation in terms of final causes, and the Neoplatonic metaphysics of the world as an expression of God in which all things in it are signatures or signs of its creator. Unlike Luther, who had no interest in nature and who

[36] *Liber de anima*, in *Corpus Reformatorum* XIII, cols. 143–144.

[37] *Ibid.*, cols. 149–150; *Erotemata dialectices*, in *Corpus Reformatorum*, XIII, cols. 616–624 and esp. cols. 647–650.

[38] The proofs of God's existence are in *Initia doctrinae physicae*, *Corpus Reformatorum* XIII, cols. 203–206, which is Melanchthon's commentary on Aristotle's *Physics*, published 1549.

readily and brusquely rejected Copernicus, Melanchthon through his expertness in astrology was quite competent to understand the new astronomy. He rejected it, but not out of hand; he seems to have regarded it (as Osiander wanted it to be regarded) as a mere hypothesis, and he rejected it as a mere hypothesis because it did not, in his opinion, fit the facts any better than the older astronomy. The facts appealed to, however, were not the neutral facts of observation, but the facts of the astronomical world as shown in biblical revelation and interpreted by the Neoplatonic view of a multi-layered world.

Melanchthon's psychology and some of his theory of knowledge are in his commentary on Aristotle's De anima (1540), but with much psychological and physiological detail drawn from current knowledge and from Galen, and with all the doctrines suitably amended to fit Christian teaching. There is an active and a passive intellect; the former has universal principles within it (e.g., the laws of logic and the axioms of the various sciences) and the passive intellect supplies the material to which the former is applied. The intellect makes a common image, or generic idea, which exists only in the mind and is indeed only the act of the mind; external real objects are always individual and particular, not universal (and Melanchthon claimed that this was the theory of both Plato and Aristotle). Experience in general does give us truth; we know this, for otherwise God would be a deceiver.

The doctrine of the soul in philosophy is taken from Aristotle. Melanchthon accepts Aristotle's definition of the soul as the "first entelechy" of the body. But in theology he goes beyond what natural reason can teach about the soul and defines the soul as spiritus intelligens, the immortal part of the substance of man. The soul is known both by revelation and by experience to be immortal; the relevant experience is the evidence of ghosts and spirits.

Discussion of the faculties of the soul, including the will, brings us to a meeting point of metaphysics, psychology, theology, and ethics. Melanchthon sees them as a central problem, and discusses them in work after work, not only in his commentary on De anima, where it would be expected, but even in his Dialectic. In the Loci communes of 1521 the freedom of the will is denied as an "impious teaching," but this was the work in which Melanchthon was least on his own and most the spokesman for Luther. On Erasmus' friendly advice he stood aside in the great debate on this question between Erasmus and Luther, but by 1528 he was developing his own theory, which was a mixture of Aristotelian, Stoic, and Christian ideas and very different from Luther's. In his Instructions for the Visitation (1528) he asserts that man has freedom in his outward works, but is weakened in its exercise by sin and impeded by the devil; and he cannot purify his heart so as to be pleasing to God.[39]

In the Loci communes of 1535 and in all later editions of that work he presented his own fully developed theory. This theory, known as the doctrine of synergism, was followed in the Formula of Concord after his

---

[39] Melanchthons Werke, ed. Robert Stupperich and Hans Engelland (Gütersloh: Bertelsmann, 1951–1965), vol. II, pt. ii, 252.

death, and became the orthodox Lutheran position on the freedom of the will.

The doctrine of synergism teaches that man had a free and unimpeded will given him upon his creation, but that his will, though remaining free, was impeded after the Fall. The problem of freedom, then, becomes not a metaphysical one of absolute impotence but the far simpler problem of the deterioration and recovery of the strength of a human faculty. To teach that human will is not free is morally dangerous; to teach that it is beset by sin and in need of divine help is morally healthful;[40] but Pelagianism is a lie and a blasphemy to be renounced.[41] The synergistic doctrine is that man in his impotence can do nothing to merit the grace of God, but that he can freely do something that inclines God to help him—even if all he does is to "faintly think that he would like to be in the grace of God again."[42] It is required of man that he not resist God's grace, and that he not think that through works he can demand it. *Praecedente gratia, comitante voluntate* (Grace guides; the will follows). The will cooperates with grace, and grace strengthens the will.[43]

Only the doctrine of synergism could bridge the gap between Lutheran theology and humanistic ethics.[44] And it could do so only when the awful mystery of the *deus absconditus* was passed over in silence. Luther's interim-ethics of man's dealing with the God preached could now be brought into positive relation with purely human ethics derived from the ancients. Melanchthon disagreed not only with the theologians who thought that ethics was an improper study since the whole end and duty of man are supernatural and revealed, but also with Aristotle, since Melanchthon held that the ultimate authority of moral law is theological. But while the connection between the divine and the natural is maintained by this doctrine, it is also important to maintain the distinction between them. Theology and ethics, then, fit and require each other. Ethics is the elaboration of natural law (*explicatio legis naturalis*) but the law of nature is God's law, which reason can discover. Ethics deals with human ends (*finis humanis*) but the end of man is *Deus ipse, communicans nobis suam bonitatem:* God himself, sharing His own goodness with us.[45]

But however important it was that Aristotle be brought into Protestant ethics (as he had been brought into Catholic), one finds little of interest to the history of philosophy in this appropriation, beyond the portentous fact that it was effected. One can easily guess at what Melanchthon is

---

[40] *On Christian Doctrine* (being an English translation of the *Loci communes* of 1555, translated by Clyde L. Manschreck [New York: Oxford University Press, 1965]), p. 54.

[41] *Ibid.,* pp. 58, 69.

[42] *Ibid.,* p. 60. [43] *Ibid.,* p. 63.

[44] Melanchthon's principal ethical treatises were *Philosophia moralis epitome* (1538), *Ethicae doctrinae elementa* (1550), and his commentary on Aristotle's *Ethics* (1529). Each went through several editions. The first-mentioned work, in the edition of 1546, is in the *Werke,* ed. R. Stupperich and R. Nürnberger, III, 149–302.

[45] Melanchthon gives a definition of God's free will which accords with this end of man, in *Definitiones multarum appellationum quarum in Ecclesia usus est* (1553) in *Werke,* ed. Stupperich and Engelland, vol. II, pt. ii, p. 784.

going to say. Naturally, because of his view of antelapsarian innocence he believed that man has an original disposition to virtue and that there is an innate knowledge of moral principles, though this knowledge has been darkened by sin. Man's will works among three forces: God's will, the devil's will, and human temperament. In natural ethics, the last-named is the most important. Knowledge of nature and human nature is essential in the day-to-day life of virtue; and knowledge of nature for Melanchthon consists not only of physics and medicine, but also of astrology. Melanchthon was a committed believer in astrology as an important part of the theory of human temperament and circumstance. Though Luther and most of the humanists chided him for his belief, they could not shake it. But Melanchthon did not believe that astrological forces were so binding on man that they denied him moral freedom.

Since nature was created by God, the law of nature is divine law. But, in addition to natural law, there is direct divine law revealed to man, pre-eminently in the Ten Commandments. There is, in addition, positive law, which varies with circumstances and is to be obeyed because it springs from the divinely instituted state. The state has the duty to strive for human welfare and to protect the church by punishing heretics. But the power of the state is not absolute: if there is a conflict between its positive law and the laws of nature or revealed law, there is an obligation to resist its encroachments.[46]

The widespread acceptance of Melanchthon's teaching in the universities and schools depended upon his skill as an expositor, his favored position as Luther's lieutenant, and the conservativism of his doctrine, which made it acceptable to those who had been trained in Catholic schools as well as those who had been affected by humanist criticism of Catholic education. Moreover, some of his imposing influence came from his position as a kind of minister of education and employment agent, with a seemingly unlimited supply of pupils, sons-in-law, nephews, and friends for whom he procured chairs in most of the universities.

Melanchthon's success as a teacher and ideologist of Protestantism while he was Luther's associate, however, did not continue when he became the successor to Luther. Though the events now to be described belong more to the history of dogma than to the history of philosophy, a knowledge of them is necessary if we are to understand the way in which monolithic Melanchthonism was broken up later in the century.

Melanchthon assumed the leadership of the Lutherans about the time of the defeat of the Schmalkaldic League by Charles V in 1547 and the promulgation of the Augsburg Interim in 1548. This was a formula which Charles V attempted to establish for all religious sects in Germany: it was Catholic in inspiration, but made a few concessions to Lutheranism. It was to be valid until a general council of the church (which Luther had demanded) could be called to settle definitively the issues in the "schism." Melanchthon, under Moritz, the Elector of Saxony who sided with the Emperor, and always anxious for peace and for reconciliation, proposed

[46] *On Christian Doctrine,* chap. xxxvi.

the Leipzig Interim, the purpose of which was to maintain the peace by what appeared to him to be unimportant concessions to Catholicism. These were mostly in matters of ritual, or *adiaphora* as he and the authors of the Augsburg Interim saw them. But neither proposal succeeded in its main purpose, while Melanchthon's hesitant efforts at compromise split the Lutheran theologians into two groups. There were the Gnesio-Lutherans, led by Amsdorf and Flacius, and the Philippists, led by Camerarius, Georg Major, and Victorin Strigel. The Philippists continued to hold and develop the views of Melanchthon on the (relative) unimportance of liturgical matters, on the importance of good works as pleasing to God (against Amsdorf's view that "good works damage holiness"), and the cooperation (synergism) of the human will and the will of God in the work of salvation. Their milder view of predestination resembled that being developed by German Calvinists (to be expressed in the Heidelberg Confession of 1563, drawn up under Melanchthonian influences in Calvinism), and on the interpretation of the Eucharist, in which Melanchthon had come (after the failure to reach agreement with Zwingli in Marburg in 1528) to follow a *via media* not unlike that of Calvin. In all these matters the Gnesio-Lutherans thought that Melanchthon had conceded too much to both Calvinism and Catholicism. After the Peace of Augsburg (1555), which provided for the continued existence side by side of Lutheranism and Catholicism under the principle *cuius regio eius religio*, according to which the religion of each state was to be that of its prince, the clear definition of dogma became essential for political and legal reasons, since the Augsburg Peace established a territorial or state church in each principality. Only two churches were recognized, the Catholic and the Lutheran, for no reigning prince was an adherent of Calvin and, in fact, an independent Calvinist church did not exist yet. (The Augsburg dictum was not extended to Calvinism until the Peace of Westphalia in 1649.) But when Frederick III, the Elector Palatine, favored Calvinist views and secured the adherence of the University of Heidelberg to them, Gnesio-Lutherans felt that the Peace of Augsburg had been betrayed. A new statement of Lutheran orthodoxy was required.

The Synod of Stuttgart of 1559 restated as official doctrine Luther's teaching concerning the Eucharist. According to it, Christ is present in the bread and wine, but the substance of the bread and wine is not transmuted into that of his body and blood. Opposing this doctrine, the Philippists in 1561 (Melanchthon having died in 1560) argued against this view and in favor of Calvinist theory that the Eucharist is a spiritual communion, neither merely symbolic (as Zwingli taught) nor quasi-physical (as Luther taught). But more important than these over-subtle distinctions was their plea, in their anonymous publication, *Exegesis perspicua*, for the right to a freer interpretation of Luther's teachings—that is, for the right to modify Luther in the direction of Melanchthon's (and Calvin's) views.

With this step, Philippists were seen to be crypto-Calvinists and were immediately subjected to strong persecution—dismissal, banishment, imprisonment, or, in one case at least, death. The victorious Gnesio-Lutherans adopted in 1577 the Formula of Concord which stamped out all the

Melanchthonian heresies except synergism. This Formula of Concord was misnamed. It produced concord only by driving leading Philippists into Calvinism and even Catholicism, and erected on the previously somewhat vague lines between Lutheran and Calvinist teachings a wall between what had become two irreconcilable churches: the Lutheran and the Reformed.

As a consequence, Lutheran theologians, unlike a few of their Calvinist counterparts, ceased to play any important part in the kind of thinking we call philosophical. Philosophy for the Lutherans became a polite name for heresy-hunting. Only one Lutheran follower of Melanchthon, Georg Calixtus (Calixt, 1586–1656), Professor in Helmstedt, argued philosophically for the realization of a dream dreamt also by two of the greatest philosophers, Nicholas of Cusa and Leibniz: agreement among all Christians.

Calvin

The philosophical differences between Luther on the one hand and Calvin and Zwingli on the other had their roots in their widely different backgrounds and education. Luther came to theology through scholastic study, Calvin and Zwingli through humanism. Calvin and Zwingli were men of the Renaissance, deeply affected by humanistic study of the ancients, especially the Stoics. Zwingli's *De providentia* was written under the influence of Cicero's *De natura deorum* and Pico della Mirandola's *Dignity of Man*. Calvin's first work was a commentary on Seneca. From these sources, Swiss Protestantism had from the beginning a very different attitude toward man and the world from that held by Luther. The peculiarly Stoic conceptions of the organic wholeness of the world, naturalistic determinism, an indwelling moral law, a positive evaluation of natural knowledge, and a sense of the autonomy of the secular were ingrained in the Swiss reformers and did not appear in Lutheran thought until they were introduced by Melanchthon. What Dilthey called "the natural system of the *Geisteswissenschaften*"[47] was brought into existence by the Swiss reformers' adapting Roman Stoicism to Christian purposes (and though Melanchthon looked more to Aristotle than to Seneca and Cicero, we have seen the Stoic elements also in his theory of knowledge). The Swiss reformers were able to carry this natural system further than the Lutherans because their Stoicism was comparatively pure, that is, not yet infected with three centuries of scholastic interpretation. Thus, while the essentially philosophical efforts of the Lutherans in their struggle against Catholic scholasticism took the form of an attempt to go back to a purified and corrected Aristotle, Calvin's need was not to find the Aristotelian kernel of truth in the established scholasticism; the Stoic philosophy in Germany from the time of Rudolf Agricola provided an alternative to the entire scholastic edifice.

Calvin's disdain of scholasticism sprang from his humanism; in contrast, Luther's arose from his detestation of everything which rationalized and systematized what ought to be directly experienced in a massive confronta-

---

[47] "Das natürliche System der Geisteswissenschaften im 17. Jahrhundert," in *Diltheys Gesammelte Schriften* (Berlin: Teubner, 1923–1936), II, esp. 153–161.

tion of man and God. To establish a theology and a church, Luther had to have a Melanchthon; Calvin was his own Melanchthon. (From this Calvinist and Melanchthonian rationalism there followed the accusations that the Philippists were crypto-Calvinists.) In spite of the humanistic elegance of Calvin, the lawyer turned theologian, there is a historical paradox in the theologies of the two men. For Luther, the monk, seems almost more interested in man than in God; Calvin, the humanist, seems more interested in God than in man. Luther's theology is man-centered to a degree quite foreign to Calvin. The central experience for Luther is a sense of paralyzing sin and impotence, from which God saves man by giving of his unmerited grace. The central experience for Calvin is the greatness and majesty of God, before whom man is nothing except insofar as he is God's creature and the receptacle of his grace. Luther found God's grace in love; Calvin was more interested in his might and justice. Both Luther and Calvin had a sense of the greatness of God and the near nothingness of man. But in Luther, one feels, the sense of sin and unworthiness is absolute, not comparative. If man were, *per impossibile,* alone in the universe, he would still be a miserable worm. Luther does not have to have a conception of the glory of God to see that there is no soundness in man. Calvin, on the other hand, begins his *Institutes of the Christian Religion* with an objective inquiry into the sources of man's knowledge of himself and of God, and a demonstration that knowledge of God is necessary for true self-knowledge. Luther's writings almost always begin with a concrete situation, a polemical difficulty, or a call to arms. Calvin begins with a proof that the knowledge of God is cognate with that of man, with a paean to the might and majesty of God and a collection of evidence that man is in the hands of an absolute deity. This difference in arrangement befits the highly systematic organization of the *Institutes,* which, in this respect, is unlike any of Luther's writings. But it is more than a rhetorical difference between two kinds of works. It permits God and the world to come into view before man; it permits man to know himself truly only by first knowing God and then descending to self-scrutiny, though it is the scrutiny of man and nature which reveals even to unregenerate man, in good Stoic fashion, his belongingness to the source of law, intelligibility, and goodness. There are for Calvin two kinds of God-knowledge. The first —and for many men, the only—knowledge of God is theological or philosophical knowledge *about* God; the second is a knowledge of God which is not theoretical or propositional but is equivalent to faith and is a gift of God.[48]

It may seem inconsistent with what has just been said about Calvin's theocentric rhetoric (should it be no more than that), to say that there is also a worldly character in his theology, God-centered rather than man-centered though this worldliness may be. It is worldly in the sense that there is worldly evidence of God and of man's place in creation quite independent of the sanctifying experience of faith and election.[49] As a

[48] *The Institutes of the Christian Religion* (trans. F. L. Battles, Philadelphia: Westminster Press, 1960), bk. I, chap. iii, § 21 and chap. xv; also bk. II, chap. ii, § 18.

[49] *Ibid.,* bk. I, chap. v, §§ 1, 2, 5.

humanist, Calvin sees man-in-the-world in a way and to a degree quite alien to Luther, as a former monk. Calvin does not draw the natural–supernatural distinction with the same self-confident dogmatism that Luther had; the things of this world and the things of God are much more inextricably interwoven than they are for Luther. It was not Luther's wish to subjugate the church to the German princes, having just saved it from the Italian, even though practical politics and the theory of divinely ordained obedience to earthly powers had this effect. It was Calvin's purpose —and one he achieved for a while—so to transform the worldly order that the division between the sacred and the political simply disappeared. Luther was content to reform the Church; Calvin tried to reform the world too.

In his theology Calvin will have nothing to do with Melanchthon's synergism.[50] He goes further even than Luther, asserting not only predestinarianism but also a rigorous determinism even in worldly events.[51] The deterministic order of the world, which does not exclude general and mysterious providence, is itself evidence of God's existence. The line between natural knowledge and mysteries is maintained, of course; yet they belong together organically—not just pragmatically, as when the Lutherans saw the practical need for secular learning in their church. There is a natural theology with which Luther would have nothing to do, but Calvin, presumably, had in mind a natural theology which was less dependent upon a theological metaphysics than Melanchthon's adaptations of Aristotle. Among Calvin's followers, therefore, there was an unquestioned assumption that it was God's world that could be studied scientifically, but also the assumption that it had to be studied without constant recourse to God's will.

God's providence is manifested in the order of nature; yet our understanding of nature, though no doubt encouraged by this faith, is not a theology of nature.[52] "However all things may be ordained by God's purpose and sure distribution," Calvin writes, "for us they are fortuitous."[53] "The Christian heart, since it has been thoroughly persuaded that all things happen by God's plan and that nothing takes place by chance, yet will give attention to the secondary causes in their proper place."[54] From this, there seems to be but a short step to a deistic conception of nature: "The several kinds of things are moved by a secret impulse of nature as if they obeyed God's eternal command, and what God has once determined flows on by itself."[55]

The worldliness of Calvin's theory effected also a naturalism and a rationalism in man's practical life. Just as nature runs under its own power and can be understood in its own terms, even though the power was created by God and the laws are God's ordinances, civil society itself is to be understood in its own terms, even though the men in it are God's subjects and the purposes are, in hidden ways, God's purposes. But God is too far above

---

[50] Ibid., bk. II, chap. v, § 9.
[51] Ibid., bk. I, chap. xvi, § 5. The Stoic origin of this teaching should not be overlooked.
[52] Ibid., chap. v, § 2.
[53] Ibid., chap. xvi, § 9.
[54] Ibid., chap. xvii, § 6.
[55] Ibid., chap. xvi, § 4.

man, his purposes too arcane, for his predestination to guide us consciously in our choices. Luther thought the denial of the freedom of the will was a comfort; Melanchthon thought it was a threat, and therefore modified it; Calvin thought it a challenge:

When man has been taught that no good things remain in his power, and that he is hedged about on all sides by most miserable necessity, in spite of this he should nevertheless be instructed to aspire to a good of which he is empty, to a freedom of which he has been deprived. In fact, he may thus be more sharply aroused from inactivity than if it were supposed that he was endowed with the highest virtues.[56]

Since man can do nothing to be saved, all the energy that formerly went into vain work for salvation seems to be now available for redirection toward the world of man. Calvinists could think they were doing God's work six days a week, and on Sundays they could think that their success was a sign of God's favor. They could do so, but I can find neither texts in Calvin nor arguments consistent with these texts which would show that they should. In ways which I cannot understand, but must acknowledge to be a historical fact, and not even a unique one, Calvin's uncompromising predestinarianism and fine-grained determinism became an energizing force in many men who held to these theories, while those who held to a synergistic theory did not, in practice, build up a dynamic and historically effective theory of the relation of work in human society to faith in God. *Prima facie*, one would have expected the *milites christiani* to have sprung from the Erasmus–Melanchthon camp; in historical fact, they came from the Calvinist exaggeration of one side of Lutheran thought. (This is a sobering thought for those who think that the way men act reflects to any significant degree the philosophy or theology they think they have embraced.)[57]

When the Philippists ceased to be dominant in Lutheran theology, and the Calvinists put down the Arminians and their deep modification of the doctrine of predestination, the differences between orthodox Lutheranism and orthodox Calvinism became greater and were legally and administratively fixed. Calvinism became a force behind political revolution in Great Britain; Calvinists first opposed, and then joined, the scientific revolution. In Germany they did neither; a milder form of Calvinism, more like Philippism and Arminianism, was followed in the Palatinate and led to

[56] *Ibid.*, bk. III, chap. ii, § 1.

[57] Even Weber, who in his *Protestant Ethic and the Spirit of Capitalism*, insisted perhaps too much upon the connection between Calvinism and capitalistic enterprise, did not think that the former was connected with the latter by a theoretical argument; and one of Weber's latest critics concludes that the relation was "perhaps one of historical preparation, but not at all of theoretical contribution" (Michael Walzer, *The Revolution of the Saints* [Cambridge: Harvard University Press, 1965], p. 303). Since this chapter was written I have been gratified to find the argument of H. R. Trevor-Roper (*The Crisis of the Seventeenth Century* [New York: Harper & Row, 1968], chap. 1) for what was merely a theoretical conjecture in the above paragraph. While thinking that the term is not entirely appropriate, he calls the attitudes which Weber thought to be primordially Calvinistic "Erasmian," and says that "the Erasmian *bourgeoisie*, if it did not renounce its Erasmian views altogether, turned to Calvinism as the only form in which it could defend them" (p. 24).

the Heidelberg Catechism of 1562. The rigors of extreme Calvinism, where they could be maintained, seem to have given it strength; and the absence of this extreme rigor in Germany may have been a factor in both Calvinistic and Lutheran Germany's being left behind in the great political and intellectual movements of the seventeenth century.

Calvinism, because of its congregational organization, never again had the monolithic dogmatic structure of early Lutheranism and the Calvinism of Geneva. The junction of Zwinglian and other elements in it gave it an elasticity that permitted it to be somewhat different in different places. On the Continent, Calvinism was largely confined to Switzerland, the Rhineland, and the Low Countries. The University of Heidelberg was a center of disputes between Philippists, Gnesio-Lutherans, and Calvinists in the 1550's; but on the death of Melanchthon and the migration of Calvinists into the Palatinate from the Low Countries during the Dutch war against Spanish rule, the Elector-Palatine Friedrich III became a Calvinist and the University of Heidelberg changed from a Melanchthonian-Lutheran to a Calvinist university, which it remained until its destruction in the Thirty Years' War (except for the period 1576–1583 when it was temporarily Lutheran, under Ludwig VI, and the Calvinist professors dismissed). Marburg, which was the first Protestant university, and a center of Philippism, became Calvinist in 1605, at which time another, Lutheran, university was established for Hessen at Giessen. In Brandenburg, Johann Sigismund became a Calvinist in 1613, but because he was a ruler of states with a large Lutheran majority, he established a rule of tolerance for both confessions. In the early part of the seventeenth century there were five Calvinist universities (or advanced schools): Heidelberg, Marburg, Herborn, Steinfurt, and Frankfurt-on-the-Oder. All the Calvinist universities except Frankfurt were in the west, whereas Lutheran schools were widely dispersed, except in the Catholic south. I mention these geographical facts because they show that the Calvinist universities were closer to the centers in which work of European importance was to be done in the seventeenth century, and that it was they, and not the Lutheran schools, that carried on the principal intellectual traffic with France and Holland.

The Philosophy of Protestant Orthodoxy

Reactions against Melanchthon's Philosophy

Melanchthon was the most important philosophical thinker in Germany during the first half of the sixteenth century. We have seen how his influence declined in Lutheran theology, and how many of his followers were hounded out of the Lutheran Church. In this chapter we shall examine the philosophical movements against his Christian humanism. There were four: (1) Ramism, an anti-Aristotelian Christian humanism; (2) a revival of metaphysics against the humanist neglect or renunciation of it; (3) the conversion of this metaphysical interest into a system of Protestant scholasticism; and (4) the development of social philosophy among the Calvinists. The first three of these movements began outside Germany, in France, Italy, and Spain, respectively.

Ramism

Peter Ramus (Pierre de la Ramée, 1515–1572) was a French humanist who was influenced by the revival of Platonism in Florence at the end of the fifteenth century, through Guillaume Budé and Faber Stapulensis (1455–1536), the editor of Nicholas of Cusa, in Paris. Through Johannes Sturm, who taught Agricola's logic in Paris, he was brought into still sharper opposition to scholasticism; through both Budé and Faber he was attracted to Calvinism.

As a student in Paris Ramus became involved in the struggles against Averroism, which had recently revived in Padua and spread to Paris, and in his famous *Animadversiones aristotelicum* he boldly stated his thesis: "Everything Aristotle said is unproved (*commentitia*)." Specifically he criticized Aristotle and the Averroists for holding the doctrine of the eternity of the world, denying the immortality of the soul and Providence, and for holding a naturalistic ethics in which the rewards were to be found in this life instead of in the hereafter. In place of this Averroistic Aristotelianism he, like a good humanist, propounded a simple "Christian philosophy" in which there would be a return to primitive Christianity and an avoidance of philosophical subtleties.

Ramus became a Calvinist in Heidelberg in 1569 and was on the point of being given an appointment in the university but was blocked by the more orthodox Calvinists. But because of the popular humanistic style of his writings, they came to be widely used in Germany either as replacements for, or additions to, the Melanchthonian corpus.

Unlike others who held that the scholastics had ruined Aristotle's logic and who wanted to go back to ancient sources and especially to the historical Aristotle, Ramus held that it was Aristotle himself who had ruined logic. Ramus did not believe that God had made man an animal and left it to Aristotle to make him rational. There is, rather, a "natural dialectic" in man, Ramus said, which begins with characters impressed on man's mind by God and not by experience and teaching. Logic is simply an image of a natural dialectic (*imago naturalis dialecticae*), and the essentials are to be found in Plato's theory of definition and division, not in the arid formalism and obscurity of Aristotle's writings. The most important features of an instrument of thought are not to be met with in a theory of exposition masquerading as a theory of proof (his criticism of syllogism), but in an art of invention (*ars inveniendi*) which will lead to discovery as well as to eloquence in persuasion. The mind has an immediate assent to truth; *inventio*, the art of finding arguments, and *dispositio*, the art of disposing them so as to "make a case" for truths already known, are more important than demonstration, which appears to imply that the truths discovered do not, as it were, stand on their own feet. Discovery is to be made by the perspicuous exposition or division of what is already known.

Logic is not a science, but an art; not a part of school-philosophy, but a propaedeutic of right thought and expression, and whatever will serve this end belongs in the study of logic. Ramus' objections to Aristotelian logic are not unlike those made today by authors of textbooks of "practical logic" against the formal sophistication of rigorous logic. He proposed a "natural logic" which included much psychology of persuasion and had an explicit epistemological foundation; and it was not so "pure" that it could not properly include discussion of appropriate gestures in debate.

Ramus divided logic into two parts: a theory of concepts, or terms and their definition and classification, and with devices for finding missing genera or species that would provide middle terms in argument (the *ars inveniendi* proper); and a theory of judgment and proof (*ars iudicandi*) which included what he had to say about demonstration. This twofold division of logic lasted until the seventeenth century, when it was replaced by a threefold division resulting from a renewed contact with Aristotelian logic. One of the first to institute this division was the Calvinist Bartholomäus Keckermann[1] who, in his *Systema logicae* (1600) distinguished *explicatio, probatio,* and *dispositio* (definition and division of concepts, their combination in judgment, and their arrangement in inference).

The Ramian twofold division could be presented formally, without the extraneous elements to be found in Ramus' own prolix presentations, and there arose in Germany various syntheses of it with the Melanchthonian conception of logic as an art. Those making these combinations were called Philippo-Ramists or Semi-Ramists or *secta mixta*.[2] The classification of various philosophers under these rubrics is by no means unanimous, in part no doubt because at various times a man might be closer to one or the other of the two poles, and in part because each was a term of abuse for one's opponents. In general, however, Lutherans (Georg Gutke and Johannes Scharf in Wittenberg, Scheibler in Giessen, and Abraham Calov in Königsberg) remained Philippists, while Calvinists like the Marburger Rudolph Goclenius (1547–1628), known for, but not the inventor of, the "Goclenian sorites", Bartholomäus Keckermann (1571–1609) in Heidelberg, and Heinrich Alsted (1588–1638) in Herborn were Ramists or Semi-Ramists. Often the decision to teach Ramist, Philippist, or a mixed logic, was not made by the teacher himself but by the magistracy, with the natural result that Ramism was almost universally taught in the few Calvinist universities; but it was sufficiently popular in the Lutheran universities to call forth official prohibitions, as in Leipzig, Helmstedt, Jena, and Wittenberg. In Hessen, whose two Landgräfe were respectively Lutheran and Calvinist, a Philippo-Ramist curriculum was required by law.[3]

All three of these sects lost in importance in the seventeenth century through a new return (yet once more!) to Aristotle.

The Revival of Aristotelian Metaphysics

The Ramists opposed Melanchthon because he had been too Aristotelian. Toward the end of the century the Lutheran complaints were exactly the reverse; he had not been Aristotelian enough, because he had neglected Aristotle's *Metaphysics*, and his logic was too far from Aristotle's. In the sectarian debates which reached a new intensity in the last quarter of the century, especially about the Eucharist, careful analysis and disciplined use of such concepts as substance, attribute, accident, locus, form, and matter

---

[1] See Wilhelm Risse, *Geschichte der Logik*, vol. I: *Die Logik der Neuzeit* (Stuttgart: Fromann, 1964), p. 446.

[2] Johannes Scharf, a Philippist, complained that they "mixed up everything in chaos, light with darkness, heaven with earth, the trunk with its branches." Quoted from H. W. Arndt's introduction to his edition of *Vernünftige Gedanken von den Kräften des menschlichen Verstandes*, in Wolff's *Gesammelte Werke*, ser. 1., vol. I (Hildesheim: Georg Olms, 1965), p. 38.

[3] See Risse, *Logik der Neuzeit*, pp. 187–188.

were required. As the only alternative to denying the validity of philosophy in theological thinking there was needed a metaphysics and a logic that had been neglected since the separation of the churches. There were those who did deny this validity and attempted to drive philosophy out of the schools. One of these was Daniel Hofmann of Helmstedt who, in his *De usu et applicatione notionum logicorum ad res theologicas* (1596), so separated the functions of philosophy and theology that philosophy was declared to be without use to theology. His colleagues in the university, Johannes Caselius (1533–1613) and Cornelius Martini, in defending philosophy from this attack, gave it a new direction in Protestant Germany. In this they were aided by an entirely different movement in other Lutheran universities. This was an open return to Aristotle.

Not only had Melanchthon neglected Aristotle's *Metaphysics*, but his compendia and commentaries on the other works, by being so widely used, had come to stand between the student and Aristotle. The same factors which had led the early reformers, even Luther, into a recognition of the importance of philosophy now forced them to make the weary pilgrimage back to the original, the pure, Aristotle. Italy gave the lead in this return as in others. In the logic of the Aristotelian circle in Padua, especially in that of Zabarella (1532–1589), there was found the inspiration and the source of all the "new" logic in Germany between Ramus and Leibniz. The important critics of Ramism in Germany were not Lutherans who were satisfied to adhere slavishly to Melanchthon, but were those who went beyond his understanding of Aristotle's logic by following the Paduan Aristotelians.

The first sign of a return to "the genuine Aristotle" among the Protestants[4] was the publication of the *Organum Aristotelicum* by Jacob Schegk in Tübingen in 1577. This marked a return, under Zabarella's influence, to the classical conception of logic as a universal instrument of reasoning, free from the humanistic conception of dialectic and rhetoric with their psychological and metaphysical content. Philip Scherb (d. 1605), the opponent of Ramus in Altdorf, was the principal representative of Italian Aristotelianism in Germany, and through him Altdorf became and remained through most of the century a center of Aristotelianism. But interest in Aristotle's logic, which rightly excluded the metaphysical problems previously handled within logic (the theory of categories, for example), forced a revival of the study of metaphysics itself. Because of the requirements of theological debate, these problems could not be ignored.

Hence Aristotle's *Metaphysics* received attention that it had not had since the humanists and Melanchthon had begun to ignore it. In 1594 Professor Daniel Cramer of Wittenberg published his *Isagoge in metaphysicum Aristotelis;* two years later Taurellus published his *Synopsis Aristotelis metaphysices,* and in 1598 the Calvinist Rudolph Goclenius in Marburg published his *Isagoge in peripateticorum primam philosophiam* which earned him the honorific title of "the Christian Aristotle."

---

[4] As a consequence of the Counter Reformation, there had been a rejuvenation of Catholic university education and a somewhat earlier turning to Aristotle; a commentary on the *Organon* by Francisco Toledo, a Spanish Jesuit, had been published in Cologne in 1574.

This great interest in Aristotle's *Metaphysics* followed three divergent paths. First was that of those who simply continued the Aristotelianism of such Italians as Pomponazzi, Caesalpinus, and Zabarella. This was the course followed by the *philosophia Altdorfina* (Scherb and his followers), characterized by a doctrine of a twofold truth and a sharp separation of Christian theology from heathen metaphysics. In pious Germany this was almost the same as a subordination of philosophy to theology. The second was the path chosen by Taurellus of Altdorf, who held that philosophy could be vindicated through a denial of the twofold truth of theology and philosophy, and an assertion of a specifically Christian philosophy which would not be at war with theology. To establish this, of course, meant to go against "the philosopher," that is, Aristotle, and to put another meta-physics in the place of his. The third path led to the establishment of a scholastic metaphysics suitable for Protestant theology by continuing and adapting Aristotelian scholasticism as it had been developed in the post-Tridentine church. This was the movement, initiated by Cornelius Martini in Helmstedt, which came to dominate Protestant university philosophy during the following century.

Taurellus

Nicolas Taurellus (original name probably Oechslein) was born in Mömpelgard in 1547 and died in Altdorf in 1606. He was a student of Schegk's in Tübingen and after taking his medical degree in Basel and teaching moral philosophy in the University of Strassburg he became pro-fessor of medicine in Altdorf. During his lifetime he was much better known as a physician than as a philosopher, and his medical works were known outside of Germany as well. His most important works in philosophy were *Philosophiae triumphus* (1573), and *Synopsis Aristotelis metaphysices* (1693). The full title of the latter work, which continues, *ad normam christiande religionis explicatae, emendatae et completae*, could serve as a statement of the program of his entire philosophical career, the program of explaining, supplementing, and correcting Aristotle by the norms of Christian thought. This was, of course, nothing new; it was not foreign to Melanchthon. But whereas the earlier attempts had been made by drawing the line between Aristotle and Christianity to coincide with that between knowledge and faith, Taurellus drew the line *within* philosophy, as a divi-sion between Aristotelian and Christian *philosophy*. Only in the light of this can the title of his chief work, *The Triumph of Philosophy*, be under-stood. The triumph of Taurellus' philosophy is to be achieved not by the theory of a double truth, the exclusion of philosophy from theology, and the primacy of faith, but by making philosophy an integral part of theology, indeed the foundation of it. A metaphysics that can serve as this foundation, however, cannot be Aristotelian metaphysics, whether in its Italian form or even in Aristotle's own work, unless it is purified of its errors. This means, in turn, that Aristotle's metaphysical views must be brought into harmony with the philosophical ideas implicit in Christianity. Christianity is the philosophical norm, not a source of an external criterion of faith and revelation to be applied to the works of reason. The truth must be one for faith and reason, and if the truths of Christianity are not the same as the opinions of Aristotle, *so much the worse for Aristotle, but without prejudice to philosophy*. Errors in philosophy are errors of philosophers, not faults of their discipline. If Aristotle is in error, he can be corrected by a better use of philosophical reason, not by an appeal to an extrarational Christian truth based upon revelation. The natural light, dimmed but not extinguished by the fall of man, is an adequate source of truth for both philosophy and theology. The philosophy which harmonizes with Christian truths will be, to be sure, an emended and corrected Aristotle; but it is Aristotelianism corrected by a philosophy, not by a theology. The triumph of philosophy, therefore, involves two victories: a victory of philosophy over those who, like Daniel Hofmann, would banish it as heathen and anti-Christian, and a victory of true philosophy over Aristotle. The triumphant philosophy was called "Christian philosophy," and its very name was a renunciation of the concept of a twofold truth and of revelation dominating reason.

There is in us, Taurellus taught, the natural light of reason, given us by God, and giving us a single, self-consistent truth. It functions in philosophy, and teaches a modified Aristotelianism. God is not the soul of the world, but a creative spirit eternally creating himself by action, and creating the world in time *ex nihilo*, endowing it with an autonomous nature, the essence of the world being a self-sustaining motion. (Taurellus adopts the metaphor, originated probably by Nicholas of Oresme, of the world as a clockwork set in motion by God but now operating under its own power without further intervention by God—a metaphor used also by Kepler at about the same time and destined to enjoy universal popularity in the following centuries.) Within the world there is no creation out of nothing, and Taurellus at least approaches an atomistic, mechanical cosmology in which all was originally created by God for man's well-being and for man's contemplation of the glory of God.

The philosophical world-view, however, can never be complete, because the fall of man did dim the natural light. Philosophy, therefore, though it teaches nothing but truth, does not teach all the truth; and there are human errors in even the best philosopher. Philosophy, therefore, does not in the long run contribute to a vain pride of intellect which might war with theology; rather, it brings us to despair and doubt: "The fruit of contemplation is hopelessness (*desperatio*)." At this point God reveals his grace and mercy to man and in revelation discloses what human powers alone are not, after the fall of Adam, sufficient to discover.

Taurellus was perhaps the most original philosophical mind in Germany, with the exception of Kepler, during the time in which he lived. Certainly he was gifted with an originality lacking in most, if not all, other university philosophers at the end of the sixteenth century. Had he had followers, the history of German philosophy during the following century might have been different, but no one seems to have appreciated him before Leibniz, who referred to him as "the German Scaliger," and Bayle, who called him one of the most skillful (*plus habiles*) metaphysicians of his time. But he came at the wrong time to be effective, and, moreover, was in the University of Altdorf where a different kind of Aristotelianism was in the ascendancy. Elsewhere, Germany was turning against anti-Aristotelians like Ramus (who was murdered the year before *Philosophiae triumphus* was published) and Taurellus, and stood at the threshold of another of its recurring periods in which Aristotle, or an established interpreter of Aristotle, would again be the master of those who know. The Aristotle emended and corrected by the norm of Taurellus' Christian philosophy was the Aristotle of theology and cosmology; the Aristotle about to be revived was the Aristotle of *philosophia prima*, who could easily be handled, if not by a theory of a two-fold truth, then at least by the division of faculties into the theological and the philosophical. German scholasticism, both Catholic and Protestant, preferred an Aristotelian ontology of forms, essences, and causes with which to dispute about the Eucharist to an Aristotelian *metaphysica realis* modified into a Christian metaphysics and cosmology.

Cornelius Martini

The beginnings of Protestant scholastic metaphysics are found in the work of Cornelius Martini (1568–1621), professor in Helmstedt. Martini was born in Antwerp and was driven into exile into Germany by the Revocation of the Edict of Nantes. After a short period of travel and teaching in Rostock he became a member of the philosophical faculty at Helmstedt in 1592. It was almost by accident that he was the first to lecture on scholastic metaphysics in Protestant Germany; the times called for it, and within a very few years it was widespread. Martini began his lectures on metaphysics in 1597 and they were published under the titles *Metaphysica commentatio* and *Compendium metaphysicum* in Wittenberg and Strassburg in 1605. His later lectures on metaphysics were published in Jena and Helmstedt in 1622. Each of these works went through many editions.

Martini was a principal participant in the polemics undertaken in the effort to keep philosophy viable under the stringent conditions imposed by the Formula of Concord, which—having carefully defined the dogmas of the established church—left many orthodox churchmen with as little feeling of need for philosophy as Luther himself had first felt. Martini was no theologian but a man of the world. He was humanistically learned and knew how to avoid the prolixity and encyclopedism of the more typical scholastic writers who came after him. Georg Calixtus was his pupil, and one can see in his irenic theology something of his teacher's provision for a philosophy that would not be narrowly sectarian but truly independent of the conflicting dogmas of the different churches.

Martini was not, of course, entirely original. Thomas Aquinas' *De ente et essentia* and Aristotle's *Metaphysics* were his models, though he was not trying to be their expositor or commentator. Metaphysics, he held, differs from all other sciences in the fact that it alone is the study of being as such, whereas the rest study the kinds of being. Being, as such, is the *summum genus*, first in the order of being, though last in the order of knowing. It is divided into beings in the mind (*entia rationis*) and real, objective beings; logic is concerned with the former, metaphysics with the latter. Often, with reference to Book V of Aristotle's *Metaphysics*, Martini does little more than define and interrelate such concepts as substance, accident, being, essence, cause, potentiality, act, form, matter, and the transcendentals. Nominalism is rejected. After metaphysics in general, Martini develops special metaphysics which deals with kinds of being, and Martini discusses God and angels. But he does so not from a theological point of view, with his sources in dogma, but philosophically, treating God simply as cause and angels simply as intelligences. The method of metaphysics is entirely that of natural reason. Three proofs of the existence of God are given, corresponding to Thomas's first, third, and fourth.

Martini must be considered the founder of Protestant scholastic metaphysics. But admirable as his work was, his somewhat exiguous *opus* was obscured by the arrival on the German scene of a full-blown, Spanish-booted (as Goethe called it[5]) system which the Protestants quickly accepted.

Scholasticism in the Age of Orthodoxy

The "Age of Orthodoxy" is a not wholly accurate name for the period of German theological thought from the time of the Formula of Concord to the time when Pietistic and Enlightenment thought began to affect German religiosity. It is not an exact term, since orthodoxy was not the only line of thought, and it neither began in 1577 nor ended in the Age of Reason. Yet, like most such terms of periodization, it would not have become a standard name unless it had important and, on the whole, correct connotations. The dividing lines between Lutheranism, Calvinism, and Catholicism were at last perfectly clear: three established churches existed side by side, engaged in theological warfare with each other and associated with internal principalities and foreign powers which, for thirty terrible years, tried to destroy each other and succeeded only in devastating Germany. The practical occupation of Germans was destroying French, Swedes, or other Germans—or merely surviving. Their theoretical occupation was to maintain purity of doctrine, whether Calvinist, Lutheran, or Catholic. It is surprising that during this time a great deal of philosophizing was done; it is not so surprising that the philosophizing that was done was of no very high order of originality or rigor. A vast body of this philosophy is called Protestant scholasticism; and what is most surprising—in fact almost incredible—is the degree to which Protestant scholasticism was neutral with respect to the sectarian differences. Scholasticism was the philosophy of the arts faculties of the exiguous universities, which themselves had only intermittent existence. It forged the tools which were used in the bitter theological debates; yet treatises on logic and metaphysics were written almost as if they were to be put to peaceful purposes. There were, to be sure, differences between Calvinists and Lutherans, but there were differences within each of these groups as well. No one in either camp distinguished himself by singular contributions to philosophical thought, such

---

[5] Though Goethe thinks of it as Jesuit logic, not Jesuit metaphysics:

> Mein teurer Freund, ich rat Euch drum
> Zuerst Collegium Logicum,
> Da wird der Geist euch wohl dressiert,
> In spanischen Stiefeln eingeschnürt,

as Mephistopheles tells the freshman (*Faust*, I, *Studierzimmer*).

as would call attention to him after three hundred years, and hence we can describe fairly well what went on without tying each statement down to a specific author or a specific date. Because of the high degree of agreement, it is possible to talk about "the scholastic philosophy of the seventeenth century" as if it were homogeneous, and without tracing, in tedious detail, the specific form in which it appeared in each writer. The interesting philosophers whose individuality made them important in their own right do not belong in this almost anonymous movement of thought and will be dealt with later.

The situation at the beginning of the seventeenth century was this. Aristotle was once again the master of those who know. But Aristotle, of course, had to be interpreted, and in a form acceptable in Christian theology— removed from the Averroism suspected to exist in the Italian Aristotelians, from whom the German interpretation had been largely borrowed. The Melanchthonian synthesis of Aristotle and Luther was outworn and had never had a fully developed metaphysics. Metaphysics was required, especially because most of the points in theological debate called for the use of Aristotelian concepts. But, as we have said, the metaphysics itself could, to a large extent, be neutral with respect to the specific use to which it was to be put by the theologians. To fight the Jesuits (and, some accounts say, to fight the Calvinists) the Lutheran majority needed a metaphysics— and both they and the Calvinists appropriated large parts of the scholasticism being imported from Spain about this time. Spanish Jesuits had been staffing the Catholic schools in Germany and Holland since about the middle of the century. The first German printing of Suarez' *Disputationes metaphysicae* occurred in 1600, and its effect was almost immediate.

Students might be, and sometimes were, forbidden to read Suarez because he was Catholic; but their teachers read and cited him. While the Catholic philosophers in Germany were content simply to use or paraphrase him, the Protestants had of course, to make some minor adaptations. The *Opus metaphysicum* (1612) of Christian Scheibler (1589–1653), professor in Giessen, was perhaps the principal Lutheran adaptation, and Scheibler won the epithet of "the Protestant Suarez." Jacob Martini (1570–1649) in Wittenberg and Henningus Amisaeus (1570–1636) in Helmstedt were other importers of Suarezian metaphysics into strongholds of Lutheranism. Clemens Timpler (1567[8]–1624), of Heidelberg and Steinfurt, was the leading Calvinist Suarezian (*Metaphysicae systema methodicum*, 1604). Thus Suarez became known to all and was used by most. All the universities now had at their fingertips the same basic scholastic vocabulary and *theoremata*. For more than half a century all German philosophers had a common starting point, and their paths were long before they came to significant partings. As occasion and sectarian needs required, additional chapters on rational, natural and revealed theology could be added; but being as being was neutral with respect to doctrinal differences, and God could be studied as a mode of being, long before the theologian took over with his divisive doctrines of God suited to each communion.

Only a few German schoolmen in the seventeenth century stood outside this common scholastic enterprise. Altdorf and Königsberg remained strongholds of non-scholastic Aristotelianism and maintained the priority of natural theology and *metaphysica specialis*, without rising to (or falling into) "first philosophy." Until efforts were made to introduce Cartesianism into scholasticism, instead of presenting it as an alternative, the internal differences among Protestant scholastics were relatively minor in comparison to their nearly universal consensus. The degree to which this kept intellectual doors open between the different churches can best be seen in the remarkable case of the last great scholastic, Christian Wolff. He, a Lutheran, taught in a Calvinist university, won his title from a Catholic prince, and had his works used as textbooks in Catholic universities.[6]

Common to all the scholastic metaphysicians was the rejection of a twofold truth—in fact, the metaphysical movement arose to meet the theological irrationalism enshrined in this ancient bugbear. To be sure, all scholastics maintained the division between revelation and reason, but no truth of reason had to be abrogated because of a conflict between it and revelation, and the transition from one to the other in the writings of Luther's followers was as smooth as it had been for Thomas Aquinas. The harmony of reason and revelation was emphasized; Occamism was rejected in favor of the reasonableness of divine truth. The Lutheran exclusion of metaphysics from theology, and the humanist exclusion of metaphysics from philosophy itself, were ended.

Logic was purified of the admixture of rhetoric and psychology which had characterized both humanistic and Protestant-scholastic logic. Its relation to metaphysics, which had been obscure because of wavering conceptions of the relation of the study of categories and causes to argumentation, was at last clarified by a definite recognition of the formal aspect of logic. While metaphysics and all the sciences dealt with terms of first intention (that is, dealt with them from the standpoint of their extra-logical meaning), logic was again seen as a sermocinal science dealing with the theory of terms of second intention. The systematic order of logic was not borrowed from metaphysics, as in earlier scholasticism, or from pedagogical considerations, as in humanism, but was thought to be strictly inherent in it as an autonomous discipline. Under the influence of Italian logicians of the school of Padua, much more attention was now given to the instrumental uses of logic—instrumental not for rhetoric but instrumental as an *ars inveniendi*. It had been the lack of such an orientation in scholastic logic which had brought about the humanists' condemnation of it as a fruitless exercise. But the humanistic logic became nearly as useless because its instrumental function lay in the arts of persuasion and not in those of discovery and proof. By the middle of the seventeenth century, the stirrings of science and mathematics in Germany were beginning to call for, and to produce, logics that were both formal and instrumental, and neither metaphysical nor rhetorical (see Chapter IX).

Yet a parallelism of logic and metaphysics was maintained. Logic is a rule of thought, while metaphysics is the science of the object of thought.

[6] See Bernhard Jansen, S. J., *Die Pflege der Philosophie in den Jesuitenorden während des 17./18. Jahrhunderts* (Fulda: Parzeller, 1938).

To show their relationship to each other the metaphor of the sun and moon was often used. Truth is given directly in metaphysics, which is like the sun; truth is given by the reflective thought of logic, which is like the moon. Logic, as *ars*, and metaphysics, as *scientia*, are related as practice to theory; but there is also a science of logic too, not restricted to working with a selection of ontological concepts.

The parallelism of, but clear distinction between, logic and metaphysics also brought changes in metaphysics. If logic and metaphysics are confused, and logic is nominalistic in intent, the stricture on metaphysics is so great that either skepticism or irrationalism results. With this stricture broken, metaphysics, at least for a time, seems to be able to go its own way or ways. For now, on the one hand, universals need no longer be regarded as mere signs or *entia rationis*, as Occamistic and humanistic logic-cum-metaphysics regarded them; while on the other hand theories of innate ideas, which were thought necessary to support logic based on metaphysics can give way to the theory that all principles are derived from experience.[7]

Metaphysics was the study of being as being. But because Catholic scholasticism had added to this Aristotelian formula the study also of the transcendentals (*unum, bonum, verum,* which applied to all being), the prime object of metaphysics was God, the One True and Perfect Being. But "being as being" was subject to two interpretations. It could be taken abstractively, and then metaphysics was ontology (and it was this ontology that was so closely paralleled by logic); or it could be the study of the most general kinds and species of beings, and then it was *metaphysica specialis*. Neither Aristotle nor the Catholic Scholastics made quite so sharp a division here as the Protestants did; and during the course of the century there was, in Protestant and especially in Calvinist writers, a repeated "spinning off" of the special parts of metaphysics from ontology and indeed from metaphysics itself. Thus it was Protestant, and more especially Calvinist, writers and university curricula which established special disciplines of natural theology and pneumatology (the study of spiritual being, including the human soul, and the spiritual attributes of God, demons, angels, and men) and prepared the way for Wolff's clear articulation of metaphysics into ontology and the special fields of rational psychology, rational theology, and rational cosmology.

The ontology left in the center was an ontology of the real existence of individuals alone, with likenesses in them discovered by experience and abstracted by the mind. How this being could become known was a problem which grew in importance during the century. New philosophical disciplines under such names as *technologia, gnosteologia,* and *noologia* made their appearance in university curricula, prefaces to metaphysics, and individual books. Valentin Fromme (1601–75), professor in Wittenberg, in his *Gnosteologia* (1631), came forward as the first German author of a comprehensive epistemology, but his proto-epistemology was modeled so closely on the current ontology that no real progress was made toward an understanding of the way we can know being. Fromme defined his gnosteology

---

[7] See Risse, *Die Logik der Neuzeit*, p. 469.

as the study of "the knowable as the knowable," in analogy to first philosophy as the study of being as being. Because of the Suarezian definition of being in terms of what it is possible to conceive without contradiction, however, the epistemological problem with respect to metaphysical truth does not arise in its full difficulty as a separate problem; or perhaps it would be better to say that the ontological problem has been subtly converted into a problem of reason instead of being (see Chapter VIII).

But the most important questions concerning the relation of reason to sense experience were neglected in the greater concern for the question concerning faith in its relation to reason. Problems agitating other contemporary Western philosophers concerning the relation of mathematics to experience, from which so much of modern epistemology has sprung, were hardly raised by the scholastic philosophers, who were more interested in the relation of our knowledge of this world to our knowledge of or faith in another world than they were of how knowledge of this world is acquired in the first place. An epistemology built around this theological question had nothing to contribute to the theory of knowledge which was to dominate modern philosophy, and which was being formulated elsewhere with mathematics and the scientific laboratory as its centers. The epistemology that had a promising future was being developed at this very time in Italy (Galileo), France (Descartes), England (Bacon, Hobbes), and Holland (Spinoza). It took its point of origin in the knowing subject—natural man with his reason and sense experience as his basis—and the understanding and control of nature as a goal at least as important as that of finding his way to blessedness. The epistemologists outside of Germany had gone against scholasticism, even when they could not completely throw off its influence. They had mathematical and scientific knowledge both as a goal and as a model; they formulated the issues clearly enough to take their stand with theses sufficiently clear to make it appear to later centuries that each man was clearly a rationalist or an empiricist.

All this was very different in Germany, where the question of how we know, when considered at all, was discussed in terms and patterns of analysis borrowed from an abstract ontology. Epistemology, far from being developed in such a way that the whole metaphysical and ontological superstructure was placed *sub judice* as in other countries, was practiced as hardly more than a handmaiden for metaphysicians or as a corollary to ontology, with its subject matter described by analogy as the science of "the knowable as knowable."

The development of such disciplines as pneumatology, natural theology, and noology as simply branches of metaphysics left German scholastics with little content and in no position to challenge the prerogatives and hegemony of speculative and critical metaphysics. "Being as being" and "the knowable as knowable" are concepts not notably rich in suggestive implications; and a tendency toward "essentialism," often attributed to Suarez in contrast to the "existentialism" of Thomas Aquinas, was continued to the point where not only critics of scholasticism accused it of being just *Wortklauberei*, but even led to the proud claim by some of its practitioners that metaphysics was lexical in subject matter and not a *scientia realis* at all. Book V of Aristotle's *Metaphysics* (the book of definitions) was the most highly esteemed part of that rich book. It was at this stage of emptiness, toward the end of the century, that satires against philosophy by such "humanists" as Christian Thomasius repeated those directed two centuries earlier against Catholic scholasticism; philosophy seemed to have made a complete circuit of fatuity in two hundred years.

The Opposition of Calvinism and Lutheranism

The foregoing summary has of necessity stressed the homogeneity of the thought of Protestant scholasticism. Now it remains to say something about its internal diversity. Generalizations about "Calvinistic" and "Lutheran" philosophy are dangerous because exceptions can be found to most of them, and differences among Lutherans are sometimes as great as those between Lutherans and Calvinists. If, however, we omit the "crypto-Calvinism" of the Philippists, and compare the hard-core Lutheranism of central Germany with the Calvinism of western Germany, some distinctive differences can be discerned. On every one of these points of difference it was the Calvinists who represented the teachings which were to lead to the distinctively modern developments in philosophy in the late seventeenth and early eighteenth centuries. Even when philosophers who were in fact Lutherans took important steps during this period, their thinking seems to have followed from what they shared with the Calvinists instead of what was peculiar to their Lutheranism.

The most important difference between the Calvinists and the non-Philippist Lutherans lay in their different estimates of the role and significance of philosophy itself. While the anti-intellectualism of Luther has been exaggerated both by historians and by his followers, it is unmistakably true that for him philosophy was of more use in secular than in sacred study; if a handmaiden to theology at all, she was a servant not only to be used but controlled, a servant to be given only menial tasks, a servant to be kept severely in her own place. Philosophy had nothing *substantial* to contribute to theology, and piety stood in no need of philosophy. In these respects Luther was a good Occamist. And though Occamism leaves philosophy free to go its own way, in a highly charged religious atmosphere that freedom is likely to be little used. The protection philosophy gains from a doctrine of twofold truth is likely to be of little worth to it if all value and interest are invested in the truth which is not that of philosophy. Twofold truth is beneficial only where the forces which would otherwise collide are of nearly equal strength. Such a near-balance of forces was not to be found in Germany until the eighteenth century; hence the disjunction between theological and philosophical truth among Lutherans did not benefit philosophy but, in fact, worked against it by robbing it of positive value.

For reasons that are not at all obvious in Calvin's own theological writings on the utter transcendence and inscrutability of God, German Calvinists did not need the strategem of a twofold truth. In Western Europe, Calvinism seemed to sanctify all the legitimate practices of life and exercise of intellect by making them contribute to the glory of God. That they contributed to the well-being of man was perhaps theologically a matter of indifference, but one whose effects on Calvinist polity and mentality cannot be ignored. Though Calvinism in Germany did not have the fructifying effect or, perhaps more accurately, was not associated with any institutions which brought about economic and political reform of the kind and magnitude which took place elsewhere, it did not separate piety and *humanitas* to quite the degree Lutheranism did. There was little or no remnant of the twofold theory of truth among German Calvinist thinkers. And for reasons which were probably not theological at all, but which lay rather in differences between Calvinist and Lutheran practices of life, the exercise of secular reason was more advanced among the Calvinists than among the Lutherans. Though Calvinist and Lutheran conceptions of God were not radically different, their conceptions of man and society, and hence their conceptions of the functions of man's natural reason, were indeed different.

Generally speaking, the Lutheran theory was that the fall of man had so clouded the natural intellect or the natural light of reason that either no metaphysics at all was possible, and profane natural knowledge had not even an ancillary role to play in theology (the view of the anti-intellectualist fanatics (*Schwärmer*) Daniel Hofmann, Johann Werdenhagen, and Wenzel Schilling),[8] or metaphysics was at best useless in comparison to the practical and factual disciplines such as the study of nature and history. Adherents of this theory were the educational reformers Johann Arndt, Johann Valentin Andrae, and, most of all, Amos Comenius (1592–1670). These held the last remnants of the twofold theory of truth of early Lutheranism; they sharply accentuated the difference in worth of the several kinds of knowledge, and did not develop full epistemological doctrines.

Where a more positive appreciation of the problems of knowledge was retained, and a theory of knowledge was regarded as an important part of philosophy, the Lutheran scholastics tended still to decry the natural light of reason and to go to—or to talk as if they should go to—extreme forms of empiricism. Georg Gutke (1589–1634) of Wittenberg and Berlin was the most important of the Lutheran epistemologists. In his *Habitus primorum principiorum seu intelligentia* of 1625 we have the most important treatment of the problem of knowledge coming out of the scholastic movement. Gutke emphasized the activity of mind in gaining knowledge, and set up a science he called *Noologia* as a special division of metaphysics dealing with the activities of *nous*, or reason. In it he sought empirically to find ontological counterparts to the rules of logic, and he anticipated, at least in one of his formulations, though not in his theory about them, the onto-

[8] In defense against such attacks, Jacob Martini (1570–1649) of Wittenberg, an author of widely used compendia of metaphysics for Lutheran schools, wrote one of the first of the few books in German to come out of the scholastic movement: *Vernunftspiegel* (1618). The details of these controversies on the legitimacy of philosophy vis-à-vis theology can be found in Peter Petersen, *Geschichte der aristotelischen Philosophie im protestantischen Deutschland* (Leipzig, 1921; reprint Stuttgart: Fromann, 1964), pp. 259–277.

logical-logical principles we shall meet with again in the writings of the Cartesian Clauberg and the Pietistic epistemologist Crusius (see Chapters IX and XVI). Noology was to be the queen of the sciences, but it was in fact an uncritical ontology phrased in a vaguely epistemological language. Not much could be made by analyses of "knowledge as knowledge," and Gutke never even raised the interesting questions of the limits and validity of knowledge. Germans must be highly filiopietistic who see in Gutke a forerunner of Kant simply because he emphasized the fact that the mind is not passive in knowing.

The Calvinist concern with epistemological problems was slightly different and began somewhat earlier than the Lutheran. In 1606 Clemens Timpler had introduced his metaphysics with a preliminary epistemological study, and there was, throughout the period, more tendency among the Calvinists to deal with various important problems, whether epistemological or theological, independently of the general ontology to which they were introductory or appendant.

In keeping with their teaching of the absolute transcendence of God, the Calvinists tacitly drew the conclusion of the independence of philosophy from theology and of the positive sciences from philosophy itself. Since they did not have the paralyzing sense of sin which was supposed to have permanently darkened the natural light of reason, they were not tempted to decry the vain pride of intellect as many Lutherans were, and for the same reason they were not thrown back upon a blind empiricism of brute fact. But it would be a gross oversimplification of the facts to see the Lutherans as proto-empiricists and Calvinists as proto-rationalists; neither had sufficiently autonomous conceptions of the factors involved in knowledge even to understand the distinction.

But the Calvinists were like the later rationalists in one respect at least: they were interested in the problems of the over-all organization of knowledge and its subdivisions. This is shown in their readiness to make internal divisions within philosophy, and to treat the problems of natural theology, cosmology, and other parts of *metaphysica specialis* as relatively independent disciplines. Even more is this synoptic sense shown in the efforts of the Herborn philosophers, Johann Heinrich Alsted (1588–1638) and Johann Bisterfeld (1605–1655), to compile a great encyclopedia which would present the "circle of knowledge." Alsted wrote perfectly conventional textbooks of scholastic metaphysics, which gradually took the field away from Timpler's, but in the encyclopedic work, Baconian, Lullian, Ramistic, Zabarellan, Paracelsan, and other Neoplatonic elements were predominant.[9] The Calvinist worldly-practical orientation—worldly-practical, of course, only in comparison to Lutheran-scholastic standards—made them stand closer to the heritage of the humanists.

Where the differences in doctrine and polity were greatest between Calvinists and Lutherans we should naturally expect the greatest differences

[9] See L. E. Loemker, "Leibniz and the Herborn Encyclopedists," *Journal of the History of Ideas*, 22: 323–338 (1961). A summary of the contents of the encyclopedia will be found in Lynn Thorndike's *History of Magic and Experimental Science* (New York: Columbia University Press, 1941) VI, 433–436.

in their respective philosophies. These differentiating characteristics are most salient, first, in their opposing views concerning the Eucharist.

There were important philosophical issues at stake in the disputes about the Eucharist. In Christ's statement, "This is my body," the "is" was interpreted in an immense variety of ways. The Catholic and Gnesio-Lutheran view (transubstantiation) held the "is" to be the "is" of identity or of conversion (the substance of the bread *is*, or is converted into, the substance of Christ's body). Zwingli, at the other extreme, held that "is" means "is a sign of," and the sacrament is interpreted only symbolically (the memorial theory). Luther held that it meant that the substance of Christ's body is in or with the bread but not identical with it (theory of real presence, variously called impanation and consubstantialization). Melanchthon seems at one time or another to have held almost every possible view; or, perhaps better, his formula in the *Variata* to the Augsburg Confession was so ambiguous that both Luther and Calvin subscribed to it, but interpreted it in different ways. According to Melanchthon's formula, *est* (is) means *est cum*, where *cum* means in or alongside of (Luther's interpretation) or *at the same time as* (Calvin's interpretation).

Calvin's full treatment of the Eucharist has more interest for the history of philosophy. Though he declared it a mystery impenetrable by human reason,[10] he developed his analysis on sophisticated philosophical terms. Briefly, he held that the "is" is metonymous and neither literal (transubstantiation) nor metaphoric (the memorial theory).[11] The physical taking of the bread, which is called, by metonymy, Christ's body, is accompanied by a spiritual partaking of the real but spiritual substance of Christ; and this partaking is made possible not by Christ's "descending" into the wafer or into the place where it is, but by man's spirit "ascending" to Christ, who is nonspatial. Against Luther's theory of the ubiquity of Christ (according to which Christ is everywhere, and hence both on the right hand of God and on the altar) and another of Melanchthon's theories ("omnivolenspresence"—Christ is wherever he wants to be), Calvin teaches that the infinite spirit cannot be contained in any finite thing (*Finitum infiniti non capax*—a thesis of Nestorian theology), but wholly transcends the physical and spatial world.[12]

The entire dispute raised fundamental ontological problems concerning substance, attribute, accident, form and matter, potentiality and actuality, cause, locus and space. Most of these concepts were worked out in comparative independence of the side of the controversy on which the apologists and polemicists would use them, since the dispute was, in the final analysis, a dispute about a mystery and not about a metaphysical problem. But any-

[10] John Calvin, *The Institutes of the Christian Religion*, trans. F. L. Battles, bk. IV, chap. xvii, §§ 1, 24, pp. 1360, 1390.
[11] *Ibid.*, § 21, p. 1385.
[12] *Ibid.*, § 30, pp. 1401–1403. See Werner Elert, "Ueber die Herkunft des Satzes *Finitum infiniti non capax*", *Zeitschrift für systematische Theologie*, XVI (1936), 500–504. (I am indebted to Professor H. A. Oberman for calling the latter reference to my attention.)

one who sided with the Calvinists in this debate would be inclined to give an important place to the science of the seventeenth century outside of Germany, and we find that some Calvinists did accept these views: (i) Space is ontologically real and absolute. Calvinists could take such a view of space since they did not have to provide physical interpretations of God's ubiquity. Lutherans, on the other hand, had a more nearly phenomenalistic or subjectivistic theory of space, since they wanted to provide for ubiquity and could not do so with a common-sense, realistic theory of space. (ii) There are two substances in the world. The Calvinists had a more definite conception of the duality of nature in God and in things (physical and spiritual) than the Lutherans had. The Lutheran consubstantiation was much closer to the Catholic transubstantiation than the Calvinistic theory was; Lutherans were close to, and commonly interpreted as holding, a theory according to which there was a miraculous change in the wafer. They never had a good answer to the charge (the accusation of "manducation") that when a unbeliever partakes of the Lord's Supper, he chews the body of Christ. For the Calvinists, however, there was no miraculous change in the bread, which is physical and remains physical; if the unbeliever takes the bread, the bread does not cease metonymously to be the spiritual body of Christ but *it* is not taken by the unbeliever for whom the metonymy is unknown. The Calvinist, therefore, had all the (semantic) advantages of the Zwinglians, and yet could maintain the doctrine of the real presence, which Zwingli could not do. They could do so because they had, or were on the way to having, a two-substance theory.[18] There is a physical world, in which bread is and remains bread and to which no miracle happens; it is in real space, and whatever is where it is is not at any other place. But, besides that, and connected with it in a mysterious way, is a nonspatial world of spirit.

I do not mean to sound as if the Calvinists were Cartesians; they fought them bitterly in Holland and Germany. I do say that their theory of the physical world and of the invisible world was not as far removed from the Cartesian conception as was the Lutheran theory, which repeatedly spawned vitalistic, Neoplatonic, nature-mysticisms—not world-views that triumphed in the seventeenth and eighteenth centuries.

The difference in the social philosophies of Calvinists and Lutherans was so great and so obviously significant that the subject deserves a section to itself.

Social Philosophy

It is to be expected that the differences between Calvinists and Lutherans would be best seen not in metaphysics and the theory of knowledge but in those parts of philosophy in which the social and political differences be-

---

[18] Bartholomäus Keckermann (1571–1609), of Heidelberg and Danzig did, in fact, formulate a two-substance theory of mind and body in his *Scientiae metaphysicae compendiosum systema* (1609). Such a theory, of course, easily grows out of the theory of substantial form. The accommodation of Calvinist scholastics to Descartes will be discussed in Chapter IX.

tween the Calvinist and the Lutheran social systems would be directly reflected.

That this expectation is fulfilled and that the religious differences made for differences in ethics, which were in turn reflected in, and in part determined, differences in the economic and political life is known as "the Weber thesis" after Max Weber's arguments[14] that Calvinism provided an ideology uniquely fitted to the development of capitalism. This has been strongly condemned by recent historians, who have pointed out the vagueness of the Weber thesis and its erroneousness when made sufficiently specific to be tested by historical data and facts. The facts against the thesis are that Calvin and his followers were as explicit in condemning practices authorized by developing capitalism as the Lutherans were; that the peculiar sense of "calling" in secular life was older than the Reformation and not markedly different in Luther and Calvin; that capitalism did not appear primarily or exclusively in Calvinist societies; and that the capitalistic system bred abuses which were condemned by Calvinists as vigorously as by Lutherans. Yet in one respect, at least, the Weber thesis is still defensible. The Lutheran polity, by assigning the principal decisions in church government and discipline to the ruling prince, did not ally religion with forces working toward social, political, and economic change, but rather opposed them; it made religious institutions instruments of social control and religion itself either a personal, sentimental, and subjective refuge from the world or an orthodoxy as rigid as the Catholic and enforced, like it, by the authority of the civil powers. "One cannot help being impressed," writes Professor Holborn,

with how neatly Lutheran social ethics, with its hankering for a static medieval society, without capitalistic enterprizes and expansionist power politics, corresponded to the general needs, particularly of central and northwestern Germany. This predominantly agrarian society, not capable of mobilizing large internal resources for external efforts—a measure which would in any case have threatened the precarious balance of internal forces—found in the Lutheran religion and ethics a natural expression of its aspirations.[15]

On the other hand, Calvinism spread in the flourishing commercial cities of the Rhineland and the Netherlands and in the free cities which were not under lords at once temporal and spiritual. If we cannot explain the diverse developments in Lutheran and Calvinist regions by reference to the theological differences, we can nevertheless see—and this was perhaps all Weber was trying to make us see—how appropriate the theologies and their ethical corollaries were to the political and economic situations of those who accepted and developed them. Each part of Germany got the theology and philosophical ethics it deserved in the seventeenth century.

---

[14] In his *Protestant Ethic and the Spirit of Capitalism*, trans. Talcott Parsons (New York: Scribner, 1930); somewhat similar views are in Ernst Troeltsch, *The Social Teachings of the Christian Church*, trans. O. Wyon, 2 vols. (New York: Macmillan, 1931).

[15] Hajo Holborn, *History of Modern Germany* (London: Eyre & Spottiswoode, 1965), I, 261.

Even in the beginning, differences in the political situation in Middle Germany and Switzerland affected, in persistent ways, the relations of the two Protestant sects with the civil powers.

The Reformation was a political as well as a religious revolt. It could not be otherwise so long as the Catholic doctrine of the civil power as divinely ordained was accepted by both the civil and the ecclesiastical powers, who, however, often drew quite incompatible practical conclusions from the doctrine of "the two swords." Any change of view concerning the authority of Rome inevitably brought with it a change of view concerning the authority of the Holy Roman Emperor. Had Rome and Charles V drawn the same conclusions from this doctrine, so that they could have acted in unison against Luther, it is likely that the Reformation would have been strangled. Since they did not, the attack on Rome was strengthened by the adherence of the opponents of the Emperor, and the complex of movements we call the Reformation became a part of the political history of the German states.

This mixture of political and religious motives must always be remembered in judging the statements made by the reformers concerning the relation of the ecclesiastical to the civil power. Luther was not interested in the state, except as a threat or a help to his movement; the political life of man was of no deep concern to him. But the help he could get from the civil power was of great importance, and as his political perils changed, so also did his statements about the nature and scope of political authority. It is therefore impossible to make up a single and consistent "philosophy of government" from Luther's often opportunistic political utterances.[16] The same is true to a lesser extent of Melanchthon and Calvin.

But to understand all the reformers, it is necessary to disabuse ourselves of the myth that the Reformation, *in theory* or *in fact*, stood for a separation of political and religious powers. The Reformation was the most important of all historical events whose effects in the very long run tended in that direction, but such was not the intention of the reformers. Early in his career, to be sure, Luther did deny the civil authorities the power to "force them to come in," the right to dictate religious beliefs to their subjects. From about 1523 to 1530 he expressed contradictory views, and from 1530 onward he consistently supported the necessity of maintaining religious institutions by force if necessary. The privacy of religion, variety of cultus, and toleration of dissent were not the professed goals of the Reformation, but rather of the Protestant Counter Reformation, which will be discussed in the next chapter.

The great battle of the early Reformation was, on the contrary, between two other views concerning the relation of the civil and ecclesiastical authority. The first was the theory that the civil magistrate had the obligation, given him by God, to support the church by the suppression of heresy and the maintenance of a proper church polity. The second was the theory

---

[16] The variety of views expressed by Luther, and the political occasions for their changes, are well recited by J. W. Allen, *Political Thought in the Sixteenth Century* (London: Methuen, 1928), pp. 23–30.

that the magistrate had the right and the authority to do so, but not the obligation. The first doctrine was a theoretical limitation on political power while, in fact, it extended the power of the political arm. The second doctrine limited the ecclesiastical claim to direct the political; it expressed the independence of the political power. In the confused state of German affairs it was the basis of actual political practice. This doctrine could be held in the moderate form in which it reflected the actual political practice of persecution of heresies and minorities when, as, and if politically convenient; or in the extreme form of Erastianism (after Professor Thomas Erastus [1524–1583] of Heidelberg) according to which the state itself had the decisive power in religious matters.

Luther and Calvin generally tended to accept the first alternative, but differences in their political situations made them interpret it in different ways. Luther could not have survived without the active support of the princes against the emperor. In the long run, the price paid for this support was a merging of the political with the ecclesiastical power, theoretically as equals but actually under the domination of the civil power. The Lutheran Church became the sacred arm of some of the North German princes; territorial churches were established with the prince as bishop (*summus episcopus*) in fact if not in name; religious duties to God became entangled with political duties to one's sovereign; obedience to earthly authority became a religious duty.

The situation in Geneva was very different from that in Saxony and Hessen. For there Calvin merged the political and ecclesiastical power in his own person, rather than subordinating the church to the state as the Lutherans had done in fact if not in a consistent theory. In Geneva the political power became the arm of the consistory, the religious governing body comprising both pastors and laymen. Theocracy rather than a near-Erastianism was attained in Geneva during Calvin's lifetime.

The Genevan situation was both unique and short-lived. A sharper separation of religious and political power followed wherever political conditions for the success of theocracy were lacking. An ecclesiastical polity which put authority in the hands of a consistory and not in those of either prince or bishop had two important consequences, both different from those of both orthodox Lutheranism and an incipient theocracy. First, religious life became more private. Second, political life became more secular.

This religious privacy, over against both political and ecclesiastical control, was an important Calvinist contribution to the spirit of Pietism. While not so important as the like contribution, in Germany, by the thinkers of the Protestant Counter Reformation (to be discussed in the next chapter) it must not be overlooked as it has been by some historians of Pietism.

From the secularization of political life came the "Protestant ethic" described by Troeltsch and Weber: In this the political and economic life is secularized because ecclesiastical institutions and doctrines no longer dominate it; but religious values are to be found in the modes of economic and political life itself. One serves God by being a good citizen; one succeeds in the economic or political competitions of life, for the glory of

God; one finds his calling in a worldly asceticism of work and thrift which are economically and politically productive.

Though the Calvinist doctrine of predestination seems incompatible with the active initiative required by worldly asceticism, another doctrine of Calvinism very much favored it. This was the Calvinist doctrine of the utter transcendence of God.[17] God is so far above the world and man that if man comes to terms with the world there can be a direct relation between man and the world, and not merely an indirect relation mediated by man's and the world's relation to God. That indirect relation between man and world exists, of course, and is the ultimate basis for the notions that man has a duty to his society. It grounds the beliefs that one should act charitably not for immediate and direct love of others but for love of God, and that success in one's world calling is a sign of God's favor. But one gets little or no guidance, in dealing with this world, from an utterly transcendent and inscrutable God; God too far transcends this world for us to base our knowledge of it upon our meager knowledge of Him.

The consequences of this doctrine of transcendence were to favor rationalism in a very broad sense, and Lutherans used the opprobrious term "rationalists" in abusing their Calvinistic brethren. A rationalist, in this sense, is one who extends reason and mundane experience into realms that, in the view of the user of this opprobrious term, should be reserved for revelation and authority. In political thought rationalism accordingly meant untrammeled political theorizing. This theorizing could be done by Calvinists because they contended that God transcends the practical political arrangements men have to make. It had to be done by them, because once the temptations of theocracy were renounced or wrested away from them, they were a political minority interested in securing their rights.

The Lutherans, on the other hand, had a somewhat more comfortable situation and did not come forth as social critics requiring a philosophy to back up their complaints about abuses or to provide a basis for social reform. They were little affected by the Stoic conception of natural law as a standard for man lying inherent in nature; they had their Aristotle. Lutheran professors in Helmstedt (Johann Caselius, d. 1613, Henningus Arnisaeus, d. 1635) and Jena (Johann Zeisold, d. 1667) edited and commented upon Aristotle's *Politics* in an effort to show its harmony with the Lutheran theory of the state. Only Calvinism developed early an original and independent political philosophy in Germany. This occurred in the writings of Althusius. Even toward the end of the seventeenth century, when the first Lutheran political thinker of any importance, Pufendorf, developed his theory, it was done under the patronage of the Calvinist Elector of Brandenburg. The social thought of the eighteenth century was, to be sure, carried on by Lutherans; but some, like Thomasius, opposed Lutheran orthodoxy, and others, like Wolff, opposed Lutheran Pietism.

17 Again, these differences cannot all be traced back to Luther and Calvin. Luther had as much a sense of God's transcendence and inscrutability as Calvin did; we have seen plenty of evidence of this in our account of Luther. But there was also something in Luther's massive piety which I must call, in default of a better name, a kind of *intimacy* with God. It was a corollary of Luther's emotional immediacy and it was lacking in Calvin.

Althusius

Johannes Althusius (= Althaus) was born in 1557 in Diedenhausen in the Wittengenstein-Berleburg Gau of Westphalia. He studied at Cologne and Basel, where he took his degree in law. Thereafter he was professor in the University of Herborn until 1604, when he was elected syndic of Emden, where he remained until his death in 1638. His most important work was *Politica methodice digesta et exemplis sacra et profanis illustrata* published in 1603.[18] The "method" to which the title alludes is that of Ramus: dichotomous divisions for the establishment of the scope of each discipline and subdivision.

Althusius' system has been called "the first complete system of political theory which was wholly based on Natural Law." [19] But this statement, though true in a sense, puts the emphasis in the wrong place, suggesting that Althusius was primarily concerned with the establishment of a system of law and finding the roots of positive law in the law of nature, whereas in fact Althusius was concerned much more with the structure of political organizations. The law of nature he appealed to, therefore, was not a "law," properly speaking, but the *facts* of nature, especially the facts about man's inherent sociality. The law of nature, understood as a set of rationally discoverable or revealed imperatives for man which governments must observe, was a very minor and unoriginal part of Althusius' theory; the nature he appealed to was the particular empirical nature of man and the purposes he has by nature which can be achieved in various kinds of associations, only some of which belong in the science of politics. Althusius was a naturalist in regard to man's whole political life, but "natural law" as a control for positive law was a minor and unoriginal part of his work.

He was a naturalist in the sense in which Aristotle was a naturalist, but he differed from Aristotle in two respects. First, he did not believe that man is by nature a political animal, and second he did not think man's goal of happiness includes only political and natural goods. In the second point, of course, Althusius was following the entire Christian tradition, which added to the Greek the Christian virtues and duties. In the first point, Althusius was much more original.

It might appear that the difference between Aristotle and Althusius is merely verbal when Aristotle defines man as a political animal and Althusius defines him as a social animal. (In fact, when explaining Aristotle's theory, one is often tempted to substitute "social" for "political.") But the difference is an important one, in the estimation of Althusius. For, he says, man is not originally a political animal but a social animal; he is a *symbioticus*, a being who must live with his fellows. Politics is the art or science of associating men together, but the primary forms of this association are not political, but natural (the family) or economic (the guild). Man becomes political

---

[18] Edited by C. J. Friedrich (Cambridge: Harvard University Press, 1932) and translated in part by F. S. Carney (*The Politics of Johannes Althusius* (London: Eyre & Spottiswoode, 1964). Each has an excellent introduction.

[19] Otto Gierke, *Natural Law and the Theory of Society*, trans. Ernest Barker (Cambridge [Eng.] University Press, 1934), I, 37.

only when these natural symbioses are associated with each other on various levels of complexity, beginning with the *polis* and reaching through the province finally to the realm or the commonwealth which is the locus of sovereignty because there is no higher locus of power. Each of these higher associations has as its constituents not the individuals but the associations below it, which are joined by a tacit or sometimes explicit contract. For this reason, Althusius is little concerned with the rights and duties of the citizen; his concern is with the relations among associations, e.g., of corporations and estates to each other and to the supervening agencies of the state. The Decalogue, which is the revealed form of what is ordinarily known as the law of nature, concerns the relation of the individual person to God and to his fellows; and though Althusius duly discusses these natural laws, they are peripheral to his main interest.

The sovereignty in the commonwealth belongs to the constituent associations, not to the collectivity of the individuals severally and not to the person of the ruler.

> . . . The people [by which he means the organized bodies of individuals, not the individuals severally] can exist without a magistrate, but a magistrate cannot exist without a people, and . . . the people creates the magistrate rather than the contrary. Therefore kings are constituted by the people for the sake of the people, and are its ministers to whom the safety of the commonwealth has been entrusted. The magistrate or prince is mortal and an individual; the realm or community is immortal.[20]

Althusius opposed the theory of "double sovereignty" (sovereignty is shared by king and people, or king and estates) as developed by the French political philosopher Jean Bodin. While anticipating Hobbes's later theory of the indivisibility of sovereignty, Althusius located it at the opposite pole to the one later chosen by Hobbes. The power of the king is restricted not so much by natural law as to what has been delegated to him, for kingship is "established for the utility of those who are ruled, not for those who rule."[21] If this power is abused, the sovereign can be removed since the contract for the delegation of administrative power has already been abrogated. In this Althusius departs from both Luther and Calvin, who denied the right of rebellion. Althusius, through the establishment of the "ephors," or magistrates, institutionalizes the right of deposition.

The sovereign has, in addition to secular duties, responsibility also for ecclesiastical administration. These duties devolve upon him by a covenant of the people and the magistrate with God; the secular administration does not require God's participation. The execution of ecclesiastical polity is to lie in the hands of the clergy, but Althusius does not spell out in any detail how the responsibility is to be divided. There should be only one religion in a realm ("and that the true one", he adds[22]). Atheists, "impious and profane men who are obstinate and incurable," epicureans and libertines, and heretics whose heresies would "tear up the foundations of faith" are not

[20] Carney, *Politics of Johannes Althusius*, p. 117; see also p. 5.
[21] *Ibid.*, p. 117. [22] *Ibid.*, p. 165.

to be tolerated, and may be banished or put to the sword. Jews and Catholics, provided they are properly segregated and have no synagogues and "temples for the practice of their idolatrous worship" may be permitted.[23] But by fifteenth-century standards, Althusius was comparatively moderate. Dissenters are to be allowed to practice their worship where forbidding them would bring peril to the commonwealth; the minor species of heresy should be discussed, not forbidden; and the power of the magistrate is peremptorily denied in "that area of the faith and religion of men that exists only in the soul and conscience."[24]

Althusius was important for his theory that government is based upon contract and consent; that sovereignty belongs to the constituents of the state, not to the person of the supreme magistrate; that the state is a natural and human institution, in its political jurisdiction largely without any religious sanction and independent of a religious covenant. Although he attributed a religious responsibility to civil government, he secularized its political functions. While he made the political realm autonomous and elevated the state above all other associations, he did not deify the state. In these respects he was followed by the political thinkers of the United Provinces, Scotland, and the American colonies; but also by the German political thinkers of the eighteenth century, who used his theories in conjunction with the Pufendorf theory of *lex naturae* in defense of the practices of enlightened despotism.

[23] *Ibid.*, p. 166.   [24] *Ibid.*, p. 168.

VIII

Occultism, Spiritualism, and Pietism[1]

Agrippa of Nettesheim

What we have been describing at distressing length was not the only philosophizing going on in the sixteenth and seventeenth centuries in Germany. Outside the universities, even sometimes outside the churches themselves, there were thinkers who did not make their peace with Aristotle and scholasticism, who did not put their philosophy at the service of the churches. They could not establish a school tradition of their own, yet they represented modes of thought which have been as characteristic of German philosophy as the articulated intellectual discipline of university philosophy. They reacted against the theological and pedagogical establishments of their time and stood against the orthodoxy of the theological and philosophical faculties of the sixteenth and seventeenth centuries, just as the mystics, the adherents of the *devotio moderna,* and Nicholas of Cusa had stood

---

[1] Lest both the title and the composition of this chapter appear arbitrary, especially in the light of the next chapter, I must explain that I have included Paracelsus here rather than in Chapter IX because (a) most of the other men dealt with in this chapter should be considered in close proximity to the Reformation, and (b) most of them resembled or were influenced by Paracelsus. Otherwise, it would be more appropriate to discuss Paracelsus in the context of natural philosophy in Chapter IX.

against the scholastic establishment of the fourteenth and fifteenth centuries. They were humanists without classical libraries, students of nature without mathematics, preachers without churches, and teachers usually without disciples; they were occultists, spiritualists, theosophists, mystics, heretics, and rebels. Consider one of these men, whose protean character was one of the richest sources of the legends of Dr. Faustus.

This was Henricus Cornelius Agrippa of Nettesheim, who was born near Cologne in 1486 and, after an adventurous life as courtier, humanist, astrologist, physician, expert on women, charlatan, pious student of the Bible, and quarrelsome critic of things in general, died in Grenoble in 1535. Agrippa differed from most of the humanists in the ancient sources he appealed to for his wisdom. It was the ancient books of occultism and orphic mysteries and hermetic writings, of medieval magic and the Jewish Cabala to which he turned, not to the humane letters of antiquity. In this respect he resembled, and was influenced by, Johann Reuchlin. Most German humanists were little interested in nature: Agrippa was devoted to Pliny and indebted to the descriptions of German nature in Albertus Magnus. And whereas most German humanists despised metaphysics, as if it were a monopoly of the schoolmen, Agrippa embraced the Neoplatonic metaphysics according to which all things, man and nature, were linked in a sympathetic relationship because of their common source in a divine emanation. Instead of mathematical science, which was slowly developing in Italy and among a few of the Occamist schoolmen north of the Alps, and which presupposed a very different metaphysics, magic was the method by which Agrippa hoped that man could gain dominance over the forces of nature. Man is a part of nature, tied to its other parts by chemical, astrological, numerological, and sympathetic mimetic relations; but he is not a passive part of it for, through his occult knowledge, he can gain control over it. In Italy Agrippa had become immersed in Neoplatonism and its magical consequences found in the writings of Marsilio Ficino and Pico della Mirandola; and he had as high an esteem for the dignity and power of man as Pico did.

By 1510 he had written *De occulta philosophia*,[2] which was published in 1531 and became the principal compendium of natural magic for the next century. In his excellent study of Agrippa, Charles Nauert writes that this book "represents the decisive moment—and foredoomed failure—of the Renaissance attempt to purge the older magic of its demonic, unorthodox, and fatalistic character by the introduction of a broader, more thoroughly Neoplatonic philosophical outlook."[3] *De occulta philosophia* presented magic as the operational science of Neoplatonic metaphysics; magic was not demoniac charlatanry but a legitimate instrument in man's efforts to fend off the blind forces of nature and to gain a free vision of the divine source of being and hence salvation. It provided an eminently plausible theoretical basis for the practice of astrology, alchemy, medicine, and other magical arts. That it could be and was used for diabolical purposes, and that

[2] Translated as *Three Books of Occult Philosophy* (London, 1651).
[3] Charles G. Nauert jr., *Agrippa and the Crisis of Renaissance Thought* (Urbana: University of Illinois Press, 1965), p. 229.

Agrippa himself seems not to have been above using it to fleece rich patrons, was more a commentary on the vice or weakness of the magi than a condemnation of the philosophical point of view itself. It was not the metaphysics and science that were destined to triumph in the next century-and-a-half; but it would have been a man more venturesome than Agrippa himself who could have said that natural magic, which he believed to be millenniums old, based on a metaphysics strengthened by the work of such men as Albertus Magnus, Dietrich of Freiberg, and Nicholas of Cusa, was not the science of the future.

Agrippa would be forgotten now, however, but for his second important book, *De incertitudine et vanitate scientiarum*, written about 1526 (but published in 1530, a year before the earlier *De occulta philosophia*). For this book was one which truly pointed to the future. It stands in a radically different intellectual tradition from his magical writings: it is one of the first popular presentations of skepticism in modern philosophy. It is the *De incertitudine* which has made Agrippa appear to be so equivocal a character, a model for the legendary Dr. Faustus, who is magician and skeptic at once. Had it been published after his *De occulta philosophia* instead of before, Agrippa's reputation as an honest man would have been higher. For, in that event, it would not have appeared that, having *already* condemned the kind of thing he did in *De occulta philosophia*, he now seemed to be practicing and promulgating teachings he must then have known to be spurious.

In the first book of *De incertitudine*, he denies the power of human reason to achieve the truth. To show this, he draws on the doctrine of original sin as having darkened the natural light in man, on ancient Academic skepticism, and on modern nominalism. While skepticism of the powers of natural human reason is not incompatible with Neoplatonism, which always insisted upon the necessity of the light coming from above, Agrippa does not have any epistemological argument for skepticism, but, in the manner later to be perfected by the French philosopher Pierre Bayle, he simply points to inconsistencies among the authorities. In chapter 54, he argues against moral philosophy, in the manner later adopted by Montaigne, by collecting examples of action approved in one society and condemned in another. Mathematics is the most certain knowledge we have—but it is only the opinions of the teachers of mathematics; physics is only "a certain art of manslaughter" which "presumes to pass under the title of philosophy" (chapter 82). Even the sciences at which Agrippa himself was an adept are not exempted. Astrology is "a science of things uncertain" and astrologists "deceive the simple sort to the end of spoiling them for their money—but then deceive themselves" (chapter 45). He turns his bitter invective against the church and the courts; he is Erasmus with a broadsword, not a stiletto. In a marvelous tour de force on the effects of the development of the arts and sciences upon culture and morality, he develops the theme with more wit than Rousseau ever used to show how knowledge corrupts manners and morals. It is a panegyric on the arts and sciences, including logic, rhetoric, arithmetic, morals, and metaphysics, as necessary to success in the arts of "bawdry and whoremongering." Finally, he presents a fideistic reaction to the skepticism of the first book and an alternative to the worldliness he has condemned in the third: an appeal to the Bible, to revelation, and to direct mystical illumination by God as the only paths to certainty and salvation.

All human learning is fictional; the best is only a likely story:

Al Sciences are nothing els, but the ordinaunces and opinions of men, so noysome as profitable, so pestilent as holsome, so ill as good, in no part perfecte, but doubtful and full of errour and contention.[4]

But magic is no more fictional than other arts, and whatever is useful to man, whether magic or something else, is to be made use of, but without any pretensions that it is more than transiently useful to man during his little while on earth.

Agrippa was in correspondence with Erasmus and Melanchthon and other humanists; his attack on monks was as scurrilous as any found in the *Letters of Obscure Men*, which had been written in defense of his own mentor, Johann Reuchlin. Though he remained a Catholic, his association with the "enemies" of the Church was no doubt responsible for some of the harrying persecution he suffered. But this association was perhaps also responsible for the positive teaching of *De incertitudine*, viz., the necessity of unrestrained faith in biblical revelation as the answer to the doubt instilled in his mind by his study of human learning.

The resemblance of Montaigne and Bayle to Agrippa has already been mentioned, and the direct influence of Agrippa on Montaigne and Bruno can be textually demonstrated. But, like Bayle, Agrippa seems in the light of history to have lost his nerve. If *De occulta philosophia* is a highwater mark in the history of magic, the *De incertitudine* represents one of the great lost opportunities in philosophy. Modern philosophy could not be born until a major effort, whether wholly successful or not, had been made to initiate a fresh beginning. At the beginning of the highest period in ancient philosophy and at the beginning of modern philosophy there stand skeptics of received knowledge—Socrates, Montaigne, Descartes, Bacon. To be called a skeptic in this sense means to say: what has been counted as knowledge is not knowledge. This skepticism is fruitful if it initiates a new effort to gain knowledge. It is fruitless if it does not; if it leads only to faith and a despair of knowledge, or to Faust's Easter morning walk.

This is why it must be said that Agrippa lost his nerve. He exchanged pseudo-science for no science at all, but only for a blind faith. In the spirit of Erasmus he was a critic of the Catholic Church, excoriating its follies and worldliness but leaving its theology unaffected. In renouncing his pseudo-science he did not make way for a rigorous observational science, and even his rejection of pseudo-science was not historically effective. For, as we shall see, others who attacked the churches continued to accept a science inspired by occultism, and the critique of orthodox theology in Germany became inextricably intertwined with a philosophy of nature which had only a distant resemblance to the emerging sciences of nature.

4 *On the Vanitie and Uncertaintie of Artes and Sciences* (London, 1575), p. 5.

For this reason the rationalistic and empiricistic critique of scholasticism and orthodox philosophy was delayed in Germany until long after it was under way in Holland, France, and England. In Germany, the principal critics of the established churches were mystics, moral reformers, and enthusiasts, not proto-scientists and mathematicians.

Paracelsus

Theophrastus Bombastus of Hohenheim (1493–1541), with characteristic presumption, took the name Paracelsus to advertise his equality and rivalry with the great Roman physician Celsus; but history borrowed his patronymic to name the unpleasant style of which he was master. Externally he resembles Agrippa in several respects. He lived the same wandering and unsettled life, creating a train of hostility and a reputation for sharp practice wherever he went; there were the same bombastic claims of superiority over all rivals, the same smell of charlatanry, the same Neoplatonic cabalistic metaphysics, and the same Faust-like rejection of the human knowledge they once professed, followed by a fideistic rejection of human vanities of which knowledge was the most vain. Apparently unlike Agrippa, however, Paracelsus had an idealism which, though impugned in his lifetime, has been authenticated by history. A genuine philanthropy for suffering mankind is discernible side by side with his scurrilous and obscene attacks on individuals who did not recognize his genius. And unlike Agrippa, Paracelsus, though a product of the same times, was groping toward ideas that had a future.

For Paracelsus is the first philosopher we have come to in German history to upset the medieval pyramid of knowledge at the apex of which stood theology. For him, medicine is the chief science and art. It is supported by natural philosophy, astronomy (astrology), alchemy, and virtue, or moral philosophy. Theology is separated from all of these, as not being a part of natural knowledge, or the sole goal for all our strivings.

Because he rejected slavish adherence to Galen and Celsus, he was intent upon reading the book of nature with his own eyes. Man himself is this book, the epitome of nature. But though this metaphor of "reading the book of nature" is to be found in many writers, it means different things at different times. For Galileo a hundred years later, the book of nature was written in mathematical characters, and Galileo is a modern scientist; for Paracelsus, it is written in the "signatures" of all things, and Paracelsus is an almost forgotten occultist.

Signatures are to occult science what functional mathematical relations are to modern science—the relations by which the mind moves from one observation to another. They are evidence of causal relations, but of relations that hold between things because those things resemble each other, not because they are contiguous and dynamically related. Signatures are qualitative and sympathetic relations between things that are found by studying the resemblances they have to each other, the resemblances being thought to represent a common origin and possession of common natures or virtues. For example, the kidney bean has, in its shape, the signature of the kidney in it; its shape, as it were, is a label indicating that it bears some essential relation to the kidney. Diseases are natural; but for every disease nature has also provided a cure. The doctrine of signatures is the clue to these natural remedies, alchemy the art of extracting the virtues from the things so signified, and medicine the art of using them for the curing of the diseased organ—hence beans for diseases of the kidney.

A medical fantasy sufficiently acute to signatures would be able to fit data of botany, alchemy, and astrology to the needs of medicine. In the search for the signatures of health and disease and of herbs and other natural products, Paracelsus developed a sensitive empiricism which was good in its observational base even when not empirically controlled in its elaborations. He condemned the empirics in medicine who worked blindly without the guide of theory, just as he condemned the authoritarians who worked only from ancient texts and did not observe kidneys and beans at all. In this way he contributed to the art of medicine even though he was working with a theory that misled him more often than not. At least he had the sound conviction that disease and its cure were natural phenomena and that a theory of medicine required also a theory of natural phenomena which was broader than clinical experience. He made almost no contribution to chemistry or alchemy, except that he tried to direct the attention of the alchemist away from the vain hope of converting lead into gold and toward the very feasible processes of extracting the medical virtues, tinctures, essences, and spirits from common substances. But he never achieved the degree of clarity and freedom from perhaps willful obfuscation that was found in his contemporary Georg Bauer (Georgius Agricola, 1495–1555), whose *De re metallica*, when compared to his own alchemical writings, seems to belong to a later age in the history of chemistry.

Behind all the appearances of quackery and offensive boastfulness, Paracelsus was a man remarkably gifted in the cure of the body, in the careful observation of the course of disease, and in the understanding of the phenomena of madness by the use of medical concepts, theory, and practice. He had a genuine social idealism which made him not only disrespectful of the intellectual and social institutions of his day, but also a courageous rebel against them.

The basis of his medical theory and practice was the microcosm–macrocosm analogy with which we are already familiar, and which was to the Renaissance what the machine model of the universe and man was to be two centuries later. But Paracelsus differed from others who used what has been called his Neoplatonic Stoic world formula in taking as his starting point the microcosm and not the macrocosm. The course of his speculation and observation is from man to an understanding of the universe and God, not in the other direction. In health, the body is an adequate reflection of the organization and balance of the forces in nature; in disease and sin, this balance is in some way disturbed. The symptoms of disease are signatures of the way in which nature is out of joint, and medicine is the art of re-establishing the lost harmony. The most important of the auxiliary sciences to medicine is alchemy, the principal task of which is not the conversion of base metals to gold but the working up of tinctures and

essences from metals, herbs, and the parts of animals which are indicated
by the signatures of disease to be able, in the human body, to redress its
disharmony. Astrology likewise helps, not because astronomical positions
represent an irresistible force which, if known, can be used to predict the
outcome of disease, but because these positions leave their signatures in
us, which, when understood, help us to mend the body. Hence we may
praise Paracelsus for using this world formula empirically, going from the
better known to the lesser known, and using it naturalistically[5] rather than
theologically. The empiricism, of course, is not very stringent; the "naturalism" of his application of it is still occult and magical; and the metaphysics he assumed was one which did not permit a sharp distinction
between the natural and the supernatural. But one cannot be expected to
step over into the modern world with one stride; it is something to be just
looking in the right direction.

The metaphysics which supports this medical theory was a quasi-ma-
terialistic version of Neoplatonism. Most Neoplatonic writing leaves something to be desired in point of lucidity. When written by a professional
mystifier and added to, no doubt, by disciples who passed off their own
lucubrations as the writings of their master—and did this so successfully
that we do not know today whether or not some of the works are genuine
—it is hardly to be expected that a wholly consistent and intelligible metaphysics can be reconstructed from them. But at least one view of the world
as given by Paracelsus pictures God, the source of all being, producing out
of nothing the prime matter (*hyle*), or the *Mysterium Magnum,* which
contains implicitly and potentially all the Special Mysteries of each thing
in the world. The Great Mystery gives rise to the Special Mysteries by what
Paracelsus called "the greatest miracle of philosophy," which he illustrated
by several analogies. As the statue emerges from a block of wood by cutting
off the superfluous parts, so do things in the world arise from the sloughing
or cutting off of parts of the *hyle*—but what is cut off is not detritus but
becomes like other statues. From alchemy, he draws the analogy of the
separation of metals from ores. All things are contained in the *hyle,* and
the elements are distilled or sublimated out of it. From medicine he draws
biological analogies: each thing is convertible into others, as grass into
flesh, and each thing reproduces its kind, as flesh becomes other flesh,
because, in a sense, all things are one. The Special Mysteries, or empirical matters (*yliade*), in their various proportions to one another constitute the gross empirical elements of earth, air, fire, and water. These are
distributed by their nature and a rule of law or justice to their proper
place in the universe—fire to the heavens, earth to the center, and air and
water between them. The fire of the heavens is compacted into stars, the
earth is compacted into stones. Air, however, has an affinity with all the
other elements, for it is full of spirits which attached themselves to various
things, such as intelligences to the stars, dryads to trees, and souls to men
and animals. Man is the last of the creatures, not made from the original

---

[5] On the meaning of "naturalistic" in the sixteenth and seventeenth centuries, see
Introduction to Chapter IX below.

arcanum but from the mixture of all Mysteries, from extracts of all creatures.

Besides the classical, Aristotelian theory of the four elements, Paracelsus also supports a theory of three substances which he sometimes thinks of as being even more fundamental. But these three substances—mercury, sulfur, and salt—are not always taken to be primal elements but rather principles which can be found in all things. Mercurcy is the principle which is present in whatever can be vaporized. Sulfur is the principle of flammability, and salt is the nonflammable and nonvaporizable principle manifested preeminently in ash. These principles are present in varying proportions in the different mixtures of the four elements, but they are not themselves self-identical materials which pass unchanged from one mixture to another. Thus all that burns is called sulfur, and burns because it contains the principle of sulfur; but sulfur is not a single material that is the same in all flammable materials. There is one sulfur for wood and another for brimstone.

The material consisting of a certain mixture of earth, air, fire, and water with the three principles constitutes man's tangible, or visible, body. But in a living body there is also, as its principle of life, another kind of body which Paracelsus calls *Geist* (spirit) or the astral or sidereal body. This subtile body also has three principles, corresponding to the principles of the tangible and visible body; these are feeling, wisdom, and art. (On the other hand, the three-principle theory is sometimes used to bridge the distinction between the various bodies of man. When this is done, the principle of salt is found in his tangible body, that of mercury in his spirit, and that of sulfur in his divine soul which is like a divine light or fire in him.)

There is a spiritual element in the world as a whole, which Paracelsus calls *archeus*; and man's spiritual nature stands to it as his chemical body stands to the chemistry of the universe. Chemically, his body is an extract of the material elements and principles in things; but spiritually in his mind is related to the hidden spirits of all other things too, especially to the stars, in which the sidereal body predominates. Hence astrology stands to man's spirit in much the same way alchemy does to his physical body.

Just as man's corporeal body is nourished by other corporeal bodies, his astral body is nurtured by the spirits in other bodies, especially the astral bodies of stellar intelligences. All wisdom and all art come to man from the stars in the form of the light of nature. Hence astrology is a useful body of knowledge, since we can learn about human temperaments and affairs from the positions of the stars. But man is a free agent and is not determined absolutely by the stellar combinations. Only the human slave is fated by the stars; the wise man can learn of them and even control the stars by his own will and make them serve his purposes.

Finally, besides the spirit there is in man alone a soul which is a direct implantation by God; it gives man the only knowledge of God he has. Paracelsus opposes Scholasticism for two errors, both of which depend upon the failure to distinguish the natural and material *spiritus* from the supernatural and immaterial *mens,* or soul: it lets theology into philosophy, and it lets philosophy into theology, to the ruination of both.

The science is primitive, the metaphysics bizarre. But Paracelsus' spirit is that of Renaissance man, bent upon asserting man's superiority over nature and even his independence of God, working out his own fate with the help of what he thinks is knowledge of the mysteries of the world. Paracelsus' unmistakable empiricism in medicine and his celebrated successes as a physician probably gave his metaphysical speculations greater weight than they would otherwise have enjoyed. A vitalistic, rather than a mathematical or mechanical, conception of nature, with alchemy—and not astronomy or mechanics—as its model, characterized German natural philosophy for the next hundred years. Paracelsian ideas, some of them adopted by the Rosicrucians, continued to be a common background for German speculation about nature down to the time of Daniel Sennert. They are very salient in the thought of Jakob Böhme.

All this, however, is only one side of Paracelsus' thought. On the other side he is by no means a typical Renaissance thinker, but belongs in the family of men whose inspiration was in the ideas which led to the Reformation and whose destiny it was to go far beyond the Reformation in the direction of an unsacramental and nonsectarian religion.

As a physician aware of what we call industrial diseases (he studied not only the chemistry of the extraction of ores, but also the diseases of miners) and of the effects of poverty, which he saw not only in his patients but intermittently in his own checkered career as an outcast driven from town to town by the jealousy of his rivals, the ingratitude of patrons, and almost universal suspicion and dislike, Paracelsus was a bitter critic of society. Against the state and estates he was an egalitarian and almost an anarchist. He argued for common ownership of property and popular sovereignty, and against war, the death penalty, and, most of all, against the pretensions of earthly power to divine right. In his political views he sympathized with the Peasants' Revolt and for a time, at least, with the Anabaptists. He may have been personally involved with the Revolt, perhaps as a pamphleteer or as a field surgeon. When it was put down, he was driven from Salzburg and many of his followers were put to death.

But though his theology was close to that of the Anabaptists, he was opposed to all sectarianism and regarded the Anabaptists—when they came to power and showed themselves to be as bloodthirsty as their oppressors —as fanatics in need of medical care. He was willing to praise men who died for their faith, but called them fools who died for a mere *article* of faith. Though remaining nominally a Catholic, he thought both the Pope and Luther were representatives of the anti-Christ and compared them to "two whores praising chastity." Like Sebastian Franck, he pled for religious toleration.

About 1532 Paracelsus underwent a life-changing religious experience. Like Agrippa, he turned against all his medical and profane knowledge. Cures come from God, he said, and knowledge does not lead to God. He became a preacher in taverns and on the roadside and called himself a professor of theology. Opposed to all sects, he preached the unity of mankind and the possibility of bringing heaven to earth before the imminently expected end of the world. He practiced a strong natural mysticism more for the sake of his soul than for the cure of his body. A change (for the better) came over his raucous personality, and when he returned in his last years to medicine he avoided in his writing the bombastic and abusive language of his earlier works. The social-religious piety of his last years resembles that of Sebastian Franck (whom he knew personally); Valentin Weigel regarded Paracelsus, the mystic, as one of his own forerunners.

The Protestant Counter-Reformation

If, as is often said, the Reformation was an essential step in the march toward tolerance and individualism, this was in spite of itself. Luther was no proponent of either, and he was violent in his denunciation of heretics from his own brand of orthodoxy. In the Revolt of 1525, he was opposed to the peasants, who confused reformation with social revolution, and to the Anabaptists, who, at least for a time, drew the logical conclusion from Luther's own conception of religious adherence as a necessary civic responsibility. His followers were as bitterly anti-Calvinist as anti-Catholic. Tolerance of religious diversity, when it came, was the result of a religious balance of forces to which continuing religious war was the only alternative. Freedom of thought, when it became possible, was favored in religion by no one of the established religious communities. For any genuine appreciation of the value of individual religious freedom in the early stages of the Reformation we have to turn to the protestants against Protestantism, to men whose theological thinking did not aim at establishing a socially and politically acceptable orthodoxy upon which only one church could be founded. They were thinkers who paid the price of dissent from Lutheran orthodoxy and found solace in more personal forms of religion than could be tolerated by the churches, which were fighting for their existence by a careful definition of theological norms used to separate sheep from goats. Both before and after Melanchthon's effort (in the controversy over the *adiaphora* in 1546) to minimize conflict by distinguishing important from unimportant doctrinal and liturgical differences, these men wanted to recapture something of the spirit of the first days of the Reformation, of the period of "normless theology" (ca. 1515–1521), before Luther's efforts at reform of the Church gave way to the establishment of an orthodoxy for a new church—a new church as compromised to the secular powers as the Roman Church was. Although the Lutheran inspiration of each of the dissenters is clear, each carried the doctrine of direct personal access to God further than Luther did, and thus cut through the ecclesiastical, and even more the political, arrangements which Luther had made for the spread of his teachings. They were the counter-reformers of the Protestant Reformation. Troeltsch calls them the left wing of Protestantism. They provided a bridge between the *devotio moderna* of the fifteenth century and the Pietism of the seventeenth. Each favored the near-mysticism of the early Luther over the established orthodoxy of his later years. Each was influenced by a Neoplatonic, cabbalistic, and occult philosophy of nature. Had they associated themselves instead with a scientific study of nature, they might have been forerunners of those who preached the natural religion of the eighteenth century. But because the nature they introduced into theological speculation was that of Agrippa of Nettesheim and Paracelsus, not that of Copernicus or Kepler, their incipient natural religion died with the death of this conception of nature.

The Protestant counter-reformation of the sixteenth and early seventeenth centuries was deeply mystical. In the seventeenth century, the principal counter-reformation reforms were not mystical, but rationalistic; and they did not have a home in Germany, but in Holland. Only Georg Calixtus (1586–1656), professor in Helmstedt, struggled to provide a minimal theology which would recommend itself to reasonable theologians of all faiths and provide a basis for tolerance and unification; but compared to the Socinians and Arminians in Holland who, though persecuted, were widely followed, German syncretism and efforts toward a rationalistic retrenchment in theological disputes were ineffectual. Only in the second half of the seventeenth century was an *institutionally* effective counter-reformation in Germany achieved. This was the work of the Pietists. In this section, then, we consider two Protestant counter-reformers, Franck and Weigel, the most important Protestant mystic, Böhme, and the Pietistic movement. Common to the first three was an ecumenical belief in the universality and continuity of revelation, a belief in the immanence of God as an active force in the world, and a symbolic interpretation of the eschatalogical drama of fall, incarnation, salvation, and the end of the world. The connection with natural philosophy is weakest in the thought of Franck, whose concern is with the history of man, and strongest in that of Böhme, who absorbed, in some way, a great deal of Paracelsian nature-wisdom. The clearest philosophical head among them was Weigel.

Sebastian Franck

Sebastian Franck, whom Luther delicately called "the devil's most cherished slanderous mouth," and whom Melanchthon helped to drive out of Germany, was born in Donauwörth in 1499, and after a life of wandering and exile he died in poverty in Basel in 1542 or 1543. Though first a Catholic and then for a time Lutheran, he was, like Kaspar Schwenkfeld (1498–1561), opposed to any organization which might stand in the way of an entirely personal and free religious life. Franck's life was, like Schwenkfeld's, one of persecution and poverty. He was personally acquainted with Paracelsus, first in Nürnberg and then Strassburg, and translated into German Agrippa's *De incertitudine et vanitate* as well as Erasmus' *Encomium moriae* (Ulm, 1534).

Franck's love of the natural world, in which God is immanent, is shown in his famous apothegm: "The bird does not really sing and fly; it is sung and flown into the air. God it is which in the bird sings, lives, nests, and flies." His geography (*Weltbuch*, 1534) was a celebrated and popular book, but his philosophical concern was not with nature and God, but with man and God. Between them he wanted to establish a more direct relation than that afforded by Lutheran doctrine, and it was characteristic of him to make a paraphrase of the *Theologia Germanica,* one of the classics of the *devotio moderna*. Luther, he held, fell into something near idolatry by taking Scripture as authoritative, and interpreting it according to the letter and not according to the spirit. Nothing can be permitted to come between God and man. Luther saw that the Roman Church could not, but he did not see that Scripture, in his own teaching, was allowed to do so. Scripture must be understood by the spirit and according to spirit (*Geist*), not by and according to the letter (*Buchstabe*).

There is in each of us, Franck contends, a natural light which is the force and power of God in us. This is spirit. Franck opposes anything which limits the freedom of this spirit, and he sets up contrasting pairs of terms which parallel the distinction he wants to make between spirit and flesh. Some of these contrasts are spirit and letter, God and Adam, faith and ritual, the New Testament and the Old Testament, love and law, the inner and the outer, nature and art (= artificial learning, scholasticism and dogma), reality and image, the church invisible and the church visible. Because human institutions, including the Lutheran Church, accept the second of some of these pairs, they ally themselves with the flesh in man and thus with evil. They allow something external to come between man and God, and they deny man's dependence upon God alone.

Salvation is solely a change in the inner man, and this occurs without sacraments and even without Christ's death, if this be considered a sacrifice for man. Salvation is universally available and is in fact achieved by "pious heathens." That the wisdom needed for salvation is not the letter of Scripture but a natural disposition of man is shown by Franck in his collections of proverbs, which are supposed to show that man need not be instructed by extraordinary means in the wisdom needed for salvation.

Franck wants to maintain a direct and primitive awareness of God and does not even want to go back to the first centuries, as Erasmus did, to capture a pristine and uncorrupted Apostolic Christianity. For he holds that the first centuries of our era were merely the childhood of Christianity, in which God spoke to his children in primitive ways (as for example, through the doctrine of the sacraments) which we have now gone beyond. Nothing, then—not even Scripture—should intervene between man and God.

Yet Franck is not for a monastic withdrawal from the world, the better to approach God. There is a mystical path and a moral path to God; they not only converge, but one cannot travel along only one. A moral work, the loving care of another, is moral only when the act is done out of the love of God; but one cannot love God except by loving his creatures. His *Little Book on War* (*Kriegsbüchlein*, 1539) is a vigorous attack on the evils of war.

The life of the spirit is inward, and it is inward works which make the outward works moral. But the "inward" for Franck is not, in more modern terminology, something subjective; it is a realm of being more real than anything outward. What a thing *is* depends upon what it is in spirit. Everything, he writes, is directed by our mind ("*na onsen mont gericht*"[6]), where "mind" refers to our moral and volitional nature. What things are

[6] *Tractaet van de Werelt* (1618), p. 23a. Quoted from Alfred Hegler, *Geist und Schrift bei Sebastian Franck* (Freiburg, 1892), p. 221n.

depends upon the spirit and upon the will that takes an attitude toward them, and this includes God. "God is for us, just as we represent him," and whatever it is that we trust in our hearts, what we love and fear, what it is that we stand on, that is, to each of us, God.[7] Franck does not intend these sentences to mean what similar statements by Ludwig Feuerbach will later mean; he is not saying that there is no God out there, but we create one in ourselves; he is not even saying that there is a God out there but we cannot know him as he is, but must create inadequate subjective images of him. That is, in fact, precisely what he thinks the church visible does. For Franck there is a union of God with man, in spirit but not in flesh, and God *is* what he shows himself to be in the inner life of man—even though he shows a different side to every man. Franck is asking us not to sacrifice the God in spirit, thus directly revealed, to the God in flesh, which is obscured by the letter, images, symbols, and dogmas.

Franck's ontology of mind and spirit is not sufficiently developed for him to know, or for us to be sure, that he is here adumbrating a thesis of later transcendental philosophy—the thesis that to be real means to be present in mind in some way. He does not and could not work this out; but his philosophical heir is Schelling, not Feuerbach, for the latter meant that there is, ontologically, no God when he likewise said that God is merely what he is in the mind of man.

Franck's life and philosophy both attest to his conception of the freedom and independence of man. In fact, he is said to have been the first to use the word *selbstständig* (independent). His theory of the will is synergistic. Though only God gives salvation, the independence of man is the limit of God's power. God's plans are realized in the world not through God's determinations of man's acts, but by his using the consequences of men's acts for his purposes. History reveals God's plans, and the motto of Franck's *Chronicle* is, "Come, behold the wonders of the wonder-working God and learn to know the way He works!"[8]

Unlike most Christian philosophies of history, Franck's is no theodicy. History is God's "carnival play." It is the drama of human folly in which man turns away from God and suffers damnation, or turns to God and thereby brings upon himself the sufferings of persecution from state and church. The Bible is one part of this history—the history of the first form of this folly in which man turns from God. Much of the Bible is only allegorical, and accepting it as literal truth is not necessary for salvation. The true salvation is available to the man with the right heart of love; all men with love in their hearts constitute the Church Invisible and will have to suffer persecution by the visible church, which is based on a literal theology and supported by the sword.

Valentin Weigel

Valentin Weigel (1533–1588) avoided the persecution and banishment that was the lot of Franck and Paracelsus only by keeping his thoughts to

[7] *Paradoxa* (1534), E 7 a (Hegler, p. 22); *Paradoxa* 277–280 (Hegler, p. 222).
[8] *Chronika, Zeitbuch und Geschichtbibel* (1531), Preface, paragraph 2.

himself. He was pastor in Tschauppau and openly accepted the Formula of Concord but with considerable reservation which he kept to himself. (His *reservatio mentalis* was published posthumously in his *Dialogos de Christianismo*, 1614.) His language is sometimes that of the *Theologia Germanica* (on which he wrote a commentary published in 1671) and the Neoplatonic metaphors of light and word:

The servant sent by God, his word, comes to all, misses none; comes not outwardly through sermons but is inward; calls and knocks at the door and waits until we open it; wants to come and sup with us . . . It is the inborn light in each of us. All knowledge comes from it and it burns in all men. Whoever walks in this light does not err. It lights him on the narrow path to life. Whoever goes against it and will not have light, he follows the high road to damnation. He must believe what others say, and is like one who puts out his sight in order to be guided by others. We cannot err and do wrong if we wander in this light, for we avoid the high road of man and follow the narrow path to eternal light; we follow the law of God and prophets, for just this light within us teaches the law and the prophets. Who follows this inborn light abides in the law of God and in the teachings of the prophets. Behold this narrow path, it is the light born in you![9]

And sometimes it is doggerel like that of the *Narrenschiff*, for example:

> The godless bunch of preachers
> Lords it over others.
> No Christian work in them,
> In everything they're against God;
> Yea, they are God's worst enemies.
> There's no shame, no vice, no sin
> That's not in them.
> They've nothing to do with Christ.
> How could any good come from them?[10]

On a more philosophical level, the influence of Nicholas of Cusa and Paracelsus is obvious; but in his thought of God as a spirit defined by actual *intelligere* his true forebear is Meister Eckhart. Like Nicholas, he thinks of God as being all things compacted together (*complicite*) and thus beyond all predicates. Only in His creation is he fully ramified (*explicite*) and personal. God's need of the world in order to attain his full perfection, which appears here again, is of course a teaching of Eckhart's.

Hegel praised Böhme as the first characteristic German philosopher because he "placed the intellectual world within one's own mind and heart" and "experienced, knew, and felt in [his] own self-consciousness all that formerly was conceived as a Beyond":[11] this was "genuinely German" (shall

---

[9] *Kirchen oder Hauss-Postill* (1611), quoted from Gottfried Arnold, *Unpartheyliche Kirchen- und Ketzer-Historie* (1741 ed.), II, 229.

[10] Appendix to *Dialogos de Christianismo*, p. 108 (*Ibid.*, p. 236). The rhymes and meter are so poor in German I do not make the apologies for my rendition that might perhaps be expected.

[11] *Lectures on the History of Philosophy*, trans. E. S. Haldane and F. H. Simson (London: Routledge & Kegan Paul, 1892), III, 191. But Alexandre Koyré, *Mystiques, spirituels, alchemistes du XVIe siècle allemand* (Paris: Colin, 1955, p. 8), specifically

we say proto-Hegelian?) and made Böhme in Hegel's judgment the original characteristically German philosopher. But if this is the test, the praise should have gone to Weigel, whom Hegel does not mention. (Weigel could perhaps not have been "characteristically" German for Hegel, for the profoundly obscure, or the obscurely profound, which is so abundant in Böhme and Hegel, is fortunately nearly absent from Weigel.)

The most original part of Weigel's philosophy is precisely this metaphysically subjective and activist theory of knowledge which Hegel singles out as Böhme's contribution. It is presented in his *Der güldene Griff. Alle Dinge ohne Irrthumb zu Erkennen* (*The Shortest Way to Knowledge* of *All Things Without Error* [1617]). He sees that there are two factors involved in all our knowledge of things—the object which stimulates the eye of the body, and the mind which responds. But the mind is a "great eye," and perception cannot be understood simply as a transaction between our body and the object. The eye of the mind, unlike that of the body, is active; it is aroused to activity by the effect of the object upon the eye of the body, but it contains both the form and the content of knowledge. Even colors are innate in the mind, not to mention the form of space and the relations of things one to another. The various levels of the soul merely reflect the world: the senses know the sense world, reason knows the arts and sciences. But error cannot be avoided in these forms of knowledge, because each mind contributes its own private activity to knowing, and what one man sees (e.g., that a wall is blue) may not be seen by another (who sees it as gray).

The way to truth, therefore, is to restrain what seems to be the activity of the mind and to make it entirely passive. We should empty it of forms and implicit contents, to make room for a supernatural knowledge wholly independent of the object and the eye of the body. Quiet and passive contemplation by the soul is necessary for it to have objective knowledge; for then, as in Luther, faith or the knowledge of God, which cannot be got by our own powers and activity, will be given as a gift by the grace of God. Weigel, in a pretty metaphor, compares our mind to a pool of water; as long as it is moved by the wind it cannot reflect clear images, but when it becomes quiet it can do so. And the metaphor continues: God moves upon the face of still waters.

The teaching of the activity of mind in all knowing, and the insistence that in our highest knowledge, that of God, the mind should be completely passive, are not really inconsistent with each other. For where the eye of the mind sees only on the occasion of the object's being presented to the eye of the body, the mind is not wholly active; it is genuinely active only where it is not thus dependent and hence passive, and the apparently passive, receptive, and contemplative knowledge of God is initiated from within the soul, to such an extent that the apparently passive mystical

warns against the tendency to see Weigel as "un précurseur méconnu de Kant et de Fichte" (and I presume he would make the same objection to Hegel's judgment of Böhme) since, he says, if you translate back into Latin you get little that was not already said by Augustine, Boethius, and Thomas Aquinas (and, I would add, Eckhart, Tauler, and Nicholas of Cusa).

knowledge of God is in fact the most active knowledge there is, and is for that very reason the most valid knowledge we have. For our knowledge of God is in fact God's knowledge of Himself.

Thus there is a consensus in divine knowledge, and all the ways of knowing God are basically one. The true church is the invisible union of all those who prepare for this unifying vision by prayer and the exercise of faith—the forms of which may be as they will, each of these forms being peculiar to the rituals and dogmas of a visible church. Thus, as in Nicholas of Cusa and Franck, as well as in the humanists, Christianity, and more especially Protestant Christianity, is only one of the many ways in which God can be known and worshipped.

Jakob Böhme

Franck and Weigel are concerned with man and God in their true relations to each other, and are inevitably polemical with respect to the established alternatives; but these established alternatives provide a framework as well as a vocabulary which makes them easily comprehensible. Nothing makes Böhme easily comprehensible, and almost every writer on him has complained of his obscurity and has been baffled and exasperated by it. Even Hegel, himself no mean head swimmer, said some parts of Böhme made his head to swim. Perhaps one should not expect clarity from a thinker in whom the word *idea* "called up the image of a very fair, heavenly, chaste virgin."[12] One cannot but suspect that Böhme's position in the history of philosophy can be attributed at least in part to the heroic stature Hegel ascribed to him; and the perfunctory and labored accounts of his thought in most histories of philosophy are not likely to generate any enthusiasm for him, or even much understanding of what he was doing.[13] But in a discussion of a philosophy and a theology which were normless—that is, systems which were not in the mainstream of thought, where established and recognized categories, distinctions, and problems determined the main line of flow—the very perversities of Böhme's thought, when combined with the recognition of his great influence in England and France and, later (in the time of Schelling), in Germany, give him an important position.

Jakob Böhme (1575–1624) was an uneducated (or, better, self-half-educated) but successful cobbler in Görlitz, who seems to have been gifted with a vivid eidetic imagination which compelled him, often against explicit prohibitions by the ecclesiastical authorities, to try to put his visions into words. These words he sometimes made up and sometimes borrowed from his smattering of knowledge of the caballa, alchemy, mysticism, and occult arts. The flow of his writings was dammed up by censorship, only to gush through in uncontrollable, or at least uncontrolled, imagery that mixes up formal and material, spiritual and earthly, properties and predicates, in

---

[12] *Encyclopedia Britannica*, 9th ed. (1894), III, 852.

[13] See, for instance, the despairing and disparaging remarks of Frederick Copleston, *History of Philosophy* (London: Burns & Oates, 1953), vol. III, pt. ii, pp. 82–83; my friend Father Copleston has my sympathetic understanding.

such chaotic confusion that one simply does not know, for many pages, what he is talking about. So far as I can tell, Böhme means something like the following.

There are three great realms of being: i) God, or the Ungrounded (uncaused, *Ungrund*), or the Abyss, which, as in all these occult philosophers, is beyond all description, definition, and predicates and is equivalent also to Nothing; ii) the Eternal Nature, which is in God but does not yet exist; and iii) Created Nature, which is not in God but which yet exists.

In mystical philosophers, from Meister Eckhart to Schelling, however, the notion of an officially inconceivable and unspeakable God does not prevent them from speaking at great length about him; and Böhme follows Eckhart in attributing an inner tension or struggle or anguish (*Qual*) to God, which results in the development of qualities out of him. (Like Hegel, Böhme is a punster but his ignorance of Latin and Greek may excuse some of his more obscure arguments based on outrageous etymologies.) The Trinity and the existent world arise from the internal tension in God. For the Trinity, this tension is between an eternal will and the internal object of that will (God willing himself), which Böhme calls the heart of the will, or the eternal mind (the Son). The tension between God's willing and that which he wills is manifested in God's power, or spirit. Thence arises the world. Out of this power comes "the first birth of nature in God," an internal differentiation of God's non-being into possible essences which do not exist but are the sources of specific kinds of existents. These possible essences are called originative spirits, or *Quellgeister*. *Quell* (= source) he thought to be derived from *Qual* (= agony) and to give rise to *Qualität*. The *Quellgeister* are the essences of elements each of which, as in Paracelsian theory, has a material, a dynamic, and a spiritual manifestation connected by a flash (*Blitz*), a word which may allude to the mystical experience Böhme had in 1600, in which a flash of light on a pewter dish revealed to him the mysteries of God and nature. The material elements are salt, mercury, and sulfur; the dynamical are the opposing forces of contraction and diffusion, uniting in rotation and oscillation; the spiritual elements are desire for *logos*, love, the fire that gives light (bringing things to knowledge), and the fire that burns (wrath and destruction of the world). It was at this point in Böhme's philosophy that Hegel noticed his head was swimming; but we are told that in a perfect harmony the three essences constitute the *Mysterium Magnum* (another Paracelsian concept), or the corporeal God which is the *Ungrund* of the created world.

Each of these elements held in harmony in the *Mysterium tremendum* has a will of its own to come into existence, to pass from possibility in God to actuality in created nature. By a fiat God permits coming into existence. Creation is a gushing out into reality of all these possibilities or material–spiritual qualities, bringing with them their essential antitheses, oppositions, and tensions. The created world, with its mixture of opposites, is thus a reflection of the internal antinomies in the eternal nature which is in God. The antinomic, competitive, dialectical struggle in the world is not something sublated in the eternal nature of God; it is a reflection in actuality of the internal and eternal conflicts within God himself. German mysticism and nature philosophy do not follow a quietistic or Spinozistic pattern in which the disharmonies and dichotomies of this world are somehow made up in the Olympian calm of the Absolute. When Meister Eckhart ascribed (in accordance with his view of the Trinity) a tension within the Godhead to which God himself owes his being, when Nicholas of Cusa made God the coincidence of *opposites*, they set a pattern which Böhme accepted and Hegel rationalized by seeing the Absolute as itself a dialectic process, not an Eleatic product of dialectic. The most extreme form of this tendency to see human conflicts and natural opposites as cosmically absolute is found in the philosophy of Böhme.

Böhme's treatment of the problem of evil in the world became more and more radical as he continued to struggle with it. Originally he held that the world was ruled by three angels; but one, Lucifer, wanted to be like God and he upset the harmony that had hitherto existed in the realm of created nature. Man must redress this balance in nature by becoming Godlike; each of us can become (literally) God's son and can (literally) sit at his right hand. That view, expressed in his first work, is modified later, and Böhme teaches—in accord with what has just been said about the internal disharmony of God in German absolutism and mysticism—that both good and evil, or the love and the wrath of God, flow directly from God into the world. But there is also a third, common, view, that all is good, and that the evil is merely incidental to it. The second of these theories seems perhaps to be the most genuinely Böhmian of the three because most consistent with that antinomic, agonal conception of God which is his most characteristic and original conception.

It is not easy to account for Böhme's historical influence. In England he was read by Robert Fludd, Henry More, and perhaps Newton. In Germany his thought merged well with Paracelsian natural speculations with their mystical and occult overtones. Leibniz and the Pietists, especially those who verged upon mysticism, admired him. Rosicrucians, Freemasons, and other secret sects fattened on his obscurities. Later Fichte, Schelling, Hegel, and Catholic romantic philosophers like Franz von Baader rediscovered him, and there was enough confusion in what they found for several of them to see him as their predecessor. The Nazis used him.[14] So far as I know, existentialists hunting for venerable ancestors have not yet rediscovered him, but I dare say they soon will.

The Pietistic Movement

Partly because these spiritualistic thinkers were not working in an established tradition but were visionaries who were persecuted or banished or kept silent, we cannot expect them to have produced a school of philosophy. But their subterranean influence was, though intermittent, great; it was felt wherever there was dissatisfaction with the rigid orthodoxy of the established churches. Until irrationalism itself again became a philosophy in the nineteenth century, its influence was more manifest in unphilo-

[14] Th. Haering, "Cusanus, Paracelsus, Böhme," *Zeitschrift für deutsche Kulturphilosophie,* II (1934), 1–36.

sophical religious practices (in England among the Quakers, in Germany among the Pietists) and in religious and devotional literature than in the hard thinking that constitutes philosophy itself. Perhaps the most satisfying expression of this enthusiastic, mystical, and vaguely pantheistical attitude in Germany is not to be found in the works of those who tried to philosophize, but in the verses of Andreas Scheffler (called Angelus Silesius, 1624–1677), who became converted to Catholicism.

The period of greatest rigidity in German religious life came in the seventeenth century, precisely at the time of the moral degeneration consequent upon the Thirty Years' War (1618–1648). Orthodoxy, which put more emphasis upon doctoral conformity than upon the emotions and the moral life, stressing correct faith instead of love and charity, satisfied less and less the religious needs of the people, especially in their suffering during and after the war. It was then that dissatisfaction with an external orthodoxy was at its peak, and the second great religious reform in Germany took place under the name of Pietism.

Pietism was the public re-emergence of a more or less continuous effort in Germany to achieve a simpler, less dogmatic, and more moralistic Christianity than that to be found in any of the established churches. The Friends of God, the Brethren of the Common Life, and the Anabaptists (in theory, but not in practice) pushed such reforms in the fourteenth, fifteenth, and sixteenth centuries respectively. Each favored the development of the religious life in an invisible church not under ecclesiastical or political control and not aspiring to become a political power. Only the Anabaptists, intoxicated with momentary success, betrayed such high reform. Reforms are naturally demanded and to be expected when churches are not noteworthy for their accessibility to the humble but pious laity. The absence of a rigorously defined theology is a source of instability in movements of this kind, and it explains their lack of continuity; but again and again reform movements, or individuals like Sebastian Franck, appeal to those whose religious motives are more emotional and moral than intellectual and ritualistic.

The first organizations of such like-minded Protestants occurred (after the Anabaptists had been put down) in the Netherlands, where there were strong Socinian (Unitarian) and Arminian interests and minorities in the Calvinist churches. In Germany the need for reform in the Lutheran Church was expressed by Johann Gerhard (1582–1637), the leading theologian of the century, and by Johann Arndt (1555–1621), whose *Wahres Christentum* (1606) was one of the most important sources of the program for revivifying lay Christianity which was later adopted by the organized Pietists.

But the real founding of Pietism is to be credited to Johann Jakob Spener (1633–1705) who, as superintendent of the ministry in Frankfort on the Main, published in 1675 his *Pia desideria*.[15] Parts of this work had been published before this time; Spener's views had become known and were, in part, already followed when this full spelling out and defense of them

---

[15] Translated into English by T. G. Tappert (Philadelphia: Fortress Press, 1964).

was made public and then widely acclaimed in Germany. The *Pia desideria*, addressed to ministers, teachers, and laymen, points vividly to the need for a moral and spiritual reform of the churches and universities. Erudite preaching in Latin and sectarian polemics are condemned. The universal priesthood of believers, Spener reminded them, was one of Luther's most essential reforms, but it had been forgotten since his time; however, since it is not knowledge of the faith but the practice of Christianity which is essential, the universal priesthood is a viable and practicable ideal. Not scholastic theology but the *Theologia Germanica* and the works of Tauler are recommended to students; meetings (*collegia pietatis*) for the reading of Scripture, prayer, self-examination and open confession are to be instituted by ministers and teachers. Religion is to be exercised unceremoniously, most of all in self-contemplation and active good works. Preaching is to be directed toward turning men inward, to the rebirth in their hearts of the love of God and their fellow men, and outward, to active philanthropy. Simplicity in clothing and manners is enjoined; enthusiasm and sentimentality are nurtured. (Both von Tschirnhaus and Thomasius were alienated from Pietism by the application of its sumptuary prohibitions to their family and social life.) "Lay monasticism" is not too strong a name for the mode of life which Pietism tried to inculcate, if we remember to add recognition of the active philanthropy of the Pietists. Not only did it not have a well-articulated theology—this, indeed, was one of its attractions, though the opponents of Pietism said that it did not turn men upward to a contemplation of God but to an autistic concern with themselves—but it did not even favor the development of the secular intellect beyond very elementary levels. But elementary schools were established, and one of the most successful of the Pietistic charities was the famous orphanage established by August Hermann Francke in Halle.

But the very success of such a movement seems to be incompatible with its maintaining the purity of its original conception, and Pietism later became so little a "normless theology" that it was the norm against which much of the revolt of the Enlightenment in the eighteenth century was directed. And when, after the death of its founders, Pietism lost its original warmth and revivalistic fervor (last seen, perhaps, in Count von Zinzendorf, who emigrated to America), it hardened into an anti-intellectual otherworldly sect whose effects on its adherents were somewhat like that of twentieth-century fundamentalism in its discouragement of open-mindedness, science, and philosophy. August Hermann Francke, one of the leading Pietists, used to say that it was impossible to make a good Christian of a young man who had studied Euclid.

When the Elector Friedrich III of Brandenburg (later King Friedrich I of Prussia) established the University of Halle in 1694, the theological faculty was peopled with Pietists under the leadership of Francke, while the philosophical faculty, as we shall see, was "rationalistic." With this move, Pietism entered higher education in Germany; and the outstanding success of the new university, which until the founding of Göttingen in 1737 had no serious rival in Germany, gave Pietism a scholarly standing it would not otherwise have had. It was commonly said in the eighteenth century that whoever went to Halle returned a Pietist or a rationalist. While the rivalry between the Pietists and anti-Pietists belongs to a later part of our story (Chapter XI), two important features of its later history must be mentioned now.

First, the triumph of Pietism over scholastic orthodoxy in the universities was an important factor in the Enlightenment. The centers of the early Enlightenment were precisely those which tolerated the Pietists. This was not just because toleration is a necessary condition for Enlightenment, but also because there were factors inherent in Pietism which made for Enlightenment. Like the *Aufklärer*, Pietists were opposed to the old order of orthodoxy; they were individualists, not agents of a rigid establishment. The lay individualism of Pietistic circles was an important ingredient in what was, comparatively speaking, the freer atmosphere of German thought in the eighteenth century. Moral practice, for the betterment of man, tended to replace theological debate as the central concern of the educated Christian. The potentiality of Pietism to become a relatively undogmatic form of religious morality gave to the entire German Enlightenment a religious tone lacking in the Enlightenment of other countries, which did not go through a religious reform at the same time they experienced the beginning of their own Age of Reason.

Second, Pietists now had to pay the price for the fact that the spiritual forebears of Pietism—men like Franck, Weigel, Böhme, even Paracelsus—in opposing the scholastic science of their time had replaced it with spiritualism, theosophy, and occult nature-mysticism. For in the eighteenth century the Pietist philosophers, almost as a corollary of their Pietism, continued to teach and practice the vitalistic philosophy of nature in opposition to the new mechanical and mathematical conceptions of the science of nature. In this respect, the Pietistic movement in the eighteenth century was philosophically anachronistic. Toward the middle of the century, when there had arisen an "Enlightenment scholasticism," many of the leaders of the revolt against the Leibniz-Wolffian philosophy (to be dealt with in Chapter XV), such as Lavater, Jacobi, Herder, and Hamann, were either Pietists or deeply influenced by Pietism. The romantic religious and natural philosophy of the nineteenth century comes from this Pietist counter-Enlightenment much more than from the Kantian philosophy. Kant's own ethics and philosophy of religion were an outgrowth of Pietism, but his philosophy of nature was not affected by the vitalism often associated with Pietism.

IX

The Natural Philosophers and the Cartesians

Introduction

The preceding chapter dealt with such a diverse group of thinkers that its title had to be almost a catalogue of its contents. This diversity regretably continues throughout this chapter too, and one is tempted simply to list the principal figures to be dealt with—Kepler, Jungius, Clauberg, and von Tschirnhaus. Yet there is a good reason for the title chosen, since all of them have been called "philosophers of nature" or have worked in, or in the ambience of, the developing sciences of nature.

The term "philosophy of nature" is difficult to define. It does not mean the same as science, even though the latter had, for a time, the name "natural philosophy." Almost any definition of "philosophy of nature" would be such that the term would have to denote the thought of men commonly called naturalists, spiritualists, occultists, or theosophists. (I have already referred, in the beginning of Chapter VIII, to an arbitrariness involved in considering Paracelsus there instead of here; had it not been necessary to present his thought before that of Böhme, it would have been easier to deal with him in the company of philosophers of nature instead of among the religious rebels.)

It is incumbent upon me, therefore, to say something in justification of the title of this chapter, and of the choice of the men considered here. This requires a preliminary explanation of the sense in which I understand the terms "nature" and "philosophy of nature"; later in the chapter I shall have to provide also a rationale for "Cartesianism" and for discussing the philosophers of nature and the Cartesians together.

The men dealt with in this chapter are thinkers more concerned with what they believed were the facts about nature than with God, man, and his destiny. No doubt their interest in nature was *ad majoram gloriam Dei*; there were few theologically indifferent, and almost no antitheological, thinkers in Germany in the seventeenth century. But it was nature, not man and God, which presented them with their most salient problems.

Yet some of the men we shall deal with were hardly aware of the distinctions we use when we call them philosophers of nature. They did not, as we do, bifurcate reality into the natural and the supernatural. Much that we would call supernatural was, for them, inherent in nature. They had a categorial conception of nature that was broader and more hospitable than ours. Those who accepted an Aristotelian, Neoplatonic, or Stoic metaphysics were not aware that they were crossing any categorial line when they first discussed observed facts and then, for example, Paracelsian *archei*, first listed the symptoms of disease and then the virtues indicated by signatures as able to cure the disease. Souls, spirits, *archei*, plastic natures, intelligences, substantial forms, hylarchic principles, and astral principles were to them just as "natural" as stars and plants.

Their world was enshrouded in mysteries—at least for us. In calling their explanatory principles mysteries we perhaps forget how mysterious our own explanatory principles would appear to them—and to us too, had we not had long familiarity with them and a dogmatic confidence in their successful use. The philosophers of nature of the seventeenth century tried to save the appearances by using concepts which the progress of science has since shown to be ineffective, and which have accordingly been excluded from the body of science. But to exclude from science means to extrude from nature. The extrusion of their philosophical principles has been an accomplishment of the scientific study of nature begun by the nominalists who undertook to give geometrical representations of phenomena, and carried to completion by Galileo and Descartes. The principles adduced by the philosophers of nature were candidates for places in the corpus of knowledge of the world. To us, however, in looking back upon them from a quite different conception (different in both denotation and connotation) of nature, theirs were not natural principles but supernatural or fictitious— because they were eliminated in the evolution of science, which we consider to be the proper study of nature as we understand that word.

The natural philosophers had explanatory principles, some of which I have listed above, which they collected under the name of "nature" or "the natures" of things. The explanations they gave seem to us to be as empty as the famous explanation of the effectiveness of opium in terms of the *vis dormitiva*, this power being "the nature" of opium. In giving this kind of explanation, they were following one of the many meanings of the word "nature" ($\phi\acute{\upsilon}\sigma\iota\varsigma$) discussed by Aristotle, the one according to which nature was "the essence of things which have in themselves, as such, a source of movement" or "the *aliquid* which intrinsically explains motion and rest."[1]

But there was another meaning of "nature." These forces, or essences, were hypostasized as universal forces—not substantial forms as in the first meaning of "nature" but as universal forces—standing, as it were, between God and the things in the world moved neither by God directly nor by inherent particular and unique essences in them. Thus there was, besides the genuine Aristotelian, also a Neoplatonic conception of nature, and these two were conflated. Some philosophers of nature adhered to one, some to the other, and some to both.

In this chapter we shall trace the gradual replacement of these conceptions by those with which we are more familiar in science. We shall see how a Neoplatonic conception of the relation of God to the world was replaced by a dualistic conception; how a qualitative, essentialist conception of the order of the world was replaced by a quantitative, instrumentalist conception; how $\Phi\acute{\upsilon}\sigma\iota\varsigma$ was replaced by $T\acute{\epsilon}\chi\nu\eta$, the organic by the geometrical and mechanical. It is regrettable that, in this long chapter, we come upon only one German, Kepler, who was a significant contributor to our modern scientific conception of nature; but Leibniz is excluded only because we shall devote an entire chapter to him and his efforts to reinstate the concept of the "natures" of things without permitting it to interfere with mechanical explanations of them.

It is only toward the end of the period under study that there are to be found clear statements of the issues. One is by Leibniz, and will be dealt with later; the other is by Robert Boyle, the English chemist who had an immediate following in Germany. Boyle's strictures on the use of the term "nature" provide a significant clue to the difference between the philosophy of nature and natural science, and an augury of what was to come.

Boyle found the word "nature" to be so equivocal that he proposed that it be dropped altogether. He gave a list of meanings then current, a list which resembles that given earlier in the century by Rudolf Goclenius of Marburg.[2] Among the meanings were substance, essence, cause, form, order, and the totality of things that exist. For some of these meanings he proposed other words or urged that both the word *and* the meaning be dropped. Among the meanings most hazardous for both science and piety was that according to which "nature" meant "creative nature" (*natura naturans*), a kind of "semi-deity or other strange kind of being" supposed to explain observable phenomena but not itself observable. Such a being, intermediate between God and the world, should not be appealed to in explaining the world or in theology; the word in this sense should be excluded from our vocabulary, since the thing referred to does not exist. The

---

[1] The first definition is from Aristotle, *Metaphysics* 1051 a 12 f; the second from Frédéric Morin, *Dictionnaire de philosophie et théologie scolastique* (Paris, 1856), II, 236.

[2] *Lexicon philosophicum* (Frankfort, 1613), p. 719.

most harmless meaning of "nature" is "the universe, or the system of corporeal works of God," which corresponds to Goclenius' "universe of things of which the world consists" (*universitas rerum, e quibus mundus constat*). For this, Boyle proposes that we use the word "world, or universe; and instead of the phenomena of nature, substitute the phenomena of the universe or of the world."[3] The world was to be explained by the mechanical properties of the corpuscles of which it is composed, God having created the matter and instituted the laws. In one sense, God was thereby alienated from the world of the natural philosophers by the exclusion of divine forces from within nature; in another, he was brought closer to the world because of having a direct, not an indirect, relation to the *systema mundi* or *machina mundi*.

Such conceptions, as we shall see, were beginning to appear in Germany even before this time. The spread of Cartesian philosophy made them widely known, though they were rejected more often than accepted. But Boyle's particular contribution of moment in the present context was that he proposed a terminological change which called attention to the fundamental issue. His terminological revisions were rejected by the Aristotelians and scholastics, but accepted by the Cartesian professor of physics in Altdorf, Johann Christoff Sturm (1635–1703), in his *De naturae agentis idolae* (1692). Sturm agreed with Boyle, saying that in all of natural philosophy there was no term more ambiguous and equivocal than "nature"; still, he was not a thoroughgoing mechanist, for he thought of God's sustaining power (*virtus divina*) as necessary for the continued existence of things and the regularity of their behavior—in this being a good Cartesian. For reasons like Boyle's, however, he did reject the putative explanatory power of a conception of an intermediate nature and did seek to explain the changes in the world in mechanical terms. However, his opponent Günther Christoff Schelhammer, in his *De natura sibi et medicis vindicata* (1697), defended the term "nature" but tried to empty it of the meanings which were characteristic of the usage of the older natural philosophers, calling nature "the complex of laws established by God for the conservation of the universe." Leibniz, as we shall see, took sides on this issue; but Walch,[4] in his famous philosophical dictionary in the following generation, looked back upon the controversy between Schelhammer and Sturm as chiefly, or only, a dispute about words.

But disputes about important words are important disputes, and the "triumph of science" at the end of the seventeenth century did not end this dispute, either about the word or the thing signified. Even Kant found it necessary to make an explicit distinction, which illuminates all that had been confused before: "Nature, taken adjectivally (*formaliter*), signifies the connection of the determinations of a thing according to an inner principle of causality. By nature taken substantively (*materialiter*), on the other

---

[3] A *Free Inquiry into the Vulgar Notion of Nature* (1686), based on *Tractatus de ipsa natura* (1682). The quotations are taken from *The Philosophical Works of Robert Boyle* (London, 1733), II, 109, 111.

[4] Johann Georg Walch, *Philosophisches Lexicon* (Jena, 1733), col. 1867.

hand, is meant the sum of appearances insofar as they stand, in virtue of an inner principle of causality, in thoroughgoing interconnection."[5]

This neat distinction permits us to state how we circumscribe our inquiry. In this chapter I consider several important German thinkers who developed theories of nature *formaliter* and several who tried to replace them with theories of nature *materialiter*. In the next chapter, we shall come to Leibniz, who tried to do justice to both conceptions; and in Chapter XI we shall see again a confrontation of proponents of the two conceptions—Thomasius and Wolff—which kept the issue alive down through the eighteenth century.

But now, back to the sixteenth!

The Astronomers

Ptolemy's astronomy became widely known in Europe in the twelfth century, Aristotle's in the thirteenth. These theories did not coincide in every detail; indeed, in many details they were inconsistent with each other. The general astronomical world-view of the educated man of the fifteenth century was based largely on Aristotle's, as modified by his Arabic Neoplatonic commentators and as adjusted to the specific requirements of the Christian architecture of the world. The universe consisted of concentric spheres of material substance, with the earth at the center. The moon rotated about the earth on the nearest sphere, and all the gross matter in the universe was in this sublunar region, the realm of the corruptible and the changeable. Above that sphere were eight others, one for each of the known planets, for the sun, for the fixed stars, and for the *primum mobile* which, like Aristotle's God, imparted motion to the inscribed spheres. Above that sphere was the immovable Empyrean, or Paradise. Below the sphere of the moon was Purgatory and the earthly paradise; on the underside of the world was hell. Each of the spheres rotated about the earth each day; in some interpretations, each was guided by a planetary intelligence, angel, or soul. Relations between these spheres and man's temperament and character formed the subject matter of astrology. Space was the interior of the outermost sphere and was therefore finite. It was not isotropic but had real differences in different directions and in its upper and lower, or outer and inner, regions. Space dynamically affected the bodies within it; the heavy matter of the universe was concentrated within the sphere of the moon, where the drag of matter and the element of chance kept mathematical harmonies and pure forms from being fully realized. Thus, superimposed on the geometrical order was a value hierarchy. It was also a thoroughly teleological order both in its original design and in its day-by-day operation. This universe, an amalgam of Aristotelian, Arabian Neoplatonic, and Christian elements was the universe of the theologian who read Aquinas and of the layman who read Dante.

The Ptolemaic astronomy was for the expert mathematician. It differed from this popular Aristotelian conception in somewhat the same way that

[5] Kant, *Critique of Pure Reason*, A 419 n = B 446 n.

popular thought nowadays about atoms and nuclei differs from the mathematical physicist's. Mathematics, not a representable series of balls, was the key to the universe of the astronomer who had to determine dates, foretell eclipses, predict oppositions and occultations of astrological importance. The general shape of the Ptolemaic and the popular Aristotelian universes was the same, but the details were different. Astronomers used and debated about the Ptolemaic; theologians, poets, and philosophers contemplated the Aristotelian, and were little concerned with, and incompetent to judge, the fine points of the Ptolemaic. The Ptolemaic, which was not for laymen, could be revised without forcing a revision in the popular conception of the Aristotelian.

The Aristotelian system of the heavens was unquestioningly accepted. The Ptolemaic system, however, did not enjoy such unquestioned acceptance because it was subjected each year to tests which it again and again failed to meet in precise detail. The most crucial of these tests was to provide the rationale of the calendar, which by the early sixteenth century was seriously askew. In 1514 the Lateran Council asked Copernicus, already a well-known astronomer, to participate in the revision of the calendar. This he declined to do because he had already given up the main features of the Ptolemaic system but had not yet worked out his alternative. There was, in fact, no alternative at that time, and astronomers continued to use the Ptolemaic system and related tables of planetary positions.

But because the Aristotelian world system was so involved with the metaphysics of Christianity, it was believed to be the true picture of the universe. The Ptolemaic could be regarded—if the discrepancies between it and the Aristotelian theory became too great—as a mere hypothesis, useful for "saving the appearances" and permitting calculations which could not be made with the grosser Aristotelian model. These discrepancies were sufficiently great to force such an instrumental or positivistic interpretation upon many astronomers. For in order to preserve two general and universally accepted cosmological principles of the Aristotelian physics there had to be serious departures from the close-fitting balls of the Aristotelian astronomical model. These two principles derived from physics were (i) all natural motion is either rectilinear or circular, and (ii) all natural motions are unaccelerated. Applied to astronomy, these principles meant that all planetary paths must be circular, and the velocity of planets must be constant. The apparent positions of the planets seemed to conflict with the second of these principles. Assuming that the planets move on a circular path around the earth, Ptolemy's astronomy had as its task the resolution of apparent motions which were not constant into circular motions which were. The method of doing so was derived from Greek and Alexandrian geometry and involved the resolution of apparently irregular circular motion into regular motion, at a constant velocity, of a point on a circle whose center was a point on another circle (epicycle and deferent). Sometimes the motion of the deferent circle had to be made eccentric with respect to the observer on earth. Every planetary motion could be fitted into this scheme; if predictions were inaccurate, they could be corrected post facto by adjusting the ratio of radii of the circles involved. Over hundreds of years of observations most of these anomalies had been smoothed out, and the Ptolemaic system was a powerful geometrical tool for converting observations into fairly accurate predictions.

But obviously a picture of the Ptolemaic system would look very different from a picture of the Aristotelian, though in their main features they were pictures of the same universe—the earth in the center, the fixed stars on the outermost visible sky, and the sun and moon and planets moving around the earth. But the two were sufficiently different and independent of each other for it to be possible to accept one and reject the other.

This was the lay of things when the Polish savant Nicholas Copernicus (1473–1543) began the study of astronomy in Italy about 1490. There he came under the influence of two modes of thought that had not previously played any great role in recent astronomical theory. One was Pythagoreanism, the other was Neoplatonism; and they were represented by many of the same men in the Italian Renaissance. The Pythagoreanism of this movement was the conviction that number is the key to nature and not merely a way to report measurements made by human beings. That is, the world-order is itself mathematical, and the world works the way it does because of the numerical and geometrical properties of things in it. This is a very much more mathematical conception than one which merely insists that phenomena may and ought to be measured; it holds that the mathematical relations are determinative of the phenomena observed. In other words, the world is rational. A geometrical or numerical ground can be found for phenomena, which are related to each other as parts of simple geometrical constructions. Reasons for one construction can be found in others; constructions are neither merely convenient inventions for saving the appearances nor merely brute physical facts. They are physical facts determined to be as they are by number and form.

Ptolemy's geometry saved the appearances and gave a geometrical *representation* of each phenomenon, but it did not tell why, for example, a certain relation existed between the radii and velocities of epicycles and deferents. Copernicus was imbued with the ideal of a mathematical *system* which would be simpler than Ptolemy's and more explanatory. For instance, the movements of all the planets had a common component of diurnal motion, and this component was simply there, for no good reason except that it was necessary to assume it to make the data fit the diagrams, i.e., to "save the appearances." To Copernicus's Pythagorean eye, looking for a rational explanation as well as a simple geometrical representation, this was intolerably uneconomical; and he had the inspiration of genius to ascribe this common component to the motion of the earth. Here was a mathematical change in the technical part of astronomy, of interest only to experts,[6] simplifying calculations and rationalizing phenomena.

---

[6] "It may fall out, too, that idle babblers, ignorant of mathematics, may claim a right to pronounce judgment on my work, by reason of a certain passage of Scripture basely twisted to suit their purpose. Should any such venture to criticize and carp at my project, I make no account of them; I consider their judgment rash, and utterly despise it." Preface to *De revolutionibus*, M. K. Munitz, ed., *Theories of the Universe* (Glencoe, Illinois: The Free Press, 1957), p. 152.

If the motions of the rest of the planets be brought into relation with the circulation of the Earth and be reckoned in proportion to the orbit of each planet, not only do their phenomena presently ensue, but the orders and magnitudes of all stars and spheres, nay the heavens themselves, become so bound together that nothing in any part thereof can be moved from its place without producing confusion of all other parts and of the Universe as a whole."[7]

By itself, as I say, this could be of interest only to mathematicians; others would not understand it. Those who accepted the Aristotelian theory as true might regard the Ptolemaic as a mere hypothesis, more useful though not true cosmologically, presented for the use of the experts. The choice of the new hypothesis, however, would strain credulity, since the Ptolemaic system was on the whole like the Aristotelian, and the Copernican required an assumption that seemed to conflict with Aristotle, common sense, and the Bible. This was the assumption that the earth moves.

It was not an original assumption with Copernicus. Nicholas of Cusa and Nicholas of Oresme, among the moderns, had entertained the hypothesis, the former accepting it on general metaphysical grounds, and the latter—though he finally rejected it on grounds of faith—giving effective answers from physics to the commonsense objections to it (as, for example, that the earth would have objects on its surface swept off if it moved). And Copernicus found that this doctrine had actually been taught by several ancient astronomers.

Copernicus was so much a rationalist that he could not accept the possibility that a system like his own could be mathematically superior and yet cosmologically false. Hence he attacked not only the Ptolemaic system but, much more portentously, the Aristotelian astronomy too. Fearful of the consequences of this, or at least anxious that the anti-Aristotelian features of Copernicus' astronomy not immediately damn it in the eyes of those who could learn from its anti-Ptolemaicism, Andreas Osiander (1498–1552) wrote the famous preface to Copernicus' book, *De revolutionibus orbium caelestium* (1543), in which the cosmological assertion of the motion of the earth was denied in favor of the assertion that Copernicus only provided a better mathematical alternative to Ptolemy. This deceptive preface helped secure a hearing for Copernicus, but it delayed the Copernican Revolution as a major event *in cosmology* until long after the death of the author. It was merely as a means for better calculations that the Copernican system was first used by other astronomers, and this they could do with impunity, not raising any difficult philosophical or theological doubts.

The other side of the Italian philosophy was less mathematical and more directly metaphysical in its Neoplatonism. This was the metaphysics of light.[8] The Copernican hypothesis that it is the sun which is the center of the universe was, as it were, the cosmological corollary of the light metaphysics, in which the giver of light and life should be put in the visible center of the universe and not in the astronomically invisible highest heaven:

[7] *Ibid.*, p. 151.   [8] See above, pp. 37–38.

In the middle of all sits Sun enthroned. In this most beautiful temple could we place this luminary in any better position from which he can illuminate the whole at once? He is rightly called the Lamp, the Mind, the Ruler of the Universe; Hermes Trismegistus names him the Visible God; Sophocles' Electra calls him the All-seeing. So the Sun sits as upon a royal throne ruling his children the planets which circle around him . . . The Earth conceives by the Sun, and becomes pregnant with an annual rebirth.[9]

Copernicus thus accomplished two great things. He put Pythagorean speculations to stunning scientific use; he put the mathematical ideal of a geometric system to successful cosmological construction. Serious science need never again be confused with numerology. Euclid is not just a picture of a universe already created, but is the blueprint for it. And he put forward a theory that, when properly developed, would provide an alternative that would finally triumph—in other countries long before Germany—over the small, neat, compact Aristotelian universe. Copernicus himself seemed to show little immodest appreciation of what he had done, and Osiander's meddling kept others from seeing it for a long time. The Copernican Revolution occurred not when Copernicus formulated his theory, but when two men understood it. They were Bruno and Kepler.

There were many obstacles in the way of the acceptance of the Copernican system, both in its anti-Ptolemaic and anti-Aristotelian features. On the side of the former, it did not provide as great a simplification of the Ptolemaic system, in its final formulation, as had been expected when preliminary accounts of it became available. Copernicus still needed some epicycles in order to save the appearances, though fewer than Ptolemy had required. There were some phenomena—for example, certain variations in the brightness of Venus—that he could not explain, for Venus appeared brightest when, by theory, it ought to have been faintest.[10] On its anti-Aristotelian side, there were other phenomena, such as the absence of parallax of fixed stars, which could not be explained without an incredible enlargement of the sphere of the fixed stars; and though Copernicus was prepared to make this enlargement, few would follow him. Finally, of course, there was the most difficult of all convictions to overcome, that of the stationary earth, which seemed required by common sense, Scripture, and Aristotle alike.

For a while the objections against its anti-Ptolemaic thesis were less serious than those against its anti-Aristotelian theses, but since the latter could be met by the Osiandrian instrumentalist theory of hypothesis, they did not delay the acceptance of the Copernican "hypothesis" by those who were engaged in making planetary tables. It was so accepted by astronomers who clearly understood that false hypotheses could give true conclusions. Hence the correctness of the predictions did little to support the anti-Aristotelian cosmology taken not as hypothesis but as physical truth. Down to the time of Galileo, the Aristotelian world picture was protected from

[9] From Munitz, *Theories of the Universe*, p. 169.
[10] This phenomenon was not explained until Galileo observed the phases of Venus, but Copernicus had conjectured the true explanation, which had to remain a conjecture until the invention of the telescope.

the Copernican by the purely hypothetical interpretation put upon the latter by Osiander and accepted by many astronomers in both the churches.[11]

In the forty years after the death of Copernicus, three events were significant for the final acceptance of the Copernican theory, in a revised form, as a cosmology. All are connected with the name of Tycho Brahe. First there was observed the new star of 1572 ("Tycho's star"), which conflicted with Aristotle's theory of the immutability of the heavens. Second, there was the great comet of 1577, which Tycho observed and convincingly argued to be outside the sublunary sphere. This interpretation, based upon the advances he had made in observational accuracy, conflicted with the assumption of planetary crystalline spheres. This discovery spoke against the Ptolemaic as well as the Aristotelian cosmology. The third was Tycho's vastly improved observations, unprecedented in accuracy and fullness, giving positions of the planets along their entire courses instead of only at specially chosen points (the points generally being determined by their astrological importance). To fit these tables, which were better than any Copernicus had had, Tycho in 1588 proposed his own theory of planetary motions as a rival to both Copernicus' and Ptolemy's.

According to this theory, the inferior planets revolve around the sun in an orbit between the earth and the sun. The superior planets revolve around both the earth and the sun, that is, in an epicycle around the sun which is larger than the deferent between the sun and the earth, around which the sun revolves. Though this theory lacked some of the symmetry and elegance of the Copernican system, it was less cumbersome than the Ptolemaic. Unlike the Copernican system, it could explain the absence of stellar parallax without making incredible conjectures concerning the distances to the fixed stars. Most important of all, it did not even ask the astronomer to act on the *fiction* that the earth moved, and certainly did not ask him to go against the Aristotelian cosmology with the wild conjecture that the earth did in fact move. It was with the hope that Kepler would confirm this theory that Tycho put his observations at his disposal.

Giordano Bruno was the first to draw truly radical cosmological consequences from the Copernican theory. The displacement of the earth from its privileged position led him to take the next step and to deny the privileged position of the sun itself: The sun is the center only of our solar system, and then it does not differ significantly from all the other fixed stars in the universe. There is an infinity of worlds; there is no Aristotelian spherical universe finite in size, but an open universe of an infinity of solar

---

[11] Luther opposed Copernicus with a brutal remark about "the fool who would upset astronomy." Melanchthon, more competent, opposed the Copernican theory in its anti-Aristotelian part because of Scripture and in its anti-Ptolemaic part because of his competent and careful but incorrect weighing of the relative advantages of the two opposing "hypotheses." He was wrong, but for the right kind of reasons. A theologian half a century later warned Kepler: "God forbid that you should try to bring your hypothesis publicly into agreement with Scripture. I bid you: act like a mathematician, and do not upset the church." (Quotation from F. W. Kantzenbach, *Protestantisches Christentum im Zeitalter der Aufklärung* [Gütersloh: Gerd Mohn, 1965], p. 27.)

systems in an infinite empty space. Bruno was inspired in this marvelous speculation by Nicholas of Cusa and Nicholas Copernicus, and in 1565 in Wittenberg he chided the Germans for neglecting these two men, who were, he said, their greatest thinkers.

The second man to push the development from the original Copernican to the modern conception of the solar system was Johannes Kepler (1571–1630). In some respects Kepler was less close to the modern conception of the universe as a whole than Bruno was, for Kepler denied the infinity of the universe of stars and the meaningfulness of a conception of an infinite real but empty space. He did so because he controlled his imagination by constant reference to exact mathematics and to empirical evidence, in a way quite foreign to Bruno's exuberant speculative imagination. Mathematically, Kepler denied the actual infinite, viz., denied that two stars could be an actually infinite distance apart. Empirically, he had good reasons, because he rejected the assumption of invisible stars and considered only the observable universe, which for him, of course, consisted of only a few thousand stars. He argued, quite convincingly upon these restrictions, that in the visible universe the solar system occupies a central position. Furthermore, he argued (correctly on the assumptions he made and with the observations at hand) that the distance of the sun to the fixed stars must be greater than their distances from each other.

In these respects, Kepler remained closer to the Aristotelian cosmology than Bruno did; in these respects, he made no advance beyond Copernicus. But he carried Copernicus' Pythagorean conception of the mathematical order of the world even farther. In his *Mysterium cosmographicum* (1596) he devised the theory that the spaces between planetary orbits correspond to the five regular polyhedrons inscribed the one within the other. He saw mathematical analogies everywhere—between planetary distances and musical scales, between the masses of the planets and the densities of metals; he saw God as the great geometer.

He also went further in his Neoplatonic metaphysics of light. Like Copernicus, he was almost a sun-worshiper and found the centrality of the sun in the physical universe a cosmological corollary of the metaphysics of the creative and generative and axiological significance of light. In his Trinitarian allegories he called the sun God the Father. While Copernicus had made the plane of the planets cut through the center of the earth (a remnant of geocentrism surviving from Ptolemy) and had therefore not been able to give a simple explanation of the divergence of the planets from the plane of the ecliptic, Kepler solved this problem by making these planes intersect at the center of the sun. Moreover, the sun was not merely the geometrical center of the solar system, as for Copernicus; it was also the dynamical center, the *primum mobile* of the great wheels of the planets. The resemblance between his quasi-mystical thought about the sun and that of his contemporary Jacob Böhme is no doubt superficial, but nonetheless marked.

But what gives Kepler his place among the great architects of nature is not these Neoplatonic speculations, but his Neo-Pythagorean conviction of a close fit between accurate observational measurements and mathematical calculations based upon the true disposition of the planets. By assuming, here and there, that Tycho had made small errors in observation, he could have fitted erroneous but easy constructions upon his data, and would have missed his greatest discoveries; this assumption he fortunately did not make. He was as convinced as Copernicus—perhaps more than Copernicus—that mathematics not only pictured, but that it explained, the structure of the world. Observational measurements were not accidentally related to each other; there was an underlying mathematical reason why even empirical measurements had to be as they were. This had led him to the false explanation of planetary intervals in terms of the regular polyhedrons; it was to lead him finally to his Third Law, which was valid. Just as the arbitrariness of all of Ptolemy's structures was an offense to Copernicus, the remnants of Ptolemaic constructions in the work of Copernicus were intolerable to Kepler.

Armed with Tycho's measurements of planetary positions along the whole path of the planet, Kepler found it necessary to surrender two cosmological assumptions which the Aristotelian, Ptolemaic, Copernican, and Tychonic theories accepted as axiomatic before this time. The first was that the planetary orbits are circular. (They can, to this day, be resolved into circular figures by the use of deferents and epicycles; but such resolution was undertaken by Ptolemy only because he accepted this axiom and then had to save the appearances by constructions of circles-upon-circles. Copernicus had, in the ideal case, made the orbits simply circular, and in other cases had had to fall back upon the Ptolemaic analysis into circles-upon-circles.) The second assumption he surrendered was that planetary motions are uniform.

In ten years of arduous labor on the orbit of Mars, Kepler found that he could save the appearances by describing its path as an ellipse with the sun at one focus, and by attributing variations in its velocity to a law which stated another uniformity: the equality of areas swept out by the planet in equal intervals of time regardless of its distance from the sun. This was shown in his *De motibus stellae martis* (1609). In *De harmonica mundis* (1619) he achieved his Third Law, relating the time of revolution of a planet with its distance from the sun, an algebraical solution to the geometrical problem of 1696.

Kepler's kinematical astronomy was one of those few transcendent achievements of the human mind accomplished single-handedly by one man so perfectly that later observations and mathematical improvements have refined but not modified it. But Kepler was not willing, like Osiander, to treat astronomical hypotheses as if their entire function were to save the appearances. He accepted the heliocentric cosmology of Copernicus and denied the infinity of the universe then being taught by Bruno. The Copernican universe was simplified; a diagram would show ellipses with the sun at the focus, not cycles and epicycles. But this cosmological revision of Copernicus' system was a lesser step forward than Kepler's hypothesis concerning the dynamics and mechanics (not merely the geometry) of the solar system. Kepler wanted to know why, physically as well as mathematically, the planets moved as they did. In answering this question he indicated the path to be followed by the great mechanists of the seventeenth century, not only by Descartes but even more by Newton himself.

He explained the motions of the planets in terms of two forces, the variations of which were related by his laws. One of these forces was originally called the *anima motrix* by which the planet is pushed in its course by rays emanating from the sun. The word *anima* suggests both the origin and the limitation of this conception—its origin in Neoplatonic speculation about planetary intelligences, its limitation in respect to being a measurable quantity which might be determined without reference exclusively to planetary motion. Kepler later called this a *vis motrix* in following his aim "to show that the heavenly machine is not a kind of divine, live being, but a kind of clockwork." [12] The other force was magnetic; it likewise radiated from the sun and regulated the distance of the planet to the sun. As a consequence of Kepler's laws, these forces varied by an inverse function, since the Second Law requires that the velocity of the planet be greater when it is nearer the sun. The former force was later to become Descartes' vortical force and, finally, Newton's centrifugal force, or the tangential component in planetary motion. The latter was to develop into Newton's central gravitational force which prevents the planet from flying off on the tangent. In the Preface to the *Astronomia nova*, indeed, Kepler was even nearer to anticipating Newton than these considerations suggest. For there he distinguishes—but notes also the resemblances—between gravity and magnetic attraction, and sees the greater generality of the former. By reference to it he suggests the proper explanation of tides, the motions of the moon, the rising of some bodies and the falling of others, without the necessity of assuming a natural position for each of the elements.

The invention of the telescope gave Galileo almost visual evidence of the truth of the Copernican and indeed Brunonian cosmology and thus brought down the Aristotelian edifice. By the end of the seventeenth century Newton had related Huyghen's and Galileo's laws of terrestrial motion to Kepler's laws of planetary motion, and the modern conception of the mechanical as well as mathematical universe was established. But Germany had made its contribution to the modern world picture by 1619. Its further elaboration and establishment was the accomplishment of Italians (Galileo), Frenchmen (Descartes, Gassendi), Dutchmen (Huyghens), and Englishmen (Hooke, Newton, Halley). The next great German contribution to our understanding of the astronomical world did not take place until 1755, when Kant formulated his mechanical conception of the evolution of the universe and did for cosmic time what Bruno had done for cosmic space.

The Atomists

Astronomy is the simplest of the sciences and, according to Comte's well-known and, on the whole, true account, it was the first to reach the

---

[12] Quoted from article "Kepler" in *Encyclopedia of Philosophy* (New York: Macmillan, 1967), IV, 331, by Arthur Koestler. The sentence occurs in a letter of 1605.

stage of being an exact science, though he underestimated how much meta-physics is left even in such a "positive science." *Prima facie*, it seems para-doxical that astronomy should be so far in advance of the other sciences; one would think rather that the very intractability of its subject matter and the sparsity of our information about heavenly bodies, even today, would have delayed its advance. But this sparsity in fact favored the astronomer over all other scientists; he did not have so much information that he could afford to pick and choose his data and therefore make wrong choices. And, even more fortunately, the data he was given were precisely those needed for the development of an exact mathematical depiction of the facts. Geometrizing was forced upon the astronomer; though for millennia he also used nongeometrical concepts from Neoplatonic or Aristotelian natural philosophy and from astronomy, it was easier—though still very difficult—for astronomers to eliminate these speculations than it was for those natural philosophers who dealt with things they could hold in their hands. Geom-etrizing was not forced upon these natural scientists and philosophers; they had to force their geometry, when the times were ripe, upon a recalcitrant material.

This difference, which to us is an accident of methodology, was given a metaphysical explanation in the Aristotelian world-view, which saw in the region of the stars the abode of intelligible, mathematical objects, while the sublunary sphere appeared to them to be only partially susceptible to rational form and mathematical treatment. Only when the metaphysical barriers between the two spheres were removed was the step taken of ex-plaining terrestrial phenomena as if they were astronomically clean. (The second momentous step was taken in the nineteenth century when the spectroscope was used by Fraunhofer, another German, to export back into the heavens the terrestrial truths of chemistry.)

Mechanics and geometrical optics were the first terrestrial sciences to achieve the virtue of astronomical cleanliness. We have seen how some of the same motives which led to the proper understanding of astronomical facts were working also in the early history of geometrical optics in Ger-many, as in the work on the rainbow by Dietrich of Freiberg. In physics, men were not so fortunate when they reasoned about mechanics of motion in a sea of air, with middle-sized bodies moving against friction. Terrestrial mechanics in the Occamist school, among such pupils of Buridan as Albert of Saxony, Marsilius of Inghen, and Nicolas of Oresme, did move away from the generalized Aristotelian theory of motions to form a conception of force and impetus which, after many refinements, was brought into concord with the pure theory of planetary motions.

Chemistry, however, had none of the advantages of astronomy. It was both too important and too complex in its observational basis to follow the path of mechanics. The chemists picked up the stick at the wrong end and observed the wrong characters, and hence made wrong theories, far longer than astronomers and mechanicians did. They began with the highly quali-tative science of alchemy, which was empirically very rich, and carried into their theoretical structures all the qualitative variety of alchemical observa-tion and speculation. While the fathers of modern science in Italy, France,

Holland, and England were doing simple and elegant experiments with balls, projectiles, and pieces of string, or cutting up human and animal bodies and applying their concepts of machinery to muscles, nerves, and blood vessels, chemists were still debating about the four elements and amassing wealth from gullible patrons whose credulous greed supported many a laboratory.

Chemistry became scientific only when measurable bodies were substituted for unmeasurable spirits and principles, and when these measurable bodies were actually measured and the measurements correlated with each other as one body changes into another. It was not likely that anyone would make this substitution as long as it was thought that chemical substances had indwelling living spirits, or that metals grew in the earth, or that chemical changes were living processes of fermentation, and that substantial forms, spirits, and imponderable principles inhered in material substances and governed their changes. For a shift from qualitative, spiritualistic, or occult science to occur, a new metaphysics of matter was required to take the place of Aristotelian or Neoplatonic or Paracelsian conceptions of the material world. Just as astronomy constructed the modern world picture by a revival of a Pythagorean metaphysics and epistemology, chemistry required a revival of a Democritean, atomic, metaphysics and epistemology.

This revival occurred in the seventeenth century in the work of Pierre Gassendi. Though Gassendi and Descartes had quite different ontologies, the mechanical and quantitative study of the chemical aspects of nature was favored by both these French savants. In Germany, however, continuation of Aristotelianism and its rival Paracelsian theory kept the Germans from taking the lead in theoretical chemistry. Though the first professorship of chemistry anywhere in the world was established in Marburg in 1609, the greatest advances in chemistry were made outside the region of Paracelsian predominance. Germans developed chemical theories of atomism, but it was a qualitative, Aristotelian corpuscular theory and not a Democritean atomic theory with a mechanical and materialistic basis.

The first formulation of a corpuscular, or atomic, theory in a form that had any relevance to alchemy or chemistry was achieved by Daniel Sennert (1572–1637). Sennert was born in Breslau and was professor of medicine in Wittenberg, where he had repeatedly to defend himself against charges of heresy. In 1619 he published his *De chymicorum cum Aristotelicis et Galenicis consensu ac dissensu*, which gave the first restatement of the ancient atomic theory that had any bearing upon the problems of chemistry. In this work, and even more clearly in his *Hypomnemata physica* of 1636, Sennert taught that matter consists of atoms, or corpuscles, (*atomi, corpora indivisibilia, atoma corpuscula*) of the four elements and of their simplest mixtures. Paracelsus' three principles he regarded as material constituents of bodies and as composed of these elements. Each atom had its own form and mode of behavior, which it retained even when in combination with others; hence atoms could be recovered from a mixture into which they had seemingly disappeared. The forms of the atoms included both geometrical forms (sizes and shapes) and substantial forms, i.e., specific and inexplicable qualitative differences. In his observations he did not apply quantitative methods, without which the conception of atoms can be only speculative and nonexplanatory.

Sennert did have great influence both in medicine and chemistry in Germany, especially through the writings of his pupil Johannes Sperrling (1603–1658), who defended the corpuscular theory in his *Institutiones physicae* (1646) which was widely used as a university textbook until the end of the century. But Sperrling made no advance in the one direction required for the progress of chemistry, that is, measurement.

The first effort to relate the corpuscular theory to the quantitative aspects of chemical substances and change was made about this time in Brabant by Jean Baptista Van Helmont (1579–1644), who attempted chemical and physical demonstrations of the indestructibility of matter by weighing his reactants and yields. He broke down the Aristotelian theory of four elements by his discovery that the "airs" resulting from different chemical changes were not identical with each other, i.e., that air was not a chemical element. Van Helmont coined the term *gas* from the Greek word *chaos* (not from *Geist* [= spirit], as sometimes said) as the name for a physical state of a substance, not for a specific subtile but material substance. The discovery of gases corresponding in their chemical constitution to solids reinforced the atomic theory, since vaporization was easily explained in its terms. Steam, for example, is simply water in which there is empty space between the atoms. It is not another chemical substance with different kinds of atoms, but a state of water which can be explained mechanically and geometrically.

Jungius

The most important German philosopher of the sixteenth century to be concerned with the problems of chemistry was Joachim Jungius (Jung) of Lübeck (1587–1657), director of the Gymnasium in Hamburg. Even before Jungius went to the university, he had become acquainted with Ramus' logic, which gave him a distaste for the Melanchthonian scholasticism of his teachers. He was a student and then, at the age of twenty-two, professor of mathematics in the University of Giessen, where his first lecture was on "The Dignity, Excellence, and Use of Mathematics." [13] He went to Italy and, in 1618, he took the medical degree at Padua, having there become acquainted with the Italian Aristotelianism of Zabarella and Cremonini. Upon his return to Germany his career as a teacher and physician was repeatedly broken into by the war which began in that year, and he lived in several different cities. In Rostock in 1619 he was associated with the disciples of Johann Valentin Andreas (1586–1654), an educational reformer who opposed scholasticism and favored the study of the *realia* (mathematics, geography, history, and modern languages) as being of greater service to Christianity than logic and metaphysics. With them, he organized in 1622 the first scientific society in northern Europe, the

---

[13] Now available in *Festschrift der Hamburger Universitat, Beiträge zur Jungius-Forschung* (1929) in German translation.

Societas ereunetica, for the purposes of opposing the Jesuits and advancing mathematics and the sciences of nature. This society lasted only three years (because of the war); thereafter, but with still other interruptions, Jungius was professor of mathematics in Rostock and then director of the Hamburg Gymnasium until his death.

During his lifetime his principal publication was the *Logica hamburgensis* (1638), but in 1662 his pupils published posthumously his most important scientific work, the *Isagoge physica doxascopica.* Many of his manuscripts were destroyed by fire, but Leibniz had in his possession a paper entitled *Noematica,* which seems to have influenced his writing of the *De arte combinatoria* in 1666. Leibniz wrote, "Among all who have ever attacked the problem of an *ars inveniendi,* I know no one who penetrated farther than Joachim Jungius of Lübeck." Leibniz praised him for his formalization of nonsyllogistic inferences and said that Jungius had a better understanding of the source of truth and of the analysis of concepts than Descartes had had.[14]

Jungius was a significant figure for two reasons. First, he opposed scholastic logic in favor of a theory—the roots of which grew in Italy—of logic as a tool of research and not solely as a reflection of metaphysics; as a propaedeutic art, not as a science cognate with metaphysics. And second, his atomic theory was, after that of Robert Boyle, the most advanced of his time.[15]

For Jungius the guiding thread of the art of discovery was not metaphysics passively reflected in logic, but experience reflected in mathematics. Against scholastic logic and Ramism, Jungius developed his logic from that of the Paduan Aristotelians, who taught him that the principles of science are to be regarded as hypotheses to be tested, not as truths evident to experience or intuitive reasoning. He learned that the method of Aristotle's science was dialectical (hypothetical) and not apodictic, as it had been misinterpreted to be by the scholastic logicians who took Aristotle's conjectures as the final answer instead of as the starting point. His emphasis upon observation and the rejection of authority was not, as we shall see, merely the normal lip service of emancipated thinkers of the time, but was evidenced in his practice. But he also clearly saw the fallibility of induction while recognizing its indispensability; the dialectical interplay between theory and observation is very patent in his investigations.

This interplay was derived from the methods Zabarella named *resolutio* and *compositio,* which were known by Jungius' time as analysis and synthesis. While Zabarella had formulated these methods as generally

---

[14] Louis Couturat, *Opuscules et fragments inédits de Leibniz* (Paris: Alcan, 1903), p. 335; Leibniz, *Philosophical Papers and Letters,* ed. L. E. Loemker (Chicago: University of Chicago Press, 1956), p. 419; *New Essays Concerning Human Understanding,* bk. IV, chap. xvii, § 4.

[15] A third important contribution of Jungius should be mentioned: his work in botany. The *Isagoge phytoscopica* (publ. 1679) proposed a taxonomic system which influenced that of John Ray and resembled that of Linnaeus so greatly that Linnaeus was charged with having plagiarized from it. This has been refuted, but Linnaeus knew of Jungius' work through Ray. Alexander von Humboldt and Goethe both praised Jungius' botanical work.

valid in logic, Galileo, Descartes, and Jungius gave them a mathematical application and made *compositio* an experimental method for testing the adequacy of an analysis. Like Galileo, who thought the book of nature was written in mathematical characters, Jungius saw the mathematical method as valid because

nature does not act the way the Chinese write, but like other peoples, i.e., with an alphabet . . . through combinations, complications, and replications of a few hypotheses, laws, or principles.[16]

Hence, when Jungius developed his atomistic theory during the period 1629–1631 (it was not published until 1639), he did so by trying to see the basis of chemical change in mixing and separating, not in the actualization of potentialities. He called his theory syndiacritic, and the Aristotelian theory he opposed he called the actupotential. He appealed to Occam's razor in his explanations and to Occam's theory that all existence is individual. Elemental substances are not continuous forms, but individuals; Jungius even called Democritus an Occamist! He denied substantial forms, i.e., reified occult properties treated as if they were discrete elemental substances. For Jungius the geometrical and physical properties—size, shape, position, and motion—of the atoms sufficed to explain all their other properties. But because Jungius fully realized and insisted upon the importance of experiment, he was not dogmatic about what specifically these elementary particles are. For example, he held properly that it was an empirical question not yet decided whether fire was an element and whether liquids and gases were continuous or made up of discrete parts. But more important than these hesitations was his specification of the way in which such questions could be decided.

The change from water to steam may take place by the addition of a hypostatic part, namely atoms of fire, to the atoms of water; this process Jungius calls *syncrisis*. Or it may be by a change without the addition of new hypostatic parts; this he calls *metasyncrisis*. *Metasyncrisis* may be explained by the addition of a principle, heat, which is syn-hypostatic, i.e., not capable of existing alone, or by a process of rearrangement of parts, which he compares to the rearrangement of the same letters to produce different words. Jungius knew that the change of a solid to a liquid, as in the process of solution, was *metasyncrisis*, since the weight of the solution is equal to the weight of the hypostatic parts, namely the solute and the solvent. He could not, however, weigh gases with sufficient accuracy to ascertain whether vaporization under heat was *syncrisis* or *metasyncrisis*. The failure to answer this question left open the way for the development of the phlogiston theory by Johann Joachim Becher (1635–1682) and Georg Ernst Stahl.[17] When the accurate measurement of the weight of

16 R. W. Meyer, "Joachim Jungius und die Philosophie seiner Zeit," in *Die Entfaltung der Wissenschaft* (Hamburg: J. J. Augustin, 1957), p. 31; no source given.

17 Stahl (1660–1734), professor of medicine in Halle, is remembered for two contributions, the theory of phlogiston (though the word itself is to be found in Sennert, but with a vaguer meaning than Stahl (attached to it) and the theory of vitalism in biology. In the latter, he rejected the Cartesian *bête-machine* theory in favor of a theory of a

gases finally became possible, phlogiston already had so secure a place in chemical theory that to explain the paradoxes to which it led in the theory of combustion it was assigned a negative weight, and Jungius' wise conviction that weight was a criterion for hypostatic substances was lost to chemistry until finally established by Lavoisier more than a century later.

What was perhaps most impressive in the intellectual conduct of Jungius was his recognition of how many questions he could not answer. He attempted to restrict his opinions to what he could experimentally confirm. Where he had no cogent evidence, he was willing to put forward alternative hypotheses. This is why one finds in his writings repetitions of older speculations side by side with the new (and at that time equally speculative) atomic hypothesis. So far from eclectically mixing up the old and the new, as Sennert and Van Helmont did, he wisely kept the old and the new side by side until one should be established. For instance, he believed that the progress of chemistry would show that it was not in fact necessary to assume the existence of synhypostatic substances. He did not decide whether all forms of matter (for example, gases and liquids) are atomic in structure. He did not profess to know how many elements there are; he simply gave an operational definition of an element, to wit, if you cannot decompose a body into substances having different properties, then it is to be treated as an element. He did not attempt to explain chemical composition by a single theory. In some cases, he asserted, it may be due to merely mechanical forces, as when the faces of atoms may be juxtaposed; but in other cases it seemed more likely to him that chemical union results from a "mutual appetite" of atoms for each other. Such caution and modesty were not the characteristic marks of most of those we are calling natural philosophers.

Stosch

The last important appearance of atomic theory in the midst of philosophical and theological debate in Germany in the seventeenth century is in the *Concordia rationis et fidei sive Harmonia philosophiae moralis et religionis Christianae* (1692) of Friedrich Wilhelm Stosch of Berlin. Stosch's atomism was derived (if we may judge by the citations) from Gassendi rather than from German sources. According to Stosch, the changes in the world are explicable by the different movements, positions, shapes, and sizes of atoms. Their differences in shape are shown by the microscope, and they may be round, cubical, or four- or five-sided, and smooth, rough, or hooked. There is no vacuum, but the atoms swim in a medium of air. Their actions are rigorously governed by laws impressed upon them by God, though anomalies are possible.

---

vital principle, to which he was brought by considerations both of Cartesian psychophysical dualism and Paracelsus' and Van Helmont's theories of *archei* in living bodies. In his *Theoria medica vera* (Halle, 1707) Stahl explained all bodily movement by actions of the soul. This theory was refuted by Albrecht von Haller (*De partibus corporis humani*, 1752) who experimentally established irritability as an inherent characteristic of muscle. This discovery, known in the early 'forties, was used both by La Mettrie in his anti-vitalistic theory (*L'Homme machine*, 1747) and by Herder in his anti-mechanistic theory of life (see Chapter XV).

Stosch combined this atomistic theory, however, with Spinozism, to which he gave a materialistic interpretation. The title of his book, *The Harmony of Reason and Faith*, indicates his opposition to scholastic and orthodox theology, which tried to keep reason and faith in concord but in separate compartments. Stosch argued not only for their harmony; he argued for the superiority of reason over faith and condemned public religious ceremonies as a form of hypocrisy. His metaphysics identified God with nature and nature with the materialistic atomic system. Included in nature is the human soul, with the consequence that mechanical determinism replaces human freedom. His Democritean views are obvious.

The aroused theologians had Stosch's book investigated by a commission which included Spener and Pufendorf, and it was condemned and burned by the public hangman in 1694. Possession of it was punishable by fine, and Stosch was forced to make a retraction.[18] (Strangely enough, Stosch was raised to the nobility in 1701 by Friedrich I.)

The atomism of the book was not, of course, the occasion for the outcry; it was the Spinozism, which was interpreted in the crassest materialistic form—the form in which it continued to be known in Germany until Lessing and Herder gave a more acceptable interpretation in the 1780's. Spinozism was represented as pantheism and fatalism by Bayle, and it was in this form that Wolff attempted to refute Spinozism; but Stosch's adding materialism to the other sins of the accursed Jew of Amsterdam certainly contributed to Spinoza's bad reputation in Germany. In these larger matters Stosch's atomism was of little moment and soon forgotten.

The Cartesians

When we trace much of modern philosophy back to Descartes, we in the twentieth century are likely to emphasize one aspect of his thought at the expense of the others, the epistemological rather than the cosmological and the metaphysical. This invidious selection was not made by those who took Descartes' Catholic orthodoxy as seriously as they did his purely philosophical contributions. There is, in Descartes' writings, an inner tension which disturbs us, but which comforted those who were most directly concerned with putting Cartesianism into the service of theology. The tension is between two poles: the first a self-guaranteeing epistemology, according to which whatever is perceived clearly and distinctly *must* be true, and the second a theological guarantee of this basic principle, namely, the purely theological doctrine that God will not deceive men. This tension is perhaps fatal to Cartesianism as a consistent theory of knowledge, since the first pole alone is supposed to suffice for the proof of the existence of God, and yet the second pole (presupposing the existence of God) must have been operative if the argument for the existence of God was to have

---

[18] A précis of Stosch's book, which is said to be very rare since only one hundred copies were printed, and a collection of the documents concerned with its condemnation, are to be found in Gottfried Stiehler, "Friedrich Wilhelm Stosch, ein früher Aufklärer in Deutschland," *Wissenschaftliche Zeitschrift der Humboldt-Universität zu Berlin, Gesell- u. Sprachwissenschaftliche Reihe*, V (1955–56), 113–122. I have not seen the original.

probative value. Such a tension invited the theologically committed to use both these theories simultaneously and, as it were, independently of each other. For the existence of God, which was not doubted, could guarantee the validity of profane reason. Yet if they felt the need for a rationalistic proof of the existence of God, Descartes provided them with that too. The "Cartesian circle," as this difficulty in his theory has been called, was to them no embarrassment but a recommendation.

There was still another tension in Descartes' philosophy. Descartes' epistemology is rationalistic and intellectualistic, but his theory of God is voluntaristic—it is the will of God, not a necessity of his nature, which keeps our natural reason from being deceptive. Hence Cartesianism at first offers a guarantee to reason but still leaves open the possibility of (revealed) truth not transparent to reason. To make Cartesianism really do the job it is supposed to do, this tension between epistemology and metaphysics, between man's reason and God's will, must be ameliorated; God must himself be made rational. The medieval doctrine that God is not bound by the logical or the moral law gives no guarantee to our rationality. If this guarantee is felt to be needed, God's will must be rationally and morally limited. Cartesianism thus leads to Spinozism, in which God's actions are determined by the (logical) necessities of his nature: God himself cannot break the law of contradiction. With Leibniz, God is not only bound by the law of contradiction, but also by the principle of sufficient reason. That the principle of sufficient reason, when applied to God, is for Leibniz the principle of the maximization of perfection, reintroduces a distinction between the will and the intellect of God which had been maintained by Descartes and denied by Spinoza. But God's freedom, for Leibniz, is not an arbitrary freedom of indifference, and man can, at least in principle, understand (give reasons for) God's creation of this world and legislation of the laws which hold within it.

This progressive rationalization of God was the long-term effect of Cartesianism in the philosophy of the seventeenth and eighteenth centuries. If the reader will recall what we have said about the general differences between Lutheran and Calvinist scholasticism (Chapter VI), he will readily see how Calvinism, at least in conjunction with its heretical but established forms, and Cartesianism seemed to be going in the same direction, and how it would appear that Lutheranism and Cartesianism had to be in opposition to each other. Yet the actual historical situation was not quite so simple. For, as we have seen, Calvinist and Lutheran philosophies were not as radically opposed in their metaphysics and epistemologies as Calvinism itself was opposed to the Socinianism and Arminianism associated with it; and what Cartesianism was to mean in the long run of modern history was by no means obvious in 1650. Few, if any, Germans saw Cartesianism as an unstable compromise between human intellectualism and divine voluntarism—a compromise so unstable that the former, under the conditions of modernity, would drive out the latter and rationalism would triumph over revelation.

For, in the seventeenth century, Cartesianism meant many things. A man might call his philosophy Cartesian (or be accused of being a Cartesian) if he accepted one of these things, while another would call his own philosophy anti-Cartesian because he rejected another. Cartesianism in Germany was any one of several brands of eclecticism, mixing a few Cartesian ideas with scholastic ideas and aspirations; as much scholasticism and as much Cartesianism were mixed as the ingenuity of the individual philosopher permitted. Among the Cartesian ingredients of this mix were: (a) the method of doubt as a prior condition of philosophy; (b) the method of mathematics (analysis and synthesis, intuition and construction, rejection of syllogism as useful) in philosophy; (c) innate ideas and common notions against nominalism and sensory empiricism; (d) a mechanistic and mathematical cosmology and rejection of substantial forms, occult properties, and internal natural teleology; (e) a two-substance theory and a Cartesian or occasionalistic psychophysical theory; and (f) acceptance of particular points in Cartesian cosmology, such as the theory of vortices, the conservation of motion, mechanistic views in physiology and optics, and denial of atomism and the vacuum.

In Holland, most or all of these could be adopted simultaneously; in Germany, a prior commitment to scholasticism excluded some of them altogether and forced a bowdlerization of the others. Perhaps the best illustration of this process of pulling the dangerous fangs of Cartesianism is seen in how the method of doubt was handled. Clauberg tried to find an Aristotelian archetype for Cartesian doubt, so that it would not lead to a skepticism of revelation, and he found it in Aristotle's statement that philosophy begins in wonder. *Dubitatio = admiratio!*[19] Descartes' method of doubt was taken as a *pia dubitatio*, and he was the true Christian philosopher because he alone was able to refute the atheists.[20]

With so vague a conception of what was truly original in the work of Descartes, it is not to be expected that he would have the emancipating effect in Germany in the seventeenth century that we attribute to him in the broad sweep of European intellectual history.

We must consider the impact of Cartesian thought upon the two chief occupations of German thinkers—natural philosophy and scholasticism.

The scientific limitations of the natural philosophers, which are obvious in all of them except Jungius, were by no means limited to German natural philosophers. It is likely that occultism, astrology, alchemy, and the witchcraft delusion were more widely practiced or accepted among the highest intellectual classes in Germany than elsewhere. But while this may be

[19] "Our defense of doubt . . . is based on this, that all philosophy begins from wonder, and that this wonder is joined with doubt."—Johannes Clauberg, *De dubitatione Cartesiana*, I, § 31 (*Opera omnia* [Amsterdam, 1691] II, 1138). Socratic and Cartesian doubt are identified, *ibid.*, pp. 1134, 1136.

[20] Said by Johann Jakob Waldschmiedt (1644–1689), professor of medicine in Marburg; see A. Angyal, "Zur Literaturgeschichte des deutschen Cartesianismus," *Germanisch-Romanische Monatsschrift* 29: 69–72 (1941). A full account of the situation in Marburg from the time of the first prohibition of Cartesianism to its acceptance (in 1692) insofar as it did not touch upon theological matters, and the role of Waldschmiedt in the quarrels, is given by Heinrich Hermelink and S. A. Kähler, *Die Philipps-Universität zu Marburg, 1527–1927* (Marburg: Elwert, 1927), pp. 309–331.

debatable, it is incontestable that Germany was later than other countries in substituting natural science for natural philosophy.[21]

Natural philosophy did not end anywhere overnight. But the change from speculation to science as we know it (speculation and all) was as dramatic and sudden as any change in an intellectual climate can be. It was accomplished in physics by Galileo and Descartes within a single generation. Both men were scientists of genius; both were writers who could be read and understood by every educated man; both, in their scientific work, were closer to the twentieth century than to the sixteenth into which they were born. Descartes, living in comparative freedom in Holland, skillful and successful as Galileo never was in recommending his doctrine to the Catholic Church, was interested in the entire range of philosophical problems. Metaphysicians had to take him into account while they might, and at their own expense did, ignore Galileo.

Descartes had the great advantage over Galileo that he not only escaped persecution himself, but lived in a country where his disciples occupied prominent positions in the universities. Their path, even in Holland, was not an easy one, and there were bans on Cartesianism; but these were ineffective. The universities of the Netherlands were the freest in Europe, and in Leyden, Utrecht, Franeker, and Groningen there were professors who adhered to Descartes. At Groningen the leading Cartesian was a German, Tobias Andreä (1604–1674). Many Dutch Cartesians were nominally Calvinists. They attempted to reconcile the Cartesian and Aristotelian cosmologies, and this forced them to undertake highly allegorical interpretations of the Old Testament. At the same time that the leader in this effort, Johan Raey[22] (or Raei), was professor of philosophy in Leyden, Cocceius (Johannes Koch, 1603–1669), the founder of "federal," or "covenant," theology, was also teaching there, and his theology also required a rather free reading of the Old Testament. In this way, the Cartesians and the Cocceians were forced into an alliance, and the condemnations of the latter by the various synods also had the effect of making Cartesianism appear to be a Calvinist heresy. But while Cocceianism was rendered ineffective in the organization of the church, both it and Cartesianism continued to be taught in the universities in spite of various prohibitions.

It has been suggested that Calvinism was more open to the Cartesian influence than Lutheranism was, and reasons for this have been found in

---

[21] For evidence of this, see F. H. Wagman, *Magic and Natural Science in German Baroque Literature* (New York: Columbia University Press, 1942), and Lynn Thorndike, *A History of Magic and Experimental Science*, vol. VII (New York: Columbia University Press, 1957), chap. xi, "Occultism in the German Universities of the Seventeenth Century." Both show the perseveration of occultism and fantastic natural philosophy, the former in the popular novels which must have reflected common beliefs, and the second among the savants themselves.

[22] Raey was one of the first of many to try to reconcile Aristotelian and Cartesian philosophy, in his *Clavis philosophiae naturalis seu introductio ad naturae contemplationem Aristotelico-Cartesianam* (1654). Jacob Thomasius suggested, and Leibniz denied, that Raey had influenced the thought of the young Leibniz on how to reconcile Aristotelian and mechanical philosophy (Leibniz, *Philosophical Papers and Letters*, p. 152; letter to Thomasius of 1669).

Calvinistic rationalism (in the broad sense that does not exclude what will later be called "empiricism"), in the Calvinist interpretation of the Eucharist, which seemed to be easily interpreted in terms of Cartesian dualism,[23] and in still other aspects of Calvinist theology and outlook. The facts, however, are rather different from what would be expected. It was far easier for a Catholic or a member of the Arminian or Socinian sect to accept Cartesian theories of the will and of the relation of God to the world than it was for an orthodox Calvinist. Yet the two minority movements could not be the vehicles for the new philosophy in Germany, where orthodox Calvinists or Lutherans were in control of the northern universities.

Yet facts were stronger than theological scruples. Calvinists were in Holland, and German Calvinists went to Holland in great numbers. And whoever went to Holland was in danger of being infected with Cartesianism. Lutheran students living in those parts of Germany not possessing a Lutheran university also went to Holland, and they brought Cartesianism back to the Lutheran parts of Germany. Nor were the Lutheran Cartesians made less welcome when they returned than the Calvinist Cartesians were; in fact, the two definite prohibitions on Cartesian teachings were enacted in the Calvinist universities of Herborn and Marburg, though not enforced in the latter. While Tübingen and Jena, among the Lutheran universities, knew how to protect themselves from the Cartesian infection, there were Cartesian professors in Altdorf (Johann Christoph Sturm, 1635–1703), Giessen (Johann Kähler, 1649–1729), Frankfort on the Oder (Johann Placentius, author of *Renatus Cartesius triumphans*), Halle (Johannes Sperlette, 1661–1725), and Leipzig (Johann Andreas Petermann, 1649–1703). At the same time, Christoph Wittich (Wittichius, 1625–1687), a Silesian educated under Racy at Leyden, was dismissed from the Calvinist University of Herborn for teaching Cartesianism instead of Ramism.

Wittich's is a good example of the difficult academic life of a Calvinist Cartesian. After he was dismissed from Herborn he took a pastorate, only to be censured by his synod in Cleves for teaching the Copernican astronomy (in its Cartesian form). He defended his views by arguing that Scripture uses only the language of common appearances and is not decisive in scientific questions. In 1655 he was back in Holland, where he had a large following among the Cocceian students at Nijmegen, but in 1656 Cartesian teaching was forbidden in all Dutch universities. This prohibition proved to be unenforceable, however, and soon Wittich was exerting a strong influence upon, and had the protection of, one important faction in the Dutch Reformed Church; in 1671 he became professor of theology in Leyden. In his theological work he remained strictly orthodox and made a sharp distinction between theological and philosophical problems. His *Anti-Spinoza* was published posthumously in 1690.

With these examples before us, we must therefore give up the notion of some effective Calvinist predilection for Cartesian ideas. We should note also that when Cartesianism passed from Holland to Germany it did not

---

[23] See above, p. 131.

have the liberating and fructifying effect it had had elsewhere. The Germans were so scholastically oriented that Descartes was assimilated into a ready-made scholastic system, and he did not have the destructive or reconstructive effects there which he had where nonscholastic students of nature were his disciples. Germans of the seventeenth century made a discovery that the rest of the world had to wait until the twentieth century to make, namely, that Descartes himself was a good Aristotelian scholastic.

The only German Cartesians of more than antiquarian interest were Johannes Clauberg (1622–1665), a Calvinist professor of philosophy in the University of Herborn until his dismissal, and thereafter professor in the new University of Duisburg; and Ehrenfried Walther von Tschirnhaus (1651–1703), a mathematician and natural scientist, who was offered, but declined, the rectorship of the new University of Halle. In the eighteenth century, Cartesianism as an independent force in philosophy ceased to be important, since it was either assimilated into other movements (e.g., its mechanism was present in Wolff, its theory of the mind–body relation was adopted by most of the followers of Wolff) or ignored. Disputes between the Cartesian and Leibnizian mechanics continued, however, until the middle of the century. When there is explicit criticism of Cartesianism in logic and metaphysics in the eighteenth century, it is very frequently directed, either tacitly or explicitly, at the teachings of Johannes Sperlette, "the last Cartesian," a Huguenot professor in Halle from 1694 to his death in 1744. Opposition to excessive rationalism is frequently aimed at his pretended "mathematical proofs" of Christian dogmas.

Clauberg and von Tschirnhaus deserve more careful study than the other Cartesians.

Johannes Clauberg

Johannes Clauberg was born in Solingen in 1622 and was educated at Groningen under Andreä and Raey.[24] After travels in England and France, where he met Cartesians, he became professor of philosophy and theology in the Calvinist University of Herborn, where he remained until 1651, when he became director of the gymnasium (then being raised to university status) at Duisburg, where he remained until his death in 1665. Clauberg was interested in developing German as a language suitable for philosophical writing and wrote at least one of his works in German.[25] In his Latin writings he frequently inserts German words and phrases, as much to help fix the German meanings as to elucidate his Latin expressions. Leibniz referred to him as only a paraphraser of Descartes (this was unjust), but speaks of him as being clearer than Descartes (this was incorrect).[26]

[24] On his relation to these men, see Paul Dibon, La Philosophie néenderlaise au siècle d'or (Amsterdam: Elsevier, 1954) I, 176–179.

[25] All of Clauberg's works in Latin or in Latin translation are in Opera omnia, Amsterdam, 2 vols. (1691), paged continuously (hereafter cited as Opera). I have not seen any of his German writings, which are not included in this edition.

[26] Letter to Jacob Thomasius in Leibniz, Philosophical Papers and Letters, trans. L. E. Loemker, I, 146.

Clauberg's philosophical works may be divided into three kinds. There are first the purely scholastic writings, then the purely Cartesian writings (generally in scholastic form), and finally the expositions of Descartes in the form of scholastic disputations and commentaries. We shall here consider only the first two.

In 1647, while still in Holland, Clauberg wrote his *Metaphysica de ente, quae rectius Ontosophia*. This is a standard scholastic textbook, showing the influence of Suarez and Clemens Timpler, the principal Calvinist scholastic philosopher of the early part of the century. The book is distinguished more by its title than by its content. Clauberg used the word *ontosophia* as a synonym for *ontologia*, which had been introduced shortly before this time as the name for the general science of being as being. While his own coinage, *ontosophia*, did not last, he no doubt popularized[27] both the concept and the name *ontologia*, and the name and concept and much of the content were fixed for Wolff's later exploitation of the whole field. Clauberg's book is primarily one of definitions and distinctions; almost no metaphysical theses are argued for, and its only unique feature is the number of French and German words he identifies parenthetically with the *termini technicis* in Latin. Gilson sees this work as providing the link between Suarez and Wolff, as being "the birth certificate of ontology as a science conceived after the pattern of theology yet radically distinct from it, since being *qua* being is indifferent to all its conceivable determinations."[28] In Gilson's well-known distinction, Clauberg is an important link in the chain of development of essential ontology out of existential ontology. In attempting to define being without regard to what kinds of being there are, Clauberg takes mere cogitability as definitive:

> Every being, whatever it is and however it is, can be thought and stated . . . I say every being can be stated, i.e., named, expressed by spoken or written word . . . Moreover, every being can be thought or known; for this reason it is called thinkable and knowable.[29]

With this there begins a rationalistic ontology in which the potentiality of being thought defines being. Since merely analytic thought obviously does not offer a sufficient condition for asserting extra-logical or extra-mental being, the potentiality of being thought is not in fact going to be limited to thought-without-contradiction; some other kind of possibility of being thought must be tacitly added to it. Thus from the consequences of Clauberg's definition of being there arises what will finally be known as the problem of the synthetic a priori. The successive steps can best be seen in

---

[27] Clauberg is often regarded as the author of the term "ontology," but this is incorrect; it had been used earlier by Rudolf Goclenius and Abraham Calov. See Jose Ferrater Mora, "On the Early History of 'Ontology'," *Philosophy and Phenomenological Research*, XXIV (1963), pp. 36–47.

[28] Étienne Gilson, *Being and Some Philosophers* (Toronto: Pontifical Institute of Medieval Studies, 1949), pp. 112–113.

[29] *Ontosophia* (1647), §§ 6–8: "Ens est quicquid quovis modo est, cogitari ac dici potest . . . Aio omne ens posse dici, hoc est, nominari, voce viva vel scripta enunciari . . . Praeterea omne ens potest cogitari seu intelligi, idcoque Cogitabile & Intelligible appellatur."

the writings of the men who did not quite know what they were doing, and therefore exposed unwittingly the weakness of their case. We shall see these steps in the writings of von Tschirnhaus, Wolff, Crusius, Lambert, and Tetens as they move toward the front Kant will attack by showing that thinkability does not define knowledge and, a fortiori, does not define being. With Clauberg's first step, however, a direction is established in German philosophy away from the classical ontological realism of scholasticism, and its primary concern with being, toward the priority of the epistemological problem which is characteristic of the Cartesian movement in modern philosophy and which triumphs in German philosophy in the eighteenth century. Kant accepts this epistemological priority but refuses to take the next step from it into ontology. He substitutes the "modest name of Analytic of pure understanding for the proud name of Ontology."[30]

But we are getting beyond our story. The most noteworthy thing about Clauberg's book is not that it set a problem that was to become central in the eighteenth century, for it did this only in the retrospective eyes of the historian. Clauberg was not actually taken as the point of departure for new directions by the men in the eighteenth century who wished to be finished with the whole scholastic tradition. It is, rather, that even in the second edition, of 1660, when Clauberg was a recognized leader of the Cartesian movement, there is so little Cartesianism in it and so much that, for a Western Cartesian, would seem to be hopelessly out of date and useless. Only the long note to Chapter III is genuinely Cartesian; it defends *cogito ergo sum* as a necessary truth from attacks by the scholastics, who preferred to make an objective, ontological form of the law of contradiction the basic principle of all philosophy. Otherwise it seems almost an accident that the *Metaphysica de ente* and some of the other works we are about to discuss were written by the same man.

A less anachronistic work was the *Logica vetus & nova* of 1558. In it, Clauberg did endeavor to combine the old and the new in a way he did not try in the *Metaphysica*. He rejects the conception, common among orthodox Protestant scholastics of the time, that logic is a mirror of metaphysics, and favors the instrumental conception of logic which had come out of the Italian school. He divided logic into two parts, a genetic and an analytic. Genetic logic deals with the origin of our ideas and knowledge. It is the logic an individual would use if he were entirely alone in the world, bent on discovering, but not communicating, truth. This part of the logic is influenced by Descartes' conception of method but with little attention to the idea of the mathematical model of certainty; rather, it deals with the traditional logical topics such as syllogism, which had been rejected as useless by Descartes himself. The analytic part is largely concerned with topics from the traditional rhetoric. The *Logica* was one of the many Cartesian and semi-Cartesian works which influenced the composition of the *L'Art de penser*, the "Port Royal Logic" which appeared four years later. There are other works which are based almost entirely on Descartes, even though their purpose is to present what Clauberg believes and not to be merely an expression of Descartes' views. The most important of the latter works are

---

[30] *Critique of Pure Reason*, A 247 = B 303.

De cognitione dei et nostri (1655) and the *Physica,* published in 1663, the last part of which is entitled *Corporis et animae in homine conjunctio.*

Almost everywhere in these works Clauberg is the faithful and accurate disciple of Descartes: There are two substances or categories.[31] There are clear and distinct innate ideas; the Scholastic statement *Nihil est in intellectu. . .* is false.[32] Animals are mere machines.[33] Doubt is the proper beginning of philosophy.[34] Error is due to the will's going beyond evidence.[35] Philosophy and theology should be sharply separated.[36] Planets are carried around the sun in vortices.[37] The quantity of motion in the world is constant. The immediate connection of mind and body is in the brain, if not in the pineal gland.[38] There are no substantial forms; all in nature is to be explained in terms of extension and motion.[39] And so on—the list could be extended indefinitely.

But in two respects Clauberg departed from Cartesian orthodoxy. First he modified the Cartesian psychophysical theory, and second he modified, in an idealistic direction, the relation of *res extensa* to God.

Clauberg must be regarded as the originator of the theory of occasionalism in the mind–body problem. He published his *Conjunction of Mind and Body* in 1663; Cordemoy and De La Forge published their occasionalistic theories in 1666, and Geulincx's was not published until after his death in 1669. There is no way to know who had the idea first, nor does it matter; apparently the idea was in the air, so dubious was the Cartesian theory, and these three men and perhaps others hit upon the same solution about the same time—all of them, of course, before Malebranche gave the theory a permanent place in the history of philosophy.

According to occasionalism, mind and body are two substances too diverse to have any causal relation to each other. We cannot explain thoughts by motions, which have only other motions as their effects; nor can we explain motions in terms of thoughts, for thoughts are causally related only to other beings which resemble them, namely, other thoughts (*Corporis et animae,* chaps. iii–iv). Yet we know, at least in the common way of thinking, that they act upon each other. This, however, does not mean that the substance of one is the cause of the substance of the other (a view Clauberg spends a great deal of time refuting) but only that their attributes, actions, and passions are in some correspondence to each other (chap. ix). This correspondence cannot be brought about by any physical contact (chap. xiii, § 4) or through the mediation of some third being, human nature (chap. x, § 8). There is, therefore, no way in the course of nature that the correspondence can be effected; but it exists; therefore the changes in each substance must be correlated with those in the other by a free and miraculous act of God (chap. xiv). A change in one is the occasion for a change in the other; one is an occasional ("procatarctic," says Clauberg [chap. xvi,

[31] *Logica, Opera omnia,* p. 787. *Differentia inter philosophiam Cartesianam,* chap. iv.
[32] *De dubitatione Cartesiana,* § 10; *Opera omnia,* p. 1182.
[33] *Theoria corporum viventium, Opera,* pp. 182–183.
[34] *Differentia, Opera,* p. 1225. [36] *Differentia, Opera,* p. 1227.
[35] *Logica, Opera,* p. 889. [37] *Physica contracta, Opera,* p. 32.
[38] *Corporis et animae conjunctio, Opera,* pp. 253–254.
[39] *Defensio Cartesiana, Opera,* p. 1067; *Physica contracta, Opera,* p. 3.

§ 10], borrowing a term from Galenic medicine) cause of the other. God, having designed the body to be a fit instrument of the soul, shows his goodness by instituting this continuous miracle without which his handiwork on the body would have been in vain.

This is two-way occasionalism. It is often said that Clauberg did not develop a two-way occasionalism but believed that the more noble (the mind) may influence the less noble (the body), but not conversely, and that he therefore rejected the symmetry of the occasionalistic relation. Yet the common interpretation of Clauberg is not wholly incorrect either. For, he says, in the angelic and in the divine minds the relation is not symmetrical (chap. xx). The divine or angelic mind is a real agent; its thoughts are dynamically related to changes in the external world but are not affected by those changes. Changes in the human mind may be occasions for changes in the body through the real agency of the divine mind; and changes in the divine mind (which correspond to changes in the body) are dynamically causative of changes in the human mind. But changes in the external world per se are not occasions for changes in the divine mind and thus are not occasions for occasions of thoughts in human minds. The dynamics of changes in both minds and bodies are divine thoughts, and therefore the human mind is conformed to the divine mind (*pereleganti ratione inter se conferuntur*—they are joined to each other by a most elegant and rational bond)[40] in a way and to a degree that it is not conformed to the body. The human mind is closer to the divine mind than it is to the human body, and closer to the divine mind than the human body is. The world itself is related to God's mind as my thoughts, not my bodily actions, are related to my own mind. The world is the creature of God's thought, just as my own thoughts, but not my bodily acts, are creatures of my own mind. Substances are to God's mind as the accidents of substances are to our own mind;[41] and just as my thoughts cannot subsist for a single moment without my thinking them, the world itself cannot exist for a single moment without God's mind. The two substances, the mental and the physical, are not, therefore, on quite the same level after all. They are mutually independent only in the case of man, not in the structure of the universe as a whole. In the latter, mind is the basic, creative force.

But it would be too much to claim that Clauberg thereby achieved a phenomenalistic interpretation of the physical world.[42] For the concept of the world as being sustained from moment to moment by God was a common thought, present also in Descartes; and at crucial points in Clauberg's argument, where an idealistic or phenomenalistic interpretation of his thesis would require reference to the sustaining power of divine thought, Clauberg draws back and asserts that things are "something" apart from God's will.[43] Not even Malebranche was willing to commit himself to a phenomenalist

---

[40] *De cognitione Dei et nostri*, chap. xxviii; *Opera*, p. 644.

[41] *Ibid.*, § 6.

[42] This is claimed by Francisque Bouillier, in his classic *Histoire de la philosophie Cartesienne*, 3rd ed., (Paris, 1868), I, 299.

[43] *De cognitione Dei et nostri*, chap. xxviii, § 6: "Quamvis res illae extra voluntatem divinam aliquid sit . . . " [Although these things, apart from the divine will, are something.]

theory; though Clauberg, like Malebranche, did quote Acts xvii:28, which was to become the motto of idealistic Cartesians: "In [God] we live and move and have our being."[44] But idealism did not build upon Clauberg's ingenious metaphysical theory, which was designed to solve the psychophysical problem and not the epistemological.

von Tschirnhaus

The last philosopher to be studied in this chapter is far removed from the other German Cartesians. He was not a metaphysician and he gave only the most perfunctory attention to the classical metaphysical and theological problems; revelation and God are mentioned only two or three times in his entire book. He referred to his work as "first philosophy," but avoided this as its title only because he said the very name was hated by most scholars. Nor would he have anything to do with scholastic logic, which makes a man no wiser than the farmer or technician who knows, without its benefit, how to solve most of his problems. Rather he insisted upon the necessity of and the joy experienced in one's own individual discovery of truths, and attacked mere learning of what others have discovered. Few books before the twentieth century have been so single-mindedly devoted to the task of working out in detail (in tedious detail, it must be admitted) the *ars inveniendi* as his was, in showing how to use it in the pursuit of truth and happiness, and in the education of children. He called it, quite appropriately, *Medicina mentis*.[45]

Ehrenfried Walther von Tschirnhaus, Freiherr von Kieslingswalde und Stoltzenberg, was born in Kieslingswalde, near Görlitz in the Oberlausitz, Saxony in 1651. In 1668 he enrolled in the University of Leyden, where Geulincx, the Calvinist Cartesian, was teaching. His studies were first interrupted by the plague, and then by the invasion by Louis XIV, against whom he served as a Dutch volunteer. In 1675 he undertook an extensive grand tour of Holland, England, France, and Italy. In Holland he knew Huyghens and Spinoza, in England Boyle and Oldenburg, and in France Leibniz and Colbert. In 1682 he was offered the chancellorship of the newly established University of Halle, but declined, and instead lived on his estate where he carried out scientific and technological studies on his own. He attained fame as a geometer (his name is preserved in mathematics in the "Tschirnhaus transformation"), and his mathematical work made it possible for him to design and make larger optical glasses and mirrors than had been feasible before his time. The Saxon glass industry was founded by him and he invented the method of glazing which made Meissen china famous all over Europe.[46] He died in Dresden in 1708.

---

[44] *Ibid.*, § 13.

[45] Amsterdam, 1687; 2nd ed., Leipzig, 1695. The second edition was photographically reproduced with introduction by Wilhelm Risse, (Hildesheim: Georg Olms, 1964) and translated, with copious notes and other documentation, by Johannes Haussleiter (*Acta historica Leopoldina*, no. 1, Leipzig, 1963). Haussleiter gives marginal pagination to the 1695 edition, and citations refer to these page numbers.

[46] A dispute concerning proper credit for this invention has raged between the descendants and partisans of Tschirnhaus and his assistant, Johann Friedrich Böttger

Tschirnhaus' correspondence with Leibniz is of some importance in mathematics, and his correspondence with Spinoza is philosophically important for understanding both his and Spinoza's philosophy. The influence of Descartes and Spinoza is obvious in all his work. On most points he agreed with Descartes rather than Spinoza, but in many details he tried to mediate between the two, carefully avoiding, however, any public adherence to Spinoza. (Spinoza's name is not mentioned even when Tschirnhaus quotes him.) Thomasius' accusation that he was a Spinozist, published in his *Monatsgespräche* in 1688, brought on a long public dispute in which Tschirnhaus minimized the Spinozistic elements in his thought and magnified the Cartesian. Tschirnhaus' chief influence in German philosophy was upon Christian Wolff. Wolff met him in Leipzig and received some professional guidance from him. Wolff was influenced by Tschirnhaus' mathematical work and attempted to follow him in basing his logic upon the methodology of mathematics set out by Tschirnhaus, but with one major departure: Tschirnhaus agreed with Descartes on the uselessness of syllogistic proof, while Wolff tried to make *all* proofs syllogistic. But their ideals were the same: to introduce a demonstrative, mathematical or quasi-mathematical method into all branches of knowledge.

The opening chapter of *Medicina mentis* is a hybrid of Spinozistic and Cartesian ideas.

After a praise of wisdom as necessary to happiness and a condemnation of what was accepted as knowledge and well-being, he makes an inventory of the contents of mind in order to find out what cannot be doubted even by the skeptic. Unlike Descartes, Tschirnhaus finds four indubitable facts:[47] that he is conscious of various things, that he finds some of them good and some evil (pleasant and unpleasant), that he has the power to conceive some things and not others and the power to distinguish the true from the false, and that he has experience of ideas of the senses and passions (*imaginum internarium & passionum*). The first of these makes him accept Descartes' theory of the individual self and its freedom of indifference and to reject Spinoza's teaching on both. The second provides him with a certain foundation for his ethics. Tschirnhaus thinks that we are not brought to choose the good and shun the evil by ethical edification but by attending to what gives us the highest pleasure. This pleasure he finds in improving the power of the intellect over the passions, in learning from philosophy that the good and evil in things are only subjective products of our imagination, and of discovering new truths. The first chapter of *Medicina mentis* is pervaded with the spirit of Spinoza's tract, *De intellectu emendatione*, which embedded epistemological and metaphysical problems in the ethical context of the discovery of what is the good life for man. Tschirnhaus lacks the spare and lean rhetoric of Spinoza, and there is lacking the Stoic fortitude of Spinoza's work, but the ethical motive of both books is equally decisive.

(b. 1682). Rudolf Zaunick, in the Haussleiter edition of *Medicina mentis*, has scrutinized the claims and reported on the extensive literature of this debate.

[47] *Medicina mentis*, Praefatio (unnumbered: Haussleiter 44–45).

The third and fourth of Tschirnhaus' indubitables are the most relevant to the remainder of his philosophy. He refers to his book as constituting "first philosophy," but it is first philosophy in a very different sense from Clauberg's; it is an epistemology and methodology, not an ontology, and Tschirnhaus contrasts it, as "real philosophy," to the "verbal philosophy" of scholasticism.

The third of these indubitables is the standard by which the fourth and the claim to the truth of specific representations of the senses are to be judged. Tschirnhaus agrees with Spinoza that there is no need for a guarantee of truth and no way in which we can appeal beyond the immediate deliverances of the natural light of the mind to determine whether they are true or not. He does not appeal to God as a guarantor of our clearest and most distinct knowledge; with Spinoza, he holds that a true judgment contains the standard both for itself and for false judgments.

To be true, for Tschirnhaus, means to be conceivable. To conceive means to have a concept of what can be clearly and distinctly perceived to be possible. He agrees with Spinoza[48] that an idea or concept is not a picture on a panel, but it contains an affirmation or a denial. It is not simple, but is a judgment based on our intellectual insight into the possibility or impossibility of thinking certain simple representations together. Possible means thinkable; impossible means unthinkable. What is possible is true; hence what we can clearly and distinctly conceive as joined together is the true. The natural light of the intellect, which is the same in all men, discovers necessary connections which can be communicated to others. Conceivability and communicability are therefore the mark of what is true. Whatever follows with logical necessity from what possesses this mark of the true is likewise true.[49]

Tschirnhaus does not, of course, distinguish between those connections of ideas which will later be called analytic from those which will be called synthetic. Like his predecessors in this venture (Descartes and Clauberg) and his contemporary Locke, he is insisting only upon there being a priori connections between clear and distinct ideas, some of which (we know by his examples[50]) are logical and others of which are not.

Since, apparently, one can form many concepts which one does not even claim to refer to actual objects, Tschirnhaus defends his theory by giving a very narrow and stringent meaning to conceivability, to the *posse concipere*. He says it is not possible to conceive of anything unreal; the unreal is that which cannot be conceived to be real (such as a whole which is not equal to its parts, or an event without a cause). That which it is *impossible to conceive*, however, cannot be equated with that which we *fail to conceive*. I can fail to conceive something now, and later be enabled to conceive it, and Tschirnhaus gives some interesting examples of this from mathematics and physics; but if I conceive that it is impossible to conceive it (instead of merely deciding that I cannot conceive it), then it is known to be impossible. Many representations which we ordinarily consider to be concepts are not reached by a process of *concipere*, but are products of imagination and

---

[48] *Medicina mentis*, p. 36.
[49] *Ibid.*, pp. 35–37.   [50] *Ibid.*, p. 34.

memory and are by no means self-certifying. *Concipere* does not mean to make an abstract concept or image of a thing, but to see how it is composed, what its simple components are, and how these components require each other. A concept then, is Tschirnhaus's equivalent for Descartes' intuition of clear and distinct idea.

Tschirnhaus, however, fails to perceive the thrust of Cartesian doubt, and makes far too simple a transition from what is conceptually necessary to what is the truth about things. He simply says that if we are to avoid a self-defeating skepticism we must assume that what is true in conceptual relations is also true in the relations between the things perceived, and that we need no more to be able to prove this than we must know the structure of the hand in order to pick something up with assurance.[51]

To conceive of something is to see how it is composed. It is to define it by showing how it is made, so that only things that can be made or constructed can be conceived and defined. A real definition not only tells us what a thing is, but that it is real.[52] To conceive of a thing is to know how it is made, to know how to make it, and to be able to tell another how he should make it. A clear but indistinct idea like blue cannot be defined; but if I know how to make something blue, I can communicate this knowledge, which is conceptual instead of perceptual, to another, no matter how much his senses may differ from mine. But if I cannot make something blue, I do not know what blue really is. Conceivability, definability, constructability, and communicability all imply one another. In a laughable example, Tschirnhaus says that anyone who can define laughter will know how to make people laugh.[53]

Things that we can conceive in this way are real. Things we cannot conceive in this way may or may not be real; they may be proper objects of faith[54] which we accept as transcending our powers of knowledge, or objects of the senses which may or may not be real. An important task of the medicine of the mind is to find out which of the latter are indeed real.

To find out, we should not look, but think; we should act as if we had no perception of a thing, to see if we could then conceive it.[55] Tschirnhaus is a more extreme epistemological rationalist than any other German philosopher of his time. Experience is useful only as setting us under way; we begin with a posteriori knowledge, to be sure, but we should then go over to the a priori method to arrive back at our dubitable starting point, now made evident.[56]

The data of imagination and sense are subject to abstraction and analysis by the power of reason (*ratio*); but only the pure intellect (*intellectus purus*) has the intuitive power of knowing whether the "concepts" made

---

[51] *Ibid.*, pp. 52–53.

[52] Leibniz wrote Tschirnhaus (May, 1678) that "when the definition is once grasped, we cannot further doubt whether the thing defined is possible or not" (*Philosophical Papers and Letters*, trans. L. E. Loemker, p. 298), and later somewhat resented that Tschirnhaus claimed this as his own discovery (*ibid.*, pp. 569–570).

[53] *Medicina mentis*, p. 68.

[54] *Ibid.*, p. 58.

[55] *Ibid.*, p. 63.

[56] *Ibid.*, p. 290.

by the reason are real concepts or not. The medicine of the mind is to raise the conjunctions of the imagination and reason to the standard of the pure intellect.

For this testing of empirical knowledge, the methods of the mathematician are exemplary. While Tschirnhaus was never convinced of the power of Leibniz's *ars characteristica*, he recognized the gain in the power of the mind from substitution of symbols for words, the introduction of algorisms and calculating machinery, and controlled experiments. But in all of this he is more Cartesian than Leibnizian, and he explicitly relates his procedures to those prescribed in Descartes' four rules of method.[57] For him they are to eliminate the dubious, define the obvious, analyze the obscure, and connect the defined obvious with the analyzed obscure. He thinks that he has only formulated Descartes' rules in a more practical way. He is here certainly more detailed than Descartes, and writes what is almost a treatise on education and how to think critically and creatively.[58]

Like Descartes, Tschirnhaus opposed abstract logical inference in mathematics and favored a direct intuition of the necessity of connections. But definition plays a much more significant role in his work than in Descartes'. The mathematician defines objects which have no existence independent of the process by which they are defined. The first parabola came into existence when the first mathematician defined it, and he defined it by giving a rule for its construction, which showed that there is indeed a curve which meets the conditions stated in the tentative definition. A mathematical definition always consists of two parts, not genus and differentia but a fixed part and a movement. For example, a line is constructed by the movement of a point, the point being the fixed meaning, and its path the changeable element. When we know what a line is, we know how to construct it; and most of the many mathematical diagrams in the book are constructions of geometrical curves, with the hands, strings, and pegs clearly shown.

When we turn to the things of sense, which we think are real independently of whether we can define or construct them, we begin with something already given. This is a phantasm of the imagination. Reason abstracts from it to get to simple sensuous elements, which are then subjected to a further abstraction until we come to the clear and distinct sensory ideas of the solid and the liquid.[59] These correspond respectively to the fixed part and the movement in the objects of a mathematical definition. We know how a thing is made if we know the combination of the liquid and solid elements in its composition. We do not know this a priori, and to find it out we have to perform experiments. We then say that a sensible thing is

---

[57] *Ibid.*, pp. 11, 158–163.

[58] Some of his ideas deeply influenced August Hermann Francke and were applied in his famous orphans' school in Halle. Tschirnhaus' chief work on education was *Gründliche Anleitung zu nützlichen Wissenschaften*. A reprint of the fourth edition (1729) has been published (Stuttgart: Fromann, 1968) with an introduction by Eduard Winter, who includes some of the correspondence between Francke and von Tschirnhaus. This book, in fact, served in the eighteenth century as a popular introduction to the *Medicina mentis*.

[59] *Medicina mentis*, p. 87.

real, and not a mere phantasm, if we are able to make it by following rules, even though these rules are discovered, at least in part, through induction.

A more powerful method of proof of existence, however, is available to the *intellectus purus*, which forms the concept of the real physical world through combinations of the basic ideas of the impenetrable solid (the fixed element) and motion (the moving element) in the definition of a physical thing. The influence of the Cartesian concept of the material as the extended is present here, as well as the Spinozistic conception of a thing as defined by its "balance of motion and rest," but Tschirnhaus adds to these the clear and distinct idea of the impenetrable solid. He does not express himself on the views of the atomists, but is clear and explicit in his renunciation of substantial forms as valid in physical explanations.[60] All the sciences are reducible to physics, which operates with only these clear and distinct ideas. The physical world so defined is the basic subject matter of all science. Physics comprises our knowledge of the direct works of God; physics contributes even more than mathematics to quietude of mind and piety. We find that in this reduced physical world the objects of our imagination are not real at all, and this frees us of fear or excessive love of them. The discovery of this truth is the greatest and most lasting happiness. Hence an epistemology or methodology for knowledge of the physical world, based upon the mathematical ideal, is the true medicine of the mind.

We shall meet these ideas again, in a less rigid and more polished and humane form, when we come to the philosophy of Christian Wolff.

Note on Erhard Weigel

The University of Jena had its own rival of Descartes in a philosopher who cannot be wholly ignored in an account of German philosophy, yet who fits into no easy historical pattern. For his ideas alone he might well be ignored, but his personality and influence deserve notice. He was Erhard Weigel (1625–1699), professor of mathematics in Jena after 1653, who was repeatedly in scrapes with his colleagues because of his philosophical and theological teaching. He wanted to reform education by an emphasis upon the *realia* and upon first-hand experience; his lectures were made popular by spectacular demonstrations (which seem more than occasionally to have gone awry). He was a skillful and ingenious engineer and inventor, but there seems to have been a good bit of inspired foolishness in some of his Goldberg machines. He was involved in the adoption of the reformed calendar in Germany, but never accepted the Copernican system of astronomy. J. C. Sturm, Leibniz, and Pufendorf were among his pupils. It is not unlikely that he contributed to Leibniz's conception of the art of combinations and a *mathesis universalis*, even though he himself went hardly beyond the Lullian art. He definitely influenced Pufendorf, and his "moral sphere" (a mechanical, or at least geometrical, representation of moral and legal concepts) occupies an important place in Pufendorf's *Elementa jurisprudentiae universalis* (1672).[61] Wolff went to Jena in order to study under

---

[60] *Ibid.*, pp. 179, 293.
[61] Republished, with an English translation by W. A. Oldfather (Oxford: The Clarendon Press, 1931); see Definition VIII, pp. 181–195.

Weigel in the semester Weigel died, but undoubtedly came under Wei-
gelian influence through his disciple Paul Hebenstreit. For all these reasons
Weigel was a man to be taken more seriously than one would infer from
only reading his works.

"God has created and ordered everything in the world according to measure and weight, and if man is to act rightly, he must imitate this" is the
basic motto of Weigel's philosophy. But it was not the simplicity and rigor
of the mathematical method which made him extol measure and weight.
He had no sense of a new beginning in philosophy and mathematics, but
of an emendation of Aristotle through Euclid in method; and a Pythagorean
metaphysics was developed at the very moment when mechanics, not numerology, was the desideratum. A very loose use of the word *rechnen* (to
reckon, to calculate) permitted him to achieve a spurious "mathematization" of human thought and action in which not much difference is seen
between counting, inferring, knowing the measure and kind (*Maass und
Weis*) of all things, and "living according to measure." In his *Arithmetische
Beschreibung der Moral-Wissenschaft* (1674) we see the not very impressive consequences of such mathematization: there are two sexes, because
there are two kinds of numbers (odd and even), and since the tetractys is
the perfect number, the perfect family must consist of four persons, viz.,
the father, the mother, the child, and one servant. The theological faculty
at Jena seems not to have been either amused or impressed by similar proofs
of the doctrine of the Trinity, and Leibniz (*Theodicy*, § 384) gives a not
very happy mathematical proof of the existence of God proposed by his
erstwhile teacher.[62]

---

[62] It is not easy to take Weigel as seriously as many of his contemporaries seem to have
taken him. His books are now exceedingly rare, and I regret especially that all my efforts
to find *Von der Vortrefflichkeit der mathematischen Philosophie gegen der* [sic]
Scholastischen und Cartesianischen (1693) were unsuccessful, for, from its title, one
would infer that it would be more interesting than those books I was able to consult.
Still, from what I *have* seen, one may perhaps be permitted to entertain a doubt as to
whether I or my reader will suffer unduly from lack of first-hand knowledge of Weigel's
other writings.

X

Leibniz

Gottfried Wilhelm Leibniz was born in Leipzig July 1, 1646. He was the son of a Lutheran professor of moral philosophy in the university. He was a precocious child and, having the run of his father's library, by the age of twelve he was something of a prodigy in pedantic erudition. He entered the university in 1661 as a student of law. One of his teachers was Jacob Thomasius, the father of Christian Thomasius, and reputed to be the first "scientific historian" of philosophy. He spent one semester (1663) at Jena where he heard Erhard Weigel. Weigel's interest in mathematics and quasi-mystical Pythagoreanism may well have influenced Leibniz' thought in these directions too.

In 1666 Leibniz stood for the degree of doctor of law but was refused it by Leipzig on account of his age. He presented his dissertation to the University of Altdorf, and his defense of it so impressed the faculty that not only was the degree awarded, but he was offered a professorship, which he declined.

For a short time thereafter he lived in Nürnberg, where he became a member and secretary of a Rosicrucian lodge and developed an interest in chemistry. Acquaintance with Johann Christian von Boineburg, a diplomat normally in the service of Johann Philipp von Schönborn, Bishop Elector of Mainz, but at this time estranged from him, led to an appointment to the court in Mainz, where he was charged with responsibility for codifying the law and was a diplomatic correspondent. His friendship with von Boineburg, now again in the good graces of Mainz, soon enabled him to become a responsible councilor on diplomatic affairs. In 1669 he published a "geometrical demonstration" concerning the Polish succession (a demonstration that history did not accept). In 1680 he composed a significant and farsighted document on the security of the Empire, arguing for a strengthening of the Empire through a confederation of the Rhineland states for protection against France. A secret plan, perhaps originating in the mind of Boineburg, was devised for the protection of the Empire and the Netherlands against France. Louis XIV was to be enticed to attack Egypt (and thus indirectly rather than directly affect Holland) without damage to the German states through which he wished to send troops.

The years in Mainz were filled by work on codifying the law and writing on the foundations of jurisprudence. Leibniz began his theological studies to find a basis for a reunification of the churches, or at least for religious peace. This was to be presented in his (unfinished) *Catholic Demonstrations*. Here also began his serious studies in physics, but until he received mathematical training in Paris his cosmological ideas were of little value. He did, however, invent a calculating machine which was in advance of that of Pascal since it could not only add and subtract but also multiply, divide, and extract roots.

In 1672 he was sent to Paris to carry out some negotiations for von Boineburg and to lay the Egyptian plan before the king. Again he failed to affect the course of history, and could not deflect Louis's attack from the German and Dutch states. But his sojourn in Paris, however little effective in the grand politics of the time, was a major turning point in Leibniz' intellectual career. He was accepted in the circles of the foremost thinkers. He became acquainted with Colbert, Malebranche, Arnauld, and Huyghens. A brief trip to London on diplomatic business brought him the acquaintance of Henry Oldenburg, the secretary of the Royal Society, with whom he had corresponded while still in Mainz, and with Robert Boyle. The Royal Society elected him Fellow in 1673. Back in Paris by March of that year, he undertook the serious study of higher mathematics under the tutelage of Huyghens and made prodigious progress. By 1676, when he left Paris, he had perfected his version of the differential and integral calculus.

Had Leibniz done nothing but this, it would have sufficed to make his name immortal. But, in fact, the circumstances surrounding the origin of the calculus have clouded his name and fame for nearly two centuries. Hailed on the Continent as the inventor of the most powerful mathematical tool, he was censured in England as a plagiarist of Newton's work. Though he had his partisans—some of whom were not blameless in stirring up the trouble—and defenders, it was only in the nineteenth and twentieth centuries that impartial scholarship distributed the blame in an equitable way, demonstrated the independent genius of both the principals, and uncovered the less than admirable actions of almost everyone concerned in the problem, not excepting Newton and Leibniz themselves.

Though this takes us beyond the point we have reached in our brief recounting of Leibniz' life, it is well to finish this sorry story at once. In

1673 Leibniz learned from Henry Oldenburg something of what Newton was able to accomplish with a new and powerful method of analysis he had developed in 1666. Newton himself, without giving away the secret, indicated in a letter to Leibniz in 1676 some of the things accomplished with his method. Within three years of the first disclosure from Oldenburg (and within a few months of receiving Newton's letter, which was delayed), Leibniz had invented his own form of the calculus. He announced this to Oldenburg in 1677 and gave a full account of his work to Newton. He published his discoveries in the *Acta eruditorum* in 1684; this was indisputably the first publication of the calculus. In 1686 Newton published his *Principia*. It is clear that he had derived many of his results by the use of his method of fluxions, but he revealed nothing of this in the publication, where he followed classical geometrical methods. In a scholium (significantly omitted from later editions of the *Principia*), Newton wrote: "In letters which went between me and that most excellent geometer G. W. Leibniz, ten years ago, when I signified that I was in the knowledge of a method of determining maxima and minima, of drawing tangents and the like . . . that most distinguished man wrote back that he also had fallen upon a method of the same kind, and communicated his method, which hardly differed from mine except in the forms of words and symbols." Leibniz in 1684, however, did not mention Newton's invention. His reason for this omission may have been that he did not know *what* Newton's invention was but only what it could accomplish; he said later that since Newton was so secretive about it, it was not proper for him to reveal anything of Newton's works. His opponents, of course, gave a less favorable explanation of his silence. But, be it noted, from 1684 to 1686 there seems to have been nothing in the relations between Newton and Leibniz that would indicate less than full propriety, nothing that gave promise of the storm that was to break.

Had the matter rested there, certain things would have been commonly admitted. Newton first made the discovery of fluxions. Leibniz first published the calculus. He knew what Newton was doing, but not how. The fragmentary information Leibniz received may have sufficed to give a direction to his own work, but he cannot be said to have known sufficient details for what he claimed as his invention to have been something that was in fact Newton's. Even had that not been so, Leibniz' method was so much more general and powerful than Newton's that, were there plagiarism, it was a kind that only a creative mathematician could have committed—which is to say that it was not plagiarism at all but a genuine new step in mathematical analysis. Finally, it must be admitted that the idea of the calculus was so much in the air that if neither Newton nor Leibniz had hit upon it, surely someone else about the same time would have done so. When mathematicians in general were more interested in getting results than in enriching the armamentorium of mathematicians in general, and when Newton himself was one of the most secretive among them, Leibniz' readiness to expose his techniques for all to see was not without its virtue, even if the desire for fame was one of his motives.

In 1693 John Wallis (1616–1703), Savilian professor of geometry in Oxford said that Leibniz' calculus and Newton's fluxions were one and the same; but by this time Leibniz was enjoying acclaim as the inventor of the calculus. Thereafter the situation rapidly deteriorated, and both sides contributed to its worsening.

John Bernoulli, in collaboration with Leibniz, in 1696 challenged mathematicians to solve a problem (that of the brachystochrone) which could be worked out, they believed, only through the use of Leibniz' method. It was hoped that Newton, who by this time had largely lost interest in mathematics, either could not solve it, or in solving it would give evidence that his method of fluxions was essentially the same as Leibniz'. Newton did solve the problem in a few hours. In 1699 Bernoulli wrote, "I do not know whether Newton had developed his method until after he had seen [Leibniz'] calculus,"[1] and Leibniz wrote in the *Acta eruditorum* in 1699 that the problem could not be solved without his method. He listed those in possession of his method and included Newton's name in the list.

This offended the *amour propre* of Fatio de Duillier, a Swiss mathematician in London, who claimed to be one who could solve the problem without Leibniz' help. Fatio insinuated that if the correspondence between Newton and Leibniz could be examined, one might find that Leibniz had got his method from Newton. In 1704, in the *Optics*, Newton made the same insinuation. In the same year Leibniz published an anonymous review of Newton's method of fluxions which had been included as an appendix to the *Optics*, and in a vaguely worded charge insinuated either that his invention antedated Newton's, or that Newton had plagiarized from him, or both. In 1710 John Keill, professor of astronomy at Oxford, made the first clear and direct charge of plagiarism, accusing Leibniz. Leibniz forced a half-hearted and ambiguous apology from him in 1711 and requested an examination of the whole question by the Royal Society. A committee was appointed, stacked strongly with Newton's backers and (we now know[2]) working under Newton's thumb. The committee, without hearing Leibniz, published the correspondence and its findings, which were expressed with a studied ambiguity sufficient to make it appear that Newton's priority entailed Leibniz' plagiarism, since the committee held that Keill's accusation "ha[d] been in no way injurious to Mr. Leibniz." Thus the committee let it appear that it had confirmed Keill's accusation, when it had in fact answered only a question not in dispute, namely, that of priority.

Leibniz counterattacked, publishing anonymously a letter from Bernoulli in his defense. But Bernoulli now wished to be on good terms with the Royal Society and tried to hide his partisanship; he failed to do so only through an error of one of the editors of the *Acta eruditorum*, Christian Wolff, who, in changing Bernoulli's letter from the first to the third person, let one personal reference slip through which revealed the secret to Newton. The arbitration failed, and by then so much damage had been done, and feelings on both sides had become so implacable, that efforts to

---

[1] Quoted from Louis Trenchard More, *Isaac Newton, A Biography*, (New York: Scribner, 1934), p. 571. Chapter xv of More's book is a large-scale, fair-minded assessment of the entire problem, and I have drawn heavily upon it. Some of the Leibniz papers relevant to the quarrel have been translated by J. M. Child, *The Early Mathematical Manuscripts of Leibniz* (Chicago: Open Court, 1920).

[2] More, *Isaac Newton*, pp. 591, 605.

reach a fair-minded decision came to nothing. Only with the coming of French savants to the Berlin Academy in the 1740's did Newton get a fair hearing in Germany, and Leibniz had to wait until the middle of the nineteenth century for simple justice from English scholars.[3]

Political issues as well as personal and national pride played their parts in this sorry affair. The rivalry between the adherents of Leibniz and Newton, and finally between the giants themselves, became entangled with that between partisans for and against the Hanoverian succession in England. When the Elector of Hanover became King George I of England, it is likely that Leibniz was left behind in Germany because of his unhappy reputation in England. Only one good thing emerged from this regrettable series of events. Leibniz wrote his friend Caroline of Anspach, Princess of Wales, to warn her against the atheism of Hobbes and the mechanism of Newton, which might threaten her religious faith. The princess revealed this to the English divine Samuel Clarke (1675–1729), who preached a sermon on the metaphyhical issues between Newton and Leibniz, and the princess then served as the intermediary in the famous Leibniz–Clarke correspondence, to which we shall come later in our exposition of Leibniz' philosophy.

But, back to Paris! Though Leibniz wished to remain in the French capital but found no suitable patronage, he accepted appointment in 1676 to the court of Braunschweig-Lüneburg as councilor to Duke Johann Friedrich. He went from Paris via London and Amsterdam (where he had conversations with van Leeuwenhoek and Spinoza) to Hanover.

The years in Hanover were incredibly busy. In engineering works in the Harz mountains, Leibniz was in charge of efforts to free the mines of water. The major official task, however, was to support the dynastic ambitions of the Guelph family, ambitions which led to the dukedom being raised to electoral status in the Empire and, finally, to the accession of Duke Georg Ludwig to the crown of Great Britain as George I. Leibniz's responsibility was to prepare a history of the family. His research into and publication of archives have given Leibniz a place among the founders of the scientific study and treatment of documents. He was in Italy from 1687 to 1690 on this mammoth work; in the last years of his life he complained about its demands on his time, and at his death he had succeeded in bringing the history and collection of documents down only to the eleventh century. Upon his return to Hanover from Italy he became the director of the ducal library at Wolfenbüttel, the position Lessing, one of his greatest admirers, later occupied.

Diplomatic and research missions took Leibniz to Munich and Vienna. In Vienna he met Peter the Great, and devised plans for an academy in St. Petersburg. He also became acquainted with Prince Eugene of Savoy, for whom the *Principles of Nature and of Grace* was written.

Philosophically more important than all these manifold occupations, however, was still another official task which had more bearing upon Leib-

[3] The turning point was Augustus de Morgan's *Essays on the Life and Work of Newton* (three papers, 1846 to 1855, reprinted Chicago and London: Open Court, 1914).

niz' career as a philosopher. Not only was Leibniz himself a man who disliked disharmony and conflict, but since Johann Friedrich was a Catholic prince in a largely Protestant state, he had political responsibilities as well as personal and philosophical motives for his activities directed to bringing about a reunification of the churches. Hanover was a focal point in the negotiations going on between Rome, Vienna, and the electors of northern Germany, by which there was hope of bringing them back into the Catholic Church. Many plans were drawn up for church union at this time. Leibniz' efforts in Mainz to demonstrate the essential agreement of Catholic and Protestant teachings on the Eucharist, and in Paris to find points of agreement with the Jansenists, were renewed in a long correspondence with the principal Catholic apologist of the time, Bossuet. (We shall examine some of the irenic points in Leibniz's theological thinking later.)

The years in Hanover were the most fruitful in Leibniz' life. While carrying a full load of official duties which required extensive travel, he was incredibly productive of published and unpublished contributions to law, history, theology, mathematics, and physics; he was an active and skillful intellectual in politics, and a clever propagandist; he carried on the largest intellectual correspondence of anyone in Europe and for this alone, had he not himself been a many-sided genius, he would have deserved Frederick the Great's apothegm, that he was an academy in himself. These were the years, too, when what the world knows as Leibniz' philosophy came to maturity. The most important writings in philosophy were the *Meditations on Knowledge, Truth, and Ideas* (1684), *Discourse on Metaphysics* (1686; unpublished until the nineteenth century), *A New System of Nature and Communication of Substances* (1695) and several replies to criticisms of it; *New Essays Concerning Human Understanding* (written in the 1690's but unpublished until 1765), *On the Radical Origination of Things* (1697), *On Nature Itself* (1698), *Theodicy* (1709), and three posthumous works: *The Monadology* and *The Principles of Nature and of Grace* (both 1714) and the *Correspondence* with Samuel Clarke (1715–16), many smaller unpublished pieces, and parts of his correspondence.

In Hanover, Leibniz' patroness was the Electress Sophie; when her daughter Sophie Charlotte became Electress of Brandenburg (later Queen of Prussia), Leibniz had a powerful and devoted friend and pupil in each court and divided his time between Berlin and Hanover. Through Sophie Charlotte, Leibniz was finally able to achieve his ambition of establishing an Academy of Sciences, and in 1700 it was founded by her husband, with Leibniz as president for life.[4] Upon the death of Queen Sophie Charlotte[5] in 1705 his connection with the Berlin court was terminated, however, and

[4] A fuller account of the Berlin Academy will be found in Chapter XIII.

[5] The admiration Leibniz felt for these two remarkable women, Sophie and her daughter Sophie Charlotte, was returned by them in full. Frederick the Great, Sophie Charlotte's grandson, described her deathbed scene. She told a weeping lady-in-waiting, "Do not grieve for me. For I go now to satisfy my curiosity about things Leibniz was never able to explain to me, about space, the infinite, being and nothing. And for my husband the king, I afford the spectacle of a funeral procession which will give him another opportunity to show off" (quoted from Kuno Fischer, *Leibniz* [Heidelberg, 1889], p. 128).

he was no longer in continuous charge of the Academy, which, like the Royal Society (but unlike the French Academy), took no notice of his death.

The last years of Leibniz' life were shadowed by ill-health and disappointment. He was a courtier, and a neglected courtier is miserable; he was peremptorily ordered to remain in Hanover to continue his work on the history when the Elector Georg Ludwig went to London to ascend the British throne. He died in Hanover on November 14, 1716.

Leibniz never succeeded in giving a comprehensive and coherent presentation of his entire philosophy. "My system," he wrote in 1696, "is not a complete body of philosophy, and I make no claim to give a reason for everything which others have sought to explain."[6] Nor has any historian of philosophy written a wholly systematic presentation that satisfies others who, with most of the same documents before them, present quite different but perhaps equally comprehensive and consistent accounts. Each reminds us that Leibniz was a mathematician, a diplomat, a theologian, a lawyer, a physicist, an engineer and inventor, a logician, and a metaphysician. A being of so many dimensions cannot be pictured without a choice of perspectives, and no man has presented as many faces to the historian of philosophy as Leibniz did. It is not to be wondered that historians do not agree about "the real Leibniz." Leibniz, more than any other philosopher, was all things to all men. His system, he says, "appears to unite Plato and Democritus, Aristotle and Descartes, the scholastics with the moderns, theology and ethics with the reason. It seems to take the best from all sides, and then it goes much farther than any has yet gone."[7] One should not be astonished that some of these apparently incompatible ingredients of his philosophy tend, when anyone "interprets" it, to precipitate out of it; and we have Leibniz the Aristotelian, Leibniz the Platonist, Leibniz the nominalist, Leibniz the logician with a derivative metaphysics, Leibniz a Pythagorean, or a Paracelsist, or a mystic, or even a neo-Kantian. Each of these pictures, like a Leibnizian monad, reflects the entire universe of his philosophy from its own point of view, and each has been taken to be the *true* picture.

We shall make no effort to show one of these to be true at the expense of the others, or to find a true Leibniz hidden rather than revealed by them. We shall see Leibniz as, I think, he saw the world itself; he was a baroque philosopher in a baroque world:

[6] Gottfried Wilhelm Leibniz, *Philosophical Papers and Letters*, trans. and ed. Leroy E. Loemker, 2 vols. (Chicago: University of Chicago Press, 1956), p. 22. All citations to Leibniz' writings, unless otherwise noted, are to this edition, indicated by the name Loemker; the pagination is continuous, and hence the volume number is omitted from the citations. The date of writing, when known, is indicated in parentheses. *Discourse on Metaphysics, Monadology*, and *Principles of Nature and of Grace*, though included in Loemker, are cited by article or paragraph number in order to facilitate the use of any of the several translations of them which exist.

[7] *New Essays on the Human Understanding*, trans. A. G. Langley (Evanston: Open Court, 1949), bk. I, chap. i, p. 66. All citations to the *New Essays* are to this translation.

I see all things regulated and adorned, beyond anything conceived of up to this time; organic matter everywhere; no sterile, neglected vacuum; nothing too uniform, everything varied but with order; and, what surpasses the imagination, the whole universe in epitome, but with a different aspect in each of its parts and even in each of its unities of substance.[8]

The very metaphor of "picture" is too static to represent Leibniz. His intellectual career resembles a fugue.

The first theme introduced is from logic; then voices from law, theology, mathematics, physics, international politics, metaphysics, biology, and psychology come in, repeating the theme from logic or varying it but living its own life. At any moment, a cross section of all his thoughts shows a marvelous harmony, with the same or analogous concepts undergoing like development in each of the staves. Strauss might compose a symphonic poem on *Also sprach Zarathustra*, but only a fugue could present Leibniz' intellectual career.[9]

The Organization of Knowledge

Leibniz' *Dissertation on the Art of Combinations* of 1666 contains one of his less important contributions to mathematics, but one both highly expressive of his dominant intellectual traits and destined to play a very important part of his later philosophical work. This was his formula for determining the number of complexions (combinations and permutations) of the components of a complex group, whole, expression, or number. While not without some arithmetical interest, this work was written by the twenty-year-old Leibniz before he became a real mathematician but was already an enthusiast for the rather elementary mathematics he then knew. His interest in it was based on the belief that the theory of combinations had an important contribution to make to various disciplines, where complete analysis and exhaustive classification of complex concepts or cases were needed. Thus among other examples of its use (one chosen from organ-playing, calculating the number of combinations of registers of an organ), Leibniz discovered that jurisconsults had omitted a possible species of cases in the law of contracts; and he recommended the calculation of the number of species of possible cases so that they could be specifically decided in legislation instead of being left to the court when a new and unexpected combination comes before it for which there is no statute law.

This essay of Leibniz belongs in a long tradition of thought which began with the Franciscan Raymond Lull (d. 1315), whose *Ars magna* Leibniz

[8] *Ibid.*, bk. I, chap. i, p. 68.

[9] This image is no doubt fanciful, but it is not fantastic. For in studying Leibniz I found it useful to use a kind of fugal schema. I took large sheets which I dated, one for each year of Leibniz' career. I divided the sheets into sections, marked off by principal concepts, and then pasted slips of paper with key sentences in these slots. It was dramatic to see an idea in one slot on one page reappear in other slots a few pages later, to see how consistent Leibniz was on any one or two pages, to see how much change there was between distant pages, and to notice how little there was in any one slot that did not have a harmonic counterpart in the other "staves."

cited. Lull, working with cabalistic and Neoplatonic number-mysticism, sketched a system wherein important ideas would be symbolized by letters and distributed in fanciful geometrical figures, which could be varied in more or less mechanical ways to show their relationships. But the choice of things to be symbolized and the manner of their combination were unsystematic, or at least the system had nothing to do with logical relationships.[10] The result is that the manipulations in the Lullian art seem to us to be more like those of word-magic and crossword puzzles than those of logic. Bruno and Agrippa of Nettesheim introduced the Lullian art into Germany, and in Herborn in the seventeenth century in the writings of Johann Heinrich Alsted it became associated also with Ramist logic in the plans for his great encyclopaedia, or *catalogue raisonné*, of human knowledge. A rigorous and not arbitrary and fanciful practice of the Lullian art, however, required more than the use of symbols and geometrical analogies for determining the relations of terms to each other. It might produce an artificial or ideal language useful as a kind of theological *lingua franca* (this was one of Lull's purposes) but it could not be an art of discovery or demonstration. In addition to the outward trappings of mathematical symbolism, there was needed also a method of combination and analysis, and this was to be sought in algebra.

It is possible that the original idea for Leibniz' dissertation is to be found in the work of Erhard Weigel, whom he heard in Jena. Weigel saw a philosophical use of mathematics in ethics, as Leibniz here sees it in the reform of law. But much more important than Weigel's rather fanciful ideas was Hobbes's conception of logic as a kind of computation. (Leibniz did not at this time see his own work in connection with the ideal of a *mathesis universalis* expressed by Descartes, whose works he did not know well until the next decade.) In the further development of Leibniz' seminal idea of an art of combination, however, Hobbes's nominalistic conception of logic was not accepted by Leibniz; the particular turn his work took must be understood as a corollary of his general commitment to a mathematical Platonism closer in spirit to Kepler and Weigel than to Hobbes. It was the ontology of mathematics as much as its methodology that appealed to Leibniz, who said: "When God calculates and exercises his thought the world (with all individuals in it) is made."[11]

During the next two decades, in which Leibniz made his greatest contributions to mathematics itself, his own conception of a *mathesis universalis* took form under the name of the *ars characteristica*. This was to be a universal mathematics of thought, an art of discovery, a universal language, and the principle of a complete synthesis of knowledge in a great encyclopaedia. No philosopher, I think, has been so confident as Leibniz was that he had discovered an intellectual panacea. In Leibniz' accounts of

[10] Leibniz, *Fragmente zur Logik*, ed. Franz Schmidt (Berlin: Akademie Verlag, 1960), p. 18 (1686).

[11] Quoted from L. E. Loemker, "Substance and Process in Leibniz," in *Process and Divinity*, ed. W. R. Reese and Eugene Freeman (La Salle, Ill.: Open Court, 1964), p. 407n) The date is 1677.

what can be accomplished by its means, he says it will increase the power of the mind just as microscopes and telescopes increase the power of the eye; it will be to the discoverer what the compass is to the sailor;[12] it will make arguments about all questions as easily resolvable as disputes in arithmetic; "If we had an established characteristic we might reason as safely in metaphysics as in mathematics."[13] It

will become the great method of discovering truths, establishing them, and irresistibly teaching them when they are established . . . When this language is once established among missionaries, it will spread at once around the world . . . Wherever it is received, there will be no difficulty in establishing the true religion, which is always the most reasonable. . . . Advantageous changes will follow everywhere in piety and morals and, in short, in increasing the perfection of mankind.[14]

In this general characteristic the art of combinations supplies the rudiments of the necessary calculus, but only the rudiments. The syntax, or calculus, of the new language is much more general than that of the theory of combinations, and, in fact, is worked out in one of Leibniz' principal contributions to thought, the conception of a systematic demonstrative symbolic logic. Instead of using the fanciful arrangements of the Lullian art or the arithmetic of combinations, Leibniz invents an algebra of thought. It is regrettable that much of Leibniz' most original and soundest contributions to this conception was unknown until the end of the nineteenth-century, after many of his discoveries had been made independently by later workers.[15]

What was newest in Leibniz' conception, and what advanced it much farther than anything found among his German predecessors (though there are some anticipations of this, without the logical calculus, in the English writers Wilkins and Delgarno) was his theory of the vocabulary, or the characters, to be used in the new language. Unlike Hobbes, Leibniz believed that we are not restricted to giving nominal definitions of concepts, so that truth is merely the consequence of an arbitrary imposition of signs and stipulated definitions of them; he does not even agree with Locke that there are no natural—in contrast to conventional and arbitrary—signs in ordinary

---

[12] Loemker, p. 344 (1679).

[13] Ibid., p. 297 (in a letter to von Tschirnhaus, 1678).

[14] Ibid., p. 402 (1679). See "Preface to the General Science" (1677) in Wiener, P. P., Leibniz Selections (New York: Scribner's, 1951), p. 51: "If someone should doubt my results, I should say to him: 'Let us calculate, Sir,' and thus by taking to pen and ink, we should soon settle the question."

[15] See C. I. Lewis, A Survey of Symbolic Logic (orig. publ., 1918; New York: Dover, 1960), pp. 5–18; William and Mary Kneale, The Development of Logic (Oxford: The Clarendon Press, 1962), pp. 320–345. The most convenient collections of Leibniz' writings on logic are Franz Schmidt, Fragmente zur Logik, and G. H. R. Parkinson, Leibniz, Logical Papers (Oxford: The Clarendon Press, 1966). The fullest study is by Louis Couturat, La Logique de Leibniz (Paris, 1901; reprint, Hildesheim: G. Olms, 1961), whose title is unduly restrictive, for the book is a valuable study of all phases of Leibniz' theory of knowledge and method.

language.[16] As a true Platonist, both in regard to the origin and the objects of our rational knowledge, Leibniz believed that we can discover real definitions and that we can know, at least partially, the real essences and not merely the nominal essences of substances.

We find real definitions by the analysis of our experiences, either internal or external; we begin with clear ideas, which we render distinct by analysis. Real definitions show that the thing defined is possible, while, on the other hand, nominal definitions can be given even of impossible things; and before we use a definition in a proof (as, for example, we use a definition of God in the ontological proof of his existence) we must show that the thing defined is possible, i.e., has a real and not merely a nominal definition. What follows from a real definition is ontologically true, while what follows from a nominal definition is only verbally true. A real definition is given when we make an analysis of the concept of the definiendum into other concepts whose possibility is already known because they are simple and contain no contradiction and are given in intuition, or when we can state the method by which the definiendum can be produced either causally, by mathematical construction, or by logical synthesis from clear and distinct intuitive and indemonstrable ideas.[17] The simple ideas into which every complex conception must be analyzed are real possibilities, essences or thoughts in the mind of God, and even, Leibniz sometimes says, attributes of the divine mind, or the forms of the valid acts of thought by the human mind.[18] Ideas are real possibilities; concepts may or may not adequately represent them. All of our thinking employs concepts in the mind, but true thinking involves also ideas or real possibilities and essences.

Now, armed with this Platonic theory of real possibilities given in real definitions, Leibniz is prepared to add to the calculus of combinations a necessary vocabulary of real characters. Let simple symbols represent simple ideas or possibilities; then use polynomial symbols or defined symbols for complex ideas, fitting the analysis of the complex ideas. Every correct name of a complex idea, so formed, will be equivalent to a definition of the idea named and a demonstration of its possibility. Algebra and geometry stand in such a relation of their characters to each other; maps and models are characters of countries and machines; but the most vivid example we have of the fruitfulness of this conception, as Loemker has pointed out, is one not known to Leibniz: the nomenclature of organic chemistry. For if a chemist is given the systematic name of a compound (e.g., *sym*-dichloroisopropylol), he can draw a structural formula (another "character" of it) and know, in most cases, whether it is a possible compound, how to synthesize it, and what some of its most important properties will be.

Leibniz at various times tried out various possibilities for systematically constructing a vocabulary available to all men in whatever science they

---

16 On Hobbes's theory of nominal definition and arbitrary truth, see Loemker, 199, 355, 371 (1670, 1679). On Locke's theory of merely conventional signs and nominal essences as objects of knowledge, see New Essays, II, vi, § 27; III, vi, §§ 24 and 32; IV, v, §§ 3–8.

17 Loemker, p. 355 (1679); p. 452 (1684).   18 Ibid., p. 452 (1684).

worked, or whatever language they spoke. The most interesting one is that in which simple ideas are symbolized by prime numbers, complex ideas by factorable numbers, and the syntax is that of ordinary arithmetic. In this scheme the proper name of a complex idea, upon factoring, gives us its definitions; convertible propositions are equations; in I-propositions (Some S is P) the subject and the predicate have a common factor, in E-propositions (No S is P) there are no common factors. In an A-proposition (all S is P) the number of the predicate is a factor in the number of the subject; this is the mathematical sense of Leibniz' assumption that the predicate is contained in the subject of a true affirmative proposition.

For the general characteristic to succeed, three things are necessary. First, we must have a complete inventory of simple ideas so that we can have a complete vocabulary of characters. Second, we must have an inventory of most of the important complex ideas and their analyses. These will be drawn largely from the sciences with a systematic structure, but much empirical and rule-of-thumb knowledge should be included too; and inspection of this inventory will show gaps in our knowledge, so that experiments can be efficiently chosen and planned. Leibniz was a maker of opulent plans; not only was he himself probably more competent than any other man who ever lived to accomplish these two tasks—and he was not competent to do so—but he saw that they would require a joint effort to an army of experts properly organized into learned academies and working on a mammoth encyclopedia. Even here, however, he minimized the stupendous difficulties of the task, believing that it was something that could be accomplished in a relatively short time if properly supported.[19] To secure this support was a principal occupation of Leibniz as the intellectual entrepreneur of Christendom, the true German heir of Bacon. It was to be the task of the academies he wished to establish to construct an ideal encyclopaedia, based on, and contributing to, international intellectual cooperation.

The third condition for success in this venture is that the underlying logic be adequate to support the superstructure. An inquiry into this condition leads to the heart of Leibniz's logic. At this point, the expositor of Leibniz is faced with the problem of having to try to say everything at once instead of giving only one thin melodic line. For *Leibniz' metaphysical conception of the world is that the world is so constituted that the ideal of the art of characteristic is achievable.* Yet the world picture is not comprehensible without the general characteristic which would be the only adequate language in which to express it. It is impossible to describe both at once, but it is impossible to make either intelligible in disregard of the other. But if the reader will remember, in what follows, that by "complete notion" Leibniz sometimes means in logic what he calls substantial form and monad in his metaphysics,[20] we may be able to follow one statement of the main theme before entry of the second voice of the philosophic fugue.

The basic thesis of Leibniz' logic is that the predicate is contained in

---

[19] Loemker, p. 344 (ca. 1679).   [20] Loemker, p. 414 (1680–84).

the intension of the subject of a true affirmative proposition.[21] This thesis was not original with Leibniz; it can be found in Aristotle and many scholastic writers as well as in Arnauld's and Nicole's *L'Art de penseé* (*Port Royal Logic*). It was almost a commonplace; but Leibniz took it more literally and more seriously than anyone else and gave it a metaphysical as well as a logical interpretation.

In logic, Leibniz is committed to the treatment of all propositions as if they were in subject-predicate form. Though he admired Jungius' work on relational propositions and relational inferences, he did not give up the view just expressed, and attempted to avoid a logic of irreducible relations by substituting a logic of relational predicates.[22] Such a restrictive logic, however, requires the addition of metaphysical assumptions that have no place in logic if well-founded inferences are to be recognized as correct. "Brutus killed Caesar" implies, in Jungius' logic, that "Caesar was killed by Brutus," by conversion of the relation "kill." But in logic restricted to subject-copula-predicate, the first is equivalent to "Brutus was 'the killer of Caesar' " and second to "Caesar was 'killed by Brutus'," and the first does not, in subject-predicate logic, entail the second; from "S is P" we cannot here infer another predicate P' for another subject S'. Leibniz can say that a world in which the first is true is one in which the second is true too; but this is because of a metaphysical harmony between the states of two substances.

A second difficulty in such a program lies in the problem of the relation of simple ideas to each other. The theory of combinations produced, naturally, combinations which were not really possible though they contained no logical contradiction, for Leibniz taught that all simple positive terms are compossible and that negative terms are not simple.[23] There can be no contradiction between "S is P" and "S is Q" if P and Q are simple terms, yet Leibniz knew full well that some combinations represented by the character "P · Q" are not really possible. For example, he eliminated some logically possible combinations of properties as complex properties of impossible chemical elements.[24] Two alternatives were open to him. He could simply, by direct intuition, see the compatibility or incompatibility of simple terms or properties, whereupon he would have to give up the hypothesis that the only relation between S and P is that of logical inclusion or exclusion. Or, second, he would have to give up the hypothesis that ideas seen to be incompatible with each other are simple. Whichever choice he made, he would have to acknowledge that first-order combinations of simple ideas

[21] Leibniz is concerned with the intensional relations of the subject and predicate and acknowledges his divergence in this respect from scholastic logic. He says that an extensional inclusion (S is contained in P) could be handled by an inversion of his own calculus, but he prefers to begin with universal concepts and their composition because they do not depend upon the existence of individuals. See Loemker, p. 365 (1679).

[22] On Jungius' theory, see Chapter IX. It should be noted that Leibniz' general characteristic and his symbolic logic are not, in principle, dependent upon this theory of the proper form of the proposition. Leibniz' preference for the subject-predicate form is based rather on the logical tradition and his metaphysical preferences, and it proves to be inconveniently restrictive both in his logic and his general characteristic. It is Bertrand Russell's view that it was determinative of his entire metaphysics.

[23] Loemker, p. 260 (1676).   [24] *Ibid.*, pp. 126, 131, 353–354 (1666, 1679).

are generically and structurally different from the higher-order combinations of complex ideas. But philosophers before Kant do not seem to have been able to see the quite different kind of necessity which may connect two simple ideas and that which connects a simple with a complex idea. Because the latter may be analytic and logically necessary, and because the first also may be known a priori, pre-Kantian philosophers repeatedly tried to reduce both to a single rubric, of the kind we find in Leibniz' maxim that all true affirmative propositions have the predicate contained in the subject. In this, he was followed by many in the eighteenth century who professed the official view that all true propositions are of the kind Kant was to call analytic, while, in fact, they recognized some non-self-contradictory combinations which "cannot be really thought together."[25] Leibniz was no clearer on this question than other pre-Kantian Enlightenment philosophers. He speaks of truths knowable *per se* and contrasts them with demonstrable truths, but then immediately seems to think that the former are only *identities*.[26] In the *New Essays*[27] he recognizes, in addition to assertions of real existence, "primitive truths of fact" such as "I think, therefore I am" and "I have different ideas" which are obviously not identities. But what was needed was a clear recognition that two concepts may be necessarily but not analytically related; this was often in fact acknowledged, but no theoretical basis for it was given, and in fact it was far too often explicitly denied.

Leibniz certainly denies it, because he thinks analysis of complex combinations will eventually lead to explicit identities, that is, to logical truths. For Leibniz, even mathematical axioms, which Kant was to argue were necessary but not analytic, are reducible to definitions and identities.[28] Where propositions are not so reducible, Leibniz says we have to do with truths of fact and not of reason, and truths of fact have a lower epistemic status and certainty than truths of reason. Leibniz' theory of judgment, according to which the predicate is contained in the subject, actually fits only the judgments in which the predicate can be found in a finite number of steps to be contained in the subject concept as part of its definition. Leibniz does not restrict his theory in this way, however, and is committed to the view that all true propositions are analytic, either virtually or explicitly. The subject contains all the predicates which hold of it. If it does not, either the judgment that S has some specific P is false, or S names only a partial concept of the true subject of the judgment. Leibniz regarded the subject-term of a true proposition as if it were the proper name of a possible or real entity (individual substance) which is related to its attributes in exactly the same way as a universal concept is related to its predicates. "It is the nature of an individual substance or complete being to have a concept so complete that it is sufficient to make us understand and deduce from it all the predicates of the subject to which the concept is

[25] We shall see many examples of this in the eighteenth century in discussions of Hoffmann, Crusius, Lambert, and others.
[26] Loemker, p. 260 (1676); similarly on "original truths" and the "natural light", *Ibid.*, 408–409 (1679) and pp. 893–894 (1704).
[27] Book IV, i, § 7 and ii, § 1.
[28] Loemker, pp. 238, 286, 348, 356 (1675, 1678, 1679).

attributed."[29] Subjects that do not designate complete concepts are incomplete symbols for mere *entia rationis*, names of abstractions which do not refer to completely determined individual things; thus mathematical objects (number, line) are not real, and their concepts are abstract.[30] Propositions containing abstract subject-terms should be reconstructed in such a manner as to contain a subject-term which does refer to an individual possibility or real thing.[31] About so-called abstract universals, Leibniz was metaphysically a nominalist in holding that all existence is individual; universals exist only *in mens*, though they are founded on the specific and individual determinations of individual essences. About *individual subjects*, on the other hand, Leibniz was—if a paradox be permitted—a Platonic or Scotist realist in the sense that there is no irreducible particularity. For the individual thing is related to its attributes exactly in the same manner that a universal is related to the predicates it contains and to the totality of which it is logically equivalent. The locus of the true universal has been shifted from the predicate to the subject position, for the subject names a completely determined individual possibility. The subject is the complete concept of the thing, not a class concept, but the representation of an idea which "determines the principle of generality adequate for an individual."[32]

Since all true propositions are actually or virtually analytic, demonstration is a series of substitutions of synonymous expressions performed until an explicit identity emerges. For Descartes, demonstration was a chain of intuitions; for Leibniz, a chain of definitions. There is no important logical difference between analysis and synthesis, for a chain of identities can be read equally well in either direction. But methodologically analysis is more important when we are solving problems which turn up accidentally, and synthesis more important in discovering truths which may be "set aside for later use when some question happens to arise."[33]

If the reduction of a nonidentical to an identical proposition takes place in a finite number of steps, the truth in question is called a truth of reason. Truths of reason are not only certain and known a priori, but they are necessary. They are true of every possible world; even God could not abrogate them in the creation of this world. Truths of fact, on the other hand, are contingent, and their opposite is possible. They cannot be reduced to identities (even by God, who cannot come to the end of an infinite series) in a finite number of steps; yet they nonetheless are said to have "a priori demonstrations of their truth which make them certain and which show that the relation of subject and predicate of these propositions has its basis in the nature of both."[34] Demonstration of these truths must be possible because of the principle of sufficient reason, to wit, "There can be found no fact that is true or existent, or any true proposition, without there being

---

[29] *Discourse on Metaphysics* § 8 (1686).

[30] Loemker, p. 873 (1704). Yet judgments relating them are explicitly analytic.

[31] "In philosophizing accurately, only concrete terms should be used." Incidentally, "No European language is better suited than German for . . . testing and examination of philosophical doctrines by a living tongue. For German is very rich and complete in real-terms, to the envy of all other languages." Loemker, pp. 195, 193 (1670).

[32] *Ibid.*, p. 515 (1686; to Arnauld).   [33] *Ibid.*, p. 287 (1678).

[34] *Discourse on Metaphysics* § 13 (1686); *Mondalogy*, § 33 (1715).

a sufficient reason for its being so and not otherwise, although we cannot know these reasons in most cases."[35] Because they can be demonstrated, they are certain; but because they are not logical truths or reducible to logical truths, they are not necessary but contingent. They are not necessary in any sense: their contradictories are not self-contradictory; nor are the propositions themselves, in their unreduced forms, contradictory to any other proposition which is necessary; nor are they true in all possible worlds.

It may well be asked, therefore, by what right does Leibniz say that they are demonstrable a priori. It is a very weak sense of "demonstrable" to use it to say merely that we know there is a reason for the proposition which is sufficient for its truth, for we could *say* this of a proposition which we believed but which was, in fact, false. The principle of sufficient reason could never show a false proposition to be false; hence it can never show a true one to be true. Unlike demonstration of necessary truths, the "demonstration" of contingent truths does not add any legitimate assurance to our assent to them.[36]

But Leibniz accomplishes two purposes with his claim for a priori demonstrations of contingent truths. First, by distinguishing between the two kinds of propositions, he is able to distinguish between truths which hold necessarily in any possible world because they express relations among real possibilities only, and truths which in fact hold only in this actual world. The first are truths in the antecedent intellect of God, the latter become true upon the contingent creation of this world. He believes that this distinction permits him to distinguish the certainty of propositions from their

[35] *Monadology* § 32 (1715); *New Essays*, III, iii, § 6; Loemker, pp. 349, 407 (1679).
[36] Presented somewhat schematically, Leibniz is arguing as follows:
(1) All affirmative judgments are either explicitly or virtually analytic, since the predicate is in the subject.
(2) If they are explicitly analytic or reducible to explicit analytic judgments in a finite number of steps, the judgment is demonstrable by the law of contradiction and is true of every possible world.
(3) If condition (2) is not met, the demonstration would involve an infinite number of steps, and neither we nor God can terminate an infinite series.
(4) But even under condition (3) there must be a reason for the judgment, since the principle of sufficient reason holds. Assuming the principle of sufficient reason and denying that the proposition has a reason would be self-contradictory.
(5) The principle of sufficient reason, however, would hold even if the contradictory of asserted truth of fact were true; hence the judgment to be demonstrated is not deducible from the principle of sufficient reason.
(6) But there is a contingent truth, to wit, that the sufficient reason for the creation of the world in which the judgment in question is true is that this world is the world of maximum perfection (see p. 227).
(7) Hence we can know that the judgment, if true at all, is in principle demonstrable from the principle of sufficient reason and the principle of maximum perfection, even though we do not know the specification of the principle of perfection that would make it possible for us to deduce the specific judgment in question from the principle of perfection.
(8) Even if we did know the detailed application of the principle of perfection, however, this would not make the judgment in question absolutely necessary, but only contingently necessary, since the principle of perfection is itself contingent.

necessity, and thus to make a contribution to the solution of the problem arising from God's foresight of evil free actions. For God can with certainty know that Adam will fall without "Adam will fall" being a necessary truth.[37] The distinction is therefore of great importance in natural theology and theodicy.

Second, because the sufficient reason of things is to be found in God's free choice of the world which contains the maximum of perfection, the principle of sufficient reason is a teleological principle which must be used to supplement the principles based on mathematical necessity. Because the best of all possible worlds is one in which the simplest laws govern the greatest variety of phenomena, the principle of sufficient reason gives rise to other more specific regulative or heuristic principles such as those of parsimony, continuity, least action, conservation of force, and identity of indiscernibles. These, while they do not demonstrate the truth of a given proposition, do often suggest it to us before we have evidence for it or render it intelligible and unsurprising once it is found. The method of "a priori demonstration of contingent truths" involves the "discovery of the interior constitution of bodies a priori from the contemplation of God" and is perhaps of use only to "superior geniuses" and "in a better life," while the method of hypothesis—of conjecture according to the regulative principles just mentioned, like a conjecture about a meaning which may lead us to discover the key to a cryptogram—may lead to "morally certain hypotheses sufficient for everyday use."[38] Attractively unlike many philosophers, Leibniz grew less dogmatic rather than more, and what was once put forward as metaphysical truths outfitted with demonstrations came later to be seen by Leibniz to be hypotheses instead of axioms or demonstrated but contingent truths.

We have now traced one line of Leibniz' thought, the logical and methodological, as far as we can while making only occasional reference to the metaphysics which was supposed to be its ontological base. We must now supplement this by considering the development of Leibniz' metaphysics from about 1666 to the end of his life. This will occupy us in the next four sections; then the two somewhat independent expositions will converge again in the section entitled "The Middle Way," where the counterpoint of the two voices will become explicit.

Substantial Form

At an early age (he says fifteen,[39] but it was probably somewhat later) Leibniz, walking in the Rosenthal in Leipzig, reached a decision between the old and the new philosophy. Was he to continue as he was being

---

[37] This distinction is not original with Leibniz; the scholastics distinguished between "necessity of consequence" and "necessity of the thing consequent" and held that the former did not entail the latter. The distinction between determining and inclining reasons was likewise a standard scholastic distinction Leibniz used to elucidate God's relation to necessary and to free actions.

[38] Loemker, p. 437 (1682–84).   [39] *Ibid.*, p. 1064 (1714).

trained, viz., as a scholastic, or was he to accept the new philosophy, which favored and was favored by mathematical and mechanical study of nature? Specifically, he had to decide what stand he would take on a central scholastic concept used in the interpretation of nature, that of substantial form.

At that time he decided in favor of the modern view. But he subsequently returned to a highly revised conception of substantial form and, in its thoroughly revised conception, it became one of Leibniz' best-known and most characteristic ideas, that of monad, the individual substance whose complete concept we have been discussing. In this section we shall trace the changes in Leibniz' attitude toward substantial form and see how he moved from a complete rejection of it first to an acceptance, and finally to an original and fruitful interpretation of it.

By "substantial form" the scholastics originally meant the essence of an individual thing; it was one of the terms also used among the natural philosophers as a specification of what they meant by "nature." It was not the universal Platonic idea which defined the genus of a thing, but the Aristotelian form embodied in matter and thus individuated by its matter (Thomas Aquinas), or individuated by its own nature whether embodied in matter or not (Duns Scotus). Though naturally the Occamists denied any such entity as a substantial form, German scholasticism in Leibniz' time had come under the influence of Suarez and largely ceased to be nominalistic and Occamistic.[40] By the end of the seventeenth century, however, substantial form meant hardly more than an occult quality reified as the virtue or power of a thing to produce its characteristic effects. The *Port Royal Logic* following Descartes' rejection[41] of substantial form referred to it as "a bizarre kind of substance . . . not body yet corporeal."[42] The notorious *vis dormativa* of opium and the striving of heavy bodies toward the center of the earth are good examples of what substantial form meant at that time. Gravity, impetus, forces, and the like,[43] are other examples of substantial forms used in physics. Descartes and the moderns[44] opposed substantial forms as principles of explanation, declaring that all natural phenomena are explicable by the magnitude, figure, and motion of matter, whose essence, which can be clearly and distinctly perceived, is extension. Leibniz' decision against the appeal to substantial forms meant a fundamental reorientation in the thought of this youth, and it was this decision, he tells us, that led him to apply himself to the study of mathematics. That may have occasioned his going to Jena to study under Weigel, where

[40] Leibniz, in rejecting substantial forms, was not overly careful in specifying what theory it was that he was opposing; it has been argued by Fritz Rintelen, "Leibnizens Beziehungen zur Scholastik," *Archiv für Geschichte der Philosophie*, 16 (1903), 157–188, 307–333) that he was not in fact well acquainted with the ins and outs of scholastic debate; but the theory of substantial form as he subsequently developed it resembled the Scotistic (Platonic) theory more than the Aquinian (Aristotelian) theory, as we shall see.

[41] *Principles of Philosophy*, § 198.

[42] *The Art of Thinking*, trans. James Dickoff and Patricia James, (Indianapolis: Bobbs-Merrill, 1964), p. 248.

[43] *Ibid.*, pp. 322, 324.

[44] The campaign against the concept of "nature" by Boyle and Sturm was part of the same program.

he came into contact with those who favored a mathematical and physical study of nature without a Cartesian metaphysical basis, or who thought, like Clauberg, that Descartes was reconcilable with Aristotle when properly interpreted, not when taken in the scholastic manner.

Leibniz' turn against the scholastic theory of substantial form did not imply that he became a Cartesian; nor did his acceptance of what he called (after Boyle) the "corpuscular philosophy" mean that he was an atomist (though reading Jungius, Sperrling, and Gassendi was one of the causes of his change). His preferred name for the new way of thought was "the re-formed philosophy," which Leibniz ascribed to Bacon and Hobbes, who, he said, were both earlier than and superior to Descartes in their conception of nature.[45] The reformed philosophy explained everything, except sense and thought, in terms of the magnitude, figure, and motion of matter, which is defined by extension and solidity, or impenetrability, without need of any appeal to substantial form.[46] Such reformed philosophy had been shown, Leibniz believed, by Jungius[47] to be consistent with Aristotle's *Physics*. We thus find Leibniz now taking the role, familiar since the sixteenth century, of the defender of Aristotle against the schoolmen. For, Leibniz convinced himself at this time, Aristotle had meant by substantial form nothing but formal cause and by formal cause nothing but figure, and consequently all change was motion in a geometrical sense. The scholastics had not seen this, and therefore they failed to see that geometry is adequate to deal with matter in motion.[48]

Leibniz' exclusive adherence to the reformed philosophy was terminated by two lines of thought, one theological and one scientific. The theological consideration was that the reformed theory could not explain transubstantiation in the Eucharist. While there is no reason to suppose that this was not a genuine motive for Leibniz' change, there can be little doubt that a theory that could be both scientific and theologically acceptable commended itself to him as a step toward an understanding between the modern scientific movement and an acceptably revised Catholic theology, with his own philosophy as the mediator.[49] In the papers preliminary to the *Catholic Demonstrations* (1668–1670), while he continued to maintain the sufficiency of magnitude, figure, and motion for purely physical explanations and rejected the appeal to substantial forms and any theological principles in physics, he argued that these primary qualities themselves, in their individual manifestation in a particular body, cannot be grounded merely in the extension of the body and hence require an incorporeal principle for their explanation.[50] The individuating principle of any specific body must be specific to it and individual. It must be unique to each thing, and not an abstract universal principle which would not individuate a particular body.[51]

Given this theory, Leibniz has an easy explanation of the possibility of transubstantiation—not a demonstration of it, of course, because its truth

[45] Loemker, p. 146 (1669).
[46] *Ibid.*, pp. 155, 166 (1669, 1670).
[47] *Ibid.*, p. 147 (1669).
[48] *Ibid.*, pp. 154–155 (1669).
[49] *Ibid.*, p. 401 (1679), p. 422 (1680).
[50] *Ibid.*, pp. 169–170 (1669).
[51] Here is an intimation of the principle of identity of indiscernibles and of the theory of the complete notion of a thing.

is a matter of faith and revelation, a mystery. Form can remain the same even though all the extensional qualities and accidents are changed; or it may be changed in any body of matter by a miraculous act of God, without occasioning any change in the magnitude, figure, and motion of the body. Hence the substance of bread and wine may be replaced by the substance of the body and blood of Christ.[52] Moreover, if the essence of body is not extension, it can then be maintained that the same body can exist in many places at once.[53]

But what does the mechanical theory gain or suffer from this theologically inspired argument? There is something here for the reformed philosophers, too. The error they condemned in the scholastic philosophy is still an error, for the scholastics used substantial form to explain changes in bodies which ought to be, and can be, explained in terms of magnitude, figure, and motion. The scholastics were correct in saying that there are intrinsic differences in bodies, which must be taken into account in explaining their changes. "Who would deny," Leibniz asked, "substantial forms, that is, essential differences between bodies?"[54] But the moderns were right in objecting to the scholastics' misuse of these intrinsic differences, for they thought that the properties of bodies can be sufficiently explained by mentioning the substantial forms without taking pains to examine the manner of their operation.[55] In physics we should give only mechanical explanations; but the mechanical explanations apply to, and presuppose, intrinsic differences or the forms of things which cannot be explained physically.

Having thus satisfied himself that he must grant the existence of substantial forms, Leibniz identified them with souls, or entelechies,[56] using these words in the Aristotelian sense of forms that are the causes of motion or change. A body, accordingly, is an extended soul or an extended agent; the phenomenal body is a manifestation of the actions of the soul.[57] The substantial form is no longer a merely logical or a merely static ontological form, but an active power.

The substantial form is identified with a Platonic idea in the Neoplatonic sense of a wholly individual, indivisible, and concrete idea in the divine mind. The particular body is thus, as a phenomenal manifestation of a substantial form, also an imitation of an idea in God's mind.[58] The substantial form is thus the cause of the thing's appearances and changes. It is the cause or total essence that differs from the appearances as a distinct concept differs from a confused one; but the idea which is identical with the soul is not itself a concept, as it were *in* the soul, but is ontologically real and basic, yet wholly individual instead of abstractly universal.[59] It is a Scotistic form,[60] having its principle of individuation inherent in it; it is not individuated accidentally by its embodiment in a particular and alien matter, but has a *materia prima* within it as its primary passive power.

[52] Loemker, pp. 182–183 (1668).
[53] *Ibid.*, p. 401 (1679).
[54] *Ibid.*, p. 289 (1768), p. 445 (1682–84).
[55] *Ibid.*, p. 474 (1686).
[56] *Ibid.*, p. 289 (1678). Later (*ibid.*, p. 416 [1680–84]) he speaks of "something analogous to the soul, which is commonly called Form."
[57] *Ibid.*, p. 580 (1680–84).
[58] *Ibid.*, p. 429 (1668?).
[59] *Ibid.*, p. 222 (1671).
[60] *Ibid.*, p. 580 (1680–84); *Theodicy* § 184.

By 1686, when Leibniz had reached the conclusions just described, he found a second reason for rejecting the Cartesian identification of body with extension. It was his discovery in mechanics that force, which is not a mode of extension, is conserved and not motion, the mode of extension Descartes had believed was conserved. He showed, in a simple *Gedanken-experiment*, that the sum of the products of mass and the square of velocity of all bodies in a system is constant, and not that the quantity of motion is constant.[61] The inertia of the bodies moved must be considered too, and inertia is the passive force of resistance to motion, thus derivative from the prime matter of the form whose active force is the agency or cause of motion.

Earlier, Leibniz had taken from Hobbes the concept of conatus as the derivative of motion at a point and instant,[62] and he had then held that bodies and minds (in the ordinary sense of the word) differed in the fact that a mind was able to retain conatus, as in memory the mind is not affected solely by the momentary present state of things. A body, being unable to retain its conatus, is only a "momentary mind." Now, however, with the conception that force, as manifested in motion or in resistance to motion, is a characteristic of an active substantial form called also a soul, Leibniz is able to connect the activity of minds (in the ordinary sense of the word) with the activities of bodies which arises from their form (which is a soul in the Aristotelian sense alone).

At this time, about 1686, it can be said that the conception of substantial form, banished in the 1660's, has been rehabilitated and has become the principal notion in Leibniz' philosophy. Since, however, in rehabilitating it, Leibniz did not have to give up any of the positive teachings of the re-formed philosophy and had, in fact, never committed himself to its particular Cartesian version, the further elaboration of the notion did not require him to turn his back on his work since the walk in the Rosenthal. For his path was not in the direction the schoolmen had followed, using substantial form as explanatory and excluding the project of knowledge based upon mathematics and mechanics.

Discourse on Metaphysics

In 1686 Leibniz, in a few days of leisure, composed his *Discourse on Metaphysics*,[63] the theses of which he communicated to Arnauld in the hope that they would provide a basis for his project of effecting a reconciliation and reunion of the churches. This work was not published until the nineteenth century, Leibniz having withheld it in his lifetime because of dissatisfaction with various parts of it; but to the modern reader it is of inestimable importance in summarizing the scattered views he had already

---

[61] Loemker, p. 457 (1686); *Discourse on Metaphysics*, § 17 (1686).

[62] Loemker, 218–20, 231 (1671).

[63] The *Discourse on Metaphysics* has been translated by Loemker (see n. 6 above); Peter Lucas and Leslie Grint (University of Manchester [Eng.] Press, 1953), and G. R. Montgomery (La Salle: Open Court, 1902). I cite by article numbers to facilitate use of any edition.

published or expressed in private and in providing a common origin for the diverse publications by which he was to be known to posterity. Much of what he said in the *Discourse* he was to repeat in the *Monadology* thirty years later, yet there are significant differences in the tones of the two short works, each meant to be a summary of his system. In the former work, Leibniz was writing for one of the most noted theologians of his day, thoroughly acquainted with scholastic and Cartesian doctrine; the orientation is theological, and the first topic discussed is the existence and nature of God. The second was written for a man of the world, perhaps drawn up in a form suitable to be versified in a new *De rerum natura.* Though plenty of attention is given to the existence and nature of God, Leibniz leads his reader to the conception of God and the kingdom of grace through a description of the world. His language is less precise; doctrines less likely to be intelligible to the man of the world than to the theologian, such as the theory of the phenomenal status of space and time, are silently omitted, and spatial and temporal terms are erroneously used to describe the metaphysical or intelligible world. But if the two works do not coincide in content, neither do they conflict in any serious way in their teaching. Because they do not coincide in content and emphasis, if one is to get a reasonably accurate conspectus of Leibniz' metaphysics it is necessary to supplement each with the other and to supplement both by reference to the works written between them.

We shall therefore proceed as follows. We shall first give a succinct summary of the teachings of the *Discourse*; then we shall give more attention to those teachings in the *Discourse* which underwent more elaborate treatment and revision in the works written after 1786, the writings of the last few years of his life being the attracting and guiding pole.

The *Discourse* consists of numbered paragraphs or sections, but for convenience may be divided into eight parts. The first, consisting of the first seven sections, discusses God. God is a perfect being, and his works are perfect. They are not perfect, however, because God created them, but he created them for the sufficient reason that this world would be the best of all possible worlds. This challenges all previous thought of the inscrutability of God's will. Though Leibniz admits that man does not in fact understand God's design in detail, and especially does not understand the occasions of his particular providence, few philosophers have written as though they had as intimate acquaintance with God as Leibniz seems to claim. Leibniz uses anthropomorphic terms in a flat, matter-of-fact tone in referring to God. He seems so much in God's counsel that it is sometimes difficult to believe that he is not, with conscious hypocrisy, talking the language of his orthodox correspondents who would not themselves claim such familiar insight into God's purposes and stratagems. The principle of sufficient reason is boldly applied to the creation of the world itself, not merely to things within it; God himself is not exempt from the principle of sufficient reason in his willing any more than his intellect is exempt from the laws of logic.

This world which God created is best because it contains a maximum of existence, that is, because it is the simplest in structure while the richest in phenomena. It is not without evil, though God did not will the evil in it;

but the evil it contains is a necessary feature of that possible world which is the best. (God could not choose the best elements of possible world A and those of possible world B and eliminate their evils, unless the resultant world, world C, was already included among the possible worlds. Since he chose the best of *all* possible worlds, we can be sure that the evil in it is minimal.) The wise man will acquiesce in God's creation and not complain about it; but the conviction that it is the best of all possible worlds does not relieve us of the necessity of deliberating and doing our own best for the general welfare, for we do not know God's ordinance for this world in detail.[64] Leibniz' determinism, therefore, is no excuse for quietism.

The second part (secs. 8–15) discusses individual substances, which correspond to the complete concept of a thing in which all the predicates (including accidents) are included. In the complete concept of a being, for example, Alexander, is included all its predicates; in that which corresponds to the complete concept, i.e., the individual substance, there must be contained all the affections of the thing. This had been intimated by those who talked about the substantial form of things, though they believed that they could account for the properties of things by appealing directly to the substantial form; whereas in truth each thing's changing affections are to be explained in terms of its *other* affections, the substantial form or substance being only the metaphysical (not efficient) cause of these changes.[65]

Leibniz then gives his objection to Descartes' theory that the substance of body consists in extension, repeating the argument about the conservation of motion and force already mentioned. In section 8 Leibniz discusses the question of whether this conception denies the difference between contingent and necessary truths and thereby destroys the possibility of freedom. He asserts that the certainty that "S is P" does not mean that "S is P" is a necessary rather than a contingent proposition. Hence a person (spirit) may freely choose P even though it is certain that he will choose P.[66]

In section 14 Leibniz presents his doctrine of the creation of substances by a "continuous emanation" of God, whereby substances in the world are said to be presentations of perspectives of the entire universe; each is independent of all other created substances, but each agrees with all the others as existing in a harmonious relation established by (chosen from among possible worlds by) God. The apparent interaction of substances is only apparent; each substance is just as it would be if only it and God existed, yet one substance seems to influence another when, in their apparent interaction, one ascends to a higher grade of perfection, to a more adequate expression of the universe.[67] Here, then, is the root of the principle of pre-established harmony.

[64] These ideas go back to at least 1671 (Loemker, p. 227), constitute later the basis of the *Theodicy* of 1709, and reappear in *Monadology* §§ 53–56 and *Principles of Nature and Grace*, §§ 10, 13.

[65] This conception of substantial form undergoes further development, and will be dealt with in the next section of this chapter.

[66] In the *Theodicy* (passim); but it is not presented in the *Monadology* or the *Principles of Nature and Grace*.

[67] *Discourse on Metaphysics*, §§ 14, 15; *Monadology*, § 50. The idea of pre-established harmony is found as early as 1678 (Loemker, pp. 318–319) and suggested even in 1671 (Loemker, p. 227).

The third part (secs. 16–22) discusses the relation of final and efficient causes, or of metaphysical and physical explanations. They are, Leibniz argues, entirely parallel, and in some instances one of them is more fruitful in the investigation of nature than the other. We find in these passages the roots of Leibniz' effort to reconcile metaphysics and physics, teleology and mechanism; and some suggestions of his final theory of phenomenalism for the objects of physics.[68]

The next part (secs. 23–29) discusses the human understanding. Sections 24 and 25 repeat the discussion of clear and distinct knowledge and the distinctions between kinds of definitions that Leibniz had published in 1684,[69] and then turn to a consideration of the nature of ideas. He argues for the innateness of ideas (Plato over Aristotle, sec. 27), identifying ideas not as contents of the minds, or permanent objects of the mind (Malebranche), or the immediate objects of thought (Arnauld, sec. 26) but as a disposition to think of objects. This disposition is, of course, a consequence of the substantial nature of the mind, which is "windowless" so that it cannot receive thoughts or sensations from without.[70]

The human will is discussed in sections 30–32, which constitute the fourth part and largely repeat the teachings of the first part and anticipate the doctrines of the Theodicy. The relation of the soul to the body, under the general conception of pre-established harmony, occupies Leibniz in sections 33–34; and the Discourse comes to an end with three paragraphs on the kingdom of God as a kingdom of spirits governed by God and in intercourse with him.[71]

After this brief survey of the Discourse, we can take up one by one the principal ideas in it as they were further elaborated and to some extent modified by Leibniz during the succeeding thirty years. These ideas are: (a) the conception of substance as power expressing the thought of God; (b) the conception of the harmony of substances; (c) the theory of the parallelism of metaphysical and physical explanations and of the phenomenalism of the perceptual and physical world; (d) the theory of the realm of grace and its practical consequences.

From Substantial Form to Monad

Leibniz' advice to avoid using the term "substantial form" in talking to Cartesians[72] reflected his own tendency to speak more of substances, entelechies, and (after 1695) monads. No doubt he wished to avoid the mis-

[68] The term "middle way" is introduced in 1682–84 (Loemker, p. 446). On the concept of parallelism between efficient and final explanations, but without the term "middle way," see Monadology, §§ 37, 54, 87; Principles of Nature and Grace, §§ 8, 10, 11. Phenomenalism is not discernible in the latter two papers, but is the basis of the correspondence with Samuel Clarke; intimations of it go back as early as 1676 (Loemker, p. 245).

[69] Loemker, pp. 448ff (1684).

[70] This view is expressed again in Monadology, §§ 7, 14, 26, 27; in Principles of Nature and Grace, §§ 2, 3, 5, 12; and is most fully developed in New Essays.

[71] This view is most fully expressed in Principles of Nature and Grace, §§ 14–18 and Monadology §§ 84–90.

[72] Loemker, p. 831 (1698).

leading connotations of the standard scholastic term. For while substantial forms were, as he said, despised, and appeal to them as occult qualities was rightly condemned, the other terms were more innocent, and he could let "monad" mean exactly what he wanted it to mean. The exoteric part of its meaning is adequately expressed in the popular *Monadology*, but much is left out of it which must be supplied if its short, numbered paragraphs are not to be either unintelligible or seriously misleading.[73] Let us, therefore, approach it through some of the less familiar writings between the *Discourse on Metaphysics* of 1686, which presented the theory as outlined in the previous section, and the popular writings of about 1715. But let us take as our text which calls for this understanding the opening sentence of the *Principles of Nature and of Grace* of 1714: "Substance is a being capable of action."[74]

By action Leibniz means a completely spontaneous action of which some other change or event is at most the occasion, but not the explanatory cause. The scholastics had thought of power as a slumbering potentiality in a thing which could be awakened only by some outer stimulus; Descartes had denied (at least to extended substance) any power to act, and traced all motion back to the one active supreme substance, God. The occasionalists had made a compromise between these two extreme views: God was the only cause of action, but he acted on substances to cause them to act only on the occasion of some other action. But for Leibniz, the capacity to act in specific ways was a definitive endowment of a thing, an enduring capacity created by God, not a momentary response to his fiat. It was a potentiality which passed over into overt action or actualization upon the mere removal of an impediment. Now overt action does not mean for Leibniz merely motion and change; what is phenomenally at rest (such as a taut bow string) is acting, exerting force all the time. The power to act, definitive of subtance, is unitary and permanent, though it manifests itself in various ways. It is not a blind stirring that, like Schopenhauer's will, does first one thing and then another for no reason at all. Action explicates and defines the substance which acts; or the substance is the sufficient reason for all its acts: *operare sequitur esse*. A substance is—if we avoid the nominalist or conceptualist interpretation of "law" and accept the Platonic—a law of activity. The nature of a soul (i.e., substance) "consists in a certain perpetual law of the same series of changes through which it runs unhindered.[75] It is "a kind of nisus or primitive force of action which is itself the inherent law impressed upon it by divine command."[76]

Leibniz' theory of the relation of possibility to actual existence, however, is somewhat more complicated and obscure than this might make it appear. Leibniz is not repeating the *Timaeus*, according to which there are independent forms or possibilities which the demiurge finds and uses in the creation of the world by putting them into the receptacle so as to generate

---

[73] See H. H. Dubbs, "The Misleading Nature of Leibniz' Monadology," *Philosophical Review*, 50:508–516 (1941).

[74] Loemker, p. 1033 (1714). But to see how little is changed, at least on the surface, see a similar statement made in 1668 (Loemker, p. 179).

[75] *Ibid.*, p. 840 (1699).   [76] *Ibid.*, p. 819 (1698).

space, time, and things. Rather, his theory is Neoplatonic; God is the ground of the possibilities, which are thoughts in his infinite intellect, just as much as by his will he is the cause of existence.

Unless God is real, there is nothing else *even possible.*[77] God, in thinking each essence, gives it an impetus to come into existence. Without this, it would be "merely imaginary."[78] But not all possibilities can be realized, for there are in God's intellect incompossible possibilities. God has a free choice of the compossibles to be realized. That God chooses the best of all possible worlds is a contingent truth; if it were not, everything in the world would be logically necessary. That the choice is contingent implies that God creates the world not by his intellect, but by his will. He freely chooses that combination of compossible possibilities which have the maximum perfection, and allows it, by a continuous fulguration[79] of his own being, to come into existence. Created monads thus "continually receive from God that which causes them to have some perfections" and real existence.[80]

The striving of essence for existence, of possibility for actuality, is the actualization of substance, and this striving appears in time as the conatus or force or appetition of an actual substance. The events in the world (the successive manifestations of the acts of substances) can be explained mechanically, in terms of other acts of the other substances, or by citing the law of change which defines that substance. But the laws themselves cannot be explained in this way.[81] Instead of physics terminating with the occult qualities considered as substantial forms, physics terminates when it comes upon its own basic and irreducible laws which define what actually exists as a selection among possible world-structures. To ask why, for instance, a certain law of physics holds (which cannot be mathematically derived from others) is to ask why this world rather than some other possible world was created.[82] The answer to every question in physics, save one, is that there is a sufficient physical reason for it; for to ask the one question which cannot be answered in this way—Why does this world, defined by these laws and containing these phenomena, exist?—is to ask for a sufficient reason that is not physical, but teleological.[83] But we never have to cite metaphysical and teleological grounds in explaining any *particular* phenomenon in the world, though parallel to every mechanical reason in the realm of nature and power there is a teleological reason in the realm of wisdom and grace. The fundamental member of this pair, however, is the teleological reason: this world, rather than any one of the infinite number of other possible worlds, exists because God, for a sufficient reason, chose it.

A substance, or monad, can be looked upon on three levels of abstractness. First of all, it is a merely logical essence or possibility. Second, it is an idea in the mind of God; he thinks it and gives it a nisus to exist. The more perfect it is, the greater the nisus. Third, it is an actual being. It is not,

[77] *Ibid.*, p. 793 (1697); *Monadology*, §§ 43, 44.
[78] Loemker, p. 793 (1697).
[79] *Monadology*, § 47.
[80] *Principles of Nature and Grace*, § 9.
[81] Loemker, pp. 722–723 (1695).
[82] *Ibid.*, p. 779 (1696).
[83] *Ibid.*, p. 780 (1696); *Monadology*, §§ 37, 54, 87; *Principles of Nature and Grace*, §§ 8, 10, 11.

however, even then a glob of brute existence. It is also a law of action, a generating function or the integral (in the mathematical sense) of all its modifications and variable values. Each state or action of a substance, like each predicate of the complete concept of the subject, is (also in a mathematical sense) a value of the variables which define it. This is the metaphysical correlate of the logical doctrine that every predicate is analytically contained in the concept of the subject: every state and action is a state and action of a substance which produces them according to the law of sufficient reason, sufficient and adequate to the complete determination of this individual substance. Even states or modifications which seem to be passions, or passive effects of modifications in other substances, are included among the actions of the substance in question. Except for their dependence on God for their actual existence, it may be said of each Leibnizian substance what Spinoza said of his one substance: it is *causa sui*. While Leibniz' substances, or monads, owe their existence to God, they are the sufficient causes of their own states, even their passive states. Hence monads are internally determined even in that which Leibniz calls their matter, or primitive passive power;[84] for a thing is characterized by its passions as well as by its actions. They also are consequences of its nature, though they seem to be caused by the actions of other substances. Just as logical accidents are really properties whose sufficient reason we do not find because we cannot completely analyze the concept of the subject, what seems to befall the substance is really an action in it which reflects the state of some other substance.

Every created monad is a law of its manifestations. It is not a bit of matter or substance which falls under its own individual law, but its substantiality is expressed in the system of predicates which define it. Every manifestation or predicate, then, expresses the monad or substance to which it pertains. But the law, which is just the necessity of this combination of states and actions, is itself integral in the harmonious system of possibilities which we call this possible world, and everything in this system of possibilities which is not logically necessary is hypothetically necessary, that is, necessary because God has chosen it for a sufficient reason. Every monad, then, expresses or represents the entire universe, or is a standpoint from which the entire universe can be surveyed. To speak in two mathematical similes, the monad in relation to its own states is like some function, say the logarithm of x, which can be expanded into a unique series of numbers; while in relation to the rest of the universe it is like one equation with an infinite number of unknowns in an infinite number of simultaneous equations. By the first, the function determines every value which, upon expansion, can be found within it. This means that the predicate is included in the subject, the attribute in the substance. The monad is pregnant with its future.[85] By the second analogy, the monad is what it is only in the context of all the others which were chosen or brought into existence along with it.

[84] Loemker, p. 607 (date uncertain).
[85] *Monadology*, §§ 11, 22; *Principles of Nature and Grace*, § 13.

As the one equation cannot be solved without simultaneously solving all the others, the monad represents (in both a mathematical and an epistemological sense) the entire universe; it is a living mirror of the universe, and is only one of an infinite number of actual perspectives of a single universe.[86] Just as the word "represents" has two senses besides the mathematical ("x represents the unknown"), there are two other senses in Leibniz' metaphor of the mirror: (a) the monad reflects the universe as a mirror reflects the face; (b) the monad is exemplary of the universe, a very image of it, an exemplar (as in the sentence, "She is the mirror of courtesy"). In short, the individual substance is a microcosm, a created God. It is itself a character of the universe; in it are found the signatures of all things.

Monads exist on all levels of perfection, perfection being defined according to the adequacy of the reflection they have of the universe or the adequacy with which they represent it. (Here the mathematical analogies just sketched out break down; "representation" now means no longer the relation in which one thing can stand for another because their structures are logically isomorphous, but it means the psychological or epistemological relation in which, for example, one photograph may give a better representation of a landscape than another.)

Every existent thing is a monad or an aggregate of monads. Monads may be "slumbering monads" of apparently lifeless and certainly unconscious matter; they may be souls which have a heightened consciousness accompanied by memory, as found in animals; or spirits endowed with reason, as found in men.[87]

Leibniz now prefers to call the first "entelechies" and reserves the name "soul" for the latter two. The entelechy is the inherent unique force of matter, active (energy) or passive (inertia). The way a bit of matter acts is dependent upon the force residing in it, either in initiating or resisting change. The laws of nature express the general features of these forces, and the uniqueness of each one is expressed in the boundary conditions which are unique for any specific instantiation of the general law.

The monads are the "true atoms of nature," but Leibniz disagrees with the physical atomists on almost every point. Matter is, for him, infinitely divisible, not particulate, for it is not substance but only phenomenon. Atoms were thought to be all alike or at least to have only a small number of species, but each monad is uniquely different from all the others, and no two differ only numerically. Atoms were supposed to interact with each other according to the laws of mechanics and chemistry; but monads stand in no metaphysically dynamic relations to each other, their changes being only correlated with each other. Atoms were supposed to be permanent; but though Leibniz denies that monads can come to be or pass away, they are permanent only in the sense in which a law of change can be permanent, and their states are in continuous flux. Atoms stood only under mechanical laws—laws which may have been instituted for the world because of God's

---

[86] *Monadology*, §§ 56, 57, 65; *Principles of Nature and Grace*, §§ 3, 12, 13.
[87] *Monadology*, §§ 18–21; *Principles of Nature and Grace*, §§ 5, 14.

purpose; but the law of the monad is inherently teleological, being a law of the striving of the created monad to represent the universe by living out of its own destiny.

The idea of living nature had not been stamped out in Germany by theories of the machinery of nature and atomism. The Paracelsian tradition favored an analogy between nature and organism; so Leibniz could read the analogy in both ways. Animals, and indeed all substances, are natural automata, the difference between a man-made machine and a natural machine being that the latter is an infinitely divisible machine while the former is not, in at least the same sense, infinitely divisible into simpler machines.[88] Read the other way, the analogy lets Leibniz deny that there is dead matter in the universe. There is a world of creatures in every drop of water.[89] This was not an unreasonable speculation then, for the microscope had just been invented, and indeed a previously unsuspected world of creatures had been laid bare to the eye.

Aggregates of matter, such as a pile of sand or even a man-made machine, are not substantial unities; but living beings are substantial unities, whose parts are entelechies or substances. (This is the sense in which *everything* is a living machine, down to its infinitely divisible parts.) Leibniz has two theories to account for the unity of substantial unities. One is the theory of a substantial chain (*vinculum substantiale*) which supervenes upon a manifold of monads making up a body, giving it "true metaphysical unity."[90] He tentatively adopted this theory since otherwise organic bodies would be, like inorganic bodies, merely well-grounded phenomena.[91] Leibniz espoused this scholastic theory in his correspondence with the Jesuit philosopher Des Bosses apparently in order to explain transubstantiation. Perhaps of less interest to Des Bosses, but of great interest to Leibniz, is the fact that this theory of organic unity supports his view maintained almost everywhere that not merely the soul but also the organic body survives death. There are no soul-monads without attendant body-monads, though no soul-monads are attached to a constant and unchanging congeries of body-monads; and while each monad is immortal, Leibniz wishes to go further and maintain that substantial unities of a plurality of monads also are ungenerated and immortal. This theory seemed to be supported by another recent discovery with the microscope, viz., the existence of "spermatic animals" having the form of the mature animal and developing into it by a series of "transformations"[92] (the theory of preformationism in embryology).

But this theory of the substantial chain, convenient as it is for these two purposes, is not consistent with the theory of merely derivative relations between monads as presented in the rest of Leibniz' work. Common to both theories is the notion of an endless gradation of monads, extending downward to "slumbering monads," or entelechies, in a state of stupor and

[88] *Monadology*, § 64; *Principles of Nature and Grace*, § 3.
[89] *Monadology*, §§ 66–69; *Principles of Nature and Grace*, § 1; Loemker, p. 416 (1679).
[90] Loemker, p. 972 (1709); p. 980 (1712).   [91] *Ibid.*, p. 976 (1710).
[92] *Monadology*, § 75; *Principles of Nature and Grace*, § 6.

possessing only *petites perceptions*,[93] but not being entirely unconscious. Some monads, however, have a heightened perception of their internal changes, which we call consciousness. This is made possible by their possessing the faculty of memory, and such a monad is called a spirit.[94] While all monads reflect the entire universe, they do not all reflect it in equal measure, and spirits reflect the universe more adequately than bare or naked monads. Even a spirit, however, does not reflect all parts of the universe with equal adequacy, and those which it reflects most adequately—so adequately that we can say that there is a direct relation of correspondence between them—are called the body of the spirit. Since monads do not interact, Leibniz' theory of the relation of mind (soul) to body is one of strict parallelism when we emphasize the differences between the spirit monad and the monads of the body; but it is a theory of panpsychism if we emphasize the ontological continuity between the kinds of substances present in the body and in the spirits, since they are all vital substances characterized by perception and appetition. But because we call a change or perception in one monad a cause of a change or perception in another if it is correlated with it and is more perfect than it, i.e., gives a better representation of the entire state of the universe, we can say that the perception in the mind is the cause of the change in the body. Leibniz thinks that his theory of the correspondence of monads meets the objections to the Cartesian theory of interaction and the occasionalists' theory that God intervenes to cause apparent interaction; his famous analogy of the two clocks to the mind and the body was designed to bring this out.[95]

In this system bodies act as if there were no souls (to assume an impossibility), and souls act as if there were no bodies, and both act as if they influenced each other.[96]

Because the spirit more adequately expresses the universe it is called the dominant monad of the body and is called "its" soul. But this dominance is only phenomenal, for the body is, after all, only a well-grounded phenomenon.[97]

The System of Pre-established Harmony

Leibniz' theory of the relation between mind and body is only a specific corollary of his general theory of the relation between substances. It was the most easily explained, and the term "pre-established harmony" was first used, with specific application to the mind-body problem, in 1696, more

[93] *Monadology*, §§ 20, 21, 23, 24; *Principles of Nature and Grace*, § 4.
[94] *Monadology*, §§ 19, 25, 26; *Principles of Nature and Grace*, § 5.
[95] Loemker, pp. 750–752 (1696).
[96] *Monadology*, § 81. Leibniz does not explain how it appears that the body influences the mind.
[97] Loemker, pp. 1013, 1017 (1696).

than ten years after Leibniz had developed the theory in all its essentials in the *Discourse on Metaphysics*,[98] and in the paper likewise unpublished, entitled "First Truths,"[99] where it is called "the hypothesis of concomitance." The first published account of his theory (without the name) appeared in 1695 in "A New System of the Nature and the Communication of Substances, as well as the Union between the Soul and Body."[100] It was this paper which attracted wide attention to Leibniz' metaphysics. It occasioned the criticisms of Pierre Bayle in the first edition of his *Dictionary* (1697), which Leibniz answered; and then more extensive criticisms by Bayle in the second edition published in 1702. The history of this controversy can be followed in Leibniz' *Theodicy*, which contains his too-prolix defense of pre-established harmony from the criticisms of Bayle and others who attacked it.

Since we have already, in discussing the theory of the relation, or union, of mind and body, introduced the main points of his theory, we can avoid many details and quickly reach the main question: Why did Leibniz develop this theory?

It is a consequence of several other theories which we have already examined, some of which were developed long before Leibniz drew this astonishing conclusion from them. The first is the theory that substance is the source of all its changes, just as the subject contains all its predicates, and that this is as true of the passions of a substance (that is, its affections when it does not seem to be acting) and the accidents of a subject as it is of actions and properties. For this view entails the dynamical and logical independence of substances one from another. Leibniz objected to the Cartesian definition of substance as that which needs nothing for its existence except God, but he agrees with Spinoza that interacting substances cannot be independent and hence that if things interact, they are not substances. While Spinoza draws from this the conclusion that there can be only one substance, Leibniz rather takes it as a good ground for asserting a plurality of noninteracting substances.

A plurality of noninteracting substances, however, would not seem necessarily to be a system of substances in harmony with each other. But the answer to the question: Why is there more than one substance? also contains the answer to the question: Why is the plurality of substances harmonious? For the answer to the first question, Leibniz appealed to two notions. (a) God, a perfect being, wills a maximum of perfections in his creation, and therefore produced as much existence as possible. Of all possible worlds, God chose the one with the maximum number of possible substances and allowed it to come into being. (b) It was a world in which the perfection which would be present in the sum of perfections was multiplied by a variety of substances, each of which expressed or reflected all the

[98] *Discourse on Metaphysics*, §§ 14, 15. The term was first used in 1696 (Loemker, p. 751), but there are intimations of the theory fifteen years before the *Discourse* (Loemker, p. 227 [1671]).

[99] Written between 1680 and 1684 (Loemker, p. 415).

[100] Loemker, pp. 739–750 (1695). This was the only application widely accepted among the Wolffians, and then finally rejected even there.

others.[101] Hence a harmonious world of substances, in which each substance represents all the others by standing in the relation of a specific variable to all the others is more perfect than one in which each substance is truly isolated from the others. Since substances cannot interact without collapsing into one, since a world with one substance is less perfect than a world with many, and since a world with many substances in no representative relation to each other is less perfect than one in which each reflects and, so to speak, replicates the perfections of the other, it follows that the best of all possible worlds is a world in which there is a pre-established harmony among all the substances in it.

The best of all possible worlds necessarily has the following characteristics by virtue of which it is the best.

(a) It is possible. There are no logical impossibilities in it.

(b) The maximum number of possibilities is actual; therefore it contains the maximum possible number of substances, each of which contains the maximum possible number of states (law of plenum).

(c) Each substance will be different from all the others; no two things or substances differ from each other only numerically (law of identity of indiscernibles.)

(d) They will fill every possible logical slot; there will be no "missing links" in the world (law of continuity).

(e) Each will multiply the perfections of the others by reflecting, representing, or expressing them.

(f) Each will be entirely active; each will therefore be completely determined by its own possibility, and all passions will be only apparent. (e) and (f) are the hypothesis of pre-established harmony.

(g) Each will go through all the states compossible with those of all the others. The states of each substance will be manifested in such a manner that incompossibles within any one and between any number of them will be avoided. Time and space are phenomena well-grounded in the compossible states of substances; two incompossible states within the single substance will be manifested as occurring at different times, and those between substances will be manifested as being at different places.

(h) But the world will not be altogether without evil; it will contain the minimum evil consistent with the preceding characteristics.

The system of pre-established harmony is the best justification for our original metaphor of the fugal structure of Leibniz' world. Unlike the typical Renaissance theorists of the harmony of the world, who were altogether too deaf to the manifest cacophonies of the world, and the mystical theorists who, as we have seen, did not hesitate to ascribe disharmony and dissension (Qual) to God, Leibniz does justice to the appearance of chaos and conflict in nature and society, yet sees the importance of and provides an arrangement for a terminal resolution in a supervening harmony.[102]

---

[101] Discourse on Metaphysics, § 9 (Loemker, p. 473).

[102] In a book published since this chapter was written, Nicholas Rescher (Philosophy of Leibniz [Englewood Cliffs: Prentice Hall, 1967] passim), has proposed the metaphor that each monad is "programmed," and the "programs," i.e., the laws of each individual development, are consonant and synchronized with each other.

Perception and the Spatial World

A monad on a high level reflects upon itself and has what Leibniz calls apperception. In apperception of its own acts, it discovers the paradigms of the metaphysical concepts of substance, existence, activity, and power.[103] These concepts it applies to other things—rightly when it is representing substances, wrongly when representing phenomenal bodies which have no substantial metaphysical unity. As we have seen, the monad also represents other monads, and those which it represents most adequately are called its body. But the monad through what is ordinarily called perception represents other things—in fact, it represents more or less adequately all substances in the universe. Those which a spirit does not represent as well as its own body, but nonetheless represents on a level of consciousness, are said to be the objects of perception.

Leibniz' formulation, in opposition to Locke, of a noncausal theory of perception is one of the most ingenious applications of the theory of pre-established harmony. Leibniz compares his epistemology to Plato's, and Locke's to Aristotle's.[104] To the Aristotelian-scholastic maxim, "There is nothing in the intellect which was not first in the senses," he adds the Platonic restriction: "except the intellect itself" (*nisi ipse intellectus*).[105] The soul itself and its functions must be presupposed. Leibniz is not asserting in any psychological sense, which would be refuted by the first book of Locke's *Essay*, that one is born with representations of things. Rather, he is saying three things that he thinks Locke cannot refute: First, if by "idea" is meant a law-like function of mind or a dispositional property, then there are innate ideas; he compares them to veins in marble which, to some extent, determine the shape of the statue before it is cut.[106] This much Locke conceded to others who had made similar criticisms; Locke did not wish to deny the inborn faculty or activity of the mind, but rejected, as a good Aristotelian, the propriety of calling it an idea. Second, Leibniz asserts that there are ideas which are not acquired by experience but are found, on the occasion of experience, in the mind; the mark of these ideas is their necessity, and their being "in the mind" is the source of their necessity.

All of this is familiar and commonplace; almost every critic of Locke could have made these criticisms. But the third thing Leibniz asserts is original and unique to his position. *All* ideas are at least virtually innate. They are in us as *petites perceptions*, or modifications of the mind, before they are brought to the full light of consciousness. For since the monad is windowless, sensible species cannot enter it "from without" by any kind of influx. A representation in my mind might be the psychical effect of a body's impinging on my sense organs—but this is only a phenomenal account of a very different process. The representation does not come from without; it was there implicitly from the beginning, and when the life of

---

103 *New Essays*, I, iii, § 19; *Discourse on Metaphysics*, § 34; *Monadology*, §§ 30, 82–3.
104 *New Essays*, Preface, p. 42.
105 *New Essays*, II, chap. i, § 8, p. 111; Loemker, p. 903 (1702).
106 *New Essays*, Preface, p. 46.

the monad is ripe for it, it will come before the monad's consciousness, just as the digit which is the 14,621st in the evolution of *e* will come up inevitably after the first 14,620 others have come up.

This is the condition of our *having* any idea; but this alone does not give any idea a cognitive reference. That must be based on the principle of harmony, whereby everything and every mode of everything represents everything else in the universe. To the mathematical sense in which everything represents everything else, there is added the psychological or phenomenological sense of representing: to represent means to stand for something in the consciousness of the monad in which the representation is a mode.

A representation in my mind is first seen as an accident of my soul, which represents immediately an accidental change in my body and mediately some accidental change in more remote substances. But we know that in actual fact there are no accidents in any of them, except in the context of only partial concepts of their underlying substances. Could I know the complete concept of my own soul, I would know, for instance, that at the moment when I represent to myself a clock-face reading twelve o'clock, I will also represent to myself the sound of a gong. If my soul is of the degree of perfection I hope it is, these representations in it will be synchronous with—and in Leibniz' sense of "character"—characters of actual changes in other substances, those which go to make up my body and the clock. When that is the case, then the position of the hands and the motion of the gong in space are well-founded phenomena, while the sounds I hear and the colors I see are confused representations which may yield to clear and distinct ideas that I may succeed in getting of the objects themselves.

The clock is a phenomenon of substances which are not material and spatial and dynamically related to each other but which seem to be related. We represent these phenomena to ourselves by means of our own ideas. It is not easy to decide whether Leibniz means to distinguish the well-founded phenomena themselves from *both* the monadic noumena *and* the representations in our soul-monads, or whether he means that well-founded phenomena are equivalent to representations in one soul of other monads *sub specie spati et temporis*. Sometimes he writes of body "as a being of reason, or, rather, of imagination"[107] and insists upon the usual distinctions between dreaming and veridical perception in terms of the orderliness of the latter. Existence, he says, is nothing but "the cause of organized sensations."[108] Leibniz puzzlingly speaks both of our organized perceptions of phenomena, and of our organized perceptions (= phenomena) of really existing things (substances) which found them.

In either case, our representations of things seem to be empirically occasioned, passively given as accidents which befall us. But in order to understand them, we may do one or more of four things with them: We may redirect our attention from the clear or unclear but in any case confused ideas of sensation to a reconstruction in terms of distinct ideas of measurable

[107] Loemker, p. 1013 (1711).
[108] *Ibid.*, p. 245 (1676); pp. 603–605 (1690?); p. 1001 (1715).

and definable qualities. We do this by measurement and analysis.[109] Second, we may make hypotheses of a scientific but still phenomenal character as a way of saving (mechanically or teleologically explaining) the appearances. Third, we may see into the necessity of these very phenomena as themselves representatives of the monadic reality which metaphysically and thus teleologically explains them. Thus, for example, we first see colors of which we have clear but not distinct ideas. Then we have distinct ideas of the angles of refraction associated with them, and with these we can construct hypotheses in physics which explain the optical phenomena while remaining wholly within the phenomenal world. But fourthly we may connect these hypotheses and well-grounded phenomena with their metaphysical base which is not physical and spatial, but which supports these phenomena in a way analogous to that in which hypothetical objects in physics support or explain the colors we see. Thus Leibniz says that we explain the phenomenal rainbow in terms of phenomenal matter which we do not see; but matter itself is to reality as the rainbow is to the phenomenal matter.[110]

Even the space we appeal to in physical explanations is a phenomenon. Space is a nonsuccessive diffusion or repetition of some substantial form; it is the form under which noncompossibles may exist at the same time.[111] Space itself is an abstraction from extended matter, which is the phenomenon corresponding to aggregates of monads. It is dependent upon things in it but can be thought without thinking of bodies in it, though we can have no image of it without representing bodies in it.[112] It is not a property or attribute of substance, nor itself a substance (as he thought Newton believed it to be).[113] For propositions about space cannot be expressed exclusively in subject-predicate form, as they would be if space were either a substance or a property of substance. Since all that truly exists is a substance or a property represented in a true analytic subject-predicate proposition, it follows that space is not real as a substance but only as a phenomenon.

But Leibniz does not mean that space is subjective or illusory;[114] certainly not illusory, for it is coherent and organized and is a principle of coherent organization of other representations; and not subjective in the Kantian sense of a form of mere human intuition. Space is a logical mapping of the representational relations among substances. For example, we generally think of my body as being in immediate proximity to my soul (if we use spatial language at all); but this means merely that my body is represented more accurately in my soul than anything else. "We can judge relations of *nearer to* and *farther from* between its terms, according as

---

[109] *Ibid.*, p. 245 (1676).
[110] *Ibid.*, p. 873 (1704); Kant uses the same analogy in *Critique of Pure Reason* A 45 = B 63.
[111] Loemker, p. 949 (1702); p. 874 (1704); p. 1010 (1711).
[112] *Ibid.*, p. 224 (1671).   [113] *Ibid.*, p. 1119 (1715–16).
[114] See. L. J. Russell, "Leibniz' Account of Phenomena," *Proceedings of the Aristotelian Society*, 54:167–186 (1954).

more or *less* middle terms are required to understand the order between them."[115]

Leibniz' theory of space is in sharp contrast to Newton's. For Newton, space is a fixed absolute receptacle in which things are placed arbitrarily by God. The space we perceive is a relative space fixed by the relations between things in it, but all these things have also a place in absolute space which can be determined, e.g., by the rotating bucket experiment. For Leibniz, on the other hand, space is wholly relative and relational. It is not an absolute, existing antecedently to the things in it; for, if it were, there would have been a sufficient reason why God put things in it in the specific positions he chose, but since all points of space are equivalent, this would require us to affirm that God acted without a sufficient reason in choosing one point rather than another.[116] It is wholly relational because, without things existing, there would be no relations which could be "mapped" spatially.

The Middle Way

In a world of maximum perfection, a maximum of phenomena are covered by or generated by a minimum of laws. If the laws were not the simplest possible, Leibniz says that God in creating the world would be like a builder who attempts to construct a building with round stones; or like a player whose purpose it is to fill, according to the rules, a maximum number of squares on the board and yet, because of his lack of skill, has to leave some of them unfilled.[117] Since an existing thing is not one thing and the laws of nature something different, but the former is only an actualization of the latter in the real dynamic relation among its own states and in a relation of representation between the states of different substances, it follows that a harmonious world of simple laws must be one in which the harmony between the different substances is pre-established, for nothing can happen after its creation to make it harmonious.

Leibniz distinguishes the two ways in which the world can be studied as the a posteriori and the a priori. As a phenomenal realm, everything in it is to be explained according to efficient causes. These causes are discovered in experience, though they may be included under mathematical and physical laws which make it possible for us to deduce the phenomena from the simple laws about the behavior of bodies, including only the variables of size, figure, position, motion, and force. As a noumenal realm, however, explicable by the reasons God had in creating it, it is to be explained by appeal to the final causes of God's creation. But since each is the same world looked at in two different ways, the two explanations can never be incompatible with each other, nor can they lead to incompatible predictions. Recognition of this permits us to use both methods and not

[115] Loemker, p. 1083 (after 1714).
[116] *The Leibniz-Clarke Correspondence* (Third Letter of Leibniz, § 5), Loemker, p. 1108.
[117] Loemker, p. 323 (1679).

to wholly exclude either. Hence Leibniz calls this the middle way,[118] and the extremes between which it is a mean are the methods of the scholastics and natural philosophers and those of mechanists or reformed philosophers. All are "right in a good part of what they propose, but not so much in what they deny."[119] The former are right in seeing the world under the architectonic aspect as a world of wisdom, grace, and final causes. But they are wrong in giving finalistic explanations to specific phenomena,[120] in their appeal to plastic and hylarchic forces in nature in the Paracelsian manner, and in their belief that they have adequately explained a phenomenon when they show it to be of benefit to man and as if designed for his purposes.[121]

The mechanists are incorrect in their total denial of final causes, which is not only metaphysically erroneous but also defeats their own purposes. It is metaphysically wrong because the mechanical principles themselves cannot be explained mechanically and are not logically necessary;[122] they are to be explained only by showing their fitness to be laws of the best of all possible worlds. In Loemker's attractive metaphor, physics is to be "a phenomenal commentary on metaphysics."[123] And it is methodologically wrong too. For though no event can be adequately explained by reference to either God's or men's purposes, sometimes we can make a right conjecture concerning a law only by thinking that the law to be discovered must be a fitting one. Thus Leibniz says that Snell and Fermat followed "the way of final causes" in their discovery of the minimum principle in optics (that light goes "by the easiest or at least most determined" path), and he suspected that Descartes would never have discovered the principle and proved it by the method of efficient causes had he not heard of Snell's discovery of it by the other method, the "way of final causes."[124]

In most cases, however, neither method can be perfectly used by men. The most perfect method, would be a "demonstration" of contingent truths of fact, beginning with a priori knowledge of the internal constitution of bodies attained by a contemplation of God and leading to mechanical laws derived from teleological premises. But Leibniz wisely points out that this method is so difficult that it is not to be undertaken except by "superior geniuses," and even they cannot hope to arrive at particular truths by it; this "absolute method" is saved for a better life.[125] But against Locke, who gave up the search for real essences and contented himself with nominal essences or the second of the two ways, Leibniz consistently holds to the ideal of knowledge which would come from our knowledge of real essences.[126]

---

[118] *Ibid.*, p. 675 (1692). For a description of the middle way without the name, see *Discourse on Metaphysics*, §§ 21, 22.

[119] Loemker, p. 1064 (1714–15).   [120] *Ibid.*, pp. 266, 444–445 (1682–84).

[121] *Ibid.*, p. 723 (1695); *Discourse on Metaphysics*, § 19. They are, however, of benefit in that they increase the perfection, and hence the happiness, of all creatures, including man.

[122] Loemker, p. 1014 (1714).   [124] *Ibid.*, p. 782 (ca. 1696).

[123] Loemker, in his Introduction, p. 37.   [125] *Ibid.*, p. 437 (1683–84).

[126] *New Essays*, III, iii, § 18; IV, vi, §§ 8–11.

In the second method, that of efficient causes, we cannot go far without having recourse to regulative or heuristic considerations proper to the "way of final causes." This we have already noticed, in Leibniz' remark about Descartes and Snell. But we cannot just juxtapose the two methods, for we do not, for the most part, have definite knowledge of God's purposes. Hence hypotheses must take the place of the a priori certainties which the perfect architectonic method of final causes would require. Hypotheses may be about either the final or the efficient causes; it does not matter which, so long as they work. They are suggested by analogies, and are to be tested by their adequacy to all the phenomena (like a key to a cryptogram) and by their predictive value.[127] All the world might be a dream, and yet if we make good use of our reason in attending to it, seeking the proper marks of objective phenomena in it, we will not be deceived by it, or confuse dreams and waking consciousness.[128] Appearances are not necessarily illusions, even though they are not metaphysically what they seem to be.

In this way Leibniz came to terms with three great movements which constitute the tide of modern science: the insistence upon a systematic, mathematical order; the insistence upon the hypothetical status of most (or all) explanations of phenomena; and the insistence upon the decisive role of observation and experiment in the empirical filling to be given to mathematical form and in the testing of the hypotheses. But another principle which modern science has explicitly rejected, even though it tacitly used it long after it was banished by Galileo, Descartes, Hobbes, and Spinoza, is also integral to Leibniz' conception of the organization of knowledge. This is the theory of the objective validity and methodological usefulness of teleological explanations of physical phenomena.

This theory, objectionable if used to permit or require specific explanations of specific events, is used by Leibniz in a less objectionable way he calls "anagogic" or "architectonic."[129] Though he maintains the validity and sufficiency of mechanical causes in intraphenomenal relations, he holds that explanation of nature is not complete when we simply give sufficient reasons for the events in its course by stating the laws by which, with proper boundary conditions, the events in question can be demonstrated to occur. In addition, according to the architectonic principle, the laws themselves must be explained in terms of *their* sufficient reason. The sufficient reason of some laws is found in others, more basic; but none of the laws, however basic, is necessary, for the existence of this frame of the world itself is contingent, and must have a sufficient condition which lies outside the complex of nature or series of natural events. Leibniz' philosophy was the longest step taken in modern philosophy toward answering the question as to why this world itself exists, instead of some other or none at all. He took this step because he assigned absolutely limitless validity to the principle of sufficient reason. Because it was applied to God himself, Leibniz did more than any other modern metaphysician since Spinoza toward rationalizing the concept of both God and nature; and because his principle

[127] Loemker, p. 288 (1678); *New Essays*, IV, xii, § 13.
[128] *Ibid.*, pp. 603–605 (1690?).   [129] *Ibid.*, p. 780 (1696).

was teleological, unlike Spinoza he moralized the concept of both God and nature.

It has been one of the paradoxes of science since the time of Descartes that the scientific control of nature for human purposes has been made possible by the denial of the legitimacy of the concept of natural purpose. This denial left man's own purposes unexplained by nature and jeopardized, at least in theory, by the expansion of natural concepts into the sphere of human conduct. Leibniz' architectonic conception of nature, based on his teleological reading of the principle of sufficient reason, bridged the chasm between cause and purpose, fact and value, and preserved a little longer in Germany than elsewhere the *possibility* of a teleological interpretation of nature, by trying to show the *necessity* of such an interpretation. A complementary relation of the two ways of looking at the world lasted through most of the eighteenth century, even though Leibniz' effort to show that it was necessary on metaphysical grounds was jettisoned in favor of a man-oriented external teleology, deistically established. When, to offset the arbitrariness of much of the physicotheology of the post-Leibniz period, the next attempt at a demonstration of their necessary complementarity was made by Kant in 1790, it was done on an epistemological basis and with metaphysical implications far removed from Leibniz'.

The Realm of Grace

Each monad reflects the entire universe from its own point of view; but the highest of created monads, spirits, reflect the system of the universe and are thus "images of the divinity itself . . . each spirit being like a little divinity within its own sphere." Spirits enter into a society with God and make up "the city of God . . . the most perfect state which is possible under the most perfect of monarchs." The city of God is "a moral world within the natural world"; it exists for the glory of God as a reflection of his distinctive goodness, while the natural world shows his power and wisdom. The harmony between the realm of grace and the realm of nature is perfect. Noble actions and vices carry their rewards and punishment with them by the order of nature; and if eschatology requires the destruction of this globe itself, its destruction and repair, or the reconstitution of another, will occur by nature.[130]

This facile optimism was attacked by Voltaire and Hume long after Leibniz' death, but from 1695 to 1709 Leibniz devoted a large part of his philosophical efforts to defending his optimism and the principle of pre-established harmony, on which it was based, from the attacks and questions of Pierre Bayle.[131] The major document, written about five years after Bayle's death, presumably at the behest of Queen Sophie Charlotte, was

---

[130] *Monadology*, §§ 83–88; *Principles of Nature and Grace*, § 15.

[131] Long before Bayle questioned the principle of pre-established harmony, Leibniz was already concerned with the problem of reconciling the freedom of man with the harmony of the world and the will of God. See Loemker, p. 227 (1671); p. 408 (1679); and *Discourse on Metaphysics*, §§ 30–31.

Theodicy: Essays on the Goodness of God, the Freedom of Man, and the Origin of Evil.[132] This was the work by which Leibniz was chiefly known, especially by nonphilosophers, during the eighteenth century, and it was the only sizable book he published. But to us it is a very unsatisfactory book. It is a work of erudition in the worst sense of seventeenth-century pedantry; it follows in tedious detail the ebb and flow of a decade-long argument, so that it is repetitious and far too long for its thin content; and, most seriously, it puts Leibniz squarely in the center—or, even worse, on the wrong side—of controversies which had begun to die out in the previous century.

Eighteenth-century optimism was to be based on man's feeling of his own power, his confidence in his own secular intellect in the service of moral and secular progress. In France, England, and Holland this confidence grew at the expense of faith in theological guarantees of the kind Leibniz tried to give. In Germany, theological support for the Enlightenment was available in Leibniz' work, and this theological support helped make the German Enlightenment less humanistic and venturesome than the Enlightenment in those countries where the spirit of Locke, Voltaire, and Diderot reigned. Leibniz' optimism was God-centered and metaphysical; in the *Theodicy* (but not in most of his other writings) it is a contemplative, not a practical, optimism. Instead of reminding man of how much remains to be done, and how much he can do, it seeks to console him by showing him that things are not so bad as they seem. Eighteenth century optimism was an optimism of hope and work, his an optimism of faith and, he claimed, of reason. Leibniz' bland acceptance of the eternity of punishment and his defense of miracles offended both the moral and the intellectual optimism of the Enlightenment. It is regrettable that Leibniz' best-known work should have been his most backward-looking, and that he was known most widely for doctrines which, though held in all sincerity, were by no means likely to put his metaphysics in the best light or to bring out the distinctively revolutionary and most original aspects of his thought. Leibniz, himself a tolerant man, was no enthusiast for the general tolerance which the Enlightenment required.

The problem of the *Theodicy* is twofold. What is the relation of faith to knowledge? And how can reason solve the old dilemma: If God could prevent evil and did not, he is not all-good; and if he could not, he is not all-powerful?

Leibniz answers the first question in the standard scholastic way. He is against Bayle, who would deny the competence of reason in the name of faith. Bayle held that reason not only conflicts with faith, but because it is in conflict with itself it cannot be maintained against faith. Bayle's fideism was a consequence of his skepticism. Leibniz was no skeptic; there was therefore no basis for agreement with Bayle's fideism. Yet Leibniz does not want to go to the opposite extreme, with Spinoza and those called rationalists in the seventeenth century, and deny the validity of revelation; he does not wish to go even so far as Locke, ordinarily considered a ration-

[132] Translated by E. M. Huggard (London: Routledge & Kegan Paul, 1951).

alist in this context, and make reason the judge of revelation (except in a highly restricted sense).

In good scholastic fashion he draws a distinction between articles of faith opposed to reason and articles of faith which are beyond reason. The first (and this is as far as he will go with Locke) are necessarily false, for they are denials of analytic truths. The second, however, are not necessarily false, even though they conflict with truths of fact, and they are to be accepted if they are attested by revelation. Truths of reason are decisive against counter-revelations and show the revelation is spurious; but truths of fact are not necessarily decisive.

To defend this view Leibniz does give a new and original twist to some old arguments. For, by his theory, *truths of faith that are beyond reason,* in the sense that their truth is not demonstrable a priori according to the law of contradiction, *are beyond reason in precisely the same sense that truths of fact are beyond reason.* Neither is in fact demonstrable; what is true in each is true because there is a sufficient reason lying in God's will, and these truths, so far as they can be attested, are never in fact contradictory to each other. A conflict between a universal statement of a truth of fact founded upon probable arguments and inductions from the normal and regular course of phenomena, on the one hand, and the occurrence of a miracle or the truth of a theological Mystery of faith on the other cannot be resolved necessarily in favor of the former. The former is based only on probable arguments drawn from the ordinary course of nature. Truths of fact are contingent truths at best, and at worst they are not true at all but only probable hypotheses. Hence there is neither any truth of reason nor of fact which prevents either God's miraculous intervention in nature or his working in ways unknown to human beings, yet working according to laws of nature he has established. Some miracles, like that of the Eucharist, are explained in the former way, and others are ascribed to the work of angels acting "according to the ordinary laws of their nature," but laws unknown to us.[133] "As Queen Christine used to say: it is enough to reject ordinary appearances when they are contrary to Mysteries."[134]

The second problem, that of evil in a world created by a perfect God, is an ancient one, and in Christianity it is involved in the complex of problems concerning the divine justice of predestination and eternal damnation. Since Leibniz' doctrine of pre-established harmony is so close to the Calvinist doctrine of predestination—it is a metaphysical formulation of that theological dogma—this family of problems was bound to concern Leibniz. Leibniz deals with it through a series of distinctions, none made up especially for this purpose but all of them originating in other parts of Leibniz' metaphysics.

The first is the distinction between certainty and necessity. God could be certain that Adam would sin, but that does not make it necessary that Adam sin. Adam's sinning is a contingent fact, certain but not necessary.[135]

---

[133] *Theodicy* § 249. Miracles of the first kind require a counter-miracle to keep the rest of nature in order.

[134] *Ibid.,* § 38. [135] *Theodicy,* §§ 20, 158, 282.

Second, there is the distinction between antecedent will and permission. For, it will be said, God not only foresaw that Adam would sin if this world were created, but by freely creating this world he thereby willed all that is in it, including Adam's sin. Not so, says Leibniz; for God willed this world for the good in it, not for the evil it contained. Therefore he only permitted Adam to sin, knowing that he would. He did not will that Adam should sin but permitted it for the sufficient reason that this world, in which Adam would sin, was better than any alternative possible world.

Third, there is the distinction between the will and the intellect of God. Not even God could create an impossible world; what worlds are possible is determined by the logical essences which are the blueprints of any world that could be created. God could, and did, choose all the perfections compossible in the best of them; but he could not have chosen, for example, a world in which I should have the pleasures of sinning *and* the bliss of innocence.

Very well, then; but in this world Adam and I cannot help sinning since the world is as it is; hence we are not blameworthy. Not so, replies Leibniz, for there is a fourth distinction: though every substance in the world acts with absolute spontaneity and, at the same time, in perfect harmony with all the others, some but not all spontaneous actions, harmonizing with the total state of the world, are free actions. Freedom is *intelligent spontaneity*, but freedom cannot require indifference or equipoise, for freedom of indifference conflicts with the principle of sufficient reason. Every action, even the freest, has a sufficient reason. But we can determine empirically, or by introspection, when an action is free in the sense that it meets, say, Aristotle's criteria of deliberateness, knowledge, and so on.

But does not this mean, even so, that Adam did not, in fact, "have any choice"? No, replies Leibniz, because there are two kinds of necessity. "Adam did not fall" is not a self-contradictory proposition even though "Adam did fall" is entailed by the complete concept of Adam. "Adam fell" is a truth of fact, which is only hypothetically necessary, and hypothetical necessity, Leibniz says, does "no harm" to the concept of freedom.[136]

Does not even hypothetical necessity make a mockery of deliberating and choosing, and induce a fatalistic resignation? No, replies Leibniz, because though we know that our future actions are determined, we do not know what they are determined to be. Hence we must deliberate and take responsibility for whatever it is that we, when the time comes, will intelligently decide to do.[137] A quietistic fatalism does not follow from knowledge that we are determined if we are ignorant of the specific determination.

Lastly, when the time comes and I choose, as I must choose, in ways foreseen by God and under the hypothetical necessities of my nature and the rest of the universe, suppose I choose to do evil; should I be punished for it, since I could not do otherwise? Yes; that I should suffer eternal

---

[136] *Theodicy*, § 132. Since "I can jump over the English Channel" is not self-contradictory, I am free to do so. How easy the case for compatibilism is! Wolff's argument is equally silly; see below, p. 274
[137] *Ibid.*, § 58.

torment if my action is in fact evil is required by "the principle of the fitness of things."[138]

Then does not one wish to rebel against so monstrous an hypothesis? No. Leibniz warns us: *We know by infallible proof that this is the best of all possible worlds.*

In consequence, all the objections taken from the course of things in which we observe imperfections are based only on false appearances. For, if we were capable of understanding the universal harmony, we should see that what we are tempted to find fault with is connected with the plan most worthy of being chosen: in a word, we should *see*, and should not merely *believe* only, that what God has done is best.[139]

It is regrettable that German philosophers did not produce a sound reply to this until long after a skeptical Scot and a cynical Frenchman had raised the obvious question: *Do we know this?*

However much Leibniz was attempting in the *Theodicy* to shore up orthodoxy against both skepticism and fideism by means of reason, this was not the only, and perhaps not the most important, aspect of his religious thinking. There are three other phases of Leibniz' piety that must be briefly mentioned.

There was his life-long effort to bring about a reunification of the churches. A Lutheran with a near-Calvinist metaphysics and sometimes in the employ of Catholic princes, Leibniz minimized the irrational factors in religious sectarianism and not only worked for, but believed in the possibility of, reunification based on a theology common to all. We can understand this illusion, which is as old as the division of the churches itself; Leibniz' was the last great effort after that of Calixtus, and after the Thirty Years' War the need for religious peace was even more obvious than it had been before. Leibniz and his forerunners had been convinced that reunification was possible so long as it was only princes and their court or academic theologians who had to be convinced that it was needed. If the cost of the division to them, and to the common culture they represented, could be shown, and if a compromise theology on which they could agree could be devised, union would be not only wise but also feasible. The cost of division was easily demonstrated. Leibniz had only to point to the divisiveness of what he thought were minor points in doctrine as a source of major weakness against two dangers that threatened them all. The first was the external danger, the Turks at the gates of Vienna. The Empire could hardly be called "Holy" as long as the Protestant princes succeeded in weakening the imperial power and were aided in this by His Most Christian Majesty in France, who favored Protestant princes over Catholic emperors. Nor would Louis XIV be pursuing a Christian policy if he made war on Christians while the Germans faced the Turks almost alone; it was worse than un-Christian, it was unenlightened. But a unification of the churches,

---

[138] *Ibid.*, § 74. This is the starting point for the important controversy between Lessing and Eberhard; see below, p. 345.

[139] *Ibid.*, § 44.

Leibniz believed, would ameliorate the tensions within the Empire and between the Empire and France and thus secure Christendom against the Turk. The decline of the Turkish threat after 1683 and the attack by the French on the Palatinate in 1688 made it obvious that a Catholic-Protestant rapprochement was politically impossible. Leibniz was rebuffed by Bossuet, and thenceforth restricted his efforts to bringing about agreement between Lutherans and Calvinists in Germany.

But there was, in Leibniz' mind at least, a second, an internal, threat. He feared an intellectual and moral, and perhaps even a political, revolution as a consequence of an erroneous secular philosophy. If nature cannot be understood in Cartesian, Spinozistic, and Hobbesian terms, how much less can human society be understood and regulated by the followers of these men. In 1678 he had warned against the consequences of Spinozism;[140] twenty years later he exculpates Spinoza himself, but warns against imitators,

who, believing themselves released from the troublesome fear of an overseeing Providence, and of a menacing future, give loose rein to their brutish passions, and turn their mind to the seduction and corruption of others; and if they are ambitious and of a disposition somewhat harsh, they will be capable . . . of setting on fire the four corners of the earth. I find also that similar opinions insinuating themselves little by little into the minds of men of high life who rule others and upon whom affairs depend, and slipping into the books of fashion, dispose all things to the general revolution with which Europe is threatened, and accomplish the destruction of what still remains in the world of the generous sentiments of the Ancient Greeks and Romans . . . If, however, this disease of an epidemic mind whose bad effects begin to be visible is corrected, these evils will perhaps be prevented; but if it goes on increasing, Providence will correct men by the revolution which must spring therefrom.[141]

The churches, at least as long as they were bitterly divided on theological questions, could make no solid front against those who now cared little for theological subtleties and who would, in the next generation, exclaim "Écrasez l'infâme." Since the differences between the churches were so much less than the differences between any church and the new ideas of the French, English, and Dutch Enlightenments, it is easy to see how Leibniz could believe in the possibility of a holy crusade against the internal enemy as well as against the external.

But quite apart from the unification of the churches against secular freethinking, Leibniz was also concerned with the religious foundation—be it ever so disputed over by the religions involved—of secular culture itself. A purely natural religion led inevitably to a purely natural law without theological sanction and thus to a general weakening of law; Pufendorf was the natural heir of Hobbes and Spinoza. But not only did Leibniz hold to the binding character of revealed divine law;[142] he also saw at least an isomorphism between divine and human law. Theology is the jurisprudence of the Kingdom of God, and the glory of God is the measure of *all* law.[143]

140 Loemker, p. 570 (1678).   142 Loemker, p. 695 (1693).
141 *New Essays*, IV, xvi, § 4.   143 *Ibid.*, p. 122 (1666).

Theological considerations are therefore inescapable even in the theory of natural law, both in the sense of the laws which the things of nature manifest and in the laws which nature seems to give to man for obedience.

The monad in its place in the established system of the world is the metaphysical vehicle of a divine vocation. Every soul carries out, if it is true to itself (and it is hard to see how it can fail to be, human sin to the contrary notwithstanding), God's purpose. The purpose of man is to increase his perfection, but this can be done only in association with all other monads. Love of man finds pleasure in the perfection of others, and furthers such perfection. Justice to others is only loving them as a wise man would love them, seeing them in all their relations to each other and to the universe and God. Duties to mankind are not accidental and man-imposed, but can be derived from our knowledge of the divine economy. Our love of our fellow man is derived from our love of God, the wise father of all of us and the monarch of the realm of grace.[144]

None of this edifying religious talk, however, has exempted Leibniz from accusations of hypocrisy. Moved, apparently, by world-historical ideals and even, perhaps, sometimes attracted by merely dynastic political expedients, Leibniz gained an unenviable reputation as more of a diplomat than a philosopher in theological questions. We are told that the burghers of Hanover called him "Lövenix"—"a believer in nothing." Efforts were made repeatedly to get him to change from Lutheranism to Calvinism or Catholicism. There was nothing unusual in that, and many of those he was associated with did go over to Rome; but the stories that he had changed his confession were widely believed. His diplomatic and irenic temperament and an apparent coldness and flatness in his emotional nature create the impression, which is hard to eradicate even today, that his religion was more a matter of words and forms than of substance. Christian sentiments flow so facilely from his pen, he so readily accomodates himself to Jesuit, Jansenist, Calvinist, Pietist, and Lutheran ways of speaking, that it may easily be thought that he had no genuine religion at all.

Yet this impression is probably incorrect. There is no decisive reason to discount the constantly repeated strains of baroque piety in his letters and publications, as if they were merely expressions of his diplomatic and not his religious make-up. Good evidence for taking them as serious and sincere expressions of his belief is to be found in his writings on religion which were *not* meant for publication and which were not seen until long after his death.[145] These show a Neoplatonic mystical piety and remind us of the fact that Protestant mysticism, in the person of Böhme (whom he often cites), and mystical naturalism and Pythagoreanism, from Paracelsus and Erhard Weigel, are present even in his metaphysics. He liked to cite St. Theresa's statement, "The soul must look at things as if only God and it existed in the world."[146] This could serve as the text for his most genuine metaphysics, and goes far beyond the requirements of a political theologizing.

[144] *Monadology*, § 90.
[145] See especially, "On the True Theologia Mystica," Loemker, pp. 608–613 (ca. 1690?).
[146] Quoted from Kurt Huber, *Leibniz* (Munich: Oldenbourg, 1951), p. 102.

Three
The Eighteenth Century

XI

Two Founders of the German Enlightenment

So long as historians divide the past into specific periods and give names to them, there will be debate about when each specific period begins and when it ends; and this will lead to debate about whether periodization has any justification at all. This pattern of debate can be seen in controversies concerning the Enlightenment.

In England it is difficult to fix the beginning of this period by answering the question, "When did a certain idea or family of ideas emerge?" Most of the ideas thought to be characteristic of the "Age of Locke and Newton" (a name which at least puts a *terminus ad quem* to the period) can be found as far back as Hobbes and even Bacon. In France, Montaigne might be claimed for the *Éclaircissement* did this not upset the chronology of other well-recognized periods too much. Faced with the problem of defining and defending two cut-off points for the purpose of choosing writers whom I considered to be representative of the Enlightenment, I elsewhere suggested the following dates: 1687–1688, the publication of Newton's *Principia* and the Glorious Revolution, and 1790–1793, the publication of Kant's last *Critique* and the Reign of Terror.[1] Locke and Newton, I said, were its mentors, Nature and Humanity its myths.

[1] *Eighteenth-Century Philosophy* (New York: Free Press, 1966), p. 1.

A large amount of arbitrariness is involved in most periodization, including this one. These myths did not come into existence in 1687 and cease to be effective in 1793. But it is easier to defend the name *Aufklärung* and such a pair of dates in Germany than it is in other countries. In fact, if there is any error it is likely to be that a date about 1690 is too early; there is a far greater perseveration of "typical" seventeenth-century modes of thought and feeling into the eighteenth century than anticipations of "typical" eighteenth-century *Weltanschauungen* in the seventeenth. This is so true that some historians of German thought prefer to see the Enlightenment as beginning about 1740, at about the time of the establishment of the University of Göttingen and the re-establishment of the Berlin Academy. Certainly Germany in, say, 1720 had very few resemblances, intellectually, to England and France, and it is hard to remember that Wolff was a contemporary of Hume and Montesquieu. Brandenburg and Hanover about 1750, however, do seem to be synchronous with Paris, London, and Edinburgh of that date, so we might well conclude that Germany joined the European Age of Reason only in the middle of the century.

But if we ignore these Europe-wide synchronies, and ask about when the greatest changes *within* Germany occurred, we must without hesitation answer: in the period of Leibniz' greatest activity, which coincided with the predominance of Pietism, the life of von Tschirnhaus, and the early careers of Christian Thomasius and Christian Wolff. Try however hard we may, we cannot find a Bacon or a Hobbes or a Descartes or a Montaigne in Germany before 1680 whom we might claim to be the "real" progenitor of the Age of Reason. We have examined the most important German thinkers, and we have found none who would qualify; we have also found no individual thoughts or works of the mind which would qualify. We have found, instead, scholastics, occultists, mystics, heresy-hunters, and witch-burners. We find no splendid courts attracting the best wits, no fearless critics of tyranny, no courageous Utopians. If there were mute inglorious Miltons, they were indeed mute in the insane clamor of the Thirty Years' War. When we compare some aspects of the thought of Wolff and Thomasius (the invincible scholastic pedantry of the former, the quasimystical natural philosophy of the latter) with the kind of thought indigenous to the seventeenth century in Germany and elsewhere, we may agree with those historians who date the beginnings of the Enlightenment only after the death of Thomasius and with the waning of Wolff's influence. Certainly if we say they were the founders of the Enlightenment along with Leibniz and von Tschirnhaus, we have not gone *too far* back. Yet Leibniz seems to me to be much more characteristic of the age that was dying than of the one that was coming to birth. He was a good European writing in Latin and French for a European audience; he was fearful of what he saw coming out of the teachings of those from whom the eighteenth century was to learn most; he contributed nothing to the *Verbürgerlichung* of culture in the eighteenth century. His direct influence on German philosophical thought from 1720 to 1765 was small. And von Tschirnhaus had no followers (except, to some extent, Wolff himself). The mentors of the German Enlightenment were two professors in the University of Halle, not von Tschirnhaus and Leibniz, the great mathematician and philosopher and man of affairs.

The German Enlightenment was unique in several respects. First, it did not spring from an upsurge of the new science coming out of England. Second, it arose at a time of religious revival, whereas in England the Methodist revival was to occur later against the Age of Reason and in France the Jansenist movement was already dying. Third, it did not have a political base; the social classes that could carry the ideology of Enlightenment were weak and ineffective.

Science, which shook the old foundations and quickly laid new ones for the universe in the seventeenth century, hardly made an impression on the German mind until the middle of the next century. Leibniz was an academy of sciences in himself, but he was best known in his own country not because of his physics and mathematics but because of his *Theodicy*, whose baroque piety seemed to belong to the previous century and was a laughing stock in France. "The battle between the ancients and the moderns," which was a conflict settled in the seventeenth century in the lands to the west, had to be fought in Germany in the eighteenth. Even in 1754, one quarter of all the books published in Germany were still in Latin.

Both Pietism and the territorial organization of the Lutheran Church in Germany kept religious innovation and criticism to a minimum. Just as German humanism, a movement against Catholic scholasticism, kept a religious orientation, so also the German Enlightenment, a philosophical movement against Protestant scholasticism, was pervaded with religious concern and sought to maintain religious attitudes and values. The cultural immaturity of German secular thought and the quiet patience of Pietism gave the German Enlightenment a religiosity and dull and pedantic sobriety not relieved by the wit, style, taste, urbanity, and intellectual courage found in France and Great Britain in this period.

Yet the Enlightenment in Germany was a part of a general change in the intellectual climate which extended from England to Russia (and, much later, under Joseph II, into Austria). As a Europe-wide movement it had some common features in each country. Everywhere it was marked by optimism, intellectualism, and a concern with human affairs and a weakening of speculation, orthodoxy, and respect for authoritarian institutions. Dilthey's classical statement is:

> The main features of the Enlightenment were everywhere the same: the autonomy of reason, the solidarity of intellectual culture, confidence in its inevitable progress, and the aristocracy of the spirit.[2]

In England its principal features were a growth in science, of toleration in religious policy, and of deism in theology; and the spread of the ideal of representative government. In France there was the new science under the influence of Newton, and an unsuccessful but persistent claim to toleration and representative ideals in government, with opposition to ecclesiastical and political forces both more extreme and less successful than in England.

[2] *Gesammelte Schriften* (Berlin and Leipzig: Teubner, 1923–36), III, 131.

Learning was put to revolutionary uses in the *Encyclopédie*. If the natural outcome of the English Enlightenment can be seen in the American Declaration of Independence and the Constitution of the United States, that of France is to be found in the French Revolution, which succeeded in establishing, though for only a short time, the ideology of the Enlightenment in the Declaration of the Rights of Man.

But in Germany nothing so dramatic issued from the Enlightenment. The reason why the Enlightenment ideals remained pious hopes and found little realization and, indeed, produced little practical activity toward their implementation, is to be found in the social structure. The losses in population, wealth, and the arts of civility resulting from the Thirty Years' War had not yet been recovered. Germany had, unlike France, no central government into which the best talents could be drawn or against which the best talents might unite. Germany was a congeries of tiny states which required bureaucratic talents for efficient administration but not broad-gauged political enlighteners; most of the states got neither. Their affairs were so frightfully mismanaged that many an intelligent man who might, in other countries, have helped remedy them preferred to move fifty miles away to a slightly better-managed state where he might think that, by contrast, he had entered an enlightened age. The states were too small to have an effective aristocratic class who might limit the arbitrariness of petty royalties, practice the arts of leisure, and develop fruitful eccentricities. Their economies were primitive, and they were too poor to have a rising middle class that might have successfully challenged particularist policies which produced economic chaos on a large scale. Even in the towns "the average citizen was . . . intensely conservative. There was something almost sacred for him in the established order of things, both in the practice of his particular craft or calling, and even in quite trivial matters of everyday life, so that his life was governed by petty rules and conventions to an extent which is now scarcely credible. A pedantic orderliness is an outstanding characteristic of almost all the good Bürger of that age."[3]

The classes from which freethinkers and *philosophes* in England and France were drawn—classes whose privileges were ideologically threatened, and classes on the way up who could threaten economically and ideologically the institutions stabilized by tradition—were weak and small in Germany. Who was to carry the burden of enlightenment? A few university professors, who might be silenced or dismissed; a few pastors, who made sure that their best works were published posthumously; here and there a misfit without followers. Reform, in the view even of Kant, would have to come from above.

Until Frederick the Great said, "Argue as much as you will, only obey!," the forces which produced enlightenment in France and England were, in Germany, not so much clandestine (for that would have required courage) as merely timid. Frederick accomplished two things. He permitted argu-

<hr/>

[3] W. H. Bruford, *Germany in the Eighteenth Century* (Cambridge [Eng.] University Press, 1935), pp. 221–222. For a more detailed study of the equivocal position of the middle classes vis-à-vis the political problems, see Leonard Krieger, *The German Idea of Freedom* (Boston: Beacon Press, 1957), esp. pp. 28–40.

ment (but was genuinely contemptuous of Germans who did argue) and inspired enthusiasm (more, though, among those who did not have to obey him than among those who did). In his time, German private scholars (*Privatgelehrter*), journalists, university professors, pastors, and even civil servants began to speak out—only to be slapped down again by Friedrich Wilhelm II. And, for better or for worse, Germans began again to feel that they belonged together spiritually and (later) politically. How the beginnings of liberal and nationalistic ways of thought came into conflict when all of Germany was faced by the threat of Napoleon belongs to a later chapter of German history; but even in the eighteenth century they did not aid and abet each other, and the forces which might have given a solid front against traditionalism, despotism, and the state churches were dispersed and ineffective. Most of the thinkers had no political program, and they had no national stage on which to complain. There was less freedom than in England, but less readiness to complain about it than in France. They never thought of trying to take things into their own hands; long habit and Pietism gave them patience with things as they were.

While in England and France "reason" and "nature" were watchwords in the struggle against dogmatic religion and, in France and America, against political absolutism, in Germany the effort was made, on the contrary, to show how reasonable and natural the religious and political powers were. "Humanity" was the ideal, for no one had any reason to fear the vague aspirations of humanity.

With unusual fervor Kant wrote in 1781: "Our age is in especial degree the age of criticism, and to criticism everything must submit."[4] A few years later he admitted that he did not live in an enlightened age, but only in an age of enlightenment, when men were just getting the courage to use their own reason, to dare to know, to release themselves from a tutelage into which they had fallen because they had not the resolution and courage to follow their own reason.[5] Courage to use their own reason and to teach others to do so too—this does not mark a new beginning in philosophy itself; but combined with school reform, the publication of moral weeklies, and philosophizing in German instead of Latin and French it did mark a new turn in German culture. Two men are preeminently responsible for this turn in Germany: Thomasius and Wolff.

Thomasius

Christian Thomasius was born in Leipzig on January 1, 1655, the son of Jakob Thomasius, professor of law in the university and later a teacher of Leibniz. He took his law degree in Frankfort on the Oder in 1679. At first, as a good Lutheran, he was strongly opposed to Pufendorf's thesis that our knowledge of natural law is independent of theology and based solely on reason even though reason must acknowledge God as its author. But reading Pufendorf's *Apologia* affected him deeply, turning him passionately

---

4 *Critique of Pure Reason*, Preface to first edition, A xi note.
5 "What is Enlightenment?" in *Kant on History*, ed. L. W. Beck (Indianapolis: Bobbs-Merrill, 1963), pp. 1, 8.

against his entire upbringing in orthodox Lutheran scholasticism. To the effect of Pufendorf on him he ascribed his entire reorientation in life: his rejection of authority, his efforts to stamp out religious intolerance, his lasting and bitter opposition to prejudices of all kinds, his thorough commitment to the conviction that he and all men should think for themselves. Not only did Pufendorf's doctrines pass over, for a time, into Thomasius, but there was a much more personal and enduring reaction: he was incensed at himself for having ignorantly taken an anti-Pufendorf position under the influence of his orthodox teachers, without having thought and investigated for himself. In turning against his former self, he also turned against the seventeenth-century orthodox education which had misled him. He described his conversion from a typical Lutheran orthodox view to an acceptance of Pufendorf's views and to a state of mind which we see as a mixture of empiricism and rationalism as opposed to dogmatism. This we learn from the preface to his *Institutes of Divine Jurisprudence* (*Institutiones iurisprudentiae divinae*, 1688).

After a journey to Holland, the source of most advanced ideas in Germany at that time, he returned to Leipzig where, about 1782, he began lecturing in the university. In 1684 he published a dissertation on bigamy, which went even further than Pufendorf, arguing that bigamy was not forbidden by natural law. In the *Institutes* of 1688 he showed his general adherence to Pufendorf's principles. He followed Pufendorf's offensive theory that our knowledge of the law is based upon reason and experience, but in the hybrid form of teaching that the source and authority of law is to be found in God as a divine legislator for nature and human nature. From this it followed both that reason can construct natural law and that the natural law includes the revealed law of the Decalogue.

The same year he broke still more openly with university traditions by announcing his lectures in German.[6] This was a step in his revolt against the sterile pedantry of those who, in his estimation, taught useless knowledge in a language the students could not understand. For these lectures he chose as his subject the Jesuit Balthasar Gracian's *Oracle and Art of Prudence*—a book for the man of the world, not a conventional text for Lutheran university students. The next year he began the publication of his literary magazine which, in articles and book reviews, under various titles continued his attack on scholasticism, Lutheran orthodoxy, religious intolerance, and, in general, the backward state of things in Germany. This was the first monthly periodical in German, the forerunner of the moral weeklies of the eighteenth century. Thomasius is often called the father of German journalism.

While appealing to the general public in his magazine, Thomasius aimed also at university reform, and for this he himself used Latin in speaking

---

[6] It is generally said that Thomasius was the first professor to lecture in German. This is not true; often German lectures were given by professors who complained of their students' inability to understand Latin. What was revolutionary in Thomasius' act was that he *announced* that he would lecture in the vernacular. He agreed with Leibniz that the backwardness of Germany was in part due to the continued use of Latin, long after the French and English had gone to the vernacular. His criticism of scholastic Latin is as satirical as that of the humanists of the preceding century.

to scholars. In 1688 he published his *Introduction to Court Philosophy* (German and Latin editions). This book, appropriately dedicated to the memory of Peter Ramus, shows Thomasius' complete break with Lutheran scholasticism. In it he proposed that philosophy should be for the "man of the world," not for theologians or academic pedants. By the man of the world Thomasius meant the *honnête homme* and the professional public man; philosophy was to be no longer handmaiden to theology so much as handmaiden to law. Already in 1687 he had described his purposes in a famous German lecture, "In What Ways Ought One to Imitate the French?" by answering that one should do so by teaching "polite learning, *beauté d'esprit*, good taste and gallantry," and by using "our native language" instead of Latin. In the *Philosophia aulica* he argued that philosophy should be eclectic, not sectarian but open to truth wherever it is to be found. It should not be metaphysics, but it should begin in self-knowledge (not in the Cartesian, but in the Socratic sense) and be directed toward the practical knowledge of men and affairs. Logic in this book is an art of discovery, not of formal proof; the epistemology is a superficial theory of common sense against the dogmatism of the scholastics and the skepticism of Descartes.

It is understandable that Thomasius made many enemies by his German lectures, his satiric attacks, his defense of unpopular causes (e.g., of Pietism and of mixed marriage—between Lutherans and Calvinists![7]), and his unconventional ways (he is said to be the first professor to wear a sword while lecturing); and on March 10, 1690, he was forbidden to write or lecture. Escaping arrest only by flight, he went to Berlin, where he was given a pension and an appointment to the Ritter Akademie in Halle by the Elector Friedrich III. This school had been founded by the Great Elector for training students in the *realia*—in fact, for training them in much the way Thomasius later proposed. When the Ritter Akademie was made the University of Halle in 1694, Thomasius became rector and professor of law.

In 1691 he published his *Introduction to Logic* (*Einleitung zu der Vernunft-Lehre*) and his *Practical Logic* (*Ausübung der Vernunft-Lehre*) both based upon his lectures. In these two works, Thomasius was even less concerned with the traditional logic than he had been in his Leipzig days, and even more explicitly committed to making logic useful for life. He had a simple correspondence theory of truth based upon an uncritical belief in a natural conformity of the mind to its object. Nominalism, a sensationistic theory of the origin of ideas, a recognition of the importance of probability in life, and a belief in healthy common sense as a substitute for speculation and subtlety were recommended in a vigorous, though often awkward, German: and again there was attack on pedantry, speculation, sophistry, and superstition. Naturally there was a polite nod in the direction of revelation as dealing with mysteries beyond human knowledge, but it was hardly more than perfunctory.

---

[7] This fine point, however, was involved in dynastic politics, namely, the opposition of the marriage of a Saxon (Lutheran) prince to a Brandenburg (Calvinist) princess. The opposition in Leipzig was stronger than in more tolerant Brandenburg, where Thomasius sought refuge when dismissed from the University of Leipzig.

It is instructive to compare the logic of Thomasius with the *Medicina mentis* of von Tschirnhaus. Both were opposing the scholastic logic; both were aiming at the improvement of the mind, at writing an *ars inveniendi*. But there the resemblance ceases. Von Tschirnhaus was an epistemologist and a practicing scientist who had gone to school to Descartes and Spinoza. Though his book has the search for happiness as its introductory and concluding theme, it finds happiness in the highest degree in the discovery of truths, especially those of science. It is a book for the thinker, who begins with Cartesian doubts and certainties and goes through geometry and physics to a somewhat perfunctory acknowledgment that he is thereby brought to the knowledge of himself and God. Thomasius, on the other hand, emphasizes how little we know from our own resources—hardly more than the simplest laws of logic—and how the development of knowledge is a social process. One cannot think alone: "Thought consists of internal discourse, but this presupposes an external discourse . . . which is a sign of the thoughts of others. Hence it follows that children first grasp what *others* think about the essence of things, and only then can they themselves think what to say."[8] Hence while education and instruction and imitation of others are essential to any thought and knowledge, they are also the source of error, of the "prejudice of authority" which arises from the unreasonable fear and love of others which is characteristic of children, but which is strengthened by the ambition and authority of teachers. The other source of error, which Thomasius calls "the prejudice of precipitancy or impatience," the eradication of which was the central theme of the step-by-step method of von Tschirnhaus, is said by Thomasius to be relatively simple to remove; it grows out of the unreasonable love of ourselves (one's own opinions) which Thomasius thinks—though he calls it paradoxical—is easier to eradicate or control than our unreasonable love of others and their opinions. In both kinds of error, the understanding is more spoiled by the will than the will depraved by bad thought. Intellectual reform depends upon moral reform, and not conversely, as von Tschirnhaus taught. In all this, one sees Cartesian, Baconian, and Pietistic maxims for self-improvement.

But the correction of error is more dependent upon the rectification of society than upon the spontaneous development of rules of method in the individual's mind. The rectification of society is predicated upon the substitution of reasonable love of self and others for the unreasonable love, which took man out of the state of innocence and made everyone miserable, even though God gave man reason and love that he might be happy. For this, freedom of speech and thought, and especially academic freedom, are essential; and the backward state of Germany in comparison with that of other countries, he says, is owing to the lack of this freedom.

In *Introduction to Ethics* (*Einleitung zur Sitten-Lehre*, 1692) is hardly more than an elaboration of its subtitle, viz., "On the art of loving rationally

---

[8] *Einleitung zur Vernunft-Lehre* (1691), chap. xiii, in the anthology, *Aus der Frühzeit der deutschen Aüfklarung*, ed. Fritz Brüggemann (Leipzig: Reclam, 1928), p. 30. This edition is hereafter cited as Brüggemann.

and virtuously as the sole way to achieve a happy, decorous, and agreeable life." The monkish virtues are condemned, a welfare ethics is expounded. The good and happy life is one led in harmony with nature. Peace of mind is the highest good of man. Epicurean and Stoic ethics are nicely balanced, but Christian elements (or at least Christian words) are present too, for the basis of man's actions is love: "The original font of all good is love. The original font of all evil is love . . . The original font of all good is *reasonable* love. The original font of all evil is *unreasonable* love, and here we have the origin of universal unhappiness. In reasonable love you have universal happiness"—which is peace of mind.[9] The principal cause for unease of mind is found in man's social nature, which makes him an imitator of others, shifting from one point to another to gain approbation of this man or that. This is the unreasonable love that we have for others. We must exercise reasonable love of others in seeking the approbation only of good men, and of ourselves in understanding our own disposition and character. Thus in the moral sphere there are the same two errors that Thomasius found in the intellectual: the prejudices of social authority and of private obstinacy, both of which are to be set aside by reasonable love.

For the good life, therefore, there must be a practical knowledge of man. The purpose of ethics is not to make Christians out of men, but to make men out of beasts. The knowledge needed to accomplish this is to be gained from social intercourse, history, and *belles lettres*. Theory is not enough; but Thomasius does have a theory as to how it can be done. This is "the science of learning, from their daily conversation and even against their will, the secrets of the heart of another man."[10] A sharp-sighted man can learn from a careless word or gesture the inner impulses of another man; and he finds that all the passions and emotions of men are the same, the same in the learned and the ignorant, the courtier and the peasant. They are the love of pleasure, of honor, and of money. The man practiced in this science is able to assign a number to each of these and thereby represent its relative importance. Thomasius draws up tables of vices corresponding to each of the principal types of character, so that a man can place himself and others under the proper rubrics and discover the vices to which he is most prone and correct them in himself and take precautions against them in others. Similarly, there are equally useful tables of virtues.

While working on his *Practical Ethics* (*Ausübung der Sitten-Lehre*),[11] in 1694 Thomasius became a Pietist of the most extreme kind. In a confession before his colleagues and students, perhaps unique in German academic history, Thomasius—always perhaps something of an exhibitionist—exposed his sins and weaknesses (chiefly ambition and the love of pleasure); he

---

[9] *Ausübung der Sitten-Lehre* (1696), chap. i. (Brüggemann, p. 50).

[10] *Erfindung der Wissenschaft anderer Menschen Gemüt zu erkennen* (Address to Friedrich III, 1692), Brüggemann, p. 68; *Fundamenta iuris naturae et gentium*, 4th ed. (1718), bk. 1, chap. ii, § iii. Thomasius criticizes Descartes' classification of passions of the soul as "totally erroneous, difficult to understand, and replete with many contradictions" (*Fundamenta iuris*, note to § i).

[11] Published in 1696 in German, 1706 in Latin. The subtitle reads: "Medicine against Unreasonable Love and the Knowledge of Oneself Needed For It."

confessed that he had not reasonable love in his heart but a mixture of sinful motives which outwardly resembled reasonable love while really being selfish and avaricious. But he went further: reasonable love itself is not able, even when it exists, to overcome sin; in fact, it is itself a mixture of sins. Here Thomasius returned to the Lutheran belief in the impotency of the moral will, going even beyond Pietism into a disabling sense of his own unworthiness. In turning still more resolutely against orthodoxy, he called Gottfried Arnold's *Impartial History of the Church and Heresy* (a main source of information about the spiritualists and theosophists we have already discussed in Chapter VI) "the best book, after the Bible," and he wrote a commendatory introduction to an edition of a work by Pierre Poiret, the French quietist and mystic.

This radical change of heart gave a markedly pessimistic strain to the *Practical Ethics*, on which he was then working. In other works he acknowledged for the first time the role of the mystical experience in the enlightenment and salvation of mankind, and saw Böhme and Sebastian Franck as his mentors and the great heretics as the true Christians. He replaced his mildly mechanistic view of man and nature with a pantheistic, vitalistic theory which borrowed much from Paracelsus. He opposed Descartes and Spinoza more than ever for their mechanism and naturalism, and he condemned the superficiality of a merely mundane ethics.

In 1699 he published his *Essay on the Essence of Spirit, or Fundamental Theory of both Natural Science and Ethics* (*Versuch von Wesen des Geistes oder Grund-Lehren sowohl der natürlichen Wissenschaft als der Sitten-Lehre*). The subtitle of this obscure and eclectic book gives sufficient evidence of its contents; it tells us that in the book it is proved "that light and air are a spiritual being, that all bodies consist of matter and spirit, and that there is one attractive force in the whole of nature, while in man there is a twofold spirit of good and evil." For the next few decades, it was this book which made Thomasius important in German philosophy, not the writings which make us remember him as one of the harbingers of Enlightenment. As we shall see in the next chapter, the epigoni of Thomasius, Pietistic opponents of Wolffianism, continued the tradition of nature-mysticism and occultism and thus opposed the intellectualism and scientific aims of Wolff and his followers.

It was in this way that Pietism, anti-intellectualistic in theology and generally indifferent to secular learning, became associated with an active opposition to the newer forms of natural science.

The extremity of the turn in Thomasius' way of thinking, while marking a public conversion to Pietism, marked also the beginning of his break with the Pietistic establishment in Halle, especially with August Hermann Francke, who had come to Halle only shortly after Thomasius and had founded the famous Halle Orphanage. This was one of the chief institutions of the Pietistic movement, and Francke had originally accepted and put into practice many of Thomasius' educational ideas. But Thomasius, always an extremist, now opposed the practical activism of Francke and the rigorous Pietistic practices he installed in the school.

In spite of his very open way of revealing himself in his writings, we do not know what led him into, or out of, the Pietistic movement. The personal influence of Francke was certainly important in both. When Francke came to Halle, Thomasius chose him as his confessor; at the end of his Pietistic period, he was offended by Francke's denunciation of Frau Thomasius' finery in Easter dress. But if we look for philosophical rather than personal reasons for his change of heart, we find the impression made upon him by Locke's condemnation of religious enthusiasm, bringing him back to his perhaps more natural and comfortable state of mind. Francke now described him as a "man of the world [*Weltkind*] from whom the spirit of God has departed." There ensued a literary and personal debate in which Thomasius made many of the objections to Pietistic education which Kant was later to express on the basis of his own experience in a Pietistic school. In trying to convert the children, Thomasius said, Francke's regimen succeeded only in making them into "monks, that is, uneducated, melancholy, fantastic, obstinate, recalcitrant, intolerant, and spiteful men."[12]

After his break with Pietism, Thomasius' activities and teaching did not recommend him to his colleagues in the theological faculty, and efforts were made to have Berlin discipline or punish him. He was ordered to refrain from trespassing in their realm, and they were ordered to desist from personal attacks on him. Neither side strictly heeded these commands, but nothing untoward happened; indeed, in 1709 to persuade him not to accept a call to return to the University of Leipzig he was given the title of *Geheimrath*.

In the successful efforts by the Pietists to have Wolff dismissed in 1723, Thomasius was strangely neutral. For though he was as opposed to Wolff's dry intellectualism as he then was to Pietistic anti-intellectualism, he had defended the *libertas philosophandi* on which Halle had prided itself and which it was now renouncing; and on the specific point which the Pietists held against Wolff (that he did not base ethics upon revelation), Thomasius was in agreement with Wolff. But the two men did not like each other, and Thomasius, so courageous in fighting intolerance and bigotry elsewhere, stood aside when the greatest scandal in Halle's history occurred.

After his break with the Pietists and after the cabinet order to desist from teaching in fields of the theological and philosophical faculties, Thomasius returned to his first profession, that of law. Most of his work in the eighteenth century was in laying the foundations of natural law and in pushing practical legal reforms. He was the principal German critic of torture and trials for witchcraft, and such progress as was made against these two evils in Germany in the eighteenth century are to be attributed to his work and influence. The work of Balthasar Bekker,[13] a Dutch theologian who adopted Cartesianism and who drew from this the conclusion that witchcraft should be dealt with as a medical problem, did not entirely convince Thomasius. So he did not attack witchcraft trials on such a specu-

[12] Quoted from "Thomasius in seinem Verhältnis zu A. H. Francke," by August Nebe in *Christian Thomasius, Leben und Lebenswerk,* ed. Max Fleischmann (Halle: Max Niemeyer, 1931), p. 404.

[13] Bekker's works were *De philosophia Cartesiana admonitio candida et sincera* (1668) and *De betooverde wereld* (1691). Thomasius' attacks on witchcraft trials were to be found in many books; see, for example, *Kurtze Lehrsatze von dem Laster der Zauberei* (1704), in Brüggemann, pp. 99ff.

lative basis. Rather, he appealed, as it were, to the professional conscience of the lawyers in pointing to the judicial abuses involved in witchcraft prosecution, namely, that the charges of witchcraft and the "evidence" admissible against witches did not meet the standards of law. By satire and by detailed historical knowledge of the precedents in witchcraft trials he made his point. Similarly, he pointed out to the judges, who were jealous of their privilege of determining punishment, that, by allowing torture, they had handed the right of punishment over to others before they themselves had decided whether it was justified by the guilt of the accused. While neither of these evils entirely ceased, Thomasius did much to reduce their frequency.

His *Foundation of the Law of Nature and Nations, Deduced from Common Sense* (*Fundamentum iuris naturae et gentium ex sensu communi deducta*, 1705) was his most important work in the theory of law and it gives a good survey of his entire psychological and ethical theory. For, as shown in the title, by this date he had given up the hybrid natural-law theory he originally accepted from Pufendorf. Law, both in the sense of moral law and in the stricter sense of *ius naturale*, is discerned by the natural light playing upon human nature; neither law nor morals, of which it is a part, concerns man's salvation but only his happiness in this life.[14] Nature, which is the source of law, is conceived independently of God's will; God is not the author or the source of the authority of the natural law, as Pufendorf had taught. Thus Thomasius goes beyond the position he and Pufendorf had shared when they believed that God was the author of laws, even of those which could be discovered by reason. Grotius had taught that natural law would be valid even if there were no God. Pufendorf and Thomasius—at the beginning of his career—had denied this; now Thomasius goes even farther and asserts that even though there is a God, God's laws are not natural laws but only divine positive laws.[15] The connection between theology and law, weakened in Germany by Pufendorf, was finally broken by Thomasius.

Instead of theology, ethics is now made the foundation of law, and ethics is a part of "special physics," that is, the empirical science of (human) nature.[16] The naturalistic and rational ethics Thomasius had already propounded provides a foundation for an equally naturalistic and rationalistic theory of law. Both are based upon a Grotian and Althusian conception of the sociality of man, not upon a Hobbesian conception of man as the natural enemy of man. The goals of morality and law are the same: the moral ideals of happiness and peace of mind become, in law, those of general happiness and external peace. The difference between law and ethics is not found in different goals, origins, or sanctions but in the question of the external enforceability of the laws. Outer freedom is the goal of *iustum*, or law, and the common good, the goal of *decorum*.[17] The basic rule of *iustum* is: do not unto others what you would not have them do unto you. The basic rule of *decorum* is affirmative: Do unto others what you would have

[14] *Fundamenta iuris*, Proem, § xix, p. 17.
[15] *Ibid.*, I, v, §§ 33, xxxvii; vi, §§ 2–4.
[16] *Ibid.*, i, § 40.
[17] *Ibid.*, iv, § 89 (p. 141).

them do unto you.[18] The first rule is strictly enforceable while the second is not, since it leaves elbow room and must take account of circumstances. Both are distinguished from *honestum,* which, concerned with inner peace and happiness, is the subject matter of ethics and is unenforceable by external authority.[19] It rule is: What you will that others should do for themselves, that do for yourself.

The resemblance of these divisions to those Kant will draw between perfect and imperfect duties and between duties of law and duties of virtue is obvious.[20] The foundation of jurisprudence in moral philosophy and the priority of the moral over the political order is to be found in both philosophers. But while Kant did not seek this foundation in human nature, Thomasius located the source and authority of the natural law in the natural human striving for peace and happiness. External law is, for him, one of the forms of the rational love of self and others. The love of God is important only in the specific duties of religion, which are a part of the positive, not of the natural law. Thomasius argued for toleration of religious differences; he argued that a superstitious man is more dangerous to the state than an atheist. But as a way of keeping religious intolerance under control, he defended a territorial theory of church polity, according to which the civil power should decide all questions of church governance, cultus, and discipline which are socially important but, from the standpoint of theology, matters of indifference (*adiaphora*). Questions of dogma should be left to the clerical authority, who would, however, be stripped of the power of punishing dissent.

Frederick the Great admired Thomasius; he said that Prussia owed more to Leibniz and Thomasius than to any other savants. But this was after 1740, when the spirit of Thomasius was returning in Frederician Prussia. We must, in fact, divide the influence of Thomasius into two periods, and on two groups of thinkers. First of all there was the period extending over part of his own lifetime, from about 1710 to about 1750, when the dominant philosophy in Germany was that of his opponent Wolff. The Thomasian influence was then felt by a few thinkers who were deeply influenced by Pietism and who continued Thomasius' psychological teachings against the intellectualism of the followers of Wolff. There was a small "Thomasian school" whose centers were Halle and Leipzig and whose leading members were Johann Budde, Andreas Rüdiger, Adolf Friedrich Hoffmann, and Christian August Crusius.

When the Wolffian influence waned about the middle of the century, the so-called "popular philosophers" in Göttingen and Berlin used Thomasius' weapons against the scholasticism of the Wolffians, and produced eclectic opinions in what has been called "half-philosophy, half-journalism." But though this group venerated Thomasius and aimed at the kinds of popular reform that he had striven for, one can hardly speak of a direct influence or continuation of "Thomasian doctrines." It is not difficult to

---

[18] *Ibid.,* vi, §§ 40–42; cf. § 21.   [19] *Ibid.,* iv, § 90.
[20] See L. W. Beck, *Commentary on Kant's Critique of Practical Reason* (Chicago: University of Chicago Press, 1962), pp. 150–152.

find the origins of an eclectic thinker's opinions but it is difficult to regard an eclectic of the turn of the century as *the* source of another eclecticism half a century later. By 1750 the ideas of the Berlin free thinkers were in the air; almost any alert and uncommitted publicist could catch and serve them up. But had it not been for Thomasius, perhaps the ideas would not have been in the air to be caught.

Even less of Thomasius' direct personal influence can be discerned in the other line of thought, initiated about 1770, which might have been traced back to him. Against both the intellectualism of the Wolffians and the superficial journalistic wisdom of the popular philosophers—at least this is the way it seemed to their opponents—irrationalistic thinkers started the movement which we shall discuss later under the title of the "Counter-Enlightenment." Irrationalistic modes of thinking historically associated with Pietism and extending far back in the natural philosophy and natural mysticism of the Protestant Counter Reformation now came to new life. Their growth led, through Herder, into the romantic natural philosophy of the nineteenth century.

What had been two strains of thought in one man, Thomasius, became separated. Each was adopted and nurtured by a different group of men. Both counter-enlighteners and popular philosophers could have looked back upon Thomasius as their progenitor. In historical fact, however, few did. Yet the roots of almost all the branches of thought of the eighteenth century in Germany which cannot have sprung from Wolff were in the philosophy of Thomasius.

Wolff

Christian Wolff was born in Breslau January 24, 1679, the son of a tanner. It was always assumed that he would become a Lutheran pastor, and his early education was in orthodox Lutheran theology. But Breslau was largely Catholic, and most of his young companions were Catholics. To carry on his theological controversies with them, he studied the writings of the Catholic scholastics, especially Thomas Aquinas and Suarez, and attended Catholic services. His skill in theological disputation with them brought him a certain local notoriety. But he was not satisfied with the orthodox theology he learned, and in his quest for certainty he turned to the study of mathematics, which seemed then to promise certainty where previously all was controversial. He enrolled in the University of Jena in 1699, the year of Weigel's death; but he worked under one of Weigel's pupils, Paul Hebenstreit (1664–1718) and he became personally acquainted with von Tschirnhaus, whose *Medicina mentis* exercised a lasting influence upon him. He received the master's degree from Leipzig in 1702 and became a *Privat-dozent* in mathematics with a dissertation on the application of mathematical methods to the problems of practical philosophy, which called Leibniz's attention to him and initiated a correspondence with Leibniz that lasted until Leibniz' death in 1716. In Leipzig he was employed also in work for the *Acta eruditorum*, Germany's first learned periodical. During his years in Leipzig he began also to give philosophical lectures, though Leibniz advised him to concentrate on mathematics. Though Wolff was not a creative mathematician, his clear style of lecturing and writing brought him some fame as a mathematician, and in 1706 he became professor of mathematics and natural science in the University of Halle with the sponsorship of Leibniz and von Tschirnhaus.

The years in Halle were the most important in Wolff's career. He was seriously dissatisfied with the popular, eclectic philosophy taught by Thomasius and N. H. Gundling, though Leibniz, always the diplomat, counseled him to make friends with them; but gradually Wolff added lectures in philosophy to those he gave in mathematics, and destroyed their influence upon the students. At first his lectures were mostly expositions of Leibniz' philosophy, or at least they were so regarded; but gradually they took on his own characteristic scholastic form, which was never Leibniz', and more and more departed from the contents of Leibniz' work. Leibniz asserted, perhaps not quite accurately, that Wolff knew no more of his philosophy than could be read in his published works, and Wolff always asserted his independence of Leibniz.[21] There was much justice in the complaints by both that the name "Leibniz-Wolffian philosophy," which was applied to Wolff's system by his opponents Budde and Rüdiger, was a misnomer, and Wolff claimed that he had taken more from Aquinas than from Leibniz. But such complaints were in vain, and the name has almost universally been applied to his philosophy since then.

During the first few years in Halle, Wolff continued to lecture on mathematics (he is thought to be the first man to teach the calculus in Germany) and to publish his mathematical works, which had great popularity as the best textbooks available. His contribution to German mathematical terminology, however, was his only lasting accomplishment, for though Wolff was an outstanding teacher of mathematics, he was no more than a teacher. The transition from mathematics to philosophy was a smooth one, both because the mathematics of the time included much of what we would now consider natural science (e.g., astronomy) and engineering (e.g., fortifications), and because Wolff regarded mathematics as the model for his logic, which he published in 1713 under the title *Rational Thoughts on the Powers of the Human Understanding* (*Vernünftige Gedanken von den Kräften des menschlichen Verstandes*—I have modernized the German spelling here and in other titles of books by Wolff), which is sometimes referred to as the "German logic" to distinguish it from the later work in Latin covering much of the same ground. With this book began a series of works with similar titles, which made him the leading philosopher in Germany. The most important were *Rational Thoughts on God, the World, the Soul of Man, and All Things in General* (*Vernünftige Gedanken von Gott, der Welt, der Seele des Menschen auch allen Dingen überhaupt*, 1719),[22] often referred to as the "German Metaphysics" to distinguish it from the series

[21] Wolff's introduction to *Leibniz' kleinere philosophische Schriften* (Jena, 1740), p. b(2).

[22] I have translated part of this in my *Eighteenth-Century Philosophy*, pp. 217–222. So far as I know, none of the other German works has been translated even in part.

of metaphysical works published separately, in Latin, on each of these topics; *Rational Thoughts on Human Actions* (*Vernünftige Gedanken von der Menschen Tun und Lassen*, 1720)—the "German Ethics"; *Rational Thoughts on the Social Life of Man* (*Vernünftige Gedanken von dem gesellschaftlichen Leben des Menschen*, 1721)—the "German Politics"; *Rational Thoughts on Causes and Effects in Nature* (*Vernünftige Gedanken von den Wirkungen der Natur*, 1723)—the "German Cosmology"; and *Rational Thoughts on the Purposes of Natural Things* (*Vernünftige Gedanken von den Absichten der natürlichen Dinge*, 1724)—the "German Natural Theology," or "German Teleology." Besides these there were four other German works of similar scope and design. None of these books is small or especially delightful to read. In reading them, one cannot forget Wolff's definition of "prolixity" in the "German Logic" (chap. 10, sec. 14): "When a book is prolix. If more of already known things is presented than is required by the purpose of the book, then the book contains superfluous things in it. Then it is prolix." He illustrates what needs no illustration. He proves (though often by proofs so invalid that the fastidious reader may squirm) what needs no proof and what admits of no proof. He defines what needs no definition. He cites, by elaborate cross-references, his other works, which all too often are found not to elucidate the passage in question but to be almost equivalent to it. He recommends his other books. He boasts of what he has accomplished. He moves with glacial celerity. He ruthlessly bores.

But these books made him famous. He was honored with membership in learned academies (Berlin, St. Petersburg, Paris, the Royal Society in London), pensions (including one from Catherine the Great), and invitations to other universities (Jena, Marburg). His philosophy began to be taught in other universities, including Jena, Tübingen (by his pupil, Georg Bernhard Bilfinger), and Königsberg.

All was not well in Halle, however. In the philosophical faculty there was opposition from Thomasius, Rüdiger, Gundling, and Budde. The Pietist theological faculty, led by Francke, who had also opposed Thomasius, strongly opposed Wolff's rationalism, which was seen as implying determinism and the denial of revelation, providence, and miracles. No doubt Wolff's popularity as a teacher and his fame as a writer aroused jealousies. He does not seem to have been an easy colleague, and his successful effort to have his pupil Ludwig Thümmig appointed to a vacancy in the faculty collided with the efforts of Joachim Lange, the theologian, to have his son appointed to the same post.

In 1721 Wolff was rector of the university, and his formal address upon relinquishing this post was "On the Practical Philosophy of the Chinese,"[23] in which he defended views already taken in his writings by using the resemblances between Chinese and Occidental ethics as evidence that the latter was not dependent upon revelation and that high culture and human happiness were possible without a religious basis. His successor as rector

---

[23] Easily available in *Das Weltbild der deutschen Aufklärung*, ed. Fritz Brüggemann (Leipzig: Reclam, 1930), pp. 173–195.

was the same Joachim Lange, who immediately called upon the theological faculty to censure Wolff for heresy. Wolff denied the authority of the theological faculty to censure him, a member of the philosophical faculty, and in this he was supported by the legal faculty. Things would no doubt have gone on much as before except for a tactical error Wolff made when he was angered by a personal attack from a former disciple. He called for vindication by the court in Berlin, which under the statutes had no more authority over his teaching than the theological faculty did. The Berlin ministry did forbid a renewal of the personal attack, and it was assumed that Wolff would be henceforth left alone; but through intrigue involving the "tobacco cabinet" of the "Soldier King," Friedrich Wilhelm I (a rough group of old military cronies with whom the king liked to smoke), Wolff was represented as teaching, in his theory of determinism, that deserters from the army should not be punished since they could not help deserting. Enraged by this, the king, without even consulting the responsible ministry, dismissed Wolff on November 8, 1723, and ordered him to leave the realm within forty-eight hours or be hanged. Thümmig was replaced in the faculty by Lange's son, other Wolffians in Prussian universties were dismissed, and in 1729 the use of Wolff's textbooks was forbidden in Prussia.

Wolff had been invited to the University of Marburg during the preceding summer, even though the statutes of the university at this time required all professors to be Calvinists and the faculty had not been consulted on this appointment. Upon his dismissal from Halle, Wolff accepted the Marburg chair, and the Marburg faculty had to accept a colleague of the other confession whose views they rejected so far as they knew them at all. His personal relations at Marburg were no better than they had been in Halle, but Wolff now had a stage from which he could address all Europe, since Marburg attracted students, including Catholic, from other countries. From 1723 to the end of his life he wrote for a European audience, and therefore in Latin, not German. His most important work had been done, but the Latin works are more scholastic,[24] more exact, than the German, and, for the philosopher, are somewhat more interesting because of his vast learning and his awareness of belonging to, and modifying, the scholastic tradition going back to Suarez. His passion for definition[25] had

[24] The principal works of the Marburg period are: *Philosophia rationalis sive Logica* (1728); *Philosophia prima sive Ontologia* (1730), *Cosmologia generalis* (1731), *Psychologia empirica* (1732), *Psychologia rationalis* (1734), *Theologia naturalis*, 2 vols. (1736–37); and *Philosophia practica universalis*, 2 vols. (1738–39). After his return to Halle he wrote *Ius naturae*, 8 vols. (1740–48); *Ius gentium* (1749); *Institutiones iuris naturae et gentium* (1750); *Philosophia moralis sive Ethica*, 5 vols. (1750–53); and *Oeconomica*, 2 vols. (1754–55). The *Ius gentium* has been translated by J. H. Drake (Oxford: Clarendon Press, 1934). The *Discursus praeliminaris de Philosophia in genere* (the introduction to the *Logica*) was published in 1728 and has been translated by R. J. Blackwell (Indianapolis: Bobbs-Merrill, 1963).

[25] This passion for definition became a crotchet adopted by others. Lucien Lévy-Brühl (*L'Allemagne depuis Leibniz* [Paris, 1890], p. 62–64) gives an example of a sermon on "Sermon on the Mount" which began, "A mount is an elevation of land; a multitude is a crowd of people"; and Schöffler, *Deutsches Geistesleben zwischen Reformation und Aufklärung* [Frankfurt: Klostermann, 1956]), pp. 214–215, quotes from a Robinson Crusoe story for children which began: "Here and there, especially outside Europe,

full scope, and though through this some clarity may have accrued to his system, his philosophy became more static, dogmatic, and encyclopedic than ever. But his works, becoming available to all Europeans during the years at Marburg, combined with his persecution, made him an intellectual hero and brought him European fame, the approbation of the Jesuits,[26] and a patent of nobility. His influence spread even to France and back into Prussia; Friedrich Wilhelm I regretted his impetuosity and in 1733 invited him to return to Prussia, an honor he declined. In 1736 a Royal Commission appointed to examine Wolff's books found no dangerous errors in them, and in 1739 there was a cabinet order requiring candidates for the ministry to study Wolff's works, especially his logic. Gottsched, in Leipzig, published his *Fundamental Principles of Philosophy* (*Erste Gründe der gesamten Weltweisheit*, 1733-34) which became the most popular textbook in Germany. Wolffian societies, such as the *Gesellschaft der Wahrheitsfreunde* ("Society of the Friends of Truth", founded in 1736, were established to carry his philosophy beyond university circles. In one such society members pledged themselves not to accept or reject any belief except for a "sufficient reason," and the motto of the "Friends of Truth" was "*Sapere aude!*" which Kant was later to call the motto of the Enlightenment. There were Wolffians in most of the German universities, even in Prussia (Kant studied under one, Knutsen, in Königsberg); the Swiss critics Bodmer and Breitinger dedicated their *Discourse of Painters* to Wolff, though they were directly opposed to the literary theories of Gottsched, also a Wolffian. The moral weeklies, following English models such as *The Spectator*, were filled with Wolffian and Lockean doctrines;[27] books were written presenting the Wolffian philosophy for the ladies.[28]

One of the first acts of Frederick the Great when he ascended the throne in 1740 was to recall Wolff, offering him a permanent fellowship in the Berlin Academy. Frederick not only wished to right a wrong done by his father and to have the leading philosophers of his day in his entourage (as he succeeded when he reorganized the Academy), but his own determinism, even fatalism, attracted him to Wolff's philosophy, and precisely to those points which had outraged his father.[29]

---

there are still some men who have been so ill-brought up in their youth that they do not even know how great a crime thievery is . . . If they practice it on land, they are called thieves or robbers; if it occurs at sea, one calls it piracy."

[26] Cf. Bernhard Jensen, S.J., *Die Pflege der Philosophie in Jesuitenorden während des 17/18. Jahrhunderts* (Fulda: Parzeller, 1938), and Robert Haass, *Die geistige Haltung der katholischen Universitäten Deutschlands im 18. Jahrhundert* (Freiburg: Herder, 1952).

[27] F. A. Brown, "On Education; John Locke, Christian Wolff, and the Moral Weeklies," *University of California Publications in Modern Philology*, 36:149–170 (1952).

[28] The most famous of these was *La Belle Wolffienne*, 6 vols. (1741–53), by the permanent secretary of the Berlin Academy, Samuel Formey. Wolff seems to have had a special attraction for the bluestockings of the time, and one wit made a rather nice pun about it: Wolff's philosophy, he said, "is so much loved by the feminine sex that a veritable lycanthropy seems to have broken out among these weak vessels" (Heinrich Hermelink and S. A. Kaehler, *Die Philipps-Universität zu Marburg 1527–1927* [Marburg: Elwert, 1927] p. 361).

[29] Later, however, Frederick saw Wolff as the source of the fatalistic errors of Holbach.

But Wolff preferred his old post at Halle. He returned in 1740 amidst great acclaim and public honor; there was even some personal reconciliation with his old opponents. But his lectures were now not successful; the Wolffians in Halle, especially Sigmund Jacob Baumgarten, had by now gone far beyond the master in their critique of revelation, and Wolff's old theological enemies, the Pietists, were no longer a strong force likely to stir up lively controversy which would attract students to the principals. He soon gave up lecturing, complaining of the poor quality of the students, saying that by his writings he could be more useful as *professor universi generis humani*. So he continued to write on natural law, moral philosophy, and private ethics, dedicating sixteen volumes to Frederick (who gently chided him on his prolixity). Full of years and honors, he died of the gout on April 9, 1754.

Wolff saw himself as the teacher of the Germans and was accorded the title of *praeceptor Germaniae*, like Rabanus and Melanchthon in their days. It is apparently characteristic of the men accorded this honorific that they are not original philosophers, but transmitters and modernizers of a tradition, adapting it for practical purposes to a changed cultural climate when the unmodified tradition would have been ineffective in the intellectual guidance of their people. As Melanchthon took Aristotelian scholasticism and humanism and made them responsive to the new requirements of the Lutheran Church, Wolff changed the Catholic and Protestant scholasticism of the Baroque period and the new mathematical methods and natural science of Leibniz and von Tschirnhaus, as well as he understood them, into a conception of philosophy as an omnicompetent instrument of public enlightenment. His goal was no longer, with the schoolmen, to make men religious, but to make them cultured and practically effective. Though few philosophers have been more completely academic than Wolff, whose pedantry, prolixity, and lack of humor became notorious, few philosophers have been more explicitly and self-consciously inspired than he toward putting philosophy in the service of nonphilosophers, toward making philosophy the basis for popular education which would end futile religious controversies and contribute directly to the well-being and happiness of mankind. Of Wolff's good will, however Philistine, there can be no doubt, and though he was a child of his times in many things—in his defense of slavery and of torture,[30] for instance—his philosophy was the first comprehensive system to be published in German and was until 1750 either the source of most of the intellectual life or the target of attack by the few who stood with the Pietism for the past or who were preparing the way for a new philosophy and the end of the intellectual dogmatism of the Enlightenment. Frederick the Great professed to have learned from him, and Kant praised him for having introduced the spirit of exactness and rigor (*Gründlichkeit*) into German philosophy. He was the principal author of the German philosophical vocabulary, and though, during the eighteenth century, much German philosophy continued to be written in Latin, German in his hands became an adequate vehicle for philosophical thought.

[30] *Vernünftige Gedanken von dem gesellschaftlichen Leben des Menschen* (1725 ed.), § 365.

Wolff's Conception of Philosophy

Using a term introduced in the late seventeenth-century, Wolff defines philosophy as *Welt-Weisheit* (world-wisdom) to distinguish it from *Gottes-Gelahrtheit* (God-learning, or theology), and thus broadens its scope to include all the human sciences. It differs from all other human and natural sciences and disciplines, however, in its goal and method. Its goal is the knowledge of why things must be as they are—why they are possible if they are possible, and why they are actual if they are actual. What things are actual is learned "historically," that is, by experience. If they are actual, they must be possible. But why they are possible and, if they are actual, why they are—that is what the philosopher claims to know. The method of philosophy is borrowed from mathematics, which is the model of our knowledge of necessities. While mathematics is knowledge of the quantities of things, more important is the fact that it is *connected* knowledge; and philosophy can imitate the connectedness of mathematics.

Wolff, however, considers mathematical knowledge to be very different from what Descartes and von Tschirnhaus thought it to be. It is significant that Wolff's only contribution to mathematics was lexicographical; for the essential feature of mathematics, as he saw it, is definition and syllogistic proof, not intuition and construction. Hence his philosophy based upon the ideal of *mathesis universalis* is very different from theirs; his is strictly scholastic, with an awesome array of definitions. Completeness requires syllogisms and not enthymemes, definitions and not intuitions. He gives a two-page polysyllogism proving that air is elastic, which he knew by an experiment he described with unwonted brevity.

For all this, Leibniz' little "Meditations on Knowledge, Truth, and Ideas" (1684) is his inspiration. He wants to begin with empirical, historical knowledge, through analysis replace unclear with clear and distinct ideas, abstract and analyze until he gets to simple ideas, combine them into definitions, and then syllogistically move back to the empirical starting point, having, he believes, picked up causes and reasons along the way. The ingenuity of this analytic-synthetic method is surpassed by its singleminded omnicompetence, a particularly pretty example of which is in the demonstration that German coffee-houses should be made like the English so that they will be comfortable for scholars.[31]

The Division of Philosophy

Wolff gives many various divisions of philosophy, but the one which was most important in the organization of his writing and most influential

---

[31] Wolff's defense of syllogism is in *Vernünftige Gedanken von den Kräften des menschlichen Verstandes* (1754 ed.), chap. iv, § 22; his long example of the elasticity of air is in *ibid.*, § 25; that of the proper arrangement of coffeehouses is in *Vernünftige Gedanken von dem gesellschaftlichen Leben des Menschen*, § 297. Unlike the last citation, citations to important points can be made almost at random, since Wolff repeats himself lovingly from book to book. He is one of the great self-plagiarizers of history. He is the largest one-man *Zitierverband* in German philosophy, his love of his own words surpassing even Schopenhauer's.

upon his followers was that into theoretical and practical philosophy, theoretical philosophy being metaphysics. Metaphysics was divided into ontology and real metaphysics, which in turn consists of rational theology, rational cosmology, and rational psychology. Corresponding to the divisions of real metaphysics were the three great divisions of empirical science: theology (based on the empirical evidences of God in nature, thus physico-theology and teleology), cosmology, or physical science, and psychology. Mathematics is the highest part of cosmology, being concerned with the measures of things. Practical philosophy was based upon theoretical philosophy, particularly ontology (with its scholastic identification of the true with the good) and psychology, which studied the cognitive and the volitional faculties of the soul. Practical philosophy was divided into general moral philosophy, politics and *lex natura*, and economics (including private ethics). Though Wolff mentions the "philosophy of the liberal arts," including "rhetorical philosophy, poetical philosophy, and so on,"[32] he does not develop them and they were not introduced into the system until later. In the order of learning, the field of logic is prior to all these divisions; but in the order of being, logic is only an organon borrowing its basic principles from ontology, since it is supposed to give knowledge of being, and from psychology, since it requires the use of the faculties of the soul.

Ontology

Wolff defines philosophy as the science of the possibles, insofar as they can be, or a science of all possible things, how and why they are possible. He defines ontology, or first philosophy, as the "science of being in general, insofar as it is."[33] Ontology, however, is the study of being in its most general signification, which for Wolff means *possible* being.

Possibility means logical possibility. A thing is a possible thing if its predicates are not contradictory. The prime and irreducible predicates of a possible being constitute its essence and can be stated in a definition. These primary predicates, or essential attributes, contain the ground or reason for all other essential predicates found in a thing. Hence from a definition all of the internal predicates of the thing follow, the definition giving the sufficient reason for all the other essential predicates. The principle of sufficient reason is the final explanation for all the possible internal predicates of a thing, and the sufficient reason of the (possibility of the) thing is that the essentials are not contradictory. Indeed, the principle of sufficient reason of why a thing is possible is simply the principle of contradiction itself.

In Gilson's famous distinction between essentialist and existentialist metaphysics,[34] Wolff's ontology is a pure example of essentialist metaphysics. There is a parallelism between, if not an identity of, a concept of a thing and the essence or possibility of a thing; if we can have a distinct

[32] *Preliminary Discourse*, trans. R. J. Blackwell, note to § 71.

[33] *Ibid.*, § 29; *Vernüftige Gedanken von den Kräften*, § 1; *Vernünftige Gedanken von Gott* (1747 ed.), § 30; *Ontologia* (1736 ed. cited here and below) §§ 1, 70.

[34] See above, p. 185.

concept of it, then it is possible. Whatever can be given a definition is possible, and if it is possible it can be defined or have a corresponding concept.

Wolff, however, does not realize that no simple predicates can be logically contradictory to one another, and hence, though he tries to make "possible" equal "non-self-contradictory," he does not in fact do so. For he has criteria of possibility other than mere non-self-contradiction. The most important are these: if the concepts entering the definition are derived by abstraction from something actual, then they constitute a possibility, for whatever is actual is possible; if the concepts are combined arbitrarily, then the possibility (i.e., that there is a real instead of a merely verbal[35] definition) is to be shown by finding an example in experience or by proof. Proof takes the form of constructing the object, as the mathematician does, or by deriving from the definition something that we know to be possible—Wolff overlooking the logical truth, known in his day, that true conclusions may follow from false premises and overlooking the other logical truth not known in his day that a self-contradiction implies everything.[36] Moreover, in Wolff's recognition that no reason can be given for essential and unanalyzed attributes or predicates (except by God, who is for this reason the only "perfect philosopher"), there is still more evidence that he does not actually believe that possibility means merely non-self-contradiction, for not every logical possibility has the kind of possibility for which his tests are designed.

Wolff does not follow Leibniz in the theory that in all true affirmative judgments the predicates are identical with all or part of the subject-concept. Judgment is for him only a connection of two or more concepts with each other, with no requirement that the predicate be contained in the subject.[37] But inasmuch as judgments are to be tested by experience or by the law of contradiction—and Wolff does not see that there is a generic difference between those tested in the one way and those tested in the other—he often writes as if a false judgment were self-contradictory or reducible to a self-contradiction, i.e., as if judgments were all analytic. When A. F. Hoffmann, Crusius, and later Kant, see that not all judgments are to be tested by reference to the self-contradictoriness of their contradictories, a long step is taken toward the discovery by Kant that there are two fundamentally different kinds of judgments. This is hidden from Wolff,[38] because his definition of judgment does not sufficiently distinguish complex concepts from judgments and therefore does not permit him to

---

[35] By a verbal definition, Wolff means merely a definition by virtue of which the thing defined can be distinguished from others somewhat like it, and by a real definition one which shows how and why the thing defined is possible (*Logica,* § 191; *Vernünftige Gedanken von den Kräften,* chap. i, § 40). He properly insists upon the necessity of not confusing verbal with real definitions just as Leibniz did; and especially of not using the former in proofs which require the latter. It is hardly necessary to say that even if one grants the distinction, most of Wolff's definitions seem to be verbal rather than real.

[36] See *Vernünftige Gedanken von den Kräften,* chap. iv, § 6.

[37] *Ibid.,* chap. iii, § 2.

[38] And it was also misunderstood by J. A. Eberhard in his controversy with Kant; see my *Studies in the Philosophy of Kant* (Indianapolis: Bobbs-Merrill, 1965), pp. 118–119, and passim. But that it was not misunderstood by either Wolff or Eberhard is argued

see the difference between the "possibility" of the one, which is purely logical, from the possibility of the other, which is meant to have something to do with existence. Wolff requires that the subject contain the "ground" of its predicates, but if "ground" means "logical ground" (and it is certain that Wolff did so interpret it), then he cannot finally test judgments except by analysis of their concepts and the search for identities and contradictions.

In discussing ground and possibility, Wolff is not much more confused than other philosophers of his day (with the exception of Leibniz and Hume). We have already seen in Clauberg the same confusion of "contradiction" with "what cannot be thought," and we shall see still later examples of it and the slowly dawning recognition that there is an important difference between the *usus logicus* and the *usus reale* of reason, between logical and real possibility, between *ratio cognoscendi* and *ratio essendi*, and between *ratio* and *causa*. Almost all of these philosophers tacitly assumed that *a priori* knowledge in the logical sense, that is, knowledge expressed in the conclusion of a valid syllogism, had some dignity lacking in an unproved "historical" proposition, and that all of the propositions whose necessity they wished to affirm had to be established by an appeal to non-self-contradiction. Only gradually did they come to see that their "axioms" could not be established in the same way the theorems were established, and that "that which cannot be thought together" is a different class of impossibles from self-contradictions. Until the *logical* distinction between analytic and synthetic judgment was made by Kant and distinguished from the *epistemological* distinction between *a priori* and *a posteriori* knowledge, this confusion was unavoidable, except in the minds of a few singularly acute men like Hume and Leibniz. That the Wolffians did not see the difference was responsible for their thinking that they could get all the advantages of a rationalistic theory of knowledge while still maintaining an empiricistic basis. When Crusius drew the necessary distinctions, the first coffin nail was driven into Wolffianism.

But to return to Wolff: we understand why we must say that whatever has an essence or a real definition is a possible substance. A substance is the bearer of, or a complex of, both constant and variable internally determined attributes. As such, it resembles a Leibnizian monad. But it is not a monad, for it does not exist in and for itself; it is only a possible subject, an object of the intellect of God, and indeed owes both its possibility and existence to its being thought by God. Thus the "essentialism" or divine conceptualism of Wolff leads him, as it earlier had led Clauberg, to an idealistic conception of the world.[39]

No possibility alone, save that of God, implies existence. For anything but God to be real, therefore, something must be added to its possibility to make it existent. Existence is the "complement of possibility."[40] There

---

in the provocative essay by A. O. Lovejoy, "Kant's Antithesis of Dogmatism and Criticism," *Mind* (1906) reprinted in M. S. Gram's *Kant: Disputed Questions* (Chicago: Quadrangle Books, 1967), pp. 105–130, who charges Kant with a misunderstanding of Wolff and, essentially, an intellectual plagiarism.

[39] *Vernünftige Gedanken von Gott* §§ 35, 975.   [40] *Ontologia*, § 174.

must be a sufficient reason of existence for anything that exists, and this sufficient reason cannot be found in the series of merely contingent beings.[41] Hence it must be found in a being which exists per se, which is God.

This ancient argument may perhaps serve as well as any argument of the time for the existence of God. But Wolff's problem (though he does not know it) is the existence of *anything* defined as the complement of its possibility. There must be a sufficient reason for the existence of anything. God is his own reason for being, for his existence follows from his possibility. But for a contingent being to exist, it must have a sufficient reason. And here is precisely the difficulty of Wolff's extravagant rationalism: the principle of sufficient reason is itself a consequence of the principle of contradiction.[42] Hence, whatever exists exists by necessity. To be sure, it is an extrinsic necessity for any being except God; but it is also a *logical* necessity (from the principle of contradiction). And he cannot make the concept of a "complement of possibility" intelligible. Kant blew away this whole fantastic structure with the very simple question: Is the complement of possibility possible? If not, existence is impossible; if so, existence is merely possibility.[43]

Knowledge of Real Existence

No possible being except God (as shown in the ontological argument) necessarily exists. To know that something other than God does exist, therefore, we have to go beyond its concept and definition and turn to experience. Sense experience gives us unclear and undistinct concepts of things; yet it does, Wolff believes, give us sufficient evidence of the existence of objects without us, and Wolff is impatient with all inquiries which, if not successfully terminated, might incline toward skepticism. "It is not much use to argue whether or not philosophy can acquire certain knowledge. I think that we should rather make the effort to see what we can and what we cannot accomplish . . . We should imitate the astronomers who, by continuous study and tireless sagacity, have discovered things beyond their highest expectations."[44]

But Wolff is not always this ingenuous; while historical (i.e., empirical) knowledge is our only source of knowledge of existence, it is not always trustworthy; not only are there errors in sense knowledge, but the entire realm of sense might be a dream. Truth is distinguished from a dream by the order of the experience; it is, in the transcendental sense, the order in the alteration of things. Without the principle of sufficient reason, therefore, there cannot be anything; nor can there be knowledge, for knowledge is to be distinguished from error by its possession of an insight into the sufficient reasons for things.[45]

Wolff's terms are so equivocal that some of his arguments seem to be little better than puns. "Reason" means both a faculty of the mind, an insight into the connection of truths, and the *ratio*, or *causa*, of judgments

---

[41] *Ibid.*, § 322.
[42] *Ibid.*, §§ 66, 70; *Vernünftige Gedanken von Gott*, § 30.
[43] *Critique of Pure Reason*, A 230 = B 282.
[44] *Preliminary Discourse*, § 139 note.   [45] *Ontologia*, § 493.

about things and things themselves. "Truth" means the agreement of concepts with the essence of things, the agreement of judgments with states of affairs (the connections of things), and the *verum* which supposedly is convertible with *esse* (being). In moving by reason, which gives logical truth, to the truth which is convertible with being, Wolff, in spite of all his definitions, has failed to make some elementary distinctions. The ground of knowing (*ratio cognoscendi*) is confused, in spite of Wolff's explicit warnings about this, with the ground of being (*ratio essendi* and *ratio fiendi*). For unless they are identified, Wolff's entire philosophy collapses. It is all very well for him, in the light of a long tradition, to identify them in the mind of God. But the trouble is: we are not gods.

Wolff never seems to have seen the difference between two sentences: (a) "This proposition is rational, because it is the conclusion of a valid syllogism"; and (b) "This proposition is known rationally to be true because there is a sufficient reason for what it says about the world." He generates thousands of propositions of which the first is true, yet he interprets what he has done as if the second were thereby shown to be true. He has missed an important distinction—the Cartesian distinction between intuition and deduction which may begin from intuitions but which may also begin from mere hypotheses or falsehoods. And he has not anticipated another important distinction—the Kantian distinction between the real use of reason (by which reason teaches us the truth of a single proposition) and the logical use of reason (by which reason moves from one proposition to another).

Wolff's philosophy is thus a confused mixture of rationalistic and empiricistic elements, and it is impossible to classify it as consistently one or the other. In his insistence that all knowledge and all principles of knowledge arise from experience,[46] he sounds like a good empiricist. But none of the fruitful consequences of this assumption, like those drawn by Locke, are so much as touched upon by Wolff. For example, he hardly sees any problem in induction, and certainly has no proper curiosity about the status of the proposition that is supposed to "solve" it: "It is certain that the same thing happens in similar cases."[47] Sometimes he seems to be an empiricist masquerading as a rationalist, sometimes as a rationalist disguising himself as an empiricist. He desires the safety of empiricism but has not the modesty of a genuine empiricist. He claims to know what he could know only if he were a genuine rationalist, but in his knowledge of real existence he emphasizes the indispensability, even in principle, of "historical" knowledge. His philosophy is intellectualism with a vengeance; but it fails as rationalism. Unlike Leibniz' philosophy, it is not even a good compromise between empiricism and rationalism. It is positively painful to see how little Wolff profited from his reading of Descartes, Leibniz, and Locke. Seldom has a man tried harder to be empirical but remained a rationalist *malgré lui*, or tried harder to be rational but found himself unable to leave the bathos of trivial experience.[48]

[46] *Preliminary Discourse*, § 107.
[47] *Vernüftige Gedanken von Gott*, § 331; see also § 374.
[48] See Hermann de Vleeschauwer, *La Déduction transcendental dans l'oeuvre de Kant* (Antwerp: de Sikkel, 1934), I, 53–54.

His psychological theory of knowing real existence is no more satisfactory than his treatment of the more strictly epistemological questions outlined in the previous paragraphs. He accepts a doctrine of pre-established harmony to explain the relations of mind to body, but goes against Leibniz in maintaining a causal theory of the relations between the sense organs and outer objects. He then sees that ideas cannot, as it were, bodily enter the soul, and thus rejects the theory of *tabula rasa*.[49]

The soul is an active substance which has one force, the *vis repraesentativa*, or power of representation. This one force manifests itself in perception, memory, imagination, understanding, reason, desire, and will. It produces sensations, images, distinct concepts, inferences, and volitions. (We shall later return to Wolff's views concerning the will.) Understanding is its faculty of producing distinct representations, or concepts, by abstraction from indistinct sensations. Pure understanding would be the faculty of producing completely distinct concepts, but the human intellect does not possess an altogether pure understanding.[50] Reason is the insight we have into the relations between concepts, or the connection of truths, and this, for Wolff, means the power to produce syllogisms (in German, *Vernunftschlüsse*, which denotes syllogisms, means literally "inferences of reason"). Thus reason can show us the causes or reasons of things. If in such inferences reason does not take any truths from the senses, it is pure (*laute*). But instead of denying, as a good empiricist might, that reason can be pure, Wolff merely warns against the hazards in reasoning which does not begin with sense experiences which are certain, while at the same time admitting that pure reason does function in mathematics.[51]

We have, then, "two ways of knowing truth": experience, which begins with the senses, and reason, which begins with the distinct concepts of the understanding.[52] The difference between the two ways of knowing shows in their issue. One gives us connected knowledge of things from knowledge of their reasons; the other gives us mere matters of fact. Yet Wolff cannot, after all, maintain this dualism of ways of knowing, for in spite of denying the doctrine of *tabula rasa*, Wolff will not admit that there are any innate concepts. He accepts Leibniz' view of innate dispositions (. . . *nisi intellectus ipse*) but also agrees with the first part of the maxim that there is nothing, i.e., no specific concept, in the intellect which was not first obscurely given by the senses. Even the purest reason we have must work with concepts abstracted from the senses. The distinction between rational and historical knowledge, therefore, is not a sharp one, and, except perhaps in mathematics, we never are able to follow one "way of knowing truth" in complete independence of the other.

But Wolff is unable to maintain his pretended radical dualism of ways of knowing because his psychology is too simple to support it. For he insists that the soul has only one faculty, and Kant and Tetens rightly pointed out that if one holds this theory, then one must either "intellectualize the senses" or "sensualize the intellect." For such a theory, differences in kinds

[49] *Vernünftige Gedanken von Gott*, § 819.
[50] *Ibid.*, § 285.
[51] *Ibid.*, § 382.
[52] *Ibid.*, § 372.

of knowledge must be interpreted simply as differences in their degrees of clearness and distinctness. When Wolff tries to insist upon two ways of knowing, his psychology will not permit it; when he tries to subordinate historical to rational knowledge he must formulate the one-faculty doctrine so equivocally that it will sometimes support one and sometimes the other mode of knowledge.

The internal tensions generated by this equivocation were to plague the Leibniz-Wolffian philosophy throughout the century. The decisive renunciation of this one-faculty theory in epistemology by Kant in 1770 marked a significant turning point not only in his life but in the career of German philosophy.

The World

We experience the world in space and time. Wolff's theory of space and time is based upon Leibniz', yet differs from it in a significant way.

For Leibniz, space and time are *phenomena bene fundatum*. They are not substances, not ontological primitives, but are dependent upon the real, though not dynamic, relations among substances. "Space is an order ... but God is its source."[53] If, *per impossibile*, we should imagine a world in which there were substances but in which conscious spirits did not exist to reflect it, it would still be a world in which the relations between substances would be real; it would be a spatio-temporal world even though there was no spirit in it with a representation of space or time. As Leibniz uses the word *phenomenon*, it does not necessarily entail the subjectivity of phenomena.

At this point Wolff diverges, or at least seems to diverge, from Leibniz. It is not certain exactly what he means, but he seems to think of space and time as representations, indeed confused representations, of the order of substances. Given a variety of things "external to one another" but simultaneous, there is an order among them, "and as soon as we represent this order we have an idea of space."[54]

Extension and continuity are phenomena; they are confused representations or—and the difficulty is that we do not know which Wolff means—are represented by confused ideas. He warns us against confusing his doctrine with that of the idealists, to whom no phenomenon has existence outside the mind; and yet in the same paragraph he says that extension and continuity are phenomena in the sense in which color is said to be a phenomenon![55] As I read Wolff, he is saying that there is an order among substances which we confusedly represent, and the representation is the manner in which we represent the order spatially, and not a representation of an intersubstantial order which is itself spatial. If this is correct—and it

---

[53] *New Essays Concerning Human Understanding*, bk. II, chap. viii, § 17.

[54] *Vernünftige Gedanken von Gott*, § 46; somewhat similarly for time, *ibid.*, §§ 94, 95, 134.

[55] *Cosmologia generalis* (1737 ed.), § 226. The first exposition of a definitely subjective (idealistic) theory of space among the Wolffians was by Gottfried Plouquet in his *Principia de substantiis et phaenomenis* (1764), but in 1752 a subjectivistic theory had been worked out by Maupertuis, an opponent of Wolffianism.

seems to be because it conforms to his phenomenalistic "consistent-dream-theory" (see above, p. 266)—then space (and time) which are at one ontological remove from substance for Leibniz, are at two removes for Wolff.

If I am correct in interpreting Wolff as holding a subjectivistic theory of space, his views are closer to Kant's mature theory than to Leibniz'. But whether this be correct or not, he is certainly closer to Kant's initial view of space, formulated while Kant was still an adherent of the "Leibniz-Wolffian philosophy," than he was to the genuine Leibnizian view. For Wolff and the young Kant, substances interact, and the spatial order is dependent upon the dynamic relations among them. For Leibniz, on the other hand, space is a mapping of a nonspatial, nondynamic set of relations. But though in this respect Wolff's theory can be seen as pointing forward to Kant's initial view, we cannot, I think, speak of Wolff's theory as having had any influence on Kant's. Too much happened in the period between Wolff's writings and Kant's dissertation of 1747 to make it possible for Wolff's somewhat confused theory to have persisted through the more solid work of those closer to Kant.

Wolff is much more clearly realistic in his theory of time, holding time to be simply "the order of things which follow one another in the world." As we shall see, many later philosophers, Lambert among them, who were willing to accept the theory of the ideality of space could not follow Kant in his analogous theory of time. If Wolff held, as I think he did, to a theory of the ideality of space, it is not surprising, then, that he was unable to follow Leibniz' view that the ontological status of time must be the same as that of space. Leibniz held that both being relational, neither could be substantial; yet the phenomenological difference between them seemed, to everyone but Leibniz and Kant, to require a different ontological status.

The ground of the existence of finite substances is force, or *Kraft*. Every substance has a potency, which may be the faculty of action (active potency) or a susceptibility to being affected by something else (passive potency).[56] With respect to active potency a substance is called an agent; with respect to the passive, a patient. But since the essence of the subject does not entail its existence, the active potency is not found in the essence of the agent, but in *force*, which is independent of the essence of the agent.[57] The grounds of the changes resulting from passive potency are forces in other substances, and we experience them in their resistance to our own actions. Force consists in "a continuous urge to act."[58] Wolff is willing to admit that this is an obscure conception, and the differences between it and Leibniz' conception of the activity of his substances are obvious.

First, Wolff's forces are not dependent exclusively upon the essences of the things exerting or suffering them, though how a thing specifically responds to or manifests forces depends upon its essence Second, force is not a power of representation or appetition, but is understood as the momen-

---

[56] *Ontologia,* § 716.
[57] *Ibid.,* § 722.
[58] *Ibid.,* § 724.

tum of inertia of bodies which macroscopically manifest the forces of the simple substances which comprise them. Third, these are transeunt forces, not immanent to the isolated substances; there is a real, dynamic interaction of Wolff's substances. And, finally, the teleological *nisus* and the logical determinism of Leibnizian substances are denied in favor of a mechanical determination of the interaction of Wolffian substances. The pre-established harmony of Leibniz' philosophy gives way to a corpuscular philosophy in which physical substances truly exist in space and interact with each other.[59] The immanent teleology in which Leibniz saw each substance fulfilling its own nature is replaced by an external teleology. For Wolff, the world is a mechanical whole whose teleology is found in its suitability for human purposes, a suitability resulting from God's design. Physicotheology replaces natural teleology.

The Soul

In his theory of the soul Wolff follows Leibniz more closely than he does in his theory of the monads of the external world. The soul is a unique monad whose power is the *vis repraesentativa*; every activity of the soul is traced back to its power to represent itself and things in the world. It is a simple substance, and therefore immaterial and immortal. It does not stand in causal relation to the body, but in a relation of pre-established harmony which explains its apparent interaction with the body.[60] All events in the soul represent changes in the body, except the supernatural events (*Wunderwercke*—miracles and revelations) which have their causes directly in God.[61] The changes in the soul occur under the principle of sufficient reason, and Wolff has nothing to add to Leibniz' theory of freedom and determinism. Like Leibniz, Wolff also teaches the doctrine of the degrees of clarity of consciousness, ranging from the *petites perceptions* of which we are "darkly conscious" to the most complete consciousness of adequate, complex, clear, and distinct ideas. All are spontanous creations in the soul, but the more sensorial our ideas, the more they seem to be mere effects of changes in the bodily sense organs.

We have earlier remarked upon the unfortunate consequences of the one-faculty theory in epistemology; similarly untoward consequences flowed more quickly from the one-faculty theory when it was not a question of knowing but of other activities of the soul. This theory required an intellectualization of the will and of artistic activity. The principal attacks on Wolff from outside his school and the principal modifications in his teachings introduced by his own disciples dealt with the inadequacy of the one-faculty theory as applied to ethics and aesthetics. The Thomasian voluntarists opposed the theory both on empirical grounds and on the ground

---

[59] Atoms of nature are distinguished from material atoms; the first are in themselves indivisible; the latter are in themselves divisible but there is no sufficient cause in nature for their actual division (*Cosmologia generalis*, § 186).

[60] *Vernünftige Gedanken von Gott*, §§ 765, 781.

[61] *Ibid.*, § 759.

that it denied freedom to the will. Wolffian disciples interested in the philosophy of art first made tentative efforts to modify the one-faculty theory (Baumgarten) in order to secure a better recognition of the non-intellectual features of artistic creation and enjoyment, and then Mendelssohn and Sulzer explicitly introduced additional faculties. Just as the epistemology of the eighteenth century was largely an effort to modify the one-faculty theory of knowledge, much of the aesthetic and ethical theorizing consisted in efforts to modify the one-faculty theory in its most radical form, according to which even will and desire, taste and pleasure, were interpreted as manifestations or corollaries of the representative faculty.

"The light in our souls makes our thoughts clear" is one of Wolff's most characteristic utterances.[62] The drive for clarity and distinctness of ideas is the only impetus of the soul, in Wolff's interpretation; it was also the main feature of Wolff's own intellectual enterprise, and the dominant trait of the philosophy of the German Enlightenment. There is a close connection, both substantive and etymological, between the act of the mind in moving from obscure to clear ideas (*aufklären*) and Enlightenment (*Aufklärung*) as a cultural phenomenon. The way in which Wolff's passion for clarification and enlightenment was extended into cultural regions into which he did not venture, the way in which his somewhat simple-minded conception of clarity was made more and more complex in order to conform better to the actual course of experience in science, morals, art, and religion, and the way in which the ideal of clarity itself was finally renounced, constitute three principal intellectual and cultural paths through German thought in the eighteenth century.

Practical Philosophy and Theology

Wolff's practical philosophy is based on his metaphysics and psychology. The will is simply the knowledge of a perfection to be attained by action. It would be self-contradictory to have a distinct perception of a perfection and not to desire it, and the thought of perfection is simply the axiological equivalent of the metaphysical notion of truth as the perfect harmony and interconnection of all essential attributes of a thing flowing from its intrinsic nature or substantial form. To know a perfection is to will an interconnection of every act so that each one supports and gives a ground for the others; it is to be independent of the accidental and obscure features of our circumstance, and when we act so as to actualize our own nature we are living "according to nature." The achievement of perfection is attended with pleasure. Men who know the organization of the entire universe see that the perfection of each is integrated with the perfection of others. Natural law, therefore, requires that each seek not only his own perfection but that of others too. Civil society is based upon contract, and the rule of natural law is the manner in which each man seeks his own happiness and that of all his fellows. No revelation of God is needed to teach men their duty; an intelligent atheist can know and fulfill his duty.

---

[62] *Vernünftige Gedanken von Gott*, § 203.

Goodness, social harmony, and happiness could subsist even if there were no God.[63] In society the citizen is bound to obey the laws of his government except when they conflict with the natural law; and the best form of government is enlightened absolutism.

In his religious theory Wolff was, of course, opposed both to Pietism, with its irrational and anti-intellectual sources of private salvation, and to orthodox scholasticism, which limited reason by revelation. Wolff admits *pro forma* the role of revelation, but like Locke requires that revelation, to be genuine, must pass the test of reason; but he does not go so far as Locke, since he admits that there may be ideas given us in revelation that could not have arisen naturally within experience. If the first truths are given by revelation, "the divine truths [have] the same order with respect to each other as other truths arising from [natural] concepts."[64] Hence there is a guarantee of perfect harmony between revelation and reason, theology and philosophy. Miracles are sometimes denied, as demeaning the perfection of God's creation, and are sometimes said, more cautiously, to be exceedingly rare. Complete freedom to philosophize is ostentatiously claimed, not only because philosophizing is inherently a spontaneous activity but also because philosophy, which seeks the truth of things, cannot even in principle produce a true doctrine that conflicts with revelation, religion, virtue, or the common well-being. But when a philosopher thinks he has discovered a truth which does conflict with genuine revelation or public virtue, it is his duty to remain silent.[65] Wolff even admits the right of a government to censor books, to require church attendance, and not to tolerate atheism.

In the fourth chapter of Part III of the *German Ethics*, Wolff speaks at great length of moral faith in God. Having proved, in the manner of Leibniz' *Theodicy*, that this is the best of all possible worlds, Wolff instructs us in a kind of quietistic patience which will make us satisfied with God's governance of the world; but then the more typical activistic strain again appears, and we are told that man's duty is to do all he can on his side for the triumph of the good. "Man must do all he can at all times, but he must keep his mind at peace, leave the outcome to God, and be satisfied with how things turn out."

Wolff uses the ontological, cosmological, and physico-teleological arguments for the existence of God. Unlike Leibniz, who sees the entire world as a living, teleological whole, Wolff sees the world-teleology as man-centered. What he sees in nature is not so much a magnificent design that could have been established only by an all-wise God, but a set of arrangements made for men's benefit: "Daylight is very useful to us, because in daylight we can do many things which we could not do at night, at least with the same ease." The sun is useful because it permits us to make sundials and determine latitude and longitude; stars are useful because they

---

[63] *Vernünftige Gedanken von der Menschen Tun und Lassen*, pt. I, chap. i, and the rectoral address of the following year (1721).

[64] *Vernünftige Gedanken von den Kräften*, chap. xii, § 8.

[65] *Preliminary Discourse*, § 163 and note.

permit us to see, to some extent, at night; and so on, from silliness to absurdity.[66]

Wolff's attempt to deal with the charge that he denied freedom is based on his adoption of the point of view of Leibniz' *Theodicy*. Actions are not (logically) necessary, but necessary only under actual given conditions in this world. A free act, different from the one I actually undertake, is not, therefore, logically impossible, for it is logically possible that I could have done the other action. If it was logically possible to have done the other action, then I was free to do it. One cannot but feel a certain sympathy for Wolff's opponents in Halle, even while condemning the threat to hang him.

One question which must arise in the mind of everyone who reads Wolff is how such a philosophy could have had the tremendous and, on the whole, beneficial influence that Wolff's did have in Germany through half the eighteenth century. Wolff is the best German representative of a general movement of thought toward deism, utilitarianism, and free thought that was sweeping over Europe as a whole, though he seems in many respects to belong to the century before Locke and Diderot. He had no peer in Germany during the formative years of the century. Three facts, apart from his lonely position, may explain his role. First, he spoke and wrote in German and was the first philosopher to give the Germans a complete system of philosophy in their own language; his works were available to the layman and the ladies as well as to hundreds of his students in Halle and Marburg. He also spoke the language of scholarship, taking over a great deal of the terminology and mode of thought of the scholastics, and thus he was also a continuer of a tradition already established. To the philosophers he spoke of things they knew—essence, contradiction, sufficient reason, property, accident, clear and distinct ideas; to the man in the street, he spoke of not smacking one's lips while eating. Second, his association with Leibniz gave him the ear of the educated world. Leibniz' philosophy was not widely known in the beginning of the century; only the *Theodicy* (published in 1709) was widely read until the *Monadology* and *Principles of Nature and Grace* were published posthumously. His prestige was tremendous yet unsupported by the philosophical writings which have become known since that time. Wolff, therefore, rightly or wrongly could be regarded as Leibniz' spokesman, and his works attracted attention they would never have got had it not been thought that there was a "Leibniz-Wolffian philosophy." Wolff's effectiveness was institutional: his position as a professor and as the hero of a *cause célèbre* gave him an audience which he would not have attracted had he been a harmless private citizen, and it kept generations of students working through an almost endless series of tedious treatises that few Frenchmen and Englishmen would have

[66] Eduard Zeller (*Geschichte der deutschen Philosophie seit Leibniz* [Munich, 1873], pp. 255–256) has collected some of the most remarkable expressions of this man-centered teleology. Other purposes of the sun are to enable us to discover the magnetic deviation and to make it possible for us to do many things that we could not so easily do in the dark. In short: "The sun exists in order that events may take place on earth; and the earth exists in order that the existence of the sun not be purposeless."

bothered to read. But in Germany for forty years, if not Wolff whom would one read? The great English and French philosophers of the Age of Reason had neither to contend with nor to continue the scholastic tradition. They addressed an urbane and sophisticated audience who had already gone through the emancipating experience of Bacon and Hobbes, Montaigne and Bayle. That we find his contemporaries in France and England still stimulating and instructive and Wolff almost unreadable, while admitting that his influence in Germany was perhaps greater than that of any one man in the other countries, throws into unmistakable relief the low state of philosophy in Germany at that time. The only philosopher of world standing in Germany in 1715 was writing in Latin and French and publishing little. Let us then give Wolff his due: he was indeed *praeceptor Germaniae*, and most good things in German philosophy in the early eighteenth century came from this prosy, pretentious, slightly comical, professor.

XII

A Generation of Epigoni

The Spread and Development of Wolffianism

We have already spoken of the popularity of Wolffianism as shown in the moral weeklies and in salon literature; but a philosophy, at least in Germany, gets established through the universities. We must therefore consider the situation in the German universities after Wolff's sudden rise to fame. German universities were orthodox Lutheran, Lutheran-Pietist, Calvinist, or Catholic in their orientation. Naturally the penetration of Wolffian ideas was easiest in the Calvinist universities, but in the centers of Pietism where the Thomasian influence was strong, Wolffian philosophy was well represented; and it even spread into the Catholic universities where, by 1770, we are told that it was no longer even resisted.[1]

We can perhaps best show the spread of Wolffianism simply by listing Wolffians who achieved important university positions. Ludwig Philipp Thümmig (1697–1728) left Halle with Wolff and then taught in Kassel. Continuously from 1738 to 1809 there were Wolffian professors in Halle:

[1] By Robert Haass, *Die geistige Haltung der katholischen Universitäten Deutschlands im 18. Jahrhundert* (Freiburg: Herder, 1952); see also J. E. Gurr, *The Principle of Sufficient Reason in Some Scholastic Systems 1750–1900* (Milwaukee: Marquette University Press, 1959).

Wolff himself from 1740 to 1755; A. G. Baumgarten from 1738 to 1740, when he became professor in Frankfort on the Oder; G. F. Meier from 1739 to 1777; S. J. Baumgarten, professor of theology from 1743 to 1772, and J. S. Semler from 1752 to 1791; Johann August Eberhard (1739–1809), noted for his controversy with Kant, after 1778. In Marburg, which Wolff left in 1740, there were few non-Wolffian professors until 1787. In neighboring Lutheran Giessen, there was J. F. Müller, a pupil of Bilfinger, and he was followed by another pupil of Wolff, Andreas Böhm, who lasted until 1790. In Helmstedt, J. N. Frobesius was professor for 1726 to 1756; he had been a pupil of Wolff's both at Halle and Marburg. In Tübingen, Georg Bernhard Bilfinger (sometimes Bülffinger) was professor from 1719 to 1725, when he was dismissed and became professor and academician in St. Petersburg. He returned in 1731 and remained until he became president of the consistorium in Stuttgart some years later. Also in Tübingen there were Israel Gottlob Canz from 1739 to 1747 and Gottfried Plouquet (1716–1790) from 1750 until his death. Plouquet was the first philosopher to take up Leibniz' project of an *ars combinatoria*, which he proposed to use against Wolff's excessive syllogizing. In Königsberg, noted then as a center of both Aristotelian philosophy and Pietistic theology, there were three Wolffians of standing. F. A. Schultz (1692–1763) was professor of theology and a patron of Kant as a child; C. F. Rast (1686–1741) was professor of medicine and converted his pupil Johann Christoff Gottsched to Wolffianism; and Martin Knutsen (1720–1756) was Kant's most influential teacher both in physics and philosophy. Leipzig, though the main center for Thomasianism, had Gottsched from 1734 to 1766 and Carl Ludovici (author of a still useful history of Wolffian philosophy[2]) from 1761 to 1768. Christian Garve, known also as a popular philosopher and for his famous review of the *Critique of Pure Reason*, was professor in Leipzig from 1770 to 1772, when he moved to Berlin. In Jena, a center of orthodox Lutheranism, there was Johann Peter Reusch from 1738 and Joachim George Darjes (1714–1792), whom Wundt[3] ranks with Fichte and Kuno Fischer as one of the three most influential men ever to teach in that university. Darjes, however, became an apostate in the 1740's and thenceforth was closer to Crusius than to Wolff. Johann Jakob Brucker (1696–1770) began as a student of Budde in Jena and seems to have been inspired by the eclectic ideals of the Thomasian attitude toward philosophy to undertake what became the first major history of philosophy, the *Historia critica philosophiae*,[4] published in five volumes between 1742 and 1744. Though episodic

---

[2] *Ausführlicher Entwurf einer vollständigen Historie der Wolffischen Philosophie*, Leipzig, 1737–38. This is an invaluable source of bibliographical information on the disputes surrounding Wolff. Ludovici says that 112 Wolffians had teaching posts in German universities and gymnasia. Ludovici was also the author of *Entwurf einer vollständigen Historie der Leibnizischen Philosophie* (1737; reprinted, Hildeshein: G. Olms, 1966).

[3] Max Wundt, *Die Philosophie an der Universität Jena* (Jena: Gustav Fischer, 1932), pp. 104–118, with portrait.

[4] Translated by William Enfield (London, 1791). Enfield does not claim to translate, but says his *History of Philosophy* was "drawn up from" Brucker. Brucker was probably Kant's chief source of information and misinformation on the history of philosophy.

rather than developmental in its structure, Brucker's work tended, nevertheless, to evaluate other systems of philosophy by the standards of Wolffianism. Even at Wittenberg, the citadel of orthodox Lutheranism, there was from 1730 to 1736 Friedrich Christian Baumeister, whose compendium of Wolffian philosophy is still useful to the student of Wolff.[5]

Most of these men were important only as teachers and authors of Wolffian textbooks. Most of them prided themselves on some slight modications they made in the teachings they passed on; some did not remain orthodox Wolffians all their lives, but adjusted to other subsequent movements. Few of them are of any importance to the historian except as examples of the power and extent of the Wolffian philosophy. But among them two groups deserve special attention because they went beyond Wolff and continued his teachings in new directions. They are the groups who developed his rationalism in religion, and who extended his theory to the arts and *belles lettres*.

The Extension of Wolffianism into the Theory of Art

Few systems of philosophy appear a priori to be less likely than Wolff's to lead to serious and sympathetic investigations of art. Not only does Wolff himself seem to have been singularly lacking in sensitivity and taste; the audience for which he was writing had, except for the great church music of Bach and Handel, little contact with art and artists. The theater was hardly above the level of Hans Wurst (Punch and Judy) shows except where it was, later in Wolff's life, producing sterile imitations of the French classic drama. Not until Klopstock was there a poet of genius. Neither Pietism nor the philistinism of Wolff and Thomasius was likely to nurture the poetic. Wolff, who had time to prove syllogistically that smacking one's lips while eating was opposed to *lex naturae*, wrote nothing on art, but he had a place for it, as for everything else: every art, he said, could have its philosophy "if it were reduced to the form of a science," and he specifically mentioned the possibility of a "poetical philosophy" side by side with the philosophy of technology and grammar.[6]

However surprising it may be, it was from the foundations of Wolff's philosophy that aesthetics became established as an autonomous part of philosophy. In fact, two lines of thought developed from Wolff toward a theory of fine art. One had its origin in the passages just cited from Wolff and came to an early and unlamented death. The other had its origin in something comparatively peripheral in Wolff and led toward the center of the independent discipline of aesthetics which was autonomous enough to survive the decline of the Wolffian philosophy as a whole and to make invaluable contributions to German philosophy and literary theory later in the century. In fact, the only part of the "Leibniz-Wolffian philosophy," so called, which was a permanently significant contribution to modern thought

---

[5] *Philosophia definitiva* (1735; many later editions).
[6] Wolff, *Preliminary Discourse on Philosophy in General*, trans. R. J. Blackwell (Milwaukee: Bobbs-Merrill, 1963), §§ 71, 72.

was the theory of fine art—which Wolff did not write. We must attempt to understand this paradox.

Gottsched

The first, and most obvious, development of a "poetical philosophy" was the work of one of Wolff's first and most faithful disciples, Johann Christoph Gottsched (1700–1766). Gottsched studied first in the University of Königsberg, then still a center of Aristotelianism, but was attracted to Wolff's philosophy by Rast. To escape the Prussian draft he went to Leipzig about the time of Wolff's exile from Prussia and withdrawal from the literary scene, at least as far as the vernacular was concerned. While Wolff was writing in Latin and his German works were forbidden as university texts, Gottsched wrote his *Foundations of All Philosophy* (*Erste Gründe der gesamten Weltweisheit* 1733–1734), which became the chief textbook of Wolffian philosophy in Germany and the means by which it became known to the general public. Unlike Wolff's tedious pedantry, Gottsched's style is a good, clear, interesting German. He modifies Wolff here and there: in his habilitation lecture in Leipzig (where he became professor of logic and metaphysics in 1734), he first defended Wolff's restricted version of the theory of pre-established harmony, but was so thoroughly defeated in the subsequent disputation that he burst into tears; this, Dessoir tells us,[7] "made a deep impression upon the young students"; and in his principal work he outlines the various possible theories of the relation of mind to body, asserts that none can be definitely proved, and favors a theory of *influxus physicus* according to which the soul possesses a "moving force."

From his position in Leipzig Gottsched exercised enormous influence; with little exaggeration historians of literature refer to him as the "literary dictator" of the middle third of the century. His *Essay Towards a Critical Poetics for Germans* (*Versuch einer critischen Dichtkunst vor die Deutschen*, 1730) and his work as critic, editor, translator, and playwright were influential until the poets Klopstock and Lessing led German literature along entirely new paths. He did much to purify the German language and to raise the level, or at least the aspirations, of German literature in its most unimaginative and uncreative period. He did almost succeed in "reducing poetry to the form of a science." That in doing so he also starved it was noticed by two other Wolffians, Bodmer and Breitinger, with the consequence that the critical disputes of the forties were an internal dispute among Wolffians, though every German literary thinker was involved. This quarrel had a permanent effect on German literary thought long after the Gottsched-Bodmer controversy was over.

Gottsched took three ideas from Wolff and built a theory of art upon them. First, he was as much a utilitarian moralist as his master, and he took Wolff's idea of the role of the man of enlightened knowledge who

[7] Max Dessoir, *Geschichte der neueren deutschen Psychologie* (Berlin: C. Duncker, 1902), I, 84.

has *vernünftige Gedanken* and extended it to encompass the role of the poet. The poet is no longer a kind of court jester or entertainer, as at the end of the seventeenth century, but is, in a most prosaic sense, a moral teacher. "A poem lies between a textbook of ethics and a true story," he said.[8] Second, he took from Wolff the theory of the imagination, according to which images are put together in the fashion of a mosaic. And third, he combined Wolff's emphasis upon the principle of sufficient reason with French literary theory on the imitation of nature, so as to establish a rule by which loose dreaming and fantasy, purely subjective and undisciplined, could be brought to conform to reality. By the confusions inherent in the doctrine of the law of nature, this conformity to reality was supposed to teach moral lessons. If one guides his imagination by adherence to the principle of sufficient reason, then he has a rational poetics (*Dichtkunst*) and will produce something natural, plausible, and morally edifying.

The principle of sufficient reason is always, in Wolff, the occasion for a syllogism, and we have seen how arbitrarily and externally he sometimes (especially in his natural teleology) used it. It is used no less mechanically by Gottsched. The purpose of art being edification, and the sufficient reason for a poem being to teach a moral lesson, the principle of sufficient reason directs the poet first to choose some sound moral theme which is to be illustrated; next to find some possible event which will in fact illustrate it; finally to decide how he will treat this illustration, whether as fable, comedy, tragedy, or epic.[9] For each of these genres there are specific rules —and taking a good idea from Aristotle and Horace, Gottsched states the rules for choosing the names and social positions of the characters proper to each literary form. No place for genius here, not much place for the charm and enjoyment of art. Taste—the power of deciding whether a work of art is good or not—is the work of understanding, of applying rules to ideas which the common man experiences only as emotion or spectacle.

The theory of art at any given time is likely to show the state of the arts of that time. Gottsched's schoolmasterly theory was perhaps the only one that could have been understood in Germany at that moment. Compared to French and English critical writings—for example, those of Boileau, Du Bos, and Shaftesbury—Gottsched's scarcely rise above the level of instruction for the young in how to compose theatricals. Yet since Germans apparently did not know how to write tragedies, Gottsched cannot be blamed for trying to teach them; it was not his fault that they required recipes. He could presuppose no cultivated taste which would have rendered mechanical rules otiose. "In France, in the middle of the century, despite all rationalism, there was no thinker who did not fully trust instinctive taste . . . [for] Du Bos' pit heard the verse of Racine, while

---

[8] Quoted from H. M. Wolff, *Die Weltanschauung der deutschen Aufklärung* (Bern: A. Francke, 1949), p. 158.

[9] The much laughed-at passage here referred to (*Critische Dichtkunst*, 2nd ed., 1737, p. 141) was not in fact original with Gottsched but, according to Joachim Birke (*Christian Wolffs Metaphysik und die zeitgenossische Literatur- und Musiktheorie* [Berlin: Walter De Gruyter, 1966], p. 39), was taken almost verbatim from P. Le Bossus' *Traité du poème épique* (Paris, 1675), p. 37.

Gottsched's bawled over Jack Pudding [*Pickelherring*]."[10] When a rival theory of art did appear in Germany, the most damning attack on it which Gottsched could make was: "Do not buy the book, for it will not teach you how to write an ode."

Bodmer and Breitinger

The book that Gottsched wished thereby to crush was the *Critical Poetics* (*Critische Dichtkunst*, 1740) by the Swiss Johann Jakob Breitinger, with a foreword in each of its two volumes by Johann Jakob Bodmer (sometimes spelled Bodemer). Since 1722 Bodmer had been the editor of an important moral weekly, the *Discourses of Painters* (*Discourse der Mahlern*) and his relations with Gottsched had not been unfriendly. Bodmer had dedicated his *Influence and Use of the Imagination in the Improvement of Taste* (1727) to Wolff. But with Breitinger's attack, which does not mention Gottsched's name, a new period in the literary history of Germany was opened, and Gottsched was not its spokesman.

The year 1740, when the *Critical Poetics* was published, is usually taken to mark the beginning of the age of sentiment in German literature and the end of bourgeois classicism based upon imitation of French writers. At this time Gottsched committed the unforgivable blunder of condemning the poet Klopstock both as artist and as religious thinker. Enthusiasm for Klopstock was so great that Gottsched's reputation and influence were irreparably damaged. With Lessing's literary successes they withered away, and after Lessing's attack on him in 1759,[11] Gottsched was done for. From that time on Gottsched was a laughingstock in philosophical and literary circles.[12] He had had nothing to say to the poets of the age of sentiment,[13] and by the time he died sentiment was going even farther, into *Sturm und Drang*. But before that there had been a long and bitter controversy between the schools of Leipzig and of Zürich. Zürich won.

The battle has been interpreted in a variety of ways: as a conflict between an aesthetic based on French (Gottsched) and an aesthetic based on English (the Swiss) models; as a dispute between an a priori aesthetic of rules and an a posteriori aesthetic of experience; as a contest between art governed by form and rule and an art growing out of a deeper psychological

---

[10] Alfred Baeumler, *Kants Kritik der Urteilskraft* (Halle: Max Niemeyer, 1923), I, 60.

[11] *Literaturbrief* 17: "Nobody will deny that the German stage has to thank Professor Gottsched for a major part of its first steps to improvement; I am that nobody, and I deny it outright."

[12] The polemical literature was large and bitter. Consider only the title of G. F. Meier's attack: *Exposition of the reasons why it appears to be impossible to carry on a useful and rational controversy with Herr Professor Gottsched* (1754).

[13] Perhaps a domestic detail will not be out of place. Gottsched was married to a gifted woman fifteen years younger than himself, and during most of their life their relation seems to have been idyllic. But Gottsched once confessed that he could not conceive why his "otherwise so talented friend," as he referred to her, "should weep over a beautiful landscape" (Fritz Brüggemann, *Gottscheds Leben- und Kunstreform* [Leipzig: Reclam, 1935], p. 14). Now anyone who could not see why a beautiful woman should weep over a landscape could not understand the new movement in German poetry from Rousseau and Klopstock to *Sturm und Drang*. Gottsched obviously could not.

insight into aesthetic content; and finally as the struggle between academic art and an anarchistic aesthetic of unregulated emotion. Gottsched himself saw it as the latter; but in fact this is the only one of the four views which is completely wrong. Both Bodmer in his preface to *Critische Dichtkunst* and Breitinger in the book itself repeatedly expressed recognition of the necessity of rules to keep sentiment from passing into ranting; both insisted on the moral function of art.[14] The Swiss had not reached the stage of *Sturm und Drang*. But compared to the Gottsched's nomothetic criticism, the very vocabulary of Breitinger's work—for instance, "the sweep of imagination," "the warmth of mental acts" (*Hitze der Gemütsbewegungen*), and even such ordinary words as "charm"—points to a new immediacy in art.

Bodmer and Breitinger found in Leibniz a different conception of imagination from that of Wolff and Gottsched. For the latter two it is the faculty of bringing forth perceptions of things which are absent from the senses,[15] but which must have once been present to the senses. For Gottsched the rules of art are the rules to be followed, self-consciously, in recalling and constructing images to illustrate some idea clearly discerned by the understanding. Leibniz, on the other hand, had emphasized the spontaneous creativity of consciousness in its representations, even in its perception of the world; the representative power (*vis representativa*), with the emphasis upon the power, has its most natural and characteristic function in the creation of images not given ready-made to the senses. Bodmer had translated *Paradise Lost*, filled with representations of things no man had ever perceived; and he was not as impressed as Gottsched was with ideal exemplars of human character and action which, according to Wolff's theory of the imagination, originate from indistinct ideas of sensation raised to the level of distinct thoughts. For Gottsched, at least in the eyes of his opponents, a work of art was a kind of mosaic, put together by rule and prescription for the purpose of moral edification.

In the explicit description Breitinger gives of the power of imagination[16] the differences from the Gottschedian conception are not so great in theory as they were in practice. In theory the poet imaginatively abstracts from the imperfections of objects in their natural existence and combines perfections which nature has distributed among many things. In making perfect images that are both abstractions from and syntheses of actual experience he transforms the images of the actual world into images of possible worlds.[17] These are then presented in a form which moves the mind in a way in which neither an abstract conception of a possible Leibnizian world nor a mosaic of bits and pieces of this one could move it. Poetry is more philosophical than history; but it is also more philosophical than painting and sculpture because it is less tied down to the actual facts of this world, and freer in its

[14] *Critische Dichtkunst* (Zürich, 1740), unpaginated preface to vol. I and vol. I, pp. 102, 105, 283, and passim.

[15] Wolff, *Psychologia empirica*, §§ 92, 144, distinguishes imagination, the faculty of producing phantasmata of physically absent objects, from the poetic faculty of combining them into objects never seen. See also *Vernünftige Gedanken von Gott*, §§ 244–247.

[16] *Critische Dichtkunst*, II, 286ff.   [17] *Ibid.*, I, 270ff.

exploration of possible worlds. In a poem there should be a perfect fit between idea, image, and word. The sensuous sound of a word and its meaning should be appropriate to each other, and if they are not the abstract fit of the word to the concept produces at best a science but never beautiful art. The Wolffians are forced by their theory of the artificiality and conventional determination of words to overelaborate systems of definitions and to a flatness of style resulting from too many abstract and sensuously indifferent words.

According to Bodmer and Breitinger, the critic may and indeed must have rules, but the poet is made a poet not by adherence to the rules of the critic but by immersing himself in experience, especially that provided by other artists. Instead of beginning with critics (Horace and Boileau, for example) and trying to learn to become poets by following their rules, Bodmer's and Breitinger's proposal was to begin with poets and to let the critical standards emerge from the study of them. In that sense their aesthetic was to be empirical, not the a priori theory of art advanced by Gottsched.

Bodmer and Breitinger's influence on German taste was profound and did much to bring both Gottsched's recipes and the slavish imitation of French models into disrepute. But Bodmer was writing more as a literary critic than as a philosopher. He was, to some extent, a Wolffian, though without the dedication of his book to Wolff one might well fail to see it; for he was not a victim of the current widespread intellectualism and narrowly utilitarian moralism of which Wolff was the chief exponent. That Bodmer was right and Gottsched wrong in their diagnoses of what was amiss with German literature is shown best by the fact that Lessing's aesthetic theories, and even more his dramas, made Gottsched's doctrines obsolete and ridiculous. It is significant that Lessing was not at all a Wolffian in his philosophy.

Baumgarten

The resources of the Wolffian philosophy should not be underestimated simply because Wolff's closest disciple was worsted in these disputes. In the works of Alexander Gottlieb Baumgarten, as thoroughgoing a Wolffian as Gottsched himself, we find an esthetic theory that is not Gottschedian and is *therefore* (given the situation at the time) Bodmerian. Baumgarten was not a highly original philosopher, but he was important because he brought together Wolffian and Bodmerian concepts into a new synthesis, instead of seeing them, as Gottsched did, in irreconcilable conflict. From Wolff he developed the idea of a logic of the lower cognitive faculty which would not be merely a propaedeutic to a logic of the understanding and reason. From the Swiss he inherited the conception of a "poetic philosophy" which was quite different from Wolff's didactic "philosophy of poetry." Merged together, these two ideas made it possible that the aesthetics he developed should be both a science and an art.

Baumgarten, the most competent—and in the long run perhaps the only philosophically important—adherent of the Wolffian philosophy, was born in Berlin in 1714. He was educated in the famous Pietistic orphanage operated by Francke in Halle and, though Francke befriended him, he soon came to accept Wolff's philosophy. His Halle dissertation, *Meditationes philosophicae de nonnullis ad poema pertinentibus* (1735)[18] and his *Metaphysica* (1739) were followed by his most important work, the *Aesthetica* (1750, 1758). Kant had high regard for his abilities, calling him "a giant among metaphysicians"[19] and regularly used his *Metaphysica* as a textbook in his lectures. From 1738 to 1740 he was professor in Halle, and from 1740 until his death in 1762 professor in Frankfort on the Oder. Like almost all other Wolffians, in most fields Baumgarten made a few changes in the original philosophy; like most of them he was dissatisfied with Wolff's solution to the mind-body problem and argued for a theory of interaction. He improved even further Wolff's important contribution to the German philosophical vocabulary, with Kant adopting Baumgarten's improvements. (It is to Baumgarten that we owe the modern distinction between "subjective" and "objective," which had the opposite meanings from their present ones as late as Descartes.) But Baumgarten's fame rests squarely on his philosophy of art (which means, for him, poetry). Not only was Baumgarten a competent Wolffian philosopher; he was also a man of sensitive taste and unusual literary learning. The latter side of his nature kept him from saying silly things which the former alone might have occasioned —and in this he differs markedly from Gottsched and from Wolff himself.

Baumgarten accomplished two things in the theory of art. He is perhaps best known for being the first man to use the word "aesthetic" as the name for the part of philosophy dealing with art, but he was no mere inventor of a new name for old ways of thinking. First, he extended the scope of a highly disciplined and architectonic conception of philosophy to an entirely new realm of phenomena that had been either ignored (by Wolff) or raped (by Gottsched), thereby enriching philosophy itself. Second, he brought to the subject of the fine arts the discipline of an established philosophical system. Certainly in the modern sense of the word Baumgarten was not the first aesthetician, and his invention of the word "aesthetics" may appear to be a trivial contribution. But he was the first to handle the subject matter of art with the apparatus of an established system that professed to have a place for everything, and to reason syllogistically with the recalcitrant material of art without distorting it beyond recognition. He thus enriched both philosophy and the intellectual concern with the fine arts. That it was the Wolffian philosophy that was thus enriched and that it was the Wolffian philosophy that accomplished this intellectual discipline and regimen of the realm of taste is the paradox to which I referred earlier.

Baumgarten made the theory of knowledge, which he called gnoseology, the basic philosophical science, just as Wolff had put logic at the foundation. But gnoseology consists for Baumgarten not only of logic, but also of another science, aesthetics. Previously, he said, only the logical side of

[18] Translated as *Reflections on Poetry* by Karl Aschenbrenner and W. B. Holther (Berkeley and Los Angeles: University of California Press, 1954.)
[19] *Nova dilucidatio* (1775), Prop. xi.

knowledge had been systematically developed and rules and criteria for it established. Sensation had been acknowledged to be the raw material which was to be worked up into concepts and judgments, to be rendered clear and distinct by abstraction and definition. The perfection of thought so guided is true knowledge. But Baumgarten, beginning perhaps from a suggestion of Leibniz', saw that there is also a perfection of the senses, a perfection achieved when the senses are regulated by their own rules, forms, and criteria. Whereas Wolff had believed that the perfection of sense is found in thought, in transcending by logic the obscurity and confusion of sense, Baumgarten believed there is an *ars analogi rationis* which is a *scientia cognitionis sensitiuae*; and this he called aesthetics.[20] "*Things known* are to be known by the superior faculty as the object of knowledge; things perceived (*aestheta*) [are to be known by the inferior faculty, as the object] of the science of perception, or *aesthetic*."[21] This perfection apprehended by perception instead of by thought is the beautiful, and therefore it follows that aesthetics is the science (or art) of the beautiful.[22] (Here arise the two different, but related, meanings of "aesthetic" which appear later in Kant: it is a general science of sensibility, and is thus separated as one cognitive discipline from the other, logic, which deals with understanding; and it is the science of taste and beauty. The first is the usage in the *Critique of Pure Reason*, the second that of the *Critique of Judgment*.)

From the definition of aesthetics we see that for Baumgarten sense perception is a kind of knowledge—knowledge given by the "lower cognitive faculty"—and as such it must have rules. If we see perception as only the preparatory phase of knowledge, the rules are those of logic. Logic leads away from the individuality and singularity of sense to clear and distinct concepts, in order that sensible knowledge be judged by the principles of contradiction and sufficient reason. But there will be another set of rules and criteria if we wish to understand or achieve the perfection of sense *as such*, which is very different from logical perfection. The forms of this perfection are not logical forms, but they are analogous to those of logic. Since the standard criteria for thought are, for all Wolffians, clearness and distinctness, there must be something similar to them as criteria within aesthetics.

A concept is distinct if it is distinguishable from every other concept; distinctness is achieved by definition; and the representations of sense are, therefore, always indistinct (confused). Hence poetry contains only confused representations.[23] A clear representation is one which has sufficient marks to be readily recognized for what sort of thing it is. It has what Baumgarten calls "intensive clarity." A *clear* representation of *confused* ideas and images lucidly represents an individual thing, person, or situation.

---

[20] *Aethetica*, Prolegomena, § 1.   [21] *Reflections on Poetry*, § 116.
[22] *Aesthetica*, §§ 14–17; *Metaphysica* §§ 521, 662.
[23] *Reflections*, §§ 14, 15. The translators rightly warn us against the pejorative use of "confused," and suggest that much of Baumgarten's meaning will be retained if we understand him to mean "fused." For example, a metaphor is better called a "fused representation" than a "confused representation."

Such a representation is said to be "extensively clear."[24] For instance, an example may be extensively clearer than a maxim which embodies the same moral truth. The maxim is an abstract proposition consisting of intensively clear and distinct ideas, while the example—e.g., the man Ulysses —presents us with a great number of indistinct (fused) ideas but does so in an unmistakable and vivid manner. An extensively clear representation may give us a sample of a perfection in the sense that any Leibnizian would understand perfection, viz., a maximum of variety without contradiction. All of the rules and skills of art are ways of making indistinct ideas extensively clear; the rules are not the rules of logic and morality, but are indigenous to the subject matter of sense perception whose highest form, as such, is the experience of beauty, not of truth. Since the perception of a perfection is pleasant, it follows for Baumgarten that the function of poetry is to arouse the affects.[25] Hence the connection of art with pleasure and feelings and judgments of delight and approbation.

Meier and Sulzer

Baumgarten is a cognitivist in his aesthetic theory; that is, he believes that beauty is a property of certain sensuously presented (or, in poetry, represented) states of affairs, just as truth is regarded (by all scholastic philosophy) as both ontological and epistemological.[26] That beauty is attended with delight is true, but less important for Baumgarten than for his former student and colleague, Georg Friedrich Meier (1718–1777). A professor in Halle from 1748, Meier published his *Foundations of All the Fine Arts and Sciences* (*Anfangsgründe aller schönen Künste und Wissenschaften*[27] in 1748, and by his urging persuaded Baumgarten to publish his own *Aesthetica*. Meier, writing in German, was important as a popularizer of Baumgarten, but he goes beyond him in recognizing the role of imagination in all intellectual activity, even in the formation and application of concepts in the process of knowing. In this he takes another important step toward Kant. (It was Meier's *Vernunftlehre* [1752] which Kant used as a textbook in his lectures on logic.)

Baumgarten and Meier moved one step away from Wolff and Gottsched by securing to aesthetic experience a perfection of its own, one not to be reduced to or raised to rational knowledge. Art is appreciated by a faculty of taste, even though taste be the "lower cognitive faculty." A more secure degree of independence of the aesthetic from the intellectual was achieved

---

[24] *Ibid.*, § 16: "When in representation A, more is represented than in B, C, D, and so on, but all are confused, A will be said to be extensively clearer than the rest." In Baumgarten's conception of extensively clear representations, we find the first gropings in German philosophy toward a theory that accounts for representation of instrinsic individuality in the object. Euler about the same time was seeing that the clear and distinct representation of space differs from an abstract concept, which has another clarity and distinctness. Both men contributed to the Kantian theory of our awareness of space, though Baumgarten's contribution has not previously been appreciated.

[25] *Ibid.*, §§ 24, 25.   [26] *Aesthetica* §§ 426–427, 558.

[27] This work has not been translated into English, but Meier's *Thoughts on Jesting* exists in a translation by Joseph Jones (Austin: University of Texas Press, 1947).

by Johann Georg Sulzer, who broke the connection between the aesthetic and the cognitive.

Sulzer (1720–1779) was a Swiss student of Bodmer and Breitinger and a member of the Berlin Academy. After his first works he can hardly be considered a Wolffian at all. But instead of building upon Baumgarten and Meier, he starts with genuine Wolffian principles less sophisticated than Baumgarten's, and then modifies them in a more radical direction by recognizing that a different faculty is active in aesthetic experience from that in cognition. Wolff was correct, he first held, in deducing all the intellectual faculties of the soul from the impetus to clarity and distinctness of ideas, but Wolff neglected to give a comparable derivation of the affective qualities of experience. This lack of Sulzer first wished to supply with his own theory of the two basic states of the soul which underlay both the cognitive and the affective life: contentment (*aisance*) and constraint. Actual pleasure, however, is an active state, not a passive state of ease, and it is experienced when the soul is agitated, so that it produces, in a lively manner, many ideas spontaneously and without constraint.[28] Pleasure in the soul is thus originally related to intellectual activity, in the experience of a multitude of ideas related to each other and arising either from the perception of a unity in variety or from the active creation of a multiplicity of ideas out of a few. "All pleasures, even those of sense, finally relate to the intellectual faculty of the soul."[29] The source of delight is in the unconstrained intellectual activity of the soul and not in the intellectual or sensible apprehension of an objective perfection. The *unitas multiplex* in which we delight is ultimately that of the operations of the soul, not that of the object itself. The variety in unity in the object is only an occasion for such a harmonious operation of the soul.

In his later works, however, Sulzer tries to erase the remnants of intellectualism in this view and puts the faculty of feeling (*Empfindungsvermögen*) on a level equal to that of ideation (*Vorstellungsvermögen*). He argues, against his own former position and that of Baumgarten, that if aesthetic experience were cognitive we should have to have a conception of the purpose of an object in order to apprehend its perfection and thus to experience it as beautiful; but since we do not in fact have to have such a conception as a basis for aesthetic delight, the aesthetic experience is not an experience of a perfection known to us. The experience of beauty is not just an emotional response to an intellectual apprehension, but is a response of another faculty of the soul to some representations which immediately arouse it. Sulzer even attempted to give a physiological explanation of aesthetic pleasure in terms of some overflow of nervous excitation from the nerves involved in perception and conception.

The entire movement of Wolffian aesthetics was an escape from Wolff's "one faculty theory," according to which both will and feeling were aspects of the faculty of representation—feeling being the confused representation

[28] "Récherches sur l'origin des sentiments agréables et desagréables," *Mémoires de l'Academie Royale des Sciences et Belles-Lettres* (Berlin, 1751–52), pt. I, p. 71.
[29] *Ibid.*, pt. II, p. 77.

of a perfection, and will the distinct representation of a perfection to be achieved or maintained by action. From the beginning, there was an ambiguity in the notion of feeling—it covered both sensation (*Empfindung*) and feeling proper (*Gefühl*). This ambiguity continued throughout the history of Wolffian aesthetics and appeared again in the two quite distinctly different meanings Kant attached to the word *Aesthetik*—the analysis of sensible cognition (intuition) and the analysis of taste. Even when aesthetic experience was differentiated from the cognitive, however, its connection with the volitional remained relatively undisturbed. Thus the break with Wolff was not complete, and Sulzer (and, as we shall see later, Mendelssohn) saw feeling, the aesthetic, related to volition and passing over into action. Because this remnant of the one-faculty theory was not eradicated, Sulzer concluded that art has a moral import which is lacking in the mere natural propensity for feeling. Art disciplines feeling, but, because of the relation between feeling and will, art falls under moral judgment.[30]

Sulzer does not even, in fact, achieve a final emancipation of the artistic faculty from the cognitive. There is a common metaphysical essence in that which is distinctly conceived (the true), clearly perceived or imagined (the beautiful), and desired or striven for (the good). To be sure, the good, the true, and the beautiful are phenomenologically far better differentiated by Sulzer than by Wolff.[31] Still, Sulzer's work was only a step, but an important step, toward the final renunciation of Wolff's one-faculty theory; he went as far as he could away from this theory without ceasing to be a Wolffian at all. The emancipation from that theory required also the work of Mendelssohn and Johann Heinrich Tetens before it was finally accomplished by Kant.

Wolffian Theology

Unlike the French and English Enlightenment, the German Enlightenment was seldom forthright and extreme in its denial of revealed Christianity. Even when revelation and dogma were denied, there was still a patina of religiosity on most eighteenth-century thought in Germany. Samuel Reimarus kept his thoughts to himself as carefully as Valentin Weigel had kept his more than a century and a half earlier. Here and there appeared explicit and courageous opponents of orthodoxy and various compromisers with it. Johann Christoph Edelmann (1698–1767) was converted from Pietism to Spinozism and rejected revelation and creeds, but he replaced them with a pantheism which must have seemed to many to be even less credible. Carl Friedrich Bahrdt (1741–1792) proceeded from deism to unrestrained attacks on the religious establishment and its dogmas, and then to a vast journalistic effort to popularize a Christianity without mysteries through popular paraphrases of the Bible which were unlikely because of their superficiality to appeal to the learned and because of their

---

[30] *Allgemeine Theorie der schönen Künste* (1774), III, 8.
[31] See A. Palme, *J. G. Sulzers Psychologie und die Anfänge der Dreivermögenlehre*, Diss., Berlin, 1905.

heresy certain not to appeal to the laity. Berlin, after the middle of the century, to be sure, was filled with village atheists in important posts, but few important thinkers, even when they were religious critics, escaped from the atmosphere of the *Pfarrhäuser* in which they were born and the orthodox or Pietistic schooling they received. It is not easy to determine what were the causes of the great difference between the intellectual-religious outlook in Germany and in France, but there were certain factors that must be mentioned as contributory to it.

First, there was Leibniz' own orthodoxy; for Leibniz not only tried to bring the churches together, but also tried to maintain his own Lutheran orthodoxy. His attacks on the Socinians, for instance, reveal a willingness to adhere to orthodox Lutheran doctrines, such as that of the eternity of punishment, which only gradually came to be opposed by leading Enlightenment thinkers; and when they did so, they had to explain away the orthodox piety of Germany's greatest thinker as hypocrisy.[32] During the early part of the century, therefore, Germany's greatest thinker was claimed by the orthodox, whereas in England, for example, Locke was at the same time a fountainhead of deism even though he explicitly disclaimed it.

A second factor was Pietism itself, together with other unorthodox movements which had existed, from the earliest days, side by side with the established churches. Socinian and Arminian groups had opposed the triumphant orthodox churches and had done so in the name, not of free-thinking antireligiosity, but rather of a deeper piety and greater purity of doctrine. Even in the heyday of orthodoxy, therefore, one could oppose orthodoxy without practicing infidelity; and the antiorthodox and anticlerical tendencies of thinkers in the eighteenth century could be seen as a continuation of a long tradition of piety.

A third factor was the existence in Germany, side by side, of three established churches. Toleration of the two Protestant sects was a political necessity, and where toleration did not exist in any one state, there was always another nearby where the oppressed sect was not oppressed but, all too often, the oppressor. Moreover, there had been a considerable sharing of ideas between the two sects, and much of the philosophical thought of the eighteenth century carried on by Lutherans seems to have been much more an inheritance from Calvinism than from Lutheranism. In this book it has been necessary to identify each thinker of the seventeenth century as a Calvinist or Lutheran; in the eighteenth, such identification would not reveal very much, even if it were not the case that most of the thinkers were publicly Lutheran. But even more important was the fact that the variety of religious views and institutions in Germany did not require a polarization of religious thought and groups into two uncompromisingly opposed forces, a religious and an antireligious one. A monolithic orthodoxy, on the other hand, calls forth an extreme reaction in the form of anticlericalism and anti-Christianity, as in France; diverse orthodoxies allow

---

[32] This was the accusation made by Johann August Eberhard in *Neue Apologie des Sokrates* (1772), which occasioned Lessing's defense of both Leibniz and the challenged doctrine. But notice how late in the century this battle occurred.

internal dissensions which do not grow into a two-party system of Christians and anti-Christians. *Libertas philosophandi* was an efficient safety valve, especially in the two leading universities, Halle and Göttingen, and there was little or no governmental interference with philosophical and philosophico-religious thought between the edict against Wolff in 1723 and the Wöllner edict of 1788.

In Prussia and Brandenburg, the situation was very favorable to religious Enlightenment. Not only had the Calvinist minority been strengthened by well-educated Huguenots who came in after the Revocation of the Edict of Nantes in 1685, but after 1740 there was a freethinking deist on the throne of Prussia. Frederick the Great was opposed to Holbach's atheism and to the radicals who might upset the balance of society by spreading atheism, but he gave refuge to hard-pressed religious dissidents and encouragement to many of those seeking to spread religious enlightenment, for he disliked the Pietists as much as he did the atheists.

Finally, and not least, there was the philosophy of Wolff with its thoroughly scholastic conception of the relation of philosophy to theology. The scholastic compromise between the claims of philosophy and theology had long since ceased to be effective in England, France, and Holland, but it was still strong in Germany thanks to Wolff. For Wolff taught three things which came to be widely accepted, even by many Pietists. He taught that a purely rational theology was possible, with proofs of the existence of God, the immortality of the soul and punishment or reward in the after life, the creation of the world, and the like. Second, he taught that the truths demonstrated in rational theology were completely in harmony with revealed theology; there could be no conflict between true revelation and reason. In effect this meant that reason was the test for revelation (as it was for Locke), but Wolff was careful to see that the test was not used in any controversial fashion, and particular dogmas of revealed religion interested him very little. And, having something for everyone, Wolff provided an empirical theology in his natural teleology, which showed the wise design and governance of the world for the sake of human beings. The freedom left to philosophy—in principle Wolff was a strong defender of academic freedom and the freedom to publish—was restricted, of course, to the teachings of "true philosophy" which, by its nature, could not teach false, and therefore harmful, political or religious doctrines. The established churches, therefore, had nothing to fear from Wolff, nor he from them after 1740, and he was equally esteemed by Catholics, Lutherans, and Calvinists.

Only the irrational, emotional, and "sentimental" aspects of religion were left out by Wolff; and as Pietism became progressively less a lay movement and developed its own regimen and dogma, these features of the religious life which had been the particular care of Pietist thought became less important, so that many Pietists were in fact Wolffian in their philosophy. The emotional inwardness of Pietism did not generally make Pietists philosophers; and among the followers of Thomasius who were both Pietists *and* philosophers, there was a rejection of Wolffian intellectualism. But during the period of Wolff's domination of German academic philosophy, the German Enlightenment was characterized by a moralistic and rationalistic view of religion;—the moralism, compatible with Pietism, and the dogmas retained (because they were thought to be rational) recommending this philosophy to the orthodox. Religion could be supported by reason and could support the humanistic and even utilitarian ethics desiderated by the enlighteners.

The history of religious thought in the eighteenth century, so far as it concerns the historian of philosophy, therefore, is a history of two principal movements. First, from the Wolffian starting point there was the encroachment of reason on the sphere of revelation and dogma. Second there was the Thomasian and Pietistic opposition to this encroachment and a sustained effort to defend the irrational and mysterious elements in the religious life. The encroaching movement, in its turn, followed two lines. The first was to criticize, rationally and internally, the contents of revelation and dogma and to exclude doctrines which were thought to be irrational or morally unworthy of an enlightened age. The second was to replace the theory of revelation altogether and to develop a religion based wholly upon reason and nature. The first involved a historical revaluation of Scripture and a marked restriction upon its authoritative content; the second a rejection of its historical authenticity and the replacement of a Scriptural by a purely rational religion.

The common source of these two Wolffian developments is to be found in the work of Siegmund Jacob Baumgarten (1706–1757), brother of Alexander Baumgarten and after 1743 a professor of theology in the University of Halle.

S. J. Baumgarten, best known as a church historian and, along with his pupil Johann Salamo Semler, regarded in Germany as a founder of *Religionswissenschaft*, preserved the Wolffian conviction of the harmony of dogma and reason, seeing in the authentic content of revealed religion a confirmation of natural religion. Through his lectures and writings on the English deists and freethinkers, and the translations of them which he inspired, Baumgarten furthered the knowledge of deism in Germany far more than he succeeded in combating it, by his continued insistence upon revealed religion as transcending it. Because of his important position (all Lutheran pastors in Brandenburg were expected to study at some time at Halle), his influence was very widespread, but because he was primarily a transmitter of Wolffian compromises, he influenced men in very diverse ways. On the one hand, there were those who inferred from his way of dealing with the deists that revelation was superior to reason: the leading figure of this "right wing" of Wolffianism was Johann Goeze, the enemy of Lessing. Or there were others who went in the opposite direction, first minimizing the importance and finally denying the validity of revelation. This path was taken by those who rationally criticized and rejected some of the revealed dogmas but accepted others, doing both for the purpose of strengthening the Christian position against an orthodoxy which embraced antirational and, in their opinion, antimoral teachings. It was followed also by those who thought that revelation and tradition were so tainted with pious fraud that they should be rejected altogether. The first were called rationalists or neologists, the second rationalists or naturalists. Both acknowledged that the essential point in the defense of Christianity was the historical authenticity and the moral and rational defensibility of revealed dogma. They differed on whether any orthodox position could be maintained against these historiographical and philosophical attacks, the neologists affirming that it could, and the naturalists denying it.

It is not possible to give in a brief space a chronological account of these two trends. If we make the lines between them sharp, we find that few important thinkers are clear cases of one or the other; if we do not, the classification of thinkers is bound to be somewhat arbitrary. Even contemporaneously, the word "neology" had sometimes a broader, sometimes a narrower, meaning, and many individual thinkers at one stage of their careers stood within, and, at another, outside the movement. Rather than try to affix labels, therefore, and classify a large number of thinkers as neologists or naturalists, it will be more instructive to take two leaders who clearly epitomize the two possible forms of left-wing Wolffianism.

Semler

The first was Johann Salamo Semler (1725–1791), pupil of Siegmund Baumgarten and after 1752 also professor of theology in Halle.

According to Semler's view, revelation is historically conditioned by God's accommodation to the local condition of those to whom he reveals himself. While this doctrine had often been taught with respect to the Old Testament—as, for example, by Spinoza—Semler held that Christ's own teachings represented an accommodation to two diverse traditions, one Jewish and one Greek. We, in a different age, Semler continued, must make allowances for this and be "relativistic" in our interpretation of Scripture. We must try to extract the divine kernel from the historical *adiaphora*. We do so not by denying revelation in favor of reason, for reason itself, in its historical development in the history of dogma, shows a high degree of relativism with respect to the personalities and interests of theologians. We use our moral reason and "sentiment" in order to find the "true Christian religion" or the "private religion" (Semler calls it both) which is the same for all Christians, though clothed in different ways by the various religious parties which are made necessary, even in God's plan, by the inequalities among men, and which are established by the not-too-divine conflicts of political ambitions and views of churchmen in all ages. Thus Semler went beyond ordinary church history and biblical exegesis, which were his professional fields, to achieve the beginnings of an understanding of the development of dogma itself. His historical insight began to penetrate into the realm of "rational" dogmatics, which can then no longer appear as a final and authoritative interpretation of a variable revelation, for *both* are historically determined.

While Semler's private religion had many resemblances to the English and French versions of natural religion, and because of its strongly moralistic emphasis even more to the older humanists' "Christian philosophy," it differed from the former in preserving some place for revelation, and from the latter in making it in principle difficult or impossible to find the norm of Christianity in any text, even in the New Testament. Most of the traditional doctrines of Lutheranism seemed to be challenged by this historical relativization, both in their putative "source" and "final" formulation.

Later in life Semler saw the instability of his position, since it gave him no grounds for putting the brake upon movements which completely subordinated revelation to reason, or completely historicized and discounted the claims of revelation. So at the price of consistency and his good standing among men who thought he was their ally, he asserted the necessity of a public and authoritative religion as a condition of public weal and of the religious welfare of the populace, and as a solid basis from which *forts ésprits* could develop their private religion. This public religion (need it be said?) was orthodox Lutheranism with a touch of Pietism. Renouncing his explicit doctrine of the sinfulness of religious compulsion, he attacked Reimarus and Lessing, defended the Wöllner Edict of 1788 against freedom of religious teaching, and led the opposition to his former colleague Karl Bahrdt, who was jailed for making fun of this edict. But he had too long alienated himself from the orthodox, and in his last years he was without significant influence except through his earlier historical works.

It is obvious that Semler's position was intellectually unstable, even if his changing stand on controversial issues is to be interpreted more as a sign of timidity than as a legitimate consequence of the unsoundness of his position, which had compromise at its very center. For it was only by an intellectually unfounded faith that Semler elevated the divine revelation in Christ above the historical accidents of Christ's historical situation, which Semler himself pointed out with great skill and learning. The march of skepticism could not be stopped by any intellectual argument Semler could mount; it could be stopped only by his own piety, and could be stopped only for him, not for those who had accompanied him that far on the road to relativism. The consistent positions which Semler could have taken, but which he in fact attacked, were three: a theory which denied reason and held fast to revealed dogma; a theory which denied the validity of revelation, and explained it away by making it relative to its historical context; and a theory that introduced a historical dimension into the very concept of revelation, and not merely into its content, without denying its validity altogether. The first was the position of Goeze and later Pietists and, in practice but not in theory, that of the old Semler. The second was that of Reimarus and Bahrdt; the third, that of Lessing.

We shall now turn to the second of these positions; we shall come to Lessing, a giant among men, in a later chapter not devoted to mere epigoni.

Reimarus

Hermann Samuel Reimarus (1694–1768), who was born and died in Hamburg, was a Wolffian who drew radical conclusions from his master's rationalism. Early in life he had been so torn between the Pietistic criticism of Wolff and Wolff's own doctrine that he retired from the higher academic world (he was *Privatdozent* in Wittenberg) in a state of indecision to become professor of Hebrew in the gymnasium in Hamburg. The conclusions Reimarus drew from Wolff were so radical that he did not publish them in his own lifetime, and when they were later published by Lessing, the name of the author was not made known and did not become known until 1814. Before looking into these radical conclusions, however, we must consider the works he did publish which established his credentials as a Wolffian.

In 1754 and 1760 he published two works which brought him fame during his lifetime: in 1754, *Essays on the Chief Truths of Natural Religion* (*Abhandlungen von den vornehmsten Wahrheiten der natürlichen Religion*), and in 1760 a treatise on natural teleology based on the study of the instincts of animals, *General Observations on the Impulses of Animals, Especially Their Craft-Impulse* (*Allgemeine Betrachtungen über die Triebe der Tiere, hauptsächlich über ihren Kunsttrieb*). He defended a Wolffian teleological view of nature as opposed to atheism, Spinozism, and materialism. As a member of Brockes'[33] circle in Hamburg, he facilely defined religion as the admiration in everything of the wisdom and goodness of God; and like other members of that group, he was avid in the search after empirical evidence for it. He found it in the study of animals, but other members of that group wrote natural teleologies and theologies based upon the study of stones ("lithotheology"), molluscs ("testaceotheology") or "ostracodermotheology") and even earthquakes ("seismotheology"). Reimarus was in good company and was respected for his work in this field. But upon his death his daughter found a manuscript of about two thousand pages entitled *Apology or Defense of the Rational Worshippers of God* (*Apologie oder Schützschrift für die vernünftigen Verehrer Gottes*), which she gave to Lessing, who published seven parts of it as the work of an unknown writer which he said he had found in the Wolfenbüttel library. The long controversy over these fragments belongs to a later stage in our history, to Lessing's rather than to Reimarus' life, so I shall point out here only Reimarus' rationalistic critique of revelation and the conclusions he drew from it.

The title of Reimarus' manuscript indicates its purpose. It is aimed at defending the "rational worshippers of God" from those who had come to condemn Christianity because of the incredibility of its historical sources and its current dogmas. It is also an apology for the freethinkers who were condemned by the orthodox, the unreasonable worshippers of God; but it is much more the latter than the former. Instead of trying to show that the historical record was in fact accurate, or that it was acceptable to reasonable men under the thesis of accommodation, Reimarus tries uncompromisingly to show that a religion based on anything but reason is in fact inadmissible to the mind of a reasonable man.

[33] Barthold Heinrich Brockes (1680–1747), whose most important work was *Irdisches Vergnügen an Gott*, was little gifted as a poet but was a genuine, if somewhat naive, worshipper of natural things (beetles, cherry blossoms, dewdrops, and roast lamb, as well as the sun and moon). He represents an earlier stage of poetic natural teleology in Germany, the later stages of which are to be found in Albrecht von Haller, who was a genuine scientist as well as poet, and Klopstock. On Haller, see below, Chapter XIII, n. 2.

Reimarus begins by condemning those who decry reason in the name of faith. The orthodox defeat their own purpose and make men un-Christian by insisting that, in order to be Christian, they must believe what rational men cannot in fact believe. The orthodox, in teaching that reason does not aid toward, and may deter one from, true Christian piety and that what does not come from faith is sinful, make it impossible for a man to be a "rational Christian." In an age of reason they thereby produce fewer Christians than unbelievers.

He then turns against the orthodox an argument which has always been used by them against rational and natural theologians. They had argued that revelation was open to all, while reason was given only to the few; and God, desiring the salvation of all mankind, has therefore revealed to all what only a few, if any, could discover by reason. Reimarus neatly turns this argument around. If revelation is necessary for salvation, then it must be available to all in accurate and indisputable form. But since even the orthodox insist that there have been "spurious revelations"—doctrines thought by their adherents to be revealed, but by the orthodox to be heretical—there must be some way in which each individual must be able to decide, and ultimately be responsible for deciding correctly, on the competing claims of various putative revelations. Hence if the plan of salvation includes the right decision on competing "revelations," each man would have been provided with what was needed for this decision: a gift for languages, a knowledge of antiquities, history, geography, and chronology, and skill in hermeneutics. In a word, the orthodox argument requires that, if true belief based on revelation is a condition of salvation, reason must be as widespread among men as ever a rational theologian could desire. Since the conclusion is false, the premise that salvation depends upon the acceptance of true revelation must be false. The acceptance of true revelation and the rejection of false cannot, therefore, have been willed by God as a condition of man's salvation.

The orthodox answer to this, of course, is to deny the first premise, and to assert that revelation is simple and straightforward. It is to be found in the Bible, where its import is clear even though it goes beyond reason. To this, Reimarus counters by trying to show two things. First, some basic orthodox doctrines are not to be found in the Bible; and second that the biblical record is historically spurious. He explains the inauthenticity of the record not merely by denying the direct inspiration of the Bible, but by accusing its human authors of being either conscious falsifiers or victims of falsification by others. The reports of miracles it contained were neither true nor binding on the Christian believer because the rational Christian neither could nor should believe them. The dogmas of the church which conflicted with the truths of natural and rational religion were derived from the spurious parts of the biblical narrative if, indeed, they were not later inventions altogether. But there is in man a natural faculty of reason, with its implanted ideas, which frees him from dependence upon such mendacious reports. This natural light has become obscured not (as believed in the previous two centuries) by the fall of man, and hence in need of a revelation to rekindle it, but by the pretensions and propaganda of the priests of positive religion. Therefore, not revelation but the exercise of natural reason is the cure for religious obscurities and obscurantism. Among the biblical reports Reimarus regarded as spurious were the parting of the Red Sea and all accounts of miracles (including those of Jesus). The disappearance of Christ's body from the tomb he attributed not to a supernatural resurrection but to a trick some of the disciples had played. Among the doctrines to be given up because they had no authentic scriptural foundation and conflicted with natural reason were those of original sin, eternal punishment, the incarnation, the Trinity, and the ascension and second coming of Christ.

The rational worshipper of God is called upon to find what is rationally and morally convincing in the teachings of "Christians, Jews, Turks, and heathens;" they will then know better what is "practical (*das Praktische*) in the universal religion of Christ" and will more gladly call themselves Christians than they now do when they are required to assume, hypocritically or in blind faith, all that which soils and obscures (*beschmutzt*) this pure practical religion." The present dispensation of dogmatism and persecution does not produce Christians, Reimarus says, but either hypocrites or victims of priestly and political persecution who are in fact "righteous worshippers of God, obedient subjects of their superiors, peaceful and useful citizens of the state, friends of humanity, and lovers of truth and virtue."[34]

The theory of revelation as unreasonable and of religion as conspiracy is the final outcome of a comparison of a rationalistic theory of "private religion" with a history of dogma based upon putatively supernatural revelation. Semler provided both factors for this comparison, but as a pious man occupying a public position as professor of theology, it is no wonder that he was shocked by this outcome of his half-rationalistic theory of accommodation. Wolff would have been no less astonished had he lived to read the Wolfenbüttel fragments and to learn that their author counted himself to be a Wolffian, for Wolff agreed with Leibniz and the scholastics that while revelation was supra-rational it could not conflict with reason.

Thomasius' Disciples

It is difficult to be a follower of a man who prides himself on being an eclectic follower of others, and especially difficult when he never succeeded in bringing his multiform borrowings into an organic unity which could be called, in spite of its eclecticism, *a* philosophy. Thomasius' "philosophy for the world" or for "the court" and his Pietism and his spiritual natural philosophy did not fit well together, and none of those who were considered his followers attempted the impossible task of uniting these widely disparate elements. At first it was the spiritualistic, peculiarly Pietistic, side of Thomasius' thought that attracted followers.

[34] The quotations in this paragraph are from previously unpublished parts of Reimarus' manuscript, to be found in Wolfgang Philip, ed., *Das Zeitalter der Aufklärung* (Bremen: Diederich, 1963), pp. 244–256. The earlier paragraphs are based on the parts published by Lessing.

Four men stand out in a direct line of succession[35] from Thomasius: Budde, Rüdiger, Hoffmann, and Crusius. Budde was a colleague of Thomasius, Rüdiger a student; Hoffmann was Rüdiger's student, and Crusius was Hoffmann's. They constitute, at least loosely, a single school. This school was characterized by three traits, even though there were some internal differences and developments. First, there was a continuing Pietistic opposition to scholasticism and to Lutheran orthodoxy, in favor of a sentimental and emotional inwardness and readiness to appeal to biblical and personal revelation and to embrace the entire inventory of Protestant mysteries. Second, there was opposition to Wolff. The school opposed Wolff's intellectualism in psychology and developed a theory of the independence of will from intellect. It opposed Wolff's intellectualism in method and favored the more informal arts of reasoning as celebrated by Thomasius. Most of all, perhaps, it fought Wolff's theory wherever it seemed to threaten the freedom of man and the authority of revelation. Finally, all four men espoused (still against Wolff) a spiritualistic, antimechanistic and antimathematical conception of nature, following the lead given by Thomasius in his venture into the philosophy of nature.

Schools of philosophy are made by joint opposition to some doctrines as well as by common agreement on others. Had there been no Wolffian school, there would have been no Thomasian. It was the opposition to Wolff and Wolffians which was shared by all the followers of Thomasius at some stage in their careers. Wolff's principal opponents in the quarrel of 1723, when Thomasius himself stood aside, were Thomasius' pupil Nikolius Hieronymous Gundling (1671–1729), professor in Halle after 1705, and Joachim Lange (1670–1744) professor in Halle after 1707. Gundling is of interest chiefly because he is one of the first to make use of Locke in Germany. Lange was more Pietistic than Thomasius and even opposed Thomasius' too great freedom in philosophizing and his treading on theological toes. But he shared Thomasius' starting point in a healthy common sense which, again in Pietistic fashion, he held to have become clouded by man's fall and to need enlightenment both by a *lumen naturale* and a *lumen supernaturale*, i.e., by worldly philosophy and revelation. In his *Medicina mentis* (1704) he developed these ideas in conjunction with Thomasius' own practical reforms in logic; a healthy reason is one that

---

[35] Only those who came out of Halle or had teachers from Halle traced their origins back to Thomasius. Hence we exclude Konrad Dippel (= Christianus Democritus) and Friedrich Christoph Oetinger, as well as the Counter-Enlighteners. Dippel (1673–1734) was a Pietistic alchemist and astrologist influenced, in his former capacity, by Gottfried Arnold and, in the latter, by van Helmont. He denied the divine authority of Scripture, but practiced an apparently intense private mysticism side by side with public charlatanry. While milking his patrons in Berlin, however, he did make some contributions to chemistry; see J. R. Partington, *History of Chemistry* (New York: St. Martin's Press, 1961–64), II, pp. 378–379. Oetinger (1702–1782) was educated in Tübingen under Bilfinger, but became a Pietist, an alchemist, and a critic of the entire modern development in philosophy since Descartes, but especially in Leibniz and Wolff. The principal intellectual influences on his thinking were those of Jacob Böhme and Swedenborg. See W. A. Schulze, "Oetinger contra Leibniz," *Zeitschrift für philosophische Forschung*, 11:607–617 (1957), and Albrecht Ritschl, *Geschichte des Pietismus* (Bonn, 1886), vol. III, chapter 46.

has been healed by medicine for the mind. It was Lange who brought the charge of Spinozism against Wolff, foreshadowing a long and bitter controversy later in the century.

Johann Franz Budde, also called Buddeus (1667–1729) professor of philosophy in Halle from 1693 to 1705, then professor of theology in Jena, is of some importance because almost all of his philosophical work was done before the rise of Wolffianism, and his works enjoyed such widespread acceptance and respect that some have suggested that Wolff should be classified as an opponent of Budde rather than Budde as an anti-Wolffian. Budde was known as a polyhistor, and in his writings we see a tendency for Thomasius' "court-philosophy" to become what Thomasius had opposed, viz., a "school philosophy" with many scholastic trimmings. In his *Elementa philosophiae practicae* (1697) Budde followed Thomasius in continuing the Grotian and Pufendorfian doctrine of natural law without a theological foundation; but in his ethics he was more Pietistic, denying even the freedom of the will and holding that only God's grace can free man's will from its bondage to earthly aims. In 1703 he published his *Institutiones philosophiae eclectica* in two parts, the first practical (*Elementa philosophiae instrumentalis*), containing a Thomasian logic; the second theoretical (*Elementa philosophiae theoreticae*), dealing with metaphysical, cosmological, pneumatic (psychological), and theological questions. In this part he offered a theoretical basis for astrology and developed an angelology. He later published a moral theology as well as several attacks on the English deists, who were then becoming known in Germany. His attack on Wolff in 1723 was influential in Jena and other universities, including Tübingen.

Johann Georg Walch (1693–1775), a son-in-law of Budde and professor in Marburg, was the author of a *Philosophisches Lexicon* (Jena, 1726; 2nd ed., 1733), a large work of erudition still useful for its compilation of the views of his contemporaries. In his judgments he generally follows Budde and, even more often, Rüdiger. The *Lexicon* gives a not unfair, but critical and well-informed, account of Wolff's philosophy. Thomasius is one of the most frequently cited authorities, but in a long and judicious article on witchcraft Walch disagrees with the master.

Rüdiger

Andreas Rüdiger (1673–1731), after study in Halle, was a physician in Leipzig, a center of Pietism and of opposition to Wolffianism. His *Physica divina* (1716), like Thomasius' cosmology, grew out of his knowledge of the natural philosophy of the previous century. In his *Physica* he rejected mechanistic theories because they could not explain the qualitative aspect of things in the world. Qualities were for him the basic, irreducible, and inexplicable facts which manifested the absolute freedom of the creator. Physics is simply a history of creation, dependent upon the arbitrary will of God. In nature, Rüdiger distinguished expansive and contractive forces, and he replaced the theory of mechanical action by contact with a theory of elastic action as these two forces played against each other, and to them he added still a third force, *spiritus*, taken from the vitalistic theories he accepted in biology.

Such a qualitative physics was the product of a crude empiricism which rejected both the mathematical-mechanical theory of nature and the mathematical and demonstrative procedures of the Wolffians. Rüdiger opposed Wolff's mathematical method in both philosophy and the sciences. Wolff's syllogisms, he held, did not lead to a conception of what actually exists, but only to logical possibilities, and even Wolff must leave demonstration for observation in order to arrive at facts. Second, Wolff overemphasized the role of syllogistic inference in mathematics, which does not, according to Rüdiger, proceed syllogistically but by inspection of particulars in counting and in geometric constructions.[36] Hence Wolff's "mathematical procedure" in philosophy is a travesty of mathematics, not an imitation of it. And, third, Wolff tried to demonstrate with certainty what in fact is at best probable in our knowledge of nature. Rüdiger saw the need for a theory of probable inference, which Leibniz has seen but which Wolff had almost completely neglected.

Rüdiger's rejection of the mathematical ideal in philosophy went hand in hand with his cosmology, which made no use of mathematics even in science. But with admirable acumen Rüdiger saw the fatally weak points in Wolff's methodology. He saw that a purely logical ontology—one based on mere logical possibility because it reduces the principle of sufficient reason to the status of a theorem derived from the law of contradiction— cannot either guide or give assurance to our knowledge of fact, which Wolff's denigrated as mere "historical knowledge." No matter how much demonstrative armament Wolff might bring up, everything finally depends upon observation; and for this, Rüdiger thought his own probabilistic methods and acknowledgement of brute qualitative fact were more honest and dependable than the highly abstract and almost silly things Wolff occasionally said about observation and experiment. But Rüdiger went too far in failing to see the positive role which reason and demonstration do serve in the organization and testing of historical, i.e., empirical, knowledge.

While Rüdiger's attacks on Wolff show a good deal of sound empiricistic good sense, he was not able to develop them into a consistent campaign for empiricism; there was too much theological inhibition for that, and where empiricism becomes most interesting, there Rüdiger is most silent or confused. For instance, he is an effective critic (though not an original one) of the theory of eternal verities and innate ideas.

We do not know, Rüdiger wrote, how it may be with God and his truths, but our truths are certainly not eternal. We know what God permits us to know, and we know it under arbitrary conditions he has established. We have no knowledge of the internal constitution of substances, but are limited merely to the apprehension of their accidents. Their accidents are not necessarily related to them, but are arbitrary signs which God has permitted us to experience. For all we know, qualities other than those we experience might have been laid before us. The signs we have are sufficient for us to know *that* they are signs of something. The question of the existence of an external world is not so much as raised by Rüdiger. The

---

[36] *De sensu veri et falsi* (2nd ed., 1722), §§ 8–12; see Ernst Cassirer, *Das Erkenntnisproblem in der Philosophie und Wissenschaft der neueren Zeit* (Berlin: Bruno Cassirer, 1922), III, 525–526.

signs are adequate for our purposes in permitting us to infer to the other observable qualities of things; but human truth is in the final analysis an intrasymbolic coherence, not a knowledge of the adequacy of the symbol to the thing.

Rüdiger's attack on innate ideas is equally truncated. All the tasks that his opponents assigned to innate ideas, he assigns to ideas that originate in an active internal sense which furnishes us—we are not told how—with ideas of God, substance, and cause. Instead of the natural light of the intellect having been dimmed by the fall of man so that we cannot clearly discern ideas implanted in Adam and his descendants, our ignorance arises from a disorder in our faculties so that *natural* reason (*bon sens*) is not to be trusted. It just as naturally errs as gives truth. To discover truth, we have to correct nature. We must replace *ratio* with *recta ratio*, and raise the ectypal logic of man to the archetypal logic of God. The natural light must be replaced by, or at least supplemented by, an acquired light. In this respect Rüdiger agreed with Thomasius and not with the ordinary Pietistic views about learning. And if his epistemology does not qualify him for the empiricistic school, at least it shows that he stood on the ground of the Thomasian Enlightenment.

Rüdiger's cosmology was too far out of step with even the admittedly slow development of science in Germany for him to have any influence at that time. But it was later of interest to the German *Naturphilosophen* of the nineteenth century who, again turning against mechanical and mathematical conceptions of nature, tried to reinstate qualitative, organic, animistic concepts even in physical science. For Rüdiger the vitalistic conception of nature was a natural corollary to an anti-intellectualistic epistemology, which in turn was based upon a voluntaristic psychology.

Rüdiger sharply rebukes Wolff for reducing the will to a mere knowledge of perfections, and against him develops a theory in which the will is a basic faculty. This voluntarism in psychology naturally accords with the quasi-empiricism of Rüdiger's theory of knowledge, since both are opposed to an overemphasis on, or exclusive recourse to, the intellectual. Such voluntarism and empiricism also go well with a Pietistic theology which opposes the excessive intellectualism of both Wolffian natural theology and the scholastic elaborations of Lutheran orthodoxy.

Thus Rüdiger's own systematic philosophy accords much better with the Pietistic faith than Thomasius' did. While it still seems odd that Thomasius ever was a Pietist and a *Naturphilosoph*, in the work of Rüdiger all these elements are brought into a harmonious relationship: nonmechanical cosmology, antirationalism in epistemology, anti-intellectualism (voluntarism) in psychology, and Pietism against natural and rational religion.

Adolf Friedrich Hoffmann

Adolf Friedrich Hoffmann (1707–1741), like his teacher Rüdiger and his pupil Crusius, was a professor in the University of Leipzig. In his earlier works[37] he was a contemptuous opponent of Wolff, laughing at Wolff's

---

[37] *Gedancken über Wolffens Logik* (1729) and *Beweisthümer derjenigen Grundwahrheiten aller Religion und Moralität* (1736).

pretentious proofs of "what any matron knows," proofs he himself recommended only to women and ten-year old boys. But he was sufficiently independent-minded not to carry on with merely the wearying Pietistic objections to Wolff. He had an unusually keen mind, little given to the speculative excesses of Rüdiger but actually attracted by Wolff's sobriety. Through him there was introduced into the Thomasian tradition some element of rigor and systematization it had hitherto lacked. His writing has the same compendious heaviness as Wolff's, the same striving for exactitude, and regrettably the same prolixity.

Hoffmann's principal work was *Logic, wherein the Characteristics of the True and the False Are Derived from the Laws of the Human Understanding*,[38] published in 1737. The emphasis upon the derivation of logical principles from psychological laws, indicated by this title, is of decisive importance in the Pietistic opposition to Wolff. Though Wolff's logic is to be found in his book on "the powers of the human understanding," his psychology was excessively simple, and the whole tenor of his logic was ontological rather than psychological. Hoffmann's logic, on the other hand, is thoroughly psychological, and his psychology of thinking much richer than Wolff's.

He opposes Wolff on almost every point with reasoned dissent. He argues that mathematics and metaphysics have radically different methods, and he even anticipates some of the distinctions between them that Kant formulated in the Prize Essay of 1763. He has a different conception of general metaphysics from Wolff's. Whereas, for Wolff, ontology was the science of the possible, for Hoffmann it is the science of the necessary, of material principles that would be true of any possible worlds. He has no extravagant claims for his special metaphysics (of minds, bodies, God, and so on), but recognizes that in much of our metaphysical knowledge we must weigh probabilities and not claim certainties. The last remnants of the doctrine of innate ideas still to be found in Wolff are rejected; everything except feelings associated with inborn drives is to be derived from experience—including the laws of logic themselves. He sees more clearly than anyone else what Wolff saw, but all too frequently forgot: that all arguments for the existence of things must have empirical premises, and that it is vain to try to draw existential conclusions from nothing but the laws of contradiction and sufficient reason. Wolff's system, instead of having a sound logical base, has no base at all, Hoffmann thinks, since Wolff never tries to justify his basic principles. Obviously they cannot be given a logical proof, for then they would not be basic; but while Wolff leaves them entirely unfounded, Hoffmann tries to give them an experiential foundation.

Whatever we may think of this extreme empiricism, it is at least a relief from Wolff's equally extreme rationalism, only occasionally tempered with the recollection that experience is, after all, important. Hoffmann, however wrong himself, was at least right in seeing that the law of contradiction and

---

[38] *Vernunft-Lehre, darinnen die Kennzeichen des Wahren und Falschen aus den Gesetzen des menschlichen Verstandes hergeleitet werden* (Leipzig, 1737). This book is exceedingly rare, and only four copies are known to exist. I am indebted to Professor Giorgio Tonelli, who is preparing a new edition of it, for the loan of a microfilm copy.

its corollary, that of sufficient reason, are insufficient bases for existential judgments. He sees in these two laws only extreme cases of more general laws having existential import and anchored in actual experiences. In general, we can say that Hoffmann takes the general phenomenon of "the inconceivability of the opposite" in a much broader sense than "the impossibility of the contradictory," articulates this broader phenomenon, and shows that Wolff's laws are only specific cases of it and are too narrow to cover all the ground Wolff claimed for their use. The basic phenomenon is not the experience of the incompatibility of *a* and non-*a*, but the experience of conviction that so and so must be the case, or that two even noncontradictory ideas may not be compatible.[39]

Hoffmann attempts to work out rules for the determination of this inconceivability, or incompatibility, so that it will not be merely a matter of introspective fact. This is one of the most interesting, and at the same time one of the least satisfactory, parts of his work. At least Hoffmann has an important problem in his hands, a problem Wolff seems never to have been aware of at all. It is the problem: How can *simple* ideas be incompatible with each other or necessary to each other? Through an elaborate division of ideas into coordinate and subordinate ideas (for the latter, the principle of contradiction supplies the criterion of incompatibility), Hoffmann comes very near to stating the rule that diverse determinants under a common determinable cannot be predicated of a thing at the same time. He never attains this degree of succinct simplicity, however, and had he done so he would no doubt have seen that his thirteen axioms (*Hauptsätze*) on incompatibility could not support the anti-Wolffian burden he put upon them. Many of his derivations are circular, and often he does no more than piece out Wolff's logic of contradictories with a logic of contraries.[40] Contradiction is, as it were, the limit of contrariety, and most of the time in empirical knowledge we have to do with decisions between contraries, not between contradictories. Since there are degrees of contrariety, there are likewise degrees of conviction that two ideas are compatible or incompatible, and this recognition leads Hoffmann far beyond Rüdiger in recognizing the necessity of measurements of qualities, and far beyond Wolff in recognizing the necessity of measures of probability in knowledge.

In Chapter IX of his *Logic* Hoffmann begins his long attempt to show how, from experience, basic laws of the mind can be discovered, and then how these laws of the mind give a guarantee of the objective validity of the judgments we produce by nature from our faculties. The formal logic of the early chapters is now developed into a psychological theory of what can and what cannot be "thought together." It cannot be said that this inquiry is successful, and there are as many question-begging arguments as one can find in Wolff. But the psychology—indeed, one can even say the phenomenology—of thought is far richer than Wolff's,[41] and what is of more importance than his proferred solution to the problem is that he has

---

[39] *Ibid.*, pt. I, chap. II, § 66.   [40] *Ibid.*, I, v, §§ 261, 269, 272, 274.

[41] Largely because Hoffmann gives a larger role to the "inventive power" (*ingenuum, Erfindungskraft; ibid.*, I, ii, § 37), the power to go from one idea to another by necessity

a clear grasp of two issues which Wolff failed to see, to wit: How can two ideas be necessarily related without being identical or contradictory? And how can ideas so related to each other give knowledge of necessary relations between their respective objects? Hoffmann has at least, and at last, asked the right questions.

The first question is: What are the sources in experience of the laws which Wolff accepted without question? Hoffmann considers first the experiential origin of our knowledge of identity. From any *Empfindung*, or sense experience, we experience what the thing is. By abstraction from it, we do not form the abstract concept of non-being, but only that of being. We form the judgment that the thing is what it is and not what it is not; hence we cannot think that a thing can both be and not be. What is, is.[42] This is a logical truth which could not be infringed even by God. From it Hoffmann believes he can derive all the other laws he needs. The claims for the principle are so great, and the arguments for it so weak, that we do no disservice to Hoffmann to allow them to remain hidden in a book of which only four copies now exist. But it should not go unmentioned that the unquestioned necessity of having *one* basic principle misled Hoffmann as seriously as it had misled Wolff; and if his proofs of other principles did require only this one, his situation would be not a bit better than Wolff's, when Wolff attempted to prove the principle of sufficient reason from the law of contradiction.

The other two basic laws are more interesting and more portentous for future philosophy: (2) "Things, one of which cannot be thought without the other, have such a relation in reality that one cannot exist without the other." (3) "A thing which cannot be thought with (*mit und neben*) another cannot exist with the other."[43] From these three principles, Hoffmann attempts to derive twenty-three "rules of inference," including the laws of contradiction and excluded middle (secs. 566–568), the principle of sufficient reason for being and knowing (secs. 613, 626), and the rule of like causes, like effects (sec. 616). In all these rules, if the basic principles are taken as referring to subordinated instead of coordinated ideas, rules of formal logic result; if to coordinated ideas of contraries, material rules of nonsyllogistic inference are supposed to result.

In Chapter XII Hoffmann finally asks: What guarantee do we have that these rules, by which we cannot avoid thinking if we are to produce conviction in our minds, have objective validity? Again, his question calls for applause, even if we greet his answer with embarrassed silence. He first tries to show that the law of identity applies to things and not merely to our thought of things. Assume the law of identity to be false. Then my assumption that it is false can be both true and false. Hence I cannot make that assumption even if I try.[44] Or, again:

---

but without syllogism, and the "power of judgment" (*judicium, Beurtheilungskraft*), the power to put ideas together into judgments. *Ingenuum* has some of the functions of the imagination among the later Wolffians.

[42] *Vernunft-Lehre*, I, xi, § 550.

[43] *Ibid.*, §§ 551–552.

[44] *Ibid.*, xii, § 671.

If it is assumed that outside our thought something can both be and not be, it is certain that we cannot think of such a being. If we say that such a thing could be outside our understanding, we would be thinking a proposition without a subject [since we cannot think such a subject], and then something would have both to be and not to be in our thought.[45]

But this is impossible, he continues, since we have granted already the validity of the law of identity for our thoughts. To think without a subject is not to think at all, but I cannot deny *cogito*. Whatever is an object of *cogitare* must either be or not be, and not both. Similar proofs are given for the other two basic laws, and then the twenty-three rules of inference are proved to be ontologically valid.

Hoffmann seems to be quite content with having crossed the psychological-ontological gap with regard to these general rules, for each of which he gives both a psychological and an ontological formulation. But he is far from overconfident in our ability to make specific application of them without error. The limits of human understanding are such that two things might very well seem to be incompatible and yet be compatible, and conversely. For this reason we ought to be guided by two principles. The first is to remember that our reasonings which appear to be certain may in fact be only probable, especially when we are thinking in terms of contraries instead of contradictions. Second, lest the previous proposition lead to skepticism, we must in obedience to God use our rational faculties as well as we can, and since they were given to us by God for our guidance, we must conclude that what seems compatible to us, when we take due precautions, *is* compatible—unless there is revelation to show us that what appears to us to be compatible is in fact not, "for God's will is worth more than demonstration."[46]

Much of Hoffmann's theory appears again in the work of Crusius, whose textbook in logic drove Hoffmann's out of the market soon after his early death. Crusius' work has an importance far beyond that of his master, however, because it was he and not Hoffmann who was the effective spokesman for anti-Wolffians and a major influence on Kant's early thought. It is therefore more appropriate to deal with him later, in the context of the development of Kant's thought. But others, even before Kant, were made aware of fundamental weaknesses in Wolffianism by the work of Hoffmann and Crusius.

On the Wolffian side, there was a formal logic supposed to have objective ontological significance, but without any link to the data of experience and the material relations between them. On the Pietist side, there was a material logic based upon psychology, but with only a weak link to objectively existing states of affairs. The Wolffians failed to see that a link was needed and contented themselves with a phenomenalistic, idealistic theory of truth while, in fact, never doubting that their well-ordered phenomena did reflect the ontological state of affairs and never ceasing to abuse the idealists. The Pietists saw the need of a link and tried to supply it. Everyone

[45] *Ibid.*, § 672.　　　　　[46] *Ibid.*, II, xii, § 692.

after Hoffmann could see the problem, and attempts to solve it led them farther and farther away from orthodox Wolffianism.

There is a very great distance between Thomasius and Hoffmann. Unlike Wolff, Thomasius was not the founder of a school to whom the epigoni repeatedly turned. His antipedanticism merged with the anti-intellectualism of the Pietists, but as genuine philosophy emerged out of this vague *Weltanschauung*, little that was distinctively Thomasian was left; anti-intellectualism became refined into antiformalism, and a voluntaristic psychology was put into the service of ontology, not of a vitalistic philosophy of nature. Thomasius' most important contributions to German intellectual life in general were little cultivated. One of these contributions was his argument for the independence of natural law from revelation and from divine law; the other was his reformative, utilitarian conception of learning, which tended toward a secularization of moral and intellectual values. It is as if the Pietistic disciples used only the thoughts Thomasius had had during his Pietistic interlude and ignored the *philosophia aulica* and the natural law theories he developed before and after this religious period. Much as Wolff and Thomasius differed intellectually, however, on these two points they were as one; and what we look back upon as Thomasius' most important contributions to the development of German culture were nurtured far more by the Thomasians' Wolffian opponents than by Crusius and his predecessors.

With the waning of Pietism in Prussia and the simultaneous satiety of the Prussians with Wolffian scholasticism, the cultural significance of each man was seen to be much the same. Enlightenment, in the broadest sense, was that which Thomasius and Wolff had in common. The quasi-mystical natural philosophy of the one and the pedantic scholasticism of the other lost adherents at the same time. What was left of both was a utilitarian *Verbürgerlichung* of education and culture, carried on in the "half-philosophy, half-journalism" of the Berlin Enlightenment. Those who opposed this "philosophy for the world" did so in two ways. They tried to maintain the rigor of philosophy against the superficial talk of things in general and, like Kant, appealed again to the spirit of *Gründlichkeit* which Wolff had represented. Or they tried to oppose the specious *clarté* of the Berlin court, Academy, and coffeehouses with a deeper and more obscure wisdom. These latter thinkers, whom we shall call the Counter-Enlighteners, however, did not find their inspiration in Thomasius the Pietist, but in Leibniz and Spinoza, both newly rediscovered and re-evaluated.

XIII

Philosophers on the Spree

The Berlin Enlightenment

The focal point of German intellectual and cultural life moved gradually eastward from the Rhineland, where it was up to the fifteenth century, into Saxony in the sixteenth and seventeenth and, finally, into Prussia and Brandenburg in the eighteenth. After the Reformation, and until the nineteenth century, the towns in South Germany, with the exception of Nürnberg and Stuttgart with their satellite universities in Altdorf, Erlangen, and Tübingen, played no great role in German intellectual life; even the universities in the Rhineland, such as Cologne, Heidelberg, and Freiburg, gradually lost in importance. The reasons are many and complicated and perhaps unknown, but probably one of the most important is the fact that, unlike the South and the Rhineland, the lands to the north and east were relatively less affected by the ravages of the Thirty Years' War, and were the home of large religious minorities who extracted toleration from reluctant rulers, permitting a freer and more varied intellectual life.

We have spoken at length of the University of Halle as one of the centers of the new mode of thought which emerged at the end of the seventeenth century. Another was the University of Göttingen, established in 1737 by the Hanoverian dynasty which had employed Leibniz. Göttingen is often considered the first modern university—modern, but not the first, in its insistence upon academic freedom (*Lehrfreiheit*). In this it had been preceded by Halle, in profession if not in fact. With the strict prohibition by the chancellor, Gerlach Adolf von Münchhausen, of interference by the theological faculty in the affairs of the other faculties, the ascent of the philosophical faculty to an autonomous, and finally to a superior, position received a great boost. Where this path was not followed, the universities disappeared from the ranks of the Enlightenment.

Münchhausen, Göttingen's first chancellor (*Kurator*) insisted upon freedom of conscience within the faculty and upon restricting the power of the theological faculty to censure the views of members of the philosophical faculty; he warned against a "Protestant papacy" and recalled the fact that the House of Hanover, the patrons of the university, had already shown its tolerance in the protection it gave Calixtus in the University of Helmstedt.[1] It is a remarkable fact that the "first modern university"—one in which the philosophical faculty was the highest, and in which *libertas philosophandi* was directly associated with the ideal of the university as a research institution—played no important role in the history of philosophy in this period. The reason is to be found in the atmosphere of the university, which concentrated on the *realia*, especially history, philology, pedagogy, science, and law. It was an "Enlightenment university" in every sense, but without any great representative of the *philosophy* of the Enlightenment. Albrecht von Haller and, later, Georg Christoff Lichtenberg were there, but not as philosophers.[2] Christoph Meiners (1747–1810) and J. G. H. Feder (1740–1820) were "popular philosophers" and lightweight opponents of Kant. Except for them, Göttingen does not appear in the history of philosophy of the eighteenth century. (Some *echtdeutsche* philosophers think that it was the "English influence" which kept Göttingen from being an important center of philosophy. This is to be put beside the superior feeling of some later important Göttingen philosophers that they were blessed with the *Sachlichkeit* and sobriety of English philosophy, for the same reason!)

[1] See Lucien Lévy-Bruhl, *L'Allemagne depuis Leibniz* (Paris, 1890), p. 77; Götz von Selle, *Die Georg-August-Universität zu Göttingen, 1737–1937* (Göttingen: Vandenhoeck & Ruprecht, 1937), p. 29.

[2] Haller (1708–77), a Swiss savant and pupil of Bilfinger in Tübingen, was professor of medicine in Göttingen from 1736 to 1753. He was known as a poet (among his works, "Die Alpen," "Unvollkommene Ode über die Ewigkeit," "Über den Ursprung des Übels") and as one of the most important scientists of his time, his *De partibus corporis humani sentientibus et irritabilibus* (1752) establishing the scientific basis on which Herder was later to construct the biological parts of his cosmology (see Chapter XV). But Haller's philosophical efforts were directed toward mitigating the naturalism his science inspired, and he defended the reasonableness of Christianity, the importance of religion to social order, the authenticity of revelation, and immortality. Lichtenberg (1742–1799) became professor of physics in 1767; his *Aphorismen* have long been justly famous. See J. P. Stern, *Lichtenberg. A Doctrine of Scattered Occasions* (London: Thomas and Hudson, 1963) for a profound study of this remarkable man. G. H. von Wright, art., "Lichtenberg" in *Encyclopedia of Philosophy* (New York: Macmillan, 1967), IV, 461–465, makes an impressive case for Lichtenberg's philosophical modernity, a modernity which keeps him from fitting into any of the patterns of eighteenth-century thought and makes comparison with Kierkegaard or Wittgenstein more fruitful than comparisons with his contemporaries.

After 1740 the most important home of Enlightenment thought in Germany was Berlin, the capital of Brandenburg and the home of Frederick II, King of Prussia. Brandenburg-Prussia was rapidly becoming the leading German state, after Austria. But whereas Austria was a Baroque Counter Reformation Catholic state into which the spirit of the Enlightenment did not penetrate until the reign of Joseph II, the roots of the Frederician Enlightenment go back into the seventeenth century. Berlin had grown commercially as a result of the wise policy of digging canals, so that it became the main trading point between Breslau and Hamburg and had access to both the North and the Baltic Seas. The Great Elector had married a Princess of Orange; the Hohenzollerns had become Calvinist; the Huguenots had been welcomed; toleration between Calvinism, Lutheranism, and Pietism had been established. The large foreign population (mostly Calvinistic, and estimated at 25 per cent in 1740) "left a permanent trace on the intellectual and social life of the town, so that its clubs on the French model, the sociability, intelligence, and political acumen of the Berliner became a source of wonder to all visitors from other parts of Germany. It was no accident that this capital became the focus of 'Aufklärung.' "[3]

None of this, however, would have been a basis of what was erected upon it had it not been for the charisma of Frederick II. And it would not have been the basis of Berlin's becoming a philosophical center had it not been for the circumstance that Frederick was a philosopher. Two weeks before his accession, he wrote Voltaire: "I assure you that philosophy appears to me to be more charming and attractive than the throne." Speaking French and thinking and writing like a *philosophe*, Frederick made Berlin a "Paris on the Spree"; and so great was his influence that Kant could call his century "the century of Frederick" as well as "an age of Enlightenment." No matter how much Frederick professed, perhaps sincerely, to admire Wolff, his admiration for French *ésprit* and his contempt for piety and Pietism introduced a tone into philosophy never before heard in Germany. Frederick the Great did for his country what Peter the Great tried but failed to do for his.

The Philosopher-King

Le hasard, que nous place ici-bas à son choix
Voulut qu'un philosophe eut le sceptre des rois.[4]

Had he not been King of Prussia, Frederick II might have merited a paragraph in histories of philosophy as a critic of Holbach, but no more. But as king and patron of the Academy, nothing he did—in verse or philosophy—could be ignored by his people; and as the wonder of Europe he contributed as much to the popular image of Germany as the land of poets and philosophers as he did to the other picture of an ambitious and disci-

---

[3] W. H. Bruford, *Germany in the Eighteenth Century* (Cambridge [Eng.] University Press, 1935), p. 173.

[4] *Oeuvres de Frédéric le Grand*, ed. J.-D. E. Preuss (Berlin, 1846–57), XII, 174.

plined military state. Of course it was an accident that the king should be one who thought of himself as a philosopher; but it was the kind of accident Prussia needed after the "iron age" of the "soldier king," Friedrich Wilhelm I.

But philosophy was not so integral a part of Frederick's mind as it was in his model, Marcus Aurelius; it is significant that Frederick did not call himself "the philosopher-king" but by the more modest, and more accurate, epithet, "the philosopher of Sans Souci." This combination of words reveals much—philosophy was saved for the carefree hours. "Distinguish the statesman from the philosopher," he wrote Voltaire, "and know that one can make war out of interest [*par raison*], be a politician because of duty, and be a philosopher by inclination." Thus while Frederick's policies show a marvelous consistency, and were successful only because this massive consistency carried them through when every military and political consideration might have dictated change and compromise, his philosophical writings are free from the enthusiasm for system; their style as well as content is that of the *philosophes,* and they belong more to belles-lettres than to philosophy as comprehensive and encyclopedic. "I love verse and philosophy very much," he wrote Voltaire, but he added: "When I say philosophy, I mean neither geometry nor metaphysics."[5] Most of his writings, then, are in the style made popular in France—but without much bite. Since French was not his mother tongue, much of his writing in that language was almost in the form of a school exercise, where attention to the style of an admired author and an effort to imitate it almost inevitably brought about also an appropriation of that author's ideas on *honnêté, tranquilité,* or whatever other "philosophical" topic was the subject of the exercise. From this body of essays, verse, and epistles it is difficult to extract *a* philosophy.

Taking them at face-value, one would conclude from some of his writings that the author was an Epicurean, as in the *Essai sur l'amour propre envisagé comme principe du morale* of 1770; from others that he was a skeptic, as in the *Dissertation sur l'innocence des erreurs de l'ésprit* of 1737; from still others that he was a Christian apologist, or a deist, or a Stoic. But one thing he was not: a systematic philosopher. He was not a professor of philosophy, but a king who liked to relax with philosophy and poetry, to forget from time to time at his palace of Sans Souci that he was king— though, it was remarked, he wanted his companions who were poets and *philosophes* to remember it always. Efforts made by some to establish the lineaments of a "Frederician system" are in vain; but since a philosophical *obiter dictum* by a king may be more weighty historically than a learned tome by a professor, we cannot pass over the philosophy of Frederick the Great as we can that of some of his courtiers.

The life of Frederick as Crown Prince in the court of his father Friedrich Wilhelm I, should not be taken as a model for how to raise a gifted son. It is to be recommended neither to fathers nor teachers nor sons that, on the

---

[5] Both quotations are from the letter of February 13, 1749. *Briefwechsel Friedrichs des Grossen mit Voltaire,* ed. Reinhold Koser and Hans Droysen (Leipzig: S. Hirzel, 1909), pt. 2, p. 245.

orders of the first, the second be beheaded before the eyes of the third. To his father's cruelty, crudity, and piety Frederick reacted by being the opposite in every respect. His brains he may have inherited from his philosophical grandmother, Sophie Charlotte, Leibniz's confidante and patroness. From his father, grandfather, and great-grandfather, the Great Elector, he inherited only ambition for Prussia and his house, the hardness without which he would never have survived the traumas of his youth, and a powerful Protestant conscience and conscientiousness.

Against his father's Pietism, Frederick revolted first by accepting Calvinist predestination. This later became theologically attenuated into fatalism, which gave a larger place to blind chance than to causal necessity and left room for the freedom of the man of action. This combination of fatalism and freedom and its ethical consequences for the man of action is one of the most pervasive themes in Frederick's writings and conversation. It is an appropriate expression of the paradox of the philosopher who is a man of deeds rather than of contemplation. Perhaps it is the only philosophy for a philosopher who happens to be a king and a military genius. The position of a man of thought and power is—at least it was felt by Frederick to be— an agonizing one: he knows that Providence has designed a plan and has an essential place in it for the powerful and responsible human leader; he is clearly called upon to cooperate in divine projects, but he does not know the plan and must improvise at the most crucial turning points in history, and he cannot see the consequences of his actions for the success of the plan. Frederick's relation to God and history is much like that of his officials and his brothers to him and to his policies, raised to a metaphysical and theological level.

The theses I have just mentioned are developed most fully in the poem, *Sur le hasard*,[6] on which Frederick worked longest, and his favorite among all his writings. While Frederick's whole body of writings did not constitute a single complex philosophical whole, starting from this poetic treatment of fatalism and freedom, very many of his ideas fall into a pattern; and since it is precisely these ideas which reappear and are skillfully argued for in the one piece of sustained "metaphysical" writing we have from his pen

[6] "*Épitre sur le hasard a ma soeur Amélie*" (1749) in *Oeuvres* (Berlin, 1840), XII, 64–79:

> Le monde est donc, ma soeur, l'empire du hasard;
> Il élève, il détruit; bizarre à notre egard,
> Il usurp les droits de notre prévoyance.
>
>   .   .   .
>
> Le philosoph sait que dans toutes les choses
> Les effets sont produit du sein fécond des causes;
> D'un pas sûr, mais tardif, par le raisonnement
> Il remonte au principe après l'événement.
> L'insolent politique, ambitieux et sombre
> Port d'un bras hardi sa lumière en cette ombre;
> Il perce l'avenir sans l'avoir apercu,
> Il règle, embrouille tout, et se trouve décu.

The poem ends with a conventional embrace of virtue. The theme fascinated Frederick, and several of his longest poems develop the same thought, among them, "Sur l'usage de la fortune" (1740), another with the same title written in 1749, and "Sur les voeux des humains" (*Oeuvres*, XIV, 88–93, X, 184–193, and X, 136–144, respectively).

(the critique of Holbach), one is perhaps justified in singling them out for special treatment and in leaving aside the rest of his work as being mere occasional writings.

The first of the ideas which gives special poignancy to the paradox of fatalism and freedom is the keen sense of historical and moral responsibility of a king. In his *Anti-Machiavell* (1740) Frederick rejected the doctrine of the king as having a divine right in favor of the view that he has a divine mission. It is his duty, he held, to secure and nurture the welfare of his people, to whom he is "the first servant." Frederick's conception of the welfare of his people was not always the same; it varied with the political situation and his own volatile estimates of human beings as beasts needing a leader and as fellow citizens in a great work of enlightenment and the glory of Prussia. Sometimes he shared the belief of the Enlightenment *philosophes* in the innate goodness of man; sometimes he saw the glory of a country in its poetic and scientific culture. But it was a French humanism he participated in, and anything that could be called "love of his people" was generally restricted to his German soldiers and did not extend to the native bourgeoisie and intellectuals. Hence, as a French-minded monarch ruling over a people he thought primitive, he was content to recommend for them ideas and doctrines he could not himself accept. While he recognized that it was easier to govern an educated and enlightened people than an illiterate nation, he was content for his subjects to practice the Christian virtues and hold to a Christian metaphysics he did not accept. His tolerance was patronizing, but he insisted upon tolerance in others as a condition of domestic peace; it did not much matter what "likely story" the masses believed, as long as they paid taxes and obeyed. Though he did very little for the improvement of popular education in Prussia,[7] this neglect did not come from any obscurantism; he just did not insist on more than education for his officials, and did little more than tolerate peaceful enlightenment among those who could manage an education on their own.

Second, there is the conception of a divine plan in the world. Frederick was through most of his life a deist.[8] We know that God exists, but we do not understand how he works or why he permits evil in the world. Frederick, the friend of Voltaire, will have nothing of Leibniz' *Theodicy*. The design of nature shows that there is a God; man's body is a chemical laboratory, and a mechanistic explanation of a blade of grass (an example Kant later used) will never be made if we do not see that it shows a wise design.[9] God is justified by his works in nature; he should not be judged, as Holbach judged him, from the abuses of priests whose conception of God cannot stand the criticism of unreasonable revelation. To be sure, Christianity is "an old metaphysical tale, full of miraculous legends, paradoxes, and nonsense";[10] but Christian morality does not require the unreasonable

[7] See Friedrich Paulsen, *Geschichte des gelehrten Unterrichts* (Leipzig: Veit, 1897), II, 68.

[8] See his account of deism and skepticism in *Histoire de mon temps*, in *Oeuvres posthumes* (Berlin, 1788), I, 92 ff.

[9] *Examen critique de la Système de la nature*, in *Oeuvres posthumes*, VI, 145.

[10] Quoted from Hajo Holborn, *History of Germany* (London: Eyre & Spottiswoode, 1965), II, 239.

parts of this metaphysics and, containing as it does the "quintessence of morality," it should be judged by its ideals and genuine accomplishments in history and not by the horror stories Holbach liked to recite.

Third, there is the skeptical strain in Frederick's conception of our knowledge of our destiny and how we should participate or intervene in it. Bayle was one of his favorite philosophers; he thought him "the best logician." After reading Bayle, no metaphysical system could be satisyfing to Frederick, but he thought that deism was so obvious that he appears not to have seen that it was a speculative metaphysical system at all.[11] Frederick carried his skepticism further than most *philosophes*, however; he had little use for or faith in science, or in what he called "the fanaticism for curves" which he found in his friend D'Alembert. Rather he thought of systems as so many likely stories, to be accepted only cautiously, with all the alternatives tolerated. But Frederick's skepticism was that of the *dilettante*, not the philosopher; it was a skepticism based on Bayle's dialectic, not on Locke's analysis of the limits of knowledge; and he justified it by citing "the sweetness of error which is preferable to the truth."[12] Except for his support of the Academy, Frederick contributed nothing to the advance of scientific thought.[13] If he had to take a stand, it would be (under Voltaire's influence) for Newton; but his failure to see that it was science and mathematics, not enlightened despotism and elegant conversation, that were to be decisive in the triumph of Enlightenment may well have had the consequence that German thought in general did not go through a scientific revolution as a stage in its Age of Reason. A scientist-king would have given a different direction to German thought.

Finally, we can gain from Frederick's view of man's plight under fate some insight into his theory of freedom. Passing beyond his early predestinarianism, he strongly argued against the Wolffian form of determinism which he found developed to its logical conclusion in Holbach's *Système de la nature*. Holbach, an Alsatian nobleman and patron of *philosophes* in Paris, published his *Système* in 1770. In it he defended a completely mechanistic and atheistic philosophy and developed, with passion and eloquence, an indictment of clericalism and political obscurantism. Frederick's examination of Holbach is his most sustained philosophical writing. Two of its parts—the defense of deism against atheism, the defense of Christianity against anticlericalism—have already been mentioned. The most interesting part is on Holbach's mechanism and denial of freedom.

Frederick argues that men love freedom and therefore must have some experience of what it is to be free. We do not experience it in our perceptions, which reveal a mechanical order and which are passively, not freely, received by our minds. But in the workings of our imagination and in the control of our passions by reason, we directly experience our active freedom.

[11] *Examen critique de la Système* in *Oeuvres posthumes*, VI, 143.

[12] *Dissertation sur l'innocence des erreurs de l'ésprit*, in *Oeuvres posthumes*, VI, 210 ff; letter to Voltaire June 1, 1739, *ibid.*, IX, 51.

[13] But in a letter to Voltaire dated February 2, 1739, he described some silly experiments with a vacuum pump. *Oeuvres posthumes*, IX, 45. Prussia's gain was not science's loss.

It is not true that man is free *simpliciter;* our freedom is intermittent, and we can learn to exercise it. Whoever denies freedom finds that he contradicts in his practice what he asserts in theory. Neither Calvin nor Holbach can convince men that they are machines. The denial of freedom comes from an enthusiasm for systems, not from an experience of life; and this is another ground for Frederick's distrust of systematic speculation.

The practice which conflicts with theory, Frederick points out, is shown by Holbach himself, in his condemnation of priests. If they are, as Holbach must believe, "tonsured machines," it is absurd to blame them for what they do; and Catiline and Marcus Aurelius are equally free from praise and blame if they are machines. No punishment would be justified if Holbach were correct; and society could not endure if Holbach's thesis were accepted. It is interesting to see how much Frederick's view of the consequences of Leibniz' and Wolff's determinism resembled his father's; but he did not have the savage intolerance of his father, and he said of Holbach, "I refute the system, but I would put out the fire that would burn him."[14]

These, I think, are ideas that a German professor of philosophy would have made into a system, repressing a vivacious and moody imagination that produced, from time to time, ideas that could not be fitted together so neatly. We would be unjust to one of Germany's greatest men if we judged him by this set of ideas that any one of his French guests could have produced in a pleasant discourse. But the kingly role required sterner stuff than parlor deism and polite skepticism. They were all very well for Sans Souci. Heroic self-mastery in the darkest days of the Seven Years' War, fortitude when his capital was occupied twice by his enemies, single-minded devotion to the interests of his kingdom, contempt for the common man combined with respect for his rights and a genuine love of his soldiers—little of this comes to light in his elegant but facile French, and yet these qualities were more characteristic of the man. Stoicism in his writings is like a stage posture; in his life, it was the nucleus of his character. Enlightened despotism was conjoined with an ethics of his station and its duties, and the despotism and personal hardness lasted even when the Enlightenment disappeared.

The king was surrounded by *emigré* philosophers and the popular philosophers in Berlin. His contempt for German letters kept Lessing and Mendelssohn at a distance, and he seems never to have heard of Kant. The Berlin Enlightenment, to the extent that the king was responsive to it, was an extension of the French, with the politically revolutionary ideas excised at the border. It did not outlive Frederick II, for Friedrich Wilhelm II differed from his uncle as much as Frederick II differed from Friedrich Wilhelm I. After 1786 Berlin was no more hospitable to philosophy, and especially free-thinking French philosophy, than it had been before 1740. The endeavor from the time of Thomasius and Gottsched to make Germany an outpost of France in the world of ideas came to an end. France will be seen, by the next generation, as the source of all that should be kept out of German thought.

[14] Wilhelm Dilthey, *Friedrich der Grosse und die deutsche Aufklärung,* in *Gesammelte Schriften,* III, 96.

Frederick II had two courts: his French companions at Sans Souci and the Berlin Academy. The popular philosophers were not admitted to the presence.

The Berlin Academy

The Berlin Academy was the creation of two men: Leibniz and Frederick the Great. Leibniz had long hoped to establish an academy under imperial auspices, as a principal part of his plan both for the cultural rejuvenation of Germany and for the cooperative endeavors which he knew the state of science required. The political situation in the Empire was not such as to enable him to do for Germany what the founders of the Royal Society or the Academie Française had done for their countries; but when Sophie Charlotte left Hanover to become Queen of Prussia, Leibniz adopted the more practical course in favor of establishing a Prussian academy. This effort was successful, and in 1700 Friedrich I formally established the Academy under the name of the Royal Prussian Society of the Sciences, with Leibniz installed as president. The Academy was endowed with the income from the calendar monopoly;[15] and though it had a philological-historical section, its principal work was in the sciences, and it supported an observatory and anatomical theater.

Upon the accession of Friedrich Wilhelm I, the Academy ceased to be an important intellectual force. It was starved for money, but even worse, it fell under the new king's ostentatious contempt for learning, and received a new name, or at least nickname, "The Society of Royal Fools." Its president was Jacob Paul Gundling, a brother of the Gundling in Halle who had participated in the vendetta against Wolff and a member of the Tobacco Cabinet partly responsible for the final sentence pronounced on Wolff. Though it was said, perhaps not quite accurately, that La Mettrie ate himself to death, Gundling is perhaps the only member *savant* to have been buried in a wine cask. Conviviality replaced philosophy; cheerfulness kept breaking through, and on the occasion of the appointment of a new vice president in 1732 the King presented its new officer with the charge to make the path of the sun around the earth a circle and not a square, and requested him to make sure that there were as many good days and as few bad days as possible in the calendar.[16]

Frederick II, however, had the reconstitution of the Academy as one of his first and dearest projects. He was dissatisfied with the state of the universities, which did not seem to him to be keeping up with the progress of

---

[15] Erhard Weigel had proposed, in 1694, that with the reform of the calendar (on which he was employed by the Regensburger *Corpus evangelicorum*) the income from the calendar monopoly be used to endow a *Collegium artis consultorum* for the Empire; but this did not prove to be feasible, so Leibniz adapted his old teacher's idea to a more modest purpose, viz., the Academy for one state rather than for the Empire as a whole. It was this connection with the calendar that not only supported the Academy, but made its observatory its most important institution.

[16] This remarkable letter patent, which reads like an appointment of a court astrologer, will be found in Adolf von Harnack, *Geschichte der Königlich preussischen Akademie der Wissenschaften zu Berlin* (Berlin, 1900), II, 233–235.

Enlightenment as he saw it developing in France and wished to have it develop in Germany. It was not easy to re-establish so moribund an institution as the Academy; but through combining the Nouvelle Société Litteraire with the old Academy (Société des Sciences), the Académie des Sciences et Belles-Lettres was constituted in 1744. Pierre Louis Morou de Maupertuis was its president, and he was undefatigable in attracting leading men to come to Berlin. It soon rivaled in prestige the academies of Paris and St. Petersburg and the Royal Society of London. Among its foreign members were Bradley (the discoverer of the aberration of light), Buffon, Helvetius, Fontenelle, Holbach, and the Bernoullis. Nonresident members included Wolff, Baumgarten, Gottsched, Bilfinger, Plouquet, and Meier among the philosophers; from the French residents in Berlin there were Voltaire, La Mettrie, D'Alembert, and Lagrange. It will be noted that there was a large representation of mathematicians and scientists as well as men of letters; but the Academy was unique in that it had a Class for Speculative Philosophy. This was in part because of Frederick's lack of interest in the natural sciences, but more because of his conviction that all parts of knowledge, and not only those of direct practical benefit, should be supported, and that they should all be in fruitful contact with each other.

The major work of the Academy was, of course, carried out by its permanent or regular members, who attended its sittings, conducted its business, and gave public lectures. The permanent secretary was Pierre Samuel Formey (1711–1797),[17] author of *La belle Wolfienne*, the most popular presentation of Wolff's philosophy, lightened here and there by borrowings from Locke and Hume. Maupertuis was followed as president by Leonhard Euler (1707–1783), the eminent mathematician, important to German philosophy for his defense of Newtonian against Leibnizian theories, and especially for his defense of Newton's theory of absolute space and time.[18]

Among the members of the Class for Speculative Philosophy, there were Johann Sulzer (president during the sixties), Nicolas de Béguelin (1714–1789), Johann Bernhard Mérian (1723–1807), who was Formey's successor as Secretary of the Academy, and André Pierre de Prémontval (d. 1764). All these writers were highly eclectic, drawing equally from Newton and Leibniz. Béguelin, for instance, attempted to prove Newton's laws of gravitation by deduction from Leibniz' monadism, attraction being a force ascribed to the monads. Mérian anticipated Kant in criticizing Leibniz for seeing sensations as confused thoughts and Locke for transforming thoughts

---

[17] About this singular man, I cannot refrain from quoting Dessoir: "The man actually produced nearly 600 books besides an even to us frightful number of reviews that were much in demand, in part because he felt happy only in his work and in part 'pour donner un peu d'aisance à ses enfants.' Besides that, he had the largest correspondence known in Germany since Leibniz'. And toward the end of his life he accomplished a stroke of genius: incapable of creative work but likewise incapable of doing nothing, he himself published his *Oeuvres posthumes*" (*Geschichte der neueren deutschen Psychologie*, p. 192).

[18] "Reflexions sur l'éspace et le temps," in *Histoire de l'Academie des Sciences et Belles-Lettres*, 1748; and *Lettres à une princesse d' Allemagne* (Eng. trans., New York, 1833). The letters are popular science at its best, and Letter 76 (1760) is a clear exposition of Euler's criticisms of Wolff.

into sensations. These men were graceful writers who lacked originality; they defended their eclecticism with the claim that an Academy should represent the best of all philosophies in the past and not be one-sided.

With one exception, Johann Heinrich Lambert, no one working under the auspices of the Academy produced an important philosophical system. The Academy, however, was more than the sum of its parts; it had able men in it whose official position gave their collegial deliberations and disputes a greater importance than the men themselves would have had. The Academy as a whole, therefore, was significant, and its principal accomplishment in philosophy was to feed into German intellectual life new ideas from France and England. This was equivalent to setting up rivals to the dominant Leibnizian and Leibniz-Wolffian systems.

We shall here describe the disputes in the Academy between the rival Leibniz-Wolffian and the Newtonian philosophies, and later, in Chapter XVI, the independent contributions to philosophy by Lambert, its most eminent philosopher-member.

The Academy was almost evenly divided between the partisans of Newton and of Leibniz and Wolff. It cannot be said that it was an impartial arbiter of the opposing claims of the two great rival systems of science and philosophy. For instance, one of the first topics announced for a prize contest was Leibniz' *Monadology* (1747). The Philosophical Class was tied in voting between two candidates for the prize, one *pro* and one *contra*, and the issue had to be decided by a vote of the whole Academy. Euler led the forces voting for Johann Heinrich von Justi, who opposed Leibniz (though Euler later confessed that the prize should have been divided because of the original tie). In 1751 there was another contest, ostensibly on the optimism of Alexander Pope, but, in fact on the Leibnizian thesis that this is the best of all possible worlds. Again, the prize went to an anti-Wolffian, A. F. Reinhard, and there were accusations of dishonest practices (Sulzer attacked Formey's honor, and said that Maupertuis could not read the papers that were submitted in German). This impelled Lessing and Mendelssohn to write *Pope a Metaphysician?*, which exposed the persiflage, saying that though Pope was named, Leibniz was meant. They argued that poetry is not the proper vehicle for philosophy and therefore Pope's *Essay* did not present the optimistic philosophy in a suitable and defensible form.

The anti-Wolffians did not have it all their own way, however. In 1751 the prize had been won by A. G. Kästner[19] for a defense of Leibniz' determinism, and in 1763 it was won by Mendelssohn, though Kant's competing essay was accepted for publication by the Academy. The subject proposed by Sulzer was: "Whether metaphysical truths generally, and in particular the fundamental principles of natural theology and morals, are capable of proofs as evident as those of geometry; and if they are not, what is the true nature of their certainty, to what degree can this certainty be developed, and is this degree sufficient for conviction?" Though the academicians were

[19] Abraham Gotthilf Kästner (1719–1800), professor in Gottingen, of whom Gauss wrote that he was the best poet among mathematicians and the best mathematician among poets (Götz von Selle, *Die Georg-August-Universität zu Göttingen 1737–1937,* p. 102).

not, in general, favorable to the "mathematical method" in philosophy, preferring a more informal, essayistic style of philosophizing, Mendelssohn won the prize with a well-presented orthodox Wolffian answer that, in principle, metaphysics could achieve the same degree of certainty as mathematics but that it could not be made as readily comprehensible. Kant's answer was his declaration of independence from Wolffianism; he argued that the method of mathematics and that of philosophy were wholly different from each other, but he did not argue that certainty in the metaphysical and moral sciences was unattainable.[20]

L'Affaire König

But we must return to 1751 for the principal scandal in the life of the Academy, which ostensibly grew out of the anti-Leibnizian views of Maupertuis and Euler, but which in fact was an expression of the overweening vanity of Maupertuis, the deep distaste for Leibniz on the part of Euler, the bitter ambition of Voltaire, and the moral outrage felt by the king.

Frederick had met Maupertuis and Voltaire in Kleve for the purpose of choosing one of them to be the first president of the Academy. He was accompanied back to Berlin by Maupertuis, whom he installed in office, though Voltaire was made an *academicien*. Maupertuis was perhaps the outstanding scientist in Europe at that time; it was he who had measured the oblateness of the terrestrial sphere and had thereby proved one of Newton's most daring conjectures. Since the Academy was also to be a scientific institution, the prestige of the "earth measurer," as Maupertuis was called, was such as to make his appointment seem (to everyone but Voltaire) entirely justified. But Maupertuis was a man of colossal vanity, and this vice led to his downfall.

Maupertuis formulated the principle of least action in 1744. This is the principle that the action involved in any natural change is always a minimum, so that the path and velocity of any natural body can be determined by finding the path and velocity which involve a minimum of force. Maupertuis did not quite correctly formulate this principle or successfully prove it; that was left to Euler and D'Alembert. But this did not prevent him from building on it both his pride and a proof (allegedly a mathematical proof) of the existence of God—God being the great mathematician. The mathematical and metaphysical elaboration of the principle was regarded by Maupertuis as yet another proof of the Newtonian system.

In 1750 Samuel König (1712–1757), professor of mathematics in The Hague and a member of the Academy, communicated to Maupertuis a paper in which he tried to show that the principle was incorrectly formulated; and he added that Leibniz had anticipated Maupertuis, having derived the same principle in a letter written to Hermann in 1707. He did not

[20] Later I shall discuss in some detail the papers submitted for this contest by Mendelssohn, Lambert, and Kant. Giorgio Tonelli has studied still other papers prepared for this competition in his "Der Streit über die mathematische Methode in der Philosophie in der ersten Hälfte des 18. Jahrhunderts," *Archiv für Philosophie*, IX, 37–66, esp. 61–63.

accuse Maupertuis of plagiarism, but rather pointed out how two great men had arrived independently at the same conclusion; his paper was polite. Maupertuis, offended by the criticism, seems not to have noticed the *clausula salvatoria*; at any rate, he returned the paper to König with a cold note that he could publish it as he saw fit. It was published in Leipzig in the *Nova Acta Eruditorum*. Then Maupertuis did read it and, enraged, challenged König to produce the letter. König replied mildly that he had only a copy of the letter, but would try to procure the original. He went to Switzerland in the summer of 1751 to try to find it.

Maupertuis was not mollified by the moderate reply from König, and in October he persuaded the Academy to demand that the letter be produced within four weeks, the penalty being that the letter would otherwise be declared a forgery. Again, König answered irenically, explaining both why he thought the copy was authentic and why he could not get the original, again disclaiming any accusation of plagiarism. Maupertuis answered hypocritically that *he* was satisfied with König's explanation but that the Academy was not; and under Maupertuis' prodding the Academy officially and unanimously declared, on April 13, 1752, that the letter was a forgery, made for the purpose of raising Leibniz and damaging Maupertuis. Euler voted for this decision. König thereupon resigned from the Academy and published his defense of the authenticity of the letter. "Maupertuis' case was won before the Academy, but was lost before Europe."[21] Maupertuis and the Academy were put, by this defense, in an unenviable, but not yet desperate, position. Then Voltaire entered the fray.

Voltaire was in Potsdam, still wanting to be president of the Academy; but added to his frustrated ambition was a new motive, the desire to test Frederick's loyalty to him, which La Mettrie, shortly before his death, had told him was not going to last a year. So Voltaire wrote an anonymous pamphlet, in the form of a letter, saying that many members of the Academy wished to resign rather than serve under a plagiarist and refrained from doing so only out of fear of displeasing the King. The King was in constant touch with Maupertuis, attempting to comfort him by assuring him of his esteem and loyalty; but when the Academy failed to censure Voltaire (it being commonly supposed that Voltaire was the anonymous author), the King himself wrote an anonymous defense of Maupertuis filled with extravagant praise; and it shortly became known that the author of this encomium was none other than Frederick.

In the meantime, Maupertuis had published a collection of short pieces on a variety of subjects, not all well thought out and not all of them even seriously meant, but by judicious selection, they provided a broad target for the greatest satiric talent in the world; not only Maupertuis but incidentally Frederick himself was made to look very silly by the satiric attack. Voltaire read it aloud to Frederick, who could not help being amused by it, but ordered Voltaire to destroy it. Voltaire did so, burning it in the royal presence.

---

[21] Adolf von Harnack, *Geschichte der Königlich preussischen Akademie der Wissenschaften zu Berlin*, vol. I, pt. i, p. 338.

Without the King's knowledge, however, Voltaire had already had the pamphlet printed. When Frederick learned this, he accused Voltaire and forced an apology from him and had the printed copies destroyed—but not before Voltaire had sent a copy out of Prussia to be published. Tricked twice, Frederick raged at Voltaire: "If your works deserve statues, your performance deserves the galleys."[22] With this condemnation, Voltaire made his exit from Sans Souci—and from German philosophy. Maupertuis, a broken man, left Germany on a two-year leave, returned still unable to take hold of things again, and died in 1759. He was succeeded as president of the Academy by Leonhard Euler.

Popular Philosophy

During the third quarter of the eighteenth century, Berlin was the center of the German Enlightenment in its most characteristic forms: the academic philosophy found in the works of the men brought to Berlin by Frederick the Great, so that the imitation of things French, desiderated by Thomasius and Gottsched, was given official status and Berlin tried to be the "Paris on the Spree"; and the popular philosophy of the literary periodicals and coffeehouses promoted by Germans who wanted to make Berlin the London or the Edinburgh on the Spree.

While there is some overlapping of these two groups, both in membership, purpose, and style, most of the popular philosophers were German-speaking Protestants one generation removed from the Lutheran *Pfarrhaus* enjoying a new and exhilarating intellectual freedom. More than the Academicians, they were explicitly committed to the doctrine that the proper study of mankind is man, and they were more antipathetic to metaphysical speculation than the Academy philosophers. Because of the royal patronage, the Academic thinkers were less concerned with social and political questions, or indeed with religious questions, than the freelance publicists of the popular group. But we must not think of even the popular philosophers as critics of their time in the manner of Diderot, Rousseau, and Voltaire. "Don't talk to me of your Berlin freedom," Lessing wrote Friedrich Nicolai on August 25, 1769. "It reduces to nothing but the freedom to hawk as many foolish jokes against religion as one wishes . . . But let someone in Berlin come forward for the rights of subjects, let someone raise his voice against exploitation and despotism (as happens now in France and Denmark), and you will soon see which country is today the most slavish in Europe." But literary criticism attained a high level in the journals edited by Nicolai[23] and Biester,[24] though each man suffered for venturing too far.

[22] *Ibid.*, p. 343. The printed copies were burned by the public hangman in the Gendarmenplatz in Berlin on Christmas Eve, 1753.

[23] Friedrich Nicolai (1733–1811), editor of the *Allgemeine deutsche Bibliothek*, the principal organ of the Berlin philosophers. Nicolai was a friend of Lessing and Mendelssohn; Kant, Schiller, and Goethe were his contemptuous enemies. See Karl Aner, *Der Aufklärer Friedrich Nicolai* (Giessen: A. Töpelmann, 1912).

[24] Johann Erich Biester (1749–1816), a secretary to Baron von Zedlitz (Frederick's minister of education, to whom the *Critique of Pure Reason* was dedicated), was editor of the *Berlinische Monatsschrift*, to which Kant was a contributor.

Political criticism, except in the writings of the Göttingen professor August Ludwig Schlözer (1735–1809), was insignificant. Educational reforms were proposed and partly carried out by Basedow.[25] There were appeals for patriotism[26] by a few and for religious toleration and freedom of the press by many. But of fundamental thinking on political questions which transcended the limits of day-to-day politics there was little, and that was done mostly by traditionalists who thought like Edmund Burke.[27]

The clandestine criticism of current institutions and ideas was practiced in secret societies like the Illuminati and the Freemasons (but with noble and even royal patronage).[28] Unlike the French *philosophes* to whom they are sometimes compared, the German popular philosophers' interests were focused on the problems of private sentiment and virtue, religion, education, and art. None of them held important positions in government, and governments had little to complain of and nothing to fear in them. Only with Kant is enlightenment seen to be a social and political process involving whole populations and nations. In a world which, as a whole, was still believed to be the best possible, the concern was with the individual who needed, perhaps, a new kind of education but not a new kind of government. Such moralistic concern found suitable expression in pretty essays, diaries, private correspondence destined to be published, and autobiographies[29] of significant and insignificant thinkers—just what one would expect from a secularized Pietistic sentimentalism and quietism. Socrates, the noble sage who reformed his disciples but suffered passively from political injustice, was celebrated in countless books.[30]

It was a period tired of polemical and encyclopedic speculation, which it banished to the Wolffian universities, but one not yet prepared for fundamental criticism of speculative pretensions. Justus Christian Hennings (b. 1731), professor philosophy in Jena, was perhaps more forthright than

[25] Johann Bernhard Basedow (1724–1790), founder of the Philanthropin in Dessau (a "progressive school" for which he wrote textbooks based on Comenius, Crusius, Locke, and Rousseau). Though a student of Crusius, his theological thinking was an extreme form of that of Reimarus, and his theory of knowledge shows the influence of Hume.

[26] By Thomas Abbt (1738–66), a friend of Lessing and Mendelssohn, in his *Vom Tode fürs Vaterland* (1761), one of the first appeals to Prussian patriotism against the current cosmopolitanism; and by Johann Georg Zimmermann (1728–1795), a gifted opportunist remembered chiefly for his popular book, *Über die Einsamkeit* (1784).

[27] The most noteworthy of them was Justus Möser (1720–1790), author of *Osnabrückische Geschichte* (1768) and *Patriotische Phantasien* (1775–1786).

[28] For an interesting account of the secret societies, see S. G. Flygt, *The Notorious Dr. Bahrdt* (Nashville: Vanderbilt University Press, 1963), chap. xxv.

[29] We have autobiographies of Semler, Nicolai, Bahrdt, Feder, Schlözer, Meiners, Edelmann, and many others. These biographies have been studied by Marianne Beyer-Fröhlich, *Die Entwicklung der deutschen Selbstzeugnisse* (Leipzig: Reclam, 1930), and selections from Nicolai's, Bahrdt's, Feder's, and Schlözer's printed in her *Höhe und Krise der Aufklärung* (Leipzig: Reclam, 1934).

[30] J. A. Eberhard, *Neue Apologie des Socrates*, 2 vols. (Berlin, 1772, 1778). Socrates is used as a model of virtue without benefit of revelation, just as Mendelssohn used him in *Phaedo*. Since revelation is not needed, those who, like Leibniz, make their peace with it are accused of hypocrisy. The work of Eberhard was the occasion for Lessing's apology for Leibniz, viz., *Leibniz on Eternal Punishments*.

most, but not essentially different even from his university colleagues and not at all different from his confrères outside the universities, when he wrote: "My purpose is not to bake the finest bread, for that often contains the least nourishment. Rather I shall serve homemade bread and popular philosophy, so far as this can be done without disadvantage to *Gründlichkeit*."[31] But *Gründlichkeit*, for which Kant praised Wolff, was indeed sacrificed. Kant wrote Lambert[32] that the popular philosophy was "the euthanasia of false philosophy." "It is perishing amid . . . foolish pranks; but it would be far worse to have it carried to the grave ceremoniously, with serious but dishonest hair-splitting." Popular philosophy is "mere misology, reduced to principles."[33]

Without going into the details of the manifold differences among most of these not very important philosophers, we can summarize some of the common and distinctive views under several characteristic headings.

They were skeptics who moderated their skepticism with eclecticism and common sense, or "sound human reason." Their eclecticism led them to extensive and influential translation of Latin, French, and, most of all, British writers.[34] Histories of philosophy[35] were written as collections of finished doctrines from which one might choose as he wished, with little or no sense of the internal dialectic of philosophical development and tradition. Sound common sense was the criterion of choice. Hume's practical and Reid's theoretical philosophy were taken as models, but Hume's theoretical skepticism, so far as it bore upon empirical and practical knowledge, was rejected.[36] Goethe described the popular philosophy not as a philosophy of "sound human reason" but as just sound human reason itself: "The philosophy was more or less 'sound human understanding' [*Verstand*] venturing into the universal and speaking about inner and outer experiences.

[31] *Kritisch-Historisches Lehrbuch der theoretischen Philosophie* (1774), quoted from M. Wundt, *Die Philosophie an der Universitat Jena*, (Jena: Gustav Fischer, 1932), p. 124.

[32] December 31, 1965; *Gesammelte Schriften* (Akad. ed.) X, 57; *Kant's Philosophical Correspondence*, trans. Arnulf Zweig, (Chicago, Ill.: University of Chicago Press, 1967) p. 49.

[33] *Critique of Pure Reason*, A 855 = B 883.

[34] Thus J. J. Spalding, a leading neologist, translated Shaftesbury; Mendelssohn translated Rousseau and Burke; Engel, Sulzer, and Mérian translated Hume; Garve translated Paley and Adam Smith. Kant, though he presumably knew no English, shows throughout his writings an extensive knowledge of English writers. G. Zart (*Der Einfluss der englischen Philosophen seit Bacon auf die deutsche Philosophie des 18. Jahrhunderts*, [Berlin, 1881]) shows that Locke was the most influential and was read and used by almost all German philosophers even when they disagreed with him; Bacon was as influential; Hume, Shaftesbury, Hutcheson, and Berkeley much less so. Hobbes was often cited, but generally opposed.

[35] J. J. Brucker (1696–1770), *Historia critica philosophiae*, 1742–1744, Dieterich Tiedemann (1748–1803), *Geist der spekulativen Philosophie von Thales bis Berkeley*, 1791–1797. See Johannes Freyer, "Geschichte der Geschichte der Philosophie im 18. Jahrhundert," in *Beiträge zur Kultur- und Universalgeschichte* (Leipzig, 1912), on these and other historians of philosophy, e.g., Garve, Feder, Tennemann, and Fülleborn.

[36] In Mendelssohn's *Gedancken von der Wahrscheinlichkeit* (1756; *Gesammelte Schriften*, I, 147–154) in which, it must be noted, he completely missed the difficulty of Hume's problem.

A clear acuteness and a notable moderation, by which one always stayed in the middle of the road and held that an even-balanced view of all opinions was correct, brought a certain respect and trust for such writings and oral expressions, and thus finally philosophers were found not only in all the faculties, but indeed in every social class."[37]

They were practicalists in religion and art. The purpose of art and of religion was, according to them, to make better men, and that meant to make happier men. The popular philosophers were deists or neologists; they propounded the ideals of religious toleration, and Mendelssohn even opposed the existence of any state or territorial church.

They were anthropologists in the empirical basis they gave their philosophy. The medical, rather than the theological and legal, faculty began to supply the philosophical.[38] Book titles, as well as their contents, show that man, not natural science or ontology or theology, was in the saddle.[39] Even physiology made its contribution to philosophy,[40] though the Germans did not go so far as La Mettrie in making man a machine.

They were essayists and aphorists, not systematic thinkers and writers. The book review, open letters (*Sendschreiben*), and collections of aphorisms[41] were the characteristic literary forms; the novel was put to philosophical purposes.[42] They were Thomasian—"philosophy for the world"[43] was the heir to Thomasius' *philosophia aulica*. They opposed systematic speculation as worthy only of pedants. Philosophy was for the practical man. The word *Aufklarung* was invented in the 1750's. Enlightenment, not just learning, was to replace the Wolffian scholastic system. An enthusiasm for

[37] *Goethe's Autobiography. Poetry and Truth from My Life*, trans. W. O. Moon (Washington, D.C.: Public Affairs Press, 1949), p. 236.

[38] Among the popular philosophers, some physicians were J. G. Zimmerman, Ernst Platner (1744–1818) in Vienna, and Marcus Herz (1747–1803), the confidant of Kant and Mendelssohn. La Mettrie, in the Academy, was also a physician.

[39] For example, *Erfahrung und Untersuchungen über den Menschen*, 4 vols., (1772–85) by Karl Franz von Irrwing (1728–1801), and *Untersuchungen über den Menschen*, 3 vols. (1777) by Dietrich Tiedemann. Not only do the titles sound like translations from Locke, but the contents are also Lockean. Wundt comments upon the whole change from Latin quartos or folios to the duodecimos of the middle of the century, which could be put into a pocket and read under a tree.

[40] Johann Christian Lossius (1748–1813), *Physische Ursachen der Wahrheit* (1775), which attempts to explain contradictions as "conflicts between nerves."

[41] Germany's best aphorist of this period (and after Nietzsche, of any period) was Lichtenberg (see the detailed study by J. P. Stern, *Lichtenberg. A Doctrine of Scattered Occasions*). Ernst Platner's aphorisms, which went through several editions after 1776 are neither short, witty, nor perceptive, and are aphorisms only in the estimation of their author.

[42] The most important philosophical novelist before Goethe was Christoff Wieland (1733–1813), whose *Agathon* has a respected place in German literature. More characteristic of the period, but of infinitely less literary worth, were Nicolai's *Sempronius Gundibert* (a burlesque on Kant) and *Sebaldus Nothanker*. Jacobi also used the epistolary novel as a vehicle of his philosophy.

[43] The name is taken from a collection of essays, *Philosoph für die Welt*, ed. Johann Jakob Engel (1741–1802), 2 vols., (1775–77). Among the contributors were Garve, Eberhard, Mendelssohn, and Engel himself. Engel was esteemed by Kant for "upholding the honor of Germany" in literary matters (letter from Kant to Engel, July 4, 1779).

enlightenment—first in the republic of letters, but then for mankind in general—was to replace the love of wisdom for its own sake:

> Der Theolog, der Duldung lehrt
> Und dürre Dogmen so behandelt
> Dass er sie in Moral verwandelt,
> Der ist und machet aufgeklärt;

but also:

> Der Landmann, der mit seinem Stande
> Vergnügt ist und im Vaterlande
> Ein nützlich Glied zu sein begehrt,
> Ist nicht gelehrt, doch aufgeklärt.[44]

and even:

If you were to find yourself in a mob of barbaric negroes on the coast of Africa and saw how wildly they dishonor the rights of mankind; if you saw a Xinga dancing around the sacrificial victim of a bloodthirsty religion, smashing his skull with an axe so that the brain spurts out, and drinking his blood with a right good thirst—O sympathetic European, would you not wish that the Xinga might be somewhat more enlightened?"[45]

The Frederician enlightenment, as the intellectual movement in north Germany from about 1740 to 1780 may be described, was short-lived. Its religious free-thinking was ended by the accession of Friedrich Wilhelm II and the Wöllner edict. Its moralistic conception of religion was ended by the *Sturm und Drang* which led into romanticism. Its mildly optimistic view of human progress through enlightenment was shaken by the French Revolution, so that most German philosophy at the end of the century was in overt opposition to the ideals of the eighteenth century. Its superficial conception of the role and scope of philosophy was destroyed by Kant. It did not understand or participate in the solidifying of the Newtonian world concept. It was indifferent to the political and ideological problems that led to the French and American revolutions. It would be forgotten but for the historic role of Frederick and the genius of two of his subjects who were excluded from his Academy but who gave voice to the ideas and tensions of his age to a much greater degree than he himself did. I refer to Mendelssohn and Lessing.

Mendelssohn was the epitome of popular philosophy at its best; Lessing stood outside and above it, and pointed beyond it. Mendelssohn expressed the ideas of popular philosophy at their best and in their best form; he had

---

[44] The first verse reads: The theologian who teaches tolerance and so treats dry dogmas that he changes them into morals is and makes others enlightened. The second: The peasant who is satisfied with his status and desires to be a useful member of his fatherland is not learned, but he is enlightened. These inimitable verses are taken from Eulogius Schneider, "Die wahre Aufklärung," in his *Gedichte* (1790); I quote from the anthology of Gerhard Funke, *Die Aufklärung in ausgewählten Texten* (Stuttgart: Koehler, 1963), p. 103.
[45] Andreas Riem, *Über Aufklärung* (1788), quoted from Funke, *ibid.*, p. 120.

gone through the Wolffian discipline without having been desiccated by it. Lessing modulated many of them into the new key in which they were to undergo still further development. To understand Mendelssohn is to know the final will and testament of popular philosophy; but to understand Lessing is to have a view into a promised land the popular philosophers did not even suspect existed.

Mendelssohn

Moses Mendelssohn was born in Dessau in 1729. He went to Berlin in 1743, where he first became tutor to the children of a rich silk manufacturer, then his bookkeeper, and finally a partner in his firm. He met Lessing in 1754 and lent him his first piece of philosophical writing, the *Philosophische Gespräche*, which so impressed Lessing that he published it without consulting the author, and Mendelssohn became famous overnight. In 1755 he and Lessing collaborated on *Pope a Metaphysician?* which we have already mentioned. In 1756 he began his long collaboration with Nicolai and Lessing on the *Allgemeine deutsche Bibliothek* and the *Briefe, die neueste Literatur betreffend*, which became the chief literary organs of the Berlin Enlightenment. From 1755 to 1757 he published his principal contributions to aesthetics, which were collected and republished in 1761. In 1763 he won the prize offered by the Berlin Academy on the degree of evidence attainable in natural theory and morals, defeating Kant. (In 1771 the Academy elected him Fellow but he was blackballed by the King.) He later enjoyed the friendship of Kant, visited Königsberg (in 1777), and attended two lectures by Kant. In 1767 he published his *Phaedo*, the work for which he was best known in his lifetime; it earned him the honorific, "the German Socrates."

In 1769 Mendelssohn was attacked by Johann Kaspar Lavater with the challenge either to refute the arguments of natural theology in Charles Bonnet's *Palingénésie philosophique*,[46] a part of which he translated and dedicated to Mendelssohn, or to become a Christian. Mendelssohn had tried to avoid religious controversy, and, though of course known as a Jew, he had not taken any distinctive stand on philosophical issues dictated by his Judaism. Now offended at Lavater's proselytizing importunity and officiousness, but not wishing to come forth as an opponent of Christianity, Mendelssohn appealed for tolerance for diverse revealed religions and agreement upon rational or natural religion. He argued that Judaism and Christianity had the same rational basis, but that while Judaism contained a revealed *law* binding only on the descendants of Jacob, Christianity also claimed revealed dogmas which went beyond the truths of rational religion. His own prize essay had contained a better presentation of rational theology than Bonnet's book; he was far from being faced with the dilemma of refuting Bonnet or becoming a Christian. Lavater had outraged many, and

---

[46] Johann Kaspar Lavater (1741–1801), a Swiss hybrid of popular philosophy and Pietism, chiefly remembered now for his *Von der Physiognomik* (1772), which was scathingly criticized by Lichtenberg. Charles Bonnet (1720–1790), a Swiss empiricistic philosopher, teacher of F. H. Jacobi.

especially Lessing, by his impudent challenge to Mendelssohn and he was finally shamed into withdrawing it.[47]

The controversy with Lavater led Mendelssohn, however, to take a more openly critical attitude toward the political and ecclesiastical oppressors of the Jews. He wished to educate the Jews to be good Germans without having them sacrifice their religion; he wanted peace between the Germans and the Jews, but not union. As an emancipated Jew (he had been made a *Schützjude*—we would say he was given a permanent visa—by the Prussian government in 1763; before that time he could have been banished at will), he tried to improve the lot of other Jews in Prussia: he befriended Marcus Herz when he first came to Berlin, having been recommended by Kant, and Solomon Maimon, whom he, in turn, recommended to Kant; he founded a school for Jewish children in Berlin and, in spite of a bitter reply to Basedow, who seems to have needed scholars *even if they were Jews*, he helped Jewish children enter Basedow's Philanthropin. He transplanted much of the Old Testament into German for the use of Jews (and earned another honorific title, "the Jewish Luther"). In 1783 he published *Jerusalem, oder über religiöse Macht und Judenthum*, in which he pleaded not only for freedom for the Jews but for religious toleration even to the point of disestablishing all state churches. (But Mendelssohn, so far in advance of other proponents of toleration in attacking the institution of the territorial church which was the instrument of intolerance, could not go all the way. Like Wolff, he stopped before the point of toleration for atheists who, he said, cannot fulfill their civic obligations, and for *Schwärmer*, who neglect this world's obligations for those of the other world.) Lessing used the Mendelssohn of the Lavater controversy and of the *Jerusalem* as the model for Nathan in his last great drama, Germany's most important literary defense of religious toleration, *Nathan der Weise*.

The last years of Mendelssohn's life were made unhappy by the death of Lessing in 1781 and by his efforts to defend Lessing from what seemed to be the calumny of Friedrich Jacobi Heinrich. Before Jacobi published his conversations with Lessing in the form of a letter to Mendelssohn, Mendelssohn had delivered to a small group of young men, including his son and the Humboldt brothers, his principal metaphysical lectures, which he published under the title of *Morgenstunden*. During the controversy with Jacobi, which we shall discuss later, Mendelssohn died, in 1786.

Mendelssohn repeatedly expressed his adherence to the Leibniz-Wolffian philosophy—so repeatedly, even toward the end of his life, that it is likely that he did not see the degree to which he actually went beyond it in his aesthetic and metaphysical writings. But there was in Mendelssohn none of the pedantic prolixity of Wolff and his university disciplines. On the other hand, there are none of the jejune commonplaces of most of the popular philosophers. In fact, a good claim might be made that Mendelssohn (who learned German only as the second of his six languages and would not venture to read his papers to the philosophical club of which

[47] For the best account in English of the controversy, see Edward S. Flajole, S.J., "Lessing's Attitude in the Lavater–Mendelssohn Controversy," *Publications of the Modern Language Association*, 73: 201–214 (1958).

he was a member because he did not trust his pronunciation) wrote the best German of any philosopher before Schopenhauer.[48] His style does not have the wit, vigor, and variety of Lessing's prose, nor the richness of metaphoric texture of Herder's, but it has a graceful simplicity and clarity. Of all German philosophers worth reading, Mendelssohn is the easiest to read.

We shall discuss his contributions to philosophy under four headings: aesthetics, ethics, theory of knowledge, and metaphysics.

Aesthetics

In his aesthetics, which was Mendelssohn's most important contribution to philosophy, he took several steps beyond Sulzer, leading in the direction from Baumgarten to Kant. While his writings show the influence of Shaftesbury and some resemblances to Burke, he had in fact formulated his theory of the sublime before he had read Burke. Most of the ideas he shares with Shaftesbury could have been found in German sources, and it is debatable whether he learned them from Shaftesbury or from his own compatriots. The dynamic, organic, plastic conception of nature's perfections is probably Shaftesbury's, but it could have been found in Leibniz. But the place ascribed to feeling and its relation to cognition and desire resembles Shaftesbury's more than anyone else's.

The Wolffian theory, as developed by Baumgarten, had held that beauty is the sensuous perception of a perfection. Baumgarten's metaphysics was Wolffian, but we have seen that his epistemology was different, because he held that senses can clearly (but not distinctly) represent a perfection, whereas Wolff had taught that clarification of the senses led to thought rather than artistic enjoyment. Sulzer added to the theory of sensuous cognition of perfection a theory of the subjective delight (*Vergnügen*) in this sensuous cognition. Mendelssohn argues against the definition of the aesthetic experience as the sensuous representation of a perfection, and replaces it with the conception of a perfect sensuous representation of anything, whether a metaphysical perfection or not.

This change is of fundamental importance. It leads to three important new views. First, it implies that art has a perfection of its own based upon the psychological experiences it engenders. Mendelssohn eliminates the cognitive conditions of aesthetic experience which had made art a lower, though in its way perfect, representation of a metaphysical or moral perfection. The human mind is too limited to perceive objectively the perfection of variety-in-unity which exists metaphysically; but experience of it is a variety-in-unity of the mind's own sensuous experiences and emotions, and this directly felt, subjective, perfection is what gives delight in the aesthetic experience. Mendelssohn does not reach the formula, which we shall find in Lessing, of art for art's sake; but we find Mendelssohn recognizing the autonomy of art. "The stage," he says, "has its own morality."[49]

---

[48] In the Introduction to the *Prolegomena*, Kant praised Mendelssohn's "depth, as well as his elegance."

[49] *Über die Empfindungen*, Letter 13, p. 94. But Mendelssohn still thinks one function of art is to awaken the "dead knowledge of reason" so that it can have an effect on

Second, and even more important: by not requiring that beauty in art be predicated upon the perfection of the object represented, Mendelssohn had a way of accounting for the aesthetic values in the ugly, the comic, the tragic, and the sublime. For though these do not represent what is in itself perfect, they produce in us "mixed feelings" which can be formed and disciplined into their own perfections. The prime subject matter of aesthetic is, then, not the object, but the subject's experience of the object.

Finally, this subjectification leads Mendelssohn to a more vivid appreciation of artistic creativity. The artist, the genius, can create what nature failed to produce, through bringing about an agreement of all the powers of his soul in creating new perfections and not in imitating natural perfections. After all, it is not the business of nature to produce beauty, but to produce perfections, whether they are enjoyed or not.[50]

The mind can experience delight in three ways. First, it can know the perfection of the object without any involvement of the bodily and perceptual processes. When it does so, the distinct representations of the perfections of the object give way to an extensive clarity of the ideas, and the soul enjoys the feeling of its own power and facility, the increase in its own perfection. Mendelssohn's example of this is the enjoyment of a mathematician who has accomplished a difficult proof, and then surveys his work, enjoying it as a well-designed whole.[51] Second, the mind can know the perfection of an object it perceives. It sees some object as useful to us in the satisfaction of some desire, even of a desire for knowledge, and it contemplates some moral achievement. This delight is called simply pleasure (Lust). Finally, there is sensuous pleasure proper, which Mendelssohn calls pleasant sensation (angenehme Empfindung)[52] or sensuous charm (sinnliche Ergötzung). For example, there is the pleasure of the taste of wine. This is not appreciation of an objective perfection; it is not analyzable into conceptions of the object. "I do not venture," Mendelssohn writes with good humor,[53] "to say with the Herr Professor [Sulzer?] that the delight in the enjoyment [Vergnügen bey dem Genusse] of a pretty woman arises merely in a mass of concepts through which the soul promises to satisfy one of its original needs."

With this general psychology of pleasure, Mendelssohn turns to the pleasure we find in the beautiful. A beautiful object, he tells us, does not cause pleasure, but only pleasant sensations. It does not cause pleasure, because the joy we find in contemplating beauty is independent of desire, and Lust is always connected with desire.[54] Rather, it causes a sensuous pleasure by enhancing the perfection of our bodily state, especially that of the perceptual organs; and it is this perfection, not the perfection of the object, which is clearly but indistinctly perceived by the soul. Therefore the physical object need not have a perfection at all if the perception of it is at-

---

moral conduct. (All page references to Mendelssohn's writings, unless otherwise indicated, are to the pagination of his Gesammelte Schriften (Berlin: Akademie Verlag, 1929–). Since this splendid edition was never completed, however, I have had to refer from time to time to earlier editions.)

50 Ibid., Letter 5, p. 61.   52 Ibid., Letters, 8 and 10, pp. 70–74, 81–84.

51 Ibid., Letter 12, p. 91.   53 Von dem Vergnügen, I, 128.

54 It is identified with Begierde (= desire) in Gesammelte Schriften I, 170.

tended with an increase of our sensuous perfection. Mendelssohn has made the transition from the sensuous presentation of a perfection (which is Baumgarten's definition of beauty) to the perfect sensuous presentation, which is his own. By that transition, art is freed from the theory of metaphysical perfections. That Mendelssohn modifies the metaphysical theory of perfection from its emphasis upon unity in variety (as in Baumgarten) to an emphasis upon organic harmony of the variety for the sake of a common end (as in Shaftesbury) is important, but less so than the fact that he has, for the first time, cut aesthetics free from metaphysics, and aesthetic value from metaphysical value.

Yet all is not clear and distinct in Mendelssohn's theory. The most obvious lacuna is his failure to distinguish adequately between the pleasant sensations in tasting the wine (his example) and those we experience when we see a beautiful object. To be sure, he discusses the ways in which the artist can produce pleasurable sensations; the line of beauty of Hogarth, he thinks, does for the eye what harmony of tones does for the ear.[55] But I cannot find in Mendelssohn's writings any clear treatment of this problem. Metaphysical perfection had provided putative standards for such distinctions. But with the perfection in question having been internalized into the nervous system and experience of the perceiver, the important distinction between mere sensuous charm and sensuous beauty, both of which please "without a concept" or have "purposiveness without purpose" (as Kant will say) is lost. It will be Kant's task to reinstate this important distinction.

A second difficulty with Mendelssohn's theory—fortunately one much more easily rectified, and one which he himself partially rectified—is found in his account of the relations between pleasure and will. In the Über die Empfindung, Mendelssohn had not yet formulated the three-faculty theory which is generally attributed to him. In discussing the relation of enjoyment (Vergnügen) to will, he says they are distinguished only in degree. "Even the will has as its basis a good, a furthering of our perfection; if it did not, we would never choose. Only in the liveliness of the desire [Heftigkeit des Verlangens] is the object of enjoyment to be distinguished from the object of will."[56] They differ only in degree, because both are contingent upon an enhancement of our perfection. Pleasure is not independent of volition or volition of pleasure; and Mendelssohn still has a two-faculty theory: volition and cognition, with pleasure dependent upon the latter.

But in the Morgenstunden, he modifies this view.[57] There he says:

One commonly divides the faculties of the soul into the cognitive and the desiderative, and counts the sensation [Empfindung] of pleasure and pain with the latter. But it seems to me that, between knowing and desiring there is approval [Billigen], approbation [Beyfall], satisfaction of mind [Wohlgefallen der Seele], which is really quite far removed from desire . . . We regard the beauty of nature and art with enjoyment and satisfaction, without their in the

[55] Über die Empfindungen, Letter 11, p. 87.   [56] Ibid., Letter 6, p. 66.
[57] Morgenstunden, 2nd ed. (Berlin, 1785), p. 118.

least inciting desire in us. It seems in fact to be a special mark of beauty, that it is observed with a restful satisfaction, that it pleases even when we do not possess it and are far from desiring to possess it.

This is the three-faculty theory, which replaces Baumgarten's one-faculty theory (one faculty, the cognitive, but having several perfections as its objects) and Sulzer's two-faculty theory (knowing and feeling).[58] This is the *Billigungsvermögen*, or faculty of approval. It becomes Kant's aesthetic faculty of judgment, and Mendelssohn's "restful satisfaction" becomes Kant's "distinterested pleasure." Until this third faculty was inserted, however, Mendelssohn could not in principle distinguish aesthetic pleasure from sensuous charm, since all the pleasures relevant to the analysis are either practical (concerned with the will, and requiring cognition of some good or perfection) or mere sense gratifications. With the insertion of the new faculty of approval as the psychological basis for judgments of taste, Mendelssohn had found the key to his problem. But by that time he was an old and sick man, more interested in his metaphysics and in saving Lessing's reputation, and it was left to Kant and Tetens to perfect this theory.

The other ideas in Mendelssohn's aesthetic writings are interesting primarily in relation to what Lessing was to make from them. There is, for example, Mendelssohn's distinction between the "fine arts" and the "fine sciences" (poetry and eloquence). They are distinguished by whether they use natural or artificial signs and whether they make an instantaneous or a successive presentation of their object.[59] This idea, of course, will be fully developed in Lessing's *Laocoön* (1766).[60] In his *Betrachtungen über das Erhabene und das Naive in den schönen Wissenschaften* (1757), written before he had read Burke, Mendelssohn distinguishes between the sublime and the naive (the simple, the graceful) and discusses the various mixed feelings in complex aesthetic experiences. He disagrees with Lessing in attributing some of the effect of tragedy to wonder instead of, with Aristotle and Lessing, finding pity and fear sufficient. He follows Shaftesbury in using the aesthetic concepts of the beautiful and sublime in describing moral characters, anticipating Kant's *Observations on the Feeling of the Beautiful and Sublime*, published in 1763.

Ethics

Mendelssohn wrote little on moral philosophy, and what he said has little or no originality. But, again, he sums up in a lucid way the basic

[58] The question as to who was the inventor of the three-faculty theory is ambiguous, since it is not clear just what is the criterion for faculties. Neither Mendelssohn nor Sulzer keeps feeling from so intimate an involvement with desire that it is unclear whether or not they are different faculties. Kant is the first to specify what it is that different mental functions must have in order to qualify as signs of distinct faculties and, consequently, to see that there must be three.

[59] *Betrachtungen über die Quellen und Verbindungen der schönen Künste und Wissenschaften* (1757), I, 175, 178, 179.

[60] Chapter XIV on Lessing's development of this idea.

Wolffian theory, its prosaic intellectualism ameliorated by the concern felt by the "philosophers for the world" with good taste and with the sentiments that function in the moral life.

Mendelssohn's important and original contribution to aesthetic theory, his separation of the criteria of beauty from the metaphysical concepts of perfection, has no counterpart in his moral philosophy. The transition from the "is" of metaphysics to the "ought" of ethics is made without hesitation, so that the solution of the problem of what I ought to do is basically reducible to a metaphysical question of increasing the ontological perfection of the world. He saw that it was not the purpose of nature to produce beauty, but to produce perfection which might or might not be aesthetically appreciated; but he did not see that the metaphysical conception of perfection is not directly translatable into the moral conception of virtue and happiness. Hume saw the impossibility of this translation, but no one in Germany saw it before Kant. The German philosophers after Leibniz had followed the Neoplatonic ontology of building so many value predicates into what truly and ultimately is that they could not see that, in finding them there, they had begged all the questions of a genuine metaphysical basis for morals.

Mendelssohn presented his ethical theory in the last part of his prize essay of 1763. It is in the form of an attempt to answer the question concerning the degree of evidence attainable in our knowledge of ethical principles. He argues that the basic principles of morals can be proved "with mathematical rigor," but that moral inferences become less certain as we move from the supreme laws of nature to specific moral decisions by a chain of practical syllogisms. The basic law of nature is found by examining human actions and sentiments to discover their hidden uniformities. This leads to a definition of a rational being, from which the basic law can be derived, he thinks, a priori. The definition is: A being is free if it can choose what gives it pleasure. Add to this the long-accepted Wolffian explanation of pleasure: Pleasure depends upon perfection, the expectation of which provides a motive for action. From this is supposed to follow the "basic law": "Make your internal and external state, and that of others in due proportion, as perfect as possible." The motives do not exert any physical coercion (*Zwang*) but constitute "moral necessities" which appear in the imperative at the end of this derivation.[61]

The moral law so derived from the nature of man as a free agent is in conformity with divine law, though independent of it. We are obligated to obey divine law not because God has the power to punish us if we do not, but because God himself wills the best possible world and his laws are devised to secure such a world. But our relation to God, as his creatures bound to obey him, to be grateful for his favors, and to fear his wrath and to hope for his approval, adds to our motives for obedience to the moral law.[62]

All specific moral laws can be derived from the basic law if we supply minor premises drawn from experience. If the minor premise is taken from

[61] *Abhandlung über die Evidenz*, in *Gesammelte Schriften*, II, 317.
[62] *Ibid.*, 320.

indubitable inner experiences, as in the premise "I desire happiness," the conclusion follows with mathematical certainty.[63] But many minor premises are only probable, and hence the moral conclusions are only probable; this is always the case where we have to estimate the consequences of our actions. On this level we cannot get the information necessary for the construction of a syllogism with certain conclusions; and even if we could, faced with the exigencies of action, we do not have time to do so. Fortunately we do not have to do so, because we are endowed with a faculty of conscience, or *bon sens*, which permits us to distinguish correctly between good and evil through an inarticulate (*undeutliche*) inference. Conscience is like taste, which permits an equally immediate judgment concerning beauty without our having to reason from the perfections its contemplation creates in our body, and like the sense of truth (*Wahrheitssinn*), which permits us, on inadequate evidence, to judge our perceptions and arguments.

Conscience directly produces a feeling of approbation and has an influence on action which clear and distinct reasons alone could never have.[64] To secure the influence of reason on conduct, we must practice virtue, multiply the variety of motives to good deeds, and associate them with the pleasant sensations produced by imagination and art. There is a beauty of right actions and virtue, as Shaftesbury saw; there is, in what Mendelssohn says about *bon sens* and taste, an allusion to Hutcheson's theory of moral sense, though Mendelssohn does not explicitly refer to either of the British philosophers. We have seen that Mendelssohn does not take a narrow, Gottschedian, view of the moral function of art; on the other hand, he does not deny the importance of art in instilling moral ideas. "Rational principles show the path to happiness, and the arts strew the path with flowers."[65]

Kant criticized the concept of perfection as being either empty of moral consequences or as tautological and empty. It is empty if moral predicates are not put into it—in which case answers to moral questions come before answers to metaphysical—or the consequences drawn from it only seem to be specifically moral.[66] The command "seek perfection" is unmoral (it might be addressed to a thief: "Be as perfect a thief as you can") or tautological (a moral agent will do the best he can). But it is noteworthy that the targets of his attack are the Stoics, Wolff, Baumgarten, and Richard Cumberland (cited by Mendelssohn), and not Mendelssohn himself. Perhaps the reason for this was that in his own essay for the competition in which Mendelssohn defeated him, Kant made precisely the same mistake. The primary formal principle in morals was, for him, "Do the most perfect thing you can." But he went further, at that time, in suggesting "moral

---

[63] *Ibid.*, 323.

[64] In his *Verwandtschaft des Schönen und Guten* (*Gesammelte Schriften*, II, 181–185) probably written about 1757, Mendelssohn discusses *bon sens* in its relation to reason and taste, anticipating the views of the prize essay. In both it and the prize essay, of course, there are suggestions of the three-faculty theory, and the theory of "sound human reason" developed only in his last writings.

[65] *Abhandlung über die Evidenz*, in *Gesammelte Schriften*, II, 327.

[66] *Foundations of the Metaphysics of Morals* (Prussian Akademy ed., IV, 443); *Critique of Practical Reason*, § 8 Remark ii; *Lectures on Ethics*, (New York: Harper & Row, 1963), pp. 24, 26, 39.

feeling" as an independent source of propositions which serve as "indemonstrable material principles of practical knowledge."[67] In 1763 Kant was as
much a disciple of Shaftesbury and Hutcheson as Mendelssohn was—perhaps more so. It may be that this is the reason why he did not make
Mendelssohn an object of his later criticisms.

Theory of Knowledge

Mendelssohn's theory of knowledge, with the exception of one part, is
found in the first three sections of his *Abhandlung über die Evidenz in
metaphysischen Wissenschaften*, which won the prize of the Academy in
1763 (published in 1764). No other single work gives so perspicuous a
presentation of the Leibniz-Wolffian epistemology; every strength of that
tradition is persuasively presented, every fault in it inadvertently revealed.
By comparison, Kant's essay, which it defeated, is groping and frequently
obscure. It is easy to see why the Academy preferred Mendelssohn's.

The essay opens with the well-known Wolffian analysis of mathematical
knowledge. In language later to be introduced by Kant we can say that
Mendelssohn believes that all mathematical judgments are analytic: they
analyze the concept of quantity or extension, all mathematical truths must
be implicit in these concepts, and mathematics teaches us to explicate
them.[68] Mendelssohn follows Wolff in comparing the analysis of a concept
to the use of a magnifying glass; it makes clear and distinct what was
obscure or invisible, but it does not bring forth anything new. There follows, then, the expected allusion to the slave boy in the *Meno* of Plato; then
the expected effort to remove the "mystical elements" from the Platonic
theory of a priori knowledge and to replace it with the Leibnizian theory
that sensuous impressions are only the occasions for the soul to bring its
innate representations to full consciousness so that they can be seen to be
logically implicated in each other.[69] Unextended quantities are rendered
susceptible to analysis by the discovery of methods of finding geometrical
representations or substitutes for them.[70]

Mathematical knowledge, however, insofar as it is analytic and therefore
certain, is not knowledge of existing things. "In the whole field of mathematics there is not a single example of an inference from merely possible
concepts to the reality of an object. Our concepts of quantity stand in
necessary relation to other concepts, but not to realities."[71] But we can trust
our senses that this or that fundamental concept (a triangle, for example)
does have a real object, and hence we can know that all the necessary consequences of the concept apply also to this object.

But can we trust our senses? Mendelssohn distinguishes two ways in
which our senses might mislead us. Our senses misinform us of the size,

---

[67] *On the Distinctness of the Principles of Natural Theology and Morals* in Kant's
Critique of Practical Reason and other Writings on Moral Philosophy, trans. L. W.
Beck (Chicago: University of Chicago Press, 1949), pp. 283–285.

[68] *Abhandlung über die Evidenz*, in *Gesammelte Schriften*, II, 273.

[69] *Ibid.*, p. 277.   [71] *Ibid.*, p. 283.

[70] *Ibid.*, pp. 279, 281.

shape, position, or color of an object, and we discover by our senses themselves that they do so. Consequently these illusions do not prove the skeptic's case, but rather tell against it, since we use the senses to discover and correct these illusions, which Mendelssohn calls "variable appearances." On the other hand, our senses might delude us by giving us representations which always and inevitably misinform us about the disposition of things we experience. In fact, they do so when they inform us that objects really are in space. If objects are really in space, then we must ascribe extension to God, as Spinoza did; but since Mendelssohn thinks this is impossible (God being a simple being), he must conclude, with Leibniz, that "extension is not among the realities" and see it as "a mere phenomenon." "There are realities in nature," he declares, "on which extension is based, but they are not at all extended but rather simple; whatever is real in them pertains to the highest degree to the highest being. But the appearances we perceive in them must be denied to the supreme being, for they are based upon the inadequacy of our knowledge. They do not apply to the things but to the way we perceive them."[72]

Let this be granted. It does not follow that mathematical knowledge does not apply to objects we experience. "The mathematician can prove that the permanent appearances [permanent because they depend upon our unchanging sensory organization, not the variable conditions of the object] stand in necessary connections with each other so that I can infer from one the presence of another."[73] Hence neither the skeptic nor the idealist can bring an argument against the certainty of mathematics. It is evident in itself, it is immediately evident to us through clear and distinct sensory perception of its objects, it is logically necessary, and it applies to empirical objects.

Philosophy is not, however, concerned with the quantities of things. It is defined as "knowledge of qualities based upon reason."[74] Pure speculative philosophy is the analysis of our concepts of the qualities of things and contains necessary propositions which can be proved by the law of contradiction. For example, "A necessary being is just to the highest degree, and a contingent being is just only to a limited degree."[75] But while such pure speculative propositions as this are as certain as those of mathematics —that is, they are evident in themselves—they are not as evident to us (fasslich). This deficiency arises from two facts. First, philosophy deals with matters of such importance that even the non-philosopher must have beliefs and opinions about them which may well be incorrect; philosophy, therefore, does not begin with a clean slate but must fight against established prejudices and deep-rooted errors.[76] Second, the symbols used by the philosopher are arbitrary. They cannot be ostensively exhibited like mathematical concepts. They must be defined in order to have any meaning at all. We cannot see their connections intuitively, as we often can between mathematical concepts even before they have been formally defined. More-

---

[72] *Ibid.*, p. 310.   [73] *Ibid.*, p. 286.
[74] *Ibid.*, p. 286; a commonplace since Wolff, and quoted from Baumgarten.
[75] *Ibid.*, p. 290.   [76] *Ibid.*, p. 295.

over, mathematical concepts can always be exhibited to the senses, but we may not always succeed in finding examples and objects for metaphysical concepts—in fact, we very seldom do so.

The task of metaphysics is more difficult than that of mathematics. It suffices in mathematics to find connections between various concepts of quantity that can be exhibited in sense experience whether that sense experience be metaphysically valid or not. But metaphysics must apply to reality, and it must do so even if sense experience is irretrievably illusory. The transition from pure speculative philosophy to metaphysics, therefore, cannot take place as the like transition in geometry does, by means of an empirical exposition of the concepts.

The transition can be made in only one way: from concepts which *must* have objects to the objects themselves. There are two such concepts, both of which were exploited for this purpose by Descartes: the concept of a thinking being, and the concept of a perfect being. Mendelssohn prefers the latter, and he gives an elaborate formulation of the ontological argument along the lines first worked out by Leibniz. If a necessary being is not impossible, it must exist. The concept of a necessary being is not impossible because it is not self-contradictory, and it cannot be contingently (hypothetically) impossible because if a necessary being exists at all it exists independently of anything else. Hence a necessary being not only exists, but exists necessarily.[77]

Having proved a necessary connection between the concept of a necessary being and its existence, Mendelssohn uses his concept of its existence and the principle of sufficient reason to establish necessary connections to other existing things of which we have concepts. To justify this, however, he must first prove the principle of sufficient reason itself. He avails himself of Wolff's argument.[78] What cannot be conceived as completely determined (every determinable determined) cannot be said to exist. A necessary being has every determinable self-determined, but a contingent being, by definition, can be conceived only if conditions external to its concept are given for each of its determinations. Hence a contingent being can exist only if there is a sufficient condition for it to be as it is and not otherwise, i.e., only if every determination of it is sufficiently determined by something else. The concept of a contingent being without a sufficient condition is, therefore, self-contradictory.

The chain of sufficient conditions for the existence of any contingent being has as its first member "the free creation and [continuing] maintenance by an independent being" for, without that, "the complete determination of a contingent being is incapable of being conceived and rationally explained."[79]

The argument for the existence of God from the design found in nature, on the other hand, lacks full demonstrative power, which the preceding argument is said to possess. Not only does it presuppose the real existence of other things, but at most it shows that God impressed order upon chaos,

[77] *Ibid.*, pp. 294, 300.
[78] Wolff, *Ontologia*, § 70; see §§ 104–109, 117.
[79] *Abhandlung über die Evidenz*, in *Gesammelte Schriften*, II, 304.

not that God created the world out of nothing.[80] But, as Kant was later to agree, the physico-theological argument possesses more power to convince than the ontological argument. "It makes a stronger impression on the mind, it awakens the mind to effective actions and brings forth the practical conviction which should be our highest goal in the contemplation of the divine attributes . . . it brings the sweetest satisfaction, the most refreshing solace, and the fire and life of knowledge which passes over into desire and which are manifest in our actions."[81]

Here, then, we have almost the last and certainly the most elegant presentation of the Leibniz-Wolffian theory of knowledge as it had developed over forty years. It is rationalistic, with due place for sense experience; it is dogmatic, moving from one well-defined metaphysical concept to another by stately formal arguments; it proves the existence of God and of a Leibnizian world of monads; it is edifying and elevating. It is all very beautiful; it is even interesting; there is nothing else like it, even in Leibniz or Wolff, for lucidity and polish.

Friedrich Heinrich Jacobi, however, argued that a rationalistic system could not stop with these edifying and harmless truths.[82] A system of philosophy that follows the method of demonstrating metaphysical truths must go all the way to Spinoza's panlogism. Spinoza's panlogism implied a monism and fatalism which was incompatible with the Leibniz-Wolffian metaphysics. Mendelssohn had, in his very first work, argued that Leibniz' doctrine of pre-established harmony had originated in Spinoza's theory of the parallelism of modes; but whereas Mendelssohn had seen Spinoza as halfway on the road which led straight from Descartes to Leibniz, Jacobi was saying that Spinozism was as far as demonstrative metaphysics could go.

Mendelssohn fought back in two ways. He gave a metaphysical answer, developing a form of "refined pantheism" that would not have the dangerous consequences both he and Jacobi saw in Spinozism. But he also changed his epistemological theory of the proper method in metaphysics. Evidence in metaphysics, a Wolffian criterion, is itself now to be judged by, or at least supplemented with, the criterion of sound common sense, which the non-Wolffian popular philosophers had used against the vagaries of speculation of all sorts.

In the heat of the controversy with Jacobi, Mendelssohn modified the speculative zeal and confidence expressed in his prize essay. If Jacobi was correct in arguing that all demonstrative philosophy tends toward Spinozism, and if Spinozism could be shown to be atheistic and fatalistic, then that was sufficient to show that speculative thought had gone wrong and stood in need of being "reoriented."

I assign to my speculation the task of correcting the assertions of sound understanding [gesunder Menschenverstand] and, so far as it is able, of converting them into rational knowledge [Vernunfterkenntnis]. So long as they

---

[80] Ibid., p. 312. [81] Ibid., p. 313.

[82] The controversy between Mendelssohn and Jacobi will be discussed more fully later. Here I consider only the effect of the controversy on Mendelssohn's own revision of his theory of knowledge. There is no better evidence of the central importance of this debate than that it must be dealt with in so many places in a history of German thought.

stand in a good agreement with each other, I follow them wherever they lead. But when they part ways, I try to orient myself and lead them back to the point from which we set out. Since superstition, priestly cunning, the spirit of contradiction, and sophistry have turned our head with so much subtlety and so many sleight-of-hand tricks and brought sound human understanding to confusion, we must seek means to help it. Metaphysical subtleties used to mislead us must be held up to the truth, compared with it, investigated and tested. If they do not stand this test, we must try to replace them with more refined concepts. For the true and genuine conviction of natural religion, for the conviction which alone can have any influence on the happiness of man, these artificial methods [of speculative metaphysics] are of no use. The man whose reason is not debauched by sophistry needs only to follow his own good sense [seinem geraden Sinne], and his happiness is unaffected.[83]

The denial of final causes and of the design of the world is an example of such a product of sophistical metaphysics developed without the guidance of the needs of human nature. Such a theory can be seriously meant by "no son of earth who does not eat of ambrosia but, like all other mortals, must eat bread, and sleep, and die." "If a philosopher comes to such a horrible conclusion, it seems to me to be high time that he orient himself and look around with mere human understanding, from which he has wandered too far."[84]

The point at issue between Mendelssohn and Jacobi was this. Jacobi rejected rational speculation because it led to the "monstrous hypothesis" of atheism and fatalism. Rejecting speculative and demonstrative metaphysics, he fell back upon mere belief and revelation. Mendelssohn held that speculation cannot validly lead to this monstrous hypothesis because its task is only to clarify and articulate the convictions of human understanding. If it seems to do so, then no matter how valid the arguments look, there must be an error in the proofs.

This is the point on which Kant entered the conflict. As so often, Kant found himself between two opponents with neither of whom he could agree because he did not accept the hypothesis on which they agreed.[85] Mendelssohn and Jacobi agreed that some metaphysical position could be maintained, and only disagreed as to what that position was and how to find it. But both parties to the controversy felt justified in citing him as an ally. For, Jacobi could ask: Had not Kant, like him, denied knowledge in order to make room for faith? But Mendelssohn could ask: Had not Kant, like

---

[83] An die Freunde Lessings, in Heinrich Scholz, Die Hauptschriften zum Pantheismusstreit (Berlin: Reuther und Reichard, 1916), p. 308; orig. ed., 1786, p. 33. How significant this change is can be seen by comparing this passage with Morgenstunden, Lecture 8, in which Mendelssohn attacked Basedow for the latter's theory of a duty to believe (Glaubenspflicht) what is necessary to our happiness. He argued against allowing the Billigungsvermögen to decide the question of the existence of God, but once the existence of God is established by a pure cognition of reason, then the Billigungsvermögen can decide what God's purposes and perfections are. This is used in Axiom VIII of his own proof, p. 148.

[84] Scholz, p. 314 (orig. ed., p. 67).

[85] See my paper, "Kant's Strategy," Journal of the History of Ideas, 37: 224–236 (1967).

him, talked of the necessary needs of reason that guide us to postulate God, freedom, and immortality.[86]

Kant entered the controversy with his essay, *What is Orientation in Thinking?* (1784). He agreed with Mendelssohn that there are practical needs of reason, but he denied that they have probative value in speculative metaphysics. What is wrong with a speculative system of metaphysics is not that it is found to contain conclusions incompatible with our practical moral needs; what is wrong is, rather, that it does not prove any conclusions at all, but only seems to. While the *Critique of Pure Reason* attempted to pull down the entire structure of speculative metaphysics, of which Mendelssohn was the outstanding living author, the essay on *Orientation in Thinking* charges Mendelssohn with defiling his own metaphysics by allowing extraneous interests to secure in it a comfortable resting place whether this could be theoretically justified or not. Jacobi, however, is wrong not because he adulterated metaphysics with common sense but because he thought that it led rigorously to a fatal end in Spinozism. Hence he rejected rational thought altogether, out of fear of being misled by metaphysics to an unacceptable conclusion. It does, in fact, lead to nowhere at all.

Metaphysics

Mendelssohn's two largest works were in metaphysics. The *Phaedo*, published in 1767, was the book which brought him the greatest fame in his lifetime. It is an adaptation of Plato's dialogue, containing some of the same arguments expressed in the language of the Leibniz-Wolffian philosophy. Socrates, Mendelssohn admits, is made to talk like an "educated Berliner," but among many other reasons for choosing Socrates as his spokesman was the fact that he wanted to avoid the entire question of revelation and hence wished to have a "heathen philosopher" to represent his views. The book is brilliantly written, though not, to be sure, quite as brilliantly as the original. But there is little in it to interest a reader today, and Kant neatly dispatched the central argument for immortality derived from the simplicity of the soul.[87]

The other work, the *Morgenstunden*, was published in 1785. The purpose of these lectures and their publication was twofold: to instruct the young men in natural religion, and to celebrate and defend the memory of his friend Lessing, who had been reported by Jacobi to be a Spinozist. Thus the setting out of his (and he believed Lessing's) attitude to Spinoza occupies an important place in the book.

Mendelssohn complains in his preface that illness has prevented him from keeping up with the advances in philosophy made by "Lambert, Tetens, Platner, and the all-destroying Kant" and confesses that his philo-

---

[86] These expressions, "postulates of practical reason" and "denying knowledge in order to make room for faith," were not used in the controversy, since they had not yet appeared in Kant's writings. But both parties to the controversy saw the relevance of what Kant had said in the *Critique of Pure Reason* (1781) to the issue that divided them.

[87] *Critique of Pure Reason*, 2nd ed. (1787), p. 413ff.

sophical thoughts stopped developing about 1765. Yet he is too modest; the book presents genuinely novel conclusions and supports some older conclusions with new arguments. Much of it will be familiar to us, because so much of it is from the standard repertory of the Leibniz-Wolffian and popular philosophy. We shall consider only the new turn his argument begins to take at the end of his life.

In the fifth lecture Mendelssohn compares the views of the idealists, who hold that our sense perceptions do not represent real and independent objects, and the dualists, who hold that they do represent independent but unperceivable objects. There is no indication of what specific philosophers Mendelssohn has in mind, but he was well-read in British philosophy, and we can well believe that he is discussing Berkeley and Hume on one side and Locke and Reid on the other.

He gives a sympathetic account of idealism, according to which a "consistent dream" is accorded all the epistemological properties of a real world. (We have seen him use this argument before in showing that idealism need not make us skeptical in mathematics.) The controversy between the dualists, who assert *simpliciter* that something exists, and the idealists who assert merely the coherence and steadiness of our experience, is declared to be a purely verbal dispute. "A thing is extended and moves" means "a thing has the characteristic that it must be thought of as extended and moving." "To be A, and to be thought as A, are, in both language and concept, exactly the same."[88] Common sense seems to speak for dualism, but since the two views reduce to exactly the same assertions and since the idealist denies no fact of experience, common sense, or sound human understanding, need not decide between them.

But while Mendelssohn has asserted that there is only a verbal difference between dualism and idealism, he now quite unwarrantably avails himself of the idealistic mode of speech to draw important conclusions which could not be got in the language of dualism. He not only asserts that all true concepts are about realities, which is a tautology perfectly acceptable to the dualist; he asserts also that all realities must be represented in concepts, which would by no means be acceptable to the dualist, though Mendelssohn taunts him for not being able to say what the really real thing is without representing it in a concept. "What no thinking being can represent as possible is in fact not possible, and what cannot be thought by a thinking subject as real is in fact not real." "A thing without a concept has no truth [true being]."[89] Possibility is not a property of things *simpliciter*, but is ascribed to a thing only as it is in thought, which leaves open the thought that it might be different. "A possibility that is not thought is a chimera [Unding]."[90] Everything possible and real must not only be thinkable; it must actually be thought by some being. Since we do not think the entire range of possibilities and actualities, we must posit another being which does so. This is a being of infinite understanding, or God.

But having used the language of idealism for this Berkeley-like conclusion, Mendelssohn still does not think he has committed himself to a

[88] *Morgenstunden*, 2nd ed. (1785), pp. 110–111.
[89] *Ibid.*, pp. 293–294. [90] *Ibid.*, p. 301.

metaphysical idealism. In fact, he seems to think that he has gone at least half the way with Spinoza. The thesis of pantheism does not require that God be an extended substance, as Spinoza held, but it adheres to the formula "All is one, one is all." This formula (which appears again in Jacobi's talks with Lessing) means that the world in its unity constitutes God, and God as unity manifests Himself in the plurality of things. Mendelssohn is willing to assert that God is the only *independent* being and is the cause of all things by thinking them. But he denies that God is the only *intrinsic* being (*Fürsichseyende*), for we have intuitive knowledge of ourselves as substances or active beings. Minds are extra-divine (*aussergöttliche*) substances, and God is a transcendent (*ausserweltliche*) substance. But all other things in nature (if Leibniz is incorrect in thinking that they are themselves minds) are God's thoughts and have no existence outside Him.

This is Mendelssohn's refined (*erläuterter*) pantheism, which he thinks is more tenable than Spinozism both speculatively and on grounds of common human understanding, for this theory does not imply mechanism and fatalism or deny natural religion. Moreover, he thinks that this was Lessing's view and quotes from Lessing's paper on the "Reality of Things outside of God," in which Lessing says he cannot understand what is meant by this expression. Mendelssohn seems to be suggesting—and we shall examine this point in the next chapter—that Jacobi has confused his and Lessing's refined pantheism with Spinozism.

XIV

Lessing

Gotthold Ephraim Lessing was born January 22, 1729, in Kamenz in the Oberlausitz (Saxony), the son of a learned Lutheran pastor. Lessing, unlike many men of letters, was fortunate in his parents, and his respect for his father was undoubtedly responsible for some of the ambivalence and double-talk which characterized his own writings on theological subjects. He attended the University of Leipzig, intending to study theology, but his interest in literature and especially the stage led him to give up this plan, and in 1755 he moved to Berlin, where he became acquainted with Nicolai, Mendelssohn, and other leaders of the Berlin Enlightenment. He was disappointed in his hope of becoming Royal Librarian and failed also to become a member of the Berlin Academy, his nomination being vetoed by Frederick the Great. From 1760 to 1765 he was in Breslau on the staff of General von Tauentzien, and during this time he wrote the *Laocoon*, his most famous aesthetic treatise, and *Minna von Barnhelm*, his most successful play. From 1765 to 1769 he was dramaturgist to the new theater in Hamburg, and during this time he produced some of his dramas and the *Hamburg Dramaturgy*. In 1769 he became librarian of the Ducal Library of Brunswick in Wolfenbüttel, where he remained until his death in 1781. The last period of his life was devoted to religious controversy.

Lessing is important in the history of German culture in four respects. First, he is the founder of modern German drama. While Bodmer and

Breitinger had opposed the imitation of French drama, it was Lessing who finally broke the French dominance by producing a native substitute for French originals and imitations. Unlike the French adaptations of classical themes in almost actionless poetic drama, Lessing's plays are on contemporary themes and his characters are German bourgeoise. Though Lessing was not a dramatist of the very highest rank, his influence on the German stage was revolutionary; if in part he substituted English models for French ones, this in itself was a factor in his success, since the realistic English was apparently more in accord with the developing taste of the times than the classical and formal French.

Second, Lessing was Germany's greatest critic and was the leading writer on aesthetics of his time—writing aesthetics and not merely art history, as Winckelmann did, and writing it in German for the ordinary reader and not in Latin for the Wolffian student, as Baumgarten did. Third, he was the principal disputant in the religious controversies of the third quarter of the century, and the debates over revelation and reason, which we have already discussed in other contexts, culminated in his theological writings. Finally, he *may have* formulated an esoteric philosophy which did not become fully known until after his death, though there are clues to it in many of his published writings. Partly Spinozistic and partly Leibnizian, and hence ambiguous and puzzling in many ways, it exercised a very great influence on the thinkers of the *Sturm und Drang* when the more typical Enlightenment ideas began to fade in the decade after his death.

Before discussing Lessing's creative philosophical work, a major source of difficulty in understanding him must be indicated. Lessing was first and foremost a polemical writer; by profession he was a critic, and a very large part of his work originated in his exercising his critical function on some writer, contemporary or long dead. Irony was his chief weapon, but one hesitates to call him a master of irony because he seems sometimes to have been mastered by it. His flaw was that he was often too clever, with the result that almost no one knew where he stood, and even now the controversy continues between those who think him a complete rationalist and those who see him as taking a major step from the Enlightenment to contemporary existential theology.[1] For his irony sometimes masqueraded as ambivalence, and he disappointed his allies as often as he outraged his enemies. "I make agreement with my obvious enemies," he wrote his brother Karl, "in order to be the better on my guard against my secret adversaries."[2] Friedrich Nicolai, saying that "Lessing could not tolerate anything that was too clear-cut," mentioned Lessing's proclivity for being a minority of one, to the point of speaking in favor of the Saxons in Prussia and of the Prussians in Saxony while he was attached to the Prussian staff. Mendelssohn accused Jacobi of naiveté in his report of conversations with Lessing, since Jacobi apparently did not realize the degree to which Lessing,

[1] Compare Karl Aner, *Die Theologie der Lessingzeit* (Halle: Niemeyer, 1929), and Henry Chadwick, *Lessing's Theological Writings* (Palo Alto, Calif.: Stanford University Press, 1957), with Karl Barth, *Protestant Thought from Rousseau to Ritschl* (New York: Harper, 1959), chap. iii. Quotations from the second of these books are identified by the name Chadwick.

[2] March 20, 1777 (Chadwick, p. 13).

even while seeming to be very positive, might be merely playing with ideas and leading his interlocutor into a trap. Lessing's strategic perfidy included outright deception, as when he not only claimed to be ignorant of the identity of the author of the Wolfenbüttel fragments (Reimarus), but even suggested that they might have been written by Lorenz Schmidt (1702–1748), a deist already well known because of the persecution he had suffered.[3] Lessing wrote most lucid and vigorous German, but often at a crucial point in an argument, or even in a summary of an argument, he practiced a kind of mystification which throws everything he has said into doubt. Lessing was one of the great masters of the art of invective and *argumentum ad hominem*, but his delight in scorning an opponent often kept him from dealing fairly with his ideas, and as his opponents changed, so also did his ideas seem to be transformed too. These considerations are important in warding off the danger of any too dogmatic or one-sided interpretation of Lessing's thought. In his aesthetic writings, he is clear and straightforward; in his theological writings, clear but devious; in his strictly philosophical (metaphysical) writings, obscure and tantalizingly brief.

Aesthetics

In his aesthetic and critical writings, which make up the largest part of his work, Lessing was a great divider, aiming to establish clear lines of division between and within the arts. In the essay on Alexander Pope, already referred to in Chapter XIII, one of his purposes was to distinguish poetry from philosophy and to pour contempt on the Academy for not having done so. He held that Pope did not even profess to be a philosopher, and that he should have been judged only on his poetry, which fell outside the scope of the question which really concerned the validity of Leibniz' optimism. In the *Hamburg Dramaturgy* he tried to state the essence of tragedy, distinguishing it from history and the other forms of poesy as sharply (and along the same lines) as Aristotle had done. And in his best-known work, the *Laocoon*, his purpose was to distinguish the critical criteria for poetry from those for sculpture and painting.

The *Laocoon* was ostensibly addressed to the question: Why does the statue of Laocoon and his sons show the father at most sighing or groaning, and not screaming in agony? J. J. Winckelmann, the historian of classical art, had used the fact that he is not screaming to buttress his argument for the noble Stoic dignity and equanimity of classical man. But Lessing, remembering that Greek and Latin authors had let heroes and gods roar and scream, argued that this fact had not a historical but an aesthetic significance: it was a clue to the difference between the purposes of the painter and the poet.

Because the painter or sculptor (Lessing uses the word "painter" generally to cover both) can, as it were, take only a snapshot of the subject, and purposes to produce a sensuously beautiful form, he must choose a moment and a gesture which will be sensuously beautiful, or he must invent such a gesture if none actually occurred. A screaming man is not beautiful

[3] See below, n. 28.

to look at; ergo. . . . The poet, on the other hand, by the temporal nature of his medium,[4] is able to portray growth and action; he does not have to single out a unique visually pleasing moment for representation. The poet is not interested in describing beautiful visual forms—and Lessing gives some fine examples chosen to show that he fails when he tries to do so—but in awakening our interest in his characters. He can sacrifice a momentary sensuous beauty for the sake of a temporal insight, whereas the external form depicted by the painter is not a significant or effective means to awaken a moral interest. The sculptor and poet, therefore, because of the differences in their media, follow completely different ends. In a sense both painter and poet are imitators; but not in the sense of the wearisome debate (which Lessing recounts) over whether the sculptor of the Laocoon group imitated a poetic description or whether the statue was older than poems describing the death of Laocoon and his sons. Rather there is one imitation of the sensuous surface, another imitation of the fulness of character. One art cannot successfully practice the imitation which is proper to the other.

But while Lessing seemed to be talking about ancient poetry and ancient sculpture, he was also talking about the contemporary French drama and the new German drama he was creating. French classical drama, he thought, had tacitly taken statuary and painting, not Greek drama, as its model. It is therefore static and does not arouse the pity and terror of true tragedy, as Shakespeare and the Greek tragedians did. Its characters are Stoic imitators of the marble Laocoön, who only sighs as he and his two sons are bitten and strangled by the serpent, not imitators of "bawling Hercules or wailing Philoctetes" who were very welcome on the Greek stage. And while Stoicism may be admired, "admiration is only a cold sentiment whose barren wonderment excludes not only every warmer passion but every other clear conception as well."[5] By writing bourgeois tragedy which goes against Aristotle's dictum (repeated by Gottsched) about the rank of personages requisite to tragedy, Lessing moved from the static Stoic perfections of Racine to the lifelikeness of the English stage, and thereby came closer also to the sentiments of his audience.

This conception gave Lessing a much freer hand than his French and German contemporaries had had. Life, movement, and humor were brought to the stage. The characteristic and the ugly, which were impermissible when the playwright was thought of as a kind of painter, prepared the way for the blood and excitement of the *Sturm und Drang*; for just as nature sacrifices sensuous beauty of the individual form for the higher purpose of the perfection of the whole of this best of all possible worlds, so also the poet, now freed from the necessity to represent superficial graces or to convert passion into Alexandrine rhetoric, can show the laughable, the ugly, and the horrible.

[4] That some arts are temporal and others spatial was not, of course, a new idea with Lessing. It was present in Mendelssohn and earlier writers; but none used it as fully as Lessing, who ties it in with another ancient problem of criticism—the merits of the treatment of the same subject in different media of art.

[5] *Laocoon, An Essay on the Limits of Painting and Poetry*, trans. E. A. McCormick (Indianapolis: Bobbs-Merrill, 1962), p. 11.

But while Lessing prepared for the next step in the history of German drama, which would be to throw off all constraint in the anarchy of the misunderstood genius, he himself was disciplined by eighteenth-century scholarship and politesse. His conception of the function of art was still that of his enemy Gottsched: moral betterment.[6] But it is moral betterment not through example and preaching, but through a catharsis of pity and terror. Also, his conception of the working of the artist is that of Bodmer and Breitinger: genius is necessary, and no man is made a poet, and no poem is produced, by rule. "What would one think of a cobbler," he asked, "who told his apprentices that all the knacks of his trade could be deduced from the one fundamental principle: each shoe must fit the foot for which it is made?"[7] But though Lessing saw the necessity of genius for art, he had no developed theory of what this genius consisted in; and, whatever it was, he seems to have had a clear and objective awareness that he did not possess it in the highest degree. After his Hamburg period, he became more exclusively historian, theologian, and philosopher. Only in *Nathan the Wise*, near the end of his life, did he return to poetry and drama as the vehicle of his creativity.

Theological Controversies

As a youth writing to his father, Lessing showed himself to be a well-schooled and precocious Wolffian. But his uncompleted and unpublished *Thoughts on the Moravians*, written about 1750, shows his sympathy with Pietism, which he praises for its undogmatic and practical character. Man, he says, was created for acting, not for speculating, and only the Pietists have properly estimated him. The effect of religious controversy is that fewer Christians are made now than in the Dark Ages, before theological debate took religion far from the heart of the practical man. Luther and Zwingli, bitterly opposed as they were, in fact were disputing about a mere nothing. A reaction against such theologizing was led by Zinsendorf, who rejected metaphysical and theological speculations which had no application to life but were built up into holy truths which had to be accepted on pain of persecution and damnation.

During the next twenty years Lessing devoted himself from time to time to what he called *Rettungen* (apologies) for Christians who had been persecuted by the orthodox churches, whether Catholic, Lutheran, or Calvinist. Again and again he argued that orthodoxy, far from making men Christian, drives some of the most intelligent and worthy of them away from Christianity altogether—his prize example being Adam Neuser, who was harried out of Christianity into becoming a Mohammedan. Some of these papers are worthy of Voltaire in their condemnation of intolerance.

[6] Thus his astonishing attitude to Goethe's *Werther*: he suggested a moralistic "cold epilogue" to prevent anyone's "mistaking the poetic truth for moral truth and believing that a character who engages our sympathy so strongly must have been good" (quoted from C. C. D. Vail, "Lessing's Attitude toward Storm and Stress," *Proceedings of the Modern Language Association*, 65: 805–823, [1950], esp. p. 817).

[7] *Gesammelte Schriften*, ed. Lachmann-Muncker, V, 152. All quotations from Lessing, unless otherwise noted, are taken from this standard edition.

Yet Lessing did not associate himself with the contemporary sentimentalists or the neologists. He attacked Klopstock, Wieland, and Basedow, all of whom, under the influence of Shaftesbury, so far rejected "cold metaphysical thought" that they were unable to distinguish between a genuine religious sentiment and mere enthusiasm.[8] And turning against the moral theology of the neologists and rationalists, Lessing attacked their tendency to identify religion with moral betterment. "Religion," he says," has far higher aims than to form righteous men. Religion presupposes the righteous man, and its goal is to elevate the righteous man to higher insights."[9]

His defense of Leibniz, entitled *Leibniz on Eternal Punishments*, follows a similar line against the neologists, seeming to defend revelation and orthodox doctrine against the rationalistic critique. J. A. Eberhard, in his *New Apology for Socrates*, had attacked Leibniz for hypocrisy in his defense of the dogma of eternal punishment, which was almost universally rejected by Enlightenment philosophers. Lessing, in his reply, advanced two arguments. First, it was in accordance with Leibniz' philosophy, and not as a concession to popular orthodoxy, that he taught that the consequences of any action, good or bad, can never terminate. Therefore man must bear some scar of sin through all eternity and can never be entirely blessed. Not even God can render undone what has been done by a free agent. But though the consequences of sin are eternal, they are not such as to destroy the hope and opportunity for betterment, since punishment is redemptive and not merely punitive. Hence, Lessing asserted, Leibniz' metaphysics was in fact harmonious with the dogma, or with its spirit if not its letter. Yet the dogma, properly understood, was not the inhuman thing which outraged the Enlightenment.

A second line of defense was found in Leibniz' clear distinction between the truths of revelation and the truths of reason. This would have permitted him to hold to doctrine of eternal punishment even if it were not in fact supported by his rational metaphysics; he should not be charged with inconsistency and hypocrisy by those who subjected all orthodox revealed doctrine to the test of human reason. With heavy irony, he wrote: "How could Leibniz have foreseen that there would soon be men who would give all explicable but not yet explained foundations (*Gründe*) a degree of strength and validity of which he had no conception? Unfortunately, because of the prejudices of his youth, he had to hold that to believe in the Christian religion merely from some or many or even all explicable reasons was the same as not to believe it at all; and that the only book which had been or could be written for the correct understanding of the truth of the Bible was the Bible itself."[10]

There seems, then, to be a clear inconsistency in Lessing's attitude. There is, on the one hand, his rejection of orthodoxy for its misinterpretation of man and for its persecution of righteous men. But, on the other side, there is his rejection of both sentimentalism (coming from Pietism) and neology (coming from Wolff) because the former dismisses theological rigor and the latter tries to substitute philosophical rigor for it by denying the dis-

[8] *Gesammelte Schriften*, VIII, 130. [10] *Ibid.*, XII, 98.
[9] *Ibid.*, p. 133.

tinction between valid revelation and reason. Neither Pietistic sentimentalism nor neological rationalism nor Lutheran orthodoxy satisfied Lessing. Yet elements of each remained permanent parts of his thought, and because they are prima facie incompatible with each other, each had to be fundamentally revised and transmuted. Lessing could be opposed to each, but on different grounds from those on which they opposed each other. Let us make specific the points of his opposition to the two principal parties to the dispute, the neologists and the orthodox.

Against the neologists, Lessing objected to their presumption that a rational theology would in fact support the substance of a theology of revelation. It does so only if one or the other theology is treated with a dishonest indulgence. Their theological scheme is not a rigorous rational system but a "patchwork of bunglers and half-philosophers," and under the pretence of making men "rational Christians" they produce only "unreasonable philosophers" (philosophers not really guided by reason, but by sentiment and tradition.)[11] And they are wrong, and can be shown to be wrong, on one point of capital importance: natural religion is not the original religion, which became submerged in a later theology of mysteries devised by a crafty priesthood, but is only a later growth from it. Revealed positive religion does not presuppose natural religion, but contains all the truths of the latter in a simple and obscure form. The return to a primitive Christianity or to a religion as old as the Creation is not to "return" to rational religion, but to go back to a religion of revelation and sentiment, more crude than its modern varieties.

Against the dogmatists, Lessing argued that much of their dogma was not actually revealed but was a later and spurious accretion. The Christian religion must be distinguished from the religion of Christ;[12] the letter of Christianity must be distinguished from its spirit. These distinctions have not been drawn by the orthodox, and those who have drawn them have not been tolerated. Their doctrine of the inerrancy of Scripture makes it impossible for an intelligent man to remain a Christian—at least a Christian by their criteria.

Of the two, it is hard to know which was the more important opponent in Lessing's estimation: both were wrong, and yet the specific way in which each was wrong kept them from coming into fruitful controversy in which the issue might be decided. The orthodox could retreat behind the wall of separation betwen faith and reason, but more often they tried to dictate in the name of faith what was in fact a matter of reason, and thus brought their entire case into disrepute. The neologists could maintain the substance of faith by trying to give rational proofs of some matters of faith, but when they did so their arguments were in fact no proofs at all but rather, indeed, brought the cause of reason itself into disrepute.

There was in neither camp a sufficiently clear-headed and consistent opponent worthy of Lessing's skill as a debater. In a marvelous *tour de force*, therefore, he decided to take *both* sides of the argument in the hope

[11] Letter to Karl Lessing, February 2, 1774 (Chadwick, p. 13).
[12] *The Religion of Christ*, (Chadwick, p. 106).

that his clear statement of the issues would force a true confrontation of the opposing views. In this way, anticipating Kant's strategy, he hoped to bring his enemies into a mutually destructive conflict and thus secure a middle position from which a reasonable hearing for both orthodoxy and free-thinking could be had. But the strategy was obviously a dangerous one, though it may have appealed to Lessing's fabulous polemical courage; it meant fighting a two-front war, with allies in neither camp.

Since the orthodox position had been skillfully stated for two centuries— Lessing seldom or never felt contempt for the great dogmatic creators of Christendom, no matter how much bitter contempt there was in his heart for such epigoni as Pastor Goeze—what was needed was an honest and uncompromising statement of the naturalist-rationalist, or antisupernatural-ist, point of view. He needed a forthright statement of a theological posi-ion which excluded not only most of the traditonal dogmas of Christianity but the very concept of revelation itself. This could be found neither in Baumgarten nor Semler; Bahrdt was beneath his notice. He found what he wanted in the manuscripts given to him by Elise Reimarus, which we have already described. Since many thought that the publication of the Reimarus fragments was itself an act of impiety, Lessing appeared to be arguing with himself in his lengthy comments on the fragments. In fact, the contro-versies which grew out of the publication were by no means as fruitful as the internal controversy between the Reimarus texts and their editor. The public debate soon degenerated into mere theological billingsgate, in which Lessing had no peer, and it was ended only by an order from the Duke of Brunswick to desist from further writing on the fragments.

Lessing conceded to Reimarus that there is in fact no revelation which is available to all men for their rational acceptance. But he denied that such revelation had ever been required by the orthodox position, and there-fore its absence was not an argument against the validity of the revelation claimed by the orthodox position. It suffices for faith to believe that God chose the manner of revelation which would in the shortest time possible make it available to the largest number of men, and that dispensation would be granted to those invincibly ignorant of it. Reimarus' argument does nothing to show that this defense of revelation is invalid.

Furthermore he conceded to Reimarus that it is impossible to deny patent contradictions in the accounts of the resurrection found in the Gospels. But he denied that the factual inaccuracy of the Bible is an argu-ment against its divine inspiration. The Bible is not religion, he proclaims (Lessing invented the word "Bibliolatry" as a term of abuse), and the certainty of Christianity does not depend on the putative infallibility of the Bible. For, granting its infallibility just for the sake of argument, even then the Bible could not support Christian theology, since no eternal truth can be based upon any contingent historical truth. There is no valid inference from "Christ rose from the dead" (even if he did) to "Christ was the Son of God."[13] There is a wide ditch between historical and metaphysical or theological truth, and Lessing confesses he does not know how to cross it.

13 *On the Proof of the Spirit and of Power*, (Chadwick, p. 54).

This, then, is a flank attack on Reimarus and on the orthodox position: it does not matter what the historical facts are, whether Reimarus or the infallibilists are correct, for no theological argument with a historical premise is valid. But the objection weighs equally against the orthodox and against Reimarus, who argued that since the historical record is spurious, its alleged theological meaning is also spurious. In this strategic *coup*, Lessing in fact strikes three sets of opponents with the same blow. As we have seen, it was a common presupposition of the orthodox, the neologists, and the naturalists that the validity of Christian doctrine depended upon the facticity of Christ's incarnation and the authenticity of our records of his revealed teachings. The orthodox asserted both and thought that they thereby saved Christian theology no matter how irrational it might seem; in fact, the more irrational the better, so long as they had authentic records of miracles and prophecy to humble human rationality. The naturalists— Reimarus, for example—denied both, and thought they had thereby destroyed the validity of Christian theology by showing it to rest upon inaccuracy, superstitition, and fraud. The neologists chose just enough of the revelation to support Christian institutions but not enough to offend rational men, thereby producing the "patchwork of bunglers" about which Lessing complained.

Lessing confronted them with a better epistemology than they had. He was simply a better rationalist than they, deriving his epistemology from Leibniz and not, as they did, from Wolff. For Wolff, all knowledge begins as empirical, or, in his words, as historical, and rational knowledge is only a polysyllogism with abstract (and thus putatively rational) premises and a "historical conclusion." But Lessing sees, with Leibniz, that truths of fact cannot be raised to the level of truths of reason. A truly rational theology cannot be based upon a historical record, no matter how accurate that record may be; and if the historical record is false, a genuinely rational theology might still be true. In fact, the rationalist–historiographical debate and its compromise are both misconceived.

While Lessing contends that the problem posed by Reimarus is an embarrassment to the orthodox theologian who has nothing but a historical record and tradition to go on, it is not in the least an embarrassment to the Christian, who does not need the proof of the text but has the "proof of the power and the spirit." "For the Christian, the Christianity he feels to be so true and in which he feels himself so blessed is simply there"—he cannot explain it, he cannot justify it, but it is there as a self-validating conviction and commitment. "When the paralytic is undergoing the beneficent electric shock, what does he care whether Franklin or Nollet or neither is right?" Some religious truths or teachings are self-validating, independent of the historical record. The redemptive power of the practice of Christian love (the religion of Christ) and not the dogmas of the religion of Christianity is the principal "fact proved in itself, not as one which can be either proved or attacked historically, but as one which is certain in itself."[14]

[14] The argument is found in *The Testament of John* and *On the Proof of the Spirit and of Power* (Chadwick, pp. 60, 55). The last quotation is from Barth, *Protestant Thought*, p. 133.

To the orthodox theologian he counsels emphasis upon the mysterious and miraculous element in faith and maintenance of a dividing line between faith and reason; for once the line is obliterated (as it is when the theologian thinks he must defend the inerrancy of Scripture even when it deals with natural, historical events which are in the territory of reason), there is no way to defend the mysteries from rational and historical criticism of the kind Reimarus wrote.

This advice to the orthodox suggests that Lessing thought the dogmatic position not merely beyond reason, as it claimed to be, but overtly unreasonable. It suggests that rational men should try to cross this line and refute dogma instead of trying to cross this line and defend it, as the neologists had done with at least some articles of faith. Or it might mean that the disputes between the rationalists and irrationalists should be permitted to go on until they destroy each other, while each Christian finds within himself a theological truth above and beyond all rational argument. Those who see the first as Lessing's counsel count him the leading rationalist in theology before Kant; those who think the latter was his message see him as the leading eighteenth-century harbinger of existential theology.

Compromise will not work. The neologists have not, he thinks, actually produced a system of rational doctrine that can be accepted by truly reasonable Christians; it is too superficially, too speciously, intellectualistic to replace the solid traditional system of orthodoxy. Lessing does not want to throw the baby of mystery out with the bathwater of historical error.[15] The orthodox, on the other hand, have solidified their position on an irrational plane which can be defended only with ever-increasingly implausible historical hypotheses.

At this impasse, Lessing's most characteristic contribution to religious controversy appears: What is wrong with both systems is that they fail to see the historical dimension of the problem of faith versus reason.

The neologists wished to establish a new orthodoxy, rendering sacrosanct the present stage of their criticism of tradition and their theory of accommodation with respect to earlier stages in religious thought. The orthodox wished to retain an orthodoxy that was already, in the eighteenth century, historically and philosophically indefensible. In method Lessing seems to agree with the neologists' theory of gradual emancipation from revelation and gradual substitution of rational for dogmatic positions. But if this was a common part of their method, their purposes were entirely different. "If [Semler] and I seem to be going along the same path," he wrote, "we certainly do not want to go to the same place."[16] Semler's goal was simply to destroy revealed doctrine so far as it was based only upon revelation, but to maintain those contents of revelation which passed the rational tests of professors in the University of Halle who had read their Wolff. Lessing's aim was to maintain a moving line between the truths of faith and the truths of reason so that faith would not be squeezed in a corner and reason would not be frozen with the dogmas and the rationalities of A.D. 1760.

[15] Lessing's rhetoric is rather more earthy than this English cliché; see his letter to Karl Lessing, February 2, 1774; *Gesammelte Werke* (Berlin: Aufbau Verlag, 1957) IX, 597 (not in Chadwick).

[16] *Gesammelte Schriften*, XVI, 492.

He wanted not only to keep the relationship between them somewhat fluid, but he also wanted to keep open the possibility of entirely new speculative inputs into each. The age was not yet completely enlightened; reason still had jobs to do. Who knows but what something related to present standards of reason, as reason is now related to obsolescent revelation, might not yet be brought forth in the fullness of time? Lessing wants to be able to say of some New Covenant, "It will come! It will assuredly come!—the time of a new eternal gospel, which is promised us in the primers of the New Covenant itself!"[17]

But both neology and orthodoxy were static, absolutistic. Each was the basis of an unchangeable dogmatism. Orthodox dogmatism was the bitter end of the open-minded tolerance of Luther, as Lessing fondly, or desperately, imagined Luther: "The true Lutheran does not wish to be defended by Luther's writing but by Luther's spirit; and Luther's spirit absolutely requires that no man be prevented from advancing in the knowledge of truth according to his own judgment."[18] But on the other side was a danger of a "new papalism of neology."

The unfinished character of theology is the consequence to be drawn from the concept of progress involved in this conception of the moving line of division. This is the outcome also of the famous parable of the rings in *Nathan the Wise*: each man is to practice his own religion (each is to believe that his ring is the genuine one) and pass it on to his descendants for a thousand years, and then some wiser judge will decide which was the true religion (the genuine ring of blessedness) by examining the moral fruits of each.[19] This is also the basis of Lessing's most famous statement, which is often quoted more for its rhetoric than for its deep philosophical meaning: "If God were holding all the truth that exists in his right hand and in his left just the one ever-active urge to find the truth, even if attached to it were the condition that I should always and forever be going astray, and said to me, 'Choose!', I should humbly fall upon his left hand and say, 'Father, give! Pure truth is only for thee alone.' "[20]

The moving line between revelation and reason is the chief theme of Lessing's best-known theological writing, *The Education of the Human Race*.[21] Just as Leibniz' sharp distinction between truths of fact and truths of reason, and his denial of the possibility of a Wolffian transition from the former to the latter, helped Lessing to attack Reimarus, Goeze, and Semler all at once, here another Leibnizian idea is invoked. It is not entirely consistent with the use of the insurmountable dogmatism of the previously used Leibnizian expedient, but it serves Lessing's purpose with equal brilliance. It is the idea of continuity in the development of the monad from a state of indistinct consciousness to a full consciousness of things, as reason, which gives knowledge of causes, brings mere historical and em-

[17] *Education of the Human Race*, §§ 85, 86 (Chadwick).
[18] *Anti-Goeze*, in Chadwick, p. 23.
[19] Act III, scene vii.   [20] *Gesammelte Schriften*, XIII, 24.
[21] How Lessing was brought to this finalistic treatment of history and its bearing upon religious enlightenment is brilliantly treated in E. J. Flajole, S.J., "Lessing's Retrieval of Lost Truths," *Proceedings of the Modern Language Association*, 74: 52–66 (1959).

pirical knowledge into the light of reason. As Kant accuses Leibniz of the error of intellectualizing the senses, Lessing exploits Leibniz by intellectualizing revelation. He does so not by applying (as the neologists did) a fully developed rational standard from who knows what source to a primitive revelation allegedly from God. Rather, he does so, in a quasi-Leibnizian manner, by seeing a continuity between the historical, empirical revelation and the more perfect reason emerging from it in the course of history and maturation. Lessing speculated that man might in the course of time have more than five senses; here, in the *Education of the Human Race*, he is speculating that what was once given only historically, in revelation and during the childhood of mankind, may later (when reason, as it were, has developed as another sense) be understood rationally. Then the historical evidence, even if it be authentic, will no longer be either sufficient or necessary.

Revelation and education give man nothing he could not get from within himself, says Lessing (*Education of the Human Race*, § 4); just as Leibniz could say that sensation could give us no knowledge which we could not, in principle, get from ourselves through the rational development of our thought. Leibniz' theory of preformation provides the vantage point from which Lessing sees "in all positive religions simply the process by which alone the human understanding in every place can develop and must still further develop" (*Education*, Preface). The analogy on which it is based is between revelation and education. "What education is to the individual man, revelation is to the whole human race" (§ 1). Just as education gives the individual nothing he could not have got himself, but gives it more quickly and more easily, revelation gives nothing that human reason could not have got alone, but gives it sooner (§ 5). Just as education must make use of the powers of the child, revelation had to take place in an order determined by the capacities of the people who were to receive it, and hence idolatry and polytheism, not natural religion, were the first stage of revealed religion (§ 7). Revelation, then, is not a monolithic body of doctrine, for later revelation supersedes the earlier (§ 36), but nothing essential is lost in this supersession and correction, only the literal truth of the vehicle of the earlier revelation is given up, as when the truth of the fall of man is preserved even if the forbidden fruit is not believed literally to have been its occasion (§ 48).

The Old Testament is the primer, suitable to a childlike intelligence; but the Jews tried to maintain this primer after the people had outgrown it, and in defense of the literal truth of what was in fact felt and seen not to be the literal truth the Jews developed their subtle and sophisticated and incredible theology. Then a new teacher, Christ, came to give the growing child a new book (§ 53); the child became a youth, and some doctrines he could not have understood as a child, e.g., the immortality of the soul and rewards and punishment after death, were revealed to him (§§ 58–60).

Now, after seventeen centuries, there are new teachers (neologists) who wish to take this second primer from the youth of mankind, but Lessing cautions against destroying this book until "these weaker fellows of yours have caught up with you," and he counsels them that the older primer may contain important truth which will be lost in their newer book (§ 69). Rather than rejecting the mysteries as the neologists threatened to do, Lessing proposes that they consider rational interpretations of them, as, for example, in his rational intepretations of the concepts of the Trinity, original sin, and salvation (§§ 73–75). But Lessing goes even farther than those who had attempted to make rational religion parasitic upon revealed religion by taking the substance of the latter and basing it upon the arguments of the former. Not only does revelation have to submit to reason in the course of man's progress, but reason itself develops under the guidance of revelation, and develops in its adequacy as a tool to go beyond what has been revealed and beyond what is, at this moment, even its own insight. To illustrate this, Lessing introduces his most daring speculation, the doctrine of metempsychosis (§ 93) to replace the doctrine of immortality in the tradition of revealed Christianity.

This speculation was meant seriously, but we do not have to take it seriously to see Lessing's polemical reason for proposing it, and it would serve its polemical purpose just as well if Lessing himself had not really accepted it.[22] For its purpose was to show a possibility the neologists had not thought of when they subjected teachings about heaven and hell to a destructive criticism. Here is a doctrine, Lessing seems to be saying, that answers many of the questions the eighteenth century raised in the field of theodicy. It answers them better than either the orthodox or the neological view, yet it has not been considered by those who wish to claim victory for a narrow and ostensibly antimetaphysical theory to replace Christian metaphysics. The neologists, especially in the doctrine of accommodation as developed by Semler, assumed the Wolffian mind of the eighteenth century to be normative for all times, and tended toward a "papacy of deism"; but Lessing tries to shock the neologists out of their naturalistic and rationalistic complacency in order to keep the various paths of religious development open for a thousand years until some wiser judge will be able to decide which religion is the correct one.

Lessing's Alleged Spinozism: the Jacobi-Mendelssohn Controversy

Spinozism in the early eighteenth century was the "monstrous hypothesis" which Bayle condemned for its antiteleological, fatalistic, atheistic, materialistic view of the world. Its pantheism was only a polite name for atheism, and eighteenth-century Germany was little inclined to be polite to "the degenerate Jew of Amsterdam," especially when his most vociferous spokesmen in Germany, Conrad Dippel (1673–1734) and Johann Christoph Edelmann (1698–1767), combined a notoriously murky presentation of Spinoza's views with an equally disreputable mode of life which shocked all right-thinking people; they seemed to be living examples of the evil consequences of Spinozism. Spinoza's biblical criticism, with its extremely ra-

---

[22] He did accept it and call it "my system" in *Dass mehr als fünf Sinne für den Menschen sein kann* (fragment from the late 1770's).

tionalistic consequences for the evaluation of revelation, offended those who had no understanding of his metaphysics; in fact, the *Ethics*, from which they could have learned the metaphysics, was a rare book, while the *Theological-Political Tractate*, which gave the religious consequences, had a considerable clandestine circulation.

Wolff, in his *Theologia naturalis* (1737), had given[23] what he considered to be a full-scale refutation of Spinozism, and this was a competent examination of the Spinozistic theory. This did not prevent his Pietist opponents, however, from making the same accusations against Wolff that Wolff was making against Spinoza. Such refutations of Wolff through affiliating him with Spinoza were written by Joachim Lange and by Johann Franz Budde.[24] What was common to Spinoza and Wolff, it appeared to their opponents, was the demonstrative, rationalistic method. To those who wished to continue to philosophize in the rationalistic way, or even to think instead of to feel in philosophy, it was important to show that the connection asserted to exist between Wolffianism and monistic pantheism, atheism, fatalism, and free-thinking did not in fact hold. The adherents of the Leibniz-Wolffian school did so not by defending Spinoza, whom they opposed as much as Leibniz and Wolff had opposed him,[25] but by trying to show that Wolffianism was not a halfway house on the road to Spinozism.

At the same time there were efforts to get a fairer hearing for Spinoza himself. One of the best defenses of Spinoza was that in Gottfried Arnold's *Impartial History of the Churches and Heresies* (*Unpartheyische Kirchen- und Ketzer-Historie*) in which Arnold (often regarded as more impartial to the heretics than to the orthodox) gave not only a commendatory account of Spinoza's life but defended him against the charge of atheism and chided Spinoza's Christian critics with acting as if they, not Spinoza, were impious atheists.[26] Mendelssohn himself tried to show that Spinoza was the true inventor of the distinctively Leibnizian theory of pre-established harmony, for which he was rebuked by Lessing.[27] Lorenz Schmidt, one of the trans-

---

[23] *Theologia naturalis*, §§ 671–716.

[24] Johann Georg Walch, the encyclopedist for the Thomasians, devoted a long article to the refutation of Spinoza in his *Philosophisches Lexicon* (2nd ed., Jena, 1733), cols. 2411–2410, and repeats Lange's criticism in col. 1401. For a full account of the accusations that Wolff was a Leibnizian, see Max Wundt, *Die deutsche Schulphilosophie im Zeitalter der Aufklärung* (Tübingen, 1945), pp. 236ff.

[25] Leibniz, (*Philosophical Papers and Letters*, trans. L. E. Loemker, p. 570, says: "I consider [the *Ethics*] dangerous for those who take pains to master it"; see also pp. 297, 300–316. Mendelssohn, in *Philosophische Gespräche*, long before the Jacobi controversy, complained about the guilt by association imputed to the Wolffians (*Gesammelte Schriften*, I, p. 11).

[26] The anonymous editor of the 1741 (Schaffhausen) edition of Arnold's work felt constrained to "tell the truth" about Spinoza and to correct some of Arnold's errors, such as the statement that Spinoza had become a baptized Christian. Among the "truths" the editor tells are: Spinoza voluntarily withdrew from the Jewish community because his income of a thousand guilders was cut off as a consequence of a fight he had upon leaving a comedy (the latter item a Calvinistic morsel picked up no doubt from Bayle's article on Spinoza). Compare Arnold's own account (*Unpartheyische Kirchen*, II, 222) with the editor's *Anhang*, pp. 1152–1153.

[27] *Durch Spinoza ist Leibniz erst auf die Spur der vorhesbestimmten Harmonie gekommen* (1763).

lators of the so-called "Wertheimer Bible,"[28] which went too far toward rationalism and antidogmatism even for other Wolffians, translated Spinoza's *Ethics* as a kind of appendix to his translation into German of Wolff's Latin refutation of Spinoza, and was commonly believed thereby to have accomplished his purpose of spreading a knowledge of Spinoza under the guise of publishing a refutation of him.

These various lines of thought about Spinozism met in the great controversy, the so-called *Pantheismusstreit*, between Mendelssohn and Friedrich Heinrich Jacobi about 1780. It was Jacobi's view that "The Leibniz-Wolffian philosophy is no less fatalistic than the Spinozistic, and leads the persistent inquirer to the foundations of the latter. Every path of demontration issues in fatalism [Spinozism]."[29] That the rationalistic, demonstrative method did lead to some kind of monism and pantheism was conceded by Mendelssohn, but he denied that Spinozism was a correct expression of this conclusion. His own pantheism, according to which space is not a real attribute of God, and the world is created by God's thought—he called "refined [*geläuterter*] pantheism,"[30] and this he believed was acceptable also to Lessing. To show this, he cited Lessing's *The Christianity of Reason*, written in 1752 or 1753 and first published in 1784. He could also have cited *On The Reality of Things Outside of God* (*Über die Wirklichkeit der Dinge ausser Gott*), written in 1762 or 1763.

The latter, as a more metaphysical and less theological work, may properly be considered first. It opens with a sentence that might sound dangerously Spinozistic: "However I define the reality of things outside of God, I must confess that I can form no concept of it." If the reality of things is taken in the Wolffian sense as the "complement of possibility," this complement is present to God in a concept or it is not. If it is, then the whole reality of a thing, and not merely its possibility, is in God; and no one would assert that God lacks a concept of the real. Granted that the *concept* is in God, might it not be of a thing which is not dependent upon God for its existence? But then its reality would be something of which God would have no concept, for in God's concept of a thing must be found everything which is in the reality of the thing itself, including its independence of God. Lessing is here involved in a problem which was to engage Kant later in his refutation of the notion of the "complement of possibility" which must itself be possible, whereupon everything ontologically possible must be ontologically real.[31] Lessing sees the difficulty, but covers it up with an argument that "to exist outside of God" means not to exist necessarily as God exists, while "to exist in God" means to exist as God himself exists,

[28] The Wertheimer Bible followed Reimarus in its naturalistic explanations of miracles and Wolff in its passion for exegetical definitions. The Spinoza translation is *B. de Spinozas Sittenlehre widerlegt von dem berühmten Weltweisen unserer Zeit Herrn Christian Wolff* (Frankfurt and Leipzig, 1744). Schmidt died in Wolfenbüttel in 1749, and Lessing allowed the belief to persist that he was the author of the Fragments.

[29] *Ueber die Lehre des Spinoza in Briefen and Herrn Moses Mendelssohn*, in H. Scholz, *Die Hauptschriften zum Pantheismusstreit* (Berlin: Reuther und Reichard, 1916), pp. 178–179. Hereafter cited as "Scholz."

[30] *Morgenstunden*, 2nd ed. (1785), pp. 233ff.

[31] *Critique of Pure Reason*, A 231 = B 284.

that is, necessarily. Spinoza's language for this distinction is *natura naturata* and *natura naturans*. But Lessing does not mention this, and his argument seems to be un-Spinozistic because it referred only to the attribute of thought. So Lessing then asks:

> If this is all that is meant [by real existence outside of God], why should not the concepts God has of real things be these things themselves? They are adequately distinguished from God, and their reality is no less necessary because they are real in God. Would there not have to be an image in God's mind [*Idee*] corresponding to the contingency they have outside God? This image is only their contingency itself; whatever is contingent outside God will be contingent in God, else God would have no concept of the contingent outside him.[32]

There is in this work, certainly, a monism, but it is unlike Spinoza's. The world is in God, as God's thoughts; God is not in the world or identical with the world, as in true pantheism. The theory Lessing is here espousing is idealistic, in the manner of Malebranche, rather than realistic, in the manner of Spinoza. For this reason it is possible for Lessing to do something impossible for a Spinozist, viz., accept the specifically idealistic Leibnizian formulation of the great chain of being and of the world as a hierarchy or society of spiritual substances. This he had done in *The Christianity of Reason* (1753), which applied these notions specifically to the interpretation of the Christian mysteries. This short essay is even less Spinozistic than the one just cited, and goes beyond even Leibniz' attempt to justify Christian doctrines. God's creation is equivalent to his having a conception of a thing (§ 3), and he can have a conception of "all his perfections at once and of himself as inclusive of them" or of "his perfections individually, one separated from another and each by itself in its own grade" (§ 4). The former is the Son of God (§§ 5–8), and the harmony between this thought and the God thinking it is the Spirit (§ 10). The thought of the perfections severally constitutes, in their totality, the World (§ 14); and each individual perfection has a place in the hierarchy of perfections in the great chain of being and Leibniz' continuum of monads. This hierarchy will eventually be seen (as Leibniz saw it) to extend even into inanimate nature (§ 21) Each simple being reflects the universe; those that are conscious of their perfections and have the power to act in accord with them are moral beings, i.e., beings who can follow a law—a law which is derived from their own nature, and can be none other than: "Act according to your individual perfections" (§§ 25–26). This essay is repeated in its entirety by Mendelssohn, and it is difficult to see why he should have boggled at § 73 of *The Education* except, perhaps, because of its obscurity.

There is obviously little Spinozism here. Yet there were in Lessing's works things that made his friends uncomfortable. There was the same attack on Scripture and orthodoxy and intolerance that one found in Spinoza. More

---

[32] These thoughts presumably grew out of conversations with Mendelssohn and are implicit in § 73 of *The Education of the Human Race*, a "crypto-Spinozistic" thesis which Lessing had not been able to explain to Mendelssohn, according to Jacobi's account of the conversation (in Scholz, p. 69; Mendelssohn's testy reply, *ibid.*, 301ff).

sinister was Lessing's repeated rejection of the freedom of the will—he even thanks his creator that he does not possess freedom by which he could interfere with the plans of the best of all possible worlds.[33] And was he not regarded by his enemies as little better than an atheist? All his talk which seemed to show he held to rational Christianity might very well be a cover for atheism. Did not Lessing himself, in *Ernst und Falk*, speak of the necessary secrecy of the true Freemason who will not say what he knows when it is wiser to remain silent? Had not Lessing been indulgent to the indisputable hypocrisy of Reimarus, whose secret was not discovered until long after his death? There were many ready to believe the worst.

The open accusation that Lessing was not just a crypto-Spinozist but that he frankly acknowledged his Spinozism was made by Friedrich Heinrich Jacobi in his *On the Teaching of Spinoza, in Letters to Mendelssohn, (Über die Lehre des Spinoza in Briefen an Herrn Moses Mendelssohn*, (Breslau, 1785). The events leading up to this publication were complicated.[34] They involved Mendelssohn's hearing of Jacobi's accusation but publicly ignoring it while replying to it by indirection in his *Morgenstunden* (1785); Jacobi's suspecting that Mendelssohn was going to reply to his charge before he made it in public, and thus rushing into print his account of his conversation with Lessing and his correspondence with Mendelssohn; Elise Reimarus' acting as go-between, transmitting information and perhaps misinformation from each man to the other; Hamann's persuading Jacobi to attack Mendelssohn. There were breaches of faith and confidence in Jacobi's handling of his end of the affair; for example, he published (anonymously) a poem of Goethe's (*Prometheus*) which Goethe had not yet published, simply because it was the first subject he and Lessing discussed, and he published Mendelssohn's letters without his permission. There were, naturally, accusations that he had not reported Lessing's conversation accurately. Some claimed that Lessing was a dying man who did not know what he was saying and was led into a trap by Jacobi; others that Lessing was in full possession of his faculties and, playing with ideas as was his wont, had led Jacobi into a trap. The tone of the controversy was not raised when Mendelssohn died early in 1786 and Jacobi was accused of having hastened his death. Much of this is only of antiquarian interest now and of little concern to the historian of the ideas under dispute; suffice it to say that Lessing dead was the subject of a dispute as lively as any he ever participated in while among the living. The dispute amongst scholars is not yet ended.

The evidence Jacobi presented for his statement; "Lessing was a Spinozist," is found in his detailed report of conversations he had with Lessing on July 6 and 7, 1780. It is presumably as accurate as a nonstenographic report of a lengthy conversation can be. It has the ring of memory, not imagination, even in the fact that Jacobi does most of the talking and that

[33] *Gesammelte Schriften*, XII, 298.
[34] A brief account with necessary details is given by Kurt Weinberg, "Pantheism Controversy," in *Encyclopedia of Philosophy*, (New York: Macmillan, 1967), VI, 35–37. A running account of the bickerings, accusations, and counteraccusations bearing upon Mendelssohn's death is to be found in Arnulf Zweig's note on it in his edition of *Kant's Philosophical Correspondence* (Chicago: University of Chicago Press, 1967), pp. 120–121n. A full account with the most important documents is in Scholz.

almost all the long speeches are by him, while Lessing seems unusually quiet and passive most of the time, agreeing with Jacobi more often than leading or disagreeing. It may not be a verbatim report, but it is certainly not made up out of the whole cloth.

Jacobi shows Lessing Goethe's *Prometheus,* a rejection of the doctrine of progress in the form of an apostrophe to Zeus by the suffering Prometheus.

Lessing. I find the poem good . . . The point of view in the poem is my own. The orthodox concepts of divinity are not mine any more. I can't appreciate (*geniessen*) them. 'Σν και Παν! [One and All—the One (God) is the All (the cosmos)—a common expression among the pantheists, found also in Mendelssohn.] I know no other; this is the tenor of the poem, and I confess I like it very much.

Jacobi. Then you would be pretty much in agreement with Spinoza.

Lessing. If I were to name myself after anyone, I know no other.

Jacobi. Spinoza is good enough for me; but what a mixed blessing [*schlechtes Heil*] we find in his name!

Lessing. Yes, perhaps so. And yet, do you know a better?[35]

The next day Lessing came to Jacobi and said he wanted to discuss his expression "One and All" which had seemed to shock Jacobi.

Jacobi. I certainly expected nothing less than to find you a Spinozist or pantheist. And you said it in so matter of fact a way. I came to you to get your help against Spinoza, more than for any other reason.

Lessing. You know Spinoza?

Jacobi. I believe I know him as very few others do.

Lessing. Then there is no help for you. You'll become his friend. There is no other philosophy than that of Spinoza.[36]

Jacobi then explains, at great length, his conception of Spinoza's philosophy, brings all the usual objections to it, and then describes his alternative to it which involves the mortal leap (*salto mortale*) of faith. Lessing says he understands the *salto mortale* very well, but does not have to make it himself. Yet

Lessing. I notice you would like your will to be free, I don't desire a free will. But in general what you say doesn't shock me. It is just a human prejudice that we regard thought as the most important and primary thing and want to derive everything else from it. But everything, including our ideas, depends upon higher principles. Extension, movement, and thought are obviously grounded in a higher power which is far from being exhausted by them. It must be infinitely more perfect than this or that effect, and there can be a kind of joy (*Genuss*) in it which not only transcends all concepts but is wholly inconceivable. That we can think nothing about it doesn't destroy its possibility.

Jacobi. You go even farther than Spinoza. For him, understanding is worth more than anything.

Lessing. For men only! He was far from thinking our miserable human acting for purposes was the best method, and far from making thought supreme.[37]

---

[35] *Ueber die Lehre des Spinoza in Briefen an Herrn Moses Mendelssohn,* (Scholz, p. 77).

[36] *Ibid.,* p. 78.   [37] *Ibid.,* pp. 82–83.

Jacobi himself, of course, believes that thought is speculatively impotent, so he now agrees with what he takes to be Lessing's meaning even if he does not attribute it to Spinoza.

Jacobi. The inquirer's ultimate goal is what cannot be explained: the irresolvable, the immediate, the simple. [When we try to explain everything] we create an illusion in our mind which blinds us and does not enlighten us. We sacrifice what Spinoza called the deep and sublime—knowledge of the highest sort [*scientia intuitiva*]—to knowledge of the lowest kind [opinion or imagination]. We close the eye of the soul with which it sees itself and God, in order to see only with the eyes of the body.

Lessing. Very good! I can use all that, but I don't have to make the same thing out of it [i.e., I don't have to fall back into blind faith]. Your *salto mortale* doesn't seem to me to be too bad. I understand how a man with brains can make this headlong plunge in order to get away from where he stands. Take me with you, if it works.

Jacobi. If you want to stand on a shaky place like mine, it just happens.

Lessing. [No], even then there must be a plunge, for which I don't trust my old legs and heavy head.[38]

The remainder of the dialogue contains little of surprise. There is a suggestion (later modified or withdrawn) that Leibniz too was a Spinozist, a praise of Spinoza's personal character, a favorable expression about personal immortality, and a few jokes (they complain about the rain; Lessing says, "Well, my dear fellow, you know it may be I who am raining.") Then Jacobi closes his report with the statement: "Lessing believed there was no cause of things distinct from the world; or, *Lessing was a Spinozist.*"

In judging this conclusion, several things should be considered. First, Jacobi may have been right; Lessing could have been as great a hypocrite as Reimarus or Lorenz Schmidt. But, second, Mendelssohn is very plausible in his argument that it is unlikely that Lessing would have revealed to a comparative stranger a conviction (at that time daring, if not dangerous) that Mendelssohn had not in thirty years of intimate talk so much as suspected.

Third, we must remember Lessing's spirit of antithesis. May he not have described exactly how he was later to deal with Jacobi when he wrote: "The more convincingly anyone tried to demonstrate to me the truth of Christianity, the more doubtful I became. The more boldly and triumphantly another wished to trample it under foot, the more inclined I felt to maintain it intact, in my heart at least".[39] Against Jacobi's irrational sentimentalism, would not a man with Lessing's love of contradiction and argument, unaware that his words were to be published, be tempted to go to the opposite extreme, especially since (as we have seen) he had already written things which were certainly pantheistic if not explicitly Spinozistic? Mendelssohn wanted to know how serious Lessing was. Was Lessing pulling Jacobi's leg?[40] Next, it must be noted that *Lessing* never said, "I am a Spinozist." He said Spinozism is the only philosophy, but he had little respect for

[38] *Ibid.*, pp. 90–91.
[39] *Bibliolatrie, Gesammelte Schriften,* XVI, 471.
[40] Letter from Elise Reimarus to Jacobi, September 1, 1783 (Scholz, p. 69).

systematic philosophy in the manner of Wolff; he did not say, "If you study Spinoza you will become a Spinozist," but in effect "If you study Spinoza and learn what he really said, you will become his friend and not beat him like a dead dog [his own expression]."[41] He said that *if* he had to "name anyone" he would name Spinoza, but he added that he hoped his Credo was not to be found in any book.[42] Moreover, it was Jacobi, not Lessing, who introduced the name of Spinoza. When Lessing said that he was familiar with the thought in Goethe's poem, he meant Aeschylus, as Hamann pointed out,[43] and it was Jacobi who ignorantly thought he meant Spinoza. Since we know what Lessing thought of "philosophical poetry" from his essay on Pope, it may well be that he had not even thought that he was engaged in a philosophical dispute when he made his favorable remark about the verse. Finally, it should be noted that Lessing really (and not just in Jacobi's judgment) went beyond Spinoza's own rationalism toward a kind of mystical naturalism that is closer to Mendelssohn's "refined pantheism" than to Spinoza's rationalistic monism. And he did not deny it when Jacobi accused him of going "farther than Spinoza."

If it was Jacobi's intention to destroy Spinozism in the various appendices to his book where he argues in detail against Spinoza, this quotation was a tactical mistake. For it was Lessing's "going farther than Spinoza" which gave Spinoza for the first time in Germany a respected place in philosophy. There were as many philosophers ready to "go farther than Spinoza" as there were those ready to give up rationalism because it led to Spinoza. *The paradox is that Spinoza's influence became strongest and most fruitful when rationalism was on the wane in Germany.* The root of this paradox is in Lessing; its fruit we shall see later in Herder.

The controversy between Jacobi and Mendelssohn can be seen as a continuation of the debate which Lessing himself had started by his publication of the Reimarus fragments. The debate against orthodoxy had, of course, been going on in Germany since Thomasius. It had become involved in historical disputes which Lessing saw were irrelevant to the philosophical problem, since no eternal truth could be derived from a historical truth, however well established. But since Lessing believed that a proper interpretation of the historical process could resolve the rationalist–orthodox dispute, he needed a confrontation of a historian who, unlike Semler, rejected the validity of the very idea of revelation, with orthodox thought that saddled itself with an impossible historiographical burden of authenticating revelation. Had Reimarus not existed, Lessing would have had to invent him in order to have a clear-cut statement of an antiorthodox position based on history and rationalism. Lessing tried to resolve the theological issue in his historical theory of revelation as education, and then tried to salve the religious wounds of the controversy with "the proof of the spirit and the power" of "the religion of Christ" and "the Christianity of reason."

Now though the disputants did not see it in this way, we can see Jacobi's philosophy of faith as a proof of the spirit and the power. The debate be-

---

[41] *Über die Lehre des Spinoza*, (Scholz, p. 88).
[42] *Ibid.*, p. 80 and note.   [43] *Ibid.*, p. cxxi.

tween rationalism and orthodoxy which Lessing had led (having largely ignored the sentimental alternative after his subsidiary attacks on Klopstock and Basedow) now gave way, after his death, to a dispute between reason and faith, not reason and dogma. Jacobi thought rationalism could not stop with neology or Mendelssohn's refined pantheism or even Wolff's compromising scholasticism; it had rather to go to the bitter end in Spinozism—and he thought he had Lessing's word to show that this was in fact where it had led. This conviction, together with his rejection of Spinozism, changed the point at issue in a radical way. The debate was no longer among the orthodox, the Wolffians, the neologists, and the naturalists and religious rationalists concerning the degree to which revelation or reason had the prerogative, for on this slippery slope there was no place to stop between Wolff's harmless scholasticism and Spinozistic atheism. The debate was now on the question of the competency of reason in general. The sentimentalists and fideists of Lessing's time were left out of the great debate between Jacobi and Mendelssohn, but they were in the center of the next stage.

If the rehabilitation of Spinoza was the first important consequence of the controversy, a renewal on the highest possible plane of the perennial conflict between faith and knowledge was the second. Kant's *Religion within the Limits of Reason Alone* was his contribution to the debate started by Lessing and Goeze, but his more important "denying knowledge in order to make room for belief"[44] and his condemnation of the philosophy of healthy common sense ("misology reduced to principle")[45] was his solution to the problems disputed by Mendelssohn and Jacobi. His *What Is Orientation in Thinking?* (1786) was his explicit reply to both Mendelssohn and Jacobi.

But what he, Hamann, and Herder said about the issues raised is examined in later chapters.

[44] *Critique of Pure Reason*, Introduction to 2nd ed., p. xxx.
[45] *Ibid.*, A 855 = B 883.

XV

The Counter-Enlightenment

If all prejudice and superstition have been banished, the question arises,
What next? What is the truth enlightenment has diffused in their place? It
has already given expression to its positive contribution in its process of ex-
terminating error; for the alienation of enlightenment [from directly purposive
action, immediacy of insight, and purity of intention] is equally its positive
reality [its treating all questions, things, and even men from the standpoint of
their external utility] . . . Faith, of course, finds this positive outcome of
enlightenment just as much an abomination as the negative attitude of enlightenment to faith is an abomination . . . Faith has a divine right against
enlightenment, and it finds itself utterly wronged by enlightenment, for enlightenment distorts all its moments, and makes them something quite different from
what they are in and for faith itself. Enlightenment [on the other hand] has
merely a human right against faith and can put in only a human claim for its
own truth . . . The wrong it commits is the right of disunion and discord; it
consists in perverting and altering, in opposition to the simple ultimate essence
or thought.[1]

This is Hegel's inimitably lucid description, written in 1806, of what went
on in Germany about thirty years earlier. But though the language may be
unfamiliar, the situation he is describing is one with which we are by now

---

[1] *The Phenomenology of Mind*, trans. J. B. Baillie, 2nd ed. (London: Allen & Unwin;
New York: Macmillan, 1931), pp. 576, 580, 581 (translation modified).

thoroughly familiar: an intellectual, self-alienating mode of thought calls forth an antithesis in the immediacy and internality of feeling which puts itself forward as direct insight into a world not alien to man's inward being but invisible to his clarified and disciplined intellectuality. Remember the historically portentous reactions against dominant intellectualisms: in the fourteenth century, the Rhineland mystics; in the fifteenth, the *docta ignorantia*; in the sixteenth, the Protestant Reformation; in the sixteenth and seventeenth, the radical reformers against Protestant orthodoxy; in the seventeenth and eighteenth, the Pietists. And at the height of the German Enlightenment there was a reaction which I shall call the "Counter-Enlightenment." The philosophical criticism of the dominant intellectual position held by the Leibniz-Wolffian and the academic *philosophes* was but a phase of a much broader dissatisfaction with the views they held: a deistic natural religion with its own orthodoxy and political protection, a moralistic view of art (which survived, in moderate form, even in Lessing), a passive acceptance of benevolent despotism, and a eudaemonistic or utilitarian optimism about the middle classes who were making their way up a Wolffian ladder of perfection. While Lessing saw the superficiality of each of these, he did not overturn the system which held them together; he manifested the Enlightenment syndrome by his bitter controversies with theologians unwilling to make any concessions to Enlightenment. But when, upon his death, his crypto-Spinozism was discovered, his position was seen to be more equivocal than had been suspected, and he ended in the unusual position of being the hero of both the Enlightenment and the Counter-Enlightenment.

The philosophical criticism of the dominant intellectual positions came only when other forces, outside philosophy, had heightened the tensions so that they could no longer be ignored and had to be dealt with epistemologically and metaphysically. These forces were a revivification of genuine Pietism, a new sentimentalism, the development of patriotism, and a vitalistic interpretation of nature.

Pietism in the early part of the eighteenth century is an excellent example of the tendency of dissident minorities who oppose an orthodox system to develop a repressive orthodoxy of their own. But toward the middle of the century, Pietism came to life again, to the kind of life it had had before it had become secure and respectable. The reviver was Count von Zinsendorf (1700–1760), who, through simple godliness and charity and the emotional power of communal music, made his followers, the Moravians (*Herrnhütte*), very different from the litigious and self-righteous critics of Wolff in the universities.

At about the same time there was also, as we have seen, a secular counterpart to this religious introversion. This was the literary movement known as sentimentalism, which grew out of the revolt against Gottsched. The rediscovery of nature as a tutelary deity in the poetic works of Albrecht von Haller (1708–1777); a novelistic exploration of Pietistic self-scrutiny and sentiment in the writings of Christian Fürchtegott Gellert (1715–1769), a pupil of Crusius and his successor in Leipzig; and, most important of all, the powerful lyric genius of Klopstock, were manifestations of a dissatisfaction with the belles-lettres associated with both rigid Pietism and Wolffian moralism. This new literary warmth was brought to Germany by the newer literary models found in France and England. The imitation of French models had earlier produced the artificialities of a culture striving for urbanity; but now Rousseau brought a cult of simplicity and naturalness into Germany. Almost equally important was the emulation of Shaftesbury and his aesthetic moralism and theory of genius, so alien to the mechanical and syllogistic morality of the Wolffian theory of perfection correlated with happiness. There was the massive (but by Gottschedian standards, formless) genius of Shakespeare, Milton, and later Ossian(!); the somber brooding of Edward Young and Thomas Gray; the tearful self-examination of *Clarissa*—every one of these imports showed Germans how much they had been leaving out of their lives and letters. Letter-writing and diary-keeping, secularized forms of Pietistic care and nurture of the soul, became major avocations; Clarissas were found in every village, waiting for Werthers. These literary imports did not fit into neat theories, nor did the new forms of life fit German conventional bourgeois morals. They brought an infection which showed in the high fever and crisis of the Storm and Stress (*Sturm und Drang*) in the 'seventies.

There was also the development of one of the most characteristic emotional attitudes of modern history: patriotism and nationalism. If we remember that Germany at this period did not exist as a political entity and that the rivalry of one German state with another was often stronger than that with another country, we can understand the long slow death of the Holy Roman Empire even during the time when no sensible man could be enthusiastic about any of the three-hundred-odd states whose area and significance varied inversely with the number of hyphens in their names. But two lines of thought and feeling, though opposed to each other, opposed also this confusion of political trifles.

The first came from Prussia. A love of fatherland among the Prussians, and a desire among non-Prussians to have a fatherland, grew in many breasts, which swelled with pride at Frederick the Great's military victories, charismatic personality, and efficient domestic government. Side by side with this nationalistic ardor was an opposition to Frederick's rationalistic and bureaucratic state and a nostalgic longing for a more organic form of political life, in communities which would have a natural style and would need no written constitutions because they were united by the traditions and historical feelings of their members. The leading spokesman for this conservatism, somewhat like Burke's in England, was Justus Möser (1720–1794) whose *Osnabrückische Geschichte* celebrated the "noble simplicity" of life in a small German state and argued against "enlightened" meddling in the organic and healthy workings of the old order. For both the Möserian feudalists and the Frederician bureaucrats and mercantilists there was now something emotional and personal to take the place of aping the French in the name of a bloodless cosmopolitanism. The opponents of Frederick favored things German to a degree which he never did understand or favor them, and opposed despotism from either the conservative point of view represented by Möser or the more liberal, constitutional point of view held by Johann Jakob Moser (1701–1785), called the father of German constitutional law, by Friedrich Karl von Moser, whose *Master and Servant* (*Herr und Diener*, 1759) was a mirror for princes, and by the Göttingen professor and journalist August Ludwig Schlözer (1735–1809), known as "the scourge of princes." The followers of Frederick—many of them not Prussians—had before their eyes a state about which they could be enthusiastic not merely for its rational organization but, even more, for its *gloire*. This is unmistakable in, for instance, the early chapters of Goethe's autobiography.

Of considerably less importance to the general public, but of perhaps more significance in the history of philosophy, was a revival of an older conception of nature. The Newtonian world picture had not been as readily accepted in Germany as in France, because the Germans had Leibniz, and the alchemistical traditions from the earlier period of natural philosophy continued to hold their own against the mathematical and mechanical conception of matter. For a time, as we have seen, the Academy was successful in furthering Newtonian views, and in the work of Lambert, Euler, and the French academicians, such as Lagrange and D'Alembert, there was spread abroad a mathematical conception of nature which seemed to many to be alien to life, supporting, at the very most, the earlier efforts at systems of physico-theology which saw evidence of God's work for man in everything from stars to conch-shells. Goethe, in his autobiography, speaks of the deadening effect of such mechanistic conceptions upon the enthusiasm of those who, like him, needed to feel at home in nature. When, therefore, the work in physiology by Albrecht von Haller, professor of medicine in Göttingen, became known, there was a conception of nature that made a "return to nature" possible and desirable—a return to a nature which was not a mechanical projection of a bureaucratic society in which everything had to be weighed and measured and each thing had its geometry, but to a nature which was imbued with life and productive of warmer beauties than those of mathematical form. The enthusiasm for Newtonian nature led to deism; the enthusiasm for Hallerian nature led to romantic identifications with nature which were almost pantheistic, with both God and man immanent in the living processes of nature.

Within the established philosophy itself, however, there was little place for any of these sentiments and enthusiasms. Philosophers, even when dealing with the exciting new subjects of the feelings of the artist and the natural man, did so from an at best urbane, and at worst a pedantic, point of view, using concepts borrowed from, or at least fitting into, a ready-made Wolffian system. Philosophy still tried to wear the "Spanish boots" of Jesuitical precision which Goethe satirized in the scene in *Faust* where Mephistopheles instructs the freshman.

But even in philosophy things were changing. We can point to two important events which brought many of these pervasive cultural trends and dissatisfactions to the point where philosophers had to deal with them epistemologically and metaphysically. I refer to the "rediscovery" of Leibniz and the effort to come to terms with Hume.

In 1765 occurred one of the most important events leading to the demise of the Leibniz-Wolffian philosophy, both in its rigorous encyclopedic form and in the diluted form articulated by most of the popular philosophers. Paradoxically, the blow against the hyphenated philosophical system came from Leibniz himself. The previously unknown *Nouveaux essais sur l'entendement humaine* was published. It must be remembered that Leibniz was best known on the basis of several of his published works, the *Correspondence with Samuel Clarke*, the *Monadology*, the *Principles of Nature and Grace*, and, most important of all in terms of ready acceptability, the *Theodicy*. A great body of his work remained available only to scholars in the Latin writings of the *Acta eruditorum*, but the largest part of it was wholly unknown. The parts of Leibniz' philosophy which were known to everyone were those present in the *Theodicy*, which readily fitted into the Wolffian system; but Wolff had not been able to make sense of the pre-established harmony, and had missed some of the main points in the theory of monads by talking of interacting physical monads or corpuscles and thus adopting a mechanical picture of the universe. While the Leibnizian theory of space and time had been accepted widely before the Academy began criticizing it, Leibniz, the dominating intellectual figure of the early part of the century, was known as one member of the Leibniz-Wolffian team. That Wolff knew that he was not representing Leibniz and that both he and Leibniz had resented the term "Leibniz-Wolffian philosophy" did not prevent Leibniz from being seen as a bourgeois rationalistic enlightener ready to compromise with orthodoxy and this or that royal highness.

The *New Essays* do not present to *us* a Leibniz of many surprises. We can see things in his other published works, available before 1765, that most writers before 1765 did not see because they were blinded by the Leibniz-Wolffian label. They ought not to have been surprised, but they were. They now found in Leibniz a sympathetic critic of empiricism, which was far more important to them than Leibniz the scholastic author of attacks on Bayle and Spinoza and the butt of Voltaire's jokes in *Candide*. But after 1765 the Wolffian excrescences were removed, and Leibniz (and, eventually through him, Spinoza) came to be more sympathetically understood; as one partner (Wolff) fell, the other (Leibniz) rose.

Another important philosopher with whom one had come to terms was David Hume. Hume, the critic of religion and the writer known for his moral theory, provided little which could not be found, and which was not actually found, in other English freethinkers and deists. Hume's epistemological writings, however, were naturally an embarrassment to any system of philosophy which did not have an answer to them. Mendelssohn had tried to answer Hume's skepticism about the causal connection by an argument concerning probabilities, but he had begged Hume's question. This early endeavor was forgotten, and for some years little effort was made to "answer" Hume. But from 1760 to about 1785 we can discern four ways in German philosophy of trying to meet Hume.

First, and least important, was the acceptance of Hume's skepticism by some of the popular philosophers in the universities, most notably J. G.

Feder (1740–1821) of Göttingen who, in his *Ueber Raum und Caussalität* [sic] *zur Prüfung der kantischen Philosophie* (1787), attempted to extend Hume's doubts[2] into the field of mathematics. Second, there were those serious epistemologists who tried, unsuccessfully, to answer Hume; Johann Nicolaus Tetens was the most important of these. Third, and best known, was the awakening of Kant from his dogmatic slumber. Kant, by generalizing Hume's problem, forced a fundamental reexamination of the entire speculative enterprise as carried out in the Leibniz-Wolffian philosophy. The fourth was paradoxical and hardly to be expected. *Hume was seen as a defender of the rights of faith against reason.* He and the Scottish philosopher Thomas Reid were interpreted as teaching the same thing, viz., that reason, or the intellectual powers generally, do not suffice to give us knowledge in the ordinary affairs of life and certainly not in religious, moral, and metaphysical questions. Several statements of Hume—that "our most holy religion is based on faith," that whoever dares to accept a miracle "becomes aware of a miracle in himself," and the like—which Hume no doubt meant ironically, were taken in dead earnest, even when it was incidentally remarked that Hume did not carry out their implications. On the authority of Hume, the hypertrophy of intellect in the Enlightenment's efforts to replace faith with reason, feeling with clear and distinct ideas, and the promptings of the heart with the search for sufficient reasons, was condemned, and the efforts declared a failure.

This was the lesson brought back to Germany on Hamann's return from his visit to London. It was readily accepted by those who are called *Glaubensphilosophen* or *Gefühlsphilosophen*, philosophers of faith and feeling.

An anti-intellectual philosophy which holds that, in some way, an unexamined belief is a priori more credible, and more creditable to the man who holds it, than an argument or proof may well disqualify a man from being called a philosopher, except in a pejorative sense. Only the most generous use of the name would cover Johann Caspar Lavater (1741–1801) or the Swedenborgian spiritualists, against whom Kant wrote the *Dreams of a Spirit-Seer* as a satire on metaphysics in general. Lavater founded the "science" of physiognomy, which was very fitting at a time when the abstract psychology of the Wolffian school was unfruitful for the greatly increased desire to understand the rich individuality of personalities, and for the desire to see man not simply as a reasonable being over against a Wolffian mechanical world but as an organic mirror of nature transcending nature by perfecting it. But Lavater was an enthusiast (*Schwärmer*) who believed, literally, that faith could move mountains, who spent time and money collecting authenticated accounts of miracles and psychic experiences, who believed in Mesmer and Cagliostro, and who wandered over Germany looking for St. John, who he believed was still alive.

I do not propose to follow some historians of philosophy and devote space to Lavater. But such laughable examples of *Schwärmerei* should not condemn, out of hand, the philosophy of faith and feeling. Each of the

---

[2] Kant, ignorant of Hume's *Treatise*, attacks Feder and exculpates Hume on this point, in *Critique of Practical Reason*, end of the Preface.

philosophers we shall deal with began with an exaggerated claim for feeling and faith against reason and Enlightenment. But in the course of argument, each of them modified his claim that there was an unbridgeable chasm between the two faculties. To be sure, the reason which emerged from this dialectic was no longer the faculty of clear and distinct ideas, systematically arranged. It became a reason not really contrasted to genuine sense and feeling, but had sense and feeling incorporated in it. Reason came to be opposed not to faith, but to understanding (*Verstand*), a purely analytical or inductive faculty which moves away from the riches of sense and feeling to become merely a useful instrument for those who must bake bread or calculate eclipses.

The opponents of the philosophy of faith and feeling, therefore, were accused of using the wrong tools for art, philosophy, religion, personal morality, and politics. They tried to make these warm human concerns take the form of mathematics or natural science; "While we are aiming at clear ideas," Hamann wrote, "the food gets cold and tasteless." The philosophers of faith and feeling wanted divided man to renounce the division of his faculties and the competition between reason and faith, for what was important was, and required, the whole man, all at once. Even understanding was not a separate faculty, but the misuse of the one creative and spontaneous power.

We shall deal with two philosophers of faith and feeling. We shall not take them in their chronological order, but consider first Friedrich Heinrich Jacobi, who opposed the intellectualism of the Enlightenment by an appeal to an orthodox theism based upon simple and immediate faith and feeling. After a brief look at Thomas Wizenmann (1759–1787), we shall consider Johann Georg Hamann (1730–1788), the most puzzling and mysterious of the Counter-Enlighteners; though he was older than Jacobi, he represents a more advanced stage of the revolt than Jacobi did. We shall not consider Herder as representing a third stage of this revolt; rather, he will be shown to move in a different direction from those taken by Jacobi and Hamann. Yet all three of them started out as Pietists, and all of them opposed "the Berlin system" of the Academy, popular philosophy, the Leibniz-Wolffian system of the universities, and Kant's critical philosophy.

Jacobi's orthodoxy disqualified him from exercising any significant influence in the next period of German thought. His quarrel with Schelling in the early nineteenth century was as notorious as his quarrel with Mendelssohn a generation earlier. But Hamann, through his personality and his mystifications, appealed to the Romantics, and the influence of Herder cannot be overestimated. Both Hamann and Herder criticized in the Enlightenment and in its greatest representative, Kant, precisely those features which the Romantics and the speculative idealists after Fichte found most blameworthy.

Eighteenth-century thought was fed into the nineteenth century through two channels: Kant and Herder. Its idealism sprang from going beyond Kant, in directions pointed out (but warned against) by him. Its naturalism, historicism, nationalism, monism, and near mysticism—in a word, its irrationalisms—were developments from Herder's ideas. If the Romantic philosophers can say, with Faust, that two souls dwell in their breast, we know how to label each: one was Kantian, the other was Herderian.

Jacobi

Friedrich Heinrich Jacobi was born in Düsseldorf in 1743, the son of a rich merchant. As a child he was deeply influenced by the Pietistic movement as revivified by von Zinsendorf, and was much given to intuitive and even mystical religious experiences. From the age of sixteen to twenty he studied in Geneva, where he was taught by Le Sage and Charles Bonnet, whose naturalistic empiricism made his commitment to an emotionalistic, unscientific concern with human experience even more pronounced and combative. In 1764 he founded, with Christoff Martin Wieland, the literary magazine *Der Merkur* and published in it (1774 and 1779) his two literary works. The first was in the form of a collection of letters, *Allwills Brief-sammlung*, which gives us a good picture of his ethical, anti-intellectualist views at this time; the second was a novel, *Woldemar*, about pure-minded ethereal people whose moral duties consisted in a sentimental care of their own beautiful souls—"everything attitude and nothing achievement" (Santayana).

In 1780 Jacobi met Lessing. We have seen some of the consequences of this meeting. In 1785 Jacobi published his *Über die Lehre Spinozas in Briefen an Herrn Moses Mendelssohn*. The storm of controversy which this occasioned—he was even accused of being a Jesuit, since he attacked rational religion which was the best defense of Protestantism!—occasioned his dialogue, *David Hume über den Glauben* (1787) with an epilogue against Kant, *Über den transcendentalen Idealismus*, and a new and much enlarged edition of his Spinoza book in 1789.

The remainder of Jacobi's life and his later work, with one exception, do not concern us here; they belong to the history of later German philosophy. But his relations to Fichte and Schelling must be mentioned. Fichte's *Vocation of Man* (1800) shows the extent to which Fichte followed out Jacobi's effort to "transcend" Kant; and Jacobi's attack on Schelling (*Über den göttlichen Dingen und ihrer Offenbarung*, 1811) is just what one would expect—an attack on Schelling's pantheism and "hypocrisy" in using Christian language to describe his conception of God. In 1807 Jacobi went to Munich where he became President of the Academy of Sciences. He resigned in 1812 and devoted the remainder of his life to preparing an annotated edition of his works, which was still incomplete at his death in 1819. From the last period of his life we must cite his introduction to the volumes devoted to his philosophical writings, since it throws light on his views in the 1780's.

Jacobi was not a systematic thinker; he did not try to form or to represent a school of philosophy. He was rightly modest about his abilities in abstract thinking, and though they did not suffice for the production of a single well-organized work which would present his views as a whole, he was a sharp critic of the views of others. He attacked the philosophy of the Enlightenment, represented by Mendelssohn, at a time when it was ripe and ready for full-scale attack. He saw the weakness in Kant's theory of the thing in itself, that was to be the point of attack by almost all of the idealists. But there was a strange irony in Jacobi's life; he attacked Spinoza, but attracted so much attention to him that Spinoza became a dominant intellectual force; and he attacked Kant for his theory of the thing in itself and opened the way for the post-Kantian development of idealism, to which he was even more opposed than he was to the equivocal realism in Kant himself. Jacobi's true heirs in the nineteenth century were Fichte, Fries, and Schleiermacher, who developed the voluntaristic, psychological, and emotionalistic criticisms of Kant initiated by him.

We have seen the controversy between Mendelssohn and Jacobi which was the historical occasion for Jacobi's first philosophical writings. The letters, replies, rejoinders, and surrejoinders make for a confusing picture of Jacobi's thought. The polemical necessities led him to take extreme and not always consistent positions. Mendelssohn's death at the height of the controversy did not encourage his friends to deal gently with Jacobi, nor was he coolly reasonable in his attacks.[3] But by concentrating our attention on the later phases of the controversy, especially as Jacobi recalled them twenty-five years later,[4] we can get a balanced view of the theory he was defending.

In his conversation with Lessing, Jacobi had said:

In my judgment, the greatest accomplishment of a philosophy is to uncover (*enthüllen*) existence, to reveal. Explanation is a means, a way to the goal, the first purpose, not the final one. The final purpose of philosophy is that which cannot be explained: the irresolvable, the immediate, the simple.[5]

Demonstrative philosophy, which seeks to replace belief with well-founded rational knowledge, leads inevitably to atheism and fatalism, as presented by Spinoza. "But all proof presupposes something already shown (*Erwiesenes*), whose first principle (origin) is revelation . . . The elemental factor in all human knowledge is belief."[6]

Hence to avoid Spinozism, which is a product of reason, and to save his Pietistic faith, Jacobi took a *salto mortale*, made a breakthrough (*Durchbruch*) from word and concept to the existence which directly reveals itself to us in faith. He began with the "learned ignorance" that is the same as firm faith.[7] He turned his back upon a philosophy which would make a complete skepticism necessary, since he could not believe what reason in philosophy would show to be true, viz., a Spinozistic atheism.[8]

It was disingenuous of Jacobi, six years later, to seem offended that he should have been accused of "teaching a blind faith and deprecating reason."[9] To reply to such charges, he wrote his dialogue, *David Hume*

---

[3] Let it be said in Jacobi's favor that he never stooped to the anti-Semitic abuse which is found in Hamann's contributions to the controversy. See Hamann's letters in Jacobi's *Werke* (Leipzig: 1812–1825), vol. IV, pt. ii, pp. 173, 184ff.

[4] *Vorrede* [to *David Hume über den Glauben*] zugleich *Einleitung in des Verfassers sämmtliche philosophische Schriften*, *Werke*, II, 3–116. Hereafter referred to as *Vorrede*.

[5] *Über die Lehre Spinozas in Briefen an Herrn Moses Mendelssohn*, in Heinrich Scholz, *Die Hauptschriften zum Patheismusstreit* (Berlin: Reuther and Reichard, 1916), p. 90. Hereafter referred to as Scholz.

[6] *Ibid.*, pp. 173, 178, 180.

[7] *Werke*, II, 20.

[8] Scholz, p. 80.

[9] *Werke*, II, 137.

Concerning Belief. In it, he appealed to Hume and Thomas Reid to justify his doctrine of the impotence of reason even in the simplest problem of knowledge, namely the perception of a physical object. Hume substituted belief for knowledge, and Reid used the word "belief" to refer to something in our knowledge that tells us there are independent objects and causal connections between them, when all that analytical reason would show was impressions and ideas that had no visible connection with each other or with objects. This was not, of course, the issue in the debate with Mendelssohn; but if he could show that belief—miraculous, because inexplicable and indefensible by reason, and revelational, because Reid and Hume said that perception "reveals" objects[10]—is essential to the very simplest knowledge, then it would be easy to show that the appeal to belief does not mean an appeal to some blind force opposed to reason.

Understanding is the faculty of analyzing and synthesizing and proving truths about the data of the senses. Its rules are based upon concepts which are derived from our immediate experiences of contact with objects and their impenetrability. These concepts apply as much to the objects as to ourselves, and Jacobi believes that this derivation of them from direct physical experience constitutes a "deduction" of these concepts which serve the same function that Kant's categories do, except that they apply to real things and not to mere phenomena.[11]

In the earlier part of the controversy with Mendelssohn,[12] he had used the word reason (*Vernunft*) to mean the faculty of concepts, judgments, and inferences, which he later called understanding (*Verstand*); and when he did so, he called the faculty of belief (*Glaubenskraft*) a faculty superior to reason. That was why, he says, he was accused of irrationalism. But, he says, the "nominal rationalists" subordinated reason to the faculty of mediate knowledge, understanding, and therefore they accused the "real rationalists," like Jacobi, of being "philosophers of feeling." Rejecting that, he now claims that by the faculty of belief he meant *reason itself*, as the highest, most immediately certain and most intuitive faculty of knowledge.

The truth of the matter is that Jacobi probably did not know what he meant. When Herder, who was opposed to any division among the various faculties of the mind, objected to Jacobi's sometimes drawing an opposition between faith and reason, as if they could never agree, and sometimes letting faith ratify the conclusions of reason, Jacobi replied only that by "belief" he meant any "groundless assent."[13] Then, of course, he could not institute any controls that would stand in the way of Lavater's foolishness.

Kant showed that reason, considered as a mere extension of understanding trying to conceive the unconditional, cannot give us any knowledge at all. Since sensibility and understanding, which Kant thought were the faculties of knowledge, give us knowledge only of appearances or phenomena which are not basically real and ontologically irreducible, these faculties cannot enable us, in Jacobi's opinion, to have any knowledge at all. Thus there appears a new alternative to Spinozistic fatalism which is just

10 *Ibid.*, 147–168.
11 *Ibid.*, II, 199–225.

12 *Vorrede*, in *Werke*, II, 9ff.
13 Scholz, p. 169.

as bad: Jacobi says that rational philosophy must lead either to Spinozism or to "Kantian nihilism."[14]

Kant saved himself from "nihilism" by two expedients. The first was his assumption that there is a thing in itself. But this theory is untenable, Jacobi declared; it is the old dualism between our experience and objects which can be bridged only by belief, but Kant cannot avail himself of this because he has denied that the categories apply beyond the phenomena. Thus, Jacobi concluded, there is a fundamental inconsistency in Kant's theory: "Without the assumption [of the thing in itself] I cannot enter the [Kantian] system, and with it I cannot remain."[15] The other Kantian expedient was to limit knowledge in order to make room for faith; Kant's greatest service to philosophy was to "save an empty place (empty for knowledge)" within which faith could be secure.[16] But because faith is not knowledge, for Kant, his entire theory is one of "absolute subjectivism" which accords well with "philosophical reason" but not with "natural belief."[17] Kant calls it a scandal that philosophers should not be able to solve the problem of whether there is an external world or not; but Jacobi says it is equally scandalous that Kant cannot show, simply by the appeal to reason, that there are objects for his transcendent Ideas.[18] He cannot do so because he has too narrow a conception of reason; it is like Jacobi's conception of understanding.

To Jacobi, Kant's fundamental error was that, in spite of denying that reason is extension of understanding, he must ultimately admit that there is only one faculty of knowledge—sensible intuition upon which understanding works its synthesis and interpretation. There are, rather, for Jacobi, two faculties: first sensibility, together with understanding, which gives knowledge of the physical world when supplemented by belief, and second, intellectual intuition. Intellectual intuition, properly understood, is more like our senses in revealing realities to us, than it is like understanding, which only analyzes and demonstrates. The reality revealed by reason is not sensible, but supersensible: the Ideas of God, providence, freedom, virtue, and immortality.

Jacobi feels justified in calling reason belief, because it is as immediate and as intuitive as sense perception, and sense perception is based upon a natural belief. Like sense perception, reason supports demonstrations, but is not itself demonstrable.[19] And he calls it feeling, because it is, like all feelings, an expression of life as a whole which cannot be grasped in distinct concepts but is given to us as an organic whole, massively present to our consciousness of ourselves as free and spontaneous substances. Like sensuous feeling, it cannot be analyzed; like belief, it cannot be demonstrated.

Feeling, therefore, which had become a faculty of the mind only in the 1760's, now, in the eighties, becomes the highest faculty of the mind,[20]

---

[14] Vorrede, in Werke, II, 19. Jacobi also accused Kant of Spinozism.

[15] Beylage zu David Hume über den Glauben: Über den transscendentalen Idealismus (1786), Werke, II, 304.

[16] Vorrede, in Werke, II, 33.

[17] Ibid., pp. 36–37.

[18] Ibid., pp. 38, 42.

[19] Ibid., p. 111.

[20] Ibid., p. 61.

superior to genuine knowledge in the ordinary sense (*eigentliches Wissen*) that we get through sense and understanding. It reveals to us an absolute in contrast to the relative, conditional existence of objects of the senses.

But here, where it would be most desirable to have precision and care, Jacobi was most equivocal. There is a fundamental ambiguity he never saw, or, if he saw it, never resolved. Is the faculty of belief identical with reason? Or is it related to reason as it is to sense, a factor which, as it were, ratifies the deliverances of reason and gives them substance and effectiveness in our conduct and world-view? Or is it an anti-rational faculty, traducing reason?

Wizenmann

An interesting effort to show how things stood between Jacobi and Mendelssohn, which convinced Kant that both men were going in the same direction and, in his opinion, a wrong and dangerous direction, was made by Thomas Wizenmann, a twenty-six-year-old Pietist and disciple of Jacobi, in his anonymous *The Results of Jacobi's and Mendelssohn's Philosophy* (1786). There was much curiosity as to who the author was, and when Kant first referred to him he did not know his name. It was believed by many that no less a man than Herder had written this book. When it became known that the author had died in February 1787, there were genuine expressions of regret by Kant, and one can still feel that Wizenmann's early death was a serious loss to German philosophy. Next to Kant he was the best debater in the entire controversy.

Wizenmann argued very effectively against Mendelssohn. He pointed out that Mendelssohn had availed himself of an appeal to faith in his debate with Lavater;[21] that his "sound human reason" differed very little from Jacobi's "faith" in its relation to speculative reason;[22] but that Jacobi's name for it was more appropriate than Mendelssohn's, since Kant had shown that no proof of the existence of God by reason was possible.[23] Wizenmann accused Mendelssohn of ignorantly, or intentionally, misinterpreting what Jacobi had meant by belief or faith: it is not "the faith of old women and miserable preachers" but faith which "converts knowledge of God directly into deed, power, and practice; a belief which is philosophically related to facts of all possible degrees of evidence, a belief that degrades man to nothing, and raises him to God."[24] It is not belief which merely ratifies some of the findings of speculative reason (and vetoes others, as Mendelssohn thought sound reason should), but it is that which takes a person out of the limited context of reason altogether, that is, out of the realm of abstract and universal truths. Faith introduces facts (*facta*) into the realm of reason; these facts are historical, single, particulars, which reason cannot gainsay, but cannot prove. These facts give religion its historical, positive form, and keep it from being abstract, natural, rational religion which is neither Christianity nor Judaism.

[21] *Die Resultate der Jacobischen und Mendelssohnschen Philosophie von einem Freywilligen* [i.e., by a volunteer] (Leipzig, 1786), p. 47.
[22] *Ibid.*, pp. 35, 36.   [24] *Ibid.*, pp. 245, 246–247.
[23] *Ibid.*, pp. 30, 83.

Either no religion, or a positive religion! Either no religious laws, or laws authorized by god! Men of Germany, can reason decide . . . ? Is there, from our side, any other possible relation to God than faith, trust, and obedience? And, from the divine side, can the laws be made effective, reasonable, and obligatory except through revelation, command, and promise?"[25]

Kant answered with an apostrophe of his own, beseeching a wider public not to dethrone reason:

Friends of the human race and of that which is holiest to it! Assume what appears most believable to you after careful and honest testing, whether it be facts or principles of reason; but do not wrest from reason that which makes it the highest good on earth, i.e., the prerogative of being the ultimate touchstone of truth. Otherwise you will become unworthy of this freedom and certainly lose it, and you will bring this misfortune on the heads of that blameless portion of mankind which wanted to make use of its freedom in a lawful manner toward the good of the world.[26]

No clearer expression of the prerogative of reason over revelation, feeling, and blind faith can be found in German philosophy, and no clearer warning of the dangers inherent in irrationalism. With acute foresight, Kant told the philosophers of faith and feeling what would be the outcome of their attacks on reason. But the attacks continued, and their outcome was the tragic one Kant foretold.

Wizenmann responded in an article in the *Deutsches Museum*, published in the month of his death, in which he argued against Kant that Kant, like Mendelssohn, moved from the existence of a need to the belief in the existence of the object which will satisfy his need. He gave as an example a man in love who fools himself concerning the perfections of the woman he loves. Kant, now apprized of who the author was ("a very subtle and clearheaded man, whose early death is to be lamented"), replied that there is a great deal of difference between believing something because one wants to (believing because of a need arising from an inclination) and believing something because one has to if he is not to go against a need arising from reason itself. He does not think that either Jacobi or Wizenmann or Mendelssohn had appealed to a "need of reason," and he does not think that *theoretical* reason has needs which require belief instead of mere heuristic principles. But because he thinks the moral law as expressed in the categorical imperative is dictated by pure practical reason, the presuppositions or the postulates which are necessary for the validity or effectiveness of the law are justified as objects of a "pure rational faith."[27]

Note carefully what Kant has done. His conception of faith is not opposed to that of reason, but only to that of knowledge. Reason is opposed to feeling too; it is not intuitive; it is not even cognitive. Reason points to what faith demands morally, not what is feigned by the dogmatic, doctrinal,

25 *Ibid.*, pp. 196–197.

26 "What is Orientation in Thinking?" *Kants Gesammelte Schriften* (Akademie Edition), VIII, 146; in Kant, *Critique of Practical Reason and Other Writings on Moral Philosophy*, trans. L. W. Beck (Chicago: University of Chicago Press, 1949), p. 305.

27 *Critique of Practical Reason*, trans. L. W. Beck (New York: Liberal Arts Press, 1956), p. 149n.

and historical faith of Jacobi and Wizenmann. It is a faith which would not satisfy the longings of either of them.

Hamann: "The Magus of the North"

In 1757 the twenty-eight-year-old Königsberg Pietist Johann Georg Hamann went to London to carry out some secret business[28] for his prospective brother-in-law, Johann Christoph Berens, an enlightened and philanthropic merchant. Hamann had attended the University of Königsberg and served as tutor in several families, including the Berens. He had published a translation, with an original supplement, of a French book on political economy; his prospects of becoming a *literatus* and a successful businessman appeared good. Another popular philosopher of the Enlightenment was in the making.

London changed all that. He was not fitted for business or diplomacy, and his negotiations were unsuccessful. He offended important people. He "gorged, drank, whored, and rushed about" and "rang the changes on debauchery and reflection, reading and knavery, industry and voluptuous idleness." Destitute and in debt to the amount of three hundred pounds and living on the charity of a humble family, he turned to prayer, praying for a friend to help and console him. He found this friend "in [his] heart, who crept in there when [he] felt most keenly its emptiness and darkness and wilderness." In exemplary Pietistic fashion, Hamann underwent a complete conversion. He read the Bible and wrote extensive commentaries on the parts which spoke most directly to his troubled mind. He wrote an autobiographical account of his sin and salvation, put the debt of three hundred pounds in the hands of God (reasoning that God had done so much for him he would do the little extra and pay this debt), and fled to Königsberg a failure. He took with him a profound and exact knowledge of the Bible and a new conception of David Hume as defender of the faith.[29]

Berens was not amused. The engagement to his sister was terminated, but if he could not save Hamann for his family and his business, at least he wanted to save him for the Enlightenment, and the London writings convinced him that Hamann had become a bigoted Christian. Berens enlisted the aid of their mutual friend Kant, and together they tried to talk sense into the eccentric who was throwing up his career and passing over to the

---

[28] The nature of the mission is unknown. It has been suggested that it was an effort to align British interests on the Russian side against Prussia. See Robert T. Clark Jr., *Herder* (Berkeley: University of California, 1955), p. 49.

[29] This account is based on *Biblical Reflections, Thoughts About My Life*, and *Fragments*, composed while he was in London. All quotations from Hamann, unless otherwise noted, are taken from R. G. Smith, *Johann Georg Hamann, 1730–1788*, (New York: Harper, 1960). In Hamann's London writings, Hume is not mentioned, but he told Jacobi that when he wrote the *Socratic Memorabilia* on his return to Germany, Hume was occupying him very much (Letter of April 27, 1787). Since the critical edition of Hamann's correspondence has not yet reached the year 1786, I shall quote Hamann's letters which are not included in Smith's translation by reference to Vol. IV of Jacobi's correspondence, included in his *Werke*.

camp of the enemy. But to no avail.[30] Their well-meaning but bungling efforts were answered in Hamann's first writing for publication, the *Socratic Memorabilia*, a witty but obscure apology for that other great misfit in a society where a "successful" thinker would have joined the Sophists instead of attacking them. The book is dedicated to Berens and Kant, the businessman and the Enlightenment philosopher, with an attempt to show that they represent, in different spheres, the same ideals. Kant's model is "Newton, the mintmaster."

Socrates, in the *Memorabilia*, is not at all the "educated Berliner" he was to be a few years later in Mendelssohn's *Phaedo*. Rather, he is the exposer of sophistry guided by his mysterious genius. It did not matter that he was ignorant of the things Berens and Kant wanted Hamann to know; he had a genius on which he could rely in knowing the things that mattered. "He is no common critic"—in a word, it is Socrates against the Enlightenment. And Hamann's other ally against Kant was David Hume, with his theory of belief:

> Our own being and the existence of all things outside us must be believed and cannot be established in any other way . . . Faith is not a work of reason and therefore cannot succumb to any attack by reason; because believing happens as little by means of reasons as tasting and seeing.[31]

Socrates' ignorance was sensibility, says Hamann, meaning that Socrates' wisdom was sensibility and a rejection of abstract rational speculation. Sensibility includes not just sensation, but a passion and feeling for the ineffable immediate experience of the concrete, a feeling which carries belief with it, a feeling whose immediacy and a belief whose credibility are destroyed by abstract reason.

Christianity and Platonism have generally been taken to be concerned with things not given, faith is the evidence of things not seen. But this combination of Christianity and speculative rational metaphysics seemed to Hamann to be radically wrong. The Enlightenment, which tried to substitute the clear ideas of reason for the obscure ideas of sense, leads away from the only revelation God makes to us, which is a sensuous revelation in the particularities of history and nature. "While we are aiming at clear ideas, the food gets cold and tasteless."[32]

Christianity and Enlightenment are antithetical. While Lessing, Voltaire, and Kant recognized the opposition between Enlightenment and the outward forms and inner mysteries of Christianity, they thought that they were thereby serving it by cracking its shell in order to find its rational kernel. But Hamann declared to the Enlighteners:

> The object of your reflections and devotions is not God, but a mere word image, like your universal human reason, which by a more than poetic license

---

[30] Hamann's shocked response is found in his brilliant letter of July 27, 1759, in *Kant's Philosophical Correspondence*, ed. Arnulf Zweig (Chicago: University of Chicago Press, 1967), pp. 35–43.

[31] *Socratic Memorabilia*, pp. 181, 182.

[32] Letter from Hamann to Jacobi, November 2, 1783 (Smith, p. 248).

you deify as a real person, making so many similar gods and persons by transubstantiation of your word images that the crassest heathendom and blindest popery in comparison with your philosophical idolatry will be justified and perhaps acquitted on the day of judgment.[33]

Not only is Enlightenment a form of idolatry, worshipping the false idols of abstract reason, but Christianity needs no philosophy. Hamann says forthrightly, "Christianity does not believe in philosophical tenets, which are nothing but alphabetical scribaceousness of human speculation, subject to the fickle changes of moon and fashion."[34]

Now no German Enlighteners or critics of Christianity had openly made such a radical distinction between the things of faith and the things of reason; it may be questioned whether they had done so even in petto. They had, rather, tried to save Christianity by purging it of unphilosophical superstition and bigotry. If the cost of doing so was to convert it into deism and natural religion, that was the price the priests had to pay for seventeen centuries of chicanery; the Christian religion might have to be sacrificed, but the religion of Christ might be saved. The Enlightenment wished to have peaceful coexistence with Christianity, and that meant disarming Christianity by removing its mysteries. This was not a peace which satisfied Hamann, the Christian spokesman; for him a war of extermination against the Enlightenment was needed.

The conviction Hamann felt arose from his discovery in Hume of the bankruptcy of reason and from his experience of the directness and simplicity of God's word.

He calls his philosophy "verbalism," not meaning what would be connoted by such a term today, but just the opposite: he means a metaphysics of the divine word (*logos*) as the explanation of nature and history, and an epistemology and psychology of language in which valid philosophy is the right use of language for the translation of the *logos*, and false philosophy is mere verbalism in the modern, opprobrious, sense of this word.

Nature and history are, in a literal sense, God's word; the Creator of the world is not a mathematician or an architect, but a Writer.[35] On the side of man Hamann asserts another identity with language:

Even if I were as eloquent as Demosthenes, I would do nothing but repeat one thing three times: Reason is language, *logos*. I gnaw on this bone full of marrow, and will do so until I die.[36]

Hamann's verbalism has four theses:

(a) Scripture, Nature, and History are the Word of God, the language by which he speaks to man.

---

[33] Hamann, *New Apology of the Letter 'H', by Itself* (Smith, p. 204).
[34] Hamann, *Golgotha and Scheblimini* (written against Mendelssohn's *Jerusalem*), p. 228.
[35] *Biblical Reflections*, p. 120.
[36] Letter to Herder, August 6, 1784 (Smith, p. 246); translation modified.

(b) The proper language of man is a language close to God's, a language of sensuous symbols reflecting naive experience and conveying God's message to us, which man must receive by divine instruction.[37]

(c) There is a human language of pseudo-reason which uses abstractions and artificial constructions, and which tries, unsuccessfully, to cut the umbilicus to sensibility, emotion, and God's world.

(d) There is a human language of prophecy and poetry which is like the divine language in that it creates its own sensuously present objects.

The first, the properly theological or metaphysical thesis, was impressed upon Hamann by the overwhelmingly direct sense of having a communication from God during his religious crisis in London. While reason can at most serve an unknown God—and ceases to do even that when this God is thought of as being really "known"—Hamann had a profound feeling for *kenosis*, for God's emptying himself into the sphere which human beings can experience, for God's "condescension to human inclinations and ideas, even prejudices and weaknesses," and not to a Voltaire, a Bolingbroke, or a Shaftesbury.[38] This revelation is not found just in the Bible, but in nature and history. "All natural events are revealed." God reveals himself "in the common events of life rather than in rare and extraordinary events." "Everything in the course of nature and its laws is directly dependent upon God." Everything is miraculous; all knowledge is revelation. Even "the tiniest actions of men" are proofs of the existence of God; they are "commentaries on the divine Word, and this Word is the only key to unravel the knowledge" of both nature and man in history.[39] In his reading of the Bible, Hamann had an uncanny sense that he was—as, for example, in the story of Cain—reading about himself; the Bible was God's way of speaking to him about himself. The Bible and the world of nature and history are full of "signatures," or hieroglyphics, whose interpretation is obvious to Hamann, however obscure they may be to his readers.

Hamann is not a pantheist. God stands outside the world and sends messages and messengers to it; his deepest condescension and humiliation were his most patent message in the incarnation and passion of Christ.

The next thesis is about human language. There is an ambiguity here, for human language means both what man understands and what he speaks and writes. The first is the sensuous, emotional content of our immediate experience, which is God's language as we directly grasp it; the second is

---

[37] Because Hamann took quite literally the notion that nature is *logos*, God's speaking to man, his theory that language must have been given to man by "divine instruction" cannot be taken quite as historically as the theorists (e.g., Johann Peter Süssmilch, a member of the Berlin Academy and the target of Herder's attack on the divine origin of language) took it. Man's learning a language is no more (and no less) miraculous than his and nature's creation. Hamann's criticisms of Herder's assertion of the natural origin of language are not meant to be taken as literally as one might suppose. See Hamann, *Des Ritters von Rosencreuz letzte Willenmeynung . . .* , in *Sämmtliche Werke*, ed., Josef Nadler (Vienna: Thomas Morus Presse im Verlag Herder, 1949–57), III, 27–33, esp. p. 32.

[38] *Biblical Reflections* (Smith, p. 121).

[39] *Ibid.*, pp. 121–135 passim; *Fragments* (Smith, p. 166).

made up of words with which we describe the world or "translate" the divine *logos* into human sounds and marks on paper. To the theories of the origin of language current in the eighteenth century—that it is a human invention or convention, and that it grew naturally out of animal sounds finally controlled by human intelligence—Hamann adds another (or rather returns to one that had been given up), viz., that language has a divine origin. God taught man to speak so that his message could be translated and communicated by human beings.

This human language proper—language in the *literal* meaning of the word—brings both death and life to thought. The language of man may move away from the immediacies of sense and emotion and deal with the *-heits* and *-keits* of things. It moves away from "the mother tongue of the human race," which is poetry, and makes the abstractions which are the marks of philosophy and mathematics. This is the fundamental error of the Enlightenment, for, in Goethe's words:

> Grau, theurer Freund, ist alle Theorie,
> Und grün des Lebens goldner Baum
>
> [Gray, dear friend, is all theory,
> But green is life's golden tree]

and

> Gefühl ist alles,
> Nahme ist Schal und Rauch.
>
> [Feeling is all,
> Name is only sound and smoke.]

The Enlightenment had emphasized only one aspect of human genius, Hamann wrote, but there are two: "The spirit of observation [of what is present] and the spirit of prophecy [of what is absent, past or future] are the wings of human genius"; the poetic genius transfigures prophecies into present experiences, but the philosopher tries to make the present as if it were absent, by abstractions which "unclothe real objects and make them naked concepts and merely thinkable attributes."[40]

In this one passage is the common root of the two important phases of Hamann's thought expressed in the third and fourth theses mentioned above: his criticism of Enlightenment philosophy for its verbalism (in the pejorative sense) and his theory of the artist who, unlike the Enlightenment poets, is not concerned with the imitation of nature and the inculcation of moral lessons but with the autonomous creativity of genius.

Developing the third of the theses, Hamann says exactly what one would expect of him in criticism of Wolff, Mendelssohn, and Lessing. But it will be more rewarding to study his attack on his neighbor and friend Kant. Out of respect and gratitude to Kant, who had secured him a livelihood as a minor official in the customs house and who permitted his son to attend his lectures *gratis*,[41] Hamann did not publish his *Metacritique of*

---

[40] *Aesthetica in nuce*, and A *Flying Letter*, pp. 196, 234.
[41] Letter to Jacobi, April 9, 1786 (Jacobi's *Werke*, IV, 205).

the Purism of Reason, with its attempt at a *reductio ad absurdum* of the *Critique of Pure Reason;* it was published after his death, in 1800, when it could no longer offend his friend and benefactor.

Reason, Hamann says in this essay, goes through two stages of purification by philosophy. The first renders it independent of tradition and of belief based upon tradition. The second tries to make it independent of all experience and even the most careful inductions from it. Kant differs from the other Enlightenment philosophers not in denying that the second purification can take place, but only in denying that the twice-distilled reason can give us knowledge. Naturally, faith must be called upon to give sustenance when all the spirits have been boiled out of reason by these two distillations. But Hamann denies that, in fact, the second purification has occurred at all, for the language Kant uses has its remote ancestry in experience or "aesthetic appearances." The concept of space, for instance, originates in "the oldest writing," which is painting and drawing, and the concept of time in "the oldest language," the cadences of music. All words and the concepts they name have an aesthetic dimension as well as a logical one; there are no pure a priori concepts, but all come, directly or indirectly from sensibility. True reason, unlike the reason of the school bench (*Schulvernunft*), is based on the unity of faith, reason, and the nature of things.[42]

Hamann then challenges Kant: if he is to write a critique of *pure reason* he must "metagrobolize"[43] transcendental philosophy by drawing the forms of intuition "out of the pure and empty quality of our inner and outer experience." In other words, he ought to try to get definite forms of intuition out of the *word,* the *mere* word *Vernunft* (= reason), without any reference to the origin of the word in the experience of *Vernehmen* (= to understand by hearing). Hamann slyly offers an ironical help as to how it might be done; after all, he says, in the form of the word *Vernunft* the first syllable is a priori and the second a posteriori.[44] If this challenge cannot be met, i.e., if we cannot move from words having no intuitive or empirical root to knowledge of their cognitive functions, then the ultimate "purism" of reason cannot be attained.

Of course Hamann thinks this second stage of purification is impossible. But even the first step away from the poetic, imaginative, emotional language of experience which condemned philosophy to futility and verbalism in the bad sense. *C'est le premier pas qui coute.* "All chatter about reason is pure wind," he wrote to Herder;[45] and to Kant, "I look upon the best demonstration as a sensible girl regards a love letter and upon a Baumgartian explanation as a witty courtesan."[46]

---

[42] Letter to Jacobi, April 27, 1787 (*Ibid.,* 347).

[43] A word which, according to R. G. Smith, he forms from a coinage by Rabelais. W. M. Alexander, in *Johann Georg Hamann, Philosophy and Faith* (The Hague: M. Nijhoff, 1966), nicely translates the verb as "meta-obscure". (This work by Alexander came to hand after the present chapter was written, but it is a pleasure to recommend it, though I was not able, in writing this chapter, to profit from its learning and sympathetic imagination except in this one point.)

[44] *Metacritique of the Purism of Reason* (Smith, p. 220).

[45] Letter to Herder, December 8, 1783 (Smith, p. 245).

[46] Letter to Kant, July 27, 1759, in *Kant's Philosophical Correspondence,* trans. Arnulf Zweig, pp. 39–40.

Philosophers like Kant "talk about reason as if it were a real thing, and about God as if he were nothing but a concept . . . If one knew what reason is, the conflict between it and revelation would cease."[47]

Philosophy must be brought down from its abstract universals; the divorce effected by Kant between reason and sense must be rescinded. "For me," he writes Jacobi,

the question is not so much What is reason? as What is language? . . . In words and ideas, no existence is possible. Existence is attached solely to things. No enjoyment arises from brooding, and all things—including the *ens entium* —are there for enjoyment and not for speculation. The tree of knowledge has deprived us of the tree of life.[48]

With the tree of life we are brought back to our starting point, the emotional and sensuous experience, the direct revelation of God which we directly receive and do not try to explain away.

Truth must be dug out of the ground, not created out of air, nor out of a technical terminology. It must be brought to light from earthly and subterraneous things, by metaphors and parables of the highest ideas and transcendent intimations . . . Nature and reason are just as much correlates as opposites.[49]

Kant was the great divider who liked sharp and dichotomous distinctions —form and content, understanding and sense, reason and understanding, the supersensible and the sensible, and so on. Once he suggested,[50] however, that there might be a common root of understanding and sensibility, though he did not develop this conjecture. For Hamann, there is this common source, and it engenders both the strengths and the weaknesses of each of the faculties which grow from it. In a metaphor of such complexity that it defies picturization, Hamann proposes:

For an image of our knowledge would not a single tree-trunk be more appropriate, with two roots, one above in the air, and the other below in the earth? The former is exposed to our sensibility, the latter, on the other hand, is invisible, and must be thought by means of the understanding . . . Without waiting, however, for the visit of a new Lucifer from the heights, or seizing the fig-tree of the great goddess Diana, the wicked snake in the bosom of ordinary language gives us the finest parable of the hypostatic union of the two natures of sense and of understanding.[51]

Nature and reason, he said to Jacobi, are correlates as much as they are opposites; Kant has treated them as opposites and forgotten their correlation. Nature and reason, sense and thought, are abstractions from a common experience, which is not either raw brute data of sense or phenomena under law (the two polar meanings Kant ascribes to experience). Experience is like art or like language—an immediately felt immediacy of form

[47] Letter to Jacobi, October 26, 1786 (Jacobi, *Werke*, IV, 291–292).
[48] Letter to Jacobi, November 14, 1784 (Smith, p. 249).
[49] Letter to Jacobi, April 22, 1787 (Jacobi, *Werke*, IV, 344).
[50] *Critique of Pure Reason*, A 15 = B 29.
[51] *Metacritique of the Purism of Reason* (Smith, pp. 217, 218).

and content: colored shapes, or geometrical hieroglyphics with sound, something felt and something thought.

We reapproach experience with the language and wings of prophecy; we approach it with genius, which re-creates it but does not just copy what it is, *hic et nunc*. Genius with the language of prophecy, parable, and metaphor—none of which is to be taken in a linguistic sense, but includes all the intimations of which art is capable—makes what is absent as if present. It can form, in a sensuous emotional language like God's own, what God does not vouchsafe to us in nature and history. The poet creates as God does, using God's language of sense. Unlike the philosopher, who moves from this language to a purely and exclusively human language, the poet translates "from the language of angels into a language of men, that is, thoughts into words, things into names, images into signs."[52] "O for a muse like a refiner's fire, or like fuller's earth. She will dare to purify the natural use of the senses from the unnatural use of abstractions, which mutilate our ideas of things as badly as they suppress and blaspheme the name of the Creator."[53]

The *Aesthetica in nuce* was written by Hamann while Herder was a student in Königsberg and at the beginning of their life-long friendship. Through Herder, his apotheosis of the artist as genius and creator fructified the dissatisfactions of poets and dramatists frustrated by Gottschedian rules and Lessing's bourgeois stiff-upper-lip to bring about the attitudes and works of the *Sturm und Drang*. No more leveling down of tragic figures into the upper middle class; no more inculcation of moral lessons; no more insipid imitation of nature or Winckelmann's praise of the quiet dignity of the Greeks; no more rules, either on or off the stage. The artist is the misfit in society—so much the worse for the society. The artist is the reformer of society by rebelling against it; the robber becomes the hero, the morally equivocal Werther the man who brings others to know themselves. Art takes its place along with—in fact, is superior to—history and nature; the theological *logos* becomes *poesis*.

Hamann has been called the most obscure philosopher since Heraclitus; certainly no German with the exception of Jacob Böhme matches him in the darkness of what he says. To read him, one must be able to swim, for his sentences are "little islands, which are not joined by any bridges or ferries in their method."[54] "My sole rule is not to have a rule."[55] His writings are cryptic and brief, unsystematic, and intensely personal. No man who loved language as much as he did, and made it the basic reality, used it so obscurely. Kant begged him to talk in human language so that he could understand him. Language is *not* life and reality, and the attempt to make it serve for life may illuminate life only if the language itself is illuminating, instead of darkening. Hamann tried to say too much, in too little. He pushed language to the point where it was as confusing as life itself instead of a clarification of it, thinking thereby that he made it like life.

---

[52] *Aesthetica in nuce* (Smith, p. 197).
[53] *Ibid.*, 199 (translation slightly modified).   [54] *Socratic Memorabilia*, 179.
[55] From the diary of the Princess Gallitzin reporting a conversation with Hamann shortly before his death (Smith, p. 110).

"The principle behind all Hamann's utterances," says Goethe, "is this: everything that man undertakes, whether it be produced in action or word or anything else, must spring from his whole united powers; all separation of powers is to be repudiated."[56] Because of this, there is a richness in Hamann that has given rise to the most various interpretations; and it is no surprise that he has been found to anticipate the teachings of two philosophers as profoundly and radically different as Kierkegaard and Ernst Cassirer.[57]

Herder

Johann Gottfried Herder was a more effective critic of the Enlightenment than Jacobi and Hamann because he provided an intellectual alternative to it, neither religious orthodoxy nor mystification. Like them, he is often considered a philosopher of faith. Herder, however, was never extreme enough in his rejection of reason to qualify for such a name. Unlike Jacobi and Hamann, he was intensely interested in the science of nature, and though he sometimes spoke the language of Hamann (though with infinitely more clarity), none of the egocentricity and obscurantism of Hamann and Jacobi is to be found in his works. His objections to the Enlightenment were not, however, unlike theirs:

A youth should learn to abstract and speculate? If he does so, he will be a miserable young old-man, an empty vessel that makes the loudest noise. If he does not, and tramples the spiderweb underfoot, how many good things will come of it! Who is it that has brought the great Diana of the German Ephesus, philosophy, to be so condemned, so despised?—Her worshippers, the fabricators not of little gold and silver temples, but fabricators of wooden compendia, theories, systems.[58]

Herder favored a more holistic view of human nature than that of either the Enlightenment philosophers or their opponents, each of whom put one faculty of the mind forward at the expense of others. Herder, like Hamann but unlike Jacobi, did not have to contrast faith and feeling with reason, and while Hamann had said that reason was, or could be, a healthy growth from sense, Herder had a detailed theory and not rhetorical asseverations of the unity of man's psyche. His philosophy begins at a level of psychological and epistemological integration toward which theirs only points, and he may therefore be seen as synthesizing the one-sided philosophy of faith and feeling with the one-sidedness of the Enlightenment philosophy. He seemed to be meeting halfway the Enlightenment philosophers who found a place

[56] *Goethe's Autobiography. Poetry and Truth from My Own Life*, trans. W. O. Moon (Washington, D.C.: Public Affairs Press, 1949), p. 452.

[57] By, respectively, Walter Lowrie, *Johann Georg Hamann an Existentialist* (Princeton: Princeton University Press, 1950), and J. C. O'Flaherty, *Unity and Language, A Study in the Philosophy of Johann Georg Hamann* (Chapel Hill: University of North Carolina Press, 1952).

[58] *Vom Erkennen und Empfinden* (1778 revision). *Herders Sämmtliche Werke*, ed. Bernhard Suphan (Berlin: Weidmann, 1877–1913), VIII, 218. All references to Herder's works not otherwise identified are to this edition.

for faith and feeling, but the efforts of Baumgarten, Meier, Sulzer, and Mendelssohn seemed to Herder to be based upon an utterly unsatisfactory psychology. If one faculty would not suffice, they would add another; if two would not, a third was added.

Herder, taking his cue from Hamann, wholly rejected such theories of faculties, and made language the basis of all of the higher psychic functions. But, unlike Hamann, he found a naturalistic rather than a supernaturalistic ground for language. He argued against the theory of the divine origin of language as presented by Süssmilch and defended by Hamann, the theory that language is an arbitrary invention of otherwise isolated men, and the theory that it grows out of animal cries rationalized and brought to order by reason. He held that it arises from man's nature as a social organism whose physique (especially his upright stature) permits, and whose physical helplessness requires, the development of a plasticity which is absent in animals whose life is governed by instinct. The question of the origin of language, which was asked by the Berlin Academy in 1772 (the prize went to Herder), is a meaningless question because it presupposes that there were primitive men who subsequently acquired a language in some way. Herder's point is that language is definitive of man, and it is as silly to ask the origin of language as to ask the origin of our prehensile thumb. (Herder was not an evolutionist, and therefore he thought the latter kind of question was indeed unanswerable.) The origin of language is divine precisely insofar as its origin is human—this was the paradox with which Herder ended his prize essay.[59]

Nonetheless, Herder did not leave the question in a theological limbo, as Hamann had done. His theory was that language, and hence reason, is natural; what "natural" meant had to be explored later, in his major works of the eighties. His answer was also opposed to Kant's; for Kant, reason was a faculty removed from the vicissitudes of time and space and even from creation,[60] and hence had a status Herder could grant to no human organ or product. Herder's reason, because it had a natural origin, also had a historical dimension and was therefore equally incompatible with Hamann's and Kant's concepts, since both of them conceived of reason in absolute terms—as a divine *logos*, or as pure, nonempirical, trans-temporal reason.

Through Herder, Hamann's conception of the world as a divine epiphany was passed on to the romantic philosophers of nature such as Schelling and Steffens. The idealists also took over the Kantian conception of reason, freed from Kantian limitations. Much of the dialectical tension in the great systems of the following century, not to mention much of the murky ob-

---

[59] *Werke*, V, 146.

[60] Kant seldom speculated about the "origin" of reason, but the suggestion that sensibility and understanding might have "a common root" (*Critique of Pure Reason*, A 15 = B 29) could point to either a Leibnizian or an Hamannian view. In the second edition of 1787 (B 167) Kant's remarks about an "epigenesis" in contrast to a "preformation" of the concepts of the understanding may, for all we know, show signs of his having read Herder. But Kant was such a voracious reader and gifted with such a phenomenal memory that he may have got the idea from the same source Herder got it, viz., Jacobi's teacher Bonnet.

scurity, derives from their authors' working with two quite opposed conceptions of reason, Harder's and Kant's.

Johann Gottfried Herder was born in Mohrungen, East Prussia, in 1744, the son of a Pietist family. As a student in Königsberg from 1762 to 1764, he was permitted by Kant to hear his lectures *gratis* because of his poverty. His genuine and almost life-long admiration for Kant was based not on Kant's original philosophizing, but on the lectures he heard in the sciences from the young *Dozent* who had not yet formulated the philosophy of which Herder was to become the most vitriolic critic. In Königsberg he was befriended also by Hamann, who made a deeper impression on his philosophical, literary, and religious views.

While the influence of Hamann on the young Herder was great, and they continued to be friends until Hamann's death, it is not correct to see Herder as the heir to Hamann's philosophy except in one important respect. For both of them, language was the central phenomenon, the key to be used for unlocking all philosophical problems. But no man can be a follower of both Hamann and Kant, and Kant's influence was to give Herder a discipline derived from the study of nature, a discipline Hamann never achieved. If Kant's influence in the sixties kept Herder from being a Hamannian enthusiast, Hamann's influence kept him from being a Kantian when Kantianism meant the critical, antinaturalistic philosophy of the eighties and nineties.

If our purpose were to give a life of Herder at all adequate to his protean activities, we should have to distinguish three periods in it—a first when he was largely in accord, at least in goals, with the Berlin philosophers; a second, the period of his greatest creative work when he was their opponent; and a third at the very end of his life, in 1803, when, disillusioned with both the classicism of Weimar (Goethe and Schiller) and the romanticism of which he had been a harbinger, he returned with greater sympathy to the ideals of the Enlighteners. We should have to see how these changes caused, or were caused by, his (temporary) break with Hamann over the origin of language, his abrupt and permanent breach with Kant over the philosophy of history (for which it must be admitted Kant deserved all the blame), and the checkered career of his friendship with Goethe (for the termination of which it must be admitted that Herder was almost wholly to blame). Of Herder's great achievements as a literary critic, biblical scholar, student and collector of folk songs, and as stimulant to the *Sturm und Drang* and the early romanticists we should have to write many pages; for so various, so complicated, so manifold, were Herder's activities that it had been seriously (but erroneously) suggested that Goethe took him as the model for his "Herr Mikrokosmos"—no less a figure than Faust himself. Finally, we should have to consider a large number of sizable and interesting works and the development of his ideas from one to another. Fortunately, none of this is necessary for understanding Herder's role in the history of philosophy, however essential it would be for understanding him as a man. For Herder was a systematic thinker who, within a few years, produced two works (*Ideas for a Philosophy of the History of Mankind*, 1784–91, and *God, Some Conversations*, 1787) for which almost all the earlier philosophical writing were preparations and to which all the subsequent ones, including the two books against Kant, were corollaries. We shall consider first the *God*, which was composed between the third and fourth volumes of the *Ideas*.

Herder's Spinozism

When Jacobi, late in 1783, wrote Herder about his conversation with Lessing, Herder was delighted to find that he had a forerunner in his admiration for Spinoza. He had known and liked Lessing in the Hamburg years, and he had been studying Spinoza for the previous eight years. He replied to Jacobi in February 1784,[61] saying that Spinozism was the only self-consistent philosophy he knew, and that since Spinoza no one, including Mendelssohn in his "refined pantheism," had done justice to the principle: All is one. He did not say, any more directly than Lessing had said, that he was a Spinozist; he found Spinoza following Descartes too closely, and he thought it would be invidious of him to call himself a Spinozist when "the seeds of Spinozism lie in the oldest of the enlightened nations in an almost clearer form." He warned Jacobi of the dangers of a *salto mortale* of blind faith, since he was completely opposed to Jacobi's (and the Enlighteners') theory of independent and competing faculties of the mind.[62] Jacobi replied with an expression of strong doubts about the possibility of a religious interpretation of Spinoza, which Herder had sketched in his letter of June 30, 1784. He took particular pains (which we may well applaud) to show his distrust of Herder's distinction between "Spinozism" and "what Spinoza actually wrote." Jacobi did not like this license in biblical exegesis, and he liked it no better in philosophy. Herder replied with a criticism of Jacobi's theory of an extra-mundane (transcendent) divine personality and further developed his own panentheistic interpretation of Spinoza which, he said, had the approbation of Goethe.[63] Jacobi replied in two appendices added to the second edition of his *Über die Lehre Spinozas*, published in 1789. With no explicit reference to the Jacobi-Lessing-Mendelssohn situation, but with a few unmistakable allusions to Jacobi (which Herder, at Jacobi's request, removed or toned down in the second edition), Herder gave his interpretation of Spinoza in *God, Some Conversations*, published in 1787.

To the debate in which Jacobi had accused Lessing of Spinozism and Mendelssohn had denied the charge, Herder brought a new strategy. He asked, "Why not Spinozism?", and the Spinozism he proposed was so consonant with his antimathematical natural philosophy that it opened a

---

[61] The letters, or the relevant parts of them, are given in Scholz, *Die Hauptschriften zum Pantheismusstreit*, pp. xc–xcii.

[62] The refutation of this view occupied Herder in three successive drafts of his essay *Vom Erkennen und Empfinden*, the last of which was finished in 1778. All are printed in Suphan, vol. VIII.

[63] Those who know Goethe's writings on nature, as in *Die Metamorphose der Pflanzen*, will easily see the degree to which they were inspired, or at least instructed, by Herder's "pandynamism" and theory of forms which grew out of his interpretation of Spinoza.

field of metaphysical speculation which Kant had tried to declare out of bounds.

Herder begins his dialogue as between a man who has read Spinoza (Theophron = Herder) and a man who has believed only what Bayle and Jacobi have said about him (Philolaus, who expresses Jacobi's views but is not modeled after Jacobi's person). Theophron argues that Bayle and all others (whom he cites at length) have misrepresented Spinoza as a pantheist, atheist, and fatalist. Theophron says he is no Spinozist, but will try to defend Spinoza's character (which he does very successfully and eloquently) and separate what was correct in Spinoza from the Cartesian and scholastic errors which made him seem a fatalist and pantheist. The "Spinozism" which results is one heavily modified in a Leibnizian direction, but one very different from the Spinozism attacked by Wolff and from the Leibnizianism appropriated by him. It is the Leibnizianism of the *Monadology,* minus the doctrine of pre-established harmony, and the *Nouveaux Essais,* not the *Theodicy.* But this reconstruction explains some of Lessing's remarks about teleology (see p. 357) which were puzzling, and therefore has the merit of seeming to be the kind of Spinozism to which Lessing expressed adherence.

Briefly, Herder's theory is this. Instead of there being one substance of which things and persons are merely modes, there are substances in the world which are somewhat like Leibniz' monads or the "point-forces" recently introduced into physics by the mathematician Boscovich. These substantial forces interact with each other, but they are created, integrated, and maintained by a supreme unitary force. The essence of each of the substances is force or power, not extension. The highest unitary force is called God: "Deity reveals himself in an infinite number of forces in an infinite number of ways." God is the primal force, "power in the highest and only sense of the word . . . the primal force of all forces, the Soul of all souls."[64] This one Force, like Spinoza's substance, manifests itself in an infinite number of ways, and those most revealing of the nature of this primal Force are life and thought. Herder denies that there is any merely *res extensa,* dead matter in space,[65] but the "parallelism of attributes" is maintained inasmuch as a thing may look like matter to the senses and yet reveal itself to thought as life. The system is more monistic than Leibniz', since God not only creates but actively, dynamically, sustains all the forces of nature; it is less pantheistic than Spinoza's, for though God manifests himself in nature, nature does not exhaust his being. But, most important of all, it differs from Spinoza's (or at least from the way Spinoza had been interpreted by everyone but Lessing) in being a thoroughly teleological system.

Lessing, it will be remembered, had asserted that Spinoza had denied teleology only from a human point of view. Herder tries to explain what Lessing meant, as Lessing had not done. He reminds us that Spinoza had warned against any kind of anthropomorphism, specifically saying that

[64] *God, Some Conversations,* trans. Frederick Burkhardt (New York: Veritas Press, 1940), pp. 97, 103, 104; Suphan, VIII, 442, 453. I shall cite both sources even when I do not exactly follow Burkhardt's excellent translation.

[65] *Ibid.,* Burkhardt, pp. 104, 105; Suphan, VIII, 453, 454.

there was no more resemblance between human and divine intelligence than between a dog on earth and the Dog Star. Spinoza's denial of teleology, his denial that God, like man, acts *sub ratione boni*, Herder writes, shows "that he preferred the stronger attack and expressed himself too drastically rather than suffer that he, who strove zealously for the worthiest and highest conception of God, should allow it to be degraded by any weak comparison with individual creatures."[66] Herder reminds us, in the manner of Hume, that we do not understand even the apparently mechanical causes at work in the world. We cannot demonstrate that there is a real, necessitating influence, but our knowledge of causes and forces is derived "from the daily experience of sound reason."[67] Even causal connections, then, can be seen only "from a human point of view," and metaphysical teleology is no more mysterious than metaphysical mechanism.

When Lessing denied that God created for a purpose, therefore, he should be understood as denying that God, like human beings and like the supreme monad in Leibniz, acted *sub ratione boni*, i.e., using his reason to survey various possibilities, and then choosing the best; but not as denying that God is the root of all good.

The world of God is the best, not because he selected it from among others less good, but because neither good nor bad existed without him, and he, according to the inner necessity of his existence could effect nothing bad.[68] . . . We have the essential law of God within us to order our limited power according to ideas of truth and goodness, as the Almighty practices them in accordance with his most perfect nature.[69]

Herder's Philosophy of History

These two quotations from *God* point to the principal thesis of the *Ideas for a Philosophy of the History of Mankind*, that man is a connecting link between two worlds, a world of nature and a spiritual world which, without man's natural being, would never come to be. But whereas the *God* was patently metaphysical speculation, the *Ideas* was meant to provide a very large empirical base for those speculations and to draw empirical and practical human consequences from the metaphysics. Almost every aspect of Herder's thought is to be found in this encyclopedic work. In wealth of empirical details and in sweep of a sovereign metaphysical eye over them, there are few books comparable to it. One thinks, in German philosophy, only of Humboldt's *Cosmos* and Lotze's *Microcosmos* as having a like scope, and it should be noted that these men, like Herder, saw man as a microcosm which, if we are to understand him, requires also an entire cosmos as his context.

Herder's book is a theodicy. In fact, Herder uses the term "philosophy of history" to mean the theory of man's harmony with the rest of creation, a theory that is supposed to confute those who "because they perceive no

---

[66] *Ibid.*, Burkhardt, p. 121; Suphan, VIII, 476. He thus associates Spinozism with Leibnizian, not Wolffian, teleology. See above, pp. 273–274.

[67] *Ibid.*, Burkhardt, p. 153; Suphan, VIII, 521–522.

[68] *Ibid.*, Burkhardt, p. 169; Suphan, VIII, 542.

[69] *Ibid.*, Burkhardt, p. 170; Suphan, VIII, 543.

plan, peremptorily deny the existence of a plan; or at least think of it with trembling dread, and doubting believe, believing doubt!"[70]

Though Herder sees a "plan" in history, he rejects several well-established and widely accepted theories of the meaning of history. He radically opposes the imposition of an external plan upon an indifferent nature; such a historical process would require the external teleology he has already rejected. He equally opposes the theory of an inevitable progress according to which the meaning and value of any historical epoch are to be found merely in what it leads to. This theory, which Herder detected in Kant and perhaps in Lessing, generally pointed to little more than a glorification of the present, though neither Lessing nor Kant had used it in this tasteless way; but it had been presented in all its baldness by Isaak Iselin, a Swiss Enlightener, in 1764, in his *Philosophical Conjectures Concerning the History of Mankind* (*Philosophische Muthmassungen über die Geschichte der Menschheit*), and when Herder attacked this philosophy of history, he thereby depreciated the Enlightenment which felt itself to be the scion of all ages. Against this degrading of the past and glorification of the present, Herder had written, "Every nation, like every age of a living being, has in itself the central point of its happiness. The youth is no happier than the innocently contented child, nor is the old man unhappier than the vigorously striving man."[71]

Now Herder is not opposed to the idea of progress itself. He goes farther than most in giving it a metaphysical and cosmological basis. Like Giambattisto Vico (who seems not to have influenced him directly), he sees various stages of natural and human history and projects higher ages yet to come. What he does oppose in the idea of progress is the hypothesis of a transcendent "finger of God" pointing out a path to mankind, as well as the opposing hypothesis that, somehow, man by himself through all ages had been striving to reach the Utopia of the mid-eighteenth century. Against these naive teleologies, which differed only in respect of the mechanisms employed, Herder insisted that there is a great organic hierarchy in which every stage is complete and represents an adequate response at that level of being; its "center of gravity" is to be found within the stage itself, and we do not need to consider a "center of attraction" at some later stage. Thus Herder anticipates Ranke's view, that each age is equally close to God; but because he does not think each one reflects the being of God with equal adequacy (as the Leibnizian monads each reflected the universe from its own partial point of view), and because he spreads out in time the great chain of being, he does hold that the later is more perfect than the earlier, at least in the large and with many temporary exceptions.

The *Ideas* is divided into four parts, published respectively in 1784, 1785, 1787, and 1791; a projected fifth part was never written. Part I deals with man in his relations to nature, especially but not exclusively his relation to the rest of the animal kingdom. Part II is anthropological and concerns the

---

[70] *Ideen* (Suphan, XIII, 8). There is a good translation by T. Churchill (London, 1800) which I shall cite even when I do not follow it verbatim. The passage just quoted is from p. viii.

[71] *Auch eine Philosophie der Geschichte* (1774), Suphan, V, 512.

pre-history of mankind. The third and fourth parts are historical, tracing the vicissitudes and fates of civilizations down to the Renaissance.

Here we shall consider in detail only Parts I and II. Both place man in his natural environment, nature being interpreted as a dynamic system of forces which express the primal force of God. Herder sometimes speaks of God's doing something, such as placing mountains in the right place for tribes to grow up in isolation; more often he personifies nature, and has her doing various things, but he begs indulgence for these verbal differences which he thinks are equivalent in meaning. Certainly there are no finger-of-God explanations in his historical account, but nature personified and deified supplies all the teleology he needs, and a great deal more "scientific" explanation of human affairs than is to be found elsewhere in the eighteenth century with the exception of the works of Montesquieu.

Harder begins with the solar system. Admitting that there may be life on other planets, he focuses in upon the earth and terrestrial life. As he comes in toward man, he indicates at each level how some difference in the physical environment ages ago would have produced differences in human life now. (For instance, had the angle of rotation of the earth to the plane of revolution around the sun been different, our seasons would be different, and this would have had such and such effects on human society.) The beasts are men's "older brothers," and many species lived and died before the human species appeared.[72]

Animal life is explained by reference to the three powers used in Albrecht von Haller's physiology: the elasticity of fibres, the irritability of muscles, and the sensibility of the nervous system.[73] These forces may be reducible to one ultimate force, as suggested in God, but Herder is content to take them as given. The various proportions of these forces and their diverse ways of modifying each other are the determinants of the specific differences we find among different organisms. All creatures are built according to the same plan, a basic formula in which these three forces are the independent variables. Herder is equally fascinated by the unity of pattern and by the diversity of execution he finds everywhere in nature. There is a good deal of sound natural history in these chapters, as, for example, in his comparisons between the anatomy of the elephant and that of the lion and between the elephant's and the lion's modes of life. One is not better or higher than the other; every creature is complete and every species has its "center of gravity" within. Every species has its "own world" in which it is completely at home and in no need of the organs or instincts of another. Each is adjusted to its own world, and the worlds are enmeshed with each other: "That creation is infinitely greater in which millions of creatures, of different senses and instincts, enjoy each its own world, pursue each its own truth, than a wilderness to be perceived by inattentive man alone with his dull five senses."[74] This is the living universe which Goethe in a letter to Herder happily described as "a compost heap, teeming with life;"[75] a Leibnizian living universe, not a Leibniz-Wolffian mechanical universe.

---

[72] Suphan, XIII, 60; Churchill, p. 35.
[73] Suphan, XIII, 81–82; Churchill, p. 48.   [74] Suphan, XIII, 85; Churchill, p. 50.
[75] Quoted in Ernst Cassirer, The Problem of Knowledge, (New Haven: Yale University Press, 1950), p. 219.

Not all creatures, however, are equally perfect. Herder takes the human organism as the standard for judging the degree of organic perfection to be found on other biological strata:

It is anatomically and physiologically true, that the analogy of one organization prevails through the whole animated creation of our globe: only the farther from man, the more the vital element of the creature differs from his, the more eternally uniform Nature must deviate from the archetype [*Hauptbild*, which is man] . . . Rejoice in thy situation, O man, and study thyself, thou noble middle creature, in all that lives around thee![76]

Man, then, is the measure of the biological world. He is the apex of the biological hierarchy because he is "the elaborated form in which the features of all genera about him are gathered into their finest summary [*Inbegriff*]." His very blood is "a compendium of the world"; he is "the great confluence of all inferior organic powers," and everything found in a less perfect form in other animals is to be seen in man in its most refined form.[77]

Man is the highest creature because he is endowed with reason, but he is endowed with reason because he is the highest creature. That is, his reason is not a gift of a transcendent God but the inevitable consequence of the changes in anatomy which made it possible for him to have speech, and speech is the organ and condition of reason. Speech can develop only as instinct, which makes for fixed mechanical response, declines in its automatic mechanisms, or is "softened down to a more delicate proportion" so that the instincts can be used or repressed as the sphere of the organism's activity becomes larger.[78]

Nature has constructed man for the use of language. Her most important gift to man is his upright posture, which permitted the use of hands for grasping and feeling and of the mouth for other purposes than tearing, grasping, and feeding. The upright stature permitted also the development of a larger brain.[79] The increased distance of the head above the ground made smell less essential, and made the eyes the most important sense organs, thereby freeing man from responses limited to that which was close to him. These changes, all brought about by his erect position, broadened man's sensory horizon, and brought with it a power to act freely. Herder does not believe in "freedom of the will" because he does not believe there is "a will"; but he does believe that human beings are free in a way in which the lower animals are not:

Brutes are but stooping slaves; though some of the nobler species carry the head erect, or at least strive after liberty with uplifted neck. Their minds, not yet ripened into reason, must be subservient to the impulses of necessity . . . Man is the first of the creation left free: he stands erect. He holds the balance

[76] Suphan, XIII, 71; Churchill, p. 41.
[77] Suphan, XIII, 168, 181; Churchill, pp. 108, 117.
[78] Suphan, XIII, 142; Churchill, p. 89.
[79] Kant published the same idea (anonymously, in a Königsberg newspaper) in 1771 and showed the importance of man's upright stature for the development of his higher faculties.

of good and evil, of truth and falsehood: he can examine, and is to choose . . .
He is, and remains, with regard to himself, a free creature, though all-compre-
hending Goodness embraces him even in his follies, and turns these both to his
own and the general good. So man, in error and in truth, in rising and in falling, is still man; feeble indeed, but free-born, if not yet rational, yet capable of
attaining reason; if not yet formed to humanity, yet endowed with the power
of attaining it.[80]

Man is the apex of the biological world, but his freedom raises him above
it. He is a connecting link between two worlds, the world of nature and that
of humanity, humanity being the scope of the uniquely human potentialities.[81] Through the upright stature which permitted the emancipation from
binding instincts, which in turn called forth the development of language,
man became a reasonable being able to act for, and communicate about,
other than immediate animal needs. But all the raw materials of humanity
have a biological origin or counterpart. The animal impulses of gregarious-
ness, sexuality, aggression, maternal love, and curiosity are sublimated or
transformed into civility, decorum, love, taste, religion, and reason.[82]

Language is the first sign of humanity and the instrument for all the rest
of humanity. The languages of mankind show their origin in the basic
biological organization of man, and their varieties bear the stamp of the
diverse character of the peoples whose modes of life varied because of their
various environments.[83] Primitive speech and poetry show this naturalness
of language better than the abstract language of sophisticated reason which
tries, but fails, to be uniform and supernational. Against it, Herder reminds
us of the natural origin of language and reason: "We are not intended to
breathe the ether, for which our machine is not adapted, but the wholesome air of our own earth."[84]

Parts III and IV of the *Ideas* trace the actual history of mankind's search
for the full manifestation of humanity, and its failures. Herder was one of
the most catholic of eighteenth-century historians, and he insisted on no
one pattern—even a pattern as complicated as those worked out by Montesquieu or Vico—to explain all the empirical facts. But many of the ideals
and ideas of the Enlightenment are illustrated in the most varied cultures,
and among the common causes of frustration and decline Herder sees some
of the *bêtes noires* of the Enlightenment: a too-sharp division of classes,
political despotism, and the political establishment of religions ("an altar
on a throne, or a throne on an altar").[85]

Thus ends our race through one of the most interesting "essays on man"
of the eighteenth century. This is not the place to compare Herder's and
Kant's philosophies of history. But while Kant missed the many virtues of
Herder's book, he did note, as we must, that Herder's "is not a logical
precision in the definition of concepts and careful adherence to principles,
but rather a fleeting, sweeping view, an adroitness in unearthing analogies

---

[80] Suphan, XIII, 147; Churchill, p. 92.   [81] Suphan, XIII, 194; Churchill, p. 127.
[82] Suphan, XIII, 154–65; Churchill, pp. 98–105.
[83] Suphan, XIII, 363; Churchill, p. 237.   [84] Suphan, XIII, 361; Churchill, p. 236.
[85] The quotation, however, is from pt. II, bk. ix, chap. v; Suphan, XIII, 390; Churchill,
p. 253.

in the wielding of which he shows a bold imagination."[86] Believing what he did, Kant could not see in Herder's ideas anything but a continuation of the attack on reason, and thus he failed to see the historical fruitfulness of what Herder attempted. Herder, to be sure, opposed the rationalism of the Enlightenment and Kant,[87] and he did so by naturalizing and relativizing reason; but this was equally effective against the excesses of irrationalism in the Counter-Enlightenment which had so denaturalized reason that it too tried "to breathe the ether" instead of the "wholesome air of our own earth." History and the philosophy of history in the next century were to breathe the air of our own earth and were to profit from Herder's effort to achieve a robust historicism, and not from Kant's more rigid and static conception of reason. Hegel's reason in history thus derived from Herder, not from Kant.

Herder's historicism was not, however, as robust as he thought. He hoped that he would not be accused of appealing to "occult qualities" when he spoke of "organic powers of creation."[88] Yet how could he escape this accusation? "Nature does so and so" is not a better explanation than "God does so and so," especially in the writings of a man who can say, "Nature is no real entity, but God is in all his works." The chief defect in Herder's philosophy of history is that he did not take time seriously enough. He gave a morphology of history but not a physiology or genetics of history. While he recognized that "animals are the older brethren of man," he did not know how to interpret this pre-eminently important fact because he did not have a theory of evolution. Until a fully temporalistic dimension is exploited in biology and cosmology, the hierarchies and stratifications of these sciences cannot provide the categories needed for history, the science which requires time.

When Herder came to history proper, he knew many of the social conflicts and tensions which bring about the rise and fall of civilizations, but he knew them in human, not in natural or organic, terms. He knew the transformative role of conflict and cooperation among men, but in spite of his metaphysical pandynamism he failed to see precisely these factors also in nature. Hence, the connection of the empirical dynamism of history with the metaphysical dynamism of nature remained a mystery which he did not uncover in his analogies between man and nature. Before nature can provide a categorial framework for history, nature herself must be made historical. Herder's abstract conception of the forces of nature was a step in that direction, but only a step. The next steps, which were to bring success nearer, remained to be taken by Hegel and Marx.

---

[86] In his review of Herder's *Ideas*, from *Kant on History*, ed. L. W. Beck (Indianapolis: Bobbs-Merrill, 1965), p. 27.

[87] Much of Herder's criticisms of Kant can be surmised from the material in this chapter; his formal attacks on Kant came near the end of his life and contributed nothing new but details and acerbity.

[88] Suphan, XIII, 9–10; Churchill, p. ix.

XVI

On the Threshold of the Critical Philosophy[1]

With the exception of Lessing, German philosophers who lived between Leibniz and Kant are now forgotten. Though I have attempted to rescue a few of them from oblivion, one may nevertheless feel that the neglect they have suffered was not altogether undeserved. Most of what they did was destroyed by "the all-destroyer," as Mendelssohn affectionately called Kant.

Yet Kant did not just destroy. Like an army— not just the German army —he destroyed some things and appropriated others. No ideas of German metaphysics or epistemology passed from the eighteenth century to the nineteenth without going through either Kant or Herder. Much of what Kant found in the corpus of German philosophy he rejected; much of what he rejected was picked up by Herder and deepened and transformed by him and then passed on.

Hume, Rousseau, Leibniz, and Newton were Kant's teachers. His language was that of Wolff and Baumgarten. But three German philosophers who preceded him had moved in his direction, raising questions, sometimes almost unwittingly, which only he was to answer. Had it not been for them, his philosophy might have been differently constructed and might not have

[1] The reader who is not familiar with Kant's philosophy may properly prefer to go directly to Chapter XVII and return to this one later.

gone as far as it did, for Kant would have had to do some of their work before he came to the point of doing what history recognizes as his own. These men—Christian August Crusius, Johann Heinrich Lambert, and Johann Nicolaus Tetens—therefore do not deserve the neglect that has befallen almost all the others.

Crusius

When Kant wrote his *Nova dilucidatio* in 1755 his esteem for Crusius was very high; in 1762, in the Prize Essay, his esteem was moderated into respect; from then on it declined steadily, and, after Kant reached the stage of his critical philosophy, he had only objections. Sometimes there was even a tinge of contempt. Yet in a fragment of unknown date, he wrote:

> The opposition and strife of systems is the only thing which has kept the human understanding, in recent times, from a complete decay with reference to the questions of metaphysics. Though the systems are all dogmatic to the highest degree, nevertheless they perfectly represent the position of the skeptic to anyone who looks at the conflict as a whole. For this reason, we can thank a Crusius as well as a Wolff, since, by the new way they took, they at least prevented the rights of understanding from becoming null and void through stupid disuse, and they preserved the seeds for more certain knowledge.[2]

Kant was correct in thus pairing Wolff and Crusius, for Crusius was the most important critic of Wolff to work within the general scholastic framework of logic and ontology as cognate sciences.

Christian August Crusius was born in Leipzig in 1715 and studied under Adolf Friedrich Hoffmann, whose views he systematically developed. He repeatedly acknowledged Hoffmann as his master. Crusius' philosophical works were published in the 1740's while he was professor of philosophy at Leipzig; in 1751 he became professor of theology and did no more important philosophical work. He died in 1775. His principal philosophical works were: *Advice for a Rational Life* (*Ausweisung vernünftig zu leben*, 1744), *Sketch of the Necessary Truths of Reason* (*Entwurf der nothwendigen Vernunftwahrheiten*, 1745), and *The Way to the Certainty and Dependability of Human Knowledge* (*Weg zur Gewissheit und Zuverlässigkeit der menschlichen Erkenntnis*, 1747).

Crusius was the most systematic and profound of the philosophers belonging to the Thomasian-Pietistic tradition of opposition to Wolff. But in him the level of philosophical thought is so deep that it is difficult to think of any indebtedness he might have to the superficial Thomasius. So far as I know, he never referred to Thomasius, but occasionally recognized the latter's position in the lineage Budde-Rüdiger-Hoffmann, and thereby indicated the provenance of his teachings in Thomasius. Crusius' works constitute a thoroughly scholastic edifice, with definitions in bold-faced type and proofs backed up by many cross-references, so that a page of Crusius looks

---

[2] Reflection 4936, in *Kants Gesammelte Schriften*, hereafter cited as *Kants Ges. Schr.* (Berlin: Preussische Akademie der Wissenschaften, 1902–), XVIII, 33.

like a page of Wolff. But in fact Crusius is opposing almost all the characteristic doctrines of Wolff. Because he did so not by cheap Pietistic polemics but by reasonable argument in favor of an alternative, which was as highly articulated and as systematic (and fortunately not so long) as Wolff's own, Crusius must be counted as the chief academic opponent of the entire Wolffian school, and as the one man who, had he written earlier, might have established a widely accepted anti-Wolffian philosophy. His close adherence to Pietism at a time when neology and orthodoxy were replacing it[3] prevented him from exercising the influence which would have been his twenty years earlier; but some of his doctrines did reappear in the works of several members of the Berlin Academy and finally contributed in important ways to Kant's thought. Because of his anti-intellectualistic—which is to say his anti-Wolffian—orientation, he may have had some influence on the writers of the period of sentimentalism which began in the forties. This is hard to estimate, but Christian Gellert (1717–1769) was at least a pupil of Crusius.

In this account of Crusius' work, I shall consider Crusius as occupying a middle point in the philosophy of the Enlightenment: as Wolff's most effective academic critic, and as the man who first developed some important ideas which were to bear fruit in the work of Kant.

Crusius begins his *Vernunftwahrheiten* by distinguishing philosophy from mathematics both in their subject matters and modes of proof. He reproves Wolff's efforts to model philosophy after mathematics and anticipates some of Kant's arguments in the Prize Essay of 1764, in which Kant set out the differences between mathematics and metaphysics.[4] He is in agreement with Kant that in philosophy we do not begin with simple ideas which we define and build up synthetically, but that we begin with experience which we analyze and try to find implicit in it simple metaphysical ideas.

Crusius sees one of the principal uses of philosophy (and in true Thomasian fashion he insists that any learning ought to be useful) in its relation to theology. While granting that philosophy is not a sufficient condition for faith and virtue, nor even for the attainment of theological truth, which can be got from Scripture, he recommends philosophy as an instrument for systematizing theology and as a weapon against sophistic objections to Christianity. Philosophy receives an accession of knowledge for this service to Christianity; since it deals only with unchangeable and universal truths, it needs to restrict some of its conclusions to the facts of this world by appealing to examples from experience, and the Bible is a record of experience, a source of truths that philosophy could not discover, or could not so easily discover, since these truths are restrictions on universal possible truths.[5] Hence revelation is much more important, and mathematics much less important, to Crusius than to Wolff.

Kant said that the "proud name of ontology" had to give way to the modest name of an "analytic of pure understanding." In this transition

---

[3] Professors in Prussian universities were forbidden by von Zedlitz to lecture from Crusian textbooks. This occurred, however, only in 1775 and probably resulted more from his efforts to modernize the curriculum than from any specific doctrinal disapproval.

[4] *Weg zur Gewissheit*, §§ 5, 9, 10.   [5] *Ibid.*, §§ 32, 33.

Crusius' "Ontology," the first book of his *Vernunftwahrheiten*, stands halfway between Wolff and Kant.

The decisive question in the historical movement from Wolff to Kant turns upon the question of the relation of logical and, more generally, epistemological concepts and principles to ontological concepts and principles. Wolff, in his German metaphysics, *Vernünftige Gedanken von Gott, der Welt, der Seele des Menschen und allen Dingen überhaupt*, began with epistemological questions. Almost in the manner of von Tschirnhaus, he began by discussing the certainty of one's own existence and of the things one experiences before undertaking an examination of the subject matters of special metaphysics (theology, psychology, and cosmology) and of ontology (*"allen Dingen überhaupt"*). Wolff's Latin *Ontologia* did not begin in this way—apparently. But indeed its stand on the question of logic vis-à-vis ontology was the same; the very subtitle describing the book as *"omnis cognitionis humanae principia continentur"* shows this. Kant himself will later use the word "metaphysics" sometimes to refer to the "science of our a priori knowledge," trading upon this Wolffian identification or near-identification of first philosophy with epistemology. Kant does so because he thinks there is no other way to get at the metaphysical problem, and *hence* ontology gives way to an analytic of pure understanding. For Wolff, on the other hand, there was nothing else to be got at, for the only basic principle of both ontological possibility and human cognition is the law of contradiction, and what is validly thought must have an ontological status. Since the principle of sufficient reason was derived by Wolff from the law of contradiction, at least in principle all ontological principles were for him logical principles. Wolff was thus radically essentialistic, not existential in his ontology and metaphysics (see p. 185). When Kant criticizes dogmatism, Wolff's misnamed *Ontologia* is a target. That it was a misnamed logic is sufficient evidence that Wolff was a dogmatist in the pejorative Kantian sense.

Crusius avoids equating ontology with logic and epistemology, but he does make explicit epistemological conditions for ontological assertions. He seems to be doing what Wolff did, but with more awareness of it. Yet this awareness keeps him from making the "dogmatic" mistake Wolff made; it keeps him from identifying epistemological criteria of knowledge with ontological criteria of real (i.e., ontological) possibility and real existence. It also immunizes Crusius against the idealistic infection. Despite his repeated renunciations of idealism, Wolff's phenomenalism and his "consistent dream theory" (see above, p. 266) seemed to show that he succumbed to it; and we shall see how hard both Lambert and Tetens had to fight it. But Crusius escapes easily, simply by not equating the conditions of knowing with the conditions of being. This refusal to identify the epistemological with the ontological is an important step in the direction of Kant. Crusius is helped to this step because he does not take the principles of contradiction and sufficient reason, which can be phrased indifferently as logical or ontological, as criteria both for valid thought and for real existence and possibility.

He accepts, of course, the principle of contradiction as ontologically and epistemologically valid. But he rejects Wolff's principle of sufficient reason.

He does so because of three objections. First, the principle conflicts with our consciousness of freedom, which requires real contingencies in the world—here is the typical Pietistic objection to Wolff. Second, it cannot be proved, as Wolff believed, from the principle of contradiction.[6] Third, it is not precise enough. In its place we need two principles, neither of which can be demonstrated to follow from the law of contradiction.

These principles were first formulated by his teacher Hoffmann, but we have seen something like them in Clauberg, von Tschirnhaus and even in Wolff, though Wolff misinterpreted them as simply forms of the law of contradiction. First, there is the law of the inseparable: "Whatever two things cannot be thought apart one from another cannot exist (or be possible) apart from one another." And, second, the law of the uncombinable: "Whatever two things cannot be thought with and beside one another cannot be possible or exist with and beside one another."[7] The law of contradiction defines only the condition of *logical possibility*; the latter two define the condition of *real possibility* and, with one addendum, the condition of actual existence.

"Can be thought" and "cannot be thought" mean more than "not contradictory" and its opposite. They sometimes refer to hardly more than an ingrained habit of thought,[8] but when Crusius is most acute, they refer to a necessity which is neither a psychological habit nor a logical necessity, but something in between. Crusius does not have a name for it, and perhaps he does not know what a deep problem it is he has touched upon; but we, who have the benefit of the later history of the problem, can see that he is working with synthetic connections known a priori. He is saying that Wolff tried to show every necessity to be ultimately logical and analytic, but that there is another necessity he overlooked.

Let us take several examples of his use of his new laws of thought, to see what was new and revolutionary in them, and what was psychological in a Thomasian, subjectivistic sense.

(a) I *cannot think* something to be true which conflicts with the possibility of my acting rationally. Hence I have a right to say that I know that there is an immaterial substance, that there are contingencies in the world, that I have a free will, and the like.[9]

(b) I *cannot think* that there is no object in the external world (the Cartesian doubt), for I have sensations and "sensation is the state of our

---

[6] Kant applauds him for seeing this, in *Nova dilucidatio*, Prop. ix, *Kants Ges. Schr.*, I, 398; English translation in F. E. England, *Kant's Conception of God* (London: Allen & Unwin, 1929), p. 226.

[7] *Entwurf der nothwendigen Vernunftwahrheiten*, § 15. (Hereafter cited as *Vernunftwahrheiten*.)

[8] Kant is emphatic that this is *all* Crusius can mean. "His criterion of truth, which is no criterion, gives free reign to enthusiasm [*Schwärmerei*]" (*Logic*, Introduction, ii, in *Kants Ges. Schr.*, IX, 21). Crusius makes mere custom and incapacity to think otherwise into an objective necessity—Letter to Karl Leonhard Reinhold, May 19, 1789, in *Kant's Philosophical Correspondence*, ed. Arnulf Zweig (Chicago: University of Chicago Press, 1967, p. 144). Crusius's theory of knowledge is based on subjective innate ideas and pre-established harmony between ideas and their objects (Reflections 4275 and 4446, in *Kants Ges. Schr.*, XVII, 492, 554).

[9] *Vernunftwahrheiten*, §§ 15, 57, 346.

understanding in which we are constrained to think immediately of the existence of a thing." Sensation is the mark of real existence and not of mere possibility; I cannot think of a sensation and not think of an object of it.[10]

(c) I *cannot think* of a thing as existing without thinking that it is somewhere and at some time. (This is the addendum to the two principles mentioned above.) Hence objects necessarily exist in space and time, even though it is not self-contradictory to speak of objects that are nowhere and exist at no time.[11]

(d) Crusius distinguishes between the real ground and the ideal ground of the possibility and existence of things. The *principium cognoscendi* and the *principium essendi* of a really possible object may be the same (as the reason why the size of one angle of a triangle, the other two being given, is necessarily what it is and is the reason why it is known to be what it is); but they are never the same in a really existing being. Existence is never a part of the essence of a thing, because existence and essence can be thought separately.[12] Thus Crusius denies the validity of the ontological argument, for while the thought of perfection is not separable from the thought of existence, the thought of perfection is separable from the thought of existence *outside thought*.[13]

(e) Finally, and most significantly, there is the corollary of (d). It is that the causal connection is not a logical connection. There is no contradiction in asserting the cause and denying the effect. Yet there is a real and a necessary connection between them because we cannot think the cause and the effect as occurring separately. The terms "cause" and "effect" are logically related; but the causal axiom does not merely state the tautology that every effect has a cause, but the "synthetic" (to use Kant's terminology) connection between independently conceivable events.[14] Crusius' reason for saying that there is a causal relation is the regular association of two events in our experience, for he admits that we have no intuitive knowledge

---

[10] *Ibid.*, §§ 16, 476.

[11] *Ibid.*, § 46. Kant objects that this principle does not distinguish between real and possible objects; later he will say that it does not distinguish between phenomenal and noumenal objects (see *Einzig möglicher Beweisgrund, Kants Ges. Schr.*, II, 76. In §§ 48–54 of the *Vernunftwahrheiten* Crusius anticipates in remarkable fashion some of Kant's conclusions concerning space and time as having a necessity that is not conceptual or logical. Space and time are neither relations, attributes of substances, substances, nor concepts, but "individual *abstracta* of existence." Unlike Kant after 1770, however, he thinks they are real, not forms of appearance. Note also, for another divergence between Kant and Crusius, the belief of the latter that mathematical propositions are (in Kant's language) analytic (*Vernunftwahrheiten* § 234).

[12] *Vernunftwahrheiten*, §§ 34–38.

[13] *Ibid.*, § 235. But in § 121 he argued that if anything is possible, something else must exist. We shall find this proposition used by Lambert and by Kant in his version of the ontological argument proposed in 1764. In Crusius, however, it has a considerably simpler meaning: possibility is the relation of something that does not yet exist to a cause which does exist (*Weg zur Gewissheit*, § 423).

[14] *Vernunftwahrheiten*, §§ 33, 72; *Weg zur Gewissheit*, § 260. J. S. Beck wrote Kant on August 24, 1793 (*Kants Ges. Schr.*, XI, 444–45), that § 260 was a better example of an early distinction between analytic and synthetic judgments than the one Kant had cited from Locke.

of causes and forces. He has a Hume-like propensity to feign, and tries to turn it, by these principles, into an objective necessity. Crusius failed to see the consequences of his discovery that all causal knowledge is empirical, not rational. But the important thing that Crusius, as opposed to Wolff, did see was that the connection between events is, if necessary at all, not logically necessary. It remained for Kant to give a "transcendental" interpretation of this principle of what can be and what cannot be thought together; neither Crusius nor, as we shall see, Tetens, had in fact gone beyond the psychological level of justification of the belief in necessary connections.

Crusius' clear recognition of the radical difference between the relation of cause to effect and that of logical ground to consequent must be considered his chief contribution to the breakdown of Wolffian logicism. Crusius recognized that the relation of cause to effect must be expressed in what Kant was to call a synthetic judgment; yet because we cannot think one without the other and because he has a general epistemological rule for such a situation, Crusius does not draw Hume's skeptical conclusion from this fact. Had he used Kant's language he would have called the causal principle a synthetic judgment known a priori—that is, known to be necessary. By Wolffian standards, at least, this means that a nonlogical but necessary element is present in all our knowledge of reality. The Wolffian identity of thought-necessities with thing-necessities is broken. Thereby another step was taken toward Kant, who carefully distinguishes between the logical necessities of thought and the necessities of existence and between logical and real possibilities.

It might appear, however, that Crusius in substituting his two laws for Wolff's single logical principle and then claiming that what cannot (not: *logically* cannot) be thought together cannot exist together made a merely subjective (not logical) principle determinative of reality. If this were the case, his theory would be in worse trouble than Wolff's. His words do suggest that he did so, but in fact he did not. For Crusius makes a distinction between intuitive and symbolic knowledge, and his laws of thought are true only for the objects of symbolic knowledge.

We can know a thing directly or absolutely, as we know, for instance, our own existence. Crusius calls this intuitive knowledge. Intuitive knowledge is knowledge that something is, but not knowledge of what it is, which always requires comparisons and relations. We can also know a thing indirectly or relatively, i.e., by knowing its relation to something else. This is what Crusius calls symbolic knowledge. For instance, we know most primitive forces by knowing their effects, and hence we have only symbolic knowledge of them; but, in the case of the primitive forces of our own souls, we know that they exist and hence know them intuitively. Since the two rules of thought apply to our association of one concept with another, they apply only to our symbolic knowledge. The objects of intuitive knowledge may be asserted to exist even if our symbolic knowledge of them should be antinomic. That is, the laws of symbolic thought are not necessarily valid in an ontological sense.

Consider two cases. (1) We cannot think of space as without a limit; hence space must be thought as finite. We cannot think of space as coming to an end; therefore it must be thought as infinite. Accepting the two propositions leads us into a conflict, which Crusius calls a "collision of principles" (and Kant will call it an antinomy). (2) We cannot think an action without a cause; therefore there is no freedom. We cannot think a moral action without freedom. Hence some actions must be both caused and uncaused. Thus our causal and moral knowledge are in conflict.[15]

Crusius proposes to resolve these antinomies which arise from not being able to think of two objects or predicates separately in one context and together in another, by what he calls a "warning rule": when such antinomies arise between the applications of the two rules, we are to attribute them to the limitation of our mind, and are not to infer that they could not be reconciled by a superior mind.[16] Since we know, intuitively, that our will is free, but do not know how it is free and do not know how to render its freedom symbolically intelligible, the antinomies of symbolic thought are insulated from metaphysics by this warning rule, and access is given to ontological statements by a nonrational (i.e., nonsymbolic) intuition. Thus in a somewhat crude form Crusius draws and uses a distinction not unlike that between noumena and phenomena in Kant. (We must remember, however, to translate properly: symbolic knowledge in Crusius becomes knowledge with an intuitive base in Kant. Crusius did not, however, use this distinction as Kant was to use it, for the purpose of limiting knowledge strictly to what can be experienced; that is, to deny knowledge of the supersensible in order to make room for a purely rational faith. Rather, being a good Pietist, he made the warning rule serve to mark out the region where revelation can afford us knowledge which we could not obtain by our investigation of the world of experience. The warning rule prepares us to recognize that what we cannot think (provided it is not self-contradictory) need not be declared impossible, and must not be declared to be impossible if this declaration would bring us into conflict with a duty laid upon us by God. Since revelation gives knowledge (and not merely the substance of faith) and gives knowledge that goes beyond, and indeed against, the knowledge we have through the use of the other principles of thought, Crusius is, in the final analysis, espousing a theory of twofold truth.[17]

After these profound adumbrations of what is to come in the history of German philosophy, the rest of Crusius' philosophy is likely to be somewhat disappointing. But there is much in the thousand pages of his *Vernunftwahrheiten* that is worthy of the attention of a historian or philosopher: his nominalism (§ 17), his denial of determining and his assertion of sufficient conditions of free acts (§ 83), his theory of the various species of perfection and analysis of the ambiguities in the concept of perfection (§§ 180–189), his theory of the interaction between mind and body (§ 363), his analysis of the concept of machine and his denial that the world is a machine

---

[15] Crusius formulates the problem of freedom more carefully than I here indicate, but I am using it only as an example of a general policy he follows.

[16] *Vernunftwahrheiten*, §§ 58, 252.

[17] *An cum B. Luthero recte negari possit, idem verum esse in philosophia et theologia* (1745), §§ 1, 10, 17; I have not seen this, but cite from Max Wundt, *Kant als Metaphysiker* (Stuttgart, 1924), p. 61n.

(§ 382), his argument for miracles (§ 340, §§ 375–378), his denial that we can know this to be the best of all possible worlds (§ 388). Though Wolff is never mentioned, most of the book is a sustained argument against Wolff's determinism, intellectualism, and optimism. But since we are interested in the paths that led to Kant, we must turn to Crusius' practical philosophy, for which he is sharply criticized by Kant.

But here again we must begin by contrasting Crusius to Wolff. Wolff had held that volition arises from our representation of a perfection, the maintenance or attainment of which is accompanied by pleasure. There is no independent faculty of will, but only various levels of clarity in the faculty of desire, depending upon the clarity with which perfections are perceived. Hence Wolff's theory of action is thoroughly intellectualistic; knowledge of a good is the necessary and sufficient condition of desiring it, and the enlightenment of our ideas is the way to virtue and happiness.

Crusius, on the other hand, appealing to the arguments of Rüdiger, holds that there are two fundamental forces (Grundkräfte) in the soul, understanding and will. Just as the understanding is studied in the science of logic, there is another science, "thelematology," which studies the will and provides the foundation for the practical sciences.

Will is defined as the power to act according to one's ideas; the power of representation does not necessarily entail any power or desire to act upon the ideas or to realize their objects. It is not, however, a blind power wholly independent of the understanding, for without ideas one cannot desire or will anything. Yet it is not subservient to the understanding for, on the contrary, thought and understanding exist only for the sake of action and the will.[18]

Crusius gives another definition of the will which he thinks follows from the one just given, and this leads into his practical philosophy. Will is the power of a rational being to desire the good and to reject the evil. But instead of defining the good in terms of an ontological perfection, Crusius holds that perfection is the achievement of the natural final goal of a thing, and the good is whatever agrees with or helps us to achieve this final goal.[19] But this final goal cannot be found if we restrict the powers of the soul to mere willing and thinking; there must be desires for various kinds of things or natural ends. The function of the intellect is to give us ideas of these goals and to show how they may be attained; the function of the will is to execute the acts which will lead to these goals, and to choose between goals when they are in conflict.[20]

Crusius gives various lists of the Grundtriebe, or fundamental desires. Besides the desire for truth, there are the Triebe for our own perfection and happiness, for the love of God, and for obedience to God's commands.[21] But since God has designed man and established his happiness as an ultimate goal,[22] we can achieve this happiness only through obedience to God's commands, which we desire to do through the Gewissenstrieb, or impulse

[18] Vernunftwahrheiten, §§ 427, 445, 453.
[19] Ibid., §§ 183–199.
[20] Ibid., §§ 446, 449–450.
[21] Ibid., §§ 452, 478.
[22] Ibid., §§ 285, 478.

of conscience. When we do so, we are in a state of virtue, and "out of obedience to God and knowledge of our obligation, we perform all acts according to the rules of the essential perfection of things and thus in accord with the moral will of God."[23]

The dependence of the moral good on God does not mean that it is an arbitrary and changeable dictate of God's will, as Kant let it appear,[24] for there are natural goods and God's will is not arbitrary but determined, rather, by the natural goals and powers and perfections of the creature. Contingent duties (if there be such) are necessary not simply because God commanded them; rather, they hold because he commanded them and one of the *natural* ends of man is to obey God. With respect to the legal, moral, and prudential aims of mankind, their material comes from human nature, and actions directed toward them are made virtuous by our seeing the actions as commanded by God, who created human nature with its natural goals. While Crusius thinks that man's happiness and blessedness are to be attained in another world, he moves from the narrowly Pietistic renunciation of the natural impulses of man, puts them into a religious context as being ends established by God in accordance with man's created nature, and gives them a this-worldly moral and political significance. In this respect, he moves from Pietism into the broad middle areas of the eudaemonism of the Enlightenment, where he and Wolff are at one; but in the details of his ethics, and the extensive duties we have to God, the spirit is still not Wolffian.

Lambert: "The Leading Genius of Germany"

Johann Heinrich Lambert was addressed by Kant as "the leading genius in Germany." C. S. Peirce called him "the greatest formal logician of those days."[25] When Frederick the Great asked him, as a candidate for membership in the Berlin Academy, what sciences he was a master of, the awkward Lambert answered, "All." When the King asked him who his teachers were, he replied, "I, myself." The King said, "Ah, another Pascal!", and Lambert modestly replied, "Yes, your Majesty." A remarkable man, now almost forgotten, but worthy of study.

Lambert is sometimes classified as a Wolffian, but he so far exceeded all the others in originality and modernity that he cannot be properly treated among Wolff's epigoni. He was less comprehensive and encyclopedic (and prolix) than Wolff, but he had one great advantage over him, especially in his logical and cosmological writings: he was an original and creative mathematician and practicing scientist, who knew from his own experience what

---

[23] *Ibid.*, § 481; *Ausweisung vernünftig zu leben*, § 26.

[24] *Critique of Practical Reason*, in *Kants Ges. Schr.*, V, 40; *ibid.*, trans. L. W. Beck (New York: Liberal Arts Press, 1956), p. 41. What Kant says is entirely correct with respect to the "contingent duties," but of the necessary moral duties his remark is not entirely fair to Crusius.

[25] Kant's letter to Lambert, December 31, 1765, in *Kant's Philosophical Correspondence* p. 47. Kant originally planned to dedicate the *Critique of Pure Reason* to him and even wrote the dedication, but changed his mind when Lambert died. Peirce, *Collected Papers*, (Cambridge, Mass.: Harvard University Press), II, § 345.

it was to do an experiment, devise an instrument, and prove a theorem.[26] This gives his writings in philosophy a substance and tone lacking since the days of Leibniz, and they make Wolff's writings on scientific method and Wolff's opponents' views on cosmology seem to belong to an earlier century.

Lambert was born in 1728 in Mühlhausen, Alsace, of poor parents who could not give him opportunities for a university education. He was apprenticed as an amanuensis and secretary to a Swiss lawyer, then worked as a private tutor and later as a surveying engineer in Switzerland. During these years he was a prodigious reader and quietly pursued his scientific investigations. In 1761 he published his *Cosmological Letters*[27] which showed his skill as an astronomical observer and mathematical astronomer, and an astronomical imagination comparable to Kant's in their somewhat similar interpretations of the Milky Way. In 1761 he wrote his first philosophical work, *Abhandlung von dem Criterium veritatis*, and he worked on a contribution to the prize essay competition of the Berlin Academy on the question whether metaphysical sciences are capable of the same degree of evidence as the mathematical, but did not complete it.[28] Desiring membership in the Berlin Academy, for which he was sponsored by Sulzer and Euler, he hurriedly published his *Neues Organon* (Leipzig, 1764) which he had written between October 1762 and November 1763. He was accepted into the Academy in January 1764 in spite of the reluctance of Frederick the Great, who had not been amused by the conversation reported in our first paragraph. He was the only member of the Academy who was permitted a seat in each of its four classes. The *Anlage zur Architektonic* was written in 1764 but not published until 1771 (with the help of Kant, and by Kant's publisher, Hartknoch in Riga). The remainder of Lambert's life —he died September 25, 1777, of tuberculosis—was spent in his scientific pursuits and lecturing in the Academy.

We can best discover what was new in Lambert's philosophy by examining some of the many statements he made about his predecessors. To Wolff, he says, belongs the honor of having introduced a correct and useful method into philosophy; but he did not go far enough in his mathematizing of philosophy. He brought half the method of mathematics into philosophy, and Lambert saw it as his own task to bring the other half of mathematics into philosophy.[29] The half which Wolff had brought in was the theory of

---

[26] Lambert first demonstrated the irrationality of π; he was the first to introduce hyperbolic functions into trigonometry; he made various conjectures about non-Euclidean space (see Roberto Bonola, *Non-Euclidean Geometry* [LaSalle: Open Court, 1938], pp. 44–51); he formulated several theorems about conic sections which simplified the calculation of the orbit of comets. He invented the first practical photometer and hygrometer, and improved the thermometer. He contributed to geometrical optics and wrote a classic work on perspective. He made several acute conjectures concerning the structure of the galaxy and covered some of the same ground as Kant's *Natural History of the Heavens*, which he had not read. His name still survives in physics in the so-called "Lambert-Beer Law" of the absorption of light.

[27] Selections from the *Letters* are published in M. K. Munitz, *Theories of the Universe* (Glencoe, Ill.: The Free Press, 1957).

[28] These works were first published by Karl Bopp in *Kant-Studien Ergänzungshefte* 36 and 42 (1915, 1918), the latter under the title *Ueber die Methode die Metaphysik, Theologie und Moral richtiger zu beweisen* (hereafter cited as *Methode*).

[29] *Anlage zur Architektonic* §§ 10, 12, 14, 23 (hereafter cited as *Architektonic*).

definition and proof; the part he neglected was the theory of postulates and constructions. Wolff took nominal definitions "as it were, gratis" and, "without noticing it, hid all the difficulties in them."[30] Nominal definitions by genus and differentia and proofs by means of syllogisms, however, have two infirmities in mathematics: they do not guarantee the truth of the premises, and hence do not lend truth to the conclusions; and they do not aid in the discovery of any mathematical truths. Lambert describes his discovery of these weaknesses as follows:

I read Euclid only long after I had read Wolff, and not so much for the purpose of learning his theorems as for the purposes of evaluating the esteem Wolff had for him because of the rigorous order and connection of his theorems. I knew already pretty well what the scholastic and mathematical methods were, and the first proposition of Euclid, in spite of that, astonished me.[31] . . . Euclid does not derive his *Elements* from the definition of either space or geometry [as Wolff did][32] but he began with lines, angles, etc., as the simple in the dimensions of space . . .[33] I saw why he began with the possibility of an equilateral triangle. He needed for this only a line, and since lines can differ only in length, he put before the eyes of those who doubted the possibility of an equilateral triangle the fact that they could refute themselves, by showing how they could make such a triangle of any size. This problem . . . served to put beyond doubt the whole theory, and prevented the inclusion of any merely imagined figure, since only possible figures are included . . . The principal point lay in this: the possibility of the equilateral triangle showed itself, or spoke for itself . . . Should not this means suffice for the proof of concepts, which one could take to be fundamental concepts? At least it seemed to me that logic had its certainty in this way.[34]

To supply the missing portion of mathematical method to philosophy, that is, to supply proofs that the theorems present real possibilities and not merely logically consistent analyses of arbitrary complex concepts,[35] Lambert turned away from Wolff to Locke and Leibniz, with a recommendation of Crusius and Darjes on the side.[36]

Locke, he tells us, gave an anatomy of our concepts and proceeded a posteriori.[37] He did discover simple ideas; and Lambert's lists of simple

30 Letter to Kant, February 3, 1766, in *Kants Ges. Schr.*, X, 64.

31 *Criterium veritatis*, § 79.

32 Wolff failed to distinguish theorems from arbitrary complex concepts, and he gave nominal definitions of the latter and thought he was proving the former. *Ibid.*, § 26.

33 Letter to Kant, February 3, 1766, in *Kant's Philosophical Correspondence*, p. 53.

34 *Criterium veritatis* § 79. See also *Architektonic*, § 12.

35 Lambert is here saying what Kant will say more clearly later, viz., that mathematical concepts are arbitrary in the sense that they are not empirical, but they are not arbitrary in the sense that one can make them up as one will, since mathematical concepts must be constructable. Thus one can give a nominal definition of a digon (a two-sided plane figure); but, since one cannot construct a digon, such a definition is of no help in any mathematical proof.

36 Joachim Georg Darjes (1714–1771; from 1735 to 1753 professor in Jena, then Baumgarten's successor in Frankfort) began as a Wolffian but later came under the influence of Crusius and attacked Wolff on the principle of sufficient reason and the pre-established harmony in the relation of mind to body. Lambert is probably alluding to Darjes' *Via ad veritatem* (1755).

37 *Neues Organon*, II, § 29; *Architektonic* § 7.

ideas, though more extensive than Locke's, included most of those which Locke considered simple: extension, solidity, movement, existence, duration and succession, unity, consciousness, moving force, and will;[38] and he later added magnitude, light, colors, sounds, warmth, being, becoming, not, like, before, because, however, and so on.[39] In his important letter to Kant on February 3, 1766, he adds space and time to this list but excludes "thing" as, "of all concepts, the most synthesized."[40] Lambert's purpose however, could not be achieved by a "plain, historical method," for he wanted to bring out the "universal possibility" of the combination of ideas—in other words, he wanted Lockean matter, but Wolffian form.[41]

This combination is possible through Leibniz' *ars characteristica*. Leibniz was not an anatomist but an analyst of concepts. By an analysis of a concept Leibniz meant the discovery of all its component concepts. Wolff had followed Leibniz part of the way, but he took a wrong turn and considered the analysis of a concept to include also relational concepts, which could be stated in nominal definitions employing *genus et differentia*. But if the latter path is followed, the evolution of a concept is infinite, and we cannot ever know whether the concept may not contain some contradiction. Leibniz' analysis was one that led to simple concepts which, because they were simple, could contain no contradiction; hence Leibniz could give proof of combinations of concepts and Wolff could not. Whether we begin as analysts or as anatomists of human reason we come to the same simple elements we are seeking.[42]

Lambert pushes the history of his problem still further back. Simple ideas, he tells us, are clear, in the Cartesian sense; but Descartes used the criteria of clearness and distinctness too broadly, applying them as criteria of the truth of all, even complex, ideas. Descartes accordingly neglected proof, and made the opposite error to that of Ramus, who ruined mathematics with his scholastic proofs which excluded construction and intuition.[43]

Lambert, therefore, saw himself as mediating between Locke and Wolff, or, by analogy, between Descartes and Peter Ramus. His most direct predecessor was Leibniz, and Lambert is the last representative of Leibniz' ideal of a Universal Characteristic: "It is the destiny of philosophy," Lambert says, "to do for quality what mathematics has done for quantity."[44] But because Lambert was very much on the side of Newton against Leibniz in the cosmological debates going on in the Academy at that time, being allied with Euler, his relation to Leibniz does not come out so clearly as that to Locke and Wolff. (When Lambert's *Architektonic* was published in 1771, its resemblance to Leibniz' treatment of Locke in the *Nouveaux Essais* was immediately noticed and commented upon; but we know that the *Architektonic* was completed before the *Nouveaux Essais* were published in 1765.)

Everything in Lambert's philosophy turns on the discovery of simple concepts, the derivation from them of propositions which are "logically

---

[38] *Neues Organon*, II, § 36.
[39] *Architektonic*, § 46.
[40] *Kant's Philosophical Correspondence*, pp. 51, 52.
[41] *Neues Organon* II, § 14.
[43] *Criterium veritatis*, §§ 4, 20.
[42] *Architektonic*, §§ 7–10, 13.
[44] *Methode*, § 5.

true," the construction of a "realm of (logical) truth," and then the proof that some of these possible truths are "metaphysically true," i.e., actual truths about existing objects. We shall take these parts of his philosophy in order.

A. *Simple concepts*. Simple, or fundamental, concepts (*Grundbegriffe*) are a subclass of empirical concepts (*Erfahrungsbegriffe*) and must be found by the Lockean method of collecting and inspecting (*Musterung*) examples. But whereas empirical concepts may be erroneous (i.e., may have no object corresponding to them) and give only a mere delusory appearance of things, the fundamental concepts are derived from the experience of the *sensu interno* and must be granted even by the skeptic (the solipsist, *der Egoist*) who denies the existence of everything except himself and his experience.[45] The simple concepts can only be ostensively defined, not nominally. They can appear as predicates in a judgment whose subject is a complex empirical concept; but in this case the subject can be analyzed into simple concepts, and the original judgment will thereby be resolved into tautologies ("white is white"), simple negative propositions like Locke's intuited disagreements of ideas ("white is not black"), or relational propositions (such as "space has length, breadth, and height" or "motion has velocity and direction").[46]

B. *Combinations of simple concepts*. Our knowledge of such propositions is a priori, for though experience is necessary if we are to have the concepts, we do not have to experience their combinations to see the truth of the propositions.[47] The various sciences are based upon some of the simple concepts (for example, geometry on that of space, chronometry on that of time, phoronomy on space and time, "agathology" on the concept of good), and Lambert builds up large and elaborate tables showing what simple concepts are involved in each of the branches of science and philosophy.[48]

But while Lambert is clear in his theory of simple concepts, his theory of their combination is no more satisfactory than that of Crusius. Lambert uses a weaker form of Crusius' criterion of what can or cannot be thought together, calling it the criterion of "thinkability" (*Gedenkbarkeit*). But while thinkability is a test for a concept, something stronger is needed as a test for judgment; "not to be thought apart," or "must be thought together" as Crusius would say, are needed. This criterion of thinkability, or inseparability, applies to propositions whose predicate is included in the subject, as Leibniz thought; but obviously it will not work for that reason on propositions connecting *simple subjects* and predicates. Lambert sometimes appeals to the law of contradiction, which in turn is based upon the incredibility (*nicht-glauben-lassen*) of contradictions[49] and sometimes to

[45] *Criterium veritatis* §§ 45, 80; *Methode*, Notanda § 14 and § 36; *Neues Organon* I, §§ 653–656.

[46] *Neues Organon* I, §§ 656, 659; II, §§ 32, 33, 72, 73.

[47] *Ibid.*, I, §§ 634–644, 656–657.

[48] "Table of the simple conceptual correlates of fundamental disciplines," *Architektonic* § 53.

[49] *Neues Organon*, II, § 162; *Architektonic*, § 273.

the mere possibility of thinking a combination of ideas under maxim that "*cogitabile* is equal to *possibile*."[50] But if *Gedenkbarkeit* is too weak a test, the law of contradiction is too stringent, and Lambert must rightly confess that the "*fons possibilitatis duos ideas combinandi* has not been fully discovered."[51] It was to remain hidden until Kant clearly distinguished the synthetic a priori from the analytic; and to explain the kind of combinations Lambert and Crusius were concerned with required the whole labor of the *Critique of Pure Reason*.

The total system of all the simple concepts and their permissible combinations constitutes what Lambert calls the realm of truth.[52] It is equally the object of logic (i.e., the science of reason, *Vernunftlehre*) and ontology, which is therefore completely a priori, since it deals with objects only insofar as they are possible. Still, Lambert does not wish the realm of truth to be defined solely in formal terms as a set of noncontradictory propositions having simple concepts as their subjects. He speaks rather of a harmony[53] reigning in the realm of truth. Harmony is what later in the history of philosophy will be called "coherence." Each proposition in the system is not only consistent with all the others, but harmonizes with it in some more intimate fashion, supporting and being supported by all the others. Every erroneous proposition can be discovered by a stepwise process (*Schritt für Schritt*, as Lambert liked to say) of testing it against each of the others; but since every proposition is ultimately reducible to simple concepts which are always logically true, every error contains some truth which we are to discover by analysis. The most harmonious system is, by definition, the logically true system: wholly unified, with no contingencies, and completely comprehensive. Any lacuna is a warning, and any dissonance a sign of error.[54]

C. *Logical and metaphysical truth*. Only one desideratum is lacking in such a harmonious system. It is concerned only with logical truth or possibility, not with actual existence. Lambert believes that anything excluded from the realm of logical truth must also be denied metaphysical truth. There can be no metaphysical truth which is not also logical truth, he says against Crusius; but the converse does not hold. There may be much in the realm of logical truth excluded from the realm of metaphysical truth.[55] Lambert does not take the last refuge of the rationalist and idealist, equating logical with metaphysical truth, as this occurs when coherence is raised from a criterion to a definition of truth. He sees that the realm of logical truth is constructed a priori, but he asks how do we find what *really* exists? How do we move from the "can exist" within the realm of truth to the "does exist" of metaphysical truth?

In the fourth book of his *Neues Organon*, entitled "Phenomenology," Lambert studies appearances of things as a way of finding what actually exists. This is one of the most interesting parts of his work, and though

[50] *Methode*, Notanda § 19, μ.   [51] *Ibid.*, μ, 1°.
[52] *Architektonic* §§ 229, 231, 273; *Methode*, §§ 23–25; but the term is not used in the *Criterium veritatis*.
[53] Compare *Neues Organon* I § 662 and II §§ 160–161 with II, § 180.
[54] *Ibid.*, II, §§ 191–240.   [55] *Architektonic* §§ 293–297.

he never mentions Malebranche it is clear that he learned much from the *Récherche de la vérité* on the discovery and correction of illusion. This was a subject close to Lambert's scientific interests, which included the design of instruments for measuring sensory qualities, eliminating the subjective and personal elements in observations, and determining the appearances of things, as in the theory of perspective (on which he wrote a major work) and stellar parallax. Lambert was repeatedly impressed with the success of the astronomers in moving from the appearances of stars to their very different actual disposition in space,[56] and much of his practical advice on the identification of errors in observation grew out of his experience in the observatory. Since the word "appearance" in German (*Schein*) is drawn from optics, Lambert calls phenomenology a "transcendent optics,"[57] a study of appearance in all its modes and not merely the visual appearance (*Bild*) of things.

Schein does not necessarily refer to illusion;[58] only the skeptic and the idealist put this narrow interpretation upon it. Since it includes the notion of illusion, however, in the sense in which Lambert is using it *Schein* has two possible objects: reality as it appears, and appearances without any corresponding reality (dreams, sensory illusions, imaginary things, and so on).[59] To be a real object, that is, to possess metaphysical truth, an object must at least conform to the rule of the realm of truth, and be harmonious with other things and orderly in its appearances, while a dream is characterized by disorder and dissonance. Here, then, is one way of locating and isolating illusion within the realm of appearance: by experiments to determine which appearances can be taken as appearances of real things and which are illusory because they depend only on us. By experience we learn what is *mere appearance* and what is the *appearance of something*. Some appearances can be explained by the medium between us and the object, some by our position or motion, some by the conditions of our sense organs, others by the state of mind we are in. Lambert gives a taxonomy, aetiology, and therapy of illusory appearance. The fifth chapter of the Phenomenology contains an account of probability—of that which appears to be true (*wahrscheinlich*).

[56] In the important letter Lambert wrote Kant, October 13, 1770, to which we shall have to revert repeatedly, he said, "In metaphysics, where the problem of appearance is so essential, the method of the astronomer will surely be the safest" (*Kant's Philosophical Correspondence* p. 65). This may well have planted the Copernican simile in Kant's mind.

[57] *Methode*, § 45; *Neues Organon*, IV, § 4. Lambert uses the word "transcendent" to mean "having reference to more than one kind of experience." Thus some simple concepts such as force are called "transcendent concepts" to indicate that they apply both to physical bodies and, at least metaphorically, to acts of will. He takes the term from the scholastic distinction between categories (modes of being) and *transcendentalia* (*unum, bonum, verum, aliquid*), which apply to all modes of being. Tetens uses the term in the same way Lambert does, but both differ from Kant. See note 105.

[58] *Neues Organon*, IV, §§ 6, 9, 14. Since *Schein* does ordinarily refer to illusion, Lambert is using the word in an unusual sense; and Kant is careful to distinguish *Schein* from *Erscheinung*, since the latter word does not have this connotation. But his *Erscheinung* is about the same as Lambert's *Schein*, except when *Schein* does mean illusion.

[59] *Architektonic*, §§ 304, 350.

Still, however, Lambert has not crossed the bridge from logical to metaphysical truth, though he has shown how not to go from logical truth to the chaos (which Lambert invariably misspells *Cahos*) of a dream-world. He was unimpressed by the "consistent dream theory" (see p. 266) which Wolff used in spite of his commitment to a nonidealistic theory; and surprisingly he showed no acquaintance with Berkeley's highly ingenious argument (accepted by his fellow academician Maupertuis) that a consistent appearance is sufficient for knowledge and with his refutation of attempts to move from the existence of ideas to the existence of material substances. In his failure to take account of Berkeley's acute criticism of material substance, Lambert avails himself of old arguments which are not up to his usual standards and, when we strip away all the scholastic apparatus, we find Lambert innocently allied with Dr. Johnson. This is one of the weakest parts of Lambert's philosophy, but also one of the most important.

He takes two simple concepts which have a transcendent meaning to be definitive of "an existing thing," and both of them he gets from Locke. These two concepts, which have and are known to have metaphysical as well as logical truth, are the solid and force. Solid in its literal sense means a material thing occupying space and excluding other things from its locus, and in its transcendent sense, any individual substance, such as a soul, which he thinks of in metaphors drawn from body. By force is meant literally the power to move or produce a change in a solid; but in its transcendent sense it refers also to that in the soul (the will) which can effect changes. It will be remembered that Locke had said that our ideas of powers make up a large part of what we understand by a substance, and Lambert is doing little more than repeating Locke here.

In their literal sense, force and solidity are simple ideas given in our immediate experience; they therefore have "logical truth," that is, they contain nothing self-contradictory because they are unanalyzable simple concepts.

Now Lambert tries to show that (a) unless something *does* actually exist, nothing *can* exist, for possibility depends upon actuality;[60] and (b) solidity and force actually exist. The first is a consequence of the proposition that real possibility is always contingent upon a condition that actually exists. (One might say, the question "Can it rain?" is meaningless unless there is either sunshine or clouds; if there were in our universe neither clouds nor rain it would not make sense to say that "it can rain, but it won't.") Now the condition under which a thing is possible is the existence of another thing and its power (which may or may not be actualized) to produce this thing. Hence we do not have to argue synthetically from the existence of one thing to the existence of another; we argue analytically from the possibility of one thing to the existence of something. Now power and solidity

---

[60] *Architektonic*, §§ 297, 471. This argument had become almost a commonplace; see Leibniz, *Monadology* § 43, and above, pp. 264 and 398 for its use in Wolff and Crusius. Kant uses this in his argument for the existence of God in *Einzig möglicher Beweisgrund*. But it does not mean at all the same thing in all its appearances; in Wolff, for instance, it has a definitely idealistic slant (possibilities are thoughts in God's mind) while in Crusius it is based upon an analysis of "causally possible." Lambert seems to follow Crusius here.

are "logically true" (their concepts are not self-contradictory) and therefore they must be logically possible; but what would make them really possible is something actual, precisely what they seem to denote, viz., a solid having power. Therefore, at least two simple ideas have metaphysical truth.[61]

Over this shaky bridge Lambert thinks he has crossed the chasm between logical and metaphysical truth. Once safely on the other side, he again returns to less scholastically subtle "proofs" and says many sensible and intelligent things about our knowledge of real existence. He follows Locke in distinguishing between sensory qualities like colors, which are only signs of the qualities and powers of solids,[62] and primary qualities which belong to objects and which "we represent not by alien images (fremden Bildern) but in themselves, sensing them as such.[63] To understand nature, we must learn to "translate the language of nature, which is optical" into the "true language," which is geometrical and mechanical. We do so under the axiom that the variations in the signs correspond to variations in their object, and that the variations in the object are dependent upon their essential features, which are solidity, force, and motion.[64] It is easy to understand the loving attention Lambert gives to these "translations" when we recall how much of his scientific work lay in devising instruments for geometrizing the language of vision; we understand how much truth there was in Lambert's obiter dictum: "What cannot be weighed and calculated is to me nothing, I understand nothing of it."[65]

Almost no German philosophy, of course, is complete without a proof of the existence of God, but Lambert gives this matter only cursory attention and points out so many objections to the proofs before he gives his own that one is astonished to find him even venturing one.[66] In the Architektonic there is a proof which professes to be a counterpart to the proof of the external world and depends upon the transcendent meaning of the concepts of force and solidity. The realm of truth, Lambert writes, would be an empty dream if there were not metaphysical truth; but it would not be even a dream were there not an existing thing which had the power to make it possible (and it is possible, because it is actual). Hence the existence or the mere possibility of a realm of truth justifies us in making a suppositum intelligens of our soul, and, since the realm of truth comprises eternal verities, it follows [?] that "a necessary, eternal, unchangeable suppositum intelligens must exist."[67]

Only very minimal use of the concept of God is to be found in Lambert's works. In the Cosmological Letters there are occasional references to the wise design of the sidereal universe, but almost never is the existence of a Designer taken as a premise for drawing any conclusions; his astronomy

---

[61] Neues Organon, IV, § 89.

[62] Ibid., IV, § 89.

[63] Ibid., § 82.

[64] Ibid., §§ 67, 68, 74, 120.

[65] Quoted by Friedrich Löwenhaupt, Johann Heinrich Lambert. Leistung und Leben (Mühlhausen: Braun, 1943), p. 15.

[66] See his caution in Methode, §§ 52 and 147. Could it be that the obvious weakness of his argument in § 52, to which he returns in the additional notes at § 147, was the reason why he did not complete the prize essay and submit it to the Academy?

[67] This proof is given in Architektonic, § 299.

is as naturalistic as Kant's. In his ethics, which is a part of "agathology," or "agathometry" ("the measurement of the good"), Lambert deals with the measurement and summation of pleasures and perfections and makes the beginnings toward a felicific calculus, but he has no place for commands and certainly none for God's commands.

In this brief account of one of the most remarkable philosophers of the mid-century, we have spoken of his relation to some of his predecessors and described some of the central features of his philosophy. Much of interest has had to be passed over; a study of his *Semiotik*, the third book of the *Neues Organon*, would be of special interest to contemporary philosophers. But we must conclude with a brief question about his influence and place in the history of German philosophy. Generally speaking, his influence was nil; no one took up where he left off. But it is often thought that he influenced Kant, and we must try to see, at least in a preliminary way, whether he did or not.

Certainly there are remarkable resemblances between Lambert and Kant up to 1770, especially in their theory of mathematical knowledge, though Kant did not pursue the mathematical or geometrical ideal which Lambert defended. Moreover, often in reading Lambert on almost any subject one finds himself reminded of somewhat similar remarks—sometimes perhaps little more than an example or turn of phrase—in the mature work of Kant. But as soon as Kant began to follow the "new path" opened by his Inaugural Dissertation of 1770, there was no more of central philosophical importance that he could learn from Lambert, and Lambert was unwilling to follow him along this new path. Lambert was the spokesman for the "men of intelligence" whom Kant mentions as objecting to the ideality of time[68] and whom he tries to answer. This means that Lambert was, in Kant's terms, still a speculative dogmatist. But, using the words in a non-Kantian sense, he was very much less dogmatic and speculative than his contemporaries, and Kant's admiration for him was genuine and justified. We shall have to advert to him again and again as we discuss Kant's intellectual development.

We have spoken of some resemblances between Lambert and Crusius on a very important point, namely, the connection between simple ideas in a necessary judgment when the contradictory would be unthinkable but not, apparently, formally self-contradictory. The distinction between formal necessities that could be proved by the law of contradiction and necessities which are *gedenkbar*, because the subject and predicate "can not be thought apart," is of the utmost importance for these men, who wanted to avoid the simple dichotomy between what Kant was later to call analytic judgments known a priori and synthetic judgments known a posteriori.

---

[68] Lambert objected to Kant's Inaugural Dissertation by saying that time must be real as the form of change (Letter to Kant, October 13, 1770; *Kants Ges. Schr.*, X, 107). Kant commented on the point in the letter to Herz of February 21, 1772 (see *Kant's Philosophical Correspondence*, p. 75), and replied formally in *Critique of Pure Reason* A 36 = B 53. (Kant repeatedly expressed his regret that he had allowed the correspondence with Lambert to lapse.)

They did not know how to do so; they did not have the terminology Kant invented to make the problem visible and manageable. But whenever they talked about these kinds of necessities, which were epistemologically the most important and novel features in their philosophies, they were talking about synthetic judgments known a priori. Perhaps their most important contribution, therefore, was to use openly a kind of connection between concepts which Wolff had used surreptitiously but which Hume seemed to show to be impossible.

Tetens

Johann Nicolaus Tetens was born in either Tetenbüll or Tönning, in Schleswig, in either 1736 or 1738. At the University of Kiel he studied under Johann Christian Eschenbach (1719–1759). Eschenbach, a pupil of Darjes and, like him, an eclectic, was the first German translator of Berkeley and introduced Tetens to British philosophy. In 1776 Tetens became professor of philosophy in Kiel, where he remained until 1789. He then entered the service of the Danish government and won a high position and honors as a farsighted and wise official in the finance ministry. He died in 1807.

His principal works were *Über die allgemeine speculativische Philosophie.* (*On General Speculative* [i.e., *Theoretical*] *Philosophy*), 1775, and the two-volume *Philosophische Versuche über die menschliche Natur und ihre Entwicklung* (*Philosophical Essays on Human Nature and its Development*), 1777–78).[69]

Herder called Lambert "the Leibniz of our age,"[70] and Tetens was called "the German Locke." After the publication of Leibniz' *New Essays*, these honorific titles did not indicate as much specific opposition between Lambert and Tetens as they would have suggested before 1765. Tetens drew an interesting comparison between what the British, since Bacon, and the Germans, since von Tschirnhaus, had done in philosophy. He thought the British had favored analysis of empirical knowledge and had interpreted all knowledge as if it were a mere collection of observations. They had minimized the role of theory and logical form in their theories of knowledge. The Germans had made the opposite mistake; they had emphasized thinking over observing, and had not worked out the empirical application and testing of their theories. Tetens wished to supplement the one by the other. Like Lambert, he saw himself as following both Leibniz and Locke —which would not have been possible before the publication of the *New Essays*—but it is obvious both here and in his longer work that Locke was his model, even though his purpose was more like that of Leibniz or the Leibniz-Wolffians.[71]

[69] Teten's first-named work, and Volume I of the second, have been reprinted by the Kant-Gesellschaft, Berlin, 1913, and I cite from that edition, but give page numbers found in the margin, which are those of the original edition. Short titles are used: *Spec. Phil.* and *Versuche*, respectively.

[70] Herder, *God, Some Conversations*, third conversation.

[71] Tetens, *Spec. Phil.*, p. 93.

The Possibility of Metaphysics

Three years before the Berlin Academy announced the topic for a prize essay on the degree of certainty attainable in metaphysics, natural theology, and morals, Tetens had published what could well have been a contribution to that contest: *Thoughts Concerning Some Causes Why There Are Only Few Established Truths in Metaphysics* (*Gedanken über einige Ursachen, warum in der Metaphysik nur wenige ausgemachte Warheiten sind,* [Butzow, 1760]). In this essay he took a position very close to Mendelssohn's. But fifteen years later, in his first major work, Tetens returned to the problem and came to quite different conclusions, for in the meantime he had read both Kant's contribution to the Academy contest and his Inaugural Dissertation of 1770. As a consequence, he could no longer hold that the superiority of mathematics to metaphysics was merely a matter of a higher degree of distinctness in mathematical concepts, and that the metaphysician could improve his science by simply working harder at attaining objectivity and clarity.

In 1775 Tetens asked a much more fundamental question than the Academy asked: *Is* metaphysics possible?

Tetens distinguishes between metaphysics, or speculative philosophy ("speculative" means much the same as "theoretical," and has no pejorative connotations), and transcendent philosophy, which he identifies with ontology, or basic science (*Grundwissenschaft*). He complains that metaphysics is a collection of various sciences without internal unity or connection, and that it cannot be put on a firm basis without a footing in transcendent philosophy. Transcendent philosophy is to do for general philosophy and metaphysics what mathematics had done for natural science, raising them from the level of common sense and common observation to that of a rigorous and disciplined investigation. Ontology is the study of principles more fundamental and more abstract than those which apply in any one body of knowledge, and it is particularly important not to confuse ontological concepts with concepts which are applicable only to minds and spiritual beings, as he thinks Leibniz did.[72] This confusion is difficult to avoid, however, since the obvious foundations of the study of nature are to be found in mathematics, not in ontology; hence ontology tends to be developed as a basis for the study of the intellectual, rather than the natural, world. But it is nonetheless a confusion; what is needed is a set of concepts and principles which apply equally to both, and some criterion by which physical and intellectual realities are to be distinguished, each with its own principles and concepts.[73]

[72] The influence of Kant's Inaugural Dissertation is unmistakable. Kant sharply divided the *mundus intelligibilis* from the *mundus sensibilis* and sought out the "forms and principles" of each. While he was not so explicitly concerned there with finding principles common to both as the subject matter of ontology, he warned against the error of trying to apply to the intelligible world concepts of space and time, which apply to the sensible, and then pointed out the errors which result when this misapplication ("subreption") is permitted.

[73] *Spec. Phil.*, p. 22.

The Psychological Turn

Transcendent philosophy is for Tetens no longer the demonstrative science of the real insofar as it *is* real;[74] the day of objective ontological definitions of reality, possibility, and actuality had passed, whether these definitions and demonstrations were projected for the construction of systems of Catholic or Leibniz-Wolffian scholasticism. The necessity which appertains to transcendent concepts must be understood, in the manner of Crusius and Lambert (and to some extent Mendelssohn), as a necessity for thought and as a necessity growing out of thought. The analysis of the necessary conditions of knowledge eventuates in knowledge of the necessary conditions of things, of whatever sort they may be, intellectual or physical.

For Tetens, to a greater extent than for the others who made epistemology prior to ontology, the determination of the conditions of knowledge was itself an empirical task; the theory of knowledge was to follow Locke's "plain, historical method." In a word, ontology previously based upon logic, or cognate with it, was now to be based upon psychology. While both Crusius and Lambert had prefaced their metaphysics with treatises on logic, Tetens followed his sketch of ontology and completed his career of creative work with a large empirical psychology. He did not take the last step, with Lossius, and base psychology upon physiology, but he did turn back from the logical and methodological interests represented by Lambert to a subjective, introspective psychology that was more like that of Crusius. He did not repeat Crusius, however; he ignored him and drew on his extensive knowledge of the accomplishments of the empiricist writers—Locke, Berkeley, Hume, Reid, Henry Home, Condillac, Diderot, and Charles Bonnet.

This was an unfortunate turn for his brilliantly critical mind to take at this critical point, for it made him write his philosophy as if it were psychology, and because of that he missed the radically critical question which led Kant from the conclusions of the Inaugural Dissertation, which resembled Tetens', to those of the *Critique of Pure Reason*, whither Tetens could not follow. Tetens' essay of 1775 was as good a starting point for a critical philosophy as Kant's own dissertation of 1770. But what followed in Tetens' career was a continuation of the genetic, empiricistic psychology in the tradition flowing from Locke. Tetens modified this psychology by discovering, or by formulating far more explicitly than his predecessors, the contribution of the active powers of the mind even to the exercise of the cognitive faculty. He explored the meaning of the expression "except the intellect itself" which Leibniz had added to the empiricists' axiom, "There is nothing in the intellect which was not first in the senses."[75] In this way Tetens wrote a psychology which could and did serve Kant as a starting point in the study of the operations of the mind, but only as a starting point. Instead of pushing forward in the direction Kant was to go in the late seventies, therefore, Tetens failed, after a brilliant beginning, to write a genuine system of transcendent philosophy, but wrote instead philosophi-

[74] *Ibid.*, pp. 58–60.
[75] But Tetens so emphasized the sensible origin of thoughts that he felt the addendum made by Leibniz was, in fact, unnecessary. *Spec. Phil.*, p. 54n.

cal essays on human nature and thereby missed the boat.[76] It is almost painful to see how, on page after page pored over by Kant,[77] Tetens dealt with the *topics* which engaged Kant, but failed to grasp the *question* to which those topics contained the answer. It is even more painful to see that in the essay of 1775 he even asked the questions which were engaging Kant at that time, before Kant had taken (or at least had given public notice that he had taken) the "new turn" resulting from his "recollection of Hume." For Kant *learned* from Hume; Tetens tried only to *answer* him. Hence Tetens stood at the end of a long series of analytical psychologists, not at the beginning of a new period in the history of epistemology.

This is not to say that the psychological interest was not obvious in his first book, or that transcendent philosophy was absent from his second. But the psychological parts of the first—original, clear, and elegant classifications of different kinds of ideas in the mind—are superseded by the much richer but less well-organized discussion of the same topics in the *Versuche*. The epistemological thesis of the two books is the same: "Those basic principles and ideas which we see objectively in metaphysics are, in ourselves, only types of subjective representations and modes of thought, which can be observed in ourselves just like other modifications and acts of our power of thinking."[78] But whereas in the *Speculativische Philosophie* the guiding thread for this observation was the systematic requirements of transcendent philosophy—just as in Kant—in the *Versuche* there was no such guidance. The interest here was psychological and genetic as well as ontological, and the former interest outweighs the latter. Discussions of cause and identity are found side by side with discussions of learning to play the piano, differences between animal and human intelligence, and functions of the nervous system. The thread is easily lost; the book is repetitious, and its parts are not all consistent with each other.[79]

The Faculties of the Mind

Tetens is sometimes considered to be the founder of the three-faculty theory (knowing, feeling, and willing). This theory was, as we have seen, formulated but not fully worked out by Mendelssohn, and it was used as if it were a ready-made truth by Kant. But Tetens' claims are valid only in part. He clearly states in a prominent place and with all the emphasis

[76] This is Kant's own estimate. "Tetens investigated the concepts of reason subjectively, I objectively. His analysis is empirical, mine transcendental." "No one considered the possibility of such a priori knowledge, although Herr Tetens could have suggested it [*hätte Anlass geben können*]."—Reflection 4901 and "Vorarbeit zu den Prolegomena," *Kants Ges. Schr.*, XXIII, 23, 57.

[77] See Hamann's letter to Herder, May 17, 1779: "Kant is at work on his Ethics [sic!] of Pure Reason and always has Tetens lying before him" (*Briefwechsel*, ed. Arthur Henkel and Walter Ziesemer [Wiesbaden: Insel Verlag, 1959], IV, 81).

[78] *Spec. Phil.*, p. 27.

[79] Even Kant, no less, complained about the style, saying that Tetens apparently published just as he wrote, hoping that if he wrote enough he would find a way out of the labyrinth; but he acknowledged that Tetens said many acute things. He was disappointed that Tetens did not review the *Critique of Pure Reason*. See *Kants Ges. Schr.*, X, 232, and *Kant's Philosophical Correspondence*, pp. 96, 103, 107.

at his command, that the three fundamental faculties, or powers, of the soul are feeling, understanding, and the active power or will.[80] Had he stopped there or had he begun there, he would have as undisputed a right to claim the invention as Mendelssohn had. But speaking against this claim are two facts: (a) this is not the only division of the faculties he gives; and (b) the terms he uses are not equivalent to the terms used in Kant's division, and it is Kant's usage of the terms, not Tetens', which is always meant when one refers to the "three-faculty theory."

First, this is not the only division Tetens gives. There is, in addition to the tripartite division just mentioned, a complex set of distinctions which can be construed from Tetens' explicit statements scattered throughout the *Versuche*. The diagram of Table 1 shows these distinctions. If we read the second line, we have the old two-power theory which goes back to Aristotle, with the interesting and important point which Tetens makes against the empiricists like Sulzer, that the cognitive faculty (*Denkkraft*) must be assigned to the active rather than to the passive power. If we read the third line, we find a "four-faculty theory" sense, feeling, thinking, and willing. We cannot make this classification, which could easily be continued for several more lines, consistent with Tetens' own "official" statement that there are three fundamental faculties; the table shows that if "fundamental faculty" (*Grundvermögen*) is taken in an unequivocal sense, there is only one, not three faculties.

Second, and far more important, is the fact that the terms used by Tetens do not have the meanings they had for Mendelssohn or were to have for Kant. The most important departure from Mendelssohn's and Kant's usage is in Tetens' understanding of what is meant by "feeling." It is hard to be sure just what he did mean, and I shall have to return to this question in the next section when I discuss the role of feeling in knowledge. But it is indisputable that he did not mean either Mendelssohn's "faculty of approbation" or Kant's "feeling," which meant "feeling of pleasure or displeasure." Rather, Tetens distinguished two aspects of feeling. There is first the receptivity to changes in the sense organs and, more generally, the inner sense of one's bodily and mental states which he calls sensations (*Empfindungen*), impressions (*Eindrücke*), and representations (*Vorstellungen*). Second, there is the receptivity to pleasant and unpleasant sensations and representations (*Empfindnisse* and *Rührungen*). Feeling, therefore, far from being a simple factor existing alongside will and thought, is made up of at least two different factors or is a faculty with two quite different functions: one is a cognitive faculty of great complexity, the other is sentiment (*Empfindsamkeit*), or the susceptibility to pleasure and displeasure. Tetens saw the important connection between feeling, in this sense of sentiment, and will. But, like Kant, and unlike Mendelssohn, he thought they were generically different, so that a high intensity or activity of sentiment does not necessarily pass over into an activity of will. Tetens' contribution was to secure the autonomy of feeling in contrast to will, and thus to go further than Mendelssohn; his failure was in not separating feeling from the cognitive faculty, and in this respect he did not go as far as

[80] *Versuche*, pp. 618, 625.

Table 1. The faculties of the mind according to Tetens

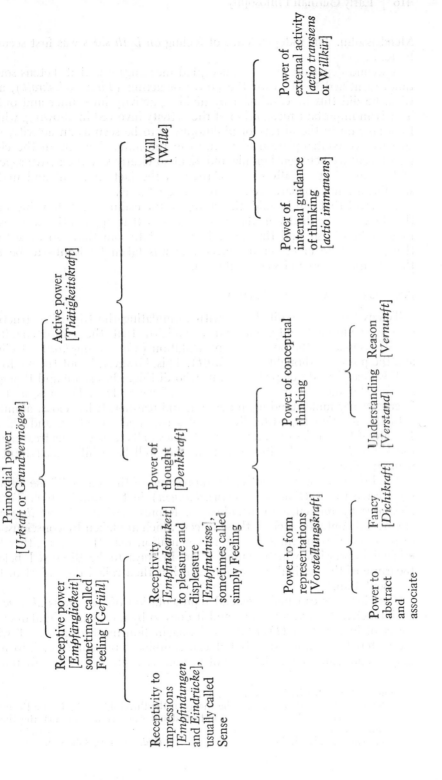

Mendelssohn. The independence of feeling *on both sides* was first secured by Kant.

A second departure from the accepted meanings was that Tetens sometimes identified "will" with the power of acting (*Thätigkeitskraft*), and when he did this he continued by dividing activity into inner and outer. This is an important recognition of the activity involved in knowing, which from now on in the history of philosophy is to be seen as an activity, not as a passive contemplation of pictures in the mind. No one in the eighteenth century between Leibniz and Kant so clearly saw the active aspects of knowing. But equally obvious, then, is the fact that will and understanding are not cognate faculties on an equal level.

The most that can be said, therefore, for the claim that Tetens invented the three-faculty theory in its perfect form is that apparently he himself thought he did so, and that he did in fact state something so close to it that it could be taken—and conceivably *was* taken by Kant—to be the three-faculty theory in its classical form.

Analysis of the Cognitive Faculty

Tetens has been credited also with formulating the tripartite structure of the cognitive faculty. He states explicitly that the entire cognitive faculty consists of the power of representation (*Vorstellungskraft*), feeling, and the power of thought (*Denkkraft*). This, however, is not the anatomy of this faculty as developed by Kant, who distinguishes sense and thought, and divides thought into the formation of concepts, judgments, and inferences[81] (by understanding, judgment, and reason). It has closer affinities with the Kantian tripartite division of sense, understanding, and reason. In spite of the confusions and inconsistencies in Tetens' various treatments, the *Versuche* is filled with ideas that may well have influenced Kant at many specific points.[82]

The human mind is receptive to impressions of the senses. These impressions leave traces (*Spuren, Nachwürkungen*) in the mind which Tetens illustrates by reference to after-images. Representations (*Vorstellungen*) are mental contents, such as these traces, which are taken by consciousness to be signs of something else. A representation may stand for either the original impression which caused it or, in ways to be discussed below, the cause of the original impression, which is then called the object of the representation.[83]

Consciousness can make general representation of "sensuous *abstracta*" or silhouettes (*Schattenwerke*), and it does so by means of a fundamental power of imagination (*Dichtkraft*).[84] Imagination must always work with the material of impressions, but it can combine representations into new simple representations which cannot be analyzed into parts but only traced

---

[81] On this tripartite division, see above, p. 117.

[82] The most obvious influences are the theory of the threefold synthesis, the theory of empirical schemata, and some aspects (and no doubt some confusions in) the theory of the inner sense.

[83] *Versuche*, pp. 11, 17, 75.   [84] *Ibid.*, pp. 129, 338–339.

back genetically to impressions which do not resemble the *new* simple representation. His not very good example of this is the synthesis of various colors in sensation into white light; with very few minor changes he could have availed himself of Hume's better example, that of the missing shade of blue which is not a copy of any simple impression of sense. Because, then, there are some representations which are not direct descendants of impressions similar to them, there can arise concepts deriving from representations but not from impressions; and he thinks Hume's mistake in his analysis of causation was that he held that all concepts had to be traced back to impressions which resembled them, whereas it is possible and sufficient to trace them back only to representations (which are like Hume's ideas).[85]

The second factor in knowing is feeling. Tetens distinguishes, as we have seen, feeling as the experience of pleasure and displeasure from feeling as a faculty having a broader cognitive competence. But to circumscribe its scope is very difficult; it seems almost omnicompetent, and he says[86] that it is "the first expression" of the undefinable fundamental faculty of which thinking and willing are others. Feeling has as its objects: sensations (*Empfindungen*) and pleasant sensations (*Empfindnisse*); representations; the acts of sensation (*Empfinden*); the given connections, changes, and modifications of consciousness; and a "dark unanalyzable core (*Boden*)" of the self which Hume had allegedly overlooked in his analysis of the self into a bundle of perceptions.[87]

All these objects of feeling, *qua* objects of feeling, have one feature in common: they are felt as "absolutes," as given unities, and not as interrelated pluralities. Feeling is always directed upon an absolute, or a single "field," even when the field contains plurality and diversities.[88] It does not necessarily change when the ingredients in the field changes. Feeling is not knowledge, but it is essential to knowledge.[89]

Is it not possible to see in this confusion an attempt by Tetens to find the mode of mind which "can accompany all of my representations" and "except in relation to which they would be nothing to me, even less than a dream?" In short, I am suggesting that Tetens' feeling, as a cognitive factor, resembles what Kant calls the unity of apperception. In favor of this interpretation is the fact that in at least one place, Tetens identified feeling with "inner sense"[90] and ascribed to it the role Kant would give to empirical apperception. The principal difference, which makes a very great deal of difference in their whole philosophies, is this: Tetens thinks feeling is a passivity of mind (though he does occasionally speak of the "act of feeling"), like the inner sense which merely surveys a field of experience as a unitary absolute before other active faculties break it up into objects and relations; Kant sees that the apparently original field (which he calls the "manifold") must be "run through" and "held together" by an act

---

[85] *Spec. Phil.*, p. 68.　　　　　　　　[86] *Versuche*, p. 737.
[87] *Ibid.*, pp. 166, 167, 186, 211, 215, 222, 615, 625.
[88] *Ibid.*, p. 203 and passim.　　　　　　[90] *Versuche*, pp. 45, 46.
[89] *Ibid.*, p. 167.

of synthesis. Therefore Kant cannot identify apperception with inner sense or feeling, as apparently Tetens did.

The third cognitive factor is the power of thought (*Denkkraft*). By abstracting and analyzing general representations it produces judgments, concepts, and inferences. The first two functions are exercised by understanding, the third by reason[91] (following a distinction made by Wolff, and standard since the Port Royal Logic.) The activities of the power of thinking are the internal activities of the *Thätigkeitskraft*, the external or bodily activities of which are called will.

The understanding works as follows. It introduces divisions and distinctions into the unitary but inwardly diverse though not yet articulated field of feeling, so that what was previously *felt* as one is now *judged* to consist of different and distinct representations externally related to each other. This relationship is expressed in judgment, and the segregated representations which become articulated in the judgment are called concepts. Tetens here points toward an important theory to be fully developed first by Kant. It is that a representation is made into a concept by the uses to which it is put. We do not have, as it were, concepts floating around in our minds which we couple into judgments. Maybe we have representations as inspectable unities, but concepts are *abstracta* of judgments, not independent ingredients in them.

When representations become distinct concepts, and their original felt association is replaced by a connection which is thought and expressed in judgment, there arises a new kind of concept, a concept of relation (*Verhältnisbegriff*) between concepts. Like feeling, which is independent of the changes in the contents of its field, thought produces concepts which are independent of the specific concepts which are carved out of the inchoate mass of feelings. These are the fundamental concepts of transcendent philosophy. This set of concepts of relation includes: sameness and difference, coexistence and succession (space and time), inherence of a property in a substance, and dependency of one thing upon another. The relations between these concepts of relation are a priori principles, for they are not derived from the specific empirical content of the representations converted into concepts and established by induction. Since they are the relations which are implicit in the formal structure of judgments, they are found in and apply to all our knowledge. These concepts which reflect the forms of judgment are the concepts of transcendent philosophy.

The resemblance to Kant's "metaphysical deduction of the categories" is unmistakable, but the difference must not be overlooked. Tetens' attempt is to show how a priori concepts arise in the mind, and his "deduction" is an empirical one. Unlike Kant, Tetens does not begin with the logical forms of judgment and infer from these what must be the relational (synthetic) acts of thought. He begins with a psychology of thought and shows the psychological derivation of possible judgments, both empirical and a priori.

[91] *Ibid.*, pp. 571, 575.

The Problem of the Objective Validity of Knowledge

It is not sufficient for either Kant or Tetens to show what are the a priori concepts in the mind; each must show how these concepts, which originally express only necessities of thought, apply also to objects, so that a priori concepts have existential reference. It is to Tetens' credit that he saw this second problem almost as soon as Kant did[92] and published an answer to it before Kant did.

We have seen how Crusius and Lambert recognized a class of necessary judgments which were not based exclusively upon the logical necessity of identity and contradiction. These were the judgments which, while their contradictories were not self-contradictory, "could not be thought otherwise." But neither Crusius nor Lambert nor the young Kant knew how to establish necessary judgments which were not logically grounded in the laws of identity and contradiction, how they could be systematically discovered, or how to justify their application to reality. Tetens was aware of each of these problems in 1776.

He explicitly rejected the Leibnizian theory that all judgments are, when fully expanded, explicable as subject-predicate judgments, and that true judgments are those in which the predicate is implicitly contained in the concept of the subject.[93] Judgments are necessary to the extent that they are independent of the specific empirical content of their subjects and predicates, and they can be independent of that without being merely formal relations between the contents. Our evidence of this is the same evidence that Kant will cite: the laws of geometry and arithmetic are not provable by the laws of identity and contradiction alone. The laws of identity and contradiction are "mere ways of thinking . . . without reference to what is peculiar to the ideas compared," whereas the laws of mathematics do deal with what is peculiar to space and time.[94] Where the necessity of a judgment does not depend upon the merely formal relationship between subject and predicate or the particular empirical contents of the two concepts, it must depend upon "what is, in respect to certain general classes of representations (or objects) necessary and natural to the understanding."[95] What these features are that are "necessary and natural to the understanding" is found by observation[96]—the kind of observation which crowds the pages of the Versuche. They cannot be found or explained as Lossius tried to find and explain them, by reference to the actions of the

---

[92] Kant was not aware of it in 1772. See below, pp. 464–465.

[93] Versuche, pp. 329–30, 365, 488.

[94] Spec. Phil., pp. 43–44. This is not consistent with what has been said above about other necessary connections being independent of the conceptual content or peculiarities of the subject and predicate or other relata. It is unclear exactly what Tetens' view here is. The logical rules are absolutely independent of the content and are indemonstrable; the material fundamental principles "express the particular ways of thinking and judging" based on universal genera of objects and representations. Spec. Phil., p. 37.

[95] Ibid., p. 37.

[96] Versuche, pp. 465–469. This basis for a theory of knowledge in observation of mental activity, meant as a modification of Kantianism and not as anti-Kantian, was further developed by Johann Friedrich Fries (1773–1843).

nervous system, because, as Tetens clearly sees, this begs the question since knowledge of the nervous system is as much in question as any other knowledge.

It does not trouble Tetens that the discoveries of such self-observation may be principles which underlie only "human truths." It is futile to say, " 'A square cannot be round' is true only for human minds," unless we can form a concept of another mind for which "A square can be round" would be a possible thought. Tetens denies that we can form the second of these concepts any more than we can form the concept of a square circle, though the latter concept is self-contradictory while the concept of the non-human intelligence is not self-contradictory. To find out how we know that our human transcendent concepts, which are known only as necessary relations between our representations, hold also as necessary relations between objects requires Tetens to answer first another question: How do we perceive objects at all, and not merely have representations which refer to other representations or impressions?

Perception (Gewahrnehmen) occurs "when the soul, as it were, says to itself inwardly 'See!' "; when the "soul grasps an object as a particular object, distinguishing it from others."[97] Perception differs from feeling in that it does not have a simple whole before it; it is the work of the faculty of thought (Denkkraft) not of feeling.[98] Perceiving differs from thinking, however, in that it occurs only in the presence of impressions and sensuous representations. The representations to which perception is the response are raised in clarity and distinctness by attention which singles them out from the mass of feeling, and this induces a forgetfulness of other present impressions and representations and especially a forgetfulness of the self as the possessor of these representations. Because of this self-forgetfulness, that which the soul tells itself to "See!" is not felt to be its own representation. Several other factors are also involved in this attribution of independent existence. For instance, in perceptions which involve the data of more than one sense organ, the representation seems less dependent upon ourselves, less subjective, than when it depends upon only one.[99] By the association of ideas,[100] a partial representation is associated with another representation resulting from the original impression, and this compound association points back to the original impression which has associated with it a propensity (Hang) to believe that it had an independent object and cause. Thomas Reid, says Tetens,[101] was correct in insisting upon the naturalness and inevitability of this belief, but wrong in not trying to analyze it but instead ascribing it only to the providence of our Creator.

---

[97] Ibid., p. 262. The thought and the rhetoric no doubt come from Condillac: "La conscience dit en quelque sort à l'âme: violà une perception"—Essai sur l'origin de la connaissance humaine, in Oeuvres philosophiques de Condillac (Paris: Presses universitaires de France, 1947), I, 24.

[98] Versuche, p. 275.   [99] Ibid., pp. 399, 407–410.

[100] Ibid., pp. 80–94. In general, Tetens strongly opposes Hartley and Condillac for overuse of the principle of association of ideas because associationism neglects the important role of the active powers of the mind.

[101] Ibid., p. 375.

All this may serve to explain how it comes about that the mind applies, or thinks that it applies, its concepts to objects that are not representations. It will serve equally well or ill, however, whether objective reference of concepts actually obtains or not. History is full of efforts made by others to resolve this problem: Locke appealed to the certainty of sensitive knowledge, Reid to belief, Dr. Johnson and Lambert to the direct sense of touch. None of these simple answers satisfied Tetens. He undertook a new and fundamental analysis of *what it means to be* objectively valid knowledge. His analysis of objectivity resembles that of Berkeley and Mendelssohn; freed from its specific psychological foundation, it is like Kant's concept of "transcendental ideality."

Tetens' question may be put schematically. Granted that I know the relation R between two representations V and V', which I take to be representations of two objects, O and O'. Do I know that R also holds between O and O'? And if so, how do I know it?

It was pretty clear by Tetens' time that if V and V' are understood as modifications of the mind, and O and O' as real substantial independent ontological objects, I cannot move from VRV' to *knowledge* of ORO', however natural and easy the movement to the belief in ORO', without some additional metaphysical assumptions of the kind made by Hoffmann (God will not deceive us) or Leibniz (my monad reflects objective relations). The alternative to such speculative assumptions is to reinterpret VRV' or ORO', or both; this is the alternative taken by Berkeley, Tetens, and Kant.

Tetens denies that V and V' are *intrinsically* subjective. They are not, to begin with, recognized as "ideas in the mind." The mind, or self, is a kind of object which must be constituted from some relation—call it R'—which when found between representations *make* them mine.[102] This relation is that of compresence and contingent and spontaneous variability. Representations may occur in the same felt manifold without having any other constant relationship to each other besides this relationship of belonging to the same mind. Let us call the relationship they have to each other by virtue of their common ingredience in one manifold R'. This relationship R' cannot fund any claim to have an objective relation as its counterpart. And if there are not some other relationships that are always present between them, V and V' will not be thought to have objects O and O', and from VR'V' *a fortiori* we do not move even to the belief in any relationship of the form OR'O'. But if R is any one of the relations of which we have specific and necessary concepts because it is independent of the specific contents of V and V', and depends only upon our thought of their possible relationships in judgment, then we say that R, being a necessary relation, is also an objective relation. To say VRV' is necessary is the same as saying ORO'. " 'The objective' means: the unchangeable subjective, while 'the subjective' means: the changeably subjective."[103] If it be objected

---

[102] *Ibid.*, p. 411. R' will become, in Kant, the relation to the transcendental unity of apperception, by virtue of which all my representations can be accompanied by the "I think" and all are synthesized into one experience.

[103] *Ibid.*, p. 540.

that this means "everything is subjective," Tetens' answer is that this accusation does not matter. No other kind of objectivity is attainable, and this is what is meant by "objective" anyway. "But it must not be forgotten," he warns,[104] "how far objectivity, which is just the same as the unchangeable and the necessary in the subjective, extends." It extends only as far "as any other beings, who have impressions of the same objects, find the same relation in themselves" and only "under the condition that their impressions also have the same character as those of our impressions which we hold to be objective."

If there is some relation, contributed by the power of the mind, to any representation whatsoever, it follows that the concept of this relation will apply to any objects of the mind whatsoever. Such a concept is transcendent,[105] and the system of such concepts constitutes the science of ontology, the "knowledge of possible objects insofar as they are possible," as Wolff defined it. Tetens has therefore, to his own satisfaction, established a foundation for an ontology like Wolff's. But more importantly he has anticipated at least a part of Kant's analytic of the understanding without seeing, as Kant did, that the latter must replace "the proud name of ontology." Tetens did not see this because he remained, at least in aspiration, a realist though his conception of objectivity is clearly idealistic in the manner of Berkeley or of Wolff's "consistent dream theory." This aspiration for realism kept him from asking the next question, which had been asked by Berkeley and was to be repeated by Kant: What must the *object* be if VRV' implies ORO'? This was the question which led Kant to the distinction between the phenomenal object, to knowledge of which the implication leads, and the thing in itself, where it breaks down.

The Critique of Hume

Kant's generalization of Hume's problem, he tells us, was the starting point of his critical philosophy. Hume showed indisputably that the causal relation is not a logical relation and that its putative necessity cannot arise from experience. Kant saw that the causal relation was not unique in these respects, but that mathematics, the foundations of physical science, and metaphysics consisted of such combinations of concepts which were not logically necessary but also not inductive. They were thus necessary in some nonlogical sense. Kant did not try to "answer" Hume by just patching up a new theory of causality, but dealt with the whole problem he suggested: How are synthetic (not logically necessary) judgments known a priori (not inductively)? He *could* have seen this problem in Crusius and Lambert, in their lists of nonlogically necessary judgments, of which the causal judgment was only a special case. In fact, however, he did not see the severity of the problem in their writings until his "recollection of Hume" showed him how radically different the logical "cannot be thought otherwise" was from the nonlogical. This was because Hume had been far clearer about the distinction between relations of ideas and matters of fact than the Germans had.

104 *Ibid.*, p. 560. 105 In Kant: "transcendental."

The failure of the Germans to understand the radical character of Hume's discovery, and therefore their failure to be awakened from *their* dogmatic slumber, can be illustrated by reference to Tetens' treatment of the causal principle.

Tetens discusses Hume's theory of causation in many places. He knows that the judgment of causation is not analytic, and he thinks most, if not all, causal judgments are contingent.[106] He thinks Hume was in error in trying to trace all concepts back to impressions, skipping over the intermediate stage of feelings and representations, and thus missing the originality and irreducibility of the feeling of striving which we can properly project into relations between things by the route outlined in the previous section on objectification.[107] On the other hand, however, Tetens is not willing to give up the notion of the "intelligibility" of the causal relation, that is, a notion which could be drawn only from the assumption that the causal relation is a logical one. He thinks that causal judgments can be seen to be necessary and intelligible provided they are embedded into a theory. For example, "One billiard ball hitting another will cause it to move" is held by Tetens to be a necessary consequence of the concepts of impenetrability and motion.[108]

This is an answer to Hume that one often hears even today. But it is not a good answer for, as Hume himself said in anticipating it,[109] it only "staves off our ignorance a little longer," until we reach the question: how do we know the fundamental statements of the theory? In Kant's language, it answers a question about the "absolutely a priori" by talking about that which is only relatively a priori.[110] In giving this answer to Hume, Tetens fails to keep in mind what was so clear to Lambert and Crusius and, usually, to himself, namely, that there is a radical difference between a logical relation and a necessary nonlogical relation. He wants to add "intelligibility" to the causal relation because, no doubt quite properly in the light of his analysis of objectivity, the logical relation is the "most objective" since surely it is the most "unchangeably subjective."

So it is correct to say of Tetens that, like Kant, he believed a necessity of thought was the basis of an ascription of an objective necessity to objects and their connections. He agreed with Kant that what is objectified is a necessity of thought, not a belief based upon instinct or custom. But he failed to remember how utterly different the synthetic and the logical "necessities of thought" are. He made the egregious mistake of trying to correct Hume, when it was the historic destiny of Hume to correct the Germans.

---

106 *Versuche*, pp. 490, 516.
107 *Ibid.*, pp. 329–330, 365.   108 *Ibid.*, p. 499.
109 *An Inquiry Concerning Human Understanding*, sec. IV, pt. 1, para. 12.
110 *Critique of Pure Reason*, B 2–3.

XVII

Kant

Kant's *Weltanschauung*

Suppose Kant had not been Professor of Logic and Metaphysics in the University of Königsberg. Suppose rather that, like his friend Berens, he had become a businessman; or like his pupil Herz a physician; or like his neighbor Hippel a civic administrator; or like his brother Johann Heinrich a pastor. Suppose, further—and this is easier to suppose—he had like the first three followed also a literary avocation. We may presume that he would have had a reputation in his time as good as that of many men we have mentioned in this book, and would now be as forgotten as they.

We may make some conjectures about what thoughts and theories this other Kant would have accepted and even what modifications he might have made in them which would stamp them as belonging to his personal *Weltanschauung*. By *Weltanschauung* I mean here: a set of philosophical ideas and opinions held together in a personal attitude, but without benefit of the technical discipline of analysis and argumentation which, it is to be hoped, raises philosophy above the merely subjective, individual, and existential and gives it some claim to more than biographical and historical interest.

For these conjectures about our hypothetical Kant, we have manifold clues. There are, first, his nonphilosophical correspondence and his table talk, from which out of *politesse* he rigorously excluded all shop-talk of philosophy. Second, there are the anecdotes and reminiscences of those who knew him but had little or no conception of his philosophy. Third, there are occasional papers written for the popular press in which he expressed views upon intellectual and moral issues of the day without drawing upon the technical resources and vocabulary of his philosophy. Fourth, there are his lectures to students on a variety of subjects (pedagogy, geography, anthropology, among them) lying outside his professional *Fach* and not presupposing any of its technical contents. Finally, and most fruitful for our purposes, are the *conclusions* of his philosophical works proper. For we find a high degree of likeness between conclusions reached in works written over five decades during which profound changes occurred in his premises and modes of argumentation. *Weltanschauungen* are likely to be more constant than philosophies in men who, like Kant, make revolutions in philosophy.

These five sets of clues point to the same family of beliefs and attitudes. The principal ones are the following.

(1) Philosophy, and more specifically metaphysics, can be "scientific." It can and should be more than loose talk about things in general. The state of philosophy in Germany is parlous because it is practiced by journalists and geniuses. One cannot expect philosophical truths from gifted but untutored amateurs writing for the ladies. But, on the other side, flights of genius have no place in philosophy. Philosophy should talk in human language, and its proper place is not "high towers around which the wind blows" but the "bathos of experience." Hence Kant opposed the superficiality of the popular philosophy and the pretensions of the *Schwärmer* and of the intellectual hippies of the *Sturm und Drang*.

(2) But philosophy is not, on the other hand, a form of pedantry and dry learning, of interest only to professors of philosophy. Philosophy is not "the monopoly of the schools" but is devoted to the "interests of humanity." Technical philosophy introduces a spirit of *Gründlichkeit* into speculation, but its great questions remain: What can I know? What ought I to do? What can I hope? What is man?

(3) The interests of humanity are the ideals of the Enlightenment: the freedom of man, the personal and legal recognition of the rights and dignity of each individual, the necessity that mankind have the freedom to improve itself through education which will fit it for self-government, the establishment of strong government which alone can afford to permit intellectual freedom among its subjects, international intercourse, and peace. The freedom of scholars to think and publish their own thoughts without fear of persecution is an essential condition for an enlightened society. From his first work, published when he was twenty-three years old, to the *Strife of the Faculties*, published when he was nearly eighty, freedom of thought is a persistent theme. A sturdy maintenance of the right of the youth to disagree with Leibniz and other great men opened his career, and he ended it claiming the freedom of the philosophical faculty from dictation by others.

(4) But in one respect Kant did not agree with a nearly universal belief of the Enlighteners. He did not hold to a eudaemonistic theory of ethics. Progress in history and improvement in man are not measured by happiness

and well being, but by the development of moral character and freedom. The *desire* for happiness is natural, but happiness itself, and certainly what is higher than happiness, cannot be built upon it. His ethics was an ethics of intention, a Stoic and not an Epicurean ethics. It derived from the Pietistic ethos of his family and school, not from the popular moral philosophy he learned from eighteenth-century thinkers. But from Pietism itself he rejected two important tenets, viz., that morality consists in servile obedience to the revealed will of God, and that the motive for morality is the love and fear of God and the hope of a future life.

(5) Not that Kant ever doubted the existence of God and the immortality of the soul. While his philosophical arguments for them varied from time to time throughout his career, and the "grounds for assent" to them were not the same at different periods, these doctrines were fixed points to which he returned again and again, by the most diverse routes.

(6) But the moral life was not, for him, predicated upon faith in God and belief in an after-life. The duties of morality were to him in no need of a theological and metaphysical backing. The most that philosophy could do was to defend allegiance to these true doctrines from the attacks of *philosophes* by showing that their arguments were unsound. To base morality upon dogma was, in his opinion, to destroy the purity of morals just as surely as basing it upon the desire for happiness would destroy it. Morality is the best support of religion; religion is a treacherous support for morality.

(7) Religion constantly threatens the purity of morals by finding the duty of man to lie in his allegiance to an alleged historical revelation of God. Religion as a putative source of morality is, rather, a source of superstition. Yet there is in the Christian tradition and, more especially, in Scripture, a representation of moral ideals which man in history would not, and probably could not, have achieved without revelation. In this sense, religion is a moral teacher of mankind; but pupils must gain and preserve their own insights, and not always remain pupils.

(8) Kant never wavered in his conviction that the will of man is free, and that everything of worth in our world is achieved by the exercise of freedom. We cannot count on God or "the provisions of stepmotherly nature" to do what only a free man, that is, a rational animal using his reason in the conduct of life, can do. (Freedom does not always mean exactly the same thing for Kant; its context varies, and arguments for it once presented are held by him at later times to be "miserable subterfuges" —but he never at any time doubted that the *will* is free, or that *man* ought to and can—also in other senses—be free).

(9) The physical world is Newtonian. It is a machine. It does not require the finger of God to keep it in running order. The phenomena of nature can be explained in terms of the basic forces of its elementary particles, and these explanations, though built upon experience, must be given a mathematical form. No scientific explanation is complete until it is a mathematical construction which fits the phenomena of matter in motion. All things in nature occur with the certainty of eclipses of the sun and moon. There is no chance, no miracle, no special providence. The Newtonian theory is essentially complete. Modifications in detail may be

required (and Kant suggested some), but mankind is now finally in possession of a world-picture that will not have to be rejected, but only improved, in the light of future research.

(10) The physical world is, by virtue of being a machine, not a product of chance. It is a teleological whole. It shows evidence of a design we cannot understand, but the evidence is the variety and harmony of its parts which show how the whole fabric results from a few simple forces and laws. We cannot explain the world by the pretensions of physico-theology, but the order and design of the world make physico-theological arguments persuasive even to Kant, who sees the logical fallacy in them. The over-all teleology of the world, however, totally excludes the homo-centric teleology of the Wolffian philosophy.

(11) Hence the science of nature, like morals, points in the direction of a metaphysical and even theological theory which illuminates the vast processes of nature and history and which satisfies the intellectual demand for a world making sense in all its parts, even if we cannot know God's over-all plan. Such a theory, also, gives ground for hope that our moral aspirations can also be achieved. The metaphysics which does all this requires the concepts of man as a metaphysical, spiritual substance endowed with freedom, of nature as the manifestation of the fundamental forces of other substances, and of God as an eternal perfect being and creator of the whole. This metaphysics is at least as old as Christian Aristotelianism, but in Kant's mind it tended to take the form of a Leibnizian theory minus the hypothesis of pre-established harmony, and the concept of God becomes less and less a functioning part of the natural and moral processes, and man becomes ever more important.

—None of these doctrines was original with Kant. Each of them has been met with somewhere earlier in our history. A good popular philosopher or a member of the Academy in Berlin or a professor in Göttingen could have held them all and made a tidy reputation by playing combinations with them in one or another *Literaturzeitung*. His stoical view of morality and his extreme Newtonism are perhaps more nearly unique than the others. In the Kantian *Weltanschauung* there is more Newton and more Rousseau than would have been found in that of any of his German contemporaries, and his whole world-picture has a stoic-Christian patina of Pietism. But most of the tenets were commonplaces, and could be put together in various combinations by anyone who had read his Leibniz, Wolff, Shaftesbury, von Haller, and Lessing. This Immanuel Kant, tax assessor for Kobbelbude-an-der-Ostbahn and occasional contributor to the *Göttinger Gelehrte Anzeigen*, would deserve a quarter of a page in Überweg.

The trouble with this *Weltanschauung* is that, like most *Weltanschauungen*, it is an eclectic mixture, not a true chemical compound. The anti-eudaemonism and the Newtonian elements in it do not form a homogeneous whole; the libertarianism necessary for Kant's moral theory goes far beyond that which is permitted by his Newtonian theory of things existing in nature. If they cannot be reconciled, Kant himself admitted, in 1788, that it would be the ethical theory which would have to be given up.

In his early life, he did not see any incompatibility between them; but when he did see it, he discovered *the* problem which could not be handled in such an indulgent *Weltanschauung*. For, as he later said, the theory of space and time (which grew out of his concern with Newtonian physics) and that of freedom of the will (which grew out of his ethics) constituted the fulcrum for his critical philosophy. So long as he held to the intellectual defensibility of the Leibnizian metaphysics of the eleventh point, his intellectual edifice was in no more danger than Leibniz's *Theodicy*. But when he found that this Leibnizian metaphysics could not be supported "as a science" (point 1), his technical philosophy underwent a profound revolution, a revolution which, if successful, would provide a foundation for the *Weltanschauung* which had become almost second nature to him. The *Weltanschauung* remained; but it was given a new foundation.

Kant's Life

Kant was born in Königsberg April 22, 1724, as the first son and fourth child of Johann Georg Cant, a harness maker, and his wife Anna Regina, née Reuter. The Cant family were Pietists, and Immanuel at the age of eight was enrolled, with financial assistance from F. A. Schultz, in the Pietistic school, the Collegium Fridiricianum, where he remained until he matriculated in the University of Königsberg in 1740. As a university student he was befriended by Martin Knutsen (1713–1751), who gave him access to his library and taught him, or at least encouraged him to learn, the works of Newton. Knutsen was a Wolffian Pietist who, like many others, rejected the Wolffian solution to the mind-body problem, favoring a theory of *influxus physicus* over that of pre-established harmony. It was no doubt because of Knutsen that Kant found it so easy to accept the theory of the interaction of substances which was present in his earliest works and perhaps never given up. In 1747 he published a dissertation entitled *Thoughts on the True Estimation of Living Forces* (*Gedanken von der wahren Schätzung der lebendigen Kräfte* [*vis viva*]),[1] which showed a detailed acquaintance with the large literature that had accumulated on this problem since the time of Descartes and Leibniz, though, like all writings on the subject except D'Alembert's, it gave an erroneous solution.

From 1747 to 1755 Kant held positions as tutor in several families near Königsberg. During these years he may have been a tutor in the family of the Graf von Keyserling near Tilsit; but whether as an employee or guest, he formed a deep and lasting friendship with its members, especially the Gräfin, and no doubt learned as much from her as the Keyserling boys could have learned from him. For when Kant gave up the relative security of his modest position to seek his fortune as a *Privatdozent* in Königsberg, he returned to his native city a polished man of the world with a refined taste for elegance in dress and manner, with attractive conversational abilities,

---

[1] Several pages of this dissertation are translated by John Handyside in *Kant's Inaugural Dissertation* (Chicago and London: Open Court, 1929).

and with a presence that recommended him to the finest houses in Königsberg. He had everything a gentleman needed except money, and had to live exiguously for fifteen years before he acceded to a professorship. In spite of his poverty, during the years that he was *Dozent* he was often called "the gallant master"—a spruce dresser, a popular teacher, and a welcome guest in the best society of his city. The popular portrait of Kant's character and mode of life is only a caricature, which projects back into his prime the crotchets of his old age.

The years with the von Keyserling family were not spent just in acquiring fashion, but must also have been years of intense study. Upon his return to Königsberg he presented two Latin dissertations: *On Fire* (*Meditationum quarundam de igne succincta delineato*, 1755) and *The First Principles of Metaphysical Knowledge, Newly Delineated* (*Principiorium primorum cognitionis metaphysicae nova dilucidatio*, 1755),[2] for which he received the M.A. degree and his lectureship. Then came one of his most remarkable works, *The General Natural History and Theory of the Heavens* (*Allgemeine Naturgeschichte und Theorie des Himmels*)[3] published in 1755. In this book he formulated the nebular hypothesis of the origin of the solar system, explained the appearance of the Milky Way, argued for the existence of an infinite number of galaxies like our own, and predicted the existence of a planet between Mars and Jupiter and of others beyond Saturn. Philosophically, the book is of interest because in it he out-Newtoned Newton. Using only Newtonian laws and forces, he provided a plausible theory of the origin and stability of the solar system, without needing to call in the hand of God at any point in astronomical evolution.

Until 1760 Kant published mostly scientific rather than philosophical works. As was then customary, however, no very sharp distinction was drawn between philosophical analysis and scientific speculation. Thus, for example, there were three papers occasioned by the Lisbon Earthquake; they are informed with solid geological learning, but also with opinions in theodicy and natural theology. There were two papers on mechanics: *Physical Monadology* (*Monadologia physica*, 1756) and *New Theory of Motion and Rest* (*Neuer Lehrbegriff der Bewegung und Ruhe*, 1758), one on the theory of winds, and, a very substantial effort to calculate the retardation of the earth's rotation by tidal friction.[4]

Kant's career falls neatly into divisions by decades, and the decade of the 1760's is more philosophical than that of the fifties. The most important works of this decade were: *The False Subtlety of the Four Syllogistic Fig-*

[2] The latter is commonly referred to as *Nova dilucidatio* and was translated by F. E. England in his *Kant's Conception of God* (London: Allen & Unwin, 1929).

[3] Translated by W. Hastie, *Kant's Cosmogony* (Glasgow: Maclehose, 1900). The work was published in Königsberg so obscurely that Hastie (p. ix) says it was not published but "simply left the press"; and neither Lambert nor Laplace knew of its existence when they came to similar conclusions. The nebular hypothesis is now called the Kant-Laplace theory.

[4] Translated by Hastie, *ibid.*, under the title: *Examination of the Question Whether the Earth has Undergone an Alteration of its Axial Rotation.*

ures (*Die falsche Spitzfindigkeit der vier syllogistischen Figuren erwiesen,* 1762),[5] *The Only Possible Premise for a Demonstration of the Existence of God* (*Der einzig mögliche Beweisgrund zu einer Demonstration vom Dasein Gottes,* 1762)[6] and his contribution to the Berlin Academy's prize contest (and hence generally referred to as the Prize Essay), *Inquiry into the Distinctness of the Principles of Natural Theology and Morals* (*Untersuchung über die Deutlichkeit der Grundsätze der natürlichen Theologie und Moral*) written in 1762 but first published in 1764.[7] In 1763 there was a short but very important work, *An Attempt to Introduce the Concept of Negative Magnitudes into Philosophy* (*Versuch, den Begriff der negativen Grössen in die Weltweisheit einzuführen*).[8] *Observations on the Feeling of the Beautiful and Sublime* (*Beobachtungen über das Gefühl des Schönen und Erhabenen,* 1764)[9] was an essay in the mode of "popular philosophy," and in 1766 Kant published a satirical work with a serious purpose. *Dreams of a Spirit-Seer, Illustrated by Dreams of Metaphysics* (*Träume eines Geistersehers, erläutert durch Träume der Metaphysik*).[10] This book was occasioned by the widespread interest (which Kant shared to the extent of spending his hard-earned money for the expensive books) aroused by the clairvoyant visions and communications with the dead claimed by Emanuel Swedenborg.[11] In 1768 Kant published a small paper rich in portents of what was to come: *On the First Ground of the Distinction of Regions in Space* (*Von dem ersten Grunde des Unterschiedes der Gegenden im Raum*).[12] Early in this decade Kant had Herder as a pupil and entered into philosophical correspondence with Mendelssohn and Lambert.

The year 1769 saw no new publications, but Kant subsequently described this year as "bringing a great light." This "great light" showed in the inaugural dissertation, *The Forms and Principles of the Sensible and Intelligible Worlds* (*De mundi sensibilis atque intelligibilis forma et principiis*),[13] written on the occasion of his finally achieving (after two disappointments) the chair of metaphysics and logic.

The decade of the seventies is often, but not quite accurately, called "the silent decade." Only a few small and not very important pieces were published by Kant during this time; but this was the decade of work on the *Critique of Pure Reason*. It is the period in Kant's life about which there is the least evidence and the most dispute, since we have large amounts of

[5] Translated by T. K. Abbott in *Kant's Introduction to Logic* (London, 1885; several reprintings).

[6] Not translated since A. F. M. Willich's edition of Kant's shorter works (London, 1798), and not now readily accessible.

[7] Translated by L. W. Beck in *Kant's Critique of Practical Reason and Other Writings in Moral Philosophy* (Chicago: University of Chicago Press, 1949), and by G. B. Kerferd and D. E. Walford in *Kant. Selected Pre-Critical Writings and Correspondence with Beck* (Manchester, England: University of Manchester Press, 1968).

[8] Hereafter cited as *Negative Grössen;* untranslated.

[9] Translated by John Goldthwait (Berkeley and Los Angeles: University of California Press, 1960).

[10] Translated by E. F. Goerwitz (London: Sonnenschein, 1900).

[11] See Ernst Benz, *Swedenborg in Deutschland* (Frankfurt: Klostermann, 1947).

[12] Translated by John Handyside (n. 1) and by Kerferd and Walford, (n. 7).

[13] Translated by Handyside (n. 1) and by Kerferd and Walford (n. 7).

undatable writings presumably done in this decade, but few hard facts to guide us in tracing the course of his thought. The most important documents of the period are the correspondence with his pupil Marcus Herz,[14] a large manuscript now called the *Duisburg Nachlass*,[15] and sets of students' notes on Kant's lectures on metaphysics and ethics.[16]

I know of no way to describe the 1780's except to say that they were the astonishing decade. Kant, fifty-seven years old at its beginning, published in nine years the following: *Critique of Pure Reason* (*Kritik der reinen Vernunft*, 1781);[17] *Prolegomena to Any Future Metaphysics* (*Prolegomena zu einer jeden künftigen Metaphysik, die als Wissenschaft wird auftreten können*, 1783),[18] written partly in response to a review of the first *Critique* by J. G. Feder and Christian Garve; *Idea for a Universal History from a Cosmopolitan Point of View* (*Idee zu einer allgemeinen Geschichte in weltbürgerlicher Absicht*, 1784);[19] *What is Enlightenment?* (*Beantwortung der Frage: Was ist Aufklärung?*, 1784);[20] reviews of Herder's *Ideas for a Universal History of Mankind* (1785);[21] *Foundations of the Metaphysics of Morals* (*Grundlegung zur Metaphysik der Sitten*, 1785);[22] *Conjectural Beginning of Human History* (*Mutmasslicher Anfang der Menschengeschichte*, 1786);[23] *What is Orientation in Thinking?* (*Was heisst sich im Denken orientieren?*, 1786),[24] his contribution to the Jakobi-Mendelssohn debate; *Metaphysical Foundations of Natural Sciences* (*Metaphysische Anfangsgründe der Naturwissenschaften*, 1786);[25] the second edition, extensively

[14] Now included in *Kant's Philosophical Correspondence*, translated by Arnulf Zweig (Chicago: University of Chicago Press, 1967).

[15] Untranslated and of uncertain date. (In my *Commentary on Kant's Critique of Practical Reason* [Chicago: University of Chicago Press, 1960], I conjectured that part of it was written in the early eighties, but the parts relevant here seem to belong in the seventies.)

[16] The lectures on metaphysics edited by C. L. H. Pölitz and others have not been translated; the *Lectures on Ethics* have been translated by Louis Enfield (London: Methuen, 1930; New York: Harper, 1963). The dates are uncertain, and one cannot be assured of the complete accuracy of the students' transcriptions of what Kant actually said.

[17] Translated by Max Müller (London: Macmillan, 1881) and by Norman Kemp Smith (London: Macmillan, 1929). Each has gone through many editions.

[18] Translated by Paul Carus (Chicago: Open Court, 1902); extensively revised by L. W. Beck (Liberal Arts Press, 1952); and translated by Peter Lucas (Manchester, Eng.: University of Manchester Press, 1953). There are several less satisfactory translations.

[19] Translated by L. W. Beck in *Kant on History* ed. L. W. Beck (Indianapolis: Bobbs-Merrill, 1963), and by Carl J. Friedrich, *The Philosophy of Kant* (New York: Modern Library, 1949).

[20] In both books referred to in n. 19.

[21] Translated by Robert Anchor, in *Kant on History.*

[22] Translated by T. K. Abbott (London: Longmans Green, 1873, with many subsequent editions), translated also by L. W. Beck (Chicago: University of Chicago Press, 1949; New York: Liberal Arts Press, 1956); and by H. J. Paton, *The Moral Law* (London: Hutchinson's University Library, 1949). There are several less satisfactory translations.

[23] Translated by Emil Fackenheim in *Kant on History* (see n. 19).

[24] Translated in Beck, *Kant's Critique of Practical Reason and Other Writings in Moral Philosophy* (see n. 7).

[25] In an unsatisfactory translation by Belfort Bax (London: Bohn's Library, 1909). A new translation by James Ellington has been announced, but has not yet appeared.

revised, of the *Critique of Pure Reason* (1787);[26] *Critique of Practical Reason* (*Kritik der praktischen Vernunft*, dated 1788 on the title page but actually published at the end of 1787);[27] *On the Use of Teleological Principles in Philosophy* (*Über den Gebrauch teleologischer Prinzipien in der Philosophie*, 1788); and *Critique of Judgment* (*Kritik der Urteilskraft*, 1790).[28]

I know of no decade in the life of any philosopher which even approaches this one in the quantity, variety, and importance of what Kant did in these nine years. When one refers to "Kant's philosophy" without modifiers or qualifications, it is these works, from the first to the third *Critiques*, which are meant.

The last decade of Kant's active life is not so easy to describe with a single adjective. The writings are even more diverse than those of the eighties, and they do not collectively show any simple integrating pattern. The systematic work of the eighties was incomplete, at least in his own conception; he had written the propaedeutic works but not the "system of transcendental philosophy" for which the *Critiques*, the *Prolegomena*, and the *Foundations* (as shown even by their titles) were to prepare the way. He had written *Foundations of the Metaphysics of Morals*, but ever since 1768, when he outlined his project to Herder, he had wanted to write—and had often spoken as if he were about to publish—a metaphysics of morals and not just the foundations for it.[29] This work was finally published in 1797.[30] Still, the remaining writings in the last decade do not clearly fall into the pattern of critical philosophy or transcendental philosophy as articulated in the *Critiques*. Some of the writings create as many problems for an integrated interpretation of Kant's thought as they solve. The fact that the major work had been done, that polemics were in full swing, that his pupils were disputing with each other about which one of them was the most faithful to the master and was his most trusted spokesman, and that major historical events impinged on Kant's heretofore quiet and uneventful life contributed to an apparent dispersal of his interests and energies.

Frederick the Great died in 1786 and was succeeded by his nephew Friedrich Wilhelm II. According to custom, the King of Prussia was crowned in Königsberg, and the coronation occurred while Kant was rector of the University. Kant had to participate in the ceremonies and was publicly praised

[26] See n. 17.

[27] Translated by T. K. Abbott (London, 1873, with many subsequent editions), and by L. W. Beck (Chicago: University of Chicago Press, 1949; New York: Liberal Arts Press, 1957).

[28] Translated by J. H. Bernard (New York: Hafner, 1951) and by J. C. Meredith (Oxford: Clarendon Press, 1952); Part I, sec. 1, bk. 1, "The Analytic of the Beautiful," has been translated by Walter Cerf (Indianapolis: Bobbs-Merrill, 1963). The *First Introduction to Critique of Judgment* was translated by James Haden (Indianapolis: Bobbs-Merrill, 1963).

[29] I have recounted Kant's repeatedly deferred plans for this work in my *Commentary on Kant's Critique of Practical Reason*, pp. 4–18.

[30] *Metaphysik der Sitten*. Part I, the *Jurisprudence*, has been translated by John Ladd (Indianapolis: Bobbs-Merrill, 1965), and Part II, the *Doctrine of Virtue*, by Mary J. Gregor (New York: Harper & Row, 1964) and by James Ellington (Indianapolis: Bobbs-Merrill, 1964).

by the king. But Kant flourished better under Frederick II, who ignored him, than under his nephew, who politely acknowledged his fame. For Friedrich Wilhelm II dismissed Kant's patron von Zedlitz and appointed in his stead Johann Christoff Wöllner (1732–1800), who had been called by Frederick the Great "a deceitful and intriguing parson." Wöllner now felt called upon both to sanction the bigamy of the new king and to stamp out religious enlightenment in his realm. The means he chose for the latter was the infamous "Wöllner Edict" of 1788 which stipulated that in Protestant churches the authority of the old tenets of faith should be enforced and that ministers were to be held strictly to orthodox doctrines. Censorship of theological writings was established.

In 1792 Kant published his *On the Radical Evil in Human Nature* (*Von der Einwohnung des bösen Prinzips neben dem guten, d.i. vom radikalen Bösen in der menschlichen Natur*), which became the first part of *Religion within the Limits of Reason Alone* (*Die Religion innerhalb der Grenzen der blossen Vernunft*, 1793).[31] This was followed in 1794 by *The End of All Things* (*Das Ende aller Dinge*),[32] an ironical attack on official Christendom represented by the forces of Wöllner, in which Kant foretells "the unnatural (perverted) end of all things for which we ourselves are responsible in that we misunderstand" the divine wisdom of things. Whereupon, on October 1, in the name of the king, there was issued a cabinet order directed against Kant and written by Wöllner: "Our highest Person has taken note, with great displeasure, of how you have misused your philosophy for the depreciation of many of the principal and fundamental dogmas of Holy Scripture and Christianity. We demand an immediate conscientious answer of you, that you will not in the future give such offence; but that you will, conformably to your duty, use your authority and talents so that Our paternal purpose towards Our realm shall be attained more and more. If this is not done, and you continue your opposition, you will certainly have to expect unpleasant consequences." Kant complied, "as Your Majesty's most faithful subject," by agreeing not to write or lecture on any religious subject.

Friedrich Wilhelm II died in 1797, and Kant (because of the *reservatio montalis* he now revealed to have lain in that innocent-sounding formula of submission) again felt free to write on religious questions. In 1798 he published *The Strife of the Faculties* (*Der Streit der Fakultäten*),[33] the first book of which defended the right to free philosophical interpretation of Scripture without liability to theological censure.

Also in the nineties there were writings on political theory: the second book of *The Strife of the Faculties*, on the historical and moral significance of the French Revolution; *On the Saying: That May Hold in Theory but Does not Work in Practice* (*Über den Gemeinspruch: Das mag in der Theo-*

---

[31] Translated by T. M. Greene and H. H. Hudson (Chicago: Open Court, 1934); republished with a new and important Introduction by John R. Silber (New York: Harper, 1960); Part I in Abbott (see note 22).

[32] Translated by Robert Anchor in *Kant on History* (see note 19).

[33] Only pt. II of this has been translated; it is in the translation by Robert Anchor in *Kant on History*.

rie richtig sein, taugt aber nicht für die Praxis, 1794);[34] and a most important book, translated and read immediately all over Europe—*Perpetual
Peace: A Philosophical Sketch* (*Zum ewigen Frieden, Ein philosophischer
Entwurf*, 1795).[35] This little work, drawn up in mock-heroic style like a
treaty, was occasioned by Kant's approbation of the signing of the Treaty
of Basel, which seemed to hold out promise of survival to the French revolutionary government. This tractate argued for the humane conduct of war
and for the establishment of an international league of republican states
which, he believed, would make war impossible. (Other German philosophers—notably Sebastian Franck, Leibniz, and Pufendorf—had opposed
war, but Kant predicated the effective banning of war upon the establishment of popular governments instead of leaving it to the good will of enlightened princes.) This, together with his enthusiasm for the French
Revolution, expressed in *The Strife of the Faculties*, made the rumor believable that he was going to Paris as an adviser to the French government!

In the same decade there were also several important polemical writings
which have never been translated into English: *Concerning a New Discovery, According to Which Every New Critique of Pure Reason is made
Unnecessary by an Earlier One* (*Über eine Entdeckung, nach der alle neue
Kritik der reinen Vernunft durch eine ältere entbehrlich gemacht werden
soll*, 1790), directed against an attack on him by J. A. Eberhard, who pretended to see a critique of pure reason in the works of Leibniz and Wolff,
and customarily called, because of its barbarously long title, *Gegen Eberhard*; *On a Newly Elevated Elegant Style in Philosophy* (*Von einem neuer-
dings erhobenen vornehmen Ton in der Philosophie*, 1796), directed against
the "philosophers of faith and feeling"; and *Proclamation of the Imminent
Conclusion of a Treaty of Eternal Peace in Philosophy* (*Verkündigung des
nahen Abschlusses eines Traktats zum ewigen Frieden in der Philosophie*,
1796), a defense of his theory of the primacy of pure practical reason over
theoretical reason.

Besides these, there were several smaller essays on a variety of subjects,
ranging from the influence of the moon on the weather to the notorious *On
an Alleged Right to Lie from Altruistic Motives* (*Über ein vermeintes Recht
aus Menschenliebe zu lügen*, 1797), a pitiful conclusion to a comedy of errors,[36] which has probably done more to damage Kant's reputation than any
piece of writing against him by his opponents and critics.

[34] Translated (in part) in C. J. Friedrich, *The Philosophy of Kant* (see n. 19).

[35] Many editions of this little book exists. The fullest study of it, with a translation,
is by C. J. Friedrich, *Inevitable Peace* (Cambridge: Harvard University Press, 1948).
I may be permitted to call attention to my translation of it (New York: Liberal Arts
Press, 1957, with analytical introduction) reprinted, without the introduction, in *Kant
on History*.

[36] Translated by T. K. Abbott (see n. 22), and by L. W. Beck (see n. 27). The "comedy of errors" alluded to arose through Benjamin Constant's saying that a "German philosopher" had denied that one had a right to lie to a would-be murderer in order to save
the life of an innocent man, and from Kant's thinking (erroneously) that Constant was
referring to him, whereupon he set out upon the extraordinary project of showing that
indeed he did believe this. But he had not said it! See H. J. Paton, "An Alleged Right to
Lie; a Problem in Kantian Ethics," *Kant-Studien*, 45: 190–203 (1953–54).

In 1797, because of the weakness of old age, Kant gave up lecturing. In 1798 he published his lectures on anthropology[37] and wrote several versions of the work, published only posthumously, he hoped to submit for a prize contest of the Berlin Academy on the progress of metaphysics in Germany since the time of Leibniz and Wolff.[38] The last years of his life were spent working on the transition from transcendental philosophy to a universal system of physics; only this last manuscript, published as the *Opus posthumum*, shows any evidence of failing powers, unless one thinks that the *Alleged Right to Lie* could not have been written by a man in full possession of his moral and intellectual powers.

Kant died February 12, 1804.

Having attempted to give the main features of Kant's *Weltanschauung* and the principal facts about his life, I may be excused from trying to give a character sketch filled out with well-known anecdotes of doubtful authenticity: how his wig fell over his shoulder again and again; how he presented a rose to the lady who helped him rise after he fell in the street; how he put fresh mustard on almost all his food and spent three hours at table; how as a young man he hesitated too long to propose and so lost the lady; how as an old man he persuaded his friend Hippel to forbid hymn-singing by prisoners in the city jail during the hours he was accustomed to work, and how—God save the mark!—the housewives of Königsberg set their clocks by his afternoon walk. But, we may ask, how did he seem to those who knew him? What was it like to be with him?

Herder, who after his break with Kant because of the reviews of his work on the philosophy of history had no reason to sentimentalize about his old teacher, remembered the *galanter Magister* thus: "He was indifferent to nothing worth knowing. No cabal, no sect, no prejudice, no desire for fame, could ever tempt him in the slightest from broadening and illuminating the truth. He incited and gently forced others to think for themselves; despotism was foreign to his nature."[39] And Ludwig Ernst Borowski, who was close to Kant later in life, wrote in his biography:

My sketch of Kant would be very unlike if a certain kindly, comfortable picture of Kant did not come before the eyes of my reader. He was certainly not one who failed to recognize his own worth, nor one who tolerated wilful neglect; but all the same he was an exceptionally good-natured, unpretentious man. He had a hundred traits which had to appeal to anyone who knew anything of human merit. They made him attractive in society, sought for by all and agreeable to everyone. I used to call him a *childish man*. Just yesterday I used the

---

[37] *Anthropologie in pragmatischer Hinsicht.* A translation of this by Mary J. Gregor is to be expected in the near future. Parts have been translated by Walter Cerf in the volume referred to in n. 28 and by Charles T. Sullivan, *The Classification of Mental Diseases* (Doylestown, Penn.: Doylestown Foundation, 1964).

[38] *What Real Progress has Metaphysics Made in Germany Since the Time of Leibniz and Wolff?* (*Welches sind die wirklichen Fortschritte, die die Metaphysik seit Leibnizens und Wolffs Zeiten in Deutschland gemacht hat?*) was prepared for the prize competition of the Berlin Academy but was not published by him. Several manuscripts in various degrees of completeness exist and have been published in the complete editions.

[39] Herder, *Briefe zur Beförderung der Humanität* (*Sämmtliche Werke*, Suphan ed.), XVIII, pp. 324–325.

word "childishness" with reference to him. "Right," cried my old friend Scheff-ner, who knew our philosoper very well indeed; "the word 'childishness' expresses the whole Kant!" Or, to sum him up in another word: humanity. Humanity in the full sense of this now so frequently used word, but best as defined by Kant himself,[40] could be ascribed to Kant in a high degree. Not only his naturally good disposition (a certain lovable simplicity), but also all his acquired maxims and principles led him to humanity. He remained true to it until his death. Here among us there was probably not a single enemy of Kant's; he certainly had more friends than ever a man in his position had.[41]

The Development of Kant's Philosophy Before 1769

Some generations ago it was the wont of biographers to divide a man's career into sharply demarcated periods. Kant seemed to be an ideal subject for an operation which should cut at the joints and not across the bones. His intellectual life was divided into two periods: the pre-critical before 1770 and the critical after 1770.

Then it was recognized that all the works in the first period were not alike, and that all the works in the second period were not alike, so several subperiods were distinguished. In the pre-critical period, dogmatic, empiricistic, and skeptical subperiods were recognized. Then the dogmatic subperiod was divided into Leibniz-Wolffian and Crusian sub-sub-periods. And so on.

Periodization, if pushed too far, changes into its Hegelian antithesis, continuity, as the number of periods increases and the length of each decreases. Styles in intellectual history change, and in reaction to the segmented Kant of the late nineteenth and early twentieth centuries, more recent scholarship has seen Kant's development as a slow, continuous growth, even to the extent of emphasizing the perservation of the thoughts across the magic dividing line of 1770. This was a healthy reaction against the almost schizoid conception of "the tragic Kant,"[42] who step by step (each step being one "period") gave up the intellectual ambitions of his youth.

But speaking against a complete homogenization of his intellectual product, there are four facts. First, even a moderately perceptive reader given the works written before 1770 and then the works written after that time, if not told that they were by the same man, would not I think discover it for himself. They are, to be sure, about the same subjects—they are understructures for the same *Weltanschauung*—but they differ in style, vocabulary, and mode of argumentation. Second, Kant himself refers to the year

---

[40] The allusion is to *Critique of Judgment*, § 60; humanity is the universal feeling of sympathy and the ability to communicate to others our inmost feelings; taken together, they constitute the characteristic social spirit of human kind by which it is distinguished from animal life.

[41] *Darstellung des Lebens und Charakters Immanuel Kants* (1804) in *Immanuel Kant, Ein Lebensbild*, ed. Hermann Schwarz, a collection of early biographies (Halle: Meiner, 1907), pp. 68–69.

[42] See Th. Haering, "Der tragische Kant. Versuch einer Ergänzung des herrschenden Kantbildes," *Zeitschrift für deutsche Kulturphilosophie*, 3: 113–140 (1937).

1769 as having "brought great light." Third, he says, his "recollection of Hume . . . interrupted [his] dogmatic slumbers and gave [his] investigations in the field of philosophy a quite new direction,"[43] and the date of this recollection was, in all probability, 1772. Finally, when Tieftrunk wished to publish a collection of Kant's smaller works, Kant told him to include nothing earlier than 1770;[44] and in Kant's own library at his death there was no copy of any work done before that date. Against these facts, a theory of continuous and slow development without a major turning point cannot be maintained.

But though the years 1769 to 1772 were marked by a sudden maturation in Kant's thought, it would be a grave mistake to name the period before them "pre-critical" and the period after them "critical." Nor would it be correct to call the first subperiod "dogmatic." Dogmatism, for Kant, is "the presumption that it is possible to make progress with pure knowledge, according to principles, from [philosophical] concepts alone."[45] With the possible exception of his Latin dissertations written for academic preferment —a genre in which even a writer of as great probity as Kant is perhaps little inclined to challenge the intellectual establishment—the writings of Kant show a continuous and persistent concern with the competency of reason to establish metaphysics as a science. Against the common conception of Kant the dogmatic slumberer awakened by Hume in 1772, I would suggest that *Kant was never an orthodox Wolffian*, and that *the dogmatic slumber from which he was aroused by Hume was a nap which did not begin until after 1766*. He may have nodded from time to time before that, but his recollection of Hume destroyed the sweet dreams which he enjoyed in 1770. From 1747 to 1770, he sometimes believed (but not blindly) that metaphysics was possible and sometimes doubted (but not despairingly) that it was possible. From 1769 to 1772 he came to see how very much more difficult the problem was than he or anyone else who wished to put metaphysics on a solid basis had thought. He saw not only that a new method was required, but that the metaphysics which could be salvaged from his own and Hume's criticisms would be a very different metaphysics from the one they had challenged. It was this recognition which brought him to perform what he perhaps rightly, even if immodestly, claimed to be "the most difficult task which could ever have been undertaken in the service of metaphysics."[46]

I shall try to confirm the conception of Kant's "pre-critical criticism" by referring to four problems with which he was occupied prior to 1770. They

[43] *Prolegomena* p. 8. All quotations from the *Prolegomena* and page citations refer to the Carus-Beck translation (see n. 18).

[44] Letter to J. H. Tieftrunk, October 13, 1797 (*Kant's Philosophical Correspondence*, trans. Zweig, p. 239).

[45] *Critique of Pure Reason*, B xxxv. (In citations of this work, "A" refers to the first edition, 1781, and "B" to the second edition, 1787.) All quotations from the *Critique of Pure Reason* are taken from the translation by Norman Kemp Smith (London, 1929), but frequently modified. Permission to quote from this work has been granted by St. Martin's Press, Inc., London, The Macmillan Co. of Canada Ltd., and Macmillan & Co. Ltd., London.

[46] *Prolegomena*, p. 8.

are the problems of the proper method of metaphysics and its scope; the nature of space; the concept of causation; and the concept of existence. (These problems overlap in part. In order to avoid unnecessary repetition, I shall deal more fully with the first problems and treat the later ones as corollaries, drawing upon considerations introduced earlier in this exposition.)

The Scope and Method of Metaphysics

A pervasive feature of German philosophy since Leibniz, indeed since Clauberg and Jungius, was the adherence to the ideal of mathematical certainty to be achieved by the imitation of the mathematical method in philosophy. Only the Pietists rejected this ideal out of hand. By the time Kant began his writing, however, some doubts were beginning to appear in the minds of a number of men otherwise sympathetic to Wolffianism.[47] Kant was not alone in his doubts, but he seems to have been independent of others who, like Maupertuis, Béguelin, Formey, Lambert, and Euler, began to feel that metaphysics and mathematics were not entirely concordant. During the fifties and sixties the relation between mathematics and philosophy was a question in many minds, but Kant had begun to entertain his doubts about the received tradition in his very first work, in 1747.

In the *Thoughts on the True Estimation of Living Forces*, Kant had come to the conclusion that the methods and contents of mathematics and metaphysics were different. He did so by reasoning from a purely physical problem, the intractable dispute between the Leibnizians and the Cartesians on whether living force (*vis viva*) was MV or MV^2. Kant argued very ingeniously that Descartes, as a mathematician, was concerned only with impressed forces and motions, for which MV is the correct function; while Leibniz was concerned with the internal, continuously manifested, force of substances which the mechanist need not recognize,[48] and that for this force MV^2 is the correct measure.

---

[47] See Giorgio Tonelli, "Der Streit um die mathematische Methode in der Philosophie in der ersten Hälfte des 18. Jahrhunderts und die Entstehung von Kants Schrift über die 'Deutlichkeit'," *Archiv für Philosophie*, 9: 37–66 (1955). E. W. Beth, in *The Foundations of Mathematics* (Amsterdam: North Holland Publishing Co., 1959, pp. 39–47) discusses the views of mathematics and its relation to philosophy held by Bernard Nieuwentyt (1654–1718) which, in his opinion, anticipated everything that was not in error in Kant's view. I have not studied Nieuwentyt's writings themselves, but I do not find Beth's case especially convincing. In the light of Tonelli's documentation I would not dispute that Kant's theory "was constructed of materials which were common property in his time," but would not go so far as to say "it contains no original contribution to the topic" except his own original errors (Beth, p. 41). The genuine originality of the Prize Essay is clearly brought out in Dieter Henrich's, "Kant's Denken 1762/3" in *Studien zu Kants Philosophischer Entwicklung*, ed. by Heinz Heimsoeth, Henrich, and Tonelli (Hildesheim: Olms, 1967), pp. 9–38.

[48] §§ 28, 65, 49, 149 (Not in Handyside abridged translation). For a brief presentation of the error in Kant's analysis, see Max Jammer, *Concepts of Force* (Cambridge: Harvard University Press, 1957), pp. 179–180. Kant's more mature theory of forces is in the *Metaphysical Foundations of Natural Science* (1786) and resembles that of Bosco-

For us, it is of less interest that Kant's attempt to mediate the dispute was vitiated by an error than that his attempt brought him to see the conflict between a physical and a metaphysical mode of thought. Kant was already, at age twenty-three, dissatisfied with the state of metaphysics but ambitious for it. Metaphysics was in trouble, he said, because it had striven to expand knowledge when it should have concerned itself with laying foundations: Men desired a comprehensive philosophy (*grosse Weltweisheit*) whereas they ought also have demanded that it be a firmly established (*gründliche*) philosophy. The lesson to be learned from the conflict between the physical and the metaphysical estimate of forces was that the tasks of the two sciences ought to be sharply distinguished; and when this was done (as Kant thought he had done it), metaphysics was brought to the threshold of truly fundamental knowledge—but "God knows when we shall see it cross the threshold!"[49]

Nine years later, in *Monadologia physica*, Kant found another incompatibility between the mathematical and the metaphysical: Monadology is incompatible with geometry, since the former denies and the latter affirms infinite divisibility. His solution to this earliest adumbration of the second Antinomy of the *Critique of Pure Reason* was to propose a division of labor: physics must begin with experience and develop its descriptions geometrically; metaphysics, on the other hand, is concerned with original causes and forces and is to complete the work which physics leaves undone.

In these two papers the methodological conclusions are of philosophical importance even though the physical issues Kant was dealing with have long since ceased to be of interest. For these papers show that Kant was a Newtonian not only in his cosmology but also in the *theory* of science. Physics saves the appearances, beginning with phenomena, generalizing from them, relating them to each other mathematically, and descending again to phenomena through new observations and experiments. *Hypotheses non fingo*, for hypotheses about the original causes and forces of things are the subject matter of metaphysics. Kant does not yet talk about the method of metaphysics, except to say that it grounds knowledge and should not aspire to expand it. It may use the paraphernalia of mathematics (axioms, definitions, proofs, and theorems)—and Kant's Latin dissertations of these years are "mathematical" in this sense—but this is a matter of style, and Kant did not delude himself into thinking that mathematics was more than an ideal of rigor which might or might not be attained in philosophy by other methods.

For the year 1763 the Berlin Academy, at the behest of J. G. Sulzer, the president of the Class for Speculative Philosophy, announced a prize for the best essay in answer to the question, "Whether metaphysical truths generally, and in particular the fundamental principles of natural theology and

---

vich; it is chiefly interesting for its replacement of concepts of impenetrability of matter and action at a distance with repulsive and attractive forces, which he had postulated as far back as the *Natural History of the Heavens* and the *Monadologia physica*.

[49] *Thoughts on the True Estimation of Living Forces*, § 19 (not in Handyside translation).

morals, are not capable of proofs as distinct as those of geometry; and if they are not, what is the true nature of their certainty, to what degree can this certainty be developed, and is this degree sufficient for conviction [of their truth]?" We have already seen the answers given by Mendelssohn and Lambert. Kant's essay was *Inquiry Concerning the Distinctness of the Fundamental Principles of Natural Theology and Morals* and is commonly referred to as the Prize Essay. It was accepted for publication (given the *Accessit*) by the Academy (actually published in 1764) but Mendelssohn's, which was more to Sulzer's Wolffian taste, won the prize. Kant's essay was not cautious at all. It marked his definitive break with the mathematical ideal in philosophy.

Mathematics begins with synthetic (arbitrary) definitions which can be shown to be real definitions by exhibiting what is defined *in concreto*, in intuition. Its proofs are performed by following simple and explicit rules of substitution and other logical operations. It begins with a few unanalyzable concepts and indemonstrable propositions whose truth is seen by the mind's eye. In each respect, mathematics differs from philosophy. In philosophy we begin with indistinct concepts and try to analyze them. We consider concepts *in abstracto* and cannot show their *denotata* in concrete experience. There are an unknown number of indemonstrable principles and simple concepts; unfortunately we do not know which principles are indemonstrable and which concepts are unanalyzable. The search for them is a major part of philosophical work. There are no paradigmatically simple procedures in philosophy, so the method of philosophy is "difficult and involved," not "easy and simple" like that of mathematics.

There are many, I know, who find philosophy very easy in comparison with higher mathematics; but they call everything philosophy which is found in books with this title. The success shows the difference. Philosophical cognitions often have the fate of opinions and are like meteors whose brilliance holds no promise of duration; they disappear, while mathematics remains. Metaphysics is without doubt the most difficult of all human insights—but a metaphysics has never been written.[50]

Kant feels, however, that he can help metaphysics over the threshold he mentioned in 1747. Science—more specifically, Newtonian science—not pure mathematics, is the model for philosophy:

The genuine method of metaphysics is, in fundamentals, identical with that which was introduced into natural science by Newton and which had such useful consequences there. It says that, by means of certain experiences and always with the aid of geometry, a search should be conducted for the rules according to which particular appearances of nature occur. Even though we do not understand the ultimate cause of appearances in bodies, it is nevertheless certain that they occur by this law [which Newton discovered], and we explain complicated natural events when we distinctly show how they are included

[50] *Prize Essay* (trans. L. W. Beck, in *Kant's Critique of Practical Reason and Other Writings in Moral Philosophy* [Chicago: University of Chicago Press, 1949]), p. 268.

under these well-proved rules. Similarly in metaphysics: through certain inner experience, i.e., self-evident consciousness, we should search for those characteristics which assuredly lie in the concept of any universal property; and, even though we may not know the entire essence of the thing, we can nevertheless make sure use of such characteristics in order to derive from them many characteristics of the thing.[51]

But we cannot now cross the threshold to a systematic, scientific metaphysics, though in principle Kant now sees how it is possible:

It is far from the time for proceeding synthetically in metaphysics; only when analysis will have helped us to distinct concepts understood in their details will synthesis be able to subsume compounded cognitions under the simplest cognitions, as in mathematics.[52]

Kant, in the later part of his essay, makes a contribution to the understanding of the method of mathematics which brings mathematics and metaphysics closer together than they seemed at the end of his first chapter, where he was more interested in pointing up their differences. Or, rather, he adopts some of Crusius' contributions to the question. He agrees with Crusius that something more than the principles of identity and contradiction is needed in mathematics. The indemonstrable principles of mathematics are not established simply by the law of contradiction and the law of identity. Besides these "formal ultimate principles" there are "ultimate material principles" too. These propositions are self-evident, though Kant does not accept Crusius' account of their certainty. But once mathematics is freed from the limitations of reasoning by formal identity and contradiction, a new resemblance emerges between its methods and the proper method of metaphysics:

Metaphysics has no formal or material basis of certainty of any other kind than geometry. In both, the formal element of judgment occurs in accordance with the laws of identity and contradiction. In both, there are indemonstrable propositions which are the foundations of inferences. But since the definitions of mathematics are the primary indemonstrable concepts of the defined things, in their stead various indemonstrable propositions must furnish the primary data [for metaphysics]. They can be just as certain, however.[53]

[51] *Ibid.*, p. 271. [52] *Ibid.*, p. 275.
[53] *Ibid.*, 280–281. The last section of the *Prize Essay* is on the principles of morals. In it Kant seeks indemonstrable principles for ethics. The method is the same as that prescribed for metaphysics, and again he moves away from Wolffianism: "In these times we have first begun to realize that the faculty of conceiving truth is intellection, while that of sensing the good is feeling, and that they must not be interchanged" (*ibid.*, p. 284). In the *Nachricht von der Einrichtung seiner Vorlesungen in dem Winterhalbjahr 1765–1766*, (*Kants gesammelte Schriften* [Berlin: Königlich Preussische Akademie der Wissenschaften, 1902–], II, 311), he elaborates the method even more, thinking now that he is following Shaftesbury, Hutcheson, and Hume (as well as Newton) in seeking for "the abiding nature of man" underlying the variety of his empirical appearances, and trying to evaluate historically and philosophically what men do before showing what they *ought* to do. On this important announcement, see H. J. de Vleeschauwer, *La Nachricht von der Einrichtung . . .* (Pretoria: University of South Africa, 1965 [in French]).

Two years later (1766) Kant wrote his most amusing work, about which there was then and has been since the greatest dispute: *Dreams of a Spirit Seer, Illustrated by Dreams of Metaphysics*. Under the guise of reporting, criticizing, and ridiculing the occult claims of Swedenborg, Kant criticizes what he thinks are the equally unfounded and fantastic claims of metaphysical speculators. In the Prize Essay he had pointed out that the metaphysician using the synthetic method might not connect his definitions at all with the problem he was trying to solve: "If I wished to arrive synthetically at a definition of time, what a fortunate accident would have to occur for this synthetic concept to be exactly that which expresses the [indistinct] idea given to us!"[54] Now, in a delicious bit of scornful satire, he ridicules the notion that the analytic (a posteriori) method of science and the synthetic (a priori) method of metaphysics can ever be *honestly* brought together:

All knowledge has two ends of which you can take hold, the one *a priori*, the other *a posteriori*. It is true, several modern scientists have pretended that one must, of necessity, begin at the latter. They think they can catch the eel of science by the tail, by first procuring enough knowledge from experience, and then ascending gradually to general and higher conceptions. But although this may not be unwise, it is not nearly learned enough, nor philosophical. For in this manner one soon arrives at a *why?* which cannot be answered, and that is just as creditable for a philosopher as it would be for a merchant to pleasantly ask one to come some other time when a bill of exchange is presented to him for payment. To avoid this inconvenience, some acute men have begun at the farthest opposite pole, the outmost point of metaphysics. But a new difficulty is here incurred, of beginning I do not know where, and of coming I do not know whither; also that the reasoning, when continued, does not seem to fall in with experience; yea, it seems as if the atoms of Epicurus, after having fallen and fallen from eternity, might sooner meet by chance some time and form a world, than that common ideas will meet and exemplify these abstract principles. When the philosopher thus clearly saw that his reasons on the one hand and actual experience or report on the other might, like two parallel lines, run alongside each other into infinity without ever meeting, he agreed with others, as by mutual consent, that each should take the starting point in his own way; each then should guide his reason not by the straight line of logic, but by giving to the lines of evidence an imperceptible twist, and so, by stealthily squinting in the direction of certain experiences or testimonies, each one should bring reason to the point of proving just what, unsuspected by the trustful pupil, he all the time had in mind as the experience to be rationally proved. Add to this that they call this road the road *a priori*, although they have imperceptibly directed it to the point *a posteriori* by following a road already staked out. They do not tell you that, of course, because it is only fair for the initiate not to betray the tricks of the profession.[55]

So much, then, for the high a priori road. But now Kant does not even want hypotheses, banished from physics by Newton, to be accepted in metaphysics. Discussing the problem of the relation of the mind to the body, Kant rejects all hypotheses about it since we do not have the data (as

[54] *Prize Essay*, p. 263.
[55] *Dreams of a Spirit Seer* (Goerwitz translation, slightly modified) pp. 98–100.

Newton did in the case of gravity) from which to form a concept of a force unlike anything found in nature.

All such opinions, as though concerning the manner in which the soul moves my body, or is related to other beings now or in the future, can never be anything more than fictions. And they are far from having even that value which fictions of science, called hypotheses, have; for with these no fundamental powers are invented; only those known already by experience are connected according to the phenomena.[56]

Causal relations and the forces underlying them can be learned only from experience, as Newton learned them.[57]

Metaphysics is, therefore, defective both in its starting point and in its methods. Fortunately, however, the complete wreckage of metaphysics is no great loss. Our moral life needs no metaphysical proof of immortality: "It seems more in accord with human nature and the purity of morals to base the expectation of a future world upon the sentiment of a good soul, than, conversely, to base the soul's good conduct upon the hope of another world."[58] Metaphysics may be important for "the applause of the schools" but not for "the future destiny of the righteous."

In spite of all this, however, Kant is not willing to give up metaphysics altogether, for, he says, "it is my fate to be in love with metaphysics, though only rarely can I boast of any favors from her."[59] Metaphysics can be salvaged, once again, by making it give up its pretensions to widen knowledge, to give us insight into what is beyond experience. Once again, the proper business of metaphysics is *Grundlegung*, not *Erweiterung*, laying the foundations, not expanding the wings of the edifice of knowledge. The task of the metaphysician "consists in discerning whether the task [of inquiring into the hidden qualities of things] be within the limits of our knowledge, and in stating its relations to conceptions derived from experience; for these must always be the foundation of all our judgments. To this extent metaphysics is *the science of the boundaries of human reason*."[60]

[56] *Ibid.*, p. 118.
[57] There is no need to suppose that Kant is here under any special tutelage from Hume. This much empiricism was a common-place, and can be found even in Wolff. But in the choice of some of his examples there is almost unmistakable evidence that Kant had read Hume (the *Enquiry* having been translated by Sulzer in 1756), and equally good evidence that he had not yet come to appreciate what he will later call Hume's *crux metaphysicorum*. Giorgio Tonelli, "Die Umwälzung von 1769 bei Kant," *Kant-Studien*, 55: 369–375 (1963), at p. 371, has said that the direct influence on Kant was from Basedow's *Philalethie* (1764) which was, in turn, influenced by Hume.
[58] *Dreams of a Spirit Seer*, p. 121. Here is the second example of Kant's anticipation of the primacy of practical over speculative reason and of the postulates of pure practical reason; the earlier one was in the final paragraph of the *Einzig möglicher Beweisgrund zu einer Demonstration des Daseins Gottes* (1762), where he wrote: "It is wholly necessary that one convince himself of the existence of God; but it is not so necessary that one demonstrate it."
[59] *Dreams of a Spirit Seer*, p. 112.
[60] *Ibid.*, p. 113. Italics added; translation slightly modified. How portentous these italicized words are! For five years later, when beginning to write the *Critique of Pure Reason*, he tells Marcus Herz (letter of June 7, 1771; not in Zweig) that he is writing a book to be entitled "The Boundaries of Sensibility and Reason" *Kants gesammelte Schriften*, X, 123. This edition hereafter referred to as *Kants Ges. Schr.*

If we look back upon the course traversed from 1747 to 1766, we find Kant moving from a moderate rationalism in metaphysics, without extravagant claims to mathematical certainty, through a moderate empiricism of the Newtonian, not Humean, variety, to a skepticism of metaphysics as knowledge of reality and to a new conception, epistemological and prophylactic, of the task of metaphysics. Writing to Mendelssohn on April 8, 1766, in answer to the latter's complaint at the tone of the *Dreams*, Kant said:

I am far from regarding metaphysics itself, objectively considered, as trivial or dispensable; in fact, I have been convinced for some time now that I understand its nature and its proper place in human knowledge and that the true and lasting welfare of the human race depends on it . . . As for the stock of knowledge currently available, which is now publicly up for sale, I think it best to pull off its dogmatic dress and treat its pretended insights skeptically . . . Admittedly, my suggested treatment will serve a merely negative purpose, the avoidance of stupidity, but it will prepare the way for a positive one.[61]

This evidence will suffice, I hope, to show that Kant was not dogmatically slumbering long before 1770, but that a critique of pure reason (not the book, but the enterprise) was a demand he made of philosophy from the beginning.

The Nature of Space

Like so many of Kant's problems, that of space arose from the fact that in his science he was a Newtonian while the metaphysical framework within which he moved was, on the whole, Leibnizian. Leibniz' and Newton's theories of space had come into collision in the correspondence between Leibniz and Clarke, and German metaphysicians had given the palm of victory to Leibniz. But when, through the decline of Wolffian philosophy and the staffing of the Academy with foreign savants like Maupertuis, Euler, and D'Alembert, Newtonism began to gain ascendancy in German thought, all the issues of 1719 were opened again.

Briefly, Newton believed that there was an infinite, absolute, uniform, isotropic space in which bodies were placed by God. Human beings could not determine the relations of bodies to absolute space except insofar as the bucket experiment showed some of them to be in absolute motion; otherwise, relative space, the relation of one body to another, had to and did suffice for all scientific purposes. For Leibniz, on the other hand, space was only a *phenomenon bene fundatum*. It was a relation holding between simultaneously compossible states of the monads; there was no absolute space which would have existed had there been no substances. This form of relating the phenomena of one substance to those of another was sufficient for all the relational or relative aspects of Newtonian space. In respect to the theory of space, Leibniz seemed to be more modestly empirical than Newton.

---

[61] *Kant's Philosophical Correspondence*, trans. Zweig, p. 55.

Kant did not take his departure in 1747 from a genuine Leibnizian starting point, but from that point as modified by Wolff. Wolff generally taught that space is only a representation of the order of compossibles; but he also taught that there are physical monads which are, like Leibniz', endowed with internal force but which, unlike Leibniz', thereby enter into *actual* dynamic relations with each other. Kant accepted the dynamic relations of substances, thus agreeing with Wolff; but he saw then that space in which these substances interact cannot be a mere subjective order. Space must be ontologically *real*, but it need not be ontologically *primitive*. Kant read Leibniz as an objective relativist and not, like Wolff, as a subjectivistic relativist. Space is not ontologically primitive, an underived basic concept, for the existence of space is a consequence of the actual, and not merely apparent, interactions of substances. It is neither prior to things in space (Newton) nor a mere representation (Wolff), but an ontological consequence of interacting substances. Bodies which do not interact are not in the same space; if there is a world not in dynamic interaction with this one, we should have to admit that there were two worlds, not one.

Kant went even further and threw out an idea so far in advance of his time that one does not know whether silently to admire his genius or to feel the hurt of the fact that neither he nor anyone else at that time knew what use to make of it. Substances interact because of the intrinsic forces. If they did not do so, there would be no extension or space. These forces decrease in space by the inverse square law. *The tridimensionality of space is a consequence of this law of physical action.* If Newton's empirically discovered law were different, space would not be Euclidean. Other kinds of space are possible, and "a science of all these possible kinds of space would undoubtedly be the highest enterprise which a finite understanding could undertake in the field of geometry."[62]

Unfortunately the twenty-three-year-old Kant did not have the mathematical equipment to develop this daring conception. It was left for others, including Lambert, to construct non-Euclidean geometries, and only after Kant's death was there again any thought that non-Euclidean geometries might have cosmological significance. Unfortunately Kant himself allowed one of his most potentially fruitful ideas to die. He never again returned to this, one of his most original ideas; and there is an irony in the fact that many philosophers think the existence of non-Euclidean geometries is a fatal objection to the theory of the mature Kant.

In the Prize Essay a new problem arises which had not troubled Kant before. The problem was not the metaphysical status of space, but the question of what it is that gives geometrical knowledge its certainty. When Kant is content to contrast metaphysical and geometrical knowledge with each other (see above, p. 442), what he says is very clear and convincing, because the contrasts he is insisting upon are so great. But let one ask the question: granting all the differences pointed out between the uncertainty of metaphysics and the certainty of mathematics and the reasons why metaphysics is so much more uncertain than mathematics, still why is

---

[62] *Thoughts on the True Estimation of Living Forces*, trans. Handyside § 10, p. 12.

mathematics *itself* certain? The mathematician is not permitted to begin with given concepts or data and to analyze them; a geometrical body is simply what the mathematician arbitrarily and synthetically defines it to be, and he finds that his definition is a "real definition" if he can find or construct the object defined. The figures which confirm our definitions are given *in concreto;* Kant sometimes says, *in intuition.* But unless we have an epistemology for "intuition," this seems to be an empirical test for a necessary truth.

And what of space itself? The mathematician does not need to define it; it is a "given concept" and only partially definable, and its definition would be of interest only to the philosopher. I analyze the "given concept" and "notice that many parts in it [sc. in space] are external to one another, and that these parts are not substances . . . [and] that space can have only three dimensions, etc. . . . Propositions of this kind can very well be exhibited [*erläutert*]; one must see them *in concreto* in order to know them intuitively; but they can never be proved."[63]

This language is so loose that it is hard to be sure what Kant means. But it may be that he is trying to say that the concepts which the philosopher analyzes and which are of use to the mathematician are not like the concepts which function in metaphysical arguments. In metaphysical arguments we consider the universal (*das Allgemeine*) *through signs* (words) *in abstracto.* Mathematics, on the other hand, considers the universal *under the signs in concreto.*[64] This suggests the difference between an intuition and a discursive concept, which will be explained in the Inaugural Dissertation and the *Critique of Pure Reason,* where it will be argued that space is *not* a universal (discursive) concept but an intuition. Kant in 1764 was still far from seeing things as he did in 1770, but if our most sympathetic interpretation of these passages is correct, then Kant by 1764 had reached one of the conclusions of 1770: space is an intuition, not a concept. (He was still far from the other conclusion of 1770: it is an a priori intuition because it is the subjective form of all empirical intuition.) This sympathetic interpretation is strengthened by the fact that Crusius in 1745, Euler[65] in 1748, and Lambert in 1766 had drawn approximately the same distinction between two kinds of representations.

But even if this is what Kant meant—and it is not certain that he was yet in possession of this distinction—it would not, by itself, help him to answer our question: how can mathematics be intuitive, yet necessary? For

[63] *Prize Essay,* p. 267.   [64] *Ibid.,* p. 264.

[65] Leonhard Euler, *Réflexions sur l'éspace et le temps,* § XIV. C. B. Garnett, Jr., in perhaps the fullest study of the problem in English, *The Kantian Philosophy of Space* (New York: Columbia University Press, 1939), emphasizes the influence of Euler, but ignores three others which I think were of equal importance: Crusius, Lambert, and Baumgarten. See Lambert's letter to Kant of February 3, 1766 (Zweig, pp. 51–52), which speaks of intuition of simple concepts like space and time and distinguishes simple concepts from generic concepts. On a more disputable but still likely stimulation from Baumgarten, I have above suggested that Baumgarten's conception of extensive clarity in sense perception points in the direction of a sensibility that has not only its own perfection but also its own form.

it would still leave open the possibility that our knowledge of space and hence our geometry are only empirical.

The next essay on space, *On the First Ground of the Distinction of Regions in Space* (1768) was written after Kant, presumably, had been re-reading the Leibniz-Clarke Correspondence, republished also in 1768. This paper can be understood only if we remember one issue in the correspondence, even though Kant does not mention it. According to Leibniz, there cannot be an absolute, isotropic, empty, and uniform space. If there were, there would be no reason why a single substance (or, for that matter, the whole world), if created, should be in *this* place rather than another; but it is impossible for it to be anywhere without a sufficient reason; hence its position cannot be in an absolute space (i.e., it does not make any sense to ask where it absolutely is). Moreover, if there were an absolute space there would be a real difference between the world as it actually exists and as it would exist if east and west were reversed. This difference, however, could not be discovered; and hence there would be two possible worlds exactly alike and there could be no sufficient reason for the creation of one rather than the other. And by the principle of identity of indiscernibles, there could not even possibly be two such worlds. There could be only one, and the putative difference between them depends only upon our "chimerical supposition of the reality of space in itself."[66]

Now by a slight modification of this argument Leibniz used against Newton, Kant defends Newton against Leibniz. For, he argues, there are spatial phenomena which show that two bodies, in the internal spatial relations of their parts (like an order of objects taken first from east to west, and then taken from west to east) are nonetheless discernibly different from each other and this difference is to be attributed to a difference in their relations to one absolute space and cannot be accounted for if space is interpreted as only relational. These are the phenomena of incongruent counterparts: two figures (e.g., spherical triangles) or two bodies (e.g., right and left hands) which are alike in all their internal spatial relations and in their reciprocal relations to each other, yet which are not congruent. He explains this puzzling situation by the hypothesis that they have different relations to absolute space. For, by the identity of indiscernibles, if *ex hypothesi* there were no differences between them, they should be identical. But they are not even superimposable. Hence there must be an absolute space to which both are related but in different ways. This ontologically real space is primitive, not dependent upon the positions and forces of the bodies in it. Kant has thus rejected his most original doctrine of 1747.

The last two paragraphs of this essay suggest, however, that Kant has done something more than merely switch his allegiance to Newton. He says:

[66] Correspondence with Clarke, Third Letter, § 5. The same passage must have been in Kant's mind also when he wrote (1786) the essay *What is Orientation in Thinking?* when he discusses how we would discover if the heavens had become reversed, though there his solution has reference to our immediate feeling of the difference between the right and the left hand, a difference which, however, is not a logically analyzable difference.

(a) Space is not an object of outer sensations; but (b) it is a fundamental concept which makes all such sensations possible; and (c) it is not a mere being of thought (*Gedankending*) but has a reality sufficiently intuitable to inner sense to be comprehended by ideas of reason. These remarks are very obscure, but very important.

Conclusion (a) is a position Kant will adhere to without change for the rest of his life. It is a sign that if he ever thought of mathematics as an empirical science, he does so no longer.

Conclusion (b) anticipates the theory, presented in 1770 and 1781, and never subsequently changed, that space is a condition of outer experience. But in calling space a concept, Kant shows that he has at least not made the terminological distinction between concept and intuition; and it is by no means clear that he has in fact developed the distinction which he adumbrated in the Prize Essay and which he might have found in Euler, Crusius, and Lambert.

The third point, (c), is a complete confusion of terminology. In Kant's mature vocabulary of the *Critique*, it makes no sense at all, and we do not know exactly what he meant in 1768. But at least it suggests that Kant was trying to distinguish here, as in the two previous points, between the mode of experience which gives us knowledge of space and the normal mode of our empirical knowledge, which is by sensation. How much simpler it would have been to say it is known by an a priori intuition! But in 1768 that would have appeared to be just as confusing as the sentence we have examined. Yet I think this is what Kant is attempting to express.

Table 2 shows how far Kant had moved in two decades. Originally he was a modified Leibnizian in his theory of space; at the end, he was a Newtonian. In 1764 he discussed in a very inadequate way the nature of mathematical certainty; in 1768 he throws out a few puzzling remarks about our knowledge of space. But it cannot be said that Kant has yet come to grips

TABLE 2. Comparison of Kant's three theories of space with those of Newton and Leibniz

	Objective or subjective	Ontologically primitive or derivative	Absolute or relational
Newton	objective	primitive	absolute
Leibniz	objective	derivative	relational
Kant (1747)	objective	derivative	relational
Kant (1768)	objective	primitive	absolute
Kant (1770)[a]	subjective	primitive, at least epistemologically	absolute

[a] Kant characteristically erected a new theory (in 1770) by denying what the other opposed theories had had in common, viz., the ontological objectivity of space. For other comparisons, see Friedrich Kaulbach, *Die Metaphysik des Raumes bei Leibniz und Kant*, Kant-Studien Ergänzungsheft 79 (1960).

with the basic problem: assuming an ontologically real, absolute space, how can it be known in such a manner that mathematical truths can be certain?

The Concept of Cause

Wolff had defined efficient cause as one species of sufficient reason,[67] and since the principle of sufficient reason was thought to be a logical truth derived solely from the law of contradiction, he could not legitimately (but did sometimes illegitimately) distinguish between a logical ground and an efficient cause. Crusius, as we have seen, criticized him for this, and Kant continued this criticism. In the *Nova dilucidatio* (1755) he objected that Wolff's definition of reason is circular. Wolff had said[68] that a reason is that by which it is understood why a thing is rather than is not. Kant argued[69] that the word "why" means "for what reason," and hence Wolff's definition becomes: A reason is that from which it can be understood for what reason a thing is rather than is not.

Kant did not at this time, however, follow Crusius to the extreme point of saying that the principle of sufficient reason, and hence any specific causal principle derived from it, is incapable of proof. Rather he tried to prove both the general principle and a more specific one. Proposition V argues that "Nothing is true without a determining reason (*ratio determinans*)," though the argument means that no *judgment* is true without a determining reason. Proposition VIII is the more specific principle: "Nothing that exists contingently can be without a reason antecedently determining its existence." The argument for the first is so lame, at least to us looking back upon it from Kant's later works instead of being involved in the thick of the fight with Wolff,[70] that I shall not reproduce it. But the second is supported by as blatant a *petitio principii* as any to be found in Wolff, depending, in fact, on nothing more than the definition of contingent existence and Proposition V. Existence is a predicate; the statement that a thing exists must have a reason (Proposition V); if the reason lay in the subject, the thing would not be contingent; but by hypothesis it is contingent; therefore it must have an antecedent condition.

Though the *Nova dilucidatio* is filled with praise for Crusius, it is quite obvious that Kant has missed the principal points where Crucius showed his greatest originality. What was potentially revolutionary in Crusius was hidden from Kant by his then adhering to the Leibnizian theory that the subject of every true affirmative judgment includes the predicate. He cannot therefore see that Crusius' important rule—i.e., that which cannot be thought together cannot be together even though it would not be contradictory for it to be together—puts the causal rule in an entirely new light.

---

[67] *Ontologia* § 886; see also §§ 71, 874, 881, 898; *Logica* § 696. For a very extensive study of the topic of this section, see Giorgio Tonelli, "Die Anfänge von Kants Kritik der Kausalbeziehungen und ihre Voraussetzungen im 18. Jahrhundert," *Kant-Studien*, 57:417–456 (1966).

[68] *Ontologia*, § 56.

[69] *Nova dilucidatio* (England trans.), p. 221.

[70] For Wolff's proof, see *Vernünftige Gedanken von den Kräften des menschlichen Verstandes*, chap. ii, § 1.

To use Kant's later language: Crusius saw that a causal judgment is synthetic, while Kant still thought it was analytic.[71]

The *Negative Grössen* (1763) marked a distinct advance over the *Nova dilucidatio*. For Kant finally saw the point Crusius had made and, in fact, now makes it far more clearly than Crusius did by pointing out various ambiguities and confusions in Crusius' own analysis of the concept of "ground." He now clearly distinguishes between logical contradiction and a real opposition of forces, and from this distinction it follows that the logical relation of ground to consequent is not the same as the ontological or cosmological relation between cause and effect. He sees that proofs of the latter based upon the former (like his own in *Nova dilucidatio*) are question-begging. He makes a significant turn in recognizing that causality is a connection between two distinctly different things. A cause is a real ground (*Realgrund*), not a logical ground, and hence a judgment of causation cannot be proved by showing the identity of subject and predicate. "The rain never follows the wind because of the law of identity."[72]

What, then, is the relation between cause and effect? Kant says he should like very much to have someone explain it to him; he has been considering it and expects sometime (*dereinst*) to publish his conclusions. He will show, he promises, "that the relation of a real ground to something else which is posited or prevented [*aufgehoben*] is not to be expressed at all by a judgment, but only by a concept, which can perhaps be reduced by analysis to simpler concepts of real grounds whose relations to the consequent cannot be made distinct."[73]

The last sentence is not without ambiguity. But the main drift of it is clear enough: judgment is a logical relation of implicit and partial identity between subject and predicate, or ground and consequence. Causality is not such a relation; a causal connection cannot, therefore, be properly expressed in a judgment but is a simple, unanalyzable concept or is a concept reducible to an unanalyzable one.

Though we can see the reason for Kant's calling causality a simple concept, he does not yet have a proper account of its use in judgments, as when one says one thing or event is the cause of another. It is the necessity of the knowledge expressed in such a judgment which is of chief importance. And there are two kinds of causal judgments which must be distinguished: the causal principle itself, that everything has a cause, and specific causal judgments such as "the wind causes the rain." Kant should have answered

[71] Kant disagrees with Crusius on two other points of some importance: (1) Crusius denies, and Kant asserts, that free actions have a determining reason. To avoid the consequences of fatalism which Crusius thought followed from determinism, Kant distinguished between unfree acts which have their causes in "some blind power of nature" and free acts where the determining reason lies in "one's own intelligent motives." His own view ("soft determinism," we would call it) he later rejected as "a miserable subterfuge", as providing the freedom only of a turnspit or marionette. See *Critique of Practical Reason*, trans. Beck (New York: Liberal Arts Press, 1957), p. 99. (2) Crusius affirms and Kant denies, that the principle of sufficient reason applies to God, Kant denying that it is possible that anything should have the reason for existence in itself. His argument for the existence of God professes to avoid the conception of *causa sui*.

[72] *Negative Grössen, Kants Ges. Schr.*, II, p. 204.   [73] *Ibid.*, p. 204.

the question of how the concept of cause enters into these judgments and the authority it gives to each.

But the Prize Essay does not fulfill the promise of the *Negative Grössen*. One would have expected Kant to list cause among the obscure ideas requiring analysis, or among the simple, unanalyzable ideas; and one would have expected to see some causal principle included among the "highest material principles" with which he and Crusius supplemented the formal principles of identity and contradiction. But for some reason Kant is silent on causality.

Three years later, in *Dreams of a Spirit Seer*, he repeats briefly the conclusions of the *Negative Grössen* and adds—what was no doubt obvious before, but not spelled out—that causes can be discovered only through experience. He states, in a few sentences strongly reminiscent of Hume, that causal connections are not intelligible but seem intelligible only when they are made familiar to us through repeated experience. But there is no whiff of Humean skepticism of our natural knowledge in this essay. While we do not have the experiences necessary for discovering the hidden powers and causes of things, the concept of causal connection itself and the validity of inductive generalizations are not problematical for Kant, as they were for Hume.

This failure to move forward in his treatment of causation is understandable when we remember that the *Dreams of a Spirit Seer* was a popular work directed against a popular delusion and arguing against metaphysical speculation. It was no part of Kant's purpose here, even had he been able to do so, to raise doubts about the epistemology of ordinary and scientific experience. Even so, it appears very unlikely that Kant had made any real progress in the understanding of causality after he had seen, under the guidance of Crusius, that the causal relation is not a logical relation. We may safely conclude that the major turning point in Kant's thought occurred when, and could not occur before, he saw further into the problem of causation. For that, he had to wait another eight years after the *Dreams*.

The Concept of Existence

For Leibniz, existence belonged to one out of an infinite number of sets of possibilities defined by the principles of identity and contradiction. Existence was granted to some of them by a free act of God, who chose that the best of all of them should realize their urge to exist. Wolff, on the other hand, because he made the principle of sufficient reason a consequence of the principle of contradiction, treated existence as not *toto genere* different from possibility, but only as the "complement of possibility."[74] Baumgarten explained Wolff's meaning here by pointing out that a possible entity has many undetermined predicates (a possible cat on my table might or might not be asleep) whereas an existent thing has only determinate predicates (the actual dog who is under my table is com-

[74] Wolff, *Ontologia*, § 174; *Vernünftige Gedanken von Gott*, § 14.

pletely determinate in every respect and, e.g., actually asleep). A completely determinate subject, all of whose predicates are fixed, exists.[75] Existing things in the world exist by a hypothetical necessity, i.e., they are completely determined by something else; but one substance must necessarily exist, i.e., must have all its predicates completely determined by its own concept, and therefore exists by the necessity of its essence.[76] This is God.

Kant's *Nova dilucidatio* of 1755 worked within this accepted framework of concepts in its discussion of the existence of God. This set of concepts seemed to be salvable from the wreckage of many parts of the Wolffian philosophy caused by the attack from the side of Crusius. So, in the theory of the existence of God at this time, Kant was closer to Wolff than to Crusius. He rejected the language of the ontological argument when this argument was interpreted to mean that God has the reason of his existence within himself; he rejected the very concept of *causa sui* as unintelligible (Prop. VI). But the substance of the ontological argument is left untouched. While God cannot be the *ratio determinans antecedenter* of himself, the existence of God is shown by the impossibility of its denial; but this impossibility of denial is only the *ratio cognoscendi* of God's existence. The actual existence of God is "prior to the very possibility of itself and of all other things" (Prop. VII). If God did not exist, not only would nothing else exist, but nothing else would even be possible. Possibility is a derivative concept and requires something actual as the "material of possibility."[77]

A very similar argument was given in the *Only Possible Premise for a Demonstration of the Existence of God*, published in 1763. But this book contains a very noteworthy advance over the more rationalistic perspective of the *Nova dilucidatio*. For though still arguing from the possibility of things to the necessary existence of something, Kant here puts his finger on the crucial error in the classical ontological argument and gives a refutation of it which will be repeated with little change in the *Critique of Pure Reason*.

This signal advance over the traditional view he had himself held is the recognition that existence is not a predicate, and hence the existence of a thing cannot be inferred from concepts alone. Existence is a semantic concept, not a syntactic one.[78] Existence, like cause, is a simple concept (in the sense of the Prize Essay), or at least one so simple that analysis can do little to render it more distinct.[79] Existence is "the absolute position of a thing" and differs from all predicates, which are posited only relatively to a thing which may equally well exist or not exist. The copulative "is" connects a subject with a predicate. The existential "is" does not add a new predicate to the subject, but posits it with all its predicates, i.e., says, in the simplest way, *it is*.[80] A nonexisting thing has exactly the same predi-

75 Baumgarten, *Metaphysica* (1750), § 55.
76 Wolff, *Vernünftige Gedanken von Gott*, § 939.
77 We have found similar arguments in Leibniz, Crusius, and Lambert.
78 *Einzig möglicher Beweisgrund, Kants Ges. Schr.*, II, p. 73 (line 3).
79 *Ibid.*, pp. 73–74.   80 *Ibid.*, p. 73.

cates that it would have were it to exist. Baumgarten was wrong in thinking that a nonexistent thing and an existent thing differ in respect to the determinateness of their predicates. If a nonexistent thing should come to exist it would not become more determinate, nor would it gain a new predicate.[81] Kant thereby shows that he is already in possession of the crucial element in the refutation of the ontological argument that is to be given in the *Critique of Pure Reason* twenty years later.

But while the *Critique* in refuting the ontological argument intended thereby to refute all possible speculative (theoretical) arguments for the existence of God, the *Only Possible Premise* repeats, with a few changes, the modified form of the ontological argument presented already in the *Nova dilucidatio*.[82] This is the argument that the possibility of anything requires the existence of something. This form of the argument is refuted (without being explicitly mentioned) in the *Critique*'s proof that possibility and actuality have a cognitive significance only in relation to the conditions of experience.[83] In 1762 the modal concepts of possibility, reality, and necessity had ontological significance and supported the judgment: if any being is possible, some being is necessary. In 1781 these concepts had only regulative significance in the organization of experience and could support no speculative metaphysical conclusion.

But the year 1762 was a significant one, for Kant reached two conclusions he was not subsequently to surrender. In the *Only Possible Premise* existence is not a predicate. In the *Negative Grössen* the effect is not a predicate of the cause, nor a logical consequence of a judgment that the cause exists. In the language of his mature philosophy: judgments of existence and judgments of cause and effect are synthetic, not analytic. Kant has at last given up the assumption which caused so much trouble: in *all* true judgments, the predicate is included in the subject.

A Conjectural "Inaugural Dissertation" of 1768

Had Kant been promoted to his professorship in 1768 and had been called upon to write an inaugural dissertation at that time, what would it have contained? By tracing the course of some of his ideas and seeing which ideas he dropped and which ones he added, we can tentatively state some of the theses he would presumably have been prepared to maintain. (I conjecture that they would be the notions he reached last along the four paths we have traced, except where final results reached on one path abrogate the final conclusions reached still earlier on another.)

1. Speculative metaphysics, in the sense of insight into things and forces lying beyond experience, is impossible.

---

[81] *Ibid.*, p. 76.

[82] This proof is here followed by an extensive presentation of the argument from the design and unity of the world, in which Kant gives a summary and draws physico-theological conclusions from the theory first published in the *Universal Natural History and Theory of the Heavens*. Through this second reporting of his astronomical theory it became better known, e.g., came to the attention of Lambert and led to their correspondence.

[83] *Critique of Pure Reason*, A 231 = B 283.

2. The proper task of metaphysics is to determine the limits of knowledge and its foundations, and not to try to extend knowledge into a realm beyond experience.

3. The proper method of knowing what exists and what the causes and forces in the world are is not by rationalistic argument, but by experience.

4. The proper method of knowing is that of science, the model for which is the procedure of Newton, and this model should be emulated by the philosopher.

5. By analysis of our experience we may find a number of unanalyzable concepts and indemonstrable principles which may later serve as the foundation for a synthetic method in philosophy; but the time is not yet ripe for that.

6. Moral philosophy should proceed in the same way, from the analysis of human conduct to discover unanalyzable concepts and indemonstrable practical propositions; but moral predicates are discovered by feeling, while truth is discovered by intellection applied to observation.

7. Metaphysics properly practiced is important, and "the true and lasting welfare of the human race depends upon it." But speculative metaphysical knowledge of God and immortality are not necessary for the practice of virtue.

8. Space is Euclidean and Newtonian: three-dimensional, absolute, and ontologically primitive. It is not subjective (*Gedankending*).

9. We do not know space empirically, through sensation, but by a "basic concept" or "intuition of inner sense" according to an "idea of reason."

10. Mathematics proceeds by a synthetical method from these intuitions. It thus differs in method from both empirical science and metaphysics.

11. The things we observe in space are completely determined in their actions according to causal laws, but we do not know their hidden powers except insofar as they have been discovered by the analysis of the relations among phenomena (as Newton discovered the fundamental law of the attraction of bodies).

12. Even human actions are under the law of sufficient reason, without infringement on freedom.

13. The unity and apparent design of the world show that the world is a teleological whole, but they speak against the doctrine of special providence and the intervention of God in the course of nature.

If we look back to Kant's *Weltanschauung*, we see how well this set of philosophical conclusions conforms to it. Having the inestimable benefit of knowing Kant's own later work, however, we can see what he himself probably did not see in 1768—how much looseness there still is in its structure, how many veiled inconsistencies there are in it. But Kant was not promoted in 1768, so he did not have to defend this combination of doctrines. A "great light" dawned on him in 1769,[84] and when he did present his Inaugural Dissertation on August 21, 1770, many things had radically changed.

[84] Reflexion 5037 (*Kants Ges. Schr.*, XVIII, p. 69).

From the "Great Light" to Hume's "Spark"

The Inaugural Dissertation as actually written, apparently in haste and while Kant was suffering from a prolonged indisposition in 1770, differs very markedly from the dissertation we have conjectured Kant would have written had he been fortunate in his ambitions for a professorship in 1768. We can determine what the "great light" which dawned upon him in 1769 disclosed by contrasting the conjectural with the historical dissertation. But it is more difficult to decide what brought the great light. Some[85] have argued (and brought external evidence to show) that Kant was reading extensively in Plato at that time, and apparently for the first time; allusions to Plato and Greek philosophy abound in the Dissertation and are almost absent from the earlier works. Others[86] have put much more emphasis upon a quite certain fact—certain, even though there is no documentary evidence for it except the Dissertation itself—that Kant must have been reading Leibniz's *New Essays*, which were published for the first time in 1765, and (less indubitably) the Leibniz-Clarke correspondence, republished in 1768. Still others[87] have seen the working of Hume during that year, but this seems to me to be highly unlikely. The first two hypotheses, however, are by no means incompatible, and there is no reason to deny one in favor of the other.

Looking for sources is a pleasant game, in which I have from time to time indulged in the writing of this book. But it is a dangerous game if played with too serious a purpose—played as if a philosopher can write only what he has read in another book. The most serious occupation of Kant in these years was the thinking of thoughts that no one had thought before.

Certainly some ideas and terminology came to Kant from his reading. The phenomenon–noumenon distinction is obviously of Platonic provenance. Though Lambert had distinguished form and matter and had demonstrated the epistemological fruitfulness of the distinction in a letter to Kant of February 3, 1766,[88] Kant made little or no use of it until 1770, and it is apparent that the extensive development of this distinction in Leibniz' *New Essays* contributed to Kant's making it basic to his new theory of knowledge. From Plato he may very well have received the stimulus to change his mind from the view of the Prize Essay and to say now that moral concepts are rational, and not derived from feeling. From Leibniz he may very well have got the compromise between empiricism and

---

[85] Max Wundt, *Kant als Metaphysiker* (Stuttgart: Enke, 1924), pp. 153–178.

[86] Vaihinger, *Commentar zu Kants Kritik der reinen Vernunft* (Stuttgart: Spemann, 1881), II, 90–95 *et passim*; Ernst Cassirer, *Kants Leben und Lehre* (Berlin: Bruno Cassirer, 1923), p. 103; Georgio Tonelli, "Die Umwälzung von 1769 bei Kant," *Kant-Studien*, 54:369–373 (1963), and personal communications.

[87] Friedrich Paulsen, *Immanuel Kant, His Life and Doctrine* (New York: Scribner, 1902), p. 99.

[88] *Kant's Philosophical Correspondence*, trans. Zweig, p. 51. Kant's reply, September 2, 1770, especially the third sentence on p. 58. Lambert is careful to point out that *he* did not get the idea from Leibniz.

rationalism, according to which form is innate and content is acquired empirically. But Kant's most important conceptions, especially his theory of the radical diversity of two sources of knowledge,[89] were wholly his own work.

We have seen Kant struggling, with an inadequate terminology, to describe our apprehension of Newtonian space. Now he is in possession of the terms he needs and he has a firm grasp of the distinctions he wants to make; he makes them so well that he never has to modify them again. He now teaches that we have a sensitive faculty of apprehension which makes it possible for us to represent an individual whole *in concreto*. This is the faculty of intuition, and such a representation of a concrete individual whole is called an intuition. We also have a faculty of thought, which represents things through abstract, general, discursive concepts. The objects of intuition are individual wholes, the objects of thought are species of things. Both permit us to move from a multitude of representations to a representation of a multitude. If the multitude is represented discursively by what its individual members have in common, with some subordinated to others (as species to genus), a concept is the unifying representation; if it is represented as a co-ordinated unity with the parts in it and not under it, the representation is an intuition (§ 12).

For us, intuition is always sensible, not intellectual. That is, we have intuitions of things upon the occasion of being affected by them through our sense organs, not by thinking their concepts. The two faculties are generically different from each other. The entire Wolffian single-faculty theory of knowledge, according to which sensation and perception are only indistinct thoughts, and thoughts are sensory representations made distinct by analysis—a theory still accepted in the textbook Kant used in his lectures, Baumgarten's *Metaphysica*—is wholly wrong. Distinctness and confusion can be found in each of the polar opposites; mathematics is intuitive and therefore sensory, but is a model of distinctness, while metaphysics is intellectual, but is a model of confusion. (Kant was no doubt helped to make this distinction and to maintain a notion of sensory distinctness by his repeated reading of Baumgarten; but he does not, until 1781, use the word "aesthetic" in his new sense, to refer to the epistemological function he is describing.)

Given this fundamental distinction, the subject matter of the Inaugural Dissertation is easily divided into three parts: (a) the forms and principles of the sensible world which we know by intuition; (b) the forms and principles of the intelligible world, which we know by thought; (c) the interpenetration and overlapping of these forms and principles—legitimate and necessary in the case of science, illegitimate and a source of error in the case of metaphysics. From (c) there follows a new division of metaphysics, both parts of which are possible and essential: a critical propaedeutic and a dogmatic system.

---

[89] In "Kant's Strategy," *Journal of the History of Ideas*, 28:224–236 (1967), I have interpreted this as the most important strategic move Kant made in his philosophical development.

In both intuition and thought Kant draws a distinction between the form and the content. The form is the unifying, structural feature of our experience; the content, or matter, is that which shows itself in this form. Form is the condition under which a variety is seen as a unity, whether of thought (through the concept of a class) or of intuition (through—to use non-Kantian terminology for a moment—a unitary sense-field in which the contents are seen "together"). Form, therefore, is the condition for the variety of representations to be seen as *a* content, whether it be content of a complex intuition or of a complex concept.

Now just as logic deals with the form of thought without attention to the specific concepts which fit into its forms, a science of sensibility (later called "transcendental aesthetic")[90] can distinguish between the form and the content of sensibility. A concept which has no content borrowed from experience is called a pure concept, and the faculty of making and using pure concepts is called pure reason. Analogously, an intuition which has no empirical content from the senses is called a pure intuition. Just as the pure forms of thought are the forms for thought which has content (as we would say that propositional functions are the forms for all propositions in which variables are replaced by constants), the pure forms of intuition are the forms for any empirical intuition whose content is sensation. With respect to any actual inference the forms of thought are a priori; with respect to any empirical intuition, the forms of pure intuition are a priori. Here "a priori" means: known to be valid prior to (independently of) the actual experience to which it necessarily applies.

There are only two forms of pure intuition: space and time. In the confusing terminology Kant uses here and never modified, he says also: space and time are pure intuitions. For they are individual wholes since there is only one space and one time, and all "spaces" and all "times" arise by divisions within the wholes. The relation of all space to the space of this room is not that of a class to its member, but of a whole to its part. Space is thus a coordinate whole, and such wholes are objects of intuition, not of discursive thought.

But how can we intuit something a priori, i.e., independently of its being given to us through affecting our sense organs? If space (and time) are real, ontologically primitive, as Newton thought, and even if they are real but not ontologically primitive, as Leibniz thought, our intuition of them would be empirical, or a posteriori. Now it is not obvious that they are not intuited in this way. If they were so intuited, mathematics would not be an a priori science, but an empirical science. But mathematical laws are independent of the empirical laws of motion; and we *know*, without waiting upon all experience, that we shall never experience a two-sided plane figure

---

[90] "Transcendental," in Kant's terminology, means "making a priori knowledge possible." Hence Transcendental Aesthetic is the study of the aesthetic (sensible) conditions of a priori knowledge. "Aesthetic" *simpliciter* is the whole study of the passive functions of the mind (sensibility and feeling). "Transcendental" must be distinguished from transcendent = extending beyond the limits of experience. "Transcendental Philosophy" is the system of all principles of pure reason to which *Critique* is the propaedeutic. (All these are distinctions in *Critique of Pure Reason*.)

enclosing a space or a non-Euclidean space (§ 15 D—this from Kant!). Hence space and time cannot be ontologically real, even if space be (as Kant maintained since 1768) absolute.

This brings Kant to the second radical discovery of 1769, to the turn which, in 1781, he compared to "the major hypothesis of Copernicus" and which has been described ever since as "the Copernican Revolution." If the forms of intuitions are forms of our sensibility, then they can be legislative of all intuitions, including the empirical perceptions we have of things. But while we find that "nature is meticulously conformed to the rules of geometry" (§ 15 E), we may ask why nature should follow laws which Kant has just concluded are "subjective." The answer is supplied by Plato: our senses (and this includes also the forms of the senses) give us knowledge only of the way in which things appear to us, not as they ontologically are, independent of us. Hence space and time are *only* the forms of the sensible world, the world of phenomena, and not forms of things as they are in themselves.

In attempting to solve the problem of innate and acquired ideas, Leibniz had said: There is nothing in the intellect which was not first in the senses, *nisi intellectus ipse.*[91] Kant sees that his own arguments refute the hypothesis that space and time are acquired ideas, for then mathematics would not be a priori; but he thinks the doctrine of innate ideas "opens the path for that lazy philosophy which declares all further research to be vain." So he says: "Nothing is innate save the law of the mind, according to which it combines in a fixed manner the *sensa* produced in it by the presence of the object." (§ 15, Corollary). He might paraphrase Leibniz: There is nothing in the senses which was not first in the sensations, except the form of intuition itself.

Turning now to the other faculty, the intellect, Kant distinguishes two functions. There is first the *logical* use of reason, by which concepts of whatever origin are subordinated one to another in inference. Second, there is the *real* use of reason, by which reason gives rise to concepts of objects and relations. The logical function of reason is to think, regardless of the sources of its concepts. These concepts may be got by abstraction from the contents and forms of our sensible experience, and by ordinary logical processes it discovers empirical laws relating these concepts to each other. This logical function of reason is to organize empirical representations, to convert mere appearances into that cognition of many appearances which is called experience (organized empirical knowledge). The most general laws of phenomena, such as Newton's, no matter how distinct and "logical" they may be, are still sensible cognitions of appearances, derived empirically, and not applicable to things as they are in themselves. Such empirical knowledge is genuine knowledge and not illusion, however, for two reasons. Phenomena bear witness to the existence of an object, a thing in itself, and hence idealism is false; and, knowledge consists in the agreement of a subject and predicate in a judgment, and if the representations of the subject and predicate arise according to and conform to common laws, there

---

[91] *New Essays Concerning Human Understanding*, bk. II, chap. i, § 81.

is that agreement of phenomena with each other which we call empirical knowledge.[92]

The second logical use of reason is the manipulation of concepts of pure intuition, and from this there arises the science of mathematics—the axioms coming from pure intuition, the proofs from the logical use of reason. Mathematics is rational in its structure, but its basic concepts are not transparent to *reason*, not logically necessary and hence not demonstrable by reason.

The third logical use of reason is to manipulate the concepts of pure reason in its real use. In its real use, reason generates concepts which could not be abstracted from experience, and the logical use of reason is to combine these concepts and make inferences in the perfectly ordinary manner of any logical operation. The logical use of reason operating with the concepts arising from the real use of reason gives us metaphysics.

Metaphysics, then, is a science of pure reason. Mathematics is the science of pure intuition. Natural science is the science of empirical intuitions organized by the logical use of reason. But while mathematics and empirical science apply only to phenomena, metaphysics applies to and gives us knowledge of noumena, the things of the intelligible world, things as they are and not as they appear.

In a brief discussion of the dogmatic system, of little interest to the reader and, apparently, of no more to Kant himself, he says that the form of the intelligible world is a cause in virtue of which there is a connection between things existing in themselves, establishing a causal *commercium* among them so that they appear in one space and time (§§ 13, 16–22). There is little in this with which we are not already familiar from the earlier Latin dissertations. In these sections, for the last time, Kant professes a system of speculative metaphysics. But there is little or nothing new in it, and it is accompanied by the caution that it is sometimes better "to hug the shore of knowledge granted us by the mediocrity of our intellect" than to "push out into the open sea of mystical inquiries" (§ 16).

If these sections tell of his somewhat tired, cautious last fling with the metaphysics with which he had confessed to be in love, the sections on the methods of metaphysics have all the bloom of young love—Kant has taken a new mistress: the propaedeutic *criticism*. Metaphysics is that part of philosophy which contains the first principles of the real use of pure reason; but there is a propaedeutic science which distinguishes sensitive from intellectual knowledge (§ 8), the goal of which is to prevent us from surreptitiously trying to apply sensitive concepts to noumena (§§ 9, 23, 24). He has already given good reasons for not trying to do so, but a series of quick, sharp attacks on Leibniz, Wolff, and Crusius shows them to have used surreptitious principles, to have committed the "fallacy of subreption," to have "intellectualized the phenomenon" (§ 24). No judgment whose interpretation requires knowledge of space or time can be metaphysical. Thus the disputes about *when* the world was created and why just then and not

---

[92] *Inaugural Dissertation*, § 11. This much Wolffianism is a permanent part of Kant's philosophy.

earlier; about Crusius' principle that "whatever is, is somewhere and some-when"; about Wolff's belief that whatever is impossible is self-contradictory (for the law of contradiction requires that a thing not have contradictory predicates *at the same time*), and the puzzles, which had earlier troubled Kant himself, about the infinite divisibility of space[93] and the simplicity of substances—all of these are illicit, because they either try to, or cannot but, use subjective forms of phenomena (space and time) as if they were objective forms of things in themselves. These errors are unavoidable (Kant will say later: there is a natural dialectical tendency to illusion in the mind) unless critical philosophy destroys the natural and naive conviction that "the limits circumscribing the mind are limits in the essence of things" (§ 1). This error is especially noteworthy in our thinking that all intuition is sensible, as ours is; but we can think of an archetypal intellect or an intuitive intellect whose concepts would have individual existing objects. Though we are not endowed with such a divine intellect, the conception of it reminds us not to take the world as it appears to us to be the only possible or, indeed, the only actual, world.

Kant does not, in spite of all his warnings, want us to think that every mixture of intuitive and intellectual concepts is unwarranted. There is the evidence of mathematics for the fruitful use of the two together. To the sensitive concepts of space and time must be added the pure intellectual concept of number, as well as the rules of the logical use of reason (§ 12). Apparently resembling the surreptitious principles, there are other "principles of convenience" which are subjective, like space and time, but which rest upon the operations of intellect instead of sense. Because they are intellectual, they seem to be "drawn from the object," but they are in fact only "rules of judgment to which we willingly submit and to which we cling as if they were axioms, solely for the reason that, if we give them up, scarcely any judgment about a given object would be possible to our intellect." There are three such principles: (1) "All things in the universe

---

[93] There is much dispute about when Kant discovered the antinomies. As far back as 1747 he saw that geometrical truths are not necessarily true in metaphysics; but that does not mean that he saw what was later to be called the antinomy. In his description of the year 1769 (Fragment 5037; *Kants Ges. Schr.*, XVIII, 69) he speaks of trying to prove propositions and their contradictories "not for the sake of skepticism, but because I suspected an illusion of the understanding and tried to find in what it consisted." This has been taken as evidence that some antinomy was discovered in that year. But if so, it is inconceivable that Kant would not have more clearly introduced it into the Inaugural Dissertation where it would have been one of the most effective arguments; in fact, however, the passages which might serve to show that he was in possession of the antinomy theory (§§ 2, 28) are no more revealing than Fragment 5037. In the datable fragments of the *Duisburg Nachlass* (ca. 1775) there is no sign of the antinomies, though the words "thetic" and "antithetic" are used once. In *Prolegomena* § 50 he says the antinomy is "a very powerful agent to arouse philosophy from its dogmatic slumber"—but he does not say it aroused him. Far from agreeing with those who think the antinomy historically initiated the critical movement, I must confess that I have no idea when the antinomies were formulated. For the best recent survey of the problem, which argues that the problem has no simple chronological answer because "antinomy" had no constant meaning, and thus draws conclusions very acceptable to me, see Norbert Hinske, "Kants Begriff der Antinomie und die Etappen seiner Ausarbeitung," *Kant-Studien*, 55:485–496 (1966).

happen according to the law of nature," accepted because otherwise "there would be no use at all for intellect." (2) The principle of parsimony, accepted not because we have any insight into the causal unity of the world either by reason or experience, but because we are driven, in true Newtonian fashion, to explain phenomena with as few principles as possible. (3) "Nothing material either comes into being or perishes," a "postulate" without which nothing stable would be left to serve in the explanation of phenomena according to constant laws.

These principles are given in the very last article of the Dissertation. Nothing is said about their derivation, but they point to some of the most significant themes to be taken up again in a few years.

Also at the end of the Dissertation (§ 29) Kant points to a "species of surreptitious axioms" which hold that it is only by the aid of the sensibly given that an intellectual concept can be applied. It took him at least three years to see that this is not a surreptitious axiom. It was the starting point of a new revolution just as profound as the one of 1769.

Some Second Thoughts—1771–1772

On September 2, 1770, Kant sent his Inaugural Dissertation to Lambert, courtesy his pupil Marcus Herz, who had been one of the participants in the public disputation the previous month. In his letter to Lambert he says that his dissertation presents a view "which, I flatter myself, I shall never have to change."[94] He says that he will complete that winter his "Metaphysics of Morals" (a book he had told Herder in 1768 he was already working on).[95] And he makes one terminological change in the Dissertation: he adopts Lambert's term, "phenomenology," to refer to the study of sensibility which he will later, and finally, call "transcendental aesthetic" (following the lead of Baumgarten, but going beyond him).

Before the end of 1770, Kant received a response from Lambert (along with disappointingly perfunctory letters from Mendelssohn and Sulzer, who had also received copies through Herz), in which Lambert applauded Kant's work in the most generous way, but made three objections. (1) Time cannot be a mere form of appearance, for then action and change would be unreal.[96] (2) There is a danger of confusing "appearance" (Erscheinung) with illusion (Schein).[97] (3) Ontology must "take up concepts borrowed

[94] Kant's Philosophical Correspondence, trans. Zweig, p. 58.

[95] To avoid complicating the history by interweaving accounts of Kant's work on two quite different books, I merely refer the reader to the history of his ethical writings in my Commentary on Kant's Critique of Practical Reason, ch. 1.

[96] Kant answered this objection, which was in fact made also by Sulzer and Mendelssohn and, in regard to space, by "honest Pastor Schultz, the best philosophical brain in this neighborhood" (Zweig, p. 74) in his letter to Herz of February 21, 1772 (Zweig, pp. 73–74), and in the Critique of Pure Reason, A 36f = B 53f. (Kant failed to answer Lambert's treasured letter, and regretted it; his esteem for Lambert was shown by his plan to dedicate the Critique to him, but did not do so because of Lambert's death in 1776).

[97] Kant replies to this in Critique of Pure Reason, B 69–71, not directly to Lambert, however, but to Garve and Feder who had objected to the idealism-illusionism of the first edition of the Critique.

from experience, since the theory must finally be applied to phenomena again."[98]

In this last point, Lambert is explicitly challenging not the radical separation of intellectual and intuitive concepts—after all, he was one of the inventors of that distinction—but Kant's insistence in § 29 of the *Dissertation* that intuition is not required in the application of the ontological concepts. The importance of this objection for the future of Kant's thinking cannot be overestimated, but it is apparent that he did not see at first how important it was, and when he did finally see it there is no evidence that there was then a "recollection of Lambert" as portentous as the "recollection of Hume."

Kant did not allude to this point until his letter to Herz on February 21, 1772, and then only indirectly, and without mentioning Lambert. He tells Herz that in writing the book—now to be called "Critique of Pure Reason"[99]—he "noticed that he [Kant] still lacked something essential," viz., an answer to the question of how a theoretical (not practical) intellectual representation *in sensu reali* (i.e., a pure concept arising from the *real* use of reason) can refer to an object. "If such intellectual representations depend on our inner activity, whence comes the agreement that they are supposed to have with objects?"[100] He rejects the answers given by Plato, Malebranche, and Crusius. Instead of giving one of his own, he abruptly turns to the question of what these concepts are. He says he has found that he can reduce them "to a certain number of categories," not in the manner of Aristotle (or, he might have added, in the manner of Lambert), but by the way they arise and arrange themselves "according to a few fundamental laws of the understanding."[101] Presumably he thinks that the answer he has found to the second question—what are the pure concepts of the intellect?—will also answer the first—how do they refer to objects? For he now expects to publish the book within three months.

Can we conjecture what the *Critique of Pure Reason* would have been had it been published in May 1772? Besides containing, in all probability, a system of the metaphysics of morals, it would have been an expansion of the Inaugural Dissertation in which the least satisfactory parts of it—those concerning the real use of reason and the dogmatic metaphysics based upon it—would have been replaced by something approaching what is called the "metaphysical deduction of the categories" in the actual *Critique of Pure Reason*, together with an ontology using these categories. The metaphysical deduction derives the system of categories from the *single* function of judgment instead of from "*several* fundamental laws of the understanding," so we would expect that there would be a part of the conjectural book which would correspond to that part of the *Critique*, though not identical with it in argument and conclusion.

But the "something essential" would still be missing. For the solution to the second problem mentioned in the letter to Herz contributes nothing

[98] *Kant's Philosophical Correspondence*, pp. 64–65.
[99] In 1771 he had referred to the book under the title "The Limits of Sense and Reason" (Letter to Herz, June 7, 1771; *Kants Ges. Schr.*, X, 123 [not in Zweig]).
[100] *Kant's Philosophical Correspondence*, p. 72.
[101] *Ibid.*, p. 73.

to the solution of the first problem. To solve it, Kant must withdraw his thesis in § 29 of the Dissertation and accept Lambert's objection. To do this is to give up the entire theoretical metaphysics of the intelligible world, which the Dissertation was supposed to establish as science. No wonder, then, that the *Critique of Pure Reason* was not published within three months, nor even at Easter of 1774 as he promised in a later letter to Herz. It took Kant nine years, and the help of Hume and Tetens, to supply that "something essential . . . that constitutes the key to the whole secret of hitherto still obscure metaphysics."[102]

The Spark Struck by Hume

We have seen that by 1763 Kant knew that causality is a "simple concept" or, in other words, that causal judgments do not express a logical relation between predicates but a nonlogical relation between the existence of one thing and that of another. This he could have learned from Crusius. Second, he knew that any specific causal judgment must be based upon experience; a fact he could have learned from Newton, had it been necessary for anyone to teach him this. No doubt he had come across similar views in Hume's *Inquiry Concerning Human Understanding*,[103] which Sulzer had translated in 1755. I remarked earlier that Kant did not clearly distinguish between specific causal judgments, which are empirical, and the general principle of causation, according to which every event has a cause. In 1770 he formulates this as the first of his "principles of convenience" which are both subjective and intellectual. He ingenuously uses it in his metaphysics of substance as if it were objective, and he does so simply because it is intellectual, not empirical and not a rule of sensibility applicable, presumably, only to the phenomenal. What he says about it—that it is a subjective principle of convenience—should have indicated that it could not be used metaphysically, as he does use it. But because it is intellectual and not sensitive and, *a fortiori*, not empirical, he erroneously uses it metaphysically as if it were a principle of the intelligible world. Only in 1772 will he come to see that there is missing "something essential" which will permit a pure concept like cause and its principle to be applied to an object, whether in experience or in the intelligible world.

It was at this point, presumably after February 1772, that Kant's "recollection of Hume" interrupted his "dogmatic slumber" and struck "the first spark of light."[104] Hume asked: "By what right does [reason] think anything could be so constituted that if that thing be posited, something else

---

[102] *Ibid.*, p. 71.   [103] But see above, n. 57.

[104] *Prolegomena*, p. 8. James Beattie's *Essay on the Nature and Immutability of Truth* was translated into German in 1772. In it, he attacked Hume's *Treatise*, quoting from it precisely those passages which had no counterpart in the *Enquiry*, which Kant already knew. Kant's words "eine Erinnerung des David Hume" may be translated "a recollection of Hume" or "a suggestion of Hume's." In my translation I chose the former; I now see merit in the latter. For a full discussion, see Norman Kemp Smith, A *Commentary on Kant's Critique of Pure Reason*, 2nd ed. (London: Macmillan, 1923), pp. xxviii–xxix, and Robert P. Wolff, "Kant's Debt to Hume via Beattie," *Journal of the History of Ideas*, 21:117–123 (1960). On the other hand, one should not ignore the radical thesis of Lewis Robinson ("Contributions a l'histoire de l'évolution philosophique de

must necessarily be posited [?]"[105] Hume demonstrated that the principle could not come from experience, for then there would be no necessity; nor could it come from reason, for then it would not be something else (something not connected with the cause by a logical relation of identity) that was posited. Hume concluded that it was not a legitimate concept at all. However necessary as a "convenience," it was "nothing but a bastard of imagination impregnated by experience, which subsumed certain representations under the law of association and mistook a subjective necessity (habit) for an objective necessity arising from [rational] insight."[106]

Kant "tried whether Hume's objection [to causation] could not be put into a general form, and soon found that the concept of the connection of cause and effect was by no means the only concept by which the understanding thinks the connection of things a priori, but rather that metaphysics consists altogether of such concepts."[107] Now, putting this discovery together with the search for "categories" mentioned in the letter to Herz in February, Kant must have continued the search for a simple rule of the understanding by which such concepts could be found ("I sought to ascertain their number"), tried to find the justification of their use ("I proceeded to the deduction of these concepts"), and then "determine[d] the whole sphere of pure reason completely and from universal principles, in its boundaries as well as its contents."[108]

Three years later[109] Kant had devised the terminology he was to use to try to solve the problem Hume had raised and he himself had generalized. He distinguished between analytic and synthetic judgments.[110] An analytic judgment is one in which there is a (partial) identity between subject and predicate. A synthetic judgment is one in which the predicate "falls outside" the concept of the subject. Next, he adapted the old terminology of a posteriori and a priori from the "logical use" to the "real use" of reason. "A priori" now means: independent of experience (and not just the inference to a conclusion from a premise), and "a posteriori" means derived

Kant," *Revue de métaphysique et de morale*, 31:269–353 [1924], esp. §§ 2–11) that Kant's statement in the *Prolegomena* is not to be taken as a report of an autobiographical fact at all; the critical influence of Hume was felt in 1760, not in 1772 (and not even, as Vaihinger, *Commentar zu Kants Kritik der reinen Vernunft* [Stuttgart, 1881], I, 343ff, argued, in both 1760 *and* 1772); Kant did not have to recall Hume's teaching in 1772, for the Humean influence had dominated the sixties when Kant "awoke from his dogmatic slumber." The passage in the *Prolegomena* as a "reconstruction" of how the problem of the synthetic a priori *might* have grown out of Hume's treatment of causation is pedagogically effective but factually false. This ingenious theory is incredible, but in arguing for it Robinson does prove (though it did not need proof) that Hume's influence was strong before 1772.

105 *Prolegomena*, p. 5.   107 *Ibid.*, p. 8.

106 *Ibid.*, pp. 5–6.   108 *Ibid.*, pp. 8–9.

109 If it is correct to date the *Duisburg Nachlass* at ca. 1775. Of the editions of the *Duisburg Nachlass* Theodor Haering's (Tübingen: Mohr, 1910) is by far the most convenient, and is provided with a valuable commentary and index.

110 There is some evidence in the Fragments that Kant had formulated this distinction in the '60's; but the dating of the Fragments is notoriously uncertain, and if he had done so it is difficult to understand why he did not use the distinction in 1770—or, rather why it did not prevent him from writing the Dissertation at all.

from experience. Third, he sharpened and modified the standard Wolffian usage of "reason" and "understanding." Understanding for Wolff was the faculty of making concepts distinct; reason was the insight into the connection of truths (i.e., the faculty of inferring). For Kant now and henceforth, understanding is the faculty of making judgments about experience using pure concepts or rules which have their "seat" in the understanding, not in reason. Reason is the faculty of inferring and is either dependent for its content upon the concepts of the understanding or, as pure reason in its *usus reale*, generates ideas which it claims to apply beyond the limits of experience.

Kant now is in possession of all of the distinctions he needs in order to ask the question of the *Critique of Pure Reason*: How are synthetic judgments a priori possible? He is not yet in possession of a full answer to this question, but he has reached several conclusions he will not have to give up.

(1) Mathematical knowledge is *synthetic* and a priori.[111]

(2) The "real use of reason" is impossible, or at least does not give knowledge.

(3) The "surreptitious axiom" of § 29 of the Inaugural Dissertation is not false, and Lambert was correct in saying that intuition is required for the application of pure concepts. The relation between sensibility and thought (understanding) is one of mutual supplementation; they do not function in isolation. Hence *a priori intellectual knowledge of what we experience* is possible.

The conclusion (1) could be simply added to the outcome of the Inaugural Dissertation's theory of space and time to produce the Transcendental Aesthetic of the *Critique of Pure Reason*. To prove (3), Kant had to write the Transcendental Analytic, and to prove (2) write the Transcendental Dialectic.

Toward the *Critique of Pure Reason*

The years 1775 to 1780 are the most silent part of the silent decade. There are student notes on Kant's lectures on metaphysics, but they are of doubtful accuracy and Kant's lectures did not keep up with his research.

---

[111] There is no evidence that Kant ever doubted that geometry was a priori, even though he *should* have doubted it when he believed that space was derivative from the powers and relations of substances; and when he gave up this theory in 1768, he was quick to point out that if Leibniz (and, incidentally, Kant in 1747) had been correct, mathematics would not be a priori. I do not know when he came to the conclusion that it was synthetic. It was implicit in the *Prize Essay*. He could not see how revolutionary this view was until he had a clear distinction of analytic-synthetic which did not coincide with the distinction rational-empirical. He did not know that Hume in the *Treatise* had made geometry empirical (which he would have rejected) and therefore synthetical (which he would have applauded). See *Critique of Practical Reason*, trans. Beck (New York, 1956), Preface, pp. 13–14. Beattie, who was presumably Kant's source for information about the *Treatise* (see n. 102), remarks that Hume did try to "involve the principles of this science [mathematics] in confusion . . . but finding, no doubt, that the public would not take any concern in that part of his system, he has not republished it in his Essays" (*Essays on the Nature and Immutability of Truth*, Edinburgh, 1773, p. 159). Kant apparently failed to see the significance of this note.

There is the statement by Hamann in a letter to Herder that Kant has Tetens' *Versuche* always on his desk; but we could have inferred that simply from the fact that much of the psychology of the *Critique* resembles Tetens'.[112] Then there is the letter from Kant to Mendelssohn of August 16, 1783, saying that though the book was "a product of nearly twelve years of reflection, I completed it hastily [*gleichsam im Fluge . . . zu Stande gebracht*] in perhaps four or five months."[113] Finally there are the hundreds of fragments presumably written in these years, though the dating of them is highly dubious.

The *Critique of Pure Reason* is not an easy book. The difficulties a reader experiences tend to increase with the number of readings he gives it. Out of this fact, which students for nearly two hundred years have confirmed, there arise two ways of reading it: One is based on the assumption that the apparent inconsistencies in it are real and are evidence of slow composition of the actual text of the *Critique*; the other is based on the assumption that the apparent inconsistencies are either trivial or disappear upon a more penetrating understanding of Kant's argument.

Those who read it in the former way argue that Kant could not have *written* the final text in four or five months; therefore he must have done a scissors-and-paste job with manuscripts written during the seventies. There is nothing improbable in this historical explanation of the origin of the final text. This conjecture is not even implausible to one who believes that the text is a stylistic and intellectual unity.

But this conjecture is of interest only if (a) the text is not a unity but does contain radical inconsistencies and (b) unified parts (strata) can be discerned in the text and their composition ascribed to different dates, so that (c) the sequence of these strata constitutes a historical development from the position of 1770 to that of 1781. The combination of these three conditions is called "the patchwork theory."[114]

It is no part of my purpose in this book to examine (a) with the detail that would be required if we were to try to affirm or refute the starting point of the patchwork theory. Those who read the *Critique* sympathetically and critically will reject (a) because they find that later study removes some of the puzzles they experienced in early reading, and that the apparent discrepancies between parts seem to conform to a pedagogical plan according to which both the problems and their solutions were unfolded

---

[112] The influence of Tetens is obviously present in the so-called "subjective deduction of the categories", more particularly in the doctrine of "the three-fold synthesis" and the role of imagination in bridging the gap between apprehension and conception. See H. J. de Vleeschauwer, *La déduction transcendentale dans l'oeuvre de Kant* (Antwerp: De Sikkel, 1934), I, 289–329.

[113] *Kant's Philosophical Correspondence*, p. 105.

[114] The principal authors of the patchwork theory were Erich Adickes, Hans Vaihinger, and Norman Kemp Smith, whose *Commentary on Kant's Critique of Pure Reason* has long been the outstanding defense of the theory in English. The principal opponent of the theory in English has been H. J. Paton. Moltke S. Gram's *Kant: Disputed Questions* (Chicago: Quadrangle Press, 1967) contains a translation of Vaihinger's paper of 1902 and a reprint of Paton's paper of 1929–1930, together with a judicious review of the controversy by Professor Gram.

gradually. Those who read the *Critique* unsympathetically and critically will accept (a), and then move on to (b) and (c) if they do not give up the *Critique* as a thoroughly bad job by a philosophical bungler.

In criticism of the patchwork theory, however, I do wish to point out a fundamental historiographical flaw, a flaw independent of the correctness or incorrectness of the philosophical judgment about condition (a). Since there is no independent evidence for the existence of multiple manuscripts, the methodology of the patchwork theory requires that these manuscripts be isolated by recutting the text and putting the cuts together in a new order. This can be done only on one assumption: *each stratum or independent manuscript was perfectly consistent in thought and terminology.* On no other assumption can we begin with only internal evidence and end with a series of reconstructed conjectural manuscripts. Condition (c) now requires that we make another assumption, to wit, that for "four or five months" the assumption underlying (b) was false.

Without the unlikely assumption[115] that in any short period of composition in the seventies Kant was *perfectly* consistent, we cannot separate these manuscripts. Without the even more dubious assumption that for four or five months in the winter of 1780–81 he threw consistency to the winds, we cannot bring these manuscripts together again.

I submit that unless we assume a near-schizoid breakdown of Kant's faculties in 1780, the recomposition of incoherent press-copy out of several manuscripts, each *ex hypothesi* perfectly coherent in thought and word, cannot be made plausible. The patchwork theory, if it goes beyond the likely statement that Kant did not actually *write* the eight hundred pages of the *Critique* in four or five months, requires *us* to make two assumptions which are as wildly divergent as any attributed to Kant himself by the patchwork theory.

The Critical Philosophy

No one has ever seriously maintained that the *Critiques* are easy books. But if one does not first look at them through a philological or philosophical microscope, they cause no more eyestrain than most other philosophical classics. In this brief account of the climactic phase of Kant's philosophizing, I shall write, so far as possible, as if Kant's views did not significantly change from 1781 to 1790, and as if the three *Critiques* were produced according to a single well-thought-out plan.[116]

---

[115] Empirical evidence against this assumption is provided by the *Duisburg Nachlass*, all of whose epistemological parts seem clearly to have been written within a very short time, even though they are not internally consistent.

[116] This simplifying assumption is historically false, and we shall not be able to adhere to it throughout. But the alternative to using it as long as possible is to destroy all proportion in what is not, after all, a book on Kant but a general history of German philosophy. Therefore I here attempt to present the "critical philosophy" as a coherent unity in the history of thought. I permit myself to do so with the encouragement of reviewers of my books on Kant who have more frequently complained of too much detail rather than of too little.

First Statement of the Problem of the *Critique of Pure Reason*

Human reason has this peculiar fate, that in one species of its knowledge it is burdened with questions which, as prescribed by the very nature of reason itself, it is not able to ignore, but which, as transcending all its powers, it is also not able to answer.

In this, the first sentence of the first *Critique*, Kant describes the state of metaphysics, once the Queen of the Sciences but now mourning like Hecuba. Where our intellect has dealt with nothing but itself and its own forms of thought, it has produced the science of logic. Where it has applied concepts of pure intuitions of space and time, it has produced the science of mathematics. Where it has applied concepts to sensible experience, it has produced the sciences of nature. In the guidance of conduct in accord with a rational law and ideal, it has produced morality or at least our knowledge of good and evil. But metaphysics differs from all of these. Unlike logic, it is supposed to deal with objects, not with mere thoughts; unlike the others, it "professes to be a completely isolated science of reason which soars far above the teachings of experience." Yet the quarrels of the schools show that in spite of pretensions, there never has been a science of metaphysics, that is, a rigorously demonstrable, systematically exhaustive, knowledge of supersensible reality.[117]

The problem of the *Critique of Pure Reason* is to determine whether or not there can be a science of metaphysics, and if so to establish at least its foundations. Reason has produced rigorously demonstrable knowledge elsewhere. But all our knowledge is truncated unless for every *therefore* it can produce a *wherefore* by giving a systematically complete answer to the last questions raised in each of the other disciplines. Metaphysics since Wolff is the science of God, the soul, the world as a whole, and things in general. Failure to establish it as a science leaves momentous issues at the mercy of skeptics; and though the ordinary man cannot be expected to be interested in the disputes of the schools, he cannot be indifferent to the outcome of philosophers' work when these interests of humanity are at stake. He will have a metaphysics, whether or not it can be scientific. If not by science, he will orient himself by "common sound reason" or take off on flights of genius:

Human reason, without being moved merely by the idle desire for extent and variety of knowledge, proceeds impetuously, driven by an inward need, to questions such as cannot be answered by any empirical employment of reason . . .
It is idle to feign indifference to such inquiries, the object of which can never be indifferent to our human nature.[118]

Here in the opening of his critical campaign, Kant has three sets of opponents: the philosophers of the schools (principally the Wolffians) who pretend already to have a system of metaphysics which answers all

---

[117] Quotations and allusions in this paragraph are to the *Critique of Pure Reason*, Preface B, ix–xv.
[118] *Ibid.*, B 21, A x.

questions; the popular philosophers who shrug off metaphysical questions as beyond the competence and legitimate concern of reason; and the Counter-Enlighteners who wish to solve them by feeling and faith. Most of the rest of the *Critique* is aimed at the first group, whom Kant respects if only for their spirit of intellectual discipline (*Gründlichkeit*).[119]

A More Precise Statement of the Problem

In the *Critique of Pure Reason* Kant at last carefully distinguishes analytic from synthetic judgments. An analytic judgment is one whose predicate is thought of as identical with all or part of the concept of the subject; it is therefore testable by the law of contradiction, inasmuch as its contradictory is self-contradictory. All other judgments are synthetic. Also, he is in possession of a new concept of a priori and a posteriori. A priori knowledge is knowledge not derived from experience and not testable by experience; it is universal and necessary, as no experiential knowledge can be. All other knowledge is a posteriori. He goes back to the Inaugural Dissertation for three other distinctions—between sensible and intellectual knowledge, between intuitive and discursive concepts, and between form and content (matter).

Any other philosopher of the eighteenth century, armed with these distinctions, would either have himself anticipated the *Critique of Pure Reason* even better than Crusius and Lambert did; or everything would have remained the same, with the following equations accepted without question:

formal knowledge = *a priori* = distinct = conceptual = knowledge resulting from the analysis and rational organization of experience = "science"
material knowledge = synthetic = *a posteriori* = confused = perceptual = knowledge of experience not yet analyzed and syllogized = "historical knowledge"

But Kant sees that the various distinctions do not overlap, and that the articulation of knowledge is much more complicated than these dichotomies represent it to be. Table 3 shows the complexities he found.

The question of the *Critique of Pure Reason* is: How are synthetic judgments possible a priori? Had he used Kant's language and consistently stuck by his commitments, Leibniz would have said there are no synthetic judgments; Crusius, with the same qualifications, would have said they are possible simply because the human mind must as a matter of fact think them. Kant's answer is close to that of Crusius, yet differs from it in ways still to be seen.

The question can be made still more articulate. Reading down the third column of Table 3, we can distinguish three sub-questions: How is mathematics possible? How are the sciences of nature possible? How is metaphysics possible? "All metaphysicians are therefore solemnly and legally suspended from their occupations until they shall have adequately answered the question, 'How are synthetic cognitions a priori possible?' "[120]

[119] *Ibid.*, B xxxvi.   [120] *Prolegomena* § 5 (p. 25).

Table 3. Kant's division of the kinds of knowledge[a]

Kinds of Knowledge	Analytic judgments		Synthetic judgments	
	Known *a priori*	Known *a posteriori*	Known *a priori*	Known *a posteriori*
Mixed knowledge containing some concepts derived from intuition, either pure or empirical	implicit tautologies	none	Mathematical axioms (concepts from pure intuition) and fundamental principles of science, applying to perceptions (A)	Empirical judgments of matters of fact (B)
Pure knowledge containing no concepts drawn from intuition, either pure or empirical	logical truths, identical judgments	none	Metaphysical judgments about the supersensible, specifically about the world as a whole and its ultimate parts, God, souls and things in general. (C)	none

[a] Note that (A) is a condition of (B) and that (C) is impossible.

The Copernican Revolution

Since human reason (in a broad sense) has accomplished its purposes in mathematics and science and failed in metaphysics, perhaps the former contain a clue to the failure, or point to a way of success, in the latter.

The true method of the mathematician had been misunderstood by Wolff. It is not to manipulate arbitrary pure concepts, but to construct concepts in intuition. The mathematician does not "inspect what he discerns either in the figure or the mere concept of it, and from this, as it were, read off its properties; but brings out what was necessarily implied in the concepts that he has himself formed a priori and has put into the figures in the construction by which he presents it to himself."[121] This procedure was described in the Prize Essay. The Inaugural Dissertation rendered it intelligible by arguing that the figures constructed were in space and time, which were not forms of reality (which we could not know a priori) but merely forms of appearances.

The true method of the natural sciences is not to collect random observations and make a posteriori generalizations from them, but, armed with principles, questions, and experiments, to approach nature "not as a pupil who listens to whatever the teacher says but as a judge who compels the witness to answer questions he has himself formulated."[122] The objects which are known by science, therefore, are conformed methodologically (Kant is not ready to say ontologically) to the requirements of the knowing mind.

But in metaphysics

it has hitherto been assumed that all our knowledge must conform to objects. But all attempts to extend our knowledge of objects by establishing something in regard to them a priori by means of concepts have, on this assumption, ended in failure. We must therefore make trial whether we may not have more success in the tasks of metaphysics if we suppose that objects must conform to our knowledge . . . We should then be proceeding precisely along the lines of Copernicus' principal thought.[123]

Initiating this procedure is the so-called "Copernican Revolution" (though Kant did not call it that). At first glance, it may appear that Kant is a counter-Copernican, a new Ptolemy in philosophy, since he seems to have put the knower in the center of the world. But properly interpreted, Kant's allusion to Copernicus is very apt. Copernicus hypothesized that the complex observed planetary motions were not real motions, but only apparent motions dependent upon the real motion of the observer. Knowing the real motion of the observer, the astronomer was enabled to foretell (in a moderately a priori manner, as it were,)[124] future apparent motions.

The Copernican Revolution occurred in mathematics in 1770. *The Critique of Pure Reason extends the Copernican Revolution into the empirical sciences of nature and into metaphysics itself.* The outcomes of the

---

121 *Critique of Pure Reason*, B xii.
122 *Ibid.*

123 *Ibid.*, B xvi.
124 See *ibid.*, B 3.

second and third stages of the Copernican Revolution are quite different. The second stage will establish a metaphysics of experience as a science. The third stage—well, that is a quite different story.

The Idea of a Metaphysics of Experience

"Metaphysics of experience" sounds like an oxymoron. Metaphysics is defined as a priori knowledge from pure concepts. Since metaphysics is not knowledge arising from experience, it was believed that it was knowledge not restricted to experience. Indeed, it might not even apply to experience, but to be knowledge only of a transcendent realm of reality we cannot experience. In 1770 Kant took the origin of metaphysical knowledge as determining its scope; a priori conceptual knowledge was knowledge of the intelligible world, not the world of sense experience. But he soon saw that this was incorrect; origin does not necessarily determine use. Metaphysics might be knowledge not arising from, yet still restricted to, experience. To this view he was brought when he saw that he had to give up the thesis of § 29 of the Inaugural Dissertation. He saw that he could not bring his a priori concepts, principles, and forms to bear upon objects without intuition:

In whatever manner and by whatever means cognition may relate to objects, intuition is that through which it is in immediate relation to them, and to which all thought as a means is directed . . . All thought must, directly or indirectly . . . be related to intuitions.[125]

Thoughts without content are empty, intuitions without concepts are blind.[126]

Hence there arise two conceptions of what metaphysics is. If metaphysics means "knowledge by means of pure reason," it turns out that such knowledge can only be a knowledge of phenomena, which are objects of intuition. If we have a priori knowledge of phenomena, this can be called a "metaphysics of experience." Knowledge of noumena (knowledge of objects proper to pure reason itself) would constitute a different kind of metaphysics, the traditional metaphysics of God, the world as a whole, the soul, and things in general.

Kant does not doubt that we have a priori knowledge of the phenomenal. The very formulation of his question, "*How* are synthetic judgments a priori possible?",[127] shows that. He has given many reasons for doubting whether we have a priori knowledge of the noumenal. He does not wish to decide, out of hand, whether we do or do not, can or cannot; but that we have a priori knowledge of the phenomenal is his Archimedean standpoint.[128] If he can find *how* we do have this kind of knowledge, then he can ask: Are (and not just how are) synthetic judgments a priori possible about the things of pure reason (noumena)? In other words, does metaphysics

---

125 *Ibid.*, A 19 = B 35.   126 *Ibid.*, A 51 = B 75.

127 *Prolegomena*, § 5; *Critique of Pure Reason*, B 19.

128 If the *Critique of Pure Reason* is interpreted as Kant's "answer to Hume," this of course begs the entire question. In my opinion, the *Critique* contains an answer to Hume, but that is by no means its main thrust. It is more obviously the purpose of the *Prolegomena,* which does indeed beg Hume's question. The entire problem of Kant's

in its classical, transcendent, sense, meet the conditions discovered for a priori knowledge in metaphysics in the new, immanent, sense?

A schematic representation of the problem will throw light on this question. In an analytical judgment, the predicate is "contained in" the concept of the subject:

$$\boxed{\;\text{S}\quad\text{is}\quad\boxed{\text{P}}\;}$$

In a synthetic judgment, it is not:

$$\boxed{\text{S}}\quad\text{is}\quad\boxed{\text{P}}$$

A judgment is a relation between S and P which is not merely an association of their ideas, but is an assertion that the connection between them holds in the object denoted by S. There must be some "third thing," which Kant calls X, to which S and P, in a synthetic judgment, are related and through which they are related to each other:

$$\boxed{\text{X}}$$
$$\boxed{\text{S}}\quad\text{is}\quad\boxed{\text{P}}$$

But what is the X? It may be any one of the following:

(1) In mathematics, it is a pure intuition or construction in space and time. Since the intuition is a priori, the connection between S and P is a priori as well as synthetic. But since space and time are mere forms of appearance, the a priori synthetic judgments of mathematics apply only to phenomena.

(2) If the S and P are empirical concepts and the X is an empirical observation of, say, a table, then by looking at the table I can say, "The table is brown," for both tableness and brownness are seen in this empirical intuition or perception. But the judgment thus formed is a posteriori, and likewise has only phenomenal meaning.

(3) If there is an X which will support a synthetic judgment having empirical content (unlike 1) and yet a priori (unlike 2), then the system of concepts and synthetic judgments known a priori on its basis will constitute a metaphysics of experience.

(4) If there is an X which will support a synthetic judgment not having intuitive (sensible) content (unlike 3) and yet a priori, then the system of concepts and synthetic judgments known a priori on its basis will constitute a metaphysics which transcends the limits of experience.

Kant will argue: there is an X which meets condition (3) and hence a metaphysics of experience is *possible*. It is, moreover, *necessary* if Humean

_____

"answer to Hume" has been snarled in controversy for a hundred years and turns in part upon the complicated relationships between the first and second editions of the *Critique* and the *Prolegomena*. My own views, too complex for presentation here, will be found in "Once More Unto the Breach," *Ratio*, 9:33–37 (1967), and in later issues in which I reply to several critics of my paper.

skepticism of matter-of-fact knowledge is to be refuted, since Hume thought that the Kantian objectively valid principles were only subjective products of habit. But Kant will also argue, as we shall see later, that there is no X which meets condition (4), and therefore the only metaphysics which can contain any knowledge is a metaphysics of experience.

The Metaphysics of Experience

In a pair of sentences Kant could almost have quoted from Leibniz' *New Essays*, he says:

There can be no doubt that all our knowledge begins with experience . . . But though all our knowledge begins with experience, it does not follow that it all arises out of experience. For it may well be that even our empirical knowledge is made up of what we receive through impressions and of what our own faculty of knowledge . . . supplies from itself.[129]

Here is the by now familiar distinction between content and form, of which Kant had made successful use in the Inaugural Dissertation. Wherever we find a priori knowledge, it indicates the existence of a form which any content of knowledge must fit.

In the Transcendental Aesthetic Kant repeats with few changes the teachings of the Dissertation. Space and time are forms of intuition. Hence we can know them a priori and know a priori that all our outer experience will be spatial and all experience whatsoever will be temporal. But they apply only to experience, not to things as they are in themselves. Space and time are empirically real (they really pertain to the things we experience, and are not mere subjective forms or illusions) but they are transcendentally ideal (i.e., not ontologically primitive, but mind-dependent). Newton and Leibniz were, in spite of their differences, transcendental realists in their theory of space; and their transcendental realism led to empirical idealism (Berkeley and Wolff) and hence to "illusionism." Kant's own theory is meant to be an alternative to both metaphysical realism and subjective idealism, against Newton, Clarke, Leibniz, Wolff, and Berkeley.[130] The Transcendental Analytic, the first part of the Tran-

---

129 *Critique of Pure Reason* B 1.

130 That Kant's own theory was not markedly different from Berkeley's, and that Kant with less than perfect ingenuousness exaggerated the differences and out of a certain animus against Berkeley criticized a theory that he accepted with few modifications, has been argued by Colin M. Turbayne in "Kant's Refutation of Dogmatic Idealism," *Philosophical Quarterly*, 5:225–244 (1955) (reprinted in my *Kant Studies Today* (La Salle, Ill.: Open Court, 1969). Kant's knowledge of Berkeley may have come from a translation of the *Three Dialogues* by Johann Christian Eschenbach, professor of philosophy in Rostock and teacher of Tetens (Rostock, 1756), or from an anonymous translation of the same work (Leipzig, 1781). Some of Kant's stranger judgments about Berkeley—e.g., that he was an "Eleatic"—are found also in Hamann's *Metacritic of the Purism of Reason*. Since the *Metacritic* was not published until 1800, Kant did not read it; and unless there is a common source which both Hamann and Kant knew, I can only suggest that this peculiar notion may have come to Kant through conversations with Hamann, who fancied himself an expert on all things British. The translation of 1781 contained "Nachrichten" about Berkeley's life and thought, and it may be that this is the source; but I have not seen the edition.

scendental Logic of the *Critique,* has the task of discovering the a priori forms of thought and knowledge of objects. The catalogue of forms of thought in general is given by general logic, which is indifferent to the distinction between mere thought and knowledge. But from general logic Kant gets a clue to the a priori forms of thought of objects, which constitute his transcendental logic. The clue is the table of judgments (properly modified, to be sure) in the general logics of his day.

A judgment is a synthesis of concepts according to a rule. For instance, if I should have, as it were floating around in my consciousness, the categorematic concepts "black" and "pipe," the rules of judgment limit the possible ways I could combine them into a unitary judgment: "the pipe is not black," "the pipe must be black," "the pipe may be black," "if the pipe is black. . . ," "the pipe is black or . . ." and so on, but not "the is pipe black." Now each of these rules corresponds to a concept of a kind or form of synthetic unity in which categorematic concepts are content. To each rule there corresponds a *pure concept of the understanding*—pure because syncategorematic concepts such as "all," "some," "not," if, . . . then," "either . . . or," "is," "may be," and "must be" are not derived a posteriori from experience. They are concepts supplied by the understanding itself, the faculty of synthesizing categorematic concepts into judgments. Since the table of judgments is (Kant believed) complete, this argument (which is now called "the metaphysical deduction of the categories") supplies us with a set of categories, systematically organized and known to be complete. Categories are concepts we apply to *any* object we judge, i.e., think of, whether we know these objects or not.[131]

Transcendental logic is thereby given a complete table of all possible pure concepts of the understanding.[132] There are four groups of categories, corresponding to the four ways in which the general logic of Kant's time classified judgments. They are the categories of quantity, quality, modality, and relation. Under each there are three specific categories. For example, under the categories of relation, there are these: of inherence and subsistence (*substantia et accidens*), of causality and dependence, and of community (reciprocity or *commercium*). These correspond, respectively, to categorical judgments (subject and predicate), hypothetical judgments (antecedent and consequent), and disjunctive judgments (either . . . or . . .). Since any judgment we make is in one of these three classes, any judgment we make about an object involves the thought of substance, cause, or mutual dependence of two things.

To have a complete set of all the pure concepts of the understanding is not the same as to show how these concepts are a priori concepts of objects, as Kant seems to have thought in 1772. They certainly are not empirical concepts. But they might not function in knowledge of objects at all. To show that they do, and that they necessarily do, is the task of the Tran-

---

131 In 1772 Kant thought he could deduce all categories from a few principles; now he deduces them from only one, that is, from the form of judging. (Kant is not always consistent as to whether the categories apply to supersensible objects we can think but cannot know; but the sentence in the text expresses, in my opinion, his most tenable view.)

132 *Critique of Pure Reason* A 80 = B 106.

scendental Deduction of the Categories. This is the most difficult of all parts of the *Critique*, and it is this Deduction which Kant says is "the most difficult task which ever could be undertaken in the service of metaphysics."[133] The reader of Kant may agree with one of the most eminent of commentators, H. J. Paton, who compares understanding the Deduction to crossing the Great Arabian Desert. In detail it is obscure and infinitely complicated, but in its underlying conception, it is of a beautiful simplicity. I shall consider here only one underlying conception.[134]

All experience in the sense of empirical knowledge (not a blooming, buzzing confusion of sense data) consists of representations of two kinds: (i) intuitions, by which an object is present to us as an appearance, and (ii) concepts, by which the object of the intuition is thought. A representation is not an intuition unless it is seen, or rather thought, as representing an object immediately; otherwise it is just a sensation or image, for no representations come to us labeled "intuition." Intuition is a role some representations play.[135] That a representation is an intuition of an object depends upon our thinking of an object and (correctly) thinking that this representation does represent it.

Categories are concepts of objects in general, and therefore thoughts of (forms of) what any object must be in order to be an object of thought and, per corollary, an object of a determinate, definite intuition. In the terminology of pp. 475–476, categories are concepts of the X by virtue of which X is the object referred to by S and qualified by P. The concept underlying the rule for the synthesis of S with P is the concept of the object X. An object is the X, the concept of which is a rule for the synthesis of representations, for choosing those that will serve as evidence that the object X exists.[136]

Reculer pour mieux sauter! I hear purring and feel something warm and furry; I see something white before me on which there are black marks; hear a clock strike, feel hungry, think of Königsberg, taste brandy, smell tobacco . . . and so on to Joycean lengths. But I attend to and associate the first three, neglect the others, and say, "There is a cat." A cat is not a sensation. Nor is the cat a concept; cats have fur, and concepts do not. Since all that is in my mind is sensations and concepts, how do I talk about cats, which are objects? The cat is that X (see p. 475) the concept of which provides a rule in accordance with which hearing the purr is constituted an empirical intuition of the cat. The cat must conform to the concept of cat; otherwise

---

[133] *Prolegomena*, Introduction, p. 8.

[134] I beg the indulgence of Kant scholars for the simplifications I must make. I have left out many important topics, but I hope that I have given a fair and understandable account of A 92–4 = B 125–27; A 110–114; B § 19. Some of the simplifications here introduced are suggested by Kant's distinction between judgments of perception and judgments of experience in *Prolegomena* § 18 which is not, as I am of course aware, entirely consistent with the deepest teachings of the Transcendental Deduction.

[135] *Note to Kant scholars:* I am perfectly aware of the fact that Kant does not *say* this, but rather talks to the contrary. But unless he *meant* this, I am convinced he could never move beyond the question of § 13.

[136] "An *object* is that in the concept of which the manifold of a given intuition is united" (*Critique of Pure Reason*, B 137).

I would have no way of finding evidence of her existence. The concept of cat is, of course, a posteriori, and cats may break my a posteriori rules of what a cat is; cats are full of surprises. Still, the concept of cat functions in the synthesis of some of my representations into judgments about her.

Now we remember that Kant has professed to show that there are pure concepts—a priori and not a posteriori concepts. By virtue of being concepts underlying rules for the synthesis of representations, some of which will be counted as intuitions of objects, they are also concepts of the objects of *any* judgments, hence of any knowledge. Any object whatsoever, if it is to be known by experience, must stand under the rule of that synthesis of representations which constitute what we call experience and not mere object-less dreaming.

The possibility of experience is . . . what gives objective reality to all our a priori cognitions. Experience, however, rests on the synthetic unity of appearances, that is, on a synthesis according to concepts of an object of appearances in general. Apart from such synthesis it would not be knowledge, but a rhapsody of perceptions which would not fit into any context according to rules of a completely interconnected possible consciousness . . . Experience, therefore, depends upon a priori principles of its form, that is, upon universal rules of unity in the synthesis of appearances.[137]

These rules being pure concepts of the understanding, we then know that every object of experience, whatever its a posteriori appearance, must conform to these categories.

Thus the Copernican Revolution has gone into its second stage. The categories apply to objects a priori only because they are the conditions under which alone objects for our intuitions can be thought. Remove the condition of intuition, and the categories remain rules for judging but are not sufficient for knowing. Since objects of intuition are not things in themselves but only appearances of them to our senses, the knowledge which the categories enable us to have of *objects in general* is valid only for *objects of the senses in general*. These are phenomena, not noumena.

Ontology was that part of metaphysics which dealt with concepts of objects in general (*alle Dinge überhaupt* in the title of Wolff's German metaphysics treatise). But now, Kant says, we must give up the "proud name of ontology" and content ourselves with the more modest "analytic of pure understanding."[138]

The second part of the Transcendental Analytic shows how we can and must combine the pure a priori concepts into synthetic judgments known to be true a priori. (Again, Kant's arguments are of fearsome difficulty; but again the pattern is fairly simple, and we shall consider only that.)

All our representations, even those of external objects, are given to us under the form of inner sense, which is time. We do not perceive time itself, but only temporal relations among our representations. Concepts can be objectively combined only be reference to some third thing, X; other-

[137] *Critique of Pure Reason*, A 157 = B 195–96.
[138] *Ibid.*, A 247 = B 303.

wise, they would be related only analytically or else accidentally, by the association of ideas. The reference of the categories to the various a priori possible temporal relations provides an interpretation—or in Kant's language, a schema—for each concept. That of causality, for instance, is "the succession of representations, insofar as that succession is subject to a rule."[139] Without a schema of causation, we judge only that one thing depends upon another, but we do not know how to "cash in" this judgment and apply "cause" to one phenomenon and "effect" to another. Without a schema, a category is only an empty form of thought. Through the schema, it is given an experiential determination so that we know how to find instances *in* experience for a pure concept which was not drawn *from* experience.

Kant is the inventor of the empirical criterion of meaning, according to which a concept has cognitive meaning only if there is an empirical test for its applicability. However much later philosophers, such as the logical positivists, condemn Kant for his belief that there are synthetic judgments known a priori, they should acknowledge that he anticipated them in asserting that no concept has cognitive meaning unless there are experiential criteria for its application. Hume had thought concepts must *come from* experience; he was a genetic, a retrospective, empiricist. Kant taught that concepts must apply to experience; he was an anticipatory empiricist. The schema is the structure of sensory experience which tells us which concept to apply and which to withhold.

Given these schemata, which involve a patterned intuition in time, we have a pure (nonempirical) X by reference to which pure concepts can be combined a priori into synthetic judgments. These synthetic judgments known a priori are the principles of a metaphysics of experience which Kant has been seeking.

The most important ones are called Analogies of Experience, the first two of which are (i) the Principle of Permanence of Substance—"In all changes of appearances, substance is permanent, and its quantum in nature is neither increased nor diminished";[140] and (ii) the Principle of Succession in Time in Accordance with the Law of Causality—"All changes in the determinations (states) of substance take place in conformity with the law of the connection of cause and effect."[141]

The "convenience rules" of the Inaugural Dissertation (see p. 462) have thus become synthetic judgments known a priori to be valid as the most generals laws of possible experience. They are, for this reason, the most general laws of nature—nature being merely "phenomena under law." Accordingly, "The understanding does not derive its a priori laws from, but prescribes them to, nature."[142]

The positive consequences of the Copernican Revolution are now before us. The (a) forms of space and time, (b) categories as pure concepts of the understanding, and (c) synthetic principles known a priori, all have objective validity for phenomena. We have seen that (b) and (c) apply neces-

---

[139] *Ibid.*, A 144 = B 183.
[140] *Ibid.*, B 224.

[141] *Ibid.*, B 232.
[142] *Prolegomena*, § 36.

sarily to objects insofar as these objects are intuited under (a). Without (a), (b) would be merely forms of thought, and (c) could not be known at all.

Classical metaphysics had little stake in (a), but it had, at the cost of its life, to preserve (b) and (c). From Aristotle to Lambert it had merely collected examples of (b) at random; and with respect to (c), it had either misinterpreted them as analytic (Wolff) or as mere subjective necessities of thought (Crusius and Tetens). For Kant, (a), (b), and (c) stand or fall together; hence the only possible metaphysics which can be established theoretically as a science is a metaphysics of experience, of phenomena under (a).

The Destruction of Speculative Metaphysics

Metaphysicians from Plato to Wolff, with few exceptions, had seen reason to be at its best when farthest removed from the confusions and subjectivity of the senses. Seeing how much reason could accomplish even when restricted by the senses, and confusing pure intuition with rational concept, they tried to extend knowledge by pure reason into realms untouched by sense.

The light dove, cleaving the air in her free flight, and feeling its resistance, might imagine that her flight would be still easier in empty space. It was thus that Plato left the world of the senses, as setting too narrow limits to the understanding, and ventured out beyond it on the wings of the ideas, into the empty space of the pure understanding.[148]

To examine the conditions of this flight, and to clip the wings of the light dove, is the sad task of the second part of the Transcendental Logic. Since dialectic was the art of specious reasoning, Kant calls his inquiry, which is to expose the illusions of pure reason, Transcendental Dialectic.

Having destroyed the classical ontology (*metaphysica generalis*) and replaced it with the more modest analytic of understanding (see note 136), Kant now turns to the second part of metaphysics, the *metaphysica specialis* of the seventeenth-century scholastics and Wolff. *Metaphysica specialis* was divided by Wolff into rational psychology, rational cosmology, and rational theology. These disciplines had the task of demonstrating the spirituality and immortality of the soul, the contingency of the world and the general features of its composition, and the existence of God. No one of these metaphysical concepts is a category, for they are not forms of thought in general and cannot be schematized (exhibited in intuition). Hence Kant chooses the Platonic name for them and calls them "ideas" or, as putative objects of pure reason, "noumena."

One might have expected Kant to think that he had destroyed all special metaphysics by his Analytic. But to have done so would have been to beg

---

[148] *Critique of Pure Reason*, A 5 = B 8–9. In *Dreams of a Spirit Seer* Kant spoke of "the butterfly wings of metaphysics." This and other metaphors in Kant have been studied by David Tarbet in a richly unusual essay, "The Fabric of Metaphor in the *Critique of Pure Reason*," *Journal of the History of Philosophy* 6:257–270 (1968).

the question. For if someone had been able to show a plausible claim that he did indeed possess rational knowledge of, say, the immortality of the soul, then the argument of the Analytic would thereby be threatened; and if such knowledge could be established, the Analytic would be destroyed. Therefore Kant had to refute the theses of the metaphysicians one by one and not by showing simply that they did not meet the conditions he had established in the Analytic.

Against rational psychology, Kant shows that there is a simple logical paralogism in arguments (like that of Mendelssohn)[144] for the immortality of the soul. The paralogism is that rational psychology uses a syllogism with four terms. The concept of substance in one premise is schematized and in the other premise is unschematized. Hence the permanence of substance in its schematized sense (immortality of the soul) cannot be attributed to substance in its unschematized sense (the soul as a supersensible being).[145]

Against rational cosmology, Kant shows that its arguments fall into antinomies. An antinomy is a pair of statements, each demonstrable but each contradictory of the other and each needed to satisfy a legitimate interest in giving explanations. Each can be demonstrated by showing that its opposite is absurd; but the opposite can be proved in exactly the same manner. Kant shows that it can be proved that the world in space and time are infinite and infinitely divisible, and that it is limited and only finitely divisible; that all changes are under the causality of nature, and that some changes have free causes; and that there is in the world a necessary being, and that there is no necessary being in the world.

The resolution of the first two antinomies argues that things in space and time are nothing in themselves; therefore they are, in themselves, neither finite nor infinite. Both the thesis and the antithesis are false; they are like the opposed propositions "a square circle is a square" and "a square circle is a circle."

The other two antinomies are handled in a slightly different way. The Third Antimony concerns freedom and determinism. Kant thinks he has already proved (Second Analogy) that causal laws are valid in nature, and that there are no events without causes. Hence one of the propositions is true. One the other side, he restates some of the classical metaphysical arguments designed to show that the series of causes of things in the world is not infinite, and hence the world is the product of the free causality of God; by showing that the concept of free cause is not self-contradictory, they strengthen the case for the belief that man's will is free.

Kant resolves this antinomy by showing that the Second Analogy is valid within experience but not known to be valid for noumenal objects, while the opposing thesis is that free causes act beyond experience without interfering with the course of nature. Restricting the scope of each removes the contradiction.

Kant is not yet ready to assert that we have any good reason for saying that there are free causes, of which man's will is one. He is content for the

144 *Critique of Pure Reason*, B 413ff.   145 *Ibid.*, A 402, B 409.

moment only to argue that if there is a good reason for doing so, the law of causality established for experience by the Second Analogy will not stand in its way. Man is determined in the order of nature, but it is not impossible that he is free in the order of noumena.

Finally, rational theology can be refuted by showing that all theoretical arguments for the existence of God (the argument from causation and the argument from design) depend upon the ontological argument, and that the ontological argument depends upon a transcendent (nonphenomenal) application of the category of necessity. It confuses logical necessity (claiming that "God exists" is analytical) with the necessity of existence, which is always synthetical and refers to the relation of things to each other and to the schematized categories of existence and necessity. "God exists" is a synthetic judgment; and the category of existence gives knowledge only when schematized and thus limited to phenomena.

Kant has done nothing to show that the soul is not mortal, the will is not free, and God does not exist. He has, indeed, shown that these ideas can be thought without contradition and argued that they can be "deduced" from the forms of syllogisms in much the way the categories were deduced from the forms of judgment.[146] They are ideas which the human mind cannot avoid thinking when it tries to complete its inquiries in the phenomenal world by extending its thought into the noumenal world. But proofs for them are fallacious, and the ideas will not support any theoretical synthetic judgments. There is no X which will connect any of them with the synthetic predicates or determinations assigned to them. Metaphysical judgments are, at best, analytic judgments masquerading as synthetic judgments or, at worst, unfounded empirical judgments.

The resemblance between Kant's program and the program of the school of logical positivism are unmistakable. A history of logical positivism should bring its Kantian provenance to light. The mediating role of the Marburg school of neo-Kantians should be given special attention. The points of resemblance are: no categorematic concept or synthetic judgment is legitimate if it cannot be exhibited, directly or indirectly, in experience; and any judgment which cannot be verified in experience can be exposed as a misclassified analytic judgment or as an erroneous empirical judgment. While the differences are as obvious as the similarities, they have been so magnified by objections to Kant's terminology of "synthetic judgments known a priori" and to his insistence upon a legitimate nontheoretical metaphysics that the resemblances have been ignored and possible historical influences little suspected.[147]

What We Can Learn from the Failure of Metaphysics?

Men are driven, Kant tells us, to extend reason as far as possible. We are pushed by the nature of our reason, to search for the simplest parts, the

---

[146] *Ibid.*, A 323 = B 379.

[147] But see Bella K. Milmed, *Kant and Current Philosophical Issues* (New York: New York University Press, 1961).

most comprehensive wholes, the first moment of time, the last boundary of space, the cause of all causes, the necessary being which supports all contingent being. The theses of classical metaphysics were proferred as demonstrated, true judgments resulting from the persistent and successful pursuit of these most distant goals of reason. Each of them is an idea or an ideal of the unconditioned premise of what would otherwise be a sorites of infinite length, which could never satisfy reason's demand for completeness of knowledge. One was the idea of an absolutely simple substance, another that of an absolutely first cause, the third that of substance possessing a maximum of perfections including necessary existence. For every *therefore* in any line of syllogisms, reason demands a *wherefore*, until it succeeds in attaining to the highest ultimate principle which terminates the otherwise endless quest of reason.

The Transcendental Dialectic shows that the pretended success is a self-delusion of reason.

But Kant was in love with metaphysics, and he never was really faithless to her; we "return to metaphysics as to a beloved one with whom we have had a quarrel."[148] So deep-rooted in man is this metaphysical urge—rooted not just in human nature, but in the very structure of his reason itself—that it is as little to be expected, Kant tells us, that men will give us metaphysics as that they will cease to breathe in order to escape the dangers of getting infections. Kant could not believe that a faculty like pure reason could have been made a part of man's endowment if it had had no proper function. "Presumably the ideas have their own good and appropriate vocation as determined by the natural disposition of our reason. The mob of sophists, however, raise against reason the usual cry of absurdities and contradictions . . . yet it is to the beneficent influences exercised by reason that they owe the possibility of their own self-assertiveness, and indeed that very culture which enables them to blame and condemn what reason requires of them."[149]

We must inquire: what is the legitimate function of reason and its use of ideas, since the most likely use (to extend knowledge into the supersensible) has been exposed as illusion? Kant has two answers to this question. The first completes his theoretical philosophy. The second introduces his practical philosophy.

The Theoretical Answer

The proper function for the ideas of reason is to serve as maxims for the conduct of inquiry. They give unity and direction to the pursuit of empirical knowledge, and they point to, but do not disclose, the supersensible

---

148 *Critique of Pure Reason*, A 878 = B 850.

149 *Ibid.*, A 669 = B 697. Though Kant did not become involved in the Mendelssohn–Jacobi controversy until he wrote *What is Orientation of Thinking?* in 1786, he has already in this and similar passages laid the foundations for his objections to popular philosophy and the philosophy of faith and feeling as guides in metaphysical matters, and he shows here and in that essay that he thinks bad metaphysics inclines toward bad morals.

foundations of the phenomenal realm. These maxims are like the rules of convenience of the Inaugural Dissertation. The ideas are regulative of our intellectual quest, not constitutive of its objects.

The search for continuity, simplicity (economy), homegeneity of species, gradation of species in every higher genera, plenitude of being, and purpose in nature and history is not guaranteed of success by reason, for we cannot establish the corresponding synthetic metaphysical judgments such as "Nature makes no leaps" and "There are no empty forms [in the hierarchy of nature]" (*natura non saltus fit* and *non datur vacuum formarum*). But the search for continuity, simplicity, and limited variety is guided by these same features and structures of reason which led metaphysicians to believe, erroneously, that they objectively knew the world to be so constituted that these goals could be achieved.

I have pointed out the resemblance between the comparatively superficial doctrine of rules of convenience in the Inaugural Dissertation and the better-founded doctrine of the first *Critique*; but the third *Critique* makes as great an advance over the first as the first did over the brief remarks of 1770.

In the *Critique of Judgment*, Kant assigns the regulative function to the faculty of reflective judgment instead of to reason. Reflective judgment does not start out with a definite concept which it applies to a given phenomenon, but it tries to produce concepts to fit empirical representations. For a priori judgment, these concepts are not empirical concepts reached by abstraction, but are structural and syncategorematic like the categories. But they are not categories, which necessarily apply in every objective experience of objects. They are concepts which have corresponding rules that we use in our endeavor, by no means guaranteed of success, to bridge the gap between the most general laws of nature known a priori and the specific observations of empirical science. They must be found by using a special a priori regulative principle.

For those concepts which have to be found for given empirical intuitions and which presuppose a special law of nature by which alone *particular* experience is made possible, judgment needs a special, equally transcendental principle for its reflection. This cannot be established in turn from previously known empirical laws so as to convert [reflective judgment] into simple comparison with the empirical forms for which one has concepts already. For the question is, how could one hope to arrive at empirical concepts embodying that which is common to a variety of natural forms by comparing perceptions if (as is quite conceivable) the immense variety of the empirical laws of nature had created so great a heterogeneity that all—or at any rate, almost all—comparison were useless for discovering a harmony and orderly ascending arrangement of genera and species?[150] All comparison of empirical representations, so as to perceive in natural things empirical laws and the corresponding specific forms, and yet through comparison of these with others to detect *generically harmonious* forms, presupposes that nature has observed in its empirical laws a certain

---

[150] Kant is here anticipating the modern principle of limited variety.

harmony, proportional to our judgment, and a similarity among forms that we can comprehend, and this presupposition must precede all comparison, being an a priori principle of judgment.[151]

This a priori principle of judgment is that of the teleological organization of nature: "Nature specifies its universal laws to empirical ones, according to the form of a logical system, for the purpose of judgment."[152] Note that this is an a priori principle of judgment, not an a priori truth about metaphysical reality. We cannot possibly know whether it is true or not.

But there seems to arise here an antinomy between a *regulative* idea and a constitutive principle, between what judgment (and reason) demand, and what understanding can deliver. Understanding, in its principle of causation, requires that all phenomena be explained by efficient and, indeed, mechanical causes. Judgment says: some must be explained by recourse to final causes. There will never be a Newton of a blade of grass.[153] Kant does not deny mechanism to make room for vitalism. Rather, he resolves this antinomy by reinterpreting the principle of causation, which in the *Critique of Pure Reason* was an a priori constitutive principle necessary for any knowledge of objective events, into a regulative maxim. The constitutive principle of the understanding that all things have sufficient mechanical causes, does conflict with the statement: some things are explicable only in terms of purposes. But the *maxim* of judging things mechanically is not incompatible with the maxim of judging them teleologically too, and Kant tries to show that the second guides us in the search for mechanical causes.

We human beings can and must follow both maxims, without having to commit ourselves to either one of the antinomic statements to the exclusion of the other.[154] This resolution of the antinomy leaves undecided "whether or not, in the unknown inner ground of nature, physico-mechanical and purposive combination may be united in the same things in one principle. We only say that our reason is not in a position so to unite them."[155]

But Kant does not leave us up in the air with two antithetic maxims. In § 77 of the *Critique of Judgment,* he argues that the human intellect must use the teleological principle as a supplement to the mechanical and not as its alternative, only because our intellect is not intuitive. If we were blessed with an intuitive intellect, whose thought would create its own object instead of having to wait upon sensuous intuition to give us a presentation of the object of thought, the teleological principle would be constitutive of experience. For purpose means only: the concept of a thing regarded as the ground of its being.[156] An intuitive intellect is not an impossible conception. We cannot say that such an intellect exists, but if it does not, it

---

[151] *First Introduction to the Critique of Judgment* (Hayden trans., n. 28) § V, pp. 17–18.

[152] *Ibid.,* p. 20.

[153] *Critique of Judgment* § 75.   [154] *Ibid.,* § 70.

[155] *Ibid.,* § 70, p. 235. All quotations are from, and page citations refer to, the translation by J. H. Bernard (see n. 28).

[156] *Ibid.,* Introduction, pt. IV, p. 17.

is not because it is logically impossible. Since it is thinkable (and many people like Hamann thought they possessed it), our own discursive intellect is not the only possible one. Therefore the limits under which we operate in our explanations of nature (viz., that mechanical causation is constitutive of our knowledge of the relations of things and events) are not known to be grounded in the actual nature of metaphysical reality. They are due only to the discursive "peculiarity" of the human understanding. Because of this peculiarity, we have to separate two concepts of causes—the mechanical and the teleological—as if they were metaphysically incompatible.

This is the highest point in Kant's theoretical philosophy. It is the final reconciliation of two views, apparently incompatible, which we found existing side by side in his *Weltanschauung*.

The Practical Answer

Kant says that the antinomies (and he could well have said the entire dialectic) are the "most fortunate perplexity" into which pure reason could ever fall.[157] Were it not that metaphysical judgments cannot be known to be true, and we asked which of the competing metaphysical judgments was the theoretically most acceptable, there could be no doubt of the answer. Thy would be the metaphysical judgments by which we project, into the supersensible, truths already established a priori for the sensible.[158] Such an extension Kant calls *dogmatism*. Dogmatism is the "presumption that it is possible to make progress with pure knowledge, according to principles, from [philosophical] concepts alone"; it is the demonstrative procedure of pure reason "without previous criticism of its own powers."[159] The dialectic fortunately stands in the way of dogmatism, and thus it "severs the root of materialism, fatalism, atheism, free thinking, fanaticism, and superstitution . . . as well as of idealism and skepticism."[160] In this respect, critique is negative.

On a cursory view of [the *Critique*] it may seem that its results are merely negative, warning us that we must never venture with speculative reason beyond the limits of experience. Such in fact is its primary use. But such teaching at once acquires a positive value when we recognize that the principles with which speculative reason ventures out beyond its proper limits do not in effect *extend* the employment of reason, but . . . principles [which it illicitly extends] properly belong [not to reason itself but] to sensibility, and when thus employed they threaten to make [us think] the bounds of sensibility [to be] coextensive with the real.[161]

---

[157] *Critique of Practical Reason* p. 111. (All page references are to the Beck translation in the New York edition of 1956; see n. 27). Kant meant this quite literally. In the *Lose Blätter zur Preisschrift über die Fortschritte der Metaphysik (Kants Ges. Schr., XX, 335)* he says that it was practical concerns which led him to the distinction between phenomena and noumena, and that the foundation of the critical philosophy lay in the concept of freedom which produced the antinomy. In *Welches sind die wirklichen Fortschritte die die Metaphysik seit Leibnizens und Wolffs Zeiten in Deutschland gemacht hat? (Kants Ges. Schr., XX, 311)* he says that the theory of the ideality of space and time and the reality of the concept of freedom were the "two angles" on which the *Critique* turned.

[158] *Critique of Pure Reason*, B xxix.   [160] *Ibid.*, B xxxv.
[159] *Ibid.*, B xxxv.   [161] *Ibid.*, B xxiv.

This is the same as to deny that reason has any function except the cognitive. If a dogmatism resulting from this apparent extension could be established, any other function of reason would be denied.

Kant asserts that reason does have another function: a practical function in morality. It needs to assent to some metaphysical judgments which not only cannot be established by theoretical reason as true, but are seemingly refuted by the dogmatic pretension of theoretical reason. Practical reason requires that we believe them even though they cannot be established theoretically. Practical reason would have no say in the matter, if theoretical reason held sway in our judgments about the supersensible reality. "Therefore," says Kant, "I found it necessary to deny knowledge in order to make room for belief."[162]

The failure of theoretical reason leaves an "empty place" into which rational belief may move.[163] There it postulates what it needs rationally to believe in order to support its moral concerns. There are three such postulates, each replacing a dogmatic assertion which theoretical reason could not support: the existence of God, the freedom of the will, and the immortality of the soul.[164] None of these is known to be true,[165] but the primacy of the practical over the theoretical reason justifies belief which can be neither established nor refuted theoretically, when that belief is judged to be rationally necessary as a foundation or a consequence of our moral concerns.

Superficially, Kant's account of belief resembles William James's theory of the will and right to believe when we face an inescapable choice between options neither of which can be theoretically established. On the other side, it seems to be just one more addition to the long list of scholastic philosophies, including that of Crusius, which have taught that when the powers of reason reach their limit, one must then be guided by faith.

In fact, however, Kant's theory is radically different from both. Unlike the scholastics, he is not contrasting faith with reason, but faith with knowledge. Reason is our guide even in these matters of faith where knowledge has reached its limit. Faith determined by putative revelations not ratified by reason is nothing but superstition. Unlike James, he does not base faith upon the demands of our passional nature but upon reason which is not limited to knowing. Faith determined by our passional nature is *Schwärmerei*, which Kant condemned in men like Jacobi.

The faith Kant is trying to establish is rational faith: rational, because it is not historical or doctrinal, but a priori; and faith, because it is not knowledge.

To support a "moral-practical metaphysics" based upon practical postulates or rational faith, Kant must first show that pure reason does have a practical as well as a theoretical function. This is the task of the major ethical writings of the eighties.

---

[162] *Ibid.*, B xxx.　　　　　　　　　　　　　[163] *Ibid.*, A 228–229 = 344–345.
[164] *Critique of Practical Reason*, pp. 126–128.

[165] Insofar as freedom is a postulate of practical reason, this statement is true. But Kant does not always maintain that it is a postulate and hence often says we know the will to be free because it is a *necessary* condition of the moral law, which we know to be valid. In this respect it differs from the other postulates.

The Rousseauistic Revolution

Kant's ethical views prior to the Copernican Revolution were not unusual for his time. He believed, with Leibniz, that freedom is self-determination in a deterministic world (soft determinism). He agreed with the Wolffians that the good is the attainment of a perfection, but with the critics of Wolff that the organ for the apprehension of the good is not reason but feeling. Shaftesbury, Hume, and Hutcheson made him aware of the necessity of understanding human nature as it is before prescribing for it. His background in Pietism and his native Stoicism produced both an active philanthropism and an inwardliness in his moral attitudes. But he rejected Pietism's basis for morality—moral law revealed by and grounded in the arbitrary will of God.

Rousseau had an immediate and profound impact on Kant. The publication of *Émile* in 1762 not only, according to legend, made him miss his afternoon walk, but it brought about a deep personal change:

> By inclination I am an inquirer. I feel a consuming thirst for knowledge, the unrest which goes with the desire to progress in it, and satisfaction at every advance in it. There was a time when I believed this constituted the honor of humanity, and I despised the people, who know nothing. Rousseau corrected me in this. This blinding prejudice disappeared. I learned to honor man.[166]

This change took place in 1762, twenty years or more before Kant showed the more important philosophical impact that Rousseau's *Social Contract*, published the same year as *Émile*, made upon him. It is as though a "recollection of Rousseau" had an effect on his moral philosophy comparable to that of the "recollection of Hume" on his theoretical philosophy. Or, even more portentously, Rousseau may have been to him in moral philosophy what Copernicus was in theoretical. Kant underwent a Rousseauistic Revolution as well as a Copernican.[167] In both, he took a principal idea of the other man and used it as the basis for an analogy which was fruitful in his own work. The analogon for theoretical philosophy was Copernicus' explanation of apparent planetary motions; for practical philosophy, it was Rousseau's conception of a self-governing commonwealth.

Rousseau had argued, on a political level, that obedience to a law imposed on a man is slavery. Disobedience to law, however, is anarchy. To avoid both, Rousseau formulated the idea of a commonwealth of self-governing citizens. The citizen in such a society qualifies as a legislator as well as a subject. He must distinguish between his private and unenlightened interests and his rational will, which is social and enlightened. The sum of the preponderant interests in a society constitutes the *volonté de tous*, while the system of rational wills constitutes the *volonté générale*. The individual participates in the general will by willing for himself what he

166 From the collection of unnumbered fragments concerning the *Observations on the Feeling of the Beautiful and the Sublime*, *Kants Ges. Schr.*, XX, 44. On Kant's relations to Rousseau, see especially Ernst Cassirer, *Rousseau, Kant, Goethe* (Princeton: Princeton University Press, 1947).

167 See L. W. Beck, *Studies in the Philosophy of Kant* (Indianapolis: Bobbs-Merrill, 1965), pp. 221–224.

wills for others, and conversely. The will of all has no moral authority unless it embodies the general will, but if it does so, then both freedom and social harmony can be attained. "Obedience to a law which one has prescribed to himself is freedom."[168] Rousseau never successfully worked out the politics of the two wills, and his work can be read as either totalitarian or democratic. Kant, in his political writings, is single-minded in his conviction that republicanism is the proper foundation for a just state, though in an unenlightened age he sees the advantages of a strong central government which requires obedience without argument but, having exacted obedience, permits the citizen to argue as much as he will.[169]

But the real importance for Kant of Rousseau's theory is not political, it is moral. Kant raises Rousseau's ambiguous political theory into the realm of moral philosophy, hoping as he goes from the difficult area of political casuistry into that of abstract moral philosophy to leave the ambiguities behind.

Practical philosophy concerns the will and its actions. The will is distinguished from impulse because it has two cognitive components: a concept of the end to be achieved, and a conception of the ways in which it can be achieved. The will, then, is nothing but practical reason or, less startlingly, reason applied to practice, disciplining and guiding desire.

If the concept of the end to be achieved is an empirical concept of an object of desire, the concept of the means by which it is to be attained is likewise an empirical concept of the relation between X, a means, and Y, the end. Then the rule a practical reason would follow is: If you desire Y, do X, for X is the cause of Y. All moral philosophy before his time, Kant says, was based upon some concept Y which was either empty or empirical: perfection (in Wolff) or the favor of God (in Crusius) or happiness (in Epicurus) and so on. For all such theories, Kant holds that (a) the law or imperative "Do X" can be abrogated by surrendering the pursuit of the goal Y: and (b) if the goal Y is one that cannot be surrendered (happiness) its concept is ambiguous, and any imperative "Do X" is based on a merely empirical generalization ("X generally produces Y") which leaves us uncertain of the effectiveness of X in producing Y.

The question is then: is this formula—"If you desire Y, do X"—confirmed by the analysis of ordinary moral consciousness as being the formula of moral constraint? Or is it merely a "product of the schools?" Kant denies that it is the formula for moral obligation. For the dictate of a moral law, "Do X," is *inexorable* (and hence [a] is wrong) and *certain* (and hence [b] is wrong).

The dictate of the moral law, "Do X," has some of the traits of a synthetic judgment known a priori: it is "universal and necessary," and hence cannot be derived from our empirical knowledge that one in fact desires Y and that in all probability X will lead to Y. Apriority here, as always, is a product of pure reason, not of experience. Hence Kant concludes that the phenomenon of inexorable and indisputable obligation requires that the

[168] *The Social Contract*, bk. I, chap. viii.
[169] *What is Enlightenment?*, in *Kant on History*, p. 5.

moral law which (under suitable conditions) commands me to do X must be a law legislated by reason, not drawn from experience (the way of the world) or revelation (the will of God).

This is the Rousseauistic Revolution in ethics. Morality is the autonomy, or self-government, of man who acknowledges no law except one he has made. Such a law can be based upon no contents of experience, which would limit its validity. Like *all* laws of reason, it is purely formal. It is a rule for choosing among the variety of maxims or policies which a man might follow. Its *application* to the particular case is through the empirical facts that one man desires this and another something else, and that (for example) aspirin cures headaches. But the form of the law is universal, prescribing a criterion by which *any* maxim, whatever its origin in our interests, can be evaluated as a rational policy of life. Kant thinks that the very concept of a categorical (apodictic, imprescriptible, inexorable) imperative tells us what it is; if "Do X" is a categorical imperative, Kant thinks that from its mere categoriality we can determine what "X" is. The form will generate the content of a supreme maxim which tells us what *other* maxims (material maxims, based upon interest and experience) may be or must be morally followed.

The supreme law, maxim, or imperative is: "So act that the maxim of your will could always hold at the same time as a principle establishing universal law."[170] It is incorrect to think that Kant believed what is obviously impossible, viz., that from this law by itself our specific duties could be derived without reference to our interests or the consequences of our actions. For this law has as its content other maxims which arise from our actual interests and intentions and purposes; it does not generate *them* out of mere abstract concepts, but it applies a rule by which we determine whether these other maxims can be morally followed. And when one follows one of these maxims, which he *might* follow out of inclination or interest, *because* it conforms to the supreme maxim, Kant says that one is acting out of respect for the supreme law and thereby shows that his will is good. Thus the categorical imperative is a test for other maxims, and can itself be a maxim which at one remove guides conduct by being held in reverence.

Any maxim we follow, however, is followed for the sake of some goal in view. While the maxims which are to be tested by the supreme maxim are maxims for the attainment of some end such as happiness, the supreme maxim itself must also have an end; and inasmuch as the supreme maxim is a priori (universal and morally necessary), it must be given by reason and not by sense or feeling. The categorical imperative, then, can be so stated as to tell us what goal we ought to pursue (and not, like other maxims, how to pursue a goal projected by our desires). This rational goal is humanity as rational nature: "Act so that you treat humanity, whether in your own person or in that of another, always as an end and never as a means only."[171] To treat humanity as an end in itself is a duty which has

[170] *Critique of Practical Reason,* § 7, p. 30.
[171] *Foundations of the Metaphysics of Morals,* trans. Beck (New York: Liberal Arts Press, 1959), p. 47.

two more specific ends in view: our own perfection, and the happiness of others.[172]

All of these, and still other formulas which Kant thinks are implicated in them, are according to him implicit in ordinary moral consciousness.[173] He finds them by making a critical regression upon the conditions of moral experience, and tries to find in them the ground of the inexorableness of duty, of the holiness of the good will, and of the imprescriptible rights of man. It is not the business of the moral philosopher to teach men these laws; and it certainly is not his job to establish moral laws by fiat. The common man is not in need of this kind of tutelage or governance; he knows very well what is right and what is wrong, and needs philosophy only in order to make this law explicit and to defend it from sophistic attack and from a "dialectic in his own mind"[174] by which he tries to convince himself, at the behest of his desires, that morality itself is only a "chimera of the brain."

"Soft determinism" might be an adequate basis for morality if the moral law were the hypothetical imperative, "If you wish Y, do X." My actions would be free if they were in fact determined by my desire for Y (and not forced upon me by someone else's wishes) and by a reasonable estimation of the relation of X to Y (and not produced by unreasoned impulse). But if the moral law is a principle known a priori and entailing no rewards or punishments as its condition, it requires the capacity to act according to a principle of pure reason without regard to the psychological conditioning which is compatible with soft determinism. Hence Kant concluded: the purity of the moral law is the *ratio cognoscendi* of the freedom of the will. The freedom of the will is the *ratio essendi* of the moral law.[175]

Theoretical reason could neither prove nor disprove the freedom of the will; practical reason, not being a cognitive faculty, cannot make it theoretically intelligible. But "if pure reason is actually practical, it will show its reality and that of its concepts [freedom] in actions, and all disputations which aim to prove its impossibility will be in vain."[176] Thus practical reason fills the empty place left by theoretical reason, and affirms the thesis of the Third Antinomy—there are free causes *in reality*—though leaving the antithesis—there are no free causes—true (at least as a valid regulative idea, if we follow the *Critique of Judgment*) of the phenomenal world.[177]

A will which follows this moral law and acts according to law out of respect for the law and not in hope of reward is a good will, and a good will is the only thing in the world (or even beyond it, Kant adds) which is good *without qualification*.[178] The good will is the metaphysical analogon to Rousseau's political general will.

---

[172] *Metaphysics of Morals*, Doctrine of Virtue, Introduction, II–V.

[173] Schiller, who is often remembered in connection with Kant's ethics only because of his satirical verses, said of this: "Concerning the ruling ideas of the practical part of Kant's system, only philosophers disagree, but men have always been unanimous."

[174] *Foundations of the Metaphysics of Morals*, p. 21.

[175] *Critique of Practical Reason*, Preface, p. 4 n.   [176] *Ibid.*, p. 3.

[177] This is most succinctly argued in part III of the *Foundations of the Metaphysics of Morals*.

[178] *Foundations of the Metaphysics of Morals*, p. 9.

A good will is not the only thing in the world which is an *intrinsic* good. There are traits of character which are intrinsically good, but not unqualifiedly good (i.e., good in every circumstance), and happiness is an intrinsic good, desired unexceptionally and for its own sake.

Because happiness is always desired and desired for its own sake, earlier philosophers had attempted to derive moral laws from it and from our observations on successful and unsuccessful ways of achieving it. Such moral laws are heteronomous, not autonomous; they are empirical but they pretend to be necessary. Thus whereas *pure* theoretical reason tends to be dialectical and to produce illusions, it is *empirical* practical reason which oversteps its bounds and produces moral illusions. Hence Kant does not call his second great work a critique of *pure* practical reason, but simply of practical reason.

Yet Kant is far from disregarding happiness as a concept in ethics. Morality is neither a sufficient nor a necessary condition of happiness, and the desire for happiness has never succeeded in making a man moral—at best, it urges him to be prudent and clever. But since "the sight of a being endowed with no feature of a pure and good will enjoying uninterrupted prosperity can never give pleasure to a rational impartial observer,"[179] happiness must bear some rational connection to morality. Kant says that morality is the condition of *worthiness* (in the eyes of an impartial rational observer) *to be happy*. Conversely, it is not satisfying to a rational impartial observer to see a being endowed with a good will not enjoying uninterrupted prosperity. Yet we see both all the time. What we rationally desire for rational beings is the *bonum consummatum*, or perfect good: moral goodness attended with proportionate happiness. But the world, unfortunately, does not seem to honor this desire. Are we then to suppose a radical disparity in the structure of the world, according to which the *bonum supremum*, or the supreme condition of all good (the good will), is only accidentally connected with (and more often disconnected from) the perfect good?

Some—for example Nietzsche, and Bertrand Russell in "A Free Man's Worship"—can stoically accept this fate. I know of no one in the eighteenth century, with the possible exception of Voltaire, who could; and Kant provides two alternatives to show that we do not have to give an affirmative answer to this ancient question of the problem of evil. One looks back to the situation in the *Critique of Pure Reason;* the other is found only in the *Critique of Judgment* and in his writings on the philosophy of history.

Looking backward, Kant sees that if we knew it to be true that the soul is immortal and that God exists as the moral governor of the universe, then the disparity between happiness and virtue would be only an accidental, empirical fact about the sensible world, to be adjusted in the next. The *Critique of Pure Reason* shows that we cannot know this. And the second *Critique* argues, in one of its most moving passages,[180] that if we did know

---

[179] *Ibid.*, p. 9.
[180] *Critique of Practical Reason*, pp. 151–154, the title of the chapter being "Of the Wise Adaptation of Man's Cognitive Faculties to his Practical Vocation."

this the purity and autonomy of morals would be threatened or destroyed by our hope for celestial rewards. But we can *postulate* them.

A postulate is "a theoretical proposition which is not *as such* demonstrable, but which is an inseparable corollary of an unconditionally valid practical law."[181] The practical law is that I must seek the *bonum consummatum*, and a law is invalid if it cannot be fulfilled. But it cannot be fulfilled by me alone, and the world does not cooperate in the attainment of the end. But it can be fulfilled if God exists and if the soul is immortal.[182] Hence I believe, as corollaries to this law which I accept, that God exists and the soul is immortal, even though I cannot prove them theoretically. The primacy of the practical reason thus fills the empty place of theoretical reason with rational belief. It does so without making any contribution to knowledge; we do not *know* any metaphysical propositions to be true which we did not know at the end of the first *Critique*. But we have a *moral guide* to take the place of common sense and revelation, which were supposed to be the metaphysical guides in the Mendelssohn-Jacobi debate.[183]

Looking forward. In the *Critique of Judgment* Kant argued that the phenomenal world as a whole must be looked upon *as if* designed. Not just a living organism, but the whole fabric of nature, is as it were designed for our intellectual comprehension and aesthetic delight. But if everything in the world has, at least in its structural relations, a purpose, *what* is the purpose? Just as theoretical metaphysics sought but could not find a confirmable condition for every conditioned thing, yet in its regulative interpretation set us the task of, and gave us a guide to, finding the unconditioned conditions, now in the *Critique of Judgment* we are set the task of finding the purpose behind all purposes, as unconditioned final cause for all final causes.[184] Such a final cause cannot be found in nature, for of every natural purpose we discern, we can ask: What is *its* purpose? But there is one being of which we cannot ask that question: man.

Of man (and so of every rational creature in the world) as a moral being it can no longer be asked why he exists. His existence involves the highest purpose to which, as far as is in his power, he can subject the whole of nature, contrary to which at least he cannot regard himself as subject to any influence of nature. If, now, things of the world, as beings dependent in their existence, need a supreme cause acting according to purposes, man is the final purpose of creation, since without him the chain of mutually subordinated purposes would not be complete as regards its ground. Only in man, and in him only as a subject of morality, do we meet with unconditioned legislation in respect to purpose.[185]

---

181 *Ibid.*, p. 127.

182 The situation with respect to immortality of the soul is somewhat different from that to the existence of God, and the argument is in fact very much more complicated. While the present text does not perhaps seriously misrepresent Kant's theory of the postulate of immortality, I must refer the more critical reader to my *Commentary on Kant's Critique of Practical Reason*, pp. 265–271, for an exact statement which I have been unable to compress into the limits of this chapter.

183 *What Is Orientation in Thinking?*, esp. p. 298 of the University of Chicago edition cited in n. 27.

184 *Critique of Judgment*, § 84, p. 284.   185 *Ibid.*, § 84, pp. 285–286.

The "unconditioned legislation in respect to purposes" is, of course, the good will. The final purpose of the world, therefore, is not man's happiness, for which, in fact, nature has only a "stepmotherly" regard. It is not even man's morality—for that is his own purpose, and nothing but man's own free decision can make him moral. It is, rather, his *culture*, his "aptitude for arbitrary purposes in general (consequently his freedom)".[186]

Thus the teleology of nature is an idea which guides our understanding of the way man has come to the point in his history when he can exercise his freedom and pass from the stage of nature to those of civilization, culture, and morality. The teleology of nature passes into a philosophy of history.

Using these ideas—they are not concepts which give knowledge, and not hypotheses that can be confirmed, but regulative ideas—Kant thinks he has a conception of a "plan of history" in which the natural and the moral can be seen in an organic connection:

Nature has willed that man should, by himself, produce everything that goes beyond the mechanical ordering of his animal existence, and that he should partake of no other happiness or perfection than that which he himself independently of instinct has created by his own reason . . . The history of mankind can be seen, in the large, as the realization of Nature's secret plan to bring forth a perfectly constituted state as the only condition in which the capacities of mankind can be fully developed, and also bring forth that external relation among states which is perfectly adequate to this end.[187]

And thus the philosophy of history leads into Kant's political philosophy and his sketch of a plan for securing universal peace.[188] This can be achieved only by the gradual attainment of republican constitutions in all states, each linked with the others in a league of nations.

The idea of such an ethical commonwealth is not only a political idea, but it also has a religious dimension. Historically, in fact, it has a religious foundation. For, as Kant wrote Jacobi, "If the gospel had not previously taught universal moral laws in their purity, pure reason would not have been able to comprehend them in such perfection; but since they are given, one can now convince anyone of their correctness and validity merely by reason."[189] But the form in which the ethical commonwealth has been achieved in history is that of a "people of God under moral laws," that is, a church, founded on ecclesiastical faith in a putative revelation.[190] Since the things of reason cannot be founded on history or instilled as dogma, as Lessing also saw, Kant foresees the gradual replacement of ecclesiastical faith by rational faith. This, however, does not mean a decline of true religion, but precisely the opposite, the "coming of the Kingdom of God,"[191] for religion is nothing but the recognition of duties as divine

186 *Ibid.*, § 83, p. 281.
187 *Idea for a Universal History of Mankind from a Cosmopolitan Point of View*, Theses III, VIII, (in *Kant on History*, pp. 13, 21).
188 In *Perpetual Peace* (1795) and *Metaphysics of Morals*, pt. I, Conclusion to part ii.
189 August 30, 1789 (*Kant's Philosophical Correspondence*, p. 158).
190 *Religion within the Limits of Reason Alone*, trans. Hoyt and Greene, p. 91.
191 *Ibid.*, p. 105.

commands.[192] Nor does he mean, of course, that God did issue these commands, for that would spell the end of autonomy and morals. Rather, for Kant *the moral law is itself holy.* Man himself is unholy enough, to be sure, and Kant shocked his contemporary fellow-Enlighteners with his argument that there is a radical principle of evil in human nature, a kind of a priori proclivity to rebel against the law. But the moral law is holy, and it is the only holy law: "Whatever, over and above good life-conduct, man fancies that he can do to become well-pleasing to God" is not only unmoral and may be evil, but "is mere religious illusion and the pseudo-service of God."[193]

The eighteenth century had several kinds of religion—in addition to revealed religion there was natural and rational religion. Kant added a new kind: moral religion. There can be no theological morals, but all valid theology is moral theology.

The Third Faculty

Since the time of Gottsched, as we have seen, a theory of taste was one of the most pressing needs of German philosophy. The history of its theory of taste reflects the history of German taste itself, from a philistine moralism and neoclassical imitativeness to the excesses of *Sturm und Drang.*

The link between them was a slow growth of an art independent of moralistic and intellectual didacticism, the development of a truly lyrical and dramatic art. This was reflected in the idea of an independent aesthetic, a philosophical theory of art, which did not borrow its categories from Wolff. The art which seems to be the objective counterpart of the aesthetic theories of men like Baumgarten, Mendelssohn, and Sulzer, is still disciplined art, the art of an orderly bourgeois world. Challenges to the orderliness of the bourgeois world by the young geniuses of the *Sturm und Drang* were the objective counterpart of challenges to the early and middle Enlightenment's theory of art. Counter-Enlightenment theory of beauty sought its foundations in the mysterious working of genius, individual or *völkisch,* which seemed to need no rules and certainly acknowledged none.

It was in this context that Kant formulated his aesthetic theory. He was opposed to *Sturm und Drang,* but instead of going back to the safe sixties, he laid foundations for the next great, the greatest, movement in German art. It is no part of my purpose to tell what happened after Kant, but in confirmation of this we have the explicit personal testimony of Goethe and Schiller.

Even in the period before the Inaugural Dissertation Kant had intended to write a "critique of taste," and did write the little *Observations on the Feelings of the Beautiful and the Sublime.* But he had to keep deferring the larger work, though he repeatedly mentioned it and made his usual sanguine remarks about its being published in the near future. When it was published, it was the first part of the *Critique of Judgment.*

---

[192] *Ibid.,* p. 142; *Critique of Practical Reason,* p. 134.
[193] *Religion within the Limits of Reason Alone,* p. 158.

This was an unfortunate position for it. Kant's aesthetic theory was, at least stylistically, forced into an alien mold. The theory of art was forced to serve the purposes of the Kantian system as a whole, but the service was not in fact needed. For the task of the *Critique of Judgment* as a whole was to show how the realm of ends can coexist with the realm of nature, and this task was brilliantly executed in its second part, the "Critique of Teleological Judgment." The connection of its first part, the "Critique of Aesthetic Judgment," to this final goal is exceedingly tenuous. But Kant had always wanted to write a "critique of taste" and here he saw a place where it could be fitted into his system as if it were an integral and necessary part of it. The critical philosophy would be impoverished were it to lack this application of some of its principles and its general method to the phenomena of art, beauty, and sublimity. The "Critique of Aesthetic Judgment" does complete, in an aesthetic sense, so to speak, the critical philosophy even if it does not do so in the logically systematic way Kant pretended.

Why, in fact, did Kant want to consider art and beauty at all? Was it just a personal interest, long delayed and now realizable? No. There is something "necessary" in the experience of beauty, and necessity is to Kant always a sign that some a priori principle is at work. A priori principles, since they cannot be confirmed by experience, must be "deduced," i.e., justified and shown to be valid, and this is the positive task of critique.

He finds the grounds of a priori judgments in science and ethics in the autonomous operations of the mind making rules for nature and for itself. No one ever thought of denying that in the creation of art there is a self-activity of some faculty, be it wit, fancy, talent, or taste. That it should follow rules was inherent in the aesthetics of Gottsched and Baumgarten. When these writers were rejected, it was freed from rules. Kant found necessity in judgments of art—the emotional ranting of *Sturm und Drang* is unartistic—but he thought his predecessors had mislocated the necessity. Their aesthetic theories were too intellectual and moralistic, too much a theory of craft. Art, Kant is saying, has rules; but they are its own rules. To show what they are requires first a phenomenological examination of art and second a transcendental justification of its conditions. The latter, in turn, requires no less than the establishment of a *third faculty of the mind* with its own a priori principles and its own operations which supply an a priori form to aesthetic and critical judgments.

Kant is the first author to maintain clearly and consistently the three-faculty theory.[194] There are three autonomous faculties, i.e., faculties irreducible to each other because each has its own irreducible (indemonstrable) principle. They are cognition, feeling of pleasure and pain, and desire. Wolff had tried to live with just one, cognition (*facultas repraesentativa*), but the Pietists added will to it. Mendelssohn, Sulzer, and Tetens (in a somewhat confused way) added feeling, or the faculty of appreciation (*Billigungsvermögen*), but neither Mendelssohn nor Tetens was able to

---

[194] It is first expressed in a letter to Karl Leonhard Reinhold, December 28, 1787 (*Kant's Philosophical Correspondence*, p. 127).

maintain its autonomy and independence, because they were not able to draw a sharp distinction between the pleasure of satisfied desire or the pleasure which spurs us to action and the pleasure of artistic excellence. An exacting phenomenological examination of the experience of art permitted Kant to draw this distinction. He saw that since aesthetic judgments are normative, not descriptive, there is something in them which is analogous to the necessity found in cognitive and moral judgments, something a priori. Now if the a priori necessities of aesthetic judgment are not the same as those of intellectual and moral judgment, then there must be a "faculty" of aesthetic judgment just as there are faculties for cognition and volition. Hence, at last, German philosophy comes to a clear criterion for discerning and distinguishing the faculties of the mind: for each distinct kind of a priori judgment there must be a specific and distinct ability (*Vermögen*) or faculty of mind.

Kant probably never saw a beautiful painting or a fine statue; he certainly never saw "shapeless mountain masses piled in wild disorder upon one another with their pyramids of ice, or the gloomy, raging sea". His taste in music seems to have been utterly philistine; and only for literature was his critical sense refined and exacting. Nevertheless, in spite of the very limited range of his aesthetic experience, he simply had a better grasp of the essential features of the experience of the sublime and the beautiful than any of his predecessors, with the possible exception of Baumgarten. Mendelssohn, Sulzer, and others saw the difference between aesthetic and intellectual worth but failed to separate sharply the aesthetic from the volitional and moral. Kant extends Baumgarten's discovery concerning sensuous perfection far enough to see that the aesthetic is not only independent of the intellectually conceptual but also of the sensuously satisfying, of the feelings of desire and the practical satisfaction of the intentions of will.

Kant believed that the establishment of the third faculty rounded out his transcendental psychology, providing a link between cognition and desire. And feeling, the third faculty, is said also to parallel the faculty of judgment as a link between the other two cognitive faculties, viz., understanding and reason. But the neat architectonic table of the faculties at the end of the Introduction to the *Critique of Judgment* is, in my opinion, hardly more than a decoration; the important thing is not that it in some important way "unifies" the Kantian philosophy but that it is solidly based upon an accurate phenomenological description of art, renders the a priori features of aesthetic judgment intelligible, and provides a psychological hypothesis as to how art is created and why it pleases.

"The beautiful," Kant writes,[195] "is that which, without any concept, is cognized as the object of a necessary satisfaction." In this definition, two things stand out: the beautiful is known (*cognized*) and is *necessarily satisfying*. The first of these relates aesthetic judgment to knowledge, and the second to that which is pleasing. We must consider each of these interfaces of experience.

(1) A cognitive judgment makes a claim upon ratification by others. I do not add to a cognitive judgment, such as "My dog is a bloodhound,"

[195] *Critique of Judgment,* § 22.

a limiting expression such as "(for me)". If it is true that he is a blood-hound, then every observer ought to agree. Everyone who knows what a bloodhound is (possesses, and knows how to apply, the concept of blood-hound) ought to agree to my judgment if it is correct. Now an aesthetic judgment makes a like claim to ratification. "He is beautiful" does not mean "He is beautiful (to me)" but implies that anyone with good taste should acknowledge his beauty.

This feature of aesthetic judgment, however, cannot be justified in the same way that the like feature of a cognitive judgment can be. For Kant also says: the beautiful is that which is cognized *without any concept.* Con-cepts are the universals in cognitive judgments, and cognitive judgments have a universal claim upon those who possess reason and know how to apply concepts. Unless I understand and know the rules for the application of the concept "bloodhound," I cannot claim that "this is a bloodhound" is normative for your judgment. But I do not have to know what descriptive concept applies to the X in "X is beautiful" when I claim that you also ought to say, "X is beautiful." If I did, the pleasure of aesthetic experience would be dependent upon possession of specific antecedent knowledge, and it would make it possible to construct (in the manner of a craftsman, Kant says) a beautiful object according to rules (say, of the imitation of nature, or moral precepts).

(2) The beautiful is necessarily satisfying. Pleasure attends the satisfac-tion of an interest, and interests are either sensuous (the interests of in-clination, as for example, the pleasures of the table), moral (the interest of the will), or intellectual (the interest in discovering and knowing the truth). All these pleasures are contingent upon the possession and satis-faction of interests, and if there are "laws of pleasure" of these kinds they are borrowed from the functioning of the interests of the senses, of the will, or of the cognitive faculty. If there is, as Kant says there is, a *necessary* satisfaction in the beautiful, then it must follow that *aesthetic pleasure is disinterested.* I can get aesthetic pleasure from a beautiful dog I do not desire to own; and if I could not, then neither could I make any claim upon your ratification of my judgment that mine is beautiful.

Baumgarten had seen that the beautiful pleases without a concept, for it is a perfection of sense and not of intellect. Mendelssohn had seen (usually) that the pleasure we take in beauty is different from that of an-ticipated satisfaction of our will or desire. Kant puts these two definitive characteristics of aesthetic pleasure together, making one support the other. And he asks: what underlies the universality and necessity claimed in a judgment of taste? How can there be a judgment which claims the agree-ment of others about an object, but applies no objective concept to it which signifies some property we might think belongs to the object as a descriptive predicate? And how can there be an object which is thought to give pleasure necessarily, regardless of the interests or lack of interest an observer might take in it?

Kant's answer is that men have a *sensus communis,* not a special organ of taste but the same *organization* of their cognitive and affective faculties. The spontaneous play of their common cognitive faculties, more especially the spontaneity of the imagination in creating and presenting images to the understanding, underlies a pleasure which is limited by neither desire, will, nor understanding. The beautiful is that which facilitates comprehension by presenting images spontaneously in which the pattern shows purposiveness (but not purposiveness *for me*) and without any conceptual representation of what the purpose is.[196]

While there is natural beauty—and natural beauty is the subjective representation of the purposes in nature, treated of in the theory of teleological judgment—the paradigm for beauty is art. Kant supplies us also with a theory of the creation of art. Fine art is the work of genius. The artist is a creator who creates a world for our contemplation and delight. The understanding creates nature itself by subjecting phenomena to law. But while the knowing subject does so by rule (categories, principles, regulative ideas), genius does so by the productive imagination operating "by nature" and not by a rule-book. "Genius is the talent, or natural gift, which gives the rule to art"[197] in a way analogous to that in which understanding "gives the law to nature."[198] Beauty points to analogies between art and knowing.

The other genre of aesthetic object, the sublime, points to analogies between artistic creation and morality.[199] In the early *Observations on the Feeling of the Beautiful and Sublime,* a rather superficial work under the obvious tutelage of Shaftesbury, Kant had used both as moral typologies (thus, courage is sublime, innocence is beautiful). In the *Critique of Judgment* § 59 he discusses "beauty as a symbol of morality." But in his full treatment of the sublime, there is much more than these rather modish commonplaces.

The basis of the experience of the sublime is not immediate pleasure, but pain or fright or terror. These are, normally, *interested* feelings; something frightens me, and I want to escape, but if I were bigger and stronger and well-armed it would not frighten me. But a raging storm at sea or a thundering cascade of water may frighten me and yet give me a disinterested pleasure. These are examples of the sublime of power, the "dynamically sublime." Lofty mountains and Pascal's "infinite silence of the universe" do not precisely *frighten* me in any ordinary sense—I can do nothing about them—but they strike awe in the soul. These are examples of the "mathematically sublime."

In the sublime, unlike in our experience of beauty, there is no easy spontaneous play of the imagination presenting images to be comprehended by the understanding, or images in which all is purposively organized without a representation of the purpose. Rather, the sublime seems counterpurposive; it makes demands upon the imagination which imagination cannot fulfill, it presents objects which seem to exceed the organizing capacities of mind. The mathematically sublime humbles my cognitive powers, the dynamically sublime my desires.[200]

[196] *Ibid.,* § 17.
[197] *Ibid.,* § 46.   [198] *Prolegomena,* § 36.
[199] See M. C. Nahm, " 'Sublimity' and the 'Moral Law' in Kant's Philosophy," *Kant-Studien,* 48:502–524 (1957).
[200] *Critique of Judgment* § 24.

How then can they be enjoyed? How explain that men seek and treasure such experiences?

The sublime gives us disinterested pleasure because it reminds us of our rational—theoretical and practical—nature. Our mind which strives to comprehend the sublime is subdued by its magnitude and might—but lifted up by the knowledge that it is only a spectacle. We attribute an infinity of magnitude and might to the world, but it really belongs to our own rational being. The pleasure in the terrifying sublimity ascribed to nature is a clue to our superiority to nature. We convert "respect for the idea of humanity in our own subject into respect for the object."[201] The sublime in nature outside us produces indirectly a feeling in us which is produced directly by the contemplation of the moral dignity of man and the moral law, which is sublime in itself, making the boldest sinner tremble.[202] The humility thus induced in man is itself sublime,[203] for the moral law which strikes down self-conceit is man's own law, given by himself, to himself.

The famous peroration of the *Critique of Practical Reason* is not just a rhetorical flourish. In lapidary inscriptions, one is not under philosophical discipline. But those who put these words on Kant's tomb chose well:

Two things fill the mind with ever new and increasing admiration and awe, the more often and the more steadily we contemplate them: the starry heavens above me, and the moral law within me.

This was a fitting epitaph for its author. Is it not also an epitome of a polarity in German philosophy itself, as, in its greatest representatives, Nicholas of Cusa, Leibniz, and Kant, it strove to bring humanity and nature together under the seamless fabric of reason?

---

[201] *Ibid.*, § 27; see also § 26.
[202] *Critique of Practical Reason*, p. 80.
[203] *Critique of Judgment* § 28; *Critique of Practical Reason*, p. 121.

An Informal Bibliography

Index

An Informal Bibliography

In this Bibliography I make no claim to exhaustiveness. I have simply listed and commented upon books and articles which have been especially instructive to me, or which, I believe, will be of interest to many readers. In a few instances, however, I have felt constrained to list works only for the purpose of warning the unwary not to make (as I sometimes did) a strenuous effort to obtain them only to be disappointed upon success. Wherever possible, I have listed writings in English and writings not difficult to procure. Works primarily relevant only to a single point have been cited in footnotes, and their titles are not repeated here.

Intellectual Histories of Germany

The literature under this heading is enormous. William J. Bossenbrook's *The German Mind* (Detroit: Wayne State University Press, 1961) is cultural history on the grand scale, synoptic but not superficial. Bossenbrook interprets German history in the light of certain conflicting, but deeply held, beliefs and attitudes already developed in the Middle Ages. (Hans Kohn's similarly titled book, *The Mind of Germany* [New York: Scribner, 1960] is much more politically oriented, but is largely confined to the nineteenth and twentieth centuries.) F. O. Hertz, *The Development of the*

German Public Mind, 2 vols. (London: Allen & Unwin, 1957, 1962), traces the development of German consciousness of nationhood. Hajo Holborn, A *History of Modern Germany* (London: Eyre and Spottiswood, 1959–), of which so far only two volumes have been published, promises to become the standard German history in English; it is rich in details, and I have constantly referred to it while composing this book. Emil Reiche, *Der Gelehrte in der deutschen Vergangenheit* (Leipzig: Diederichs, 1900) is richly illustrated. Friedrich Paulsen, *Geschichte des gelehrten Unterrichts*, 2nd ed., 2 vols. (Leipzig: Veit, 1896–97), is an essential work, especially for the specific orientation of this book; Paulsen's *The German Universities and University Study* (New York: Longmans Green, 1906) is much less informative. J. E. Spenlé, *La Pensée allemande de Luther à Nietzsche* (Paris: Armand Colin, 1934) is brief but perceptive.

Histories of German Philosophy

There are, surprisingly, very few such histories. Eduard Zeller, *Geschichte der deutschen Philosophie seit Leibniz* (Munich, 1873) is the standard work, but out of date. Émile Brehier, *Histoire de la philosophie allemande* (Paris: Collection Payot, 1921) is too brief to be of much value. R. O. Gropp, *Das nationale philosophische Erbe* (Berlin: Deutscher Verlag der Wissenschaften, 1960) is in a series of small volumes reinterpreting the history of German philosophy in Marxist terms but is otherwise of no value. A. Richter, "Grundlegung einer Geschichte der deutschen Philosophie," *Philosophische Monatshefte*, 23:385–421, (1887), is of some value on problems of periodization.

In the *Encyclopedia of Philosophy*, ed. Paul Edwards (New York: Macmillan, 1967, III, 291–309) I have an article, "German Philosophy," which may be regarded as a trial run for the present book; the main themes are the same in the two writings.

But the lack of comprehensive treatments of German philosophy does not mean that any inch of German philosophy has not been examined microscopically. Germans have been the great historians of philosophy, and their quite understandable preference for their own countrymen has had the effect that many of their standard histories give special attention to German philosophy and contain accounts of men not usually considered by historians of other nationalities. Outstanding in this respect, and absolutely indispensable, is *Friedrich Überwegs Grundriss der Geschichte der Philosophie*, 12th ed., vols. II and III, ed. respectively by Bernhard Geyer and by Max Frischeisen-Köhler and Willy Moog, (Berlin: Mittler, 1924). I have found J. E. Erdmann's *History of Philosophy*, trans. W. S. Hough, 2 vols. (New York: Macmillan, 1890) the most useful of the German histories translated into English.

Reference Works

The standard bibliographies are both old: V. P. Gumposch, *Die philosophische Literatur der Deutschen von 1400 bis um 1850* (Regensburg, 1851), and J. S. Ersch and C. A. Geissler, *Bibliographisches Handbuch der philosophischen Literatur der Deutschen von der Mitte des 18. Jahrhunderts bis auf die neueste Zeit* 3rd ed. (Leipzig, 1850). Each is now available in reprint by Stern Verlag, Düsseldorf, 1967 and 1965 respectively. Gumposch's book is more than a bibliography, but less than a history; it is rationally (not merely chronologically or alphabetically) organized, and contains, in addition to rich bibliography, essential biographical data and sometimes short summaries.

Two other reference works have been indispensable: the great *Allgemeine deutsche Biographie*, 56 vols. (Leipzig, 1875–1912, with later addenda), and the *Evangelisches Kirchenlexikon*, ed. Heinz Brunotte and Otto Weber, 4 vols. (Göttingen: Vandenhoeck & Ruprecht, 1956, 2nd ed. 1961).

The Encyclopedia of Philosophy, edited by Paul Edwards, was published too late for me to make full use of it, but I was permitted to see many articles in it before publication, and they were of great value to me. The *Enciclopedia Filosofica*, 4 vols. (Venice & Rome: Istituto per la Collaborazione Culturale, 1957) was a source of information not to be found elsewhere. *Philosophen-Lexikon*, ed. Werner Ziegenfuss and Cortrud Jung, 2 vols. (Berlin: De Gruyter, 1949), was at best a convenience, for most of the older information in it seems to have been taken from Überweg. The *Sachwörterbuch der Deutschkunde*, ed. Walter Hofstaetter and Ulrich Peters, 2 vols. (Leipzig and Berlin: Teubner, 1930) was of use on nonphilosophical topics.

It is to be understood that most of the books listed above contain material bearing on the contents of each chapter of the present History. But I have not listed them again at each of the many places where they might well be consulted.

Chapter 1. A National History of Philosophy?

Since the theory of the historiography of philosophy has been neglected, anyone who ventures upon the formulation of organizing and heuristic concepts for the history of philosophy is largely on his own. But nationalism as an organizing category in the history of philosophy has been studied by Marcell Grilli in "The Nationality of Philosophy and B. Spaventa," *Journal of the History of Ideas*, 2: 339–370 (1941); the first part of this interesting paper (down to p. 346) deals with the origins of the conception of the "nationality of philosophy" and the transition from it, in Germany, to the "philosophy of nationalism."

Glowing descriptions of the essence or spirit of German philosophy can be found in Fichte (*Reden an die deutsche Nation*, vii) and Schelling (*Ueber das Wesen der deutschen Wissenschaft*). A less flattering picture is given in Nietzsche's *Beyond Good and Evil*, § 244.

World War I produced Wilhelm Wundt's *Die Nationen und ihre Philosophie* (Leipzig: Kröner, 1916) and, on the Allied side, less commendatory treatments in J. H. Muirhead's *German Philosophy and the War* (London: J. Murray, 1916), John Dewey's *German Philosophy and Politics* (New York: Holt, 1915), and George Santayana's *Egotism in German Philosophy* (New York: Scribner, 1916). Between the wars there was the comparatively temperate work by Gustav Lüddemann, *Entgegengesetzte Denkwelten* (Halle: Buchhandlung des Waisenhauses, 1925).

But all stops were pulled in the philosophical literature of the Third Reich. The following is only a sample to indicate the state of mind supporting the kind of propaganda referred to on p. 3, though usually the works have no other value: Franz Böhm, *Anti-Cartesianismus, Deutsche Philosophie im Widerstand* (Leipzig: Meiner, 1938); August Faust, "Wesenszüge deutscher Weltanschauung und Philosophie," *Zeitschrift für deutsche Kulturphilosophie*, VIII (1942), 81–165; Hermann Glockner, *Vom Wesen der deutschen Philosophie* (Stuttgart: Kohlmann, 1941); Theodor Haering, *Was ist deutsche Philosophie?* (Stuttgart: Kohlmann, 1936); *Die deutsche und die europäische Philosophie* (Stuttgart: Kohlmann, 1943); and a book of essays edited by Haering, *Das Deutsche in der deutschen Philosophie* (Stuttgart: Kohlmann, 1942). Also August Menzer, "Deutsche Philosophie als Ausdruck deutscher Seele," *Kant-Studien*, 39: 271–283 (1934); Erich Rothacker, "Das Problem einer Geschichte der deutschen Philosophie," *Deutsche Vierteljahrschrift für Literaturwissenschaft und Literaturgeschichte*, XVI (1938), 161–183; Hermann Schwarz, *Grundzüge einer Geschichte der artdeutschen Philosophie* (Berlin: Junker und Dunnhaupt, 1937); Friedrich Seifert, *Schöpferische deutsche Philosophie* (Köln: Schaffstein, 1936); Max Wundt, *Die Wurzeln der deutschen Philosophie in Stamm und Rasse* (Berlin: Junker und Dunnhaupt, 1944). On this book, see my comment, p. 3n. There are warrantedly censorious essays in G. P. Gooch, ed., *The German Mind and its Outlook* (London: Chapman and Hall, 1945), in which the essay by Morris Ginzberg on the Germans' own characterizations of their thought is not unfair even when most depressing.

C. G. Gustavson's "German Lutheranism. A Psychological Study," *Journal of the History of Ideas*, 11: 140–158 (1950), in spite of its modest title, is an attempt to explain much of German cultural life, including German philosophy, in terms of the inwardness and world-alienation of the Lutheran life-form. See also: Mario Pensa, *Il Pensiero Tedesco. Saggio di psicologica della filosofia tedesca* (Bologna: Zanichelli, 1938); German translation, *Das deutsche Denken*, trans. W. Meckauer (Erlenback-Zürich: Ernst Rentsch, 1948); Magdalena Aebi, *Kant's Begründung der deutschen Philosophie* (Basel: Recht und Gesellschaft A.-G., 1947).

PART ONE: GERMAN PHILOSOPHY BEFORE THE REFORMATION

Chapter II. From the Beginnings to Albertus Magnus

The Beginnings

H. Weniger, "Das deutsche Bildungswesen im Frühmittelalter," *Historische Vierteljahrschrift*, 30: 446–492 (1935); H. Henning, *Der Ursprung der nordischen Philosophie* (Berlin: Junker und Dunnhaupt, 1933); and A. Richter, *Der Uebergang der Philosophie zu den deutschen im VI.–XI. Jahrhundert* (Halle, 1879–80). Michael Seidlmayer, *Currents of Medieval Thought with Special Reference to Germany* (Oxford: Blackwell, 1960), though brief, is very valuable for the connections indicated between philosophy and other phases of culture.

See also E. Aergetter, "Gottschalk et le problème de la prédestination," *Revue de l'histoire des religions* (Paris), 116: 186–233 (1937). Erich Dinkler's *Gottschalk der Saxe* (Stuttgart: Kohlhammer, 1936) is marred by tendentious arguments about the possibility of reconciling *Deutschtum* with Christianity. Paul Th. Hoffman, *Der mittelalterliche Mensch gesehen aus Welt und Umwelt Notkers des Deutschen* (Gotha: Perthes, 1922) is excellent.

Hugo of St. Victor

In addition to translations cited in the text, there are: *Soliloquy on the Earnest Money of the Soul*, trans. Kevin Herbert (Milwaukee: Marquette University Press, 1956); *Selected Spiritual Writings* in an anonymous translation (London: Faber & Faber, 1962); and selections in R. C. Petry, ed., *Late Medieval Mysticism* (Philadelphia: Westminster, 1957). See also P. J. Kleinz, *The Theory of Knowledge of Hugh* [sic] *of St. Victor* (unpub. diss., Catholic University of America, (Washington, D.C. 1944); Martin Grabmann, *Geschichte der scholastischen Methode*, II, 229–309 (Freiburg: Herder, 1911). Jerome Taylor, *The Origins and Early Life of Hugo of St. Victor* (Notre Dame, Ind.: Notre Dame University Press, 1957), discusses the disputed questions of whether Hugo was a Saxon and comes to an affirmative conclusion.

The *Peripatetici* and Their Critics

J. A. Endres, "Die Dialektiker und ihre Gegner im XI. Jahrhundert," *Philosophisches Jahrbuch*, 19: 20–33 (1906), and M. T. Stead, "Manegold von Lautenbach," *English Historical Review*, 29: 1–15 (1914). Georg Misch, *Geschichte der Autobiographie* (Frankfurt: Schulte-Bulmke, 1959), vol. III, pt. ii, pp. 57–107, discusses Ottloh of St. Emmeram.

Otto of Freising

The translation is cited in the text. See also Fritz Fellner, "The Two Cities of Otto of Freising and Its Influence on the Catholic Philosophy of History," *Catholic Historical Review*, 20: 154–174 (1934); and J. Schmidlin, "Die Philosophie von Otto von Freising," *Philosophisches Jahrbuch*, 18 (1905), 156–175, 312–323, 407–423. The first of Schmidlin's articles gives a good survey of the sources of Aristotelianism in the twelfth and thirteenth centuries.

Albertus Magnus

Works
Opera omnia, ed. August Borgnet, 28 vols. (1890–99). A new edition of forty volumes under the editorship of Bernhard Geyer has been in preparation since 1951 (*Opera omnia*, Monasterii Westfalorum, Aschendorff). There is little in English. *Liber sex principiorum*, trans. J. P. Mulally, in *Medieval Philosophy*, ed. H. Shapiro (New York: The Modern Library,

1964), pp. 264–293; *De intellectu et intelligibili*, from *Parva naturalia*, trans. Richard McKeon, in *Selections from Medieval Philosophy* (New York: Scribner, 1929) I, 315–335.

Studies

Étienne Gilson, *History of Christian Philosophy in the Middle Ages*, pt. vii, chap i (New York: Random House, 1955), is perhaps the best in English. T. M. Schwertner, *St. Albert the Great* (Milwaukee: Bruce, 1932) is too simple. I am much indebted to the paper by Robert G. Miller, C.S.B., "An Aspect of Averroes' Influence on St. Albert," in *Medieval Studies*, 16: 57–71 (1954). B. J. Muller-Thym's, *The Establishment of the University of Being in the Doctrine of Meister Eckhart*, chap. 2 (a) is penetrating, but difficult. Martin Grabmann's *Der Einfluss Alberts des Grossen auf das mittelalterliche Geistesleben* (Innsbruck: Rauch, 1928) is sketchy.

Albertists

Geschichte des Albertismus by Gilles Meersseman, O. P. (Dissertationes historicae, Institutum historicum f.f. praedicatorum Romae ad S. Sabinae [Paris, R. Haloua], fasc. III, V, 1933, 1935) traces the relations between Thomists and Albertists in Paris and Cologne and their common opposition to the Occamists and includes texts of the polemics between the first two groups. Later volumes were to continue the study of the situation in other universities, but seem not to have appeared. The Cologne faculty is treated in G. M. Löhr, "Zur Geschichte der Kölner Dominikanerschule im XIV. Jahrhundert," *Divus Thomae*, 22: 57–84 (1945). A short survey is given in Grabmann's *Der Einfluss Alberts des Grossen*. Individual Albertists are treated in: Walter Eckert, "Berthold von Mosburg," *Philosophisches Jahrbuch*, 45: 210–233 (1957), and in Grabmann's *Mittelalterliches Geistesleben* (Munich: Hueber, 1926), pp. 147–221 (on Ulrich of Strassburg and Dionysius the Carthusian [1402–1471]. Biographies and short accounts of these and many other Albertists will be found, of course, in *Überwegs Grundriss der Geschichte der Philosophie*, ed. Bernhard Geyer, vol. II.

On Dietrich of Freiberg: W. A. Wallace, *The Scientific Method of Theodoric of Freiberg* (Fribourg, Switzerland: The University Press, 1959); Pierre Duhem, *Système du monde*, VI, 181–205 (Paris, 1954–59); and Wilhelm Preger, *Geschichte der deutschen Mystik im Mittelalter* (1874); reprint, Aalen: Zeller, 1962), I, 292–305, which contains some errors corrected by later scholarship.

North-European Thomists (Johannes of Sterngassen, Gerhard of Sterngassen, Nicholas of Strassburg, Jacob of Metz, and Heinrich of Lübeck) are treated in "Forschungen zur Geschichte der ältesten deutschen Thomistenschule des Dominikanerordens" in Grabmann's *Mittelalterliches Geistesleben*, pp. 392–431, and, of course, in Überweg.

Chapter III. Mysticism

Works of Meister Eckhart and Translations

Die deutschen und lateinischen Werke (Stuttgart: Kohlhammer, 1936–   ); Josef Quint, *Deutsche Mystikertexte des Mittelalters* (Bonn,

1929); Franz Pfeiffer, *Meister Eckhart* (1857; reprint Göttingen: Vanden-hoeck und Ruprecht, 1924; German works only); C. de B. Evans, *Meister Eckhardt* (London: J. M. Watkins, 1924, 1957), 2 vols., of which the first is largely a translation of Pfeiffer; R. M. Blackney, *Meister Eckhart, A Modern Translation* (New York and London: Harper, 1941); J. M. Clark, *Meister Eckhart, An Introduction to the Study of His Works with an Anthology of His Sermons* (Edinburgh and London: Thomas Nelson and Sons, 1957); good exposition as well as translations.

Studies

J. M. Clark, *The Great German Mystics* (Oxford: Blackwell, 1949), has especially interesting material on "The Friends of God." See also G. M. Gieraths, *Reichtum des Lebens; Die deutsche Dominikanermystik des XIV, Jahrhunderts* (Düsseldorf: Albertus Magnus Verlag, 1959), with texts; Martin Grabmann, *Die Kulturwerte der deutschen Mystik des Mittelalters* (Augsburg: Filser, 1923); and M. A. Lücker, *Meister Eckhart und die Devotio moderna* (Leyden: J. J. Brill, 1950). B. J. Muller-Thym, *The Establishment of the University of Being in the Doctrine of Meister Eckhart of Hochheim* is concerned primarily with Eckhart's scholastic philosophy. Wilhelm Preger's *Geschichte der deutschen Mystik im Mittelalter*, I, 309–488, contains documents on Eckhart's trial. See also Martin Grabmann, "Die deutsche Frauenmystik des Mittelalters," in *Mittelalterliches Geistesleben*, pp. 469–488.

Chapter IV. Nicholas of Cusa

Works and Translations

Opera, 3 vols. (Paris, 1514; reprinted, Frankfurt, 1962; *Opera omnia*, being published by the Heidelberg Academy of Science (Leipzig: Meiner, 1932–), and *Schriften* in a bilingual edition edited by Paul Wilpert (Hamburg: Felix Meiner, 1964–), are still incomplete.

See also *Of Learned Ignorance*, trans. Germain Heron (New Haven: Yale University Press, 1954); *The Vision of God*, trans. Emma G. Salter, with an Introduction by Evelyn Underhill (London: J. M. Dent, 1928). *Unity and Reform*, trans. and ed. J. P. Dolan (Notre Dame, Ind.: Notre Dame University Press, 1962) contains selections from the previous two works and *On Wisdom, On Concord in Religion*, and *On an Experiment in Weight*. Two sermons are translated in *Late Medieval Mysticism*, ed. R. C. Petry (Philadelphia: Westminster Press, 1957).

Studies

Henry Brett, *Nicholas of Cusa* (London: Methues, 1932) is the most comprehensive and best balanced study in English. Ernst Cassirer, *The Individual and the Cosmos in Renaissance Philosophy* (New York, Harper & Row, 1963), is a splendid study of the entire period, seeing Nicholas as a central figure in it (perhaps a bit too much so). Karl Jaspers, *Nicolaus Cusanus* (Munich: Piper, 1964), is a deep work showing both Jaspers and Nicholas at their best. Paul E. Sigmund, *Nicholas of Cusa and Medieval*

Political Thought (Cambridge: Harvard University Press, 1963), is good on this phase. Edmond Vansteenberghe, *Le Cardinal Nicolas de Cues* (Paris: Champion, 1920), is perhaps the most comprehensive study. Eduard Zellinger, *Cusanus-Konkordanz* (Munich: Hueber, 1960), is highly useful as a reference book. An especially beautiful book containing facsimiles and fascinating illustrations is Gerd Heinz-Mohr and W. P. Eckert, *Das Werk Nicolaus Cusanus* (Cologne: Wienand Verlag, 1963). W. H. Hay, "Nicolaus Cusanus: The Structure of His Philosophy in "*Philosophical Review*, 41: 14–25 (1952), is instructive on the theory of remission of forms. Rudolf Stadelmann, *Vom Geist des ausgehenden Mittelalters* (1929; reprint, Stuttgart: Fromann, 1966), pictures Nicholas of Cusa's philosophy as symptomatic of a breakdown of the great medieval syntheses and intellectual confidence, and traces his influence (or at least the perseveration of his "type") in the continued "waning of the Middle Ages" in the writings of Agrippa of Nettesheim and Sebastian Franck, where it appears in the characteristic phases of subjectivism, pessimism, and a sense of crisis. Stadelmann's theses have been examined in *Coincidentia oppositorum* (Witten: Luther Verlag, 1961), by Erwin Metzke, who argues that Stadelmann has overemphasized the negative, backward-looking passive factors in the writings of these men. On the Platonism of Nicholas of Cusa and the mystics, see the short paper by Maurice Gandillac, "Le Platonisme en Allemagne aux XIVe et XVe siecles," in *Actes du Congrés de Tours et Poitiers* (Paris: Société d'édition "Les Belles Lettres," 1954) pp. 372–375.

Chapter V. Nominalism and the Rise of University-Philosophy

Ernest A. Moody, "Empiricism and Metaphysics in Medieval Philosophy" *Philosophical Review*, 67: 145–163 (1958), disputes the widespread identification of the "decline of scholasticism" with the "rise of nominalism." The thesis of this stimulating paper affected the composition of Chapter V.

On the Founding of the Universities

Herbert Grundmann, *Vom Ursprung der Universitäten im Mittelalter* (Darmstadt: Wissenschaftliche Buchgesellschaft, 1960), is a brief exposition of specifically secular elements in early university history. Georg Kaufmann, *Geschichte der deutschen Universitäten*, 2 vols. (Stuttgart, 1888–96), and Friedrich Paulsen, *Geschichte des gelehrten Unterrichts*, are standard studies. Most universities have their own histories; those of Heidelberg and Tubingen are most relevant to the subjects of this chapter: Heinrich Hermelink, *Die theologische Fakultät in Tübingen vor der Reformation* (Tübingen: Mohr, 1906), is especially valuable. For a general survey of philosophical curricula, see F. W. Dediger, *Über die Bildung der Geistlichen im späten Mittelalter* (Leiden: E. J. Brill, 1953), especially chap. ii.

On the *Viae*

The standard work is Gerhard Ritter, *Studien zur Spätscholastik. I. Marsilius von Inghen und die Okkamistische Schule in Deutschland. II. Via Antiqua und Via moderna auf den deutschen Universitäten* (*Sitzungsbe-*

richte der Heidelberger Akademie der Wissenschaften, Phil.-Hist. Klasse, 4. and 7. Abh., 1921–22.) Volume II has been published as a separate work (Darmstadt: Wissenschaftliche Buchgesellschaft, 1963). See also Franz Ehrle, S.J., *Der Sentenzkommentar Peters von Candia* (Münster: Franziskanische Studien, 1925). Karl Prantl, in *Geschichte der Logik* (reprint, Leipzig: Fock, 1927), has much information which must be taken account of, but I have disagreed with his interpretation. Three important books came to hand too late for me to make full use of them in my discussion of the *viae*. Gilles Meersseman, O.P., *Geschichte des Albertismus*, already referred to in the bibliography to Chapter II, discusses the controversies among the *antiqui* in Paris (vol. I) and Cologne (vol. II), where Thomists, Albertists, and Occamists were engaged in a three-way controversy. K. A. Sprengard's *Systematisch-historische Untersuchungen zur Philosophie des XIV. Jahrhunderts* (Bonn: Bouvier Verlag, 1967), published too late to be of use to me, carefully delineates (in chap. vii) the diversity of movements called "nominalism" and describes and assesses various historical conceptions of the *viae* (by Duhem, Hermelink, Ritter, and Prantl). Less instructive, but of some interest because of its detailed and vigorous critique of Prantl and Hermelink, is Friedrich Benary, "Via antiqua und Via moderna auf den deutschen Hochschulen des Mittelalters mit besonderer Berücksichtigung der Universität Erfurt," in *Zur Geschichte der Stadt und der Universität Erfurt am Ausgang des Mittelalters* (Gotha: Perthe Verlag, 1919), pp. 1–72. The somewhat unclear and not wholly convincing distinction between the *viae* as coinciding with that between the "a priori method" and the "a posteriori method" mentioned in the text on p. 80, is found in this work.

On scientific work by German nominalists, see Pierre Duhem, *Système du monde* (Paris: Hermann, 1954–59), passim. For a less favorable estimation see Anneliese Maier, *Ausgehendes Mittelalter* (Rome: Edizioni di storia e letteratura, 1964), I, 413–424.

On the theology, see H. A. Oberman, "Some Notes on the Theology of Nominalism," *Harvard Theological Review*, 53:46–76 (1960), and his magisterial study of Gabriel Biel, *The Harvest of Medieval Theology* (Cambridge: Harvard University Press, 1963). Bengt Hägglund's *Theologie und Philosophie bei Luther und in der Okkamistischen Tradition* (Lund: Gleerup, 1935) is excellent.

PART TWO: FROM LUTHER TO LEIBNIZ

Dependable histories of the entire period are Hajo Holborn, *History of Modern Germany*, vol. I, and G. R. Elton, *Reformation Europe* (London: Collins, 1963). Wilhelm Dilthey's *Weltanschauung und Analyse des Menschen seit Renaissance und Reformation* and *Das Erziehungssystem und die pädogogischen Theorien der modernen europäischen Völker*, vols. II and IX (*Gesammelte Schriften*, Leipzig and Berlin: Teubner, 1923–) are the classical studies of the *Weltanschauung*, but now somewhat dated. On church history, the English books I have profited most from are K. D. Macmillan's *Protestantism in Germany* (Princeton, N.J.: Princeton University Press, 1917), and A. L. Drummond's *German Protestantism Since Luther* (London: Epworth Press, 1951), though each must be supplemented by more detailed work on each specific topic. On the philosophers of the entire period, Peter Petersen's *Geschichte der aristotelischen Philosophie im protestantischen Deutschland* (1921; reprint, Stuttgart: Frommann, 1964) is an indispensable work.

But in contrast there are the views of John Herman Randall, Jr., in his comprehensive history, *The Career of Philosophy* vol. I (New York: Columbia University Press, 1962). In his well-known rubrics, Randall gives the Augustinian-Neoplatonic theme a nuclear position in the German intellectual history of this period, especially among the reformers themselves. In this connection, see also the article by Maurice de Gandillac referred to at the end of the Bibliography to Chapter IV above.

Chapter VI. Philosophy of the Reformation

Humanism

A standard, richly illustrated, older work, is Ludwig Geiger, *Renaissance und Humanismus in Italien und Deutschland* (Berlin, 1882), vol. II. The most comprehensive recent work in English is L. W. Spitz, *The Religious Renaissance of the German Humanists* (Cambridge: Harvard University Press, 1963). On the religious uniqueness of German humanism, see Gerhard Ritter, *Die geschichtliche Bedeutung des deutschen Humanismus* (1923; reprint, Darmstadt: Wissenschaftliche Buchgesellschaft, 1965), and Paul Mestwerdt, *Die Anfänge des Erasmus: Humanismus und Devotio moderna* (Leipzig: R. Haupt, 1917). H. A. Enno van Gelder, in *The Two Reformations of the Sixteenth Century* (The Hague: Nijhoff, 1964), argues, on the other hand, that the "humanist reformation" was the major intellectual event of the century and had little to do with Luther's "minor reformation." Heinrich Hermelink's thesis (*Die theologische Fakultät in Tübingen vor der Reformation*, p. 97 and passim) that humanism was a continuation along the *via antiqua* and that its opposition to scholasticism was primarily to the *via moderna* is implausible. Humanists opposed the "scholastic enterprise" altogether, and not just one set of its partisans. At least in the terminology of some humanist polemics against the Cologne *antiqui*, some humanists even associated themselves with the other enemies of the Cologne faculty, viz., the *moderni*. See the documentation in K.-H. Gerschemann, "'Antiqui-Novi-Moderni' in den 'Epistolae obscurorum vivorum'," *Archiv für Begriffsgeschichte*, vol. II (1967), pt. 1, pp. 23–36.

On the concept of renaissance and humanism, see Wallace K. Ferguson, *The Renaissance in Historical Thought* (Boston and New York: Houghton Mifflin, 1948) and Paul Oskar Kristeller, *Renaissance Thought, The Classic, Scholastic, and Humanist Strains* (New York: Harper, 1961).

Luther

Works

The standard edition of Luther's works is the still incomplete *Kritische Gesamtausgabe* in over ninety volumes (Weimar, 1883–   ). The best translation, still incomplete, is *Works*, ed. by Jaroslav Pelikan (St. Louis: Concordia, 1966–). Since it is incomplete I have had to cite several other editions in the footnotes. A good selection in German is in vol. II of the series, *Classiker des Protestantismus*, ed. Franz Lau (Bremen: Dieterich, 1964).

Studies

Bengt Hägglund, *Theologie und Philosophie bei Luther in der Okkamistischen Tradition*, contrasts Lutheran and Occamistic conceptions of the role of reason in theology. The fullest study of this problem in English is B. A. Gerrish, *Grace and Reason* (Oxford: Clarendon Press, 1962), which defends Luther from the accusation of "irrationalism." Two studies of Luther's place in the history of philosophy are Heinrich Bornkamm, *Luther im Spiegel der deutschen Gesistesgeschichte* (Heidelberg: Quelle und Meyer, 1955), and Erwin Metzke, "Lutherforschung und deutsche Philosophiegeschichte," *Blätter für deutsche Philosophie*, 8:355–382 (1934–35).

Melanchthon

The complete works are in *Corpus Reformatorum*, 36 vols. (Halle, 1834–). The few works translated into English are identified in the text. Life and works are surveyed in Karl Hartfelder, *Philipp [sic] Melanchthon als Praeceptor Germaniae* (1889; reprint, Nieuwkoop: de Graaf, 1964), and more briefly in J. W. Richard, *Philip Melanchthon, the Protestant Preceptor of Germany* (New York: Putnam, 1907). Charles L. Hill, *Exposition and Critical Estimate of the Philosophy of Melanchthon*, unpubl. diss., Ohio State University, 1938, is available only on microfilm but repays study. Petersen, *Geschichte der aristotelischen Philosophie. . .* , is unsurpassed in exposition; Wilhelm Risse, *Geschichte der Logik*, vol. 1: *Die Logik der Neuzeit* (Stuttgart, 1964), chap. ii, is instructive in relating Melanchthon to other logicians. Wilhelm Mauer, "Melanchthon und die Naturwissenschaft seiner Zeit," *Archiv für Kulturgeschichte*, XLII–XLIII (1961–62), pp. 199–226, explains Melanchthon's attitude to Copernicus. Quirinus Breen, "The Two-fold Truth Theory in Melanchthon," *Review of Religion* 9:113–136 (1944–45), is important in all discussion of the relation of philosophy to theology during this period. Though Robert Stupperich is the leading Melanchthon scholar, his *Melanchthon: The Enigma of the Reformation*, trans. R. H. Fischer (London: Lutterworth Press, 1960), is regrettably without value to the student of philosophy.

Calvin

I do not know of any good and comprehensive study of Calvin's philosophy and it has been denied that he had one. But see five works which indicate that a full study of Calvin as a philosopher would be a valuable contribution: Quirinus Breen, *John Calvin, A Study of French Humanism* unpubl. diss., University of Chicago, 1931; E. A. Dowey, Jr., *The Knowledge of God in Calvin's Theology* (New York: Columbia University Press, 1952); T. F. Torrance, *Calvin's Doctrine of Man* (London: Lutterworth, 1949); François Wendel, *Calvin, sources et évolution de sa pensée re-*

ligieuse (Paris, 1950; trans. P. Mairet, New York: Harper & Row, 1963); and Josef Bohatec, *Budé und Calvin* (1943; reprint Graz: H. Böhlaus, 1950). The last-named work, pp. 263–270, discusses Calvin's views on natural science and much-disputed question concerning the relations between Calvinism and the scientific revolution. I found Schneckenburger [no first name on title page], *Vergleichende Darstellung des lutherischen und reformirten Lehrbegriffs* (Stuttgart, 1855) instructive. John T. McNeill, *The History and Character of Calvinism* (New York: Oxford University Press, 1954), gives the most essential historical facts about the spread of Calvinism.

Chapter VII. The Philosophy of Protestant Orthodoxy

Inexhaustible sources of information on philosophy in the Age of Orthodoxy are Petersen's *Geschichte der aristotelischen Philosophie im protestantischen Deutschland* and Max Wundt's *Die deutsche Schulmetaphysik des 17. Jahrhunderts* (Tübingen: Mohr, 1939). More restricted in scope is Wilhelm Risse's *Die Logik der Neuzeit.* Risse's *Bibliographica logica:* vol. I: *Verzeichnis der Druckschriften zur Logik mit Angabe ihrer Fundorte, 1472–1800* (Hildesheim: Olms, 1965), is essential for further *Quellengeschichte.*

Ramus

The standard study in English is W. J. Ong, S.J., *Ramus, Method and Decay of Dialogue* and *Ramus and Talon Inventory* (both Cambridge: Harvard University Press, 1958). F. P. Graves, *Peter Ramus and the Educational Reform of the Sixteenth Century* (New York: Macmillan, 1912) is good. Some material on Ramus and Ramists in Germany will be found in Neal W. Gilbert, *Renaissance Concepts of Method* (New York: Columbia University Press, 1960), esp. chaps. v, vi and x. Most instructive for the purposes of this book was Jürgen Moltmann, "Zur Bedeutung des Petrus Ramus für die Philosophie und Theologie im Calvanismus," *Zeitschrift fur Kirchengeschichte*, 68:295–318 (1957).

Taurellus

Petersen, *Geschichte der aristotelischen Philosophie in protestantischen Deutschland,* pp. 219–258, is the most complete account and makes Taurellus a real hero of Aristotelianism. Hans-Christian Mayer, "Ein Altdorfer Philosophen-Porträt," in *Zeitschrift für bayerische Kirchengeschichte,* 29:145–166 (1960), gives more attention to his theology and thus minimizes his Aristotelianism.

Protestant Scholasticism

F. A. Tholuck, *Vorgeschichte des Rationalismus*, 2 vols. (Halle, 1853 and 1862) is old but very comprehensive. Another old but still instructive study is "The Rise of Protestant Scholasticism" in Charles Beard's *The Reforma-*

tion of the Sixteenth Century (1883; reprint, Ann Arbor: University of Michigan Press, 1962), though Beard was more concerned with the "scholasticization" of Protestant theology itself than with the development of a scholastic philosophy as an underpinning for theology. Closer attention is given to the interplay between philosophy and theology in Hans Leube, *Calvinismus und Lutherthum im Zeitalter der Orthodoxie* (1928; Aalen: Scientia, 1965), and Paul Althaus, *Die Prinzipien der deutschen reformierten Dogmatik im Zeitalter der aristotelischen Scholastik* (Leipzig: Deichert, 1914; reprint, Darmstadt: Wissenschaftliche Buchgesellschaft, 1967). The standard and indispensable history of the philosophy of the movement is Wundt's *Die deutsche Schulmetaphysik des 17. Jahrhunderts.* Good, but without Wundt's inexhaustible detail is Emil Weber, *Die philosophische Scholastik des Protestantismus im Zeitalter der Orthodoxie* (Leipzig: Quelle und Meyer, 1907). How things went in a single university is described in Max Wundt's *Die Philosophie an der Universität Jena* (Jena: Gustav Fischer, 1932).

The Spanish influence has been extensively studied. The most important works on it are: Jose Ferrater Mora, "Suarez and Modern Philosophy," *Journal of the History of Ideas.* 14:528–547 (1953); Karl Eschweiler, *Die Philosophie der spanischen Spätscholastik auf den deutschen Universitäten des 17. Jahrhunderts,"* (*Spanische Forschungen der Görresgesellschaft,* Münster, 1928); Ernst Lewalter, *Spanisch-Jesuitische und Deutsch-Lutherische Metaphysik des 17. Jahrhunderts* (Hamburg, 1935; Darmstadt: Wissenschaftliche Buchgesellschaft, 1967); and Paul Mesnard, "Comment Leibniz se trouve placé dans le sillage de Suarez," *Archives de philosophie,* 18:7–32 (1949). H. J. de Vleeschauwer, "Cornelius Martini en de ontwikkeling van de protestantsche Metaphysica in Duitschland," *Mededeelingen van de Koninklijke Academie voor Wetenschappen, Klasse der Litteren,* I (1940), 3–22, is somewhat unrewarding.

Giorgio Tonelli has shown in "Das Wiederaufleben der deutsch-aristotelischen Terminologie bei Kant" (*Archiv für Begriffsgeschichte,* 9:223–242 [1964]), that Kant preferred "to call upon an old and honorable tradition, the Aristotelian, whose terminology was no longer current but still quite well known in the schools," and thus how, through Kant, the terminology of the Protestant scholastics entered upon a new life in philosophy long after the movement itself had died.

Social Philosophy

Besides Weber's work, cited in the text, the fullest study of social philosophy is Ernst Troeltsch, *The Social Teachings of the Christian Churches,* trans. Olive Wyon (New York: Macmillan, 1931), vol. II, and his *Aufsätze zur Geistesgeschichte und Religionssoziologie* (*Gesammelte Schriften,* vol. IV [Tübingen: J. C. B. Mohr, 1925]). On the Weber thesis, see R. W. Green, ed., *Protestantism and Capitalism: The Weber Thesis and its Critics* (Boston: D. C. Heath, 1959), and Michael Walzer, *The Revolution of the Saints* (Cambridge: Harvard University Press, 1965); H. R. Trevor-Roper, *The Crisis of the Seventeenth Century* (New York: Harper & Row, 1968).

J. W. Allen, *Political Thought of the Sixteenth Century* (London: Longmans Green, 1928), is standard and encyclopedic.

Otto Gierke's *Natural Law and the Theory of Society*, trans. Sir Ernest Barker, 2 vols. (Cambridge: The University Press, 1934), is the work in which Althusius was, so to speak, rediscovered. Besides the translation by C. J. Friedrich (Cambridge: Harvard University Press, 1932), see the abridgment and introduction in *The Politics of Johannes Althusius* by F. S. Carney (London: Eyre and Spottiswood, 1964). Erich Cassirer, *Natur- und Völkerrecht im Lichte der Geschichte* (1919; reprinted, Aalen: Scientia Verlag, 1963), chap. iii on Althusius.

Chapter VIII. Occultism, Spiritualism, and Pietism

Rudolf Stadelmann's *Vom Geist des ausgehenden Mittelalters* (Halle: Fromann, 1929) is of utmost importance on the entire subject of this chapter. See the note on this book and the criticism by Metzke in the bibliography to Chapter IV. On Franck, Paracelsus, and Valentin Weigel see Alexandre Koyré, *Mystiques, spirituels, alchimistes* (Paris: Colin, 1955); on Cusanus, Paracelsus, and Kepler see Rudolf Eucken, *Beiträge zur Einführung in die Geschichte der Philosophie*, vol. 1: *Forschungen zur älteren deutschen Philosophie* (Leipzig, 1906).

Agrippa of Nettesheim

Charles G. Nauert, Jr.'s "Magic and Skepticism in Agrippa's Thought," *Journal of the History of Ideas*, 18:161–182 (1957), and *Agrippa and the Crisis of Renaissance Thought* (Urbana: University of Illinois Press, 1965) render everything else in English obsolete. See also the review of Nauert's book by L. W. Spitz in *Journal of the History of Ideas*, 27:464–469 (1966), which shows only that Nauert's book is not *quite* perfect, and R. H. Popkin, *History of Skepticism from Erasmus to Descartes* (New York: Humanities Press, 1964). Erwin Metzke, *Coincidentia oppositorum* (Witten: Luther Verlag, 1961) gives more emphasis (too much, in my opinion) to religious motives in Agrippa. On the early history of the Faust legend, see E. M. Butler, *The Fortunes of Faust* (Cambridge [Eng.] University Press, 1952).

Paracelsus

The literature is so large, and most of it so poor, that one hesitates in making recommendations. Works: *Hermetical and Alchemical Writings*, 2 vols., trans. A. E. Waite (New Hyde Park, N.Y.: University Books, 1966); *Selected Writings*, ed., Jolande Jacobi (New York, Bollingen Series no. 28, 1958); *Sozialethische und sozialpolitische Schriften*, ed., K. Goldhammer (Tübingen: J. C. B. Mohr, 1952). Studies: J. M. Stillman, *Paracelsus* (Chicago: Open Court, 1920), and H. M. Pachter, *Paracelsus* (New York: Schumann, 1951), are somewhat unsophisticated. Most rewarding to me personally was J. R. Partington, *A History of Chemistry* (New York: St. Martin's Press, 1961), vol. II, chap. iii, and Heinz Heimsoeth, "Paracelsus als Philosoph," *Kant-Studien Ergänzungsheft* 82:111–119 (1961).

Sebastian Franck

Gesamtausgabe, ed. W. Zeller (Stuttgart: Hertzberger, 1966–). Selections have been translated by G. H. Williams in *Spiritual and Anabaptist Writers* (Philadelphia: Westminster Press, 1957). There are good accounts in Rufus Jones, *Spiritual Reformers of the Sixteenth and Seventeenth Centuries* (London: Macmillan, 1914), and G. H. Williams, *The Radical Reformation* (Philadelphia: Westminster Press, 1962). The most penetrating single study is Alfred Hegler's *Geist und Schrift bei Sebastian Franck* (Freiburg, 1892). More recent scholarship is reported in Eberhard Teufel, "Sebastian Franck im Lichte der neueren Forschung," *Theologische Rundschau,* n.s., XII (1940), 99–129, but Hegler's work still stands.

Valentin Weigel

Sämmtliche Schriften, ed. Willerich Peuckert and Winfried Zeller (Stuttgart-Bad Cannstadt: Fromann, 1962–). Selections have been translated in G. H. Williams, *Spiritual and Anabaptist Writers;* and Jones, *Spiritual Reformers of the Sixteenth and Seventeenth Centuries,* has a good chapter. H. Längin, "Grundlagen der Erkenntnistheorie Valentin Weigels," *Archiv für die Geschichte der Philosophie,* 41:435–478 (1932), was essential in my study of Weigel's theory of knowledge.

Böhme

Sämmtliche Schriften (Amsterdam, 1730) has been reprinted in 11 volumes (Stuttgart, 1955–61). About a dozen works have been translated into English. The best studies are Alexandre Koyré, *La Philosophie de Jacob Böhme* (Paris: Urin, 1929); J. J. Stoudt, *Sunrise to Eternity* (Philadelphia: University of Pennsylvania Press, 1957); and Rufus Jones, *Spiritual Reformers of the Sixteenth and Seventeenth Centuries,* chaps. ix–xi.

Pietism

The standard work is Albrecht Ritschl, *Geschichte des Pietismus,* 3 vols. (Bonn, 1880), which emphasizes too much the Dutch-Calvinist influences. A. L. Drummond, *German Protestantism since Luther* (London: Epworth Press, 1951), ch. iii, is perhaps the best in English. Marianne Beyer-Fröhlich's anthology, *Pietismus und Rationalismus* (Leipzig: Reclam, 1933), contains some important later texts. Ernst Troeltsch's well-known critical views on the Pietistic movement can be found in his *Social Teachings of the Christian Churches,* II, 714–21, 784–88, and passim.

Chapter IX. The Natural Philosophers and the Cartesianism

There seems to be no comprehensive history of natural philosophy and early German science. Carl Siegel, *Geschichte der deutschen Naturphilosophie* (Leipzig: Akademische Verlagsgesellschaft, 1913), is much too brief on the early period. Chapters here and there in Lynn Thorndike's *History of Magic and Experimental Science,* 7 vols. (New York: Columbia Univer-

sity Press, 1940–) contain vast amounts of not very well-digested information, so that no clear over-all picture of the situation in Germany
emerges. Martha Ornstein's *The Role of Scientific Societies in the Seventeenth Century*, 3rd ed. (Chicago: University of Chicago Press, 1938),
contains interesting but somewhat peripheral information in chaps. vi, vii,
and viii; it has the merit of bringing out quite definitely the geographical
and political factors.

The most difficult concept in this chapter is that of nature, and the
changes in this concept have been fully studied in other countries. An
article which fortunately deals with the developments in Germany leading
to the Sturm-Schelhammer controversy is by H. M. Nobis, "Frühzeitliche
Verständnisweisen der Natur und ihr Wandel bis zum 18. Jahrhundert,"
Archiv für Begriffsgeschichte, 11:37–58 (1967). The immediately following
article, "Genetisches zum Naturbegriff des 18. Jahrhunderts" by Robert
Spaemann (*ibid.*, pp. 59–71) continues the story but also contributes to
the understanding of the debate in the 1690's.

The Astronomers

Works of Copernicus have been translated in *Three Copernican Trea-
tises*, trans. Edward Rosen (New York: Columbia University Press, 1957);
Source Book of Astronomy, ed. Harlow Shapley and Helen E. Howarth
(New York: McGraw Hill, 1929); and *Theories of the Universe*, ed. M. K.
Munitz (Glencoe: The Free Press, 1957). The latter two contain transla-
tions also from Kepler. Kepler's *Somnium* has been translated by Edward
Rosen (Madison University of Wisconsin Press, 1967). Important studies
are: Thomas S. Kuhn, *The Copernican Revolution* (Cambridge: Harvard
University Press, 1957); Alexandre Koyré, *From the Closed World to the
Infinite Universe* (Baltimore: Johns Hopkins Press, 1957); Ernst Cassirer,
*Das Erkenntnisproblem in der Philosophie und Wissenschaft der neueren
Zeit* (Berlin: Bruno Cassirer, 1922), I, 271–377; and E. A. Burtt, *The Meta-
physical Foundations of Modern Physical Science* (New York: Harcourt
Brace, 1927), especially chap. ii. See also N. R. Hanson, "The Copernican
Disturbance and the Keplerian Revolution," *Journal of the History of Ideas*,
22:169–184 (1961), of which the title indicates the thesis. Arthur Koestler's
life of Kepler, *The Sleepwalkers* (New York: Macmillan, 1959) and his
article on Kepler in *The Encyclopedia of Philosophy* should be consulted,
the first with pleasure but also some caution. On Bruno, see Heinz Heimsoeth, "Bruno and die deutsche Philosophie," *Blätter für deutsche Philosophie*, 15:396–433 (1942).

The Atomists

Kurd Lasswitz, *Geschichte der Atomistik vom Mittelalter bis Newton*,
2 vols. (1st ed. 1890; reprint, Hildesheim: G. Olms, 1963), is the standard
work. J. R. Partington, *A History of Chemistry*, vol. II, is accurate and
detailed. Walter Böhm, *Die Naturwissenschaftler und ihre Philosophie:
Geistesgeschichte der Chemie* (Vienna: Herder, 1961), has valuable material in a somewhat dilute solution.

Jungius' *Logica hamburgensis* exists in a modern reprint (Hamburg, 1957); it has been studied by Earline Jennifer Ashworth in *The Logica Hamburgensis of Joachim Jungius*, unpubl. Diss., Bryn Mawr College, 1964, and in "Joachim Jungius and the Logic of Relations," *Archiv für die Geschichte der Philosophie*, 49:72–85 (1967). *Die Entfaltung der Wissenschaft* (Hamburg: J. J. Augustin, 1957) contains several papers which survey the many-sided work of Jungius. See also Adolf Meyer-Abich, "Joachim Jungius, ein Philosoph vor Leibniz," in *Beiträge zur Leibniz-Forschung*, ed. Georgi Schischkoff (Reutlingen: Gryphius Verlag, 1947), pp. 138–152.

The Cartesians

Joseph Bohatec, *Die Cartesianische Scholastik in der Philosophie und reformierten Dogmatik des 17. Jahrhunderts* (Leipzig, 1912; reprinted Hildesheim: G. Olms, 1966), is the essential work but unfortunately only volume I was ever published. Paul Althaus, *Die Prinzipien der deutschen reformierten Dogmatik im Zeitalter der aristotelischen Scholastik*, chap. vii, is good on the impact of Cartesianism on Calvinism. Herbert Schöffler, *Deutsche Geistesgeschichte zwischen Reformation und Aufklärung* (Frankfort: Klostermann, 1956), is important for its study of intellectual connections between Leyden and the Eastern parts of Germany. Moritz Hagemann's *Descartes in der Auffassung durch die Historiker der Philosophie* (Winterthur: Keller, 1955) is detailed on the eighteenth century but is not without value for the seventeenth in Germany.

On Clauberg, see Francisque Bouillier, *Histoire de la philosophie cartesienne*, 3rd ed. 2 vols. (Paris, 1868), and A. G. A. Balz, *Cartesian Studies* (New York: Columbia University Press, 1951), pp. 158–194. On the small effect of Cartesian on scholastic ontology, see Italo Mancini, "L'Ontosofia di Clauberg e i primi tentativi di sostituzione cartesiana," in *Festschrift H. J. de Vleeschauwer* (Pretoria: University of South Africa, 1960), pp. 63–83.

On Sturm, Georg Baku ,"Der Streit über den Naturbegriff am Ende des 17. Jahrhunderts," *Zeitschrift für Philosophie und philosophische Kritik*, 98:162–190 (1890), is of considerable interest, though I diverge from his interpretation. See also the articles by Nobis and Spaemann referred to in the second paragraph of the Bibliography on this chapter.

von Tschirnhaus

The editions and translations of the works of von Tschirnhaus are cited on p. 189. Studies of his life and philosophy are: Ernst Cassirer, *Das Erkenntnisproblem* . . . , II, 191–201; Johannes Verweyen, *E. W. von Tschirnhaus als Philosoph* (Diss., Bonn, 1905); Eduard Winter, ed., *E. W. von Tschirnhaus und die Frühaufklärung in Mittel- und Ost-Europa* (Berlin: Akademie Verlag, 1960); and Giorgio Radetti, "Cartesianismo e spinozismo nel pensiero del Tschirnhausen [sic]," *Travaux du IXᵉ Congrès de Philosophie* (Paris, 1937), III, 32–36. Unfortunately Risse, in his *Die Logik der Neuzeit*, has not yet reached Clauberg's and von Tschirnhaus' logics.

Erhard Weigel

The only works I could procure are *Arithmetische Beschreibung der Moral-Wissenschaft* (1674) and *Philosophia mathematica theologica naturalis* (1693). Georg Wagner, *Erhard Weigel, ein Erzieher aus dem XVII. Jahrhundert* (Diss., Leipzig, 1903), deals in great detail with Weigel's theory of education, in which mathematics was to be the basic discipline, but gives very little of his philosophy; this dissertation contains a valuable bibliography from which one must begin in searching for his works. F. Bartholomai, "Erhard Weigel, Ein Beitrag zur Geschichte der Philosophie auf den protestantischen Universitäten im 17. Jahrhundert," *Zeitschrift für die exakte Philosophie*, 19:250–275 (1871), gives a rather meager account of Weigel's philosophy and makes one suspect that there is not much more to be said; but the still briefer report in Max Wundt's *Die Philosophie an der Universität Jena* (Jena: Gustav Fischer, 1932), with a nice portrait, whets one's appetite.

Chapter X. Leibniz

Editions

There is no complete edition of Leibniz' work, and vast amounts of his writings have never been published in any form. The edition of the Prussian (now "German") Academy of Sciences (Darmstadt: Reichl, 1923–) had reached thirteen volumes by 1967. Until the completion of that vast work, the standard edition will remain C. J. Gerhart, *Die philosophischen Schriften*, 7 vols. (Berlin, 1875–90). Other useful editions are Artur Buchenau and Ernst Cassirer, *Philosophische Werke*, 6 vols., (Leipzig: Meiner, 1924–1926; now in paperback), and H. H. Holz, *Philosophische Schriften* (Darmstadt: Wissenschaftliche Buchgesellschaft, 1961– ; 2 vols. by 1968).

Translations

The most comprehensive translation of Leibniz' works is that of L. E. Loemker, which has been repeatedly cited in the text. There are many collections of works in translation, largely overlapping, by G. M. Duncan (New Haven: Yale University Press, 1908), Robert Latta (Oxford: Clarendon Press, 1898), G. M. Montgomery (Chicago: Open Court, 1902, 1924), Mary Morris (London: Dent, 1934), Paul Schrecker (Indianapolis: Bobbs-Merrill, 1965), and P. P. Wiener (New York: Scribner, 1951). Translations of the *Correspondence with Samuel Clarke* and the *New Essays* have been cited with full bibliographical details in the text; a new translation of the *Correspondence* by H. T. Mason has been published since this chapter was written (Manchester, [Eng.], Manchester University Press, 1967); also, since this chapter was completed, there has been a translation of Leibniz' logical works by G. R. H. Parkinson (Oxford: Clarendon Press, 1966).

Bibliography

Émile Ravier, *Bibliographie des œuvres de Leibniz* (Paris: Alcan, 1937), is essential on the publication history of each piece of Leibniz' writings.

Kurt Müller, *Leibniz Bibilographie* (Frankfort: Klostermann, 1967), covers less fully the vast secondary literature. Two critical surveys of recent literature are L. E. Loemker, "Leibniz in Our Time," *Philosophische Rundschau*, 13:81–111 (1965), and E. Cione, "La fortuna postuma di Leibniz," *Filosofia e Vita*, 5:45–63 (1964); 6:74–96 (1965), the latter containing some less useful surveys of the older literature.

Studies

G. E. Guhrauer, *Gottfried Wilhelm Freiherr von Leibniz*, 2 vols. (Breslau, 1842), is the standard biography but now out of date. Kuno Fischer's *Gottfried Wilhelm von Leibniz*, especially in the fifth edition (1920) with new material added by Willy Kabitz, is now the best source on Leibniz' life, and is excellent also on all aspects of his thought. A sumptuous volume, *Leibniz, Sein Leben–Sein Wirken–Seine Welt*, ed. Wilhelm Totok and Carl Haase (Hanover: Verlag für Literatur und Zeitgeschehen, 1966), came too late to be of help to me but should be a source of information and delight to others. The paper on Leibniz as metaphysician is by Wolfgang Janke.

The great classical studies of Leibniz' philosophy are: Ernst Cassirer, *Leibniz' System in seinen wissenschaftlichen Grundlagen* (Marburg: Elwert, 1902); Fischer, cited above; Bertrand Russell, *A Critical Exposition of the Philosophy of Leibniz* (London: Allen & Unwin, 1900, 1937); and Louis Couturat, *La Logique de Leibniz* (Paris, 1901; reprint, Hildesheim: Olms, 1961) –the last having a far too restrictive title. All except Fischer emphasize the logical and methodological aspects of Leibniz' philosophy.

More recent surveys of Leibniz' philosophy as a whole are Pierre Burgelin, *Commentaire du Discours de métaphysique* (Paris: Presses Universitaires de France, 1959), which, because of the central place of the *Discourse* of 1686, serves as a valuable study of all parts of Leibniz' metaphysics; Kurt Huber, *Leibniz* (Munich: Oldenbourg, 1951), written in a Nazi prison while Huber was awaiting execution for anti-Nazi activities; Gottfried Martin, *Leibniz: Logik und Metaphysik* (Cologne, 1960; Eng. trans. by K. J. Norrott and P. G. Lucas as *Leibniz: Logic and Metaphysics* [Manchester: Manchester University Press, 1964]). The second edition (Berlin: De Gruyter, 1964) contains important new material on the relations of Wolff and Kant to Leibniz' theory of judgment. See also G. R. H. Parkinson, *Logic and Reality in Leibniz' Metaphysics* (Oxford: Clarendon Press, 1965); Nicholas Rescher, *The Philosophy of Leibniz* (Englewood Cliffs, N.J.: Prentice-Hall, 1967); and Ruth Lydia Saw, *Leibniz* (London: Penguin Books, 1954). The beginner will find the last two most instructive. H. H. Holz, *Leibniz* (Stuttgart: Kohlhammer, 1958) is unique in seeing adumbrations of dialectical materialism in Leibniz.

Works that make important contributions to our understanding of Leibniz in his historical position are the classical work of Dilthey, *Leibniz und sein Zeitalter* (*Gesammelte Schriften*, vol. III) which must, however, be read with caution because of new information now available on Leibniz' background, especially in scholastic philosophy; R. W. Meyer, *Leibniz and the Seventeenth Century Revolution,* trans. Peter Stern (Cambridge [Eng.], Bowes & Bowes, 1952) which also must be read with caution because of many small errors, though the over-all value is high; H. W. Barber, *Leibniz in France* (Oxford: Clarendon Press, 1955); a stimulating essay, "Der Zeitgeist der Barock und seine Verewigung in Leibnizens Gedankenwelt" by Dietrich Mahnke in *Zeitschrift für deutsche Kulturphilosophie,* I (1936).

Leibniz' relations to scholasticism are dealt with in Fritz Rintelen's "Leibnizens Beziehungen zur Scholastik," *Archiv für die Geschichte der Philosophie,* 26:157–188 (1903), and in Paul Mesnard's "Comment Leibniz se trouve placé dans le sillage de Suarez," *Archives de philosophie,* 18:7–32 (1949). While Rintelen is concerned to point out how little detailed knowledge Leibniz seems to show concerning the twists and turns of scholastic thought, Mesnard, not at all inconsistently with Rintelen, pictures the pervasiveness of the Suarezian influence on the seventeenth century and at least indirectly on Leibniz.

Short papers on Leibniz' religious philosophy and attitudes are: Walter Kühnert, "Die Krisis des deutschen Protestantismus um 1700," *Zeitschrift für systematische Theologie,* 23:259–288 (1954), and Ernst Troeltsch, "Leibniz und die Anfänge des Pietismus," in *Gesammelte Schriften,* IV, 488–531.

A new periodical, *Leibniz-Studien,* has been announced for publication. Each important anniversary of Leibniz brings forth a large number of collected memorial volumes or issues of philosophical periodicals devoted to his life and work. A typical one for the 300th anniversary of his birth is Giorgi Schischkoff, ed., *Beiträge zur Leibniz-Forschung* (Reutlingen: Gryphius Verlag, 1947); for the 250th anniversary of his death, *Revue internationale de philosophie,* nos. 76–77 (1966) and *Zeitschrift für philosophische Forschung,* XX, 3–4.

The reader of this chapter will readily see the degree to which I have learned, or failed to learn, from the Leibniz researches of my first teacher, Professor L. E. Loemker. Besides the articles repeatedly referred to in the text, I would call attention to the long introduction to his Leibniz edition, and the following papers: "Leibniz's Judgments of Fact," *Journal of the History of Ideas,* 7:397–410 (1946); "Leibniz's Doctrine of Ideas," *Philosophical Review,* 55:229–249 (1946); "Leibniz and Boyle," *Journal of the History of Ideas,* 16:22–43 (1955); "A Note on the Origin and Problem of Leibniz' Discourse of 1686," *ibid.,* 8:449–466 (1947); "Leibniz und die Grenzen des Empirismus," *Kant-Studien,* 56:315–328 (1965–66); and "Leibniz's Conception of Philosophical Method," *Zeitschrift für philosophische Forschung,* 20:507–524. (1966).

PART THREE: THE EIGHTEENTH CENTURY

All histories of thought in the eighteenth century, of course, have material on Germany. But since the German Enlightenment is generally considered to be less interesting than the English and the French, and is often regarded as a mere alien import, it tends to be neglected in general works on the European movement as a whole. The following either do not make that mistake, or are important for German studies in spite of it: Ernst Cassirer, *The Philosophy of the Enlightenment* (Boston: Beacon Press, 1951); Paul Hazard, *The European Mind 1680–1715* (London: Hollis and Carter, 1953), and *European Thought in the Eighteenth Century* (New York: World Publishing Co., 1963); Robert Anchor, *The Enlightenment Tradition* (New York: Harper & Row, 1967); and Peter Gay, *The Enlightenment, An Interpretation* (New York: Knopf, 1967). Of the two books by Hazard, the former is the more valuable, though the latter has more bearing upon what was happening in Germany.

The first volume of Gay's work, with the subtitle "The Rise of Modern Paganism," is a sustained attack on interpretations of the Enlightenment (such as Carl Becker's, in *The Heavenly City of the Eighteenth-Century Philosophers*) which see in the Enlightenment a perseveration, albeit a secularization, of Christian values and traditions. It will, I think, be far more difficult to maintain Gay's thesis (if indeed he attempts to do so) when he comes, perhaps in a second or later volume of his history, to deal with the German Enlightenment. See Roger Emerson, "Peter Gay and the Heavenly City," *Journal of the History of Ideas*, 28:383–402 (1967). A radically different interpretation, in which the roots of Enlightenment are found in the development of physicotheology (as an exploitation of natural knowledge for theological purposes) is given in Wolfgang Philipp's *Das Werden der Aufklärung in theologiegeschichtlicher Sicht* (Göttingen: Vandenhoeck und Ruprecht, 1957). Philipp's anthology, *Das Zeitalter der Aufklärung* (vol. VII of Klassiker des Protestantismus [Bremen: Dieterich, 1963]) is constructed in part to bring out this connection.

The following books are more directly on the German Enlightenment. Cay von Brockdorff, *Die deutsche Aufklärungsphilosophie* (Munich: Reinhardt, 1926) is somewhat pedestrian. Exhaustive on the university-philosophy and encyclopedic is Max Wundt, *Die deutsche Schulphilosophie im Zeitalter der Aufklärung* (Tübingen: Mohr, 1945). The most complete survey in English is Frederick Copleston, *A History of Philosophy*, vol. VI: *Wolff to Kant* (London: Burns & Oates, 1960). Max Dessoir's *Geschichte der neuren deutschen Psychologie*, 2nd ed. (Berlin: C. Duncker, 1901; vol. I, all published) is not entirely dependable in all details but very comprehensive. See also F. W. Kantzenbach, *Protestantisches Christentum im Zeitalter der Aufklärung* (Gütersloh: Gerd Mohn, 1965), and Hans M. Wolff, *Die Weltanschauung der deutschen Aufklärung* (Bern: A Francke, 1949), which is a perceptive interpretation through philosophy, literature, and religion.

The social and political factors are brought out in Lucien Lévy Bruhl, *L'Allemagne depuis Leibniz. Essai sur le développement de la conscience nationale en Allemagne 1700–1848* (Paris, 1890). Leonard Krieger, *The German Idea of Freedom* (Boston: Beacon Press, 1957), especially pp. 1–125, is a deep study of the failure of German political and philosophical thinkers (from Pufendorf through Kant) to provide a "liberal ideology" against the doctrines of the organic or absolutistic state, a failure which is partly to be explained through the peculiarly weak position of the middle class and the isolation of the intellectual.

W. H. Bruford, *Germany in the Eighteenth Century* (Cambridge University Press, 1935), has comparatively little on the strictly intellectual life, but provides useful background material on social and cultural life. A most interesting study in the sociology of knowledge of the eighteenth century is Herbert Schöffler, *Deutsches Geistesleben zwischen Reformation und Aufklärung* (Frankfurt: Klostermann, 1956). In general, and of course with many exceptions, the center of philosophical life in Germany has slowly moved eastward, from the Rhineland in the fourteenth century of Prussia and Saxony in the eighteenth. Saxony was centrally important toward the end of the seventeenth century, and many of its leading men of letters came from neighboring Silesia. Schöffler explains this as follows. Silesia was a Catholic state, and Silesian Lutherans to pursue their university education had to go elsewhere. Theologians went in large numbers to Wittenberg, and arts students went to Leiden, where they became acquainted with Dutch thought which had been influenced by Descartes. Upon their return to Silesia, the school teachers introduced modern western philosophy which was still being strongly resisted in the Lutheran and Calvinist states. Schöffler sees this as a reason for the origination of *Aufklärung* in Silesia and its neighboring Saxony and Brandenburg.

Chapter XI. Two Founders of the Enlightenment

Thomasius

There is no collected edition and few if any modern printings of Thomasius' works. A convenient selection is in Fritz Brüggemann, *Aus der Frühzeit der deutschen Aufklärung* (Leipzig: Reclam, 1928). A complete bibliography is by Rolf Lieberwirth, *Christian Thomasius. Sein wissenschaftliches Lebenswerk* (Weimar: Böhlaus, 1955). The fullest study of his thought is a collection of essays edited by Max Fleischmann, *Christian Thomasius, Leben und Lebenswerk* (Halle: Max Niemeyer, 1931). W. R. Jaitner, in *Thomasius, Rüdiger, Hoffmann, und Crusius* (Cologne Diss., 1958; Bleicherode, 1939), discusses Thomasius' anthropological views, but is disappointing. The only treatment in English I know is in Andrew D. White, *Seven Great Statesmen in the Warfare of Humanity with Unreason* (New York: Century, 1910), chap. iii. White deals with Thomasius' campaign against witchcraft trials. The best treatment I know of Thomasius' political and legal thought is in Leonard Krieger's *The German Idea of Freedom*, pp. 59–66. I know of no general study of Thomasius' philosophy in English.

For an understanding of Thomasius, some knowledge of Pufendorf is helpful. Leonard Krieger, *The Politics of Discretion; Pufendorf and the Acceptance of Natural Law* (Chicago: University of Chicago Press, 1965), is highly recommended. Some Pufendorf exists in English translation, e.g.: *De officio humanis et civis*, trans. F. G. Moore (New York: Oxford University Press, 1927), and *Elementa jurisprudentia universalis*, trans. W. A. Oldfather [Oxford: Clarendon Press, 1931]). On the concept of natural law throughout German history, the profound paper of Ernst Troeltsch, "The Idea of Natural Law and Humanity in World Politics," printed in Otto Gierke's *Natural Law and the Theory of Society* (Cambridge: Cambridge University Press, 1934), I, 201 ff, should be consulted and taken with utmost seriousness. Troeltsch explains how the theory of natural law, which had revolutionary implications in England, Holland, and France, was used in Germany to bolster despotism. See also chap. vi of Erich Cassirer, *Natur- und Völkerrecht im Lichte der Geschichte*.

Wolff

Wolff's principal works, in German and Latin, together with the few English translations, have been listed on pp. 257 and 259. A splendid modern edition is now being published in Hildesheim by G. Olms Verlag, but by July 1968 only four volumes had appeared. Fritz Brüggemann's anthology, *Das Weltbild der deutschen Aufklärung* (Leipzig: Reclam, 1930) gives a good selection from the German works.

The most complete study of Wolff is Mariano Campo's *Christian Wolff e il razionalismo precritico*, 2 vols. (Milan: Vita e Pensiero, 1939). So far as I know, the only book on Wolff in English is John V. Burns, *Dynamism in the Cosmology of Christian Wolff* (New York: Exposition Press, 1966). Wolff and his pupils are described, with copious quotations, in C. G. Ludovici, *Ausführlicher Entwurf einer vollständigen Historie der Wolffischen Philosophie*, 3 vols., (Leipzig, 1737–38). Clara Josten, *Christian Wolffs Grundlegung der praktischen Philosophie* (Leipzig: Meiner, 1931), important also for the study of Kant's ethics, Hans Lüthje, "Christian Wolffs Philosophiebegriff," *Kant-Studien*, 30:39–56 (1923). H. J. de Vleeschauwer, "La genèse de la méthode mathématique de Wolff," *Revue Belge de philologie et d'histoire*, 11:651–677 (1931), traces in detail the influence of Descartes, Leibniz, Erhard Weigel, von Tschirnhaus and a Cartesian *milieu* in Silesia on the young Wolff.

Interest in Kant's ontology, or perhaps we should say ontologists' interest in Kant, has naturally directed attention to Wolff's ontology, and has led to worthwhile studies. The most instructive is Heinz Heimsoeth's "Wolffs Ontologie und die Prinzipienforschung Kants," in his *Studien zur Philosophie Immanuel Kants* (Cologne: Kölner Universitätsverlag, 1956), pp. 1–92.

Since Wolff's vocabulary was standard throughout most of the century, Julius Baumann's *Wolffsche Begriffsbestimmungen* (Leipzig: Meiner, [1935]) is in spite of its regrettable brevity (54 pp.) useful in reading all philosophers of that time. E. A. Blackall, *The Emergence of German as a Literary Language* (Cambridge: University Press, 1959), provides a great deal of information on the philosophical vocabulary of Wolff and Thomasius.

Richard J. Blackwell's translation of *Discursus preliminaris de philosophia in genere* (Indianapolis: Bobbs-Merrill, 1963) contains, in addition to an informative introduction, a useful but brief bibliography of recent publications—brief because Wolff is not at this time an object of insatiable historical curiosity.

Chapters XII and XIII. A Generation of
Epigone and Philosophers on the Spree

Much of the literature on this period has been cited in the text or in the Bibliography under Book III and Chapter XI. Max Wundt's *Die Philosophie an der Universität Jena* gives a very full picture of characteristic but minor figures in one university. Marianne Beyer-Fröhlich, ed., *Pietismus und Rationalismus* (Leipzig: Reclam, 1933), contains selections from the autobiographies of Francke, Christianus Democritus, J. J. Moser, and J. S. Semler. Carlo Antoni, *Der Kampf wider die Vernunft* (Stuttgart: Koehler, 1951), is important on the contribution of the philosophers and historians to the development of national feeling at this time. Johann Burkhard Mencke (sometimes Mencken), *The Charlatanery of the Learned* (original 1713; English translation by H. L. Mencken, New York: Knopf, 1937) is an amusing book by the editor of the *Acta eruditorum* on the foibles of the learned; it could have been written by his friend Thomasius or his descendent H. L. Mencken.

The Wolffian school's history is given in Carl Günther Ludovici's *Ausführlicher Entwurf einer vollständigen Historie der Wolffschen Philosophie*, 3 vols. (Leipzig, 1737–38) which gives a great deal of information on the minor figures because they did not seem minor at the time. The religious philosophy of the school is reported in Karl Hagenbach, *German Rationalism in its Rise, Progress, and Decline* (Edinburg, 1865). Kantzenbach's and Wolfgang Philipp's book listed at the beginning of the Bibliography for Book III, and Karl Aner, *Die Theologie der Lessingzeit* (Halle: Niemeyer, 1929) are widely divergent in interpretation but instructive on the theological Wolffians.

J. S. Baumgarten's *Geschichte der Religionsparteien*, in the edition of 1766, with preface by J. S. Semler, is in a modern reprint (Hildesheim, Georg Olms, 1966). Semler's own *Anhandlung der freien Untersuchung des Kanons* (1771–1775) has not had a later edition. For a good account of Semler, see S. G. Flygt, *The Notorious Dr. Barhdt* (Nashville, Vanderbilt University Press, 1963), and Leopold Zscharnack, *Lessing und Semler* (Giessen, Töpelmann, 1905). The fullest study of Reimarus is David Friedrich Strauss's *Hermann Samuel Reimarus und seine Schutzschrift* (Bonn, 1861; 2nd ed., 1877). On the whole Strauss' book is somewhat tendentious, since it argues that "the deepest conviction of the eighteenth century was: all positive religions, without exception, are works of deceit" (p. 175). A complete edition of works of Johann Christian Edelmann, the most notorious freethinker of Berlin, is being published now in thirteen volumes, under the editorship of Walter Grossmann (Stuttgart: Fromann, 1968–).

The aesthetic theory of the time is surveyed in meticulous detail in the first (and unfortunately the only) volume of Alfred Baeumler's *Kant's Kritik der Urteilskraft* (Halle: Neimeyer, 1923; reprinted under the title *Das Irrationalitätsproblem in der Aesthetik und Logik des 18. Jahrhunderts*, Darmstadt: Wissenschaftliche Buchgesellschaft, 1967); and very competently, but more briefly, in Armand Nivelle, *Les Theories esthétiques en*

Allemagne de Baumgarten à Kant (Paris: Société d'édition 'Les Belles Lettres,' 1955). Alberto Martino's *Storia delle teoria drammatiche nella Germania del settecento (1730–1780)*, vol. 1, *La drammaturgia dell'illuminismo* (Pisa: Università de Pisa, 1967 [actually 1968]) was published too late for me me make use of it, but it would have saved me much labor and corrected my judgment on several points. It should be noted that the title is too restrictive to indicate the broad scope of the work. I have not been able to consult the following book but have reason to believe that it would be rewarding: Ernst Bergmann, *Die Begründung der deutschen Aesthetik durch A. G. Baumgarten und G. F. Meier* (Leipzig: Röder und Schunke, 1911), which is said to make a good case for the originality and effectiveness of Meier. Gottsched's writings can be found in the modern reprints cited in the text and in Fritz Brüggemann's *Gottscheds Lebens- und Kunstreform* (Leipzig: Reclam, 1935). On Gottsched's relation to Wolff and to the aesthetics of music of his time, see the monograph of Joachim Birke, *Christian Wolffs Metaphysik und die zeitgenossische Literatur- und Musiktheorie* (Berlin: de Gruyter, 1966).

The Thomasians have been far less fully studied than the Wolffians. Except for Old Faithful, Max Wundt's *Die deutsche Schulphilosophie im Zeitalter der Aufklärung*, some of them would now be hardly more than names to modern readers (and writers!). There is an excellent study of Rüdiger: Heinrich Schepers, *Andreas Rüdigers Methodologie und ihre Voraussetzungen* (*Kant-Studien, Ergänzungsheft* 78 [1959]); his treatment of the *Voraussetzungen* did much to make his study of Rüdiger's logic useful for our present studies. W. R. Jaitner's Cologne dissertation, *Thomasius, Rüdiger, Hoffmann und Crusius* (1938), in spite of its promising title, is a disappointment. Jaitner discusses only the ethics and anthropology of these writers, and on Hoffmann, the most neglected of them, he has almost nothing to say.

The neglect of the work of A. F. Hoffmann is especially to be regretted, and can be accounted for only by the extreme rarity of his books. It is to be hoped that the new edition of Hoffmann now being prepared by Giorgio Tonelli will permit wider attention to this interesting philosopher; I am indebted to Professor Tonelli for the loan of microfilms of Hoffmann's *Vernunftlehre*. Apparently much of what has been thought to be original in the works of his most outstanding pupil, Crusius, is present *in ovo* in Hoffmann's writings.

An interesting account of the intellectual life of Berlin during this period is to be found in Ludwig Geiger, *Berlins geistiges Leben* (Berlin, 1893) vol. I. On Frederick the Great, consult Eduard Zeller, *Friedrich der Grosse als Philosoph* (Berlin, 1886), and the more perceptive work by Eduard Spranger, *Der Philosoph von Sans Souci*, in *Abhandlungen der Preussischen Akademie der Wissenschaften zu Berlin*, Phil.-Hist. Klasse, 1942, as well as the classical work by Dilthey, *Friedrich der Grosse und die deutsche Aufklärung* (*Gesammelte Schriften*, III, 53–208).

The standard history of the Berlin Academy is Adolf von Harnack's *Geschichte der Königlich preussischen Akademie der Wissenschaften zu Berlin*, 4 vols., (Berlin, 1900). Von Harnack's account of the Maupertuis controversy is in vol. I, with the documents in the case in vol. II, pp. 381–410, together with an analysis of the specific issue in physics involved, by Hermann von Helmholtz. Pierre Brunet, *Maupertuis* (Paris, Blanchard, 1929), vol. II, chap. v, and *Étude historique sur le principe de la moindre action* (Paris, Hermann, 1938), also discusses the mathematical and physical questions involved. In the latter work Brunet comes to the conclusion that though Maupertuis did not succeed in formulating or proving the principle of least action in an acceptable form, he did in fact go beyond both what Leibniz had published (in *Specimen dynamicum* [1695] and *Concerning Nature Itself* [1698]—both in *Philosophical Papers and Letters* [trans. Loemker], pp. 711–27 and 808–25) and what was contained in the copy of the letter (the original of which has never been found) submitted by König. The source of the copy and indeed the identity of the addressee are disputable, but König has been cleared of any guilt.

Other studies of the case, with an emphasis upon the personal politics and not the physics involved, will be found in Dilthey's *Friedrich der Grosse und die deutsche Aufklarung* and in Pierre Brunet's *Maupertuis*, I, 4, which is an apology for Maupertuis.

Maupertuis was certainly a significant thinker whose administrative effect on German philosophy was important through his constructive work in the Berlin Academy (treated in detail and justly praised by Brunet). But otherwise, with the exception of his unhappy role in *l'affaire König* (which D'Alembert, in the *Encyclopédie*, compared to a religious controversy "in its acidity and in the number of people involved who spoke without understanding"), little that he did as a thinker belongs specifically to a history of German philosophy. It would be wholly different, of course, if Schopenhauer's conjecture (*World as Will and Idea*, vol. II, ch. iv) were plausible that Maupertuis' doctrine of the ideality of space and time was, in some sense other than merely the chronological, the "precursor" of Kant's; but this is highly unlikely, and Maupertuis' own doctrine seems to have been taken from Berkeley. It is odd, in fact, that Schopenhauer seems puzzled about the provenance of the theory. Among the works of Maupertuis which are not restricted by the German context assumed here, see the comprehensive *Maupertuis* by Pierre Brunet and, in English, the brief essay by Harcourt Brown, "Maupertuis *philosophe*," in *Studies in Voltaire and the Eighteenth Century*, ed. Theodore Besterman (Geneva, *Institut et Musée Voltaire*, 1931), I, 255–270.

Formey has been studied by Eva D. Marcu in *Formey and the Enlightenment* (unpubl. diss., Columbia University, 1952, available as University Microfilm AC–1, no. 3904). The only Formey I have found in English is *A Concise History of Philosophy and Philosophers* (London, 1766), which ends with Wolff.

There is unfortunately less material on Mendelssohn than he deserves. The *Gesammelte Schriften* (Berlin, Akademie Verlag, 1928–) could not be completed; this should be undertaken and finished. See H. M. Z. Meyer, *Moses Mendelssohn Bibliographie* (Berlin, De Gruyter, 1965). The principal biography is M. Kayserling, *Moses Mendelssohn, Leben und Wirken* (Leipzig, 1888). Also of interest is Beate Berwin, *Moses Mendelssohn im*

Urteil seiner Zeitgenossen (*Kant-Studien Ergänzungsheft* 49 (1919). Heinrich Scholz includes in *Die Hauptschriften zum Pantheismusstreit* (Berlin, Reuther und Reichard, 1916) the essential documents concerning the Mendelssohn-Jacobi controversy.

Chapter XIV. Lessing

The edition of Lessing's works used is Lachmann-Muncker (Stuttgart, 1886–1924) in 23 volumes. Much of Lessing's literary work, of course, has been translated into English, but little of the philosophical writing. The most important, but by no means the whole, of the theological writings are in Henry Chadwick, *Lessing's Theological Works* (Stanford: Stanford University Press, 1957). E. A. McCormack has translated *Laokoon* (Indianapolis: Bobbs-Merrill, 1962).

Studies

A brilliant re-creation of Lessing's character and work is in a lecture by E. H. Gombrich in *Proceedings of the British Academy*, 43:133–156 (1957). Karl Ancr's *Die Theologie der Lessingzeit* (Halle: Niemeyer, 1929), is the most authoritative work on all the theological controversies. Carl Schrempf *Lessing als Philosoph*, 2nd ed. (Stuttgart: Fromann, 1921) covers all of his work. Hans Leisegang, *Lessings Weltanschauung* (Leipzig: Meiner, 1931), is unique in the emphasis it puts upon Lessing's use of the German mystical and natural-philosophy tradition. Ernst Kretzschmar, *Lessing und die Aufklärung* (Leipzig: Richter, 1905) is a historical commentary on *The Education of the Human Race*. H. B. Garland, *Lessing, Founder of Modern German Literature* (London: Macmillan, 1937) is a brief account of his literary work. Karl Barth, *Protestant Thought from Rousseau to Ritschl*, trans. B. Cozens and H. H. Hartwell (New York: Harper, 1959), chap. iii, has the expected emphasis upon "the proof of the spirit and the power."

[Since this chapter was completed, Henry E. Allison's *Lessing and the Enlightenment* (Ann Arbor: University of Michigan Press, 1966) appeared. It is gratifying to find so many of my interpretations and conjectures confirmed in this learned and original book, which emphasizes even more than I have the Leibnizianism of Lessing.]

Chapter XV. The Counter-Enlightenment

Two important studies of the over-all situation in Germany as expressed by the Counter-Enlighteners are: Roy Pascal, *The German Sturm und Drang* (Manchester: Manchester University Press, 1953), which contains much on the literary work and influence of this group of thinkers and *poseurs*; and Carlo Antoni, *Der Kampf wider die Vernunft* (Stuttgart: Koehler, 1951), which studies the growth of nationalistic and historical sentiment from Haller through Herder and Hamann, with a good chapter on Kant's conception of Enlightenment. Mme. Janine Buenzod, in "De l'*Aufklärung* au *Sturm und Drang*, continuité ou rupture?," in *Studies on*

Voltaire and the Enlightenment, ed. Theodore Besterman (Geneva, 1963) I, 289–313, argues that *Sturm und Drang* was a natural consequence of the philosophical and moral individualism of the Enlightenment, and would no doubt oppose the sharp division made in this book between Enlightenment and Counter-Enlightenment.

On the relation of German philosophers to the French Revolution, which frightened many of them but not Kant, "the old Jacobin," out of their Enlightenment optimism, there have been many studies. G. P. Gooch, *Germany and the French Revolution* (London: Longmans Green, 1920), is the most complete.

The influence of Spinoza is treated by M. Grunwald in *Spinoza in Deutschland* (Berlin, 1897), which is disappointing in the amount of undigested information it presents, but useful because of its raw data. David Baumgardt's "Spinoza und der deutsche Spinozismus," *Kant-Studien,* 32:182–192 (1927), deals too briefly with the period in question. An old Breslau dissertation, Moses Krakauer, *Zur Geschichte des Spinozismus in Deutschland* (1881), is brief but contains valuable information on minor figures (e.g., Dippel and Edelmann). The essential work is the collection of documents in Heinrich Scholz's *Die Hauptdokumente zum Pantheismusstreit.*

Jacobi

Werke, edited by himself, Leipzig: 1812–1825. I know of no translations.

Jacobi has been neglected by English and American writers. I know only Norman Wilde, *F. H. Jacobi. A Study in the Origin of German Realism* (Columbia University Contributions to Philosophy, Psychology, and Education, vol. I, no. 1, 1894) and Alexander W. Crawford, *The Philosophy of F. H. Jacobi* (Cornell Studies in Philosophy, no. 6 [New York, 1905])— both doctoral dissertations in the old, informative style without much imagination. O. F. Bollnow, *Die Lebensphilosophie F. H. Jacobi's* (1933; reprint, Stuttgart: Kohlhammer, 1966) is very much more comprehensive, and, coming out of the Dilthey tradition, sympathetic in its reconstruction. Alfred Hebeisen, *F. H. Jacobi und seine Auseinandersetzung mit Spinoza* ("Sprache und Dichtung," no. 5; Bern: Haupt, 1960), argues that Jacobi overemphasized the rationalism of Spinoza, failing to understand and to give due weight to Spinoza's intuitive knowledge, with which, Hebeisen thinks, he would be more congenial; the author insists Jacobi was not a "fideist."

Herder

The standard edition of Herder's work is that of Bernard Suphan (Berlin: Weidmann, 1881–1913; 33 vols.). See also, *Ideas for a Philosophy of History* (London, 1800); *God, Some Conversations,* trans. Frederick Burkhardt (New York: Veritas Press, 1940; reprint, Indianapolis: Bobbs-Merrill, n.d.); *Essay on the Origin of Language,* trans. J. H. Moran and Alexander Gode in *On the Origin of Language: Rousseau and Herder* (New York: Frederick Ungar, 1966).

Unlike that on Jacobi, the literature on Herder in English is very extensive. The best life and overall study I know is Robert T. Clark, Jr.'s *Herder, His Life and Thought* (Berkeley and Los Angeles: University of California Press, 1955). Briefer: Frank McEachran, *The Life and Philosophy of Johann Gottfried Herder* (Oxford: Clarendon Press, 1939). Also brief, but highly perceptive, is Sir Isaiah Berlin, "Herder and the Enlightenment," in *Aspects of the Eighteenth Century*, ed. E. R. Wasserman (Baltimore: Johns Hopkins University Press, 1965), pp. 47–104. If one is to limit his reading on Herder, this should not in any circumstances be omitted. Herder's aesthetics has recently been treated by J. K. Fugate in *The Psychological Basis of Herder's Aesthetics* (The Hague: Mouton, 1966).

The most important and widely discussed part of his philosophy is his philosophy of history, and the following are only a few of the many interesting studies in English. A. O. Lovejoy's "Herder and the Enlightenment Philosophy of History," in *Essays in the History of Ideas* (New York: Braziller, 1955, pp. 166–182), discusses the internal contrasts in Herder between progressivism and the fixedness of historical processes; similarly, G. A. Wells, "Herder's Two Philosophies of History," *Journal of the History of Ideas*, 21:527–537 (1960), and "Herder's Determinism," *ibid.*, 19:105–113 (1958); see also F. M. Bernard, "Herder's Treatment of Causation and Continuity in History," *ibid.*, 24:197–212 (1963). On Herder's social and political theory and his contributions to the German theory of the folk and nation, see R. R. Ergang, *Herder and the Foundations of German Nationalism* (New York: Columbia University Press, 1931); R. J. Schmidt, "Cultural Nationalism in Herder," *Journal of the History of Ideas*, 17:407–417 (1956); F. M. Barnard, *Herder's Social and Political Thought from Enlightenment to Nationalism*, (Oxford: Clarendon Press, 1965), and Robert Anchor, *Community and History in Johann Gottfried Herder* (unpubl. diss., University of Rochester, 1965).

The relations between Herder and Kant have received special attention in G. A. Wells, *Herder and After* (The Hague: Mouton, 1959), especially chap. iv. Theodor Litt, *Kant und Herder als Deuter der geistigen Welt* (Leipzig: Quelle und Meyer, 1930), Heinrich Springmeyer, *Herders Lehre vom Naturschönen im Hinblick auf seinen Kampf gegen die Aesthetik Kants* (Jena: Diederichs, 1930), and Gottfried Martin, "Herder als Schüler Kants," *Kant-Studien*, 41: (1936), 294–306. Wolfgang Harich, "Ein Kantmotiv im philosophischen Denken Herders," *Deutsche Zeitschrift für Philosophie*, I (1954), 43ff, traces Herder's evolutionary theory back to the *Natural History of the Heavens*.

Hamann

Werke, 6 vols., Joseph Nadler (Vienna: Thomas Morus Presse im Verlag Herder, 1949–57. *Briefwechsel*, ed. Walter Ziesemer and Arthur Henkel (Wiesbaden: Inselverlag, 1955–) is still incomplete. The few English translations are indicated in the text, with the exception of J. C. O'Flaherty's translation of *Socratic Memorabilia* (Baltimore: Johns Hopkins Press, 1967) which appeared, with its splendidly informative introduction and notes, too late for me to make use of it.

The Lowry and O'Flaherty monographs cited in the text are radically different interpretations of this most mysterious thinker; W. M. Alexander's *Hamann, Philosophy and Faith* (The Hague: Nijhoff, 1966) is the most comprehensive study in English, but it also appeared after my chapter on Hamann was completed. But Alexander's "J. G. Hamann, Meta-critic of Kant" in *Journal of the History of Ideas*, 27:137–144 (1966), was fortunately at hand. Hamann has been studied as an intermediary between Hume and Kant by Philip Merlan in "Hamann et les Dialogues de Hume," *Revue de la métaphysique et de moral*, 59:285–289 (1954), and in other articles under the collective name "Parva Hamanniana"; see also C. W. Swain, "Hamann and the Philosophy of Hume," *Journal of the History of Philosophy*, 5:343–353 (1967)—again an important paper whose benefits were denied me by later publication.

A full study of Hamann is Erwin Metzke's "Hamanns Stellung in der Philosophie des 18. Jahrhunderts" in the *Schriften der Königsberger Gelehrten Gessellschaft*, X (1933–34), 121–266; a briefer account will be found in some of the essays included in the same author's *Coincidentia oppositorum* (Witten: Luther Verlag, 1961).

Chapter XVI. On the Threshold of the Critical Philosophy

All three men discussed in this chapter have received attention in Ernst Cassirer's *Das Erkenntnisproblem in der Philosophie und Wissenschaft der neueren Zeit*, 3rd ed (Berlin: Bruno Cassirer, 1922), vol. II.

Crusius

The German works exist in a modern edition by Giorgio Tonelli (Hildesheim: G. Olms, 1964–   ). The Latin works are earlier and are now rare. The best studies of Crusius that I have found are Heinz Heimsoeth's "Metaphysik und Kritik bei Crusius," in his *Studien zur Philosophie Immanuel Kants* (Cologne: Kölner Universitätsverlag, 1956), and Max Wundt's *Kant als Metaphysiker* (Stuttgart: Enke, 1924), pp. 52–81.

Lambert

Lambert's *Neues Organon* and *Architektonic* are in a modern reprint (*Gesammelte Philosophische Schriften*, ed., H.-W. Arndt (Hildesheim: G. Olms, 1965–   ). For the other works not yet reprinted in this edition, see *Kant-Studien Ergänzungshefte* 36 and 42 (1915, 1918), edited by Karl Bopp. Lambert's correspondence with Kant, important for an understanding of both men, will be found in *Kant's Philosophical Correspondence*, trans. Arnulf Zweig (Chicago: University of Chicago Press, 1967). I have not seen the volume of Lambert's complete scientific correspondence published by Johann Bernoulli (1782–85).

The essays edited by Friedrich Lowenhaupt, *Johann Heinrich Lambert, Leistung und Leben* (Mühlausen: Braun, 1943), are more biographical than philosophical. In English, there seem to be only Harold Griffing's "J. H. Lambert: A Study in the Development of the Critical Philosophy," *Philo-*

sophical Review II (1892), 54–62, where it is argued that Kant's theory of mathematics was affected by Lambert's views; and Norman Kretzmann's account of Lambert's semantic theory in *Encyclopedia of Philosophy*, VII, 386–87.

Tetens

On Tetens there is even less. Except for *Versuche*, volume I of which has been reprinted in a modern edition, Teten's works are rare. Wilhelm Uebele has written the most comprehensive study in *Kant-Studien Ergänzungsheft* 24 (1911). In "Herder und Tetens" (*Archiv für Geschichte der Philosophie*, 18:216–249 [1905]), Uebele compares Herder and Tetens in their theories on the origin of language.

Chapter XVII. Kant

Works

There are several more or less complete editions of Kant (von Kirchmann, Hartenstein and Schubert, Vorländer, Cassirer, Grossherzog Wilhelm Ernst, Weischedel) which are in various degrees satisfactory for many purposes, but the edition which is most complete and destined to replace all others is *Kants Gesammelte Schriften* (Berlin: Königlich Preussische Akademie der Wissenschaften, 1902–   ; later volumes published by Georg Reimer and Walter de Gruyter). Not only does this edition contain all the published works, letters, and fragments, but it will, when complete, contain all the extant transcripts of lectures. An index to Kant's writings is being prepared, based on this edition, by the Kant Archiv in Bonn, under the general editorship of Gottfried Martin. An inexpensive reprint of the Academy edition is now being published by de Gruyter in Berlin.

Books about Kant

The literature about Kant is formidable in size. Erich Adickes' *Bibliography of Kant* (Ithaca, N.Y.: *The Philosophical Review*, 1893) lists 2832 titles and stops at the year 1802. Books and articles on Kant are being published now with such rapidity that an open-ended bibliography would have to be revised monthly. In view of all these indigestible riches, I have restricted my recommendations to a small fraction of the writings which I have found valuable. I have arbitrarily limited the list to fifty books and excluded all articles and have preferred, wherever feasible, works in English over those in other languages. These fifty books should suffice to give the beginner a fair introduction to Kant.

Biographies

The only good life is that by Karl Vorländer, *Immanuel Kant, der Mann und das Werk*, 2 vols. (Leipzig: Meiner, 1924). J. W. H. Stuckenberg, *The Life of Immanuel Kant* (London, 1882), is about the only one in English. Kurt Stavenhagen, *Kant und Königsberg* (Göttingen: Deuerlischer Verlag,

1949), is fascinating social-intellectual history of Königsberg and its greatest thinker.

Reference Books

Rudolf Eisler's *Kant Lexikon* (1930; Hildesheim: Olms, 1964) is of considerable use but is unfortunately not based on the Academy edition. Heinrich Ratker, *Handlexikon zu Kants Kritik der reinen Vernunft* (Leipzig: Meiner, 1928) is much briefer and covers only the first *Critique* and the *Prolegomena* but most of the things one wants to find in Kant can be more easily located here than in Eisler. (The index to the Akademie edition, in preparation by the Kant-Archiv in Bonn will render both of these now essential books obsolete.)

Books on Kant's Intellectual Development

H. J. de Vleeschauwer, *The Evolution of Kantian Thought*, trans. A. R. C. Duncan (London: Nelson, 1962), is based on the author's three-volume work cited below, which is a full-scale commentary and not merely an intellectual biography. The fullest histories are Mariano Campo, *La genesi del criticismo kantiano* (Varese: Magenta, 1953; two parts published thus far); Georgio Tonelli, *Kant: dall'estetica metafisica all'estetica psico-empirica* in *Memorie della Academie delle Scienze di Torino* (1955; the title is too restrictive for its rich contents), and *Elementi methodologici e metafisici in Kant dal 1747 al 1768* (Turin, 1959; only volume one published thus far); Paul Menzer, *Kants Aesthetik in ihrer Entwicklung* in *Abhandlungen der deutschen Akademie der Wissenschaften* (Berlin, 1950); and Paul Arthur Schilpp, *Kant's Pre-Critical Ethics*, 2nd ed. (Evanston, Ill.: Northwestern University Press, 1960). Alfred Baeumler, *Kants Kritik der Urtheilskraft*, vol. I: *Das Irrationalitätsproblem* (Halle: Miemeyer, 1923) is as much a history of eighteenth-century aesthetics as of Kant's thought, and the author reaches Kant only near the end of the book; vol. II was never published. *Studien zu Kants philosophischer Entwicklung*, ed. Heinz Heimsoeth, Dieter Henrich, and Giorgio Tonelli (Hildesheim: Olms, 1967), unfortunately appeared too late for me to make use of it in my account of Kant's development.

General Works on Kant's Philosophy as a Whole

The following books differ widely, but none could be classified under any of the narrower headings introduced below. For those who wish to read only *one* book about Kant and that a short one, there are A. D. Lindsay (i.e., Lord Lindsay of Birker), *Kant* (London: Oxford University Press, 1934), Friedrich Paulsen's *Immanuel Kant, His Life and Doctrine* (New York: Scribner, 1902), John Kemp, *The Philosophy of Kant* (London: Oxford University Press, 1968), and, from a very different point of view, Stephan Körner's *Kant* (London, Penguin, 1955). Karl Jasper's *Kant* (translated and published as a separate from his *Grosse Denker*; New York: Harcourt Brace, 1966) is perhaps less instructive. For an Hegelian orientation to Kant, see Edward Caird, *The Critical Philosophy of Kant*, 2 vols. Glasgow, 1889). A good introduction to the "Marburg" (purely *wissenschaftstheoretisch*) way of reading Kant is Ernst Cassirer, *Kants Leben und Lehre* (Berlin: Bruno

Cassirer, 1923; being the last volume in the Cassirer-Buchenau edition of *Kants Werke*); the best introduction to the contrasting "Heidelberg" way (emphasis upon ethics) is Richard Kroner's *Kant's Weltanschauung*, trans. John E. Smith (Chicago: University of Chicago Press, 1956). It should be noted that Kroner uses the word *Weltanschauung* rather differently from the way it is used in this chapter, and much of what Kroner considers Kant's *Weltanschauung*, I here consider to be a part of his "professional" philosophy. The "metaphysical" way of reading Kant which is predominant now in Germany will be found in Max Wundt, *Kant als Metaphysiker* (Stuttgart: Enke, 1924), Heinz Heimsoeth, *Studien zur Philosophie Kants* (Cologne: Kölner Universitätsverlag, 1956), and Gottfried Martin, *Kant's Metaphysics and Theory of Science*, trans. P. G. Lucas (Manchester: Manchester University Press, 1955). Less typical of this movement and least informative, but important in its own right, is Martin Heidegger, *Kant and the Problem of Metaphysics*, trans. J. S. Churchill (Bloomington: Indiana University Press, 1962). Papers on theory of knowledge, ethics, and aesthetics in R. P. Wolff ed., *Kant. A Collection of Critical Essays* (New York: Doubleday, 1967). My *Studies in the Philosophy of Kant* (Indianapolis: Bobbs-Merrill, 1965) contains essays on Kant's ethics and theory of knowledge, and I shall soon publish a large anthology of others' writings on Kant under the title *Kant Studies Today* (Evanston: Open Court, 1969). An older collection of essays is *The Heritage of Kant*, ed. G. T. Whitney and D. F. Bowers (Princeton: Princeton University Press, 1939).

Last, but by no means of less than pre-eminent value, are the three volumes of *La Déduction transcendentale dans l'œuvre de Kant* (Antwerp: De Sikkel, 1934–   ) by H. J. de Vleeschauwer. In spite of its apparently restrictive title, it is perhaps the most comprehensive single presentation of Kant's thought that exists.

Kant's Theory of Knowledge

There are no less than eleven commentaries in English on all or major parts of the *Critique of Pure Reason*. The most venerable ones in English are Norman Kemp Smith's *Commentary on Kant's Critique of Pure Reason* 2nd ed. (London: St. Martin's Press, Macmillan & Co. Ltd.; Macmillan Co. of Canada Ltd. 1929) and (radically different) H. J. Paton's *Kant's Metaphysic of Experience*, 2 vols. (London: Allen & Unwin, 1936; only on the Aesthetic and Analytic). An extreme example of Teutonic thoroughness is Hans Vaihinger, *Commentar zu Kants Kritik der reinen Vernunft* (Stuttgart, 1881), of which only two large volumes were published. He could not push his examination beyond p. 70, but the treatment of these 70 pages was not marked by hasty superficiality. Since no commentator has ever yet reached the Transcendental Dialectic with sufficient reserves of energy to do it justice, Heinz Heimsoeth in his eightieth year embarked upon it with the ingenious plan of beginning his commentary *Transzendentale Dialektik* [Berlin: De Gruyter, 1966–   ]) with the Dialectic; of the projected four volumes, three have been published. Other studies and commentaries, a few of which show more philosophical sophistication than exegetical faithfulness are Peter Strawson, *The Bounds of Sense* (London: Methuen, 1966);

Jonathan Bennett, *Kant's Analytic* (Cambridge [Eng.] University Press, 1966); R. P. Wolff, *Kant's Theory of Mental Activity* (Cambridge: Harvard University Press, 1963); T. D. Weldon, *Kant's Critique of Pure Reason* (Oxford: Clarendon Press, 1945; 2nd ed., 1958; the first edition is recommended in preference to the second); Graham Bird, *Kant's Theory of Knowledge* (London: Routledge, Kegan Paul, 1962); and A. C. Ewing, *A Short Commentary on Kant's Critique of Pure Reason* (Chicago: University of Chicago Press, 1950). Ewing's book is the best *vade mecum* for the first venture into the *Critique of Pure Reason*. D. P. Dryer's *Kant's Solution for Verification in Metaphysics* (Toronto: University of Toronto Press, 1967) is a very large commentary, marked by unusual sympathy with Kant's position and a pugnacious readiness to dispute all his critics. Moltke S. Gram has an interesting anthology, *Kant: Disputed Questions* (Chicago: Quadrangle Books, 1967), which, because of its worthwhile introductions to pairs of antithetical interpretations, must be counted as an original contribution to Kant-scholarship.

Kant's Ethics

H. J. Paton's *The Categorical Imperative* (Chicago: University of Chicago Press, 1948) is in my opinion the best book on Kant's ethics. My *Commentary on Kant's Critique of Practical Reason* (Chicago: University of Chicago Press, 1960) is perhaps the longest in English. Mary J. Gregor's *The Laws of Freedom* (Oxford: Blackwell, 1963) is the only full study of the *Metaphysics of Morals*. A. R. C. Duncan, *Practical Reason and Morality* (Edinburgh: Nelson, 1957), presents an unusual reading of the *Foundations of the Metaphysics of Morals*, about which there has been much dispute. W. T. Jones, *Morality and Freedom in the Philosophy of Kant* (London: Oxford University Press, 1940), deals with the difficult problem of the relation between the second and the third *Critiques*.

Aesthetic Theory

Baeumler hardly reaches the third *Critique* in his mammoth, yet truncated, commentary, but provides all the needed background. See also the books by August Menzer and Giorgio Tonelli listed above under "Kant's Intellectual Development." The works on aesthetics cited in the Bibliography to Chapter XII naturally contain material on Kant's theory of art. While the periodical literature in English contains many studies of Kant's aesthetics, there are only few books, to wit, Israel Knox, *The Aesthetic Theories of Kant, Hegel, and Schopenhauer* (New York: Humanities Press, 1958), and H. W. Cassirer, *A Commentary on Kant's Critique of Judgment* (London: Methuen, 1938). The latter is perhaps the fullest work in English but is of uneven quality. A new commentary of the magnitude of those now available on the other *Critiques* is needed.

Other Topics

On Kant's political philosophy, there is even less; see Carl Joachim Friedrich, *Inevitable Peace* (Cambridge: Harvard University Press, 1948), and the collection *La Philosophie politique de Kant* (Annales de philosophie politique, no. 4; Paris: Presses Universitaires de France, 1962).

On Kant's philosophy of religion, there are four recommendable books: C. C. J. Webb, *Kant's Philosophy of Religion* (Oxford: Clarendon Press, 1926); F. E. England's more metaphysical *Kant's Conception of God* (London: Allen & Unwin, 1929); and, on a very much more exegetical level, Joseph Bohatec, *Die Religionsphilosophie Kants in der 'Religion innerhalb der Grenzen der blossen Vernunft' mit besonderer Berücksichtigung ihrer theologisch-dogmatischen Quellen* (Hamburg: Hoffmann und Campe, 1938); Allen Wood, *Kant's Moral Religion* (to be published in 1969 by Cornell University Press), which is a very important and original defense of the consistency of Kant's ethical and religious writings. I here break my own self-imposed rule in order to recommend one article: W. H. Walsh, "Kant's Moral Theology," *Proceedings of the British Academy*, 49:263–289 (1963).

For a very thorough study of Kant's scientific work, see Erich Adickes, *Kant als Naturforscher*, 2 vols. (Berlin: De Gruyter, 1924).

I regret that the self-imposed limitation on the length of this bibliography (which I find that I have already slightly exceeded) restrains me from naming many other worthwhile books and articles in the extremely rich periodical literature. Those who wish to keep up with the vigorous contemporary study of Kant should be familiar with *Kant-Studien* (Bonn), and its associated series of monographs, the *Ergänzungshefte*.

Index